UNLIKELY HEROES

ALSO BY DEREK LEEBAERT

*Grand Improvisation: America
Confronts the British Superpower, 1945–1957*

*Magic and Mayhem: The Delusions of American
Foreign Policy from Korea to Afghanistan*

*To Dare and to Conquer: Special Operations and
the Destiny of Nations, from Achilles to Al Qaeda*

*The Fifty-Year Wound: How America's
Cold War Victory Shapes Our World*

UNLIKELY HEROES

Franklin Roosevelt,
His Four Lieutenants,
and the World They Made

★

DEREK LEEBAERT

St. Martin's Press
New York

First published in the United States by St. Martin's Press, an imprint
of St. Martin's Publishing Group

www.stmartins.com

Library of Congress Cataloging-in-Publication Data

Names: Leebaert, Derek, author.
Title: Unlikely heroes : Franklin Roosevelt, his four lieutenants, and the
   world they made / Derek Leebaert.
Other titles: Franklin Roosevelt, his four lieutenants, and the world they made
Description: First edition. | New York : St. Martin's Press, 2023. | Includes
   bibliographical references and index.
Identifiers: LCCN 2022045421 | ISBN 9781250274694 (hardcover) |
   ISBN 9781250274700 (ebook)
Subjects: LCSH: United States—Politics and government—1933–1945. |
   Roosevelt, Franklin D. (Franklin Delano), 1882–1945—Friends and
   associates. | Hopkins, Harry L. (Harry Lloyd), 1890–1946. | Perkins,
   Frances, 1880–1965. | Ickes, Harold L. (Harold LeClair), 1874–1952. |
   Wallace, Henry A. (Henry Agard), 1888–1965. | Cabinet officers—United
   States. | United States—Social conditions—1933–1945 | United
   States—Economic policy—1933–1945. | New Deal, 1933–1939. | World War,
   1939–1945—United States.
Classification: LCC E806 .L44 2023 | DDC 973.917—dc23/eng/20220927
LC record available at https://lccn.loc.gov/2022045421

Our books may be purchased in bulk for promotional, educational, or
business use. Please contact your local bookseller or the Macmillan Corporate
and Premium Sales Department at 1-800-221-7945, extension 5442, or by
email at MacmillanSpecialMarkets@macmillan.com.

First Edition: 2023

10 9 8 7 6 5 4 3 2 1

For Angela Lindsay Kingue, and her mom

Suffering produces endurance, and endurance produces character, and character produces hope, and hope does not disappoint us.

Romans 5: 3–4

CONTENTS

INTRODUCTION

One of Franklin Roosevelt's favorite poems was Kipling's *If*, which presents life as a continuous test. Roosevelt too had passed through endless tests of endurance, of waiting, of repeated disappointment, of triumph and disaster, certainly since summer 1921 when he was stricken by polio. He came to feel truly at ease only among the world's castoffs, as his wife, Eleanor, observed.

Only four people served at the top echelon of Roosevelt's presidency from the frightening early months of spring 1933 until he died in April 1945 and, in their different ways, they were as wounded as he. This was no coincidence.

Himself "crippled," Roosevelt had overridden the prejudices of that era toward those who were thought to be damaged. These three men—and, unprecedentedly, one woman—were peculiar outsiders rather than actual castoffs. He could sense their despairs even as they built the great institutions being raised against the Depression, implemented most of the projects and reforms known as the New Deal that remade their country, and proved themselves vital to victory in World War II.

They were his key lieutenants—the tough, constructive, enduring core of his government. In an era when unmatched concentrations of power gathered in Washington, they rammed their priorities through—FDR willing, of course.

Up to 1933, none of these four would ever have been considered for high office. Yet each riveted the nation during the celebrity-crazed 1930s and towered as world figures when, a long twelve years later, the adventure ran down. They called one another friends, if often through gritted teeth, and were bracketed together by the press and by their swarms of enemies. Their suffering intensified the relationships among themselves, and with their president. Like Roosevelt, each had much to hide, and all lived on the edge of calamity, as did their country.

The best way to come to terms with Franklin Roosevelt, I believe, as well as to penetrate the maze of his presidency, is to take the synoptic view that arises from examining their lives. To this end, my book sheds new light on Roosevelt and on his dangerous times, and now is the moment to do so. The 2020s raise uncomfortable parallels with those most world-changing of years during the last century: social upheavals, climate extremes (the Dust Bowl), an urge to rebuild, and furious politics (the cry of "America First" in both epochs), while world disorder threateningly increases.

Harry Lloyd Hopkins, son of an itinerant harness maker from Iowa, was forty-one when Roosevelt took office. He lends himself to fiction, as do all the others, but only Hopkins has figured in a novel—the Pulitzer-winning dramatist Jerome Weidman's *Before You Go* (1960)—as the thinly fictionalized Benjamin Franklin Ivey, the sickly, self-promoting assistant director of a settlement house who ascends ruthlessly from the Lower East Side to the peaks of decision-making in Washington. Such had been Hopkins's path in real life as he leapt from running boys' baseball games to being called the nation's largest employer as the New Deal fought overwhelming joblessness—and, even more surprisingly, to then becoming the president's "Number 1 adviser."[1]

Yet Hopkins's self-destructive habits tore through his life; he also suffered from ulcers and the complications of a major cancer operation. Much of his death-defying agony could have been avoided. Nevertheless, his illness cast him as a grievously wounded hero who refused to leave the field. This became a source of power, and it drew him closer to FDR.

Harold Ickes, fifty-nine at the start, was the abused son of an alcoholic father. He had worked his way through law school to become a "people's counsel" in Chicago for causes such as the newly founded American Civil Liberties Union and the city's Indian Rights Association, which he organized. He had sought to be a kingmaker in progressive Republican politics, and failed humiliatingly. A long, wretched marriage to a rich divorcée only turned worse after he seduced his stepdaughter. By 1932 he was describing himself as a loser, continuously self-medicating a torturous insomnia and constant headaches with Nembutal and whiskey, his moods swinging between rage and unrestrained joy. Some days he literally could not speak. A white-shoe Wall Street lawyer he had never been. Roosevelt appointed him from nowhere to be secretary of the interior. This position

merely became his base as he accumulated so many responsibilities—not
least, as the country's unrivaled builder of public works, its "Secretary
of Negro Affairs," its energy czar, and czar as well of all U.S. territories, such as Alaska—that he functioned basically as the chancellor of
an ever-watchful monarch. He was the first U.S. official to be denounced
by Hitler, in 1939, and he itched for war. Once it erupted, he proved a
formidable war administrator, and central to Allied victory.

Frances Perkins, fifty-two, had known Franklin Roosevelt in the days
when, she remembered, he could vault casually over a chair, like a "beautiful, strong, vigorous, Greek god king of an athlete."[2] She reinvented
herself as a Boston Brahmin, dedicating herself to God, to workers' rights,
and to putting an end to the horrors of child labor. She brought Hopkins
into Roosevelt's orbit and, in Washington, served as FDR's far-ranging
secretary of labor. She was an essential force behind Social Security, minimum wage laws, unemployment insurance, and the rights of workers to
organize. Less known are the terrible mistakes from which she saved the
Administration and, because she also headed the Immigration Service,
how hard she fought on behalf of refugees. As hostilities loomed, it was
she who provided FDR with the sharpest assessments of the crumbling
European balance. Then, often working closely with Ickes, she became
pivotal to the war effort.

Her husband, Paul Caldwell Wilson, was a cameo version of Franklin
Roosevelt: handsome, upper-class Episcopalian, Dartmouth, delightful in
manner, and a rising star in New York progressive politics. They had
a daughter, and Perkins yearned for more children. However, Paul was
gripped by manic depression, as bipolar disorder was known in his lifetime, and he squandered his inheritance. Finally she had to institutional-
ize him, at enormous expense to herself, at "the Haven," in Westchester
County. The time would come when her daughter also had to be hospitalized, and the money drained away.

Perkins was ever moved by a deep sadness. Several times she tried
to escape Washington for "a proper place in life," as she told FDR, who
would not hear of it, and she "suffered pain" even from seeing her picture
in the news. Ultimately, her sacrifice left its enduring marks, including
commemoration by the feast day of Frances Perkins, "Public Servant and
Prophetic Witness," in the calendar of the Episcopal Church.

Henry Wallace, a crisp forty-five, was driven by an intellect *The New*

York Times would describe as "freakish."[3] Surely, he was the foremost agronomist in the Western Hemisphere, though his vibrant intellect was of a sort that left little room for human intimacy. He embodied intellectual strength but often failed to comprehend where that might take him, or the costs of his decisions.

For three generations, Wallace's staunchly Republican family had run the important weekly *Wallace's Farmer* out of Ames, Iowa. The Depression drove this paper into the hands of creditors while he was struggling simultaneously to keep alive what today would be called a biotech startup.

Any man who combined brilliance, lonely idealism, involvement with the land, and being trapped was likely to appeal to Franklin Roosevelt. Wallace became secretary of agriculture at a time when nearly 30 percent of the nation made its living from farming. Then, in 1940, FDR told the Democratic Party Convention, in words conveyed through Frances Perkins, that Wallace would be his third-term running mate. For several years Wallace was a uniquely influential vice president as he rallied the country for war and then illuminated the vision of a postwar world worth fighting for.

Throughout, Roosevelt wanted those upon whom he depended most to be able to "take it."[4]

Unlike other statesmen, as Cabinet officers were considered in those days, each of the four arrived in Washington with well-crafted plans and all had primary, hands-on responsibility for executing what they had largely conceived. Along the way, they would come to see FDR close-up, and indeed acutely, for a dozen years, and they often pooled their impressions.

To be sure, Roosevelt was watching them too. He understood them in ways that proved crucial to making real the "action, and action now" that he demanded of every specific New Deal initiative and that, when war began, cut through the disarray caused by his approach to ruling.

Within months of his inauguration in 1933, our four were taking shape as a group. This cadre was utterly political and versatile, phenomenally visible, yet composed of individuals who were God-given targets for their enemies. They were by no means a unified board of directors. Roosevelt was incapable of tolerating any such consolidation of power. Besides, historian Arthur M. Schlesinger, Jr., notes, so lonely a man as Roosevelt could best find "the intimacy of exchange" with a single person, or—in this case—in varying combinations of two or three, less often with all four.[5]

To be secretary of the interior or of labor, or to be the president's special assistant, meant far more in American life during the Depression and the Second World War than those offices do today. Roosevelt did not mind the prominence these four received from newsreels, magazine profiles, and books. Quite the reverse. Had his own face instead been plastered on every enormous program, he would indeed have looked like Mussolini—as Republicans charged anyway. Mere ubiquity might fade his aura, and no one doubted who made the final decisions.

He never avoided having strong, uninjured presences around him: he would face plenty in his military circle, but he took the deference of the brass for granted. When it came to high civilian authorities, he preferred those whom he could shape, and he knew that Hopkins, Ickes, Perkins, and Wallace would each soar yet remain loyally in hand. It would have been exceedingly difficult for Roosevelt to have mastered Washington's turbulent and centrifugal system without them.

Several prominent men served at the heights for nearly as long as these four, including Secretary of State Cordell Hull and Secretary of the Treasury Henry Morgenthau, Jr. Several White House aides in fact stayed straight through from 1933 to 1945, along with speechwriters and counselors—many of them eloquent and shrewd—who served for intermittent periods. Yet none were the Administration's big, long-standing operators.

Early on, Roosevelt had identified the large established government departments that he believed vital to recovery: Agriculture, Interior, Labor, and Treasury. That meant counting on Wallace, Ickes, and Perkins, and then largely on Hopkins as de facto "Secretary of Public Welfare." For the Treasury Department, he came to have other uses. And the confidence he developed in each of these four during the valiant struggle for recovery carried over into the intensities of war.

If the Roosevelt Administration had an "inner cabinet"—meaning the center of power, not necessarily those gathering around a long mahogany table—it consisted of Hopkins, Ickes, Perkins, and Wallace. They held power over a far longer and more transformational epoch than did President Lincoln's famous "Team of Rivals," including years when the life of the Republic was equally in peril. Unlike Lincoln's "team"—his secretaries of state, treasury, and war, and his attorney general, none of whom could abide one another—our four were strange outsiders. Nor did any of them look down on FDR, or think they could do a better job, as did Lincoln's subordinates. In different ways, Hopkins, Ickes, Perkins, and Wallace each stood in awe of Roosevelt until the end—despite, by then, having been exposed to most every chilling defect of his character.

Myths abound about the Roosevelt years, against which I offer many new findings. Just to begin, two big misconceptions must first be cleared away.

One is that "no two members of the Roosevelt cabinet were ever real friends." Such was the opinion of FDR's office secretary, Grace Tully, in her ghostwritten memoir of 1949; and she added, "The contacts between cabinet members were largely of an official character."[6] Tully had neither the stature nor the range of access to look more closely, yet Roosevelt's biographers have repeated this mistake ever since.[7]

Another fallacy is that the Cabinet itself was insignificant at the start and thereafter did not "serve any good purpose."[8]

For us, a pattern will emerge—a strong, wounded, large-hearted core of builders (Ickes, Perkins, Wallace, and essentially Hopkins) with others in the room for the most part being politically necessary placeholders, at least until 1940. As for the Cabinet's usefulness overall, this assembly will prove indeed to have been quietly significant.

Today, left and right alike insist that America is changing irrevocably, though such has always been the case in this most proudly changeable of nations. Calls for "a New Deal" arose in the plague years of 2020–2021, and the president who came to office citing FDR as a model for uniting this troubled country will be the last born in Roosevelt's lifetime. Above the fireplace in the Oval Office presides the portrait of a somber FDR. But to invoke the New Deal is implicitly to summon larger-than-life saviors—surely not how America at its best should work.

Meanwhile, an unyielding opposition is distinctly less interested in heroizing FDR. Still, he towers over the nation, although not far below him, in terms of lasting achievement, come Hopkins, Ickes, Perkins, and

Wallace. As we shall see, they grappled in their curious ways with issues that confront us today. Some were existential, such as the yawning gaps between rich and poor, and the racial violence that, during the Roosevelt presidency, ran pretty much unchecked from state to state, highlighted by lynching. Other issues were structural, such as how to handle a politically asymmetrical Supreme Court. Yet still more might as well come from headlines of the 2020s: healthcare, a minimum wage, the nation's infrastructure, anguished choices on immigration, Lend-Lease, and America's altering role in the world.

Overlying these comparisons is the fact that our nation's breadth and diversity provide rich terrain for brushfire fears of conspiracy. At the time, many of Roosevelt's foes—who also singled out Hopkins, Ickes, Perkins, and Wallace for attack—discerned the hidden hands of un-American interests underway. Primarily it was the red fist of "socialism," which, we again hear, endangers our fractious land.

During those years, the peril of revolt—whether from left or right—was far graver than is remembered. Like today, a president spoke to his intimates of losing the country to violence.

Yet, by the time Roosevelt and his four lieutenants completed their journeys, America had largely been made anew, and with it much of the world. An index of what occurred may be found by simply recalling how we once commonly referred to our country.

A morning service at St. John's Episcopal Church, across from the White House on Lafayette Square, preceded the inauguration ceremonies of 1933, Roosevelt's old headmaster, the Reverend Endicott Peabody, offering a closing prayer. He sought God's grace for "Thy servant, Franklin, about to become President of these United States," using the plural in a then familiar way for the Republic.[9] When Roosevelt's presidency ended, the adjective would be dated, and *the* United States stood triumphant in 1945.

PART I

★

Suffering

1

STEPPING FORWARD

From Inauguration as Governor, January 1, 1929, to the October Crash

There never was a nicer man to work for.
Irvin McDuffie, Franklin Roosevelt's valet

Those attending Franklin Roosevelt's inauguration as governor of New York that New Year's afternoon saw an enviable man. Standing six feet two inches, the handsome new chief executive, nearly forty-seven, took his oath on a 240-year-old Dutch family Bible—matters Dutch being close to his heart out of a long Hudson Valley bloodline. He could indeed carry on a simple conversation in the language, though this came from his study of German. Also, he was fluent in French, and read Spanish easily.[1] People sensed a cosmopolitan air about him.

Observers would have noticed the impeccable cut of his morning dress; his suits and jackets covered the well-muscled shoulders and flat belly of an athlete. Old friends in the chamber could remember him racing ice yachts down the frozen Hudson.

His youthful presence had equally dazzled Washington during Woodrow Wilson's administration, in which he had served from 1913 to 1920 as assistant secretary of the navy. And together with Eleanor—President Theodore Roosevelt's niece, whom Franklin married in 1905—he had brought glamour to the nation's still provincial capital. In fact, T.R. was Franklin's fifth cousin, and both sides of the Roosevelt family enjoyed the quiet authority that accompanies a century or two of wealth. Everyone knew that Franklin Roosevelt possessed a 1,500-acre estate along the Hudson at Hyde Park, which he occasionally opened to political receptions. He was also known to receive lawmakers in his neo-Georgian town house on

East Sixty-Fifth Street in Manhattan when he was not spending summer months on Campobello Island, off the New Brunswick coast.

Roosevelt had walked to the microphone while leaning on a cane and supported by the arm of his eldest son, James, a student at Harvard as had been his father (Class of '04). His other four children sat whispering with a radiant Eleanor on the dais. At forty-four, and five feet eleven inches tall, Eleanor was athletically fit with a long neck and sloping shoulders, and still wore her long blond hair in great coils or braids. Her detractors could only snipe that this prevented her from donning stylish hats.

The inaugural address took less than half an hour, even allowing for frequent applause. The new governor wore a pince-nez as had T.R., but, unlike the former president's memorable squeak, he spoke in a rich tenor.

His listeners knew of the courage it had taken for him to overcome polio, or largely so, since being carried off Campobello in agony in August 1921. His return to politics appeared heroic, and he still visited often with his fellow sufferers at Warm Springs, the polio rehabilitation center he had founded in 1926. His physical therapist, Helena Mahoney, had received her own gold-foil invitation and had traveled north with other staff from west Georgia.

Throughout the ceremony, onlookers could feel the charm for which Roosevelt was already famous. His credentials sparkled. While at Navy, during the World War, he had visited the most exposed of bloody front lines in France and returned from Europe sick on a stretcher. Soon thereafter, in 1920, he was the Democratic candidate for vice president when only thirty-eight. Four years later, after being stricken, he riveted his party's convention in New York City with a truly powerful speech, from crutches, in which he endorsed his state's governor, Al Smith. At the 1928 convention in Houston, he then thrillingly placed Smith's name once again in nomination. That time, Smith had indeed gotten the nod—only to lose to Herbert Hoover.

Rarely before had the chamber been so filled on such an occasion by assemblymen and state senators. They were a motley crowd—hundreds of beefy men, roughnecks, merchants, and farmers from places like Lowville, Bath, and Buffalo. Given all the deplorables being drawn to the trough, Louis Howe, fifty-seven, was not entirely out of place. He had been Roosevelt's innermost adviser since 1912, when his hero was just a state senator, and followed him to Washington the next year as his secretary. This former newspaperman from Saratoga had become obsessed with the success of "his Franklin."

Howe was sickly, with hollowed cheeks, a scarred face, and brown protruding eyes. He grew bent with age and never weighed more than a hundred pounds, which is why the *Boston American,* for instance, styled him a "medieval gnome."[2] Slowly dying—very slowly, as it was to prove—he seemed to distill the enfeeblement that the new governor had overcome. He chain-smoked Sweet Caporals, drank hard, and hacked out asthmatic coughs while playing a ruthless political game—the pieces of which included large stacks of cash from who-knew-where. Still, when even Roosevelt had doubts about himself, as he could not avoid having after 1921, there was Howe, ready by his side with plans to carry them headlong to the White House.

Viewing this gray eminence, as he slouched in the back, makes it clear that something far more complicated was under way that day in the Assembly. Little was as it seemed about this new governor.

Roosevelt's seventy-five-year-old widowed mother, Sara, also sat on the dais, near a stone-faced ex-governor Smith and her son's incoming state officials. She wasn't fond of such company, even if lovingly proud of her only child. Nonetheless, she and her financial advisers controlled most of his money, and the money had strings. A decade earlier, she had threatened to cut him off when, after having been caught in an affair, he had talked of giving Eleanor a divorce. Nor had "Mama" wanted him to return to politics after the catastrophe at Campobello. She had intended for him to retire as an invalid squire to what was really her Hyde Park home.

Roosevelt's own record of moneymaking in the Roaring Twenties had been, at best, mixed. In 1921, he earned the first serious income of his own by becoming vice president of an insurance broker, Fidelity & Deposit. Then in 1924, while struggling to recover, he left one small law partnership to establish a more venturesome one at 120 Broadway. As a rainmaker, he also got into promoting a half dozen dubious startups in this age of hot speculation. But none of these bets compared to the attainments of his peers at white-shoe law firms or the House of Morgan. And making money is the prime American standard of achievement.

Roosevelt still felt an emotional bond with Eleanor, the unhappy child of an alcoholic father, who had been orphaned at nine. However, they had kept to separate beds since his affair came to light, and they maintained a professional arrangement warmed by some affection, as she threw herself into Democratic and humanitarian causes. Those didn't necessarily involve him.

Nor were the children of this winning couple a joyful brood. People close to the situation already detected "problems" among these offspring, who increasingly felt excluded from their parents' preoccupied lives. Altogether, the Roosevelt family was full of secrets, as in an Edith Wharton tale of patrician New York. There were many pretenses, as there had been with Franklin Roosevelt's parents, who had felt they were being pushed aside by waves of richer if less wellborn people as a Gilded Age of enormous wealth swelled around them.

Yet Roosevelt's smile was ever on display. So, too, was his "unfailing good humor," as his speechwriter Sam Rosenman noted. To some, that smile seemed inauthentic. Cultural critic H. L. Mencken called it his "Christian Science smile." It showed a denial of pain as he willed himself forward. Edmund Wilson, the literary artist, went further in saying that this smile "fairly makes one's flesh creep."[3] Just so, the "unfailing good humor" might not be convincing: the *unfailing* part of this happy description was unlikely.

And acuter eyes might detect the subtly altered tailoring of his morning dress, from Rinaldi & Scogna in Washington. His trousers were actually cut wide at the bottom to disguise the heavy, black-painted long steel braces that had to be snapped tight to let him stand. The extrawide open-button cuffs on the jackets he bought from Savile Row and Brooks Brothers made it easier to help him dress, a process that started with him lying on his back. His shoes also had to be bespoke, by Peale (of London). Paralyzed virtually from the waist down, he was far more impaired than he admitted.

Already Roosevelt was a lonely man, as his only daughter, Anna, would remind her mother after he died; and already he was the coldest of men as, sixteen years hence, his sharp-eyed vice president, Harry Truman, would conclude. Roosevelt had few illusions about himself, and might say he was "mean at heart," though such candor depended on whom he was talking with, and on what he was trying to pull off.[4]

He always cherished the regard of Endicott Peabody, his headmaster at Groton. Peabody's influence meant more to him than that of anyone besides his mother and his father, the latter dying when he was eighteen. The rector expected his boys to harbor the boarding school virtues of public service and opposition to injustice. These qualities his pupil had in spades.

Reporting on the inauguration, a front-page article in the conservative Democratic *New York Times* described an unusual scene: "The crippled condition of the new Governor made it impossible for him to proceed to his place on the rostrum by coming down the aisle of the Assembly chamber," and "a system of ramps had been constructed to enable him to reach the platform in his wheel chair."[5]

On the one hand, Roosevelt could not avoid being seen in a wheelchair that day—and it was better to have people see him as a courageous invalid on the mend than as an embarrassed sneak who might have slipped onto the dais earlier. Alternatively, his act of somehow being able to walk was improving over time. There would be many ways for a governor, then for a president, to conceal whatever it was he wanted to hide.

Later in 1929, when reflecting on his ordeal, Roosevelt would tell Frances Perkins, whom he would appoint the state's industrial commissioner (in effect labor secretary), that "God had abandoned me."[6] Much was boiling inside a man who could never again stride along the Hudson or plant poplar seedlings, as he liked to watch his tenants doing in the fields of Hyde Park. Nor, because of infidelity, could he enjoy an intimate marriage—that experience having been nearly equal to the polio in making him feel that part of his life was broken. And so, he was already drawing near to him other people whom God was forsaking.

Initially, of course, there was Louis Howe. Also, he had recently retained a valet, Irvin McDuffie, who had been a barber in Atlanta until scalding water ruined his legs.[7] But there would be no self-pity for Roosevelt. Such feelings had been drilled out of him by his parents, by Groton, by an iron will, and by knowing the public could detect unhappiness, and would loathe it.

Roosevelt had won the governorship in 1928 by 25,608 votes out of more than four million, whereas Smith—running for president—had conclusively lost his home state. Had it not been for that 0.6 percent margin, as Smith said later, there would have been no Franklin Roosevelt.

From the moment of victory, Louis Howe was already looking ahead. "His Franklin" would run for president, ideally in 1936. If any Democrat had a shot, it would most likely be a man from New York—the richest and most populous state—like Governor Grover Cleveland in 1884 and again in '92. Furthermore, Howe argued, T.R. had surely been no typical Republican in '04, and had bolted the party in 1912 to finish second as a Bull Moose progressive. That said, it still seemed doubtful that Franklin Roosevelt could reach the White House from Albany.

The Republican platform of 1928 tells why. "Nominees of Republican National conventions have for 52 of the 72 years since the creation of our party been the chief executives of the United States," it boasted.[8] And so people believed it would remain. Woodrow Wilson, who Roosevelt served under while at Navy, had been the only sitting Democratic president to be reelected between 1832 and, as it would prove, 1936. Since the Civil War, control of both houses of Congress had usually been in Republican hands as well. Furthermore, this GOP hammerlock meant that Republican presidents had appointed most justices of the Supreme Court.

Despite the clout of New York State, Albany was no more a waystation to the presidency than it had been for former Republican governor Charles Evans Hughes in 1916—let alone for Democrat Al Smith in '28.

The two parties were also different from today regarding the loyalties of Black Americans. Republicans called themselves the "Party of Lincoln" and counted on keeping the Black vote—outside the South, that is. Not that the Republican Party concerned itself with issues of racial justice anymore, other than proposing an anti-lynching bill in 1922, which Southern Democrats filibustered to death.

Democrats, in turn, depended on the eleven states of the Old Confederacy as a voting bloc. Those had stuck together, at least until '28, when religious bigotry and Smith's alleged radicalism split the Solid South. Additionally, the South's old bull legislators had a grip on party machinery. Ultimately, the Democratic Party's most reliable base rested on unspoken violence. Terror kept Black Americans from voting in the South, while lesser modes of suppression such as the poll tax negated the vote of poor whites. The worst atrocities and insults to the Constitution were not enough to refute states' rights.

For example, just three days before Governor Roosevelt's inauguration, "a negro," as reported, had been burned at the stake in Mississippi.

(*The New York Times* wouldn't capitalize "Negro" until March 1930.) This savagery was extreme, even for Sunflower County in the Delta. A storm of telegrams from around the nation, including from queasy Southerners, poured into Governor Theodore Bilbo's office, demanding that he investigate. However, the inquiring governor pronounced the cause of death unknown.

America was split by enormous divides. Al Smith said that he'd seen blazing effigies of himself wherever he campaigned in the South in '28. Not only was he a "catlicker" (i.e., Catholic, in the parlance of a resurgent Ku Klux Klan), but a half-Irish, half-Italian from New York's Lower East Side. When near a microphone, the way he pronounced "rad-ee-oo" identified him as a member of the coastal proletariat.

Alternatively, President Coolidge in 1928 was delivering a high-tech and industrial "Coolidge boom," which people naturally wanted to roar on.

Herbert Hoover was Coolidge's famous secretary of commerce. Once he was inaugurated, and if the proud GOP platform were correct, he would likely be in the White House for eight shining years, likely to be succeeded by another Republican. Nonetheless, Louis Howe knew that boomtimes don't last, and he yearned for a timely recession, perhaps around 1935.

Meanwhile, Roosevelt had to govern, which he did as a hands-on chief executive who built on Smith's liberal record. He also pushed his own farsighted legislation, such as a bill to abolish mandatory life sentences for four-times-convicted felons. Even critics granted that he was a more empathetic and insightful man than had been the callow striver of his early Washington years—the type of raw careerist who told jokes about his mild-mannered superior, the landlubberly Navy Secretary Josephus Daniels. Polio—that mysterious virus known as "the gray death"—had indeed changed him.

The second-toughest job in Albany went to Frances Perkins as "industrial commissioner," basically the head of the state's labor department. On January 14, she was sworn in by an admiring judge who was a family friend. "Your qualifications and fitness were the only reasons you were selected," he assured her. "Not because you were a woman."[9] Her twelve-year-old daughter stood alongside; her husband was notably absent.

Perkins had first met Roosevelt when he was a state senator. On that New Year's Day 1929 inauguration, as a snowstorm howled outside, he had placed her next to his mother on the dais, where Perkins chatted away with the formidable Sara Delano Roosevelt.

Perkins was of medium height, with olive skin and vivid dark-brown eyes. To appear serious, she already wore austere black dresses, which would become as familiar as her tricorne hat—an echo of colonial times— perched on short-bobbed hair. The hat, her mother had instilled into her as a child, might offset her round, unappealing face. Her father was a store clerk who opened a stationery business in Worcester, Massachusetts, and she used her family's old yet modest lineage to don a grander persona. The changes were slight—born a Congregationalist, then being confirmed Episcopalian—except, her enemies would hiss during the battles to come, might not she really be Jewish?

Fanny Coralie Perkins, as christened, graduated from Mount Holyoke ('02, chemistry) and had taught science from 1904 to 1907 at the exclusive Ferry Hall girls' school in Lake Forest, outside Chicago. While teaching, she worked part-time at the Chicago Commons settlement house and volunteered at the social reformer-activist Jane Addams's Hull House on the city's West Side.

She moved to Philadelphia in 1907 to work at an interfaith organization founded by the Episcopal Diocese, where she fearlessly rescued immigrant girls from pimps at a time when "immigrant" included Black girls fleeing the South. She studied at the University of Pennsylvania, social work becoming her profession in the heyday of Theodore Roosevelt's Progressive Era. Thereafter, she moved to New York to live in settlement houses and earn a master's degree (in sociology and economics) from Columbia in 1910.

The National Consumers League hired Perkins to fight child labor and press the state legislature for a law imposing a maximum fifty-four-hour workweek for women and children. On Saturday, March 25, 1911, she stood aghast in Washington Place to see the Triangle Shirtwaist Company's sweatshop consumed by flames. One hundred forty-six people, mostly young immigrant women, were burned to death or jumped hopelessly from ten stories up. She never shook off the feeling of being part of the horror.

Perkins appeared as an expert witness before the city's investigating commission, and thereafter headed a citizens' Committee on Safety in the workplace—although she was still not allowed to vote. Such efforts for social well-being were privately funded, and the financier R. Fulton Cutting, the "First Citizen of New York," a descendant of Livingstons and Schuylers, donated $100,000.

Testing fire escapes and walking factory floors, she helped introduce the country's broadest range of health and safety laws. After 1918, she became Governor Al Smith's adviser on labor issues. All along she was meeting eminent New Yorkers, such as the self-effacing William Woodin, head of that huge family-controlled enterprise, the American Car & Foundry Company. She also encountered a newer elite, including Henry Morgenthau, Sr., an honest, openhearted real estate operator who owned large tracts of Manhattan, and soon of the Bronx. She made his twenty-something son, Henry Jr., a factory inspector. To her annoyance, this "problem child" would last only two months.

She married Paul Caldwell Wilson in 1913 and all seemed perfect for a while. He was among the gallant young men who had become public-spirited aides to New York City's progressive Mayor John Purroy Mitchel, and, appropriately, a top-ranked bridge player at the Whist Club. Tragically, bipolar disorder struck him in early 1918. He became withdrawn and nearly unemployable. Such a misfortune in one's family was compromising—emphatically so for a woman who should anyway be home with her ailing husband, who let it be known that she did not cook, and whose absence at work, people whispered, might have caused his breakdown in the first place. And why had she not taken his name?

Perkins would always be clouded by a deep sadness. For years to come, she struggled to maintain the appearances of the upper-class life into which she had married. She needed to pay for the care of her husband and then, when her daughter suffered a nervous breakdown, for more doctors. Moreover, unlike her wellborn friends, Perkins was compelled to work her entire life. To be sure, she had earned impressive degrees. But, when reminiscing, she would insist that she had never wanted an actual career, in contrast to a traditional family of the time, and lament that "all this forced me into a professional life which married women . . . don't ordinarily undertake."[10] Regardless, she was devoutly religious, and felt an undying sense of duty to an Episcopalian God.

Franklin Roosevelt already knew her story because he grasped the fine gradations of New York and New England society, relished gossip, and had an unsurpassed network of eager informants.

Just before his inauguration, he had invited Perkins to Hyde Park to discuss her becoming industrial commissioner. He laughed heartily, she recalled, and asked if she didn't think it funny that Governor Smith had cautioned him that men would find it hard to take orders from a woman. "No, I don't think it's funny," she replied.[11]

She accepted and moved fast, threatening to jail employers who evaded workers' compensation insurance, which New York progressives had enacted in 1914. No longer, she warned, would the state Labor Department just monitor health and safety regulations. She would use its police powers to haul violators of all these codes into court, too. Among such laws was the "one-day-rest-in-seven" proviso to counter the ruthless employers' jingle, "Don't come in Sunday, don't show up Monday."

She headquartered herself at the Labor Department's offices on East Twenty-Eighth Street in Manhattan. After all, New York City held four-fifths of the state's factories and their workers, plus Manhattan gave her better access to experts. Her office was a fairly quick drive from the large, sunny fourth-floor apartment she loved on the corner of Madison and Eighty-Ninth Street. Working in the city also meant that she could dash home to attend to the emergencies of her tormented husband.

Another social worker was toiling six blocks away, at 244 Madison Avenue. Harry L. Hopkins had been running the New York Tuberculosis and Health Association since 1924. He too looked much like he would when known worldwide: six feet one inch tall, 160 pounds, dark-brown eyes, hair thinning. He wore the same shirt for two or three days, his rumpled suits stained and spattered from fueling himself on black coffee and Lucky Strikes.

Perkins had known his sister, Adah, since around 1915 when they had met at the Charities Building, which still stands near Gramercy Park. At the time, it served as a twenty-four-hour-a-day hub for numerous, mostly Protestant federations, such as the Children's Aid Society and the Association for Improving the Condition of the Poor (AICP). *Charities Review,* for which Adah wrote, was located there as well. When Adah's "kid brother," as she called him, came east after graduating from Iowa's Grinnell College in 1912, she found him work directing activities for boys at Christodora House ("Gift of Christ") on the Lower East Side's Avenue B. Harry had studied Applied Christianity and been class president. He fit well at Christodora, then advanced just as quickly to professional social work at AICP.

Adah and Harry were the plucky children, among six, of a harness maker in Sioux City at a time when, early in the century, harness making was an admired, skillful calling. Once in New York, however, Harry proclaimed himself a son of the proletariat. He soon married Ethel Gross, a Hungarian-born "poor, struggling Jewish girl," as he later described her, whom he met through Christodora. Ethel was well connected too. She had lived in France as secretary to the rich American founder of the Equal Suffrage Association, helpfully knew the director of Christodora, and had many friends among the city's bohemian artists and actors.

In 1917, Hopkins joined the Red Cross's Division of Civilian Relief to aid the families of servicemen as America moved toward war. Disqualified from military service by bad eyesight, he remained at the Red Cross to again rise fast, this time to run all southeastern U.S. operations. He lived alone in New Orleans and then in Atlanta, and responsibilities became grueling once the influenza pandemic struck in 1918–1919. By 1921 he was back in New York, and the following year, he accepted the directorship of New York's tuberculosis association, a critical piece of the city's public health infrastructure. The uncurable disease claimed five thousand New Yorkers a year, with Blacks dying at about twice the rate of whites.

As with Perkins, his charitable work enabled him to meet such of the city's benefactors as Thomas Lamont of J.P. Morgan & Co. Already Hopkins was visibly on the make. He was drawn by the glitter of Manhattan's theaters and speakeasy nightclubs and the Louis XIII *hôtels particuliers* along Vanderbilt Row. With no chips on his shoulders, he was so transparent that few seemed to mind.

In 1926, he launched into an office affair with Barbara Duncan, a fair-haired nurse ten years younger than he, from an upper-middle-class family in Michigan. This betrayal involved imaginative deceptions. In summer 1928, he sailed for Europe for the first time, sponsored by the Milbank Fund, to study conditions in the London slums. He wrote passionately to Ethel on stationery from the fancy Royal Palace Hotel in Kensington, while returning secretly to New York ten days earlier than claimed to spend time with Barbara. On what little money he possessed, he promoted himself to first-class travel throughout.

That year Hopkins's father died, leaving him and Adah one dollar each. For all Hopkins's fine salary, he was a spendthrift as had been his father. It was not the home in suburban Yonkers or the small country place in Woodstock, let alone support for Ethel and their three boys, that drained him. Extravagant restaurants, top hotels, and the racetrack ensured that money ran through his fingers. Once it was gone, he borrowed from Ethel's brothers. He hadn't a cent to contribute to Roosevelt's campaign during fall 1928, merely getting a handshake at a rally.

Guilt over his marriage drove him into psychotherapy at $2.50 an hour, and he was diagnosed with "nervousness." His analyst apparently heard Hopkins explain how he only married Ethel to "shock the good Methodists back in Iowa"—an explanation hard to believe even from Hopkins. Anyway, by March 1929, he and Ethel were separated, his debts unpaid. He was already "an ulcerous type," observed a physician at the Tuberculosis and Health Association.[12] Moreover, he was sinking into more self-destructive habits.

By 1929, America had passed through a fevered history of boom and bust, at least as far back as Charles Dickens's Ebenezer Scrooge, who fears that the riches the Ghost has shown him are mere "United States securities." The country experienced repeated financial excesses, including the near decade of rampant speculation after the Civil War and the crisis of 1893, followed by the populist Democrats' ringing calls for inflation. At the time, a traveler could not expect the dollar to always be a dollar. A $50 check deposited in St. Louis, for example, got a premium of $3 if drawn on a New York bank.

Demands for serious reform followed; a seminal one was the Federal Reserve System that Congress created in 1913 to steady the economy.

"Progressivism" is a term that keeps redefining itself, as with all major political movements. Early in the century, progressives backed an unembarrassed growth of the state by urging the government to intervene against the excesses of big business, at a time when the Democratic Party remained nervous about reaching much beyond Jeffersonian self-restraint. The face of the Progressive Era in the fifteen years before World War I had been that of Theodore Roosevelt, especially after he left the White House in March 1909. When he returned to the arena in 1912 to fight again for the presidency, Jane Addams seconded his nomination.

T.R. inspired only one weighty political figure of the New Deal more than he did Cousin Franklin and Frances Perkins. This was Harold Ickes, a troubled, apparently mediocre Chicago lawyer who had been steeped in progressive politics since his twenties.

Ickes, born in 1874, had grown up poor near Altoona, Pennsylvania, of Scottish-German ancestry. At age thirteen, he hid a pistol under his pillow should he need to kill his brutal father. Three years later, the boy fled to Chicago after the death of his adored mother. He lived with an aunt and uncle and spent seven years working his way through John D. Rockefeller's newly endowed University of Chicago, from which he graduated in 1896. He thereafter got by as a $12-a-week reporter for the *Chicago Tribune,* branching out to manage quixotic political campaigns in the city. His candidates inevitably lost.

Finally, in 1907, at the age of thirty-three with a law degree from Chicago, he felt ready to defend the weak and humble the strong. Ickes, a five-foot, seven-inch bespectacled fireplug with sandy hair and blue eyes, was always set for a fight, ever ready to turn the merest slight into a scalding enmity.

Right away Ickes sought out such noble, unpopular cases as representing the Women's Trade Union League and advocating for Hull House when it became enmeshed in a tragedy no other lawyer would touch—a Russian Jew, an alleged anarchist, shot in the back by the Chicago PD. Ickes got the body disinterred to make his stunning case.

Come 1911, he married Anna Wilmarth, the social-activist daughter of an alcoholic Chicagoan who had made a fortune in the gaslight fixtures business. Having honeymooned in Europe for three months, they entered a miserable twenty-five-year marriage. Money was no concern, a good thing because Ickes never earned much anyway from his year upon year practice as the informal "people's counsel" in Chicago, litigating angrily for then remote causes like the ten-hour workday.

Ickes met his idol, T.R., in Chicago during 1912, donated a munificent $1,000 to his Progressive Party campaign (which turned out to just be for time and services), and soon visited him in Oyster Bay. Better still, in 1916, the former president—while speaking in Chicago for military preparedness—agreed to be the guest of honor at a luncheon party Mr. and Mrs. Ickes were hosting at their substantial new house, Hubbard Woods, in the posh suburb of Winnetka.

The couple must have been on their best behavior. In private, their physical combat was rough. Ravenous lovemaking ensued, which we know from Ickes's unpublished 1,117-page memoir that discloses the deepest intimacies of his disordered life. They did have a son, Raymond, born in 1912, whom Ickes loved.

In 1918, at age forty-four, Ickes got his chance to flee Anna by serving as a wartime administrator with the YMCA, based in Paris. His twenty-two-year-old stepdaughter, Frances, was already there as a volunteer nurse in a Red Cross hospital near the Bois de Boulogne. He seduced her in his suite at the Hôtel Seville. Anna, smoldering in Winnetka, learned of the incident. Even so, there would be no divorce once he was home. Enraged and depressed, he would write, "I did not care if I lived or died."

These were among the crippling aspects of Ickes's life, further tortured by insomnia. Depression bore down on him and, absent the range of medications available today, his endless disappointments only inflamed it.

At Jane Addams's insistence, Ickes chaired the Chicago branch of the NAACP for a year early in the twenties. Otherwise, he championed foredoomed causes, such as suing the city utilities monopoly on behalf of his self-styled People's Traction League, and the banning of literacy tests for immigrants as a requisite for voting.

He also doted on his now-teenage son, Raymond, whom he trained as a marksman and as a welterweight boxer, but Ickes never ceased his bitter struggle with Anna. She sent him letters—while they lived under the same roof—about her humiliation before the servants. In response, he could only bring up his "wrecked ambitions . . . my friendlessness and lonlinness [sic]," which she was compounding.[13]

He diverted himself from his misery in several ways. During the mid-1920s, he took up stamp collecting, which became a lifelong passion, and patronized the nation's top dealers. In 1928, moreover, he finally managed a successful political campaign to elect Anna as a Republican reformer to the Illinois state legislature in happily distant Springfield. His energetic support, she scolded, sprang only from his desire to be rid of her.

Most of all, Ickes took his first steps to immortality—in this case as a gardener. For his work in that gentlemanly pastime, he has ever after been honored by the American Dahlia Society.[14] As always, he had to be number one, and nearly got U.S. Plant Patent Number 1 for a flower, only to be edged out by a rose grower. Nonetheless, he was first to patent a dahlia, the "king of flowers." All in all, he suggests in his 1943 autobiography, he would rather have been a florist than a fighter for justice.[15] Maybe so, but before coming to Washington, he was quick to sue anyone who violated the patent of the "Anna W. Ickes Dahlia."

In spring 1929, Ickes referred to himself as a "has-been." On the upside, at least he was making money in the stock market, as was everyone else.

For the first time, Ickes had been able to pick up some of the bills for Hubbard Woods and indulge Anna with extravagances that could run up to $10,000 a year. By summer 1929, he was deep into equities, backed by assets from Anna's fortune.

Life in Winnetka, then as today, was a different world from much of an America that had been adjusting painfully to the shift from an agricultural economy to an industrial one. Farmers had long demanded what the weekly Corn Belt newspaper *Wallace's Farmer* dubbed "parity" with the earnings of industrial workers: a farmer should receive roughly the same for selling his goods as he needed to pay for buying the manufactured products essential to his labors. In the heartland, the roar of the 1920s was that of a gale fanning the flames of rage.

Wallace's Farmer affirmed midwestern hopes and grievances alike. Henry Agard Wallace, born in 1888, grew up with the paper and became the last of his family to control it. Even before Iowa State College—Class of '10, and a whiz at math—he had been fascinated by the growth of corn. After graduation, he wrote for the *Farmer*, kept experimenting with corn, and in time, would develop a hybrid called Copper Cross.

He married the daughter of an Indianola real estate broker. They had three children, the last born in 1920, the year when he published the first of eleven books. It is one of the earliest works on econometrics, *Agricultural Prices*. Meanwhile, there was much he did not share with his wife, Ilo, and he was often so remote as to appear indifferent to his sons.[16] It was statistical tables and calculations about exact quantities of produce that danced through his head.

Politicians in Washington valued *Wallace's Farmer* as a listening post for midwestern opinion. Henry Wallace's father—Henry Cantwell Wallace, or "Harry"—made the most of that.

The father was a Republican power broker in Iowa as well as a journalist.

President Warren Harding appointed him secretary of agriculture in 1921 to a Cabinet ruled by big business. When Harding died suddenly in 1923, to be succeeded by Calvin Coolidge, Harry Wallace was kept in office. So was Herbert Hoover, the secretary of commerce. In 1924, amid a vicious battle with Hoover over raising farm incomes, Harry died after a gall-bladder operation. For the rest of his life, his son believed that Hoover had killed his father as plainly as if he had shot him.

Young Henry Agard maintained his family's Republican loyalties, and kept editing *Wallace's Farmer,* which gave him a pulpit to excoriate Hoover, and even to support Al Smith's doomed Democratic candidacy in 1928. By the following summer, he was also struggling with a money-losing business he had launched three years earlier on his wife's small inheritance, the Hi-Bred Corn Company.

It is unlikely that Henry Wallace lost sleep over Hi-Bred, nor, for that matter, over what soon befell his paper. He was preoccupied with finding the right formula or philosophy to help impose order upon a fallen world. Throughout, observed the historian Arthur M. Schlesinger, Jr., who had occasion to meet him, "neither mysticism nor rhetoric could abolish the fissure, the emptiness, at the core of [Wallace's] personality."[17]

He always seemed odd, mused bankers in Des Moines. Yes, he might look like a solid man of the soil: nearly six feet tall, weighing 175 pounds, lean face, chiseled features, blue eyes, thick reddish-brown hair, a starchy voice, and the mild untidiness of a man who was happiest in his fields. The press called him "taciturn," or "remote."

Nonetheless, he appeared an authentic Hawkeye, and like most farm families, the Wallaces loathed Wall Street. Ultimately, the debts from farm country ended up in the hands of anonymous people at the lower tip of Manhattan. Businessmen in Chicago—and good-government types like Ickes—were equally bitter. Chicago was the central creditor to the Midwest, though locked into a banking system swayed by Eastern financiers, or "money changers" as Franklin Roosevelt was about to paint them.

Roosevelt visited Cambridge for his twenty-fifth reunion in mid-June 1929, during Harvard University's commencement. He spoke of "The Age of Social Consciousness," which outlined the themes behind his re-forming efforts at Albany. A quarter century later, the *Harvard Crimson,* of which he had been president, recalled that joyful day in "a beautifully tranquil world in which happy boys and girls romped under a gentle sun while the stock market rose in an always ascending curve."[18]

The prevailing wisdom throughout that enticing summer could be heard from the normally grim registrar of the U.S. Treasury. "A fool is someone who doesn't believe Radio will reach 500," this official told a skeptical Robert Maynard Hutchins, the new, thirty-year-old president of the University of Chicago. "Radio," as everyone knew, being RCA, the hottest stock of 1929.[19]

In July, Eleanor Roosevelt left with her youngest children on a trip through France, Germany, and Belgium, having shipped over two Buick Roadsters for their vacation. Her journey reflected the moment as well. This would be the last time—for at least twenty years—that the family of an elected official could so traipse around Europe. Soon enough, voters would find the very notion intolerably extravagant.

Roosevelt had become governor at exactly the right juncture—the start of 1929, before the market crashed in late October. Had he run for governor a term or two later, in 1930 or 1932, voters would have taken his patrician charm, Groton-Harvard enunciation, and apparent wealth rather differently. As it was, he had slid, during the best of times, into an essential victory.

Trees don't grow to the sky, moneymen say on the Street, except 1929 was one of those years when many investors insisted *this time* was different—as, in a way, it was. America was enjoying an authentic surge of scientific and technological creation: Nobel Prizes, Ford's newly completed River Rouge complex, plus a slew of entrepreneurial airlines and ever-taller skyscrapers. In such a world, men like Henry Ford, aviator-entrepreneur Eddie Rickenbacker, and self-made millionaire Herbert Hoover, above all, seemed the more likely figures to take America into the future than, say, the grandson of a highborn New Yorker whose clipper ships had plied the China trade.

President Hoover was determined to uphold "the individual and local sense of responsibility and self-reliance," and Republicans hailed the economy that summer of '29 for its record-breaking successes.[20] So, what could go wrong?

By any standard, Wall Street's business culture was unlikable: anti-Semitic, anti-Catholic, anti-most-people. From its heights gazed men like

Winthrop Aldrich, forty-four, who was crafting a merger early that fall to make Chase National the world's largest bank, which he would of course chair. Known as "Mr. Wall Street," his columns in *Who's Who* exuded power: graduate of Harvard College, commodore of the New York Yacht Club, member of seventeen other clubs, son of a thirty-year senator from Rhode Island, and director of America's biggest corporations who, on financial matters, spoke for his brother-in-law, John D. Rockefeller, Jr. Aldrich was easy to underestimate, and he found these aristocratic trappings effective camouflage for a sharp mind (top of his class at Harvard Law).

Men such as he were glad to buy you a drink at the Down Town Association before ruining you. It was a culture that had always irritated Roosevelt—and that would repulse Ickes and Wallace, the more they learned of it—while offering a way of living large that tantalized Harry Hopkins.

To Perkins, this culture was familiar. Women of the social circles into which she had made her way comprised the wives or daughters of such masters of the universe. Harriet Aldrich, for instance, was a friend from the settlement-house movement—not only the wife of "Mr. Wall Street" himself but a granddaughter of Charles Crocker, a builder of the Central Pacific Railroad.

Other friends included Caroline Love O'Day, a widow who served on the state board of social welfare and whose father-in-law had been an associate of John D. Rockefeller; and Florence Lamont, wife of the acting head of J.P. Morgan & Co. when the witching hour struck. Perkins's closest friend of all, Mary Harriman Rumsey, was the daughter of the railroad baron E. H. Harriman. A Barnard alumna, Rumsey had founded the Junior League for the Promotion of Settlement Movements (today simply the Junior League) and moved easily between helping the poor and giving magnificent parties.[21]

The fathers and husbands of these women were generous enough, too. Winthrop Aldrich and his Bankers Club, for instance, wrote large checks to the State Charities Aid Association. Yet settlement houses, the Community Chest, and civic groups altogether were about to be submerged. In 1929, the U.S. government was less prepared than that of any modern nation to provide necessities for its suddenly destitute citizens—as would be the case again in 2020. Earlier panics could not compare to what was about to descend, and no one imagined the worst.

2

ECONOMIC PLAGUE

October 1929 to Campaign Summer 1932

We are all waiting, waiting for something to turn
up . . . but why this paralysis of the intellect?
Anne O'Hare McCormick, correspondent, *The New York Times*

In October 1929, even before the Crash, more than 60 percent of people in the United States were living at or below the margin of a decent existence, and one-tenth of the 1 percent of the families at the top of the economic scale received about as much income as 42 percent of the families further down that scale. Such numbers suggest why much of the country yearned for more than a return to "the American standard of living."[1]

The economic breakdown exposed many ailments that had appeared normal to American life—and those included how great fortunes had shaped all forms of policy in a nation whose labor unions were "dead," and capital markets uncontrolled.[2]

Three long years dragged on between the collapse and Roosevelt's arrival as president, by which time more than a quarter of Americans were out of work, and national income had fallen by half. Contrary to myth, a decent man like Herbert Hoover was not bound by laissez-faire passivity.[3] In 1930, his White House pressed for action at a moment when the country spent a larger part of its GDP on infrastructure than it did in 2020. He boosted public works and, eventually, set up the Reconstruction Finance Corporation to offer credit intended to "trickle down"—said that great industrialist, Treasury Secretary Andrew Mellon—to railroads, banks, and corporations. A larger role for government, argued Hoover, risked "socialism and collectivism."[4]

Moreover, during his presidency, it was an almost subversive notion to assume that American citizens could be as at risk of danger in peace as in war, and that Washington had to help. Eminent businessmen, including Winthrop Aldrich, condemned government aid to the unemployed, only to demand federal assistance once their own enterprises teetered.

Franklin Roosevelt observed all this unfold while completing his first year as governor. His accomplishments seemed promising even to opponents. In private, however, he told Frances Perkins—whom he was drawing close—that "I haven't got my full strength." She believed such "sickness and crippledness" made him determined to show he could operate alone.[5] That said, she recognized one of his best qualities—an openness to new ideas.

Such receptivity was going to be vital, given the times. He would need to grasp that being poor in America was a soul-destroying experience—as it remains today, and to a degree unknown in other prosperous countries. In a system geared for individual success, and with far too few safety nets, the down-and-out stand accused of lacking self-reliance. These feelings can whip up terrifying resentments all around.

In the run-up to the Crash, as today, a relatively small number of wealthy families owned the vast majority of shares controlled by U.S. households, and—also like today—financial markets were detached from events on Main Street. Soon after taking office in Albany, Perkins saw red lights flashing from her state's unemployment statistics. Requesting additional research, she tracked the rising joblessness. Months before Black Tuesday, October 29, 1929, she knew what was incubating.

People had always been unemployed during America's booms and busts, though not in such catastrophic numbers. In New York State, layoffs occurred everywhere, and, as during the actual pandemic of our own day, employers frequently took advantage of the relatively few who were hanging on to their jobs. Perkins's Factory Inspection Division counted half a million industrial accidents just in 1930. Immigrants were easiest to exploit, and she insisted that workers who had "funny names like Jablowsky" be compensated just as seriously as were the Joneses for losing toes, fingers, or limbs.[6]

She urged Roosevelt to launch a committee to stabilize industry and prevent mass unemployment. Its remedies included the five-day workweek, something largely unknown, though even here it was a recommendation of despair. Maybe a shortened week could enable companies to keep more workers on the payroll. Another approach was to reduce work hours as well. For men, those were unlimited; for women in New York, the workday was eight hours, in theory.

Perkins also studied Roosevelt. She noticed an expression on his mouth, "where he pulled his lips down, making a sort of long lip." When he did this, she remembered, she "always knew that something phony was going on inside of him."[7] She had much more to discover.

Harry Hopkins was on the front lines as well. The Crash initially motivated benefactors to write bigger checks. Then slowly these generosities tightened, which pulled Hopkins into politics. The Association for Improving the Condition of the Poor (AICP), after all, was the hub of a public health network that included state hospitals and mitigation programs, extending into preventoriums—boarding schools for children without tuberculosis yet who had menacing family histories.

Among others, Hopkins cultivated Henry Bruère, a former protégé of the singular R. Fulton Cutting. Bruère had lived in a settlement house (after Harvard Law) and aspired to be a junior Mr. Cutting: banker, philanthropist, public servant. In the teens, newsmen had called Bruère the "real mayor of New York"—days when he had worked alongside his best friend, Perkins's husband Paul Caldwell Wilson, in city government. Now Bruère consulted Hopkins, and shared Hopkins's ideas in Albany as well as with Perkins, of whom he was a longtime friend.

Hopkins was not on her new unemployment committee, although they crossed paths in the state capital and at her Labor Department's Manhattan offices. In Albany, he would appear with other social workers to convene in groups of ten or twenty with Governor Roosevelt. To be sure, Hopkins was not like other social workers, as Perkins knew, and she realized that he could help with her plan to work the governor toward a different perspective on business.

Details of manufacturing, hiring, sales, and other operations were foreign to Roosevelt. His key adviser, Louis Howe—a political wizard, not a businessperson—was equally unaware. At this time, economics itself was a mystery, given what is still being learned of the discipline. And so Perkins needed to bring to her tutorials a practical knowledge, a command of statistics, and, especially, verve as a storyteller.

"Hopkins knew that my idea was to educate the Governor," she recounted.[8] When the three of them met, she would raise a question, and Hopkins would bat back an answer, or vice versa. Roosevelt naturally became curious. For bitter reasons, she could not march him through paper mills and canning factories as she had his predecessor, Al Smith. Hence the tactic of well-choreographed Q&A. Roosevelt, in turn, developed quick, astute responses for the press.

Hopkins therein had a perfect opportunity, given that he could connect with anyone, slum-dweller or millionaire. To this extent, he was a frail, lower-middle-class version of Roosevelt himself. He loved to experiment, never shouted, and was unfailingly bright, quite funny, and appealing to women. If a yeti had walked into the room, he and Roosevelt alike would have found things in common with it.

Hopkins effused energy as he clarified the efforts of those people equally intelligent, whether bankers or social workers, who lacked his magic. During 1930, he helped privately raise an initial $75,000, under the auspices of the AICP, to subsidize relief work on city properties. Men were paid five dollars a day to maintain city parks, and he made sure that the ensuing publicity emphasized self-help. America's comfortable classes were already alarmed at the dreaded word "dole"—the British slang for government handouts.

Hopkins's ties with Perkins were cordial, the more so as worsening conditions intertwined their duties, and her statisticians handed him the best information on the crisis.

During 1930 and 1931, Perkins held hearings in the most blighted parts of the state. At these literal town halls, where starving bricklayers and debt-burdened farmers vented their fury, she would hear it all. When the minutes came to be written, she nevertheless asked her staff to assume a calmer tone for the record, to avoid panicking both those with money and those without. She backed public works projects as the greatest source of hope, and shared her gospel on the war-level casualties of industrial safety with faculty and students at Harvard Business School. It was both Christian and productive, she held forth, to guarantee decent working conditions.

Her tutorials with Governor Roosevelt continued. She tried to engage him every ten days, when possible, for at least an hour. At one point in her life, Perkins had studied speechmaking. She resorted to Principle One—to make your key point at the opening of a meeting, in the middle, and at the end. His memory for what she had said was then startling.

It was like "Mama tell me a story," she could say after Roosevelt died, and her tales drew on the sorry lives of people and the highest qualities of drama. Who would have thought that dust from the manufacturing of pearl buttons could explode? She described hovels that surrounded the western New York salt mines and mob-run urban sweatshops and told Roosevelt of how toiling children were scalped by heavy machinery. "That's *barbarous*," he would interrupt.[9] Everything was personalized. Old families with whom he was acquainted, such as the Villards, might own some of those mines. She selected businessmen to join her for these briefings, including the owner of the Manning Paper Company in Troy, with whom Roosevelt shared friends.

When working late in Albany, Perkins often stayed at the governor's Italianate mansion rather than take the midnight train to Grand Central. She came to know the Roosevelts informally. A whirl of people attended the governor's lunches, and guests for dinner often stayed the night. She and Eleanor frequently spent hours talking in a bedroom they shared. Roosevelt's secretaries, the quietly formidable Missy LeHand and her assistant Grace Tully, were forever present. In the background, Perkins might glimpse Louis Howe, who had become the governor's behind-the-scenes chief of staff, though his usual lair was Manhattan—where, to her approval, he sang in the choir of St. Thomas Episcopal Church.

Hopkins also came to know Eleanor because of their common preoccupations with emergency relief, even if he was not part of this high-spirited circle at the executive mansion. He was in Albany frequently, though not invited, and unlike Perkins, when he took the New York Central's Empire State Express up from the city, his tickets had to be first class.

For everyone, part of the agony of these years was radically false recoveries, notably the bull market of spring 1930. As during a real plague, what seemed to be the worst was only followed by the yet worse.

The White House and Wall Street incited further distrust by promises of an imminent revival. Such was heard in June from Richard Whitney, the forty-one-year-old president of the New York Stock Exchange. He was an imposing, cold-blooded figure, one more product of Groton and Harvard. He rode to the Essex Fox Hounds in New Jersey, served under Winthrop Aldrich as treasurer of the Yacht Club, and his firm, R. H.

Whitney & Co., was broker for the House of Morgan. In a speech to an investors' association in June 1930, Whitney had looked back on the lessons learned from the October Panic. His belief in what he said was audible. The Exchange had done well in handling that unfortunate mishap; though, he conceded, the stock-ticker system needed to be improved.[10]

Hopkins initially accepted the conceit of men like Whitney, who argued that the Crash was the merest bump in the road, until Perkins convinced him otherwise. She also nudged the cautious Roosevelt to the point where he asked, "Why shouldn't Government act to protect its citizens from disaster?"[11] Nonetheless, during his years as governor, Roosevelt suspected outright aid of being "character-destroying."[12] Perkins took a different approach when bringing Hopkins, and often Henry Bruère, into these colloquies. She spoke of a novel use of the term "insurance" as it applied collectively to unemployment.

Perkins believed property to be an essential part of a free society that government had a responsibility to protect. To her, reform need not undercut the ordinary human right to prosperity. Indeed, she empathized with small businessmen. It was likely to be harder for the owner of, say, a one-hundred-man tool-and-die works in Elmira to meet her department's inspection orders than for DuPont's vast electrochemical plant at Niagara Falls. She did not condemn such giant corporations, but she knew how America's third-largest industrial enterprise could easily deflect regulatory costs onto consumers rather than waste time in court.

Perkins couldn't fathom why critics labeled her anti-employer. Nor, in coming years, did she grasp why Roosevelt would be denounced as anti-business. Many of his political friends were employers, and good ones, whether brewers in Poughkeepsie or felting manufacturers in Rensselaer.

His feelings toward Wall Street moneymen like Aldrich and Whitney were another matter.

On September 12, 1929, some six weeks before Black Tuesday, Henry Wallace sailed for England. He had been to Europe once before, on an agricultural tour after college, and two of his sisters had married diplomats, one Swiss, the other Swedish.

This was a time when overseas travel was rare, except for the rich, and Wallace was to attend a conference in Devon of the world's top thirty-five agricultural economists. He gave two presentations. One was a deeply technical paper on regression theory; the other anticipated a global economic collapse.

After the conference, Wallace traveled through the peaceful and relatively prosperous Germany of the Weimar Republic. He knew German, as did all students of science in those days, and from there he meandered into Hungary, which was under feudal strongman rule. He met with scientists in Budapest before taking the train to Prague, where his sister Mary was living with her husband, Switzerland's ambassador to the new state of Czechoslovakia. He planned to journey on to Japan, via Russia, until he got a telegram. His uncle, who held controlling interest in *Wallace's Farmer*, was about to assume an unsustainable, two-million-dollar debt by acquiring a rival paper. Feeling disaster on his heels, Wallace hurried home in October—though too late to prevent the deal, which was proudly announced in Des Moines on the twenty-sixth, just three days before the Crash.

Soon *Wallace's Farmer* was forced to become a biweekly and—as the heartland's total farm income fell by two-thirds between 1929 and 1932—the paper's sales agents had to accept chickens in lieu of cash. As the family business collapsed, Wallace hung on as editor, and wrote essays about so-called anti-national selfishness and other anguishing topics. Moreover, his startup, Hi-Bred Corn Company, had no employees, no office, and its research and development division filled his basement. But he was possessed by the greatest of visions: there must be a better way of feeding the world than just to grow corn by random pollination.

Meanwhile, Wallace never stopped his political jousting in speeches and editorials. He also explored new vistas, such as trying to find a correlation between the weather and positions of the planets. He used an IBM tabulating machine to squeeze data from thousands of punch cards.

Wallace's fascination with the uses of tomorrow's technology was shared by Perkins—all of which underscores how our four were so often thinking in parallel even before they combined in Washington. For instance, IBM was then headquartered in Endicott, New York, and the achievements of its factory complex featured in her stories for the governor. "International Business Machines has got to invent us a way of keeping these records," she told Roosevelt, referring to the state's expandingly convoluted unemployment files. That might not be easy, she added. The governor would need "to get Tom Watson and stir his conscience." She believed IBM's founder to be ungenerous to his workers.[13]

Around the same period, in early March 1930, *The New York Times* first noticed Wallace. Apparently, wrote the *Times* in a tiny article, Mr. Wallace, "under modern methods of corn breeding," could enhance plants to the degree that cattle could be finely bred.[14] What if he were able to boost America's corn crop 10 percent or more? And what if hybridizing other commodities brought an end to humankind's history of famine?

Another midwestern idealist was sitting some three hundred miles east in Chicago, though Ickes's dreams of changing the world were fading. At least he enjoyed a financial cushion to help ride out the Crash—Anna's downtown real estate interests.

The only passion he and Anna shared besides domestic violence was the Native American. Anna had become a self-taught expert on the Indian cultures of the Southwest, and Ickes had his Indian Rights Association in Chicago, which he ran for a decade. It wasn't hard to mobilize him for any good cause. He liked to dislike people, and his crusades gave him a license to fight.

Anna had bought a second home ten miles from Gallup, New Mexico, adjacent to the 28,000-square-mile Navajo reservation, which she explored with guides between her travels back and forth to Winnetka. Tutored in the language, she worked on completing *Mesa Land* (1933), a deeply informed account of the arid domains of both the Pueblo and the neighboring Navajo. The book is dedicated to "H. L. I." (Harold LeClair Ickes).[15]

Summer 1930 found Mr. and Mrs. Ickes in the dry desert heat of their adobe residence. He chafed at being idle while Anna wrote and spent time with Native American friends. He began to truly worry about the stock market, and by summer's end, could no longer deceive himself that he had escaped unscathed. His losses mounted to around $250,000, roughly $4 million today. He wasn't ruined. On the other hand, he couldn't cover such an amount demanded by his investment firm, Slaughter & Co.

Once back in Chicago, he tried to resolve the mess. Having managed Anna's money for years, he decided to reinterpret the will of his deceased father-in-law. Doing so tripled Anna's income from her Chicago properties while undercutting the inheritances of her two children—Frances, whom he had seduced, and her brother Wilmarth, an attractive, fast-living thirty-one-year-old ne'er-do-well. The stepdaughter didn't care. After the war, she had the good sense to keep the family at a healthy distance. Better still, Harold successfully got Anna reelected to the Illinois General Assembly in November 1930.

As usual, Ickes lived on a checkerboard of misery and undue elation, swinging between times of enormous energy and fits of wearying anger. A prime target of his fury was big business, in which unlike Perkins, he gave employers no benefit of the doubt. Corporations were dishonest and mostly enemies of the Republic. His was a fiercely Jacksonian vision of America, and until the day he died, he was convinced a corporation could never refrain from pursuing anything but its primitive self-interest. A deeper hatred was reserved for those companies that raped the earth of its timber, oil, water, and mineral wealth.

To think of someone like Ickes finding himself trustee of a million square miles of the nation's lands—with a viselike grip on its oil and coal industries—might chill members of Chicago's Union League Club, though the very idea was preposterous.

Loneliness was also stalking each of these four. Ickes could admit his suffering. For him, loneliness was the isolating discovery of himself being solely right while everyone else was wrong. Men he befriended and law partners with whom he tried to work dropped away.

Perkins without a doubt enjoyed people and had long been a public figure. As New York's industrial commissioner, she liked to join farmers at the State Fair in Syracuse during August. Except to her, an authentic affection went to what she called a "private friend." Her loneliness is apparent in the "very, very few friends" she admitted to having, in her despondent marriage, and eventually in her estrangement from her troubled daughter.[16] As a child, Perkins had been intensely shy, and this emotion would return once she broke all barriers by joining the Cabinet of nine men and one very unusual president.

Wallace, guarding his deep empty core, endured another type of loneliness. He consulted an astrologer and spiritualists in 1929, after he had turned to theosophy; then he called upon an occultist and a Native American medicine man in 1930. The following year, he joined the Episcopal Church, having dropped Presbyterianism after reading William

James. Wallace wasn't just on a "spiritual treasure hunt."[17] He felt desperately isolated and was seeking spiritual support. The intensity of this quest pushed away people who tried to get close to him.

As for Hopkins, his isolation might seem least apparent because of the delight he took in café society, the love he shared with his three boys, and his finding of a new life with Barbara Duncan. However, his friends were the people whom he found useful. Loneliness had shaped him during his rise. Early on, his powers had gone unrecognized, and social work could only take him so far.

In 1930, as he turned forty, he might be briefing the governor of New York. Yet as he bantered with one Roosevelt, somewhere in his mind he was aware that another Roosevelt, T.R., had been president at forty-two. The people from whom he sought donations were grandee bankers, lawyers, philanthropists. And where was Harry Hopkins?

Nonetheless, each of these four up-and-comers embodied hope. That was true even of Ickes, who chronicled his "brain fog" over these dozen years, not seeing a psychiatrist until 1945. And most hopeful of all appeared to be Roosevelt.

Still, Perkins, herself deeply lonely, had observed Governor Roosevelt's isolation since their first months together in Albany. He was "a peculiarly lonely person," she reminisced, though one who had countless political friends.[18] His friends outside politics were ones of "propinquity," as she put it—chums from boarding school and Harvard or Yale, perhaps with roots in the Hudson Valley, the sort of men who did not bother themselves with the sordid doings of Albany or Washington.

Then again, he enjoyed exceedingly close ties to a number of women and longed for women in his life other than the busy, distant Eleanor. Above all, there was Missy LeHand, whose keen instincts made her a unique tactical adviser on personnel and policy. Her clicking high heels, flashing blue eyes, and adoration brought them together. Still, neither LeHand nor FDR's cousin, Daisy Suckley, with whom he would form another deep relationship, could be his equals, and there were limits to the emotions he would convey about the men's business of governing. In his last year of life, there would be the newly widowed Lucy Mercer Rutherfurd, his former lover from navy days, to whom he might admit, as he did to the bright, beautiful heiress Dorothy Schiff, that he was lonely. But this he disclosed to very few more. His was a largely self-built enclosure. Had he been an open man, it could have been seen that he was deeply hurt.

Given a boss who would soon call the entire country "mah frens," Perkins concluded that he possessed very few. Missy LeHand, who knew him probably better than Eleanor, determined he "was really incapable of personal friendship with anyone."[19]

By necessity, Roosevelt had to reveal himself to Louis Howe, who shuffled alongside him, wearing a ponderous truss, as FDR's marriage collapsed, as he struggled to regain his life after being stricken with polio, and as he tried and usually failed in business. No one better understood his ambition. Even so, as Perkins also observed, Howe was "more in the category of a high-grade intellectual servant."[20] Howe was devoted to both the Roosevelts, having spent scores of hours coaching Eleanor on the arts of speechmaking. Except here too was a lonely figure, a man who simply acknowledged that most people regarded him with indifference or hatred.

An epoch of surprises arrived with the Crash of 1929. Suddenly Roosevelt, Howe, and the men around them, such as the tall, hearty campaign manager James Farley, saw the opening of a path to greater power. Perkins would be drawn in too. Roosevelt's reelection in November 1930 (two-year terms were extended to four years in 1938) with an impressive majority—in contrast to his previous squeaker—made the path wider. Nationally, the Republicans barely held the Senate and the Democrats had gained a rare slim margin in the House, though progressives of both parties could proclaim a qualified victory.

Roosevelt seemed more physically confident on the campaign trail in 1930 than two years before, and he felt secure when standing in his leg braces while a tall, strong, dependable man or two was near for him to lean on. Soon he was to propel himself in an armless wooden kitchen chair on wheels—a wordless assertion that he was not an invalid, just a strong man in a chair.

State policemen managed his needs. They knew which speaking halls had steps to avoid and what back entrances to use. Concealment was becoming routine; no photos exist showing him being carried from his chair to his car.

Perkins had campaigned for him in the industrial areas that other

leading figures avoided, although when possible she dodged the wearisome ladies' lunches that women's groups tried to arrange in better-off
towns such as Binghamton and Ithaca.

Roosevelt's second two-year term was much like his first, other than
that an organization was being put together to win the presidential nomination in 1932. On one hand, little of such planning directly involved
Perkins. When political pros like Farley and the speechwriter Sam Rosenman plotted, they shut her out as being purely a social worker. On the
other, she was useful, as voters hailed her for delivering widows' pensions,
employment offices, and other services.

Groundwork for the presidential campaign was being laid amid 1931's
even greater banking crisis including, in January, the biggest bust in the
country's history of booms and busts, at New York's Bank of United States.

That month as well, President Hoover announced that employment
had risen the previous month by 4 percent. If trends should continue, all
would be well by May or June. No national unemployment statistics then
existed, but it did not require Perkins's expertise to detect that Hoover's
claim reflected Christmas retail sales. Surely, he could not have made so
basic a mistake.

"I think that was bully," Roosevelt said, channeling Cousin Theodore,
adding that a "bunch of swindlers in Washington" had surely concocted
the illusion.[21] Perkins had given him an argument against the Republicans
anyone could understand.

Hopkins was for now shuttling between the city and Albany while
his personal affairs grew ever more dire. "I am financially bankrupt,"
he wrote Ethel, some months before she divorced him in May 1931. He
could not manage his salary and was penniless. Car and dental bills went
unpaid.[22] In the months before his divorce, overwork laid him open to
bouts of influenza and a collapse into pneumonia.

By June, he was well enough to marry Barbara at the city clerk's office.
Half of his income would go to alimony, and no matter how hard he worked
or modest his home, he lived large when out and about. Ethel had the children, though payments got skipped. Unlike his society friends, moreover,
his marriage had not been dissolved cleanly by a decree in Reno, "divorce
capital of the world." A so-called New York divorce labeled him, on that
state's strict terms, as an adulterer, which might cloud dreams of high office.

There remains no record that he ever saw Ethel again, though they kept up a long, mostly tender correspondence. Few gentiles were married to Jews in those days, nor was divorce common, let alone devoting hours to psychotherapy. Hopkins was a modern man in a hurry.

Now he was beginning to rise incredibly fast. New York State became the first in the country to provide for its destitute citizens, and Hopkins used his contacts to be executive director of Governor Roosevelt's $23 million Temporary Emergency Relief Administration. TERA initiated employment projects as well as dispensed assistance for local welfare agencies. Its very name suggested a hopeful transience.

That summer of 1931, Roosevelt encouraged Perkins to attend a conference on labor policy held in Amsterdam. Combining the trip with a holiday, she booked passage for herself and daughter Susanna on the SS *Rotterdam* to Southampton. In London, headlines blared of the government's imminent collapse under the Labour Party's unbalanced budgets, compounded by a run on gold and talk of cutting never abundant jobless benefits.

For Perkins, vacations often included research, with daughter in tow. She studied how Britain was handling unemployment insurance, and also dug into government archives at Somerset House, where she discovered a will from 1692 by one John Francis Perkins. Such apparent proof of ancient lineage was comforting. Once in Amsterdam, she slipped off from her conference to tour the Rijksmuseum with Susanna, and they visited Haarlem to see Frans Hals paintings. They took the train to Paris, where effects of the Depression were still mild, while the dollar went far. Finally, they sailed home from Le Havre in early September. Perkins's husband Paul was, for the moment, well enough to be waving a handkerchief from the New York pier.

Back in Albany, she saw Governor Roosevelt. "Well, how about unemployment insurance?" he asked. "Are you sold on it? Remember, I'm against the dole."

"I looked at this entirely as a project that would not have the dole," she responded, in what sounds like a cool reply.

"That's the way it went down in Franklin Roosevelt's memory and mind," she would recall in her vast oral history. "We were all opposed to the dole and so was he. To manufacturers who came in to see him on this, he would say, 'I'm opposed to the dole as much as you are.' Whether their minds ever met as to what the dole was, I don't know."[23]

As for Hopkins, he was not the type of man whom Roosevelt would have encountered close-up before he became governor—shabbily dressed, an "ulcerous type" with ruinous personal habits, who touted his plebeian bona fides. Hopkins was certainly unusual, though no more so than Louis Howe, and hence Roosevelt came to recognize Hopkins's gifts as well.

Among these gifts was Hopkins's capacity to handle big, unprecedented tasks by organizing people and resources. He harmonized unlikely factions, such as the state's different religiously based charities. In the northern counties, he used TERA's money to help country churches hire the jobless. Dusty pews and naves needed scrubbing. For New York City, he recruited boys from the slums to plant trees upriver on Bear Mountain and persuaded the state's apple growers to unload their surplus crop on TERA so that he could organize needy men to resell them on the street for five cents each. He also started a public works program for building schools. But as treasuries dwindled, it was difficult to persuade cities such as Rochester or Corning to come up with cash, and enough critics soon coined the term "made work."

The plight of America's second-largest city, Chicago, was as bad as anywhere in New York State. Chicago's teachers were being paid in IOUs and, shockingly at the time, fourteen hundred families were recorded as having been evicted in the first half of 1931 (a far lower rate than today).[24] Ickes had resolved to be rid of politics, always excepting the effort required to keep Anna in Springfield. Nonetheless, he couldn't remain aloof when, as Edmund Wilson reported, "there is not a garbage-dump in Chicago which is not diligently haunted by the hungry."[25]

Ickes urged his fellow T.R. progressive, California senator Hiram Johnson, sixty-five, to challenge Hoover for the nomination. Once Johnson finally declined, Ickes instead committed himself to electing Anton Cermak, a Democratic reformer, as Chicago's mayor, while keeping up his flow of venomous letters to the newspapers.

Wallace was using his pen to better effect. He remained at *Wallace's Farmer* to editorialize that America's path to the Promised Land was blocked by "ignorance, prejudice and hatred."[26] Having discovered how to multiply nature's bounty by hybridization, he saw worthless Iowa corn being used for fuel. Hunger and poverty were sickening a plentiful land,

and ever a knight errant, he arranged a food drive for drought-stricken Arkansas. He reached into his threadbare pocket to pay $420 for three freight cars of corn and oats at a time when average annual income was $1,368, and a fraction of that in the South.

In the darkness of 1931 America, some light was still showing. Word came on December 10 that Jane Addams had received the Nobel Peace Prize. A spokesman in Oslo added that he had visited Hull House where, "in the poorest districts of Chicago, among Polish, Italian, Mexican, and other immigrants," Addams had created a community to uplift them all.[27] Congratulatory telegrams from Ickes and Perkins arrived simultaneously.

Did Americans have to accept depressions as "inevitable," just as people had accepted plagues as part of their cruel lives centuries earlier?[28] Hoover appeared to think so, and his treasury secretary—old, thin, icy Andrew Mellon—certainly did. Roosevelt did not know the answer, though he was inclined to experiment when he avowed his candidacy in January 1932.

Hoover had popularized the term "rugged individualism" during his first presidential run. He exemplified the social mobility for which America was renowned before, in our own day, hopes of rising from the bottom to the top plunged to the lowest ranks among high-income countries. Still, notions of "rugged individualism" did not fit a time when people felt trapped.

Coming down from New York, Perkins testified before the U.S. Senate Committee on Education and Labor about the malnourishment of hundreds of thousands of families. The statistics she displayed on easels looked like fever charts of the nation's health.

In the depths of the Great Depression, 1932 was the only year until 2020 when the stock market declined at least 20 percent in one quarter to bounce back by at least 20 percent in the next. Hopkins used his skills and contacts to ride this roller coaster. In April, he became TERA's president; his work now touched the lives of 40 percent of New Yorkers. The Tuberculosis Association was struggling, in part, due to his absence. Mortality had been dropping steadily, but in Depression conditions, cases of the disease began to climb.[29] Private charities, and even state-by-state improvisations such as TERA, were overwhelmed.

Equally inadequate were plans for recovery heard at the governors' conferences for which Perkins helped Roosevelt prepare. The forty-eight states were confronting the economic plague with a mishmash of uncoordinated approaches.

Between April and December 1932, Hopkins conferred with Roosevelt a dozen times, four by telephone. Hopkins was showing how public relief could be accomplished better than hoped. Meanwhile, a by now well-honed campaign organization was zeroing in on the Democratic National Convention, to be opened at Chicago Stadium on June 27.

Capable adversaries were vying for the presidential nomination. They included former governor Al Smith, who was eager for another shot and backed by many serious men, such as Dean Acheson, a prominent Washington lawyer and future secretary of state. Another contender was Newton Baker, previously a reform mayor of Cleveland and the secretary of war from 1916 to 1921. "He was the greatest man I've ever known," reflected General George C. Marshall years later, who made the point after having worked hand-in-glove with Roosevelt and Churchill to win World War II.[30]

Only on the fourth ballot in Chicago did Speaker of the House John Nance Garner, the fifteen-term congressman from hilly Uvalde, Texas, throw his state's delegates to Roosevelt, which set off an avalanche that brought in California. Not far away at the Congress Hotel, Louis Howe had lain racked by strangling asthma on the floor of his room as Big Jim Farley kneeled to hear him croak out the winning strategy. In turn, the delegates would unanimously acclaim a reluctant Garner—the nation's top Democrat—for vice president.

The convention adjourned on July 2, and one week later, stocks hit bedrock, down 89.2 percent in less than thirty-five months.

Once nominated, Roosevelt's election was assured, and definitely so after July 28, when Hoover deployed the army against civilian protesters in Washington. Veterans of the World War were demanding early payment of a congressionally enacted bonus for their services. Like most of the nation, Washington's police superintendent was appalled when the beribboned army chief of staff, General Douglas MacArthur, deployed cavalry and tear gas to clear out some ten thousand men, women, and children from the Bonus Marchers' encampment.

Over these months, Perkins would occasionally stop at Hyde Park to deliver documents when on her way between Albany and the city, as she did one day that summer. Roosevelt wasn't home, so she sat talking with his mother, Sara, on the terrace overlooking the Hudson. On that languid sunny afternoon, Perkins also stepped through the long French windows into the 22,000-volume library of Springwood—name of the family's actual house. She was curious about Roosevelt's reading habits.

Roosevelt was "always interested in any kind of book," his learned White House aide, William Hassett, would reminisce, and he could often be found browsing.[31] To Perkins, Roosevelt was a walking American history lesson, with much of his knowledge passed down from grandfathers and great-grandfathers, as well as through books—an awareness she believed they had in common.

In later years, when burdened by the presidency, he would pick up anything, including detective novels. While trying to recover after Campobello, however, he read deeply. These books were among the volumes she examined.[32] She knew of his interests in geography and history, so to find Alfred Thayer Mahan's *The Interest of America in Sea Power* was no surprise, nor were various biographies, including several of Bonaparte. He read maps as if they were books, and, splayed on a table, lay big colorful atlases and sagas of exploration such as *Arabia Deserta*.

She saw well-thumbed books on sailing, of course, though what intrigued her were the novels. He did not read modern fiction but loved familiar and dramatic human accounts of great issues in which the hero strides forth, as in *A Tale of Two Cities*. Much historical fiction and tales of exciting political careers were there, too, including Trollope's *The Duke's Children,* among sixteen other volumes by Trollope.

For these novels to be in the library of a Hudson River estate indicates how attached the American gentry remained to the motherland, although Roosevelt never regarded England as his place of origin. The "homeland," as he called it to Dutchmen, was the Netherlands, and somewhere in this library were children's books written in Dutch, which, in time, he would show visitors from Holland, including Queen Wilhelmina.

As the race for president took off early in September, Roosevelt had already found Perkins and Hopkins, as he had found Louis Howe long before. On the advice of a campaign aide, and to court the farm vote, he had also written Henry Wallace in Des Moines, inviting him for lunch at Hyde Park. They met on a Saturday, August 13, which gave Roosevelt more time than usual. Wallace remembered having been suspicious of a typical rich Easterner who didn't know how ordinary people lived.

Although they had never spoken, Roosevelt picked up immediately on how to handle the taciturn, introspective Wallace. They did not discuss politics, but rather the travails that came with farming the rocky Hudson Valley. The conversation went well, and Wallace recognized a stout, generous heart. While en route, however, he had stayed overnight in Albany and heard personal accounts of the governor's shiftiness, which reinforced his original sense that Roosevelt might not be a man with whom to do business.[33]

At that point Roosevelt knew three of our four. Not until the following February, only weeks before Inauguration Day, would he encounter Harold Ickes, every bit as wounded as the others.

3

SURGE TO POWER

November Elections 1932 to Roosevelt's Inauguration, March 1933

In the midst of war and crisis, nothing is as clear
or as certain as it appears in hindsight.
Barbara Tuchman, *The Guns of August*

Mary Harriman Rumsey knew that her close friend Frances Perkins would never accept an invitation to her daughter's debutante ball for the late summer evening of September 16, 1932. Perkins rarely came to extravagant events, though other friends, including Caroline Love O'Day, would not think of missing it. To be sure, Harry Hopkins didn't attend, although Rumsey knew him from her relief projects in the city, such as the Emergency Exchange Association. The trouble was Harry always looked sloppy, and anyway, his new wife was expecting a child in November.

Otherwise, everyone gathered at Rumsey's Sands Point estate on Long Island. Her thousand guests included Winthrop Aldrich, "Mr. Wall Street" himself, and his wife, Harriett; the Richard Whitneys; the Edgar Auchinclosses; the August Belmonts; Nelson Doubleday; Mr. and Mrs. William Randolph Hearst, Jr.; Marshall and Evelyn Field; Tommy Hitchcock, Jr. (the ten-goal polo star) and his wife, Margaret Mellon; Rumsey's younger brother Averell (with his new wife, Marie); Count and Countess László Széchenyi; and a swarm of the junior set.

Women's pages of every major newspaper chronicled the Rumsey ball. Guests were asked to come in overalls rather than white tie. The mansion's splendors were offset by cornstalks and vegetables. Ham, eggs, and applesauce were served for supper. Mary Rumsey wanted to bring attention to farmers who were between the teeth of what by then was being called the Great Depression.

Before the dancing, the hostess startled her guests by setting up a voting machine with two big pictures of the contenders above it. Ballots were cast. Roosevelt hadn't a chance.

Upholding the tradition of playing poor going back at least to Marie-Antoinette, Rumsey was doing so at a time when, in big cities, "people were flopping on the streets from hunger."[1]

President Hoover's assurances of imminent recovery made cynics chortle. The Democrats, they said, would win even with a Jew and a Negro atop the ticket. In contrast, Republicans didn't believe the contest hopeless. Therefore, toward summer's end, Wallace knew he needed to throw himself into the campaign, and Perkins was busy assembling position papers, stumping New York, and speaking in Chicago and in Boston, where she befriended the city's former mayor, John F. "Honey Fitz" Fitzgerald.

Hopkins's ambition had been brought to a "roiling boil" after the Chicago convention, according to his granddaughter's impressive biography. Still, there was little he could contribute. Barbara was expecting, they had no money, and he was frantic to get New York State a loan (not grant) from the federal emergency relief program belatedly launched by Hoover in July.[2]

That same month, Ickes and Wallace—both Republicans—met for the first time over lunch in Chicago at the introduction of Louis Howe, Roosevelt's intimate "gnomish" adviser. He was launching a "Progressives for Roosevelt" group, although, as it turned out, Wallace preferred to work alone. Democratic Party headquarters finally persuaded Ickes to go ahead anyway and to organize a "Western Independent Republican Committee," which made him responsible for ten *mid*western states. Come September, he was also managing Anna's third Republican campaign for the Illinois General Assembly—all while she complained he was embarrassing her by backing a Democrat.

Iowa was one of Ickes's states, though when he visited Des Moines, no one had heard of him or his committee. After all, Iowa had voted Democratic only once—for Woodrow Wilson, when the Republicans split in 1912. Wallace told an envious Ickes of having recently visited Hyde Park and amiably assured him that Roosevelt understood the heartland's despair. Moreover, he added, Roosevelt would surely sweep all of Ickes's ten states, which Ickes took as an implication that he wasn't making much of a difference.

In 1932, after skating the edge of insolvency, *Wallace's Farmer* finally reverted to its principal debtholder, who kept both the name and Wallace as editor. Not wasting a moment, Wallace turned the paper into a megaphone for Roosevelt. He saw the candidate once more before the election, in Sioux City on September 29. There Roosevelt, while whistle-stopping through the Midwest, addressed a convention of two thousand fellow Shriners.

So much had been "lost in the smash of an economic system that was unable to fulfill its purposes," declared Roosevelt.[3] When Hoover arrived in Des Moines five days later, *Wallace's Farmer* eviscerated him as the most dangerous man in America for falsely proclaiming that he had "turned the tide."[4]

In New York, Perkins knew that Hoover had turned no tide, and in early fall, she relished opportunities to say so. She by now had committed her husband, Paul, to "the Haven"—then as today an exclusive, and expensive, psychiatric hospital in White Plains, its Victorian buildings set in well-tended gardens. Insurance covered none of it. Even so, this agonizing decision gave her more freedom than relying on home nurses.

She seldom encountered Hopkins, who for almost a year had been directing Albany's relief administration, TERA, with an intensity stoked by his horror over malnourishment throughout the state and actual deaths from starvation in New York City. He was caring for Barbara and barely eating, yet money kept slipping through his fingers. That September, he wrote his brother to say he had seen little of Roosevelt, but insisted that rumors of the candidate's poor health—implying that a "cripple" couldn't handle the strain of a presidential race, let alone the presidency—were "utter nonsense."[5]

At this moment, Roosevelt was grinding through a nine-thousand-mile odyssey over an enormous transcontinental loop he would call "the circuit." Wherever he was he read a half dozen newspapers—and in mid-September he was zipping through Wyoming in his seven-car "Roosevelt Special" packed with aides and newsmen. (Only as president would he insist his train keep a steady 35 mph during the day.) He likely smiled over Rumsey's spectacle in one or more of these sheets for he enjoyed the society columns, and anyway found Mary amusing. She was also writing big checks for the campaign.

By and large, he did not enjoy the company of most of her thousand closest friends. Hers was an elite of tycoons and trade, less of those New Yorkers who were members of the lineal Holland Society, which embraced only descendants of settlers in what had been New Amsterdam. Nor, technically, was Roosevelt a "millionaire," even with his mother's capital. People did not think of him as such, as they did of the Vanderbilts and Mellons. He had no personal luxurious needs or tastes, as displayed by residents along Mary Rumsey's Gold Coast, and, except for a few times as an observer, his fondness for sailing did not include ocean racing with the New York Yacht Club off Newport.

Roosevelt stood apart from the class he had been brought up to dismiss as merely moneyed. He avoided "Commodore" Aldrich. Nor did he wish to have much to do with the progeny of William Randolph Hearst, Sr., let alone with Hearst himself. The Wall Streeters and industrialists, the lighthearted polo players and sportsmen, weren't quite his kind, nor did he find them interesting. As for the Democratic-leaning Hearsts, he was pleased they had finally endorsed him—not that he would enjoy supping with the proprietors of the world's biggest newspaper-magazine-radio conglomerate.

In Wyoming, Roosevelt was addressing Americans significantly different from those who dwelt along the Hudson or in the breezes of Long Island Sound. Speaking from his railcar's rear platform, he extemporaneously evoked "equality" (Wyoming's motto) in Laramie and Hanna. On a siding in Cheyenne, he took his son James's arm to step directly from the train onto an improvised stage. Standing tall, looking as fit as when inaugurated governor nearly four years earlier, he addressed the crowd cheerfully. He recalled his last visit to Wyoming in his "Navy days," and reminded his audience he was still a sailor. Why, he even needed to keep telling himself not to call the end of his train "the stern."[6]

Nonetheless, campaign manager Farley, éminence grise Louis Howe, and party officials, as well as a council of senators and representatives, had urged him not to brave this western trip. His "physical condition" made it too risky when speaking impromptu from the back of railcars, they insisted.[7] Roosevelt overruled them, and brought himself to exhibit such heroic vigor in every whistle-stop of each campaign.

It is worth recalling how physically challenged people were regarded at this time. To support the disabled in the abstract, as by donating to the Community Chest, was different from, say, noticing a victim of polio beside you in a shop. Richard L. Dougherty, *The Los Angeles Times*' bureau chief in New York, recalled the difficulty of funding the first Special Olympics in 1968. Generous folk who routinely sponsored the main Olympics recoiled from the thought of packing "a stadium with cripples."[8] Of course, the Special Olympics went on to triumph. Among its offshoots is the wheelchair division of today's New York City Marathon. Still, within memory, such openheartedness was impossible.

Yet in 1932, two blind men were serving as U.S. senators: Thomas Gore of Oklahoma, sightless since childhood, and Minnesota's Thomas Schall, blinded at twenty-eight by a cigar lighter. They were admired, and each had been reelected. But had Gore or Schall crazily sought the presidency, their fellow senators no less than voters would have found the effort unnatural. There were limits to what disabled people could get the public to believe.

In Wyoming that September, as in the other thirty-three states he visited, Roosevelt denounced Washington's "stand pat" Republicans, repeating the charge as the Roosevelt Special steamed through Illinois, Wisconsin, and Michigan, to head east back to Albany.

Throughout the campaign, he consumed policy papers, introductions to specialists, and speech drafts from a tight circle of experts. They regarded themselves originally as "the little general staff," to become known to the press as Roosevelt's "Brain Trust." It was a turn-of-the-century term: soldiers had applied it contemptuously to elite brother officers serving on the U.S. Army's real General Staff.[9]

In this case, it applied mostly to stars from Columbia University's faculty, such as Adolf Berle, thirty-seven, coauthor of that vastly influential work *The Modern Corporation and Private Property* (1932), which insisted that CEOs must serve what today are called "stakeholders," who include employees and the wider community. All were terrific idea men, except they were not "indispensable" to educating Roosevelt on the issues of the day, as they have been canonized ever since by fellow intellectuals.[10]

Another Brain Truster was Rexford Tugwell, forty-one, an urbane professor of economics who had met Wallace during the Chicago convention and introduced him to Governor Roosevelt in August. Tugwell specialized in agriculture and was otherwise known for his movie star looks. An authentic insider like Perkins would recall that she knew few of these Brain Trusters, nor even recognized the term before they descended on Washington in March 1933.

The Brain Trust was the first professorial clique to shower a presidential candidate with ideas, though Al Smith had tried something like it in 1928. Nonetheless, Roosevelt always held to his own clarity of purpose. His plans, it is all too often said, "remained largely unknown to the public" or contained "no larger philosophy or grand design"—or, even, that they were similar to Hoover's.[11]

In fact, he was laying out, coast-to-coast, most every important step to be taken in office: farm relief, securities regulation, commodity subsidies, minimum wage and maximum hours, old age insurance, labor's right to organize, and public works—the latter, it was yet to be revealed, being achieved through an immense government-financed construction agency to build dams, bridges, hospitals, airfields, and schools. There was little need to debate foreign affairs. Voters were not interested.

In 1932, the Democratic Party was, for once, well organized. The presence of Perkins's friend Mary "Molly" Dewson—a "New England spinster of the blueblood," said Perkins, and also head of the party's Women's Division—was among the reasons why.[12] Her millions of color-coded, one-sheet flyers were aligned with the themes of Roosevelt's speeches and the messaging of his surrogates, including editorials in *Wallace's Farmer,* Ickes's attacks on the status quo, and Perkins's speeches, which won praise even from Honey Fitz.

Hoover was swept from office—going by modern party arrangements, the only president until 2020 to preside over the loss of the White House, the House, and the Senate in a single term. His defeat made Roosevelt just the third Democrat to be elected since James Buchanan (1857–1861), a long lifetime earlier. Democrats took both houses of Congress, and thirty-four governorships. The vital center had done more than change its mind. Voters had felt the American system was breaking up under their feet.

Among our four, only Perkins was with Roosevelt on election night when she came alone to campaign headquarters at New York's Biltmore Hotel. Victory had been apparent by nine o'clock, and Roosevelt was accepting congratulations in a small room on the hotel's first floor. He received Perkins and also a distinguished figure whom they both knew, the elderly Henry Morgenthau, Sr., a generous Democratic contributor who from 1913 to 1916 had served as President Wilson's strong-nerved ambassador in Istanbul, doing his best to save the Armenians.

Morgenthau had brought along his twenty-year-old granddaughter to witness history in the making, and he introduced her. This was Barbara Tuchman, as she would later be known when writing epic histories, including the Pulitzer-winning *The Guns of August*. Tuchman recalled the meeting to friends.[13] Roosevelt was sitting in a regular stiff-backed chair and did not stand when they were introduced, which surprised her for a split second. He gripped her hand firmly and, looking up, locked her into his gray-blue eyes, rumbling "Why, ah am SO glad." For another split second, it was if he had insisted that this night would mean nothing to him had she not just taken the train down from Radcliffe.

November 8, 1932, shows how, in America, outsiders repeatedly emerge as great doctrines collapse. The decks are cleared for strange, unexpected people, such as that prodigy of otherness, Abraham Lincoln, on the edge of civil war. So, too, the ruin of the Great Depression had thrust up Franklin Roosevelt, a man unusual in so many ways—and, equally odd, Hopkins, Ickes, Perkins, and Wallace. During prosperous times, none of Roosevelt's up-and-coming lieutenants could have ventured far beyond political suburbia. Then the Great Depression changed everything.

Four terrifying months of delay preceded Roosevelt's inauguration on March 4 and the swearing in of the Seventy-Third Congress. Banks were failing, Wall Street swindles crowded the front pages, and Perkins's roll of jobless numbers kept climbing.

The traditional, uniquely American scramble for political spoils also began, on a scale found in no other advanced democracy. Then, as today, thousands of government jobs were up for grabs. ("Thousands," at that time of fewer government posts, because the spoils system encompassed postal clerks, tax collectors, and other functions now under civil service.)

Of course, while presidents themselves select Cabinet officers, ambassadors, and other top officials, as Roosevelt did, it was left to party operatives to decide who should fill the innumerable lesser slots. Once the Democrats held power, the man responsible was bald, bluff Jim Farley, a forty-four-year-old New Yorker from rural Rockland County who was among the first Irish Catholics to achieve national fame in politics. Roosevelt had installed him as chairman of the Democratic Party after Farley had done much to win him the nomination.

Also toiling on the transition was Louis Howe, the heroic wreck who had so much to do with the rise of Franklin Roosevelt. Farley and other backslapping politicos found his wizened looks disconcerting. Howe didn't mind. He preferred to hatch conspiracies in the darkest corners.

Howe and Perkins were friends. "I always thought Louis wanted above everything to be loved," she would recall—knowing that, as a boy, people had found him "repulsive."[14] Like Molly Dewson, Howe wanted to see Perkins reach the heights, and so they floated trial balloons in the *Times* and prompted Jane Addams to call for Perkins to be appointed secretary of labor.

Not that she was the first to be tapped for office among the four. The president-elect, vacationing amid the tall pines and buoyant waters of Warm Springs, invited Wallace down to Georgia. He arrived early on Monday morning, November 28, after a long train journey from Iowa. For more than an hour they discussed agriculture in Roosevelt's brand-new six-room, one-story wooden cottage. Roosevelt at first sat in a bathroom chair shaving with a safety razor (Missy LeHand hovering nearby), saying nothing about Wallace's going to Washington.

Roosevelt then passed him off to Raymond Moley, a self-satisfied Columbia University professor who had organized the Brain Trust. In the evening, after a dozen or so people had gathered around the president-elect for a still-illegal cocktail hour, it was nevertheless back to the station for Wallace (who didn't drink) and a long trip home.

Roosevelt might have appeared blasé that morning, and restless to drive away in his hand-controlled Plymouth Phaeton, but he recognized there could be no on-the-job training at Agriculture. Henry Morgenthau's son, Henry Jr., forty-one, yearned for the post. His father had bought him a farm near Hyde Park, and both Roosevelts liked the younger man, who had advised the governor on farm issues. Ambassador Morgenthau had also bought his son a specialty newspaper, *American Agriculturalist*. Regardless, the stakes were too high to hazard that top slot.

In Kansas and Nebraska, as elsewhere in the heartland, sheriffs risked being shot when, for instance, they tried to foreclose a $15,000 mortgage on a farm worth $80,000–90,000. The long-experienced senator Hiram Johnson actually feared revolution. "If these farmers with their love for law and order ever united with the disorderly and anti-government spirit of the cities," he wrote his son, the countryside might indeed break into

rebellion.[15] And, in 1932 and 1933, "the countryside" meant thirty million farmers and the workers who depended directly on farming.

Ickes spent these eternal weeks commuting on the Chicago & North
Western between Winnetka and his fading downtown law office. Often,
he would dash to Harrison Street to snag the Capitol Limited sleeper to
Washington. Once there, he set out to buttonhole his best contacts on the
Hill. They included Senator Johnson and another formidable progressive
Republican, Senator Bronson Cutting of New Mexico, forty-four-year-old
scion of the New York philanthropist.

Ickes yearned to reap his deserved spoils, so these were trying months.
Between legislative sessions in Springfield, Anna was back in Winnetka,
and Ickes kept telling her he was in line for something big—maybe even
director of Indian Affairs within the Department of the Interior. She
doubted it. He was getting nowhere, and suffering migraines from the
anxieties of stalled ambition.

Instead, it was Henry Wallace who received a letter from Roosevelt,
dated February 6, 1933, asking him to join what was then called the
president's "official family"—i.e., one of the ten members of the Cabinet.
Would he agree to be nominated secretary of agriculture? For months,
farm organizations had been telegraphing Roosevelt to appoint him. Everyone knew of his intelligence and his tireless quest to rescue the belea-
guered farm sector. Yet Wallace hesitated. It's not unfair to say that he was
busy, at this pivotal moment, seeking, in his own words, "the religious key
of the new age."[16] (And not for the last time.)

Harry Hopkins also painfully awaited word as he scooted between
Albany and New York City, trying to catch spare hours with Barbara
and their three-month-old daughter. He heard nothing from the president-
elect, despite knowing that Roosevelt loved to use the phone and was on
it one third of the day. Hopkins longed to roll out New York State's first-
in-the-nation TERA relief program across the entire country. Money for
doing so, he wrote his brother, would come from raising income, inheritance, gift, and other taxes on "the big boys."[17]

Nor did Hopkins see Perkins between the election and Roosevelt's
swearing in. Starting in December, reporters were hounding her over rumors that the president-elect might prove so radical as to place a woman
in his Cabinet.

Perkins dreaded what was coming. Already she spent tension-filled days confronting the casualties of a plummeting economy. Additionally, each Saturday, without fail, she drove an hour from midtown Manhattan to White Plains to spend the afternoon with Paul. On some days, he was ebullient, and they'd walk through the Haven's gardens. On other days, he was immobile in bed. Susanna was a junior at Brearley, the expensive private girls' school on East Eighty-Third Street, not far from Perkins's apartment. For this little while, mother and daughter were close.

The cost of an exclusive psychiatric hospital, and Brearley, and the rented Madison Avenue flat—plus paying for maid, cook, and part-time governess—was nearly overwhelming. Perkins might earn $3,000 more from a Cabinet post in Washington, though to accept the offer seemed impossible, no matter the urgings of Molly Dewson, Mary Rumsey, Caroline O'Day, and many other friends.

She was Louis Howe's candidate too. Yet, ever politic, he was willing to lie about how essential her work had been in Albany, as he did that February in *The Saturday Evening Post,* if such falsehood could glorify the man he would always call "Franklin."[18] In any case, Perkins had heard nothing directly.

Roosevelt's February 6 letter to Wallace had asked him to reply through channels that were ultimately to reach the president-elect by U.S. Navy radio. He was to embark on an eleven-day fishing trip from Jacksonville, Florida, aboard Vincent Astor's yacht *Nourmahal.* When nothing was heard from Wallace, Professor Moley made a short, sharp call to Des Moines telling him to decide.

Meanwhile, Roosevelt had gone to sea. His enduring quality of physical courage included the leaderlike ability to put such courage to use. Ulysses Grant had done so at Cold Harbor as he continued to write orders when a shell shrieked past his head. He never looked up. Within hours, the entire Army of the Potomac knew that "Ulysses don't scare worth a damn." Grant was distilling courage into an army-wide virtue. Thus, an army and its general come to bind together—and so too for a president and his nation. Roosevelt understood this completely. During times of extremity, courage at the top somehow communicates itself far and wide, as it would in Miami on February 15, just after he came ashore from the *Nourmahal.*

Astor's yacht had steamed into Biscayne Bay near sunset to berth at the city pier. Having stayed aboard for dinner, Roosevelt was wheeled down a covered gangway around eight thirty. Once his braces were snapped into place, he walked haltingly the fifty feet, on the arm of a steward, to a reception committee of reporters and city officials on the dock. Tan and robust, he promptly cut off talk about possible Cabinet appointments, while cheerfully conceding that he had gained weight.

A crowd of some fifteen thousand waited in nearby Bayfront Park for what Roosevelt told reporters would be an "inconsequential speech."[19] He was then to be driven to Union Station, to board his special railcar attached to the ten o'clock for New York.

He left the pier by motorcade to speak from an elevated area near the bandstand while sitting himself atop the back seat of a Buick convertible. He spoke for ten minutes, then slid back down into the car. At 9:24, a self-described anarchist—a naturalized citizen from Italy—standing ten yards away, fired five shots at him from a .32-caliber pawnshop revolver. None hit Roosevelt, though Anton Cermak, the mayor of Chicago, who was talking to him while standing beside the car, was mortally wounded.

Bullets struck four other people, including one of Roosevelt's seven Secret Service agents. Roosevelt shouted, "I'm all right. I'm all right," which likely saved his would-be assassin from being beaten to death. The bleeding Cermak was pulled into the car, and Roosevelt cradled him as they sped to Jackson Memorial Hospital. Later, he checked on the other casualties, wheeling himself into their rooms. Then he returned to the *Nourmahal* to spend the night under heavy guard.

The attempt is one of history's great "what ifs." If Roosevelt had been the one killed, Vice President Elect John Garner would have entered the White House on March 4.

Ickes, who would see Garner close-up and often during the coming years, believed him to embody mean-spirited reaction. John L. Lewis, head of the United Mine Workers, would dismiss Garner as "a labor-baiting, poker-playing, whiskey-drinking, *evil* old man."[20] Both were utterly wrong. Even so, the Speaker of the House, as he still was, might not have been America's best hope in 1933.

Within days of that bloody evening, word was spreading out that Roosevelt was a leader without fear.

The attempt on his life was a brutal test of character, albeit in preposterous circumstances. At the very depths of that fearful winter of 1933, the entire country learned of his cruising the southern seas aboard a plutocrat's yacht so enormous as eventually to be commissioned as a warship. In the television age, the optics might have proved ruinous. Even so, the forty-two-year-old Astor was a friend, although one of those whom Perkins termed of "propinquity." He was a distant relative of Roosevelt's, with a 2,600-acre Hudson River estate, and a descendant of one of America's first millionaires. As a result, Astor was not the sort of man to have put on dungarees for Mary Rumsey's debutante ball, liking her though he did. All in all, Roosevelt simply did not notice any contradiction of fishing with him in the Bahamas.

Roosevelt was convinced that he had been saved by God. His faith rested on a Navy Hymn view of the Deity: "For those in peril on the sea." When you face dangers that seem to wither your strength, you can offset them by calling on a higher power. "And he had perfect trust" in God, Hopkins and Perkins agreed one day. Hopkins wondered why. "There is a star" over him, concluded Missy LeHand after the bullets somehow missed.[21] And it is startling to observe how Roosevelt could bend others into thinking him a superior being.

The president-elect possessed the abiding faith of the Episcopal vestryman he was. At the same time, he was deeply superstitious. The number thirteen alarmed him. A man's death could be read as an omen, as occurred when one of his Cabinet choices fell dead three days before the inauguration. He would delay ships and trains so as not to travel on Fridays, and "three on a match"—lighting three cigarettes off a single flame—chilled him. He wore the same lucky Italian felt hat throughout his campaigns, and insisted that one particular man, a nondescript judge, be always on the Roosevelt Special for good luck.

Superstition is common among sailors and keen athletes, both of which Roosevelt had been before he lost use of his legs. He was forever calling on powers beyond his understanding, as when they more or less brought him through paralysis.

Once safely back in New York, on February 18, he needed to finalize his Cabinet and announce it to the nation. He asked Perkins to meet him on Wednesday evening, the twenty-second, at his house in town. She knew what was afoot, and agonized over her response, telephoning Molly Dewson, who, blunt as usual, said, "I'll murder you if you don't!"[22]

Perkins was content in New York. She liked working for the new Democratic governor; she could manage her husband's health crises; and her daughter, now sixteen, seemed happy at Brearley. In fact, on February 1, Perkins had sent FDR a handwritten note saying that "grave personal difficulties" would make it hard to accept a Cabinet post.[23]

Roosevelt's quiet, usually stately house on East Sixty-Fifth Street seems to have been a mess when Perkins arrived for an 8:00 P.M. appointment. Aides, police, and Secret Service men, who milled around smoking, directed her upstairs to wait in a book-filled room outside Roosevelt's study. A stout, odd-looking man with gold-rimmed glasses and sandy hair turning gray slumped in another chair also waiting, and never looked up. "I put him down as no New York City bird," she remembered. "He didn't have any of the elegance that you're accustomed to."[24]

At that point, an aide opened the study door and they both entered. Roosevelt sat behind his desk. The "Governor," as she still called him, expressed surprise that she didn't know "Harold," and asked her to wait a while longer in the anteroom. She obliged, and the door closed.

After a long wait, Harold emerged, wishing her a "good evening" as he headed downstairs. She then entered and first asked who "Harold" might be. Startled, Roosevelt replied "Ickes"—a name she did not recognize, itself a reminder of how disconnected America still was in the 1930s. The name sounded like one of those "funny" ones, she said, probably Polish. Roosevelt roared with laughter, and then promptly asked Perkins to join his Cabinet, at which she feigned surprise.

"Oh, come on now, don't say 'surprised.' You're no fool. What did you think I wanted to see you for?"

Perkins had, in fact, arrived bearing a list of programs for which she hoped to win his support, such as insurance against old age and unemployment. To all this, he agreed in principle, and gave her twenty-four hours to decide.

Another account, from Professor Moley, differs markedly, while offering as much fun at this crossroads of history. When Ickes appeared that day, Farley, Moley, and a mob of other aides were bustling around downstairs. Moley remembered taking him up to the study where Perkins was already sitting with the president-elect, who indeed was amazed that Ickes and Perkins were strangers. "It is nice to have the Secretary of Labor meet the Interior Secretary here tonight," boomed Roosevelt.[25]

Unlike Perkins, Ickes had been stunned to the point of incoherence.

How did he get it? A week earlier, Moley had invited him to New York to attend a morning meeting of ten or so people at East Sixty-Fifth Street. They were to advise the president-elect on economics, of which Ickes—like Roosevelt—knew little. Ickes joined, and seldom spoke. Nevertheless, he noticed that Roosevelt was watching. As the group disbanded, Rexford Tugwell stopped Ickes at the head of the stairs. Would he stay? Telling Ickes to pull up a chair near his desk, Roosevelt confided his difficulty in filling the Interior slot. By now, he suspected Mr. Ickes of Chicago might fit the bill. Should Mr. Ickes kindly return that evening at eight, he would let him know.

Louis Howe was mystified. "There isn't any such name as Ickes," he muttered. "There must be some mistake." Moley was equally baffled: It was "one of the most casual appointments to a Cabinet position in American history."[26]

That said, Roosevelt's decisions about people were never so casual as he let on. In those days, the FBI did not vet candidates, and he would not have trusted others to do such work for him anyway. Instead, he drew on his innumerable listening posts and his deep intuition. Where it came to Ickes, the president-elect simply told Moley that there had been no time to investigate. Here he invoked the ultimate nautical acclaim: he just "liked the cut of his jib."[27] In fact, groundwork had been done, and Roosevelt had been hearing about Ickes for several years.

Roosevelt excelled at reading people. He could single out the useful, the potentially loyal, and the dangerous. He would have understood much about Ickes by observing this "people's counselor" during that hour's colloquium with experts who included Professors Moley and Tugwell, banker James Warburg, and Bernard Baruch, the investor and bankroller of Democratic candidates. Plus Roosevelt knew what he was looking for.

One element was to call in a progressive Republican from beyond the East. In fact, as an empty gesture of goodwill, he had offered Interior to the venerable senator Hiram Johnson, knowing that Johnson—long a national figure in his own right—would take no subordinate position. Then, passing to the serious, he offered Interior to the tubercular Bronson Cutting, a boyhood friend and one more alumnus of Groton and Harvard, and also well known as a bachelor and an aesthete. Cutting declined as well. The choice triangulated onto Ickes.

Whatever feedback Roosevelt had picked up about Ickes must have been disturbing. In the months ahead, even after Ickes himself had been sworn in, any other president would have gotten rid of him fast. Yet Ickes's truculence proved to be an exercise ground for the master's charm.

No celebration awaited Ickes when he returned to Winnetka, and the great hall of Hubbard Woods lay still. Anna agreed to attend the inauguration, then added that she had not decided if she would spend time in Washington as the mere wife of a Cabinet secretary. After all, she held responsibilities in the Illinois General Assembly.

Neither was Perkins's situation joyful, having immense obstacles to face.

In New York, she had been accepted for her achievements. The great city boasted every variety of talent: Jewish adventurers and streetwise Italians, or mixtures thereof—like the irascible Episcopalian Republican congressman Fiorello Henry La Guardia, who was running for mayor. Not so in Washington, still Southern and sleepy. Moreover, she feared that, on any given day, some political foe might accuse her of abandoning her sick husband or pry about the left-behind daughter.

"Do it for the sake of other women," urged Dewson and O'Day as Roosevelt's twenty-four-hour deadline neared. If she didn't accept, they argued, it would take a hundred years until such an opportunity reopened. Perkins had already spoken with her bishop, who counseled that she would be fulfilling a duty to God. Nonetheless, she still drove to the Haven to discuss her decision with an uncomprehending Paul. She grew so distraught as the hours passed that she never would be really sure if she had telephoned Roosevelt to refuse as she intended. Whether or not there had been a call, she knew what he would have answered: "Don't be such a baby, Frances." And so she agreed.[28]

Perkins never cried, except when someone unexpectedly gave her a kind word. On this occasion, as we know from her correspondence and reminiscences, she was overcome by days of tears.

Roosevelt announced his final Cabinet picks from Hyde Park late on February 26—just six days before the inauguration. The roll included of course Ickes, Perkins, and Wallace. One discordant note, to our twenty-first-century ears, came from *The New York Times,* which initially described Perkins's selection, unlike those of the other two, as a "personal" decision of Roosevelt's born of a long twenty-three-year acquaintance. A later edition came round to emphasizing her experience.[29]

To some mysterious degree, Roosevelt's intuition had brought him to assemble these three—and soon enough Hopkins—for the adventure ahead. In a phrase of the time, people close to him said his instincts were downright "feminine intuition." To be sure, he combined catlike attention and unsleeping observation with uncanny listening skills. These are the abilities of a fine mimic, which he was, and such talents can interlock with an expertise in birdsongs (and he could evoke the notes of two dozen different northeastern species). These powers were germane to the ways he dealt with those around him. The most cerebral columnist of the day would conclude that he governed by ear.[30]

Roosevelt gleaned information daily from gossip, but also from a host of political informants and favored journalists. In parallel, he interpreted personalities, and did so out of the union of his intellect and his long or-deal of griefs, above all his disability. He had a particularly sharp eye for people who stood outside the crowd.

Instead of avoiding such people, Roosevelt could grasp opportunities to reach deeper and tap a common sorrow. He imparted energy and mo-tivation, and sensed how he could craft each of these curious figures to his purpose: Hopkins, the wildly ambitious social worker; Ickes, who was by his own account too nervous to give a decent speech; Perkins, at this moment diffident and tearful, soon to shred apart CEOs and labor bosses alike; and the remote, solitary genius, Wallace.

On Saturday, March 4, at eight minutes past one, on the Capitol's East Portico, Roosevelt stood tall in morning dress. He had removed his silk hat again to take an oath on the family's 1686 Dutch Bible. When he then delivered a fifteen-minute address under a cold gray sky, climaxing in "The only thing we have to fear is fear itself," he evoked his life, with the rest of that sentence—warning against "the terror which paralyzes needed efforts"—mirroring what he had endured and the paralysis with which he still lived.[31] The children from Warm Springs whom he had invited to the ceremony knew terror and incapacity, and he had ensured that they, as well as his valet, Irvin McDuffie, himself crippled, were close in the audience.

Roosevelt also set out to rally a "great army of our people dedicated to a disciplined attack" upon the dark realities of the moment. Comparing public struggles to war is by now a standard trope, but it was then uncommon to hear metaphors of war from a peacetime president. His words took for granted a vast national undertaking, likely to unfold with little care for any single individual, as in war, and investing enormous authority in (civilian) commanders.

Some sixty million Americans listened on radio, as did Harry Hopkins in his office. By this season of the nation's ordeal, people were afraid. Few expected any imminent recovery. Anyhow, most of Roosevelt's 123 million fellow citizens were ready to believe. For the time being, their faith overrode political hatreds.

The new president reviewed the three-hour inaugural parade from a grandstand built along Pennsylvania Avenue. He was brought inside the White House at six o'clock to take the elevator to what today is known as the Yellow Oval Room on the second floor, above the South Portico. This became his study, soon taking on a nautical look with naval prints and model ships, plus his tall overstuffed mahogany bookcases. That evening, from behind a big flat-topped desk, he watched Justice Benjamin Cardozo, a Republican friend from New York, swear in Cabinet officers one by one on the Roosevelt family Bible. "You won't be able to read a word of it," he teased them, which implied that *he* could. They would become familiar with his one-upmanship, and in this instance, given his childhood Dutch, he was roughly correct.

The nation's emergency had brought about both this unique oath taking and the Senate's decision to confirm the entire Cabinet in a single swoop without debate that afternoon. A White House buffet and three inaugural balls followed. After midnight, Roosevelt and Louis Howe sat reminiscing back in the study, from which a side door opened on what was now to be Roosevelt's bedroom. At last McDuffie limped in to help the president undress and lift him into bed.

On Sunday morning, the Roosevelt family worshipped at St. Thomas church near Dupont Circle. After lunch, he met with his new-fledged Cabinet—and the press took notice. This was no formal Cabinet meeting per se, and everyone gathered again in his study. "FDR," as the president had become known, wanted the country to realize he was talking freely with his "official family." Panic withdrawals had brought a good half of the nation's banks to the edge of collapse. Many others were already bust. At this point, a decision so grave as closing every bank in the country—which he did by executive order at 1:00 A.M. on

Monday, March 6—had to be shown to involve a pooled wisdom from throughout America.

The first actual Cabinet meeting fell on Tuesday afternoon, in the Cabinet Room adjoining the Oval Office, looking out over the Rose Garden. The purpose of this body, as it then stood, was utterly different from today. Cabinet officers were the government's only high-visibility political appointees. No ambassadors and only the highest-level jurists had any such prominence. Much would change with the New Deal.

In 1933, the Cabinet still served to legitimize the party in power. Every substantial region of the country, interest group, or political faction could be assured that "Your man is here, and he is carrying weight." As a lifetime's bitterness after the Civil War faded, it became statesmanlike to add one or two men from the opposing party. In a nation so large and diverse, a high proportion of these officials had never met one another. Perkins, for instance, recognized Henry Wallace only from photos in *The New York Times,* and Ickes scrambled to learn something useful about the secretaries of war and navy.

At this juncture, the Cabinet was also called the "board of directors of the nation."[32] The magnitude of the New Deal, about to arrive, gave it additional prominence. Before long, it wasn't unusual for a visiting secretary of This or That to receive a motorcycle escort even in so jaded a city as New York. Nineteen-gun salutes, the correct number for greeting governors and Cabinet officers, might follow. And often this president would dispatch some trusted figure from his Cabinet to negotiate on Capitol Hill over issues that had nothing to do with the visitor's remit.

In Washington, where protocol is nearly as important as gossip, Cabinet officers were also ranked by seniority. The secretary of state was preeminent, largely because his department was the oldest, created in 1789, and from 1886 until 1947, he was second in line of succession. The newest was Labor, as of 1913, its secretary therefore ranking lowest. This affected the courtesies of who spoke first in meetings, or who stood where around the president. Past presidents had dealt with their Cabinets in various ways. Lincoln, who found Cabinet meetings unhelpful, condoned voting, except (goes the story, which Roosevelt enjoyed) when the result came to seven "No's" to his "Yes"—and the ayes had it.

Traditionally, the Cabinet had not included the vice president. When Roosevelt, running for the office in 1920, had asked Ohio governor James

Cox, who led the ticket, if he might attend should they win, Cox said firmly no. The amiable Warren Harding had welcomed his vice president, Calvin Coolidge, into the Cabinet, and Coolidge similarly accommodated his number two. Hoover kept up the practice with his VP, though he rarely held meetings. It would have been difficult for Roosevelt to break this now established practice because he owed a big political debt to John Garner, who had an open invitation. Notwithstanding, he allowed no one to take notes or make transcripts. What came about in the Cabinet Room was what he said had occurred.

Around the table on March 7 sat only two hard-hitting politicos among the ten appointees. One was Jim Farley, Democratic Party chairman and now postmaster general. He wasn't the best man for delivering letters, yet the historic purpose of this role was to dispense small-grade patronage as the president's representative. There he excelled. The other was Attorney General Homer Cummings, a famed prosecutor from Connecticut. Roosevelt knew a strong AG would be essential.

Otherwise, the Cabinet appeared to be, at most, merely diligent. Secretary of Commerce Daniel Roper from South Carolina had been President Wilson's commissioner of internal revenue. He represented the deeper South, even if, being obscure outside the Palmetto State, he did not represent the South too strongly—just as his chief wished.

Secretary of War George Dern, previously Utah's governor and considered briefly for Interior, stood in for the West, except he knew nothing of the military and shared his state's historic suspicion of federal troops. Claude Swanson, the elderly secretary of the navy, had been born in Swansonville, Virginia, Confederate States of America. Even if he needed help getting into his chair, he at least had led the Senate's Naval Affairs Committee and was aware of the subject. However, a seafaring president who casually spoke of "my" navy would likely rule the fleet.

Cordell Hull, secretary of state, was a crusty mountaineer from Olympus, Tennessee, and a graduate of Cumberland School of Law. He might remind you, should debates get heated, that his father had hunted a man down and killed him. Tall, dignified, and fine-featured under a shock of white hair, Hull had been one of the weightiest Democrats in Congress during the years of exile, culminating in two years as a senator, after twenty-two in the House. Everyone on both sides of the aisle genuinely liked him, so his appointment pleased the Hill. His remitting-relapsing sarcoidosis was a deep secret—except who knew what was secret from Franklin Roosevelt?

Hull's global concerns were limited to neutrality and free trade. That was OK with Roosevelt, who would basically limit Hull's authority to trade, Latin America, and Japan. He placed William Phillips, whom he knew from Groton and Harvard, as Hull's undersecretary. This nominal second-in-command would be followed in 1937 by Sumner Welles, once more from Groton and Harvard, who had been a page at Roosevelt's wedding. Each was a career diplomat of immense wealth who relieved Hull from expensive diplomatic entertainment.

For Treasury, Roosevelt turned to the industrialist and unlikely campaign benefactor William Woodin, whose presence reassured Big Business, and who enjoyed additional standing as a director of the Federal Reserve Bank of New York.

The elfin, low-key Woodin doubted that he was prepared for the job. In this he was far too modest. However, he was receiving medical care and soon dying before the eyes of his undersecretary, Dean Acheson—who, at age forty, had switched his loyalties from Al Smith to Roosevelt fast enough in Chicago to claim this role. Acheson got the second job in mid-May.

Like Wallace and Ickes, Secretary Woodin was a Republican apostate. With his resignation in December, that left just two Republicans in the Cabinet. Had the need come, FDR would have found it easier to throw either of them to the wolves than to drop some Democratic stalwart.

These unevenly assorted officers, united only by their commitment to Roosevelt, were in no sense a team, but together they evinced a humanitarian streak that few had detected in Hoover's hard-faced coterie. Everyone had been immersed in high national politics except for Ickes, Perkins, and Wallace. All were long acquaintances of Roosevelt's—again except for Ickes and Wallace. Critics, such as Arthur Krock, Washington correspondent of *The New York Times,* complained about the absence of national figures—men like Newton Baker or Al Smith—and, ever since, historians have believed that there was nothing distinctive about this Cabinet.

Instead, FDR's motives are revealed in his first real choice for secretary of the interior, Bronson Cutting. This handsome aesthete was not only tubercular; he was, in the polite term of the day, "sensitive"—which meant he was gay, as FDR surely knew.[33] And under the cultural standards of the time, being gay meant one lived a life always subject to shame. In different ways, Cutting was as wounded as Ickes and burdened by just as many secrets. It is no surprise that FDR had hoped to pull Cutting into the "family," except Cutting was both rising in politics under his own steam and knew Roosevelt too well to consider working under him.

Leaving aside the peculiarities of Roosevelt's Cabinet, an administration was being formed in the typically American way—by the winner taking the spoils. When it works well, this approach pulls people with fresh perspectives into public life. It builds on the countless abilities offered by a continent-sized nation, and awakens unexpected talents, as it did in our four. The absence of both a mandarin-grade civil service and a lordly diplomatic corps fosters such openness too.

To be sure, other nations co-opt unconventional talents from outside the political establishment, yet America turns such ad hoc selection into a routine. At the time—as can occur today—there was no telling who one might encounter. That phenomenon became the more apparent as Hopkins, Ickes, Perkins, and Wallace each arrived in a shaken Washington.

4

ACTION NOW

The Hundred Days, March–June 1933

The President took the position that many of us did
things prior to 1929 that we wouldn't think of doing now;
that our code of ethics had radically changed.
Harold Ickes, diary entry of May 26, 1933

Most of America's great fortunes, although made in less than a lifetime, had, by 1929, bestowed on their owners a mystique of irresistible weight resting on dollars and status. Wealth of this size had largely survived the Crash—not just that of the Harrimans, Hearsts, and Aldriches but also the capital of less moneyed people, including Anna Wilmarth. Yet the sense of such persons being surrounded by a magical aura of privilege had vanished, at least for the time being. All at once, Americans who had labored to make these fortunes, such as the twelve-hour-a-day ironworkers in Andrew Mellon's Pittsburgh furnaces, were, in theory, enabled to organize and push back.

However, better-off Americans also had reason to demand change. They too had felt the malignancy of unchecked markets, as at the hands of the National City Bank of New York, predecessor of Citigroup. Had not National City profited by pushing $90 million in Peruvian bonds onto trusting customers, while its own agents in Lima warned that those securities would soon be worthless?

Progress on such issues as trade unionism and securities regulation had stalled during the twenties. With the Crash, a surge of public feeling began reworking economic plague into opportunity. Roosevelt's inaugural address had pledged "action and action now," and he intended to strike while his opponents lay humbled, and Congress was raring to go.

Hoover's outgoing secretary of state, Henry Stimson, back at his white-shoe law office in New York, denounced Roosevelt's "weasel words" to his diary. Perhaps so, but by March 15, one of Stimson's former assistants, who remained at State, wrote him of the president that "the outside public seems to behave as if Angel Gabriel had come to earth."[1]

Today, politically attuned film buffs have rediscovered a movie, *Gabriel Over the White House*, which MGM and William Randolph Hearst had rushed into theaters by spring 1933. Hearst, who had yet to turn against Roosevelt, offered advice on public policy, conveyed through Walter Huston, FDR's favorite actor.

Hearst believed America needed a dictator, and the movie parallels the incipient violence and frantic legislating of Roosevelt's first months in office. At the White House, the president screened a working print in the second-floor hallway outside his study. He wrote Hearst that the film should "do much to help" in the crisis.[2] America was shown to be pulling itself together. Ickes, who also enjoyed movies, saw it, as likely did Hopkins, forever eager to know what people at the top were seeing and doing.

Today, it's hard to understand the fun. In the film, the United States Party has replaced the all-too-alike Republicans and Democrats, which leads *Gabriel* into a wish fulfillment for martial law in the face of economic collapse. Thanks to divine intervention, the newly elected party-hack president (Huston, as Judson Hammond) becomes an inspiring leader who dissolves Congress, overrides the Constitution, and, as a dictator, ends unemployment to achieve world peace. He alone can save us.

Some five million Americans viewed *Gabriel* at a time when the nation was simmering with an unfocused anger driven by fear. Once fear takes hold, the worst nightmares can possess decent minds. Had the economy been reopened in less than a reassuring way, calamity would have followed, and absent sweeping reforms, life could easily have imitated art.

As today, banks were the source of credits and stored assets that upheld modern life. Teachers were being paid in IOUs, and Andrew Mellon simply gave his miners scrip. Had banks totally failed to function, the value of a dollar in New York would again have been at a premium in St. Louis. And who was to reinvent a banking system during the worst of the Great Depression? A grievously disconnected nation seemed imminent.

"I had kept my eyes open for anything that might open the way for a military coup," Wallace recalled, "if President Roosevelt turned out to be weak."[3] And so were others.

With heroic skill, and a dying man's resolve, William Woodin set to work at Treasury while the long inaugural parade was still marching up Pennsylvania Avenue. Even before being sworn in, he built quickly on designs left by Hoover's people to close the nation's banks and assess their solvency. Weak banks were liquidated, and regulations devised to underpin the resumed operations of stronger ones. Roosevelt stood even taller once the healthier banks reopened on March 13, and the stock market two days later.

In July, Roosevelt would coin the term "the first 100 days" for what followed the bank emergency—a term he likely took from Bonaparte.[4]

During this time, government action was so intense that the columnist Stewart Alsop recalled seeing congressmen substitute a rolled-up newspaper for the draft of a bill being rushed through committee. Fifteen major laws were enacted, supported by two (radio) "fireside chats" and thirty press conferences. Prohibition—an issue of such immense cultural significance that Mencken had expected it to dominate the '32 campaign—was soon swept from the Constitution.

New ventures were waiting to be launched, such as the Civilian Conservation Corps, which most involved Perkins, Ickes, and Wallace; the Federal Emergency Relief Administration, to be run by Hopkins; the Agricultural Adjustment Administration, driven by Wallace; the Tennessee Valley Authority, which helped pull into modernity poor, malaria-ravaged Americans who clung to eighty thousand square miles of the rural Southeast; and the across-the-board National Industrial Recovery Act that empowered labor and initiated a massive public works program, to be helmed by Ickes.

To succeed, FDR needed lieutenants able to raise and undertake huge offensives against national ruin. Brain Trusters could be helpful in drafting legislation and shaping policy, doing so in tandem with young lawyers down from Harvard, who would go on to staff the bureaucracies. Except these were not the type of hardened, tenacious operators who could stay at the top from beginning to end and deliver victory.

There is always a current of emergency in government. The challenge is knowing how to navigate from day to day. Like Roosevelt, his four lieutenants had formed in their painful earlier years the right qualities for command. All were undismayed and set to persevere.

None of the four had lived in Washington, although each had traveled overseas, unlike several Cabinet members, including Secretary of War Dern. They discovered the capital to be a foreign country—utterly strange in its protocol and racial segregation. In those days, every government directory published one's home address and phone number, and people enjoyed guessing an official's wealth and ambitions.

Harold and Anna Ickes, and their twenty-one-year-old son, Raymond, had taken a suite at the Mayflower Hotel for the inauguration, as did the Roosevelts for the two nights before March 4. Three days later Anna returned to Illinois, not before holding what *The New York Times* called "her first 'press conference.'" She had a "fighting glint in her eye," said *The Washington Herald,* as she laughingly explained that the secretary of the interior had come to Washington to escape her.[5]

Ickes stayed at the Mayflower until April, then rented a modest furnished house in Georgetown, which was not yet the completely opulent neighborhood of today. In the fall, with Anna's approval, he leased a recently built six-bedroom fieldstone residence with parklike grounds in Washington's new Spring Valley development. While Ickes was still at the Mayflower, however, and within moments of Anna's departure, he started an exceedingly risky affair.

Perkins began her Washington years just as much in character. She and her daughter took a room at Willard's, the Civil War–era hotel on Pennsylvania Avenue that, like the Mayflower, flourishes in renovated form today. In 1933, it was declining and inexpensive. After the ceremonies, Susanna returned to school in New York to live at home with a full-time governess. Perkins still had not made domestic plans for herself. She considered boarding at a Catholic convent near Georgetown University, to discover the nuns were already lodging four elderly ladies. There wasn't the space—and, besides, it might look odd for a Cabinet secretary to live in a convent.

During the campaign, Perkins had seen lost children clinging to life in the Kansas City rail yards, and, when home in Manhattan, would bring leftovers from dinner to the haggard inhabitants of Central Park's homeless camp, located near the East Ninety-First Street entrance not far from her apartment. Sick at heart over ostentation amid misery, she believed that an embrace of simplicity would prove another common passion with

Roosevelt. Anyway, she had to watch every penny. She therefore moved to spartan rooms at the Women's University Club.

Nonetheless, it wasn't easy for Perkins to live simply. She enjoyed moving in rarefied social circles, which she also found practical. Rich friends helped subsidize her life. In late April, Mary Rumsey asked her to share a relatively small house in Georgetown for two months before they moved for the summer to "Uplands," cousin Daisy Harriman's colonial mansion on Foxhall Road, between Georgetown and Spring Valley. Come fall, the two women would return to a larger place in Georgetown, well suited to the intellectually intense receptions they began hosting.

Perkins and Rumsey lived as partners, though no details exist, such as impassioned letters, about their intimacy. Thanks to Rumsey, Perkins's costs were nominal—and a Depression secretary of labor didn't want to be seen as living in luxury. Their Georgetown home, despite Chippendale and Chinese objets d'art, might not have been luxurious. Rumsey's two-thousand-acre estate, "Grasslands," in Virginia hunt country, was another story, and Perkins would often be chauffeured there on such Sundays as she needn't dash to New York to check on Susanna and Paul.

The slim, dark-eyed Rumsey is "the pretty woman in a brown riding habit" of *The Great Gatsby*. In real life, her campaign donations brought her a significant appointment in June: to head the federal government's first consumer rights board, and she sought Perkins's help.

That spring, the austere Wallace and his wife, Ilo, began to visit the spectacular farming spread of Grasslands, up Route 50 from Middleburg, Virginia, then a village ninety minutes west by car from Washington. Wallace was the first Cabinet colleague whom Perkins had met on Inauguration Day. They liked each other immediately. Perkins was happy to have him at Grasslands, and Rumsey welcomed his advice about running her large agricultural operation.

In town, the Wallaces had moved into the Wardman Park, adjacent to Rock Creek. Built in 1917, it was the world's fifth-largest hotel, and then one of the most famous, like New York's Waldorf or San Francisco's Sir Francis Drake. Year by year, as grand hotels and fancy neighborhoods emerged, Washington was shedding its provincial beginnings.

Many high government officials, such as former vice president Charles Curtis, lived at the Wardman. A Cabinet secretary's salary of $12,000 placed those who enjoyed it among America's 1 percent. It would cover such an apartment, except Wallace too had to be frugal. Hi-Bred lost money in 1932, and he received only $622 from the company in 1933. Yet the Wardman was perfectly situated for his brisk three-mile walks in all sorts of weather through Rock Creek Park to his department on Independence Avenue, along the plowed-up Mall.

Hopkins arrived in Washington two months later, thanks to Perkins. In March, she had brought him and a New York coworker to the White House to show FDR how their state's TERA emergency relief efforts could be a model for the nation's—and deliver swift action coast-to-coast. Roosevelt approved and identified Hopkins as the more dynamic of his two briefers. Congress passed the Federal Emergency Relief Act, and Hopkins became the program's administrator on May 22. "It was as simple as that," recalled Perkins, "and the beginning of Hopkins' rise."

She would also remember that he "immediately began thinking about how he could make greater inroads on the President's mind." And one way, according to what she saw, was to flatter Eleanor by asking, "What would you advise us to do?"[6]

Hopkins met Henry Wallace right away. Nearly the same age, they knew some of the same people in Iowa. Meanwhile, after a month at the Cosmos Club on Lafayette Square, he rented a redbrick house in Georgetown, soon to be filled with books, when Barbara and their baby joined him in early summer. The little family later moved to the recently opened, chic, and widely advertised art deco Kennedy-Warren apartment building on Connecticut Avenue, which even had an air-cooling system.

Hopkins could afford none of this. His salary as an agency administrator was $8,000, half of this going in alimony, much of what remained squandered in high living. Earlier in 1933, he had turned down lucrative positions in New York—not only Perkins's vacated role as industrial commissioner but a $25,000 per year executive slot at Macy's. "I'd rather have a small job with the President of the United States," he told people in Albany, echoing Caesar, "than a big job with the Governor of New York."[7]

During the Hundred Days, Ickes, Perkins, and Wallace were developing stronger ties among themselves than they did with the rest of the Cabinet. Roosevelt soon began to use them as a foursome, though he more often deployed them in combinations of two or three.

At the first Cabinet meeting, on March 7, for example, he instructed Ickes and Wallace to resolve the vexing problem of abandoned farmland in Florida. Then, three days later, he told them to explore how to put a half-million unemployed men to work on government projects, which was easier said than done. With input from George Dern, whose War Department hoped to benefit, Ickes and Wallace also explored the possibility of creating a multibillion-dollar public works system. Other cooperation was informal, such as Ickes agreeing to hire Wallace's eldest boy for a job in Grand Teton National Park.

No Executive Office of the President would exist until 1939 and, in addition to clerks, Roosevelt had just two White House aides, or assistant secretaries, on whom to rely. Both were journalists from what he always called his "Navy days": Marvin McIntyre of Kentucky handled appointments and burly Stephen Early of Virginia juggled the press (the Black press being excluded from news conferences until 1944). The title of secretary to the president—the highest staff position—went to Louis Howe. Roosevelt had a military and a naval aide, plus Grace Tully and the omnicompetent Missy LeHand. All in all, the coordinating, implementing, and policy making—and even the initiating roles—of government were largely shouldered by the jumble of department chiefs.

This made it important for Ickes, Perkins, and Wallace to anticipate one another's moves. Everything was in play as America clamored for drastic controls on the economy, and of a scale that even this administration had not dared to contemplate. Such cries arose from leaders of industry, not least the nation's coal barons, who, as Roosevelt put it, rushed to Washington as to "an emergency hospital . . . to cure the disease."[8]

At the start, these three officials had to assert control over their domains. To different degrees, each had to re-create a whole federal department. The challenge was greatest for Perkins, who walked into a criminal enterprise at the decrepit rented building on G Street that housed her office. (The big new Labor Department building on Constitution Avenue would not open until 1934.)

At this point, there was very little federal labor legislation. In fact, two-thirds of the department's budget went to the bureaus of immigration and naturalization. Entry into the United States had been the department's key "labor" issue from the start. Originally, large U.S. employers had hired, say, five hundred men at a time in Dublin, who were then shipped over to work in America, thereby undercutting local wages, which is why immigration functions were located at Labor.

Hoover's labor secretary, William Doak, had found ways to profit by cooperating with what Perkins called "the gangster world."[9] The secretary could lawfully deport people who might become public charges, who had a communicable disease, or who were labeled subversive. Generous fees poured in for Doak and his henchmen from shakedowns and blunt threats of deportation to quell labor troubles for businesses.

What Perkins labelled a "despotic" nationwide squad conducted warrantless raids on immigrants' homes, social clubs, and church halls. "The brutality of the immigration service was beyond words," she recalled, and some nine thousand people had just been deported, with no right to appeal.[10] This was all under federal authority, while Doak was also complicit in local outrages such as the city fathers of Los Angeles repatriating "Mexicans" (many being U.S. citizens). Throughout, he was well funded by Congress. Legislators nodded sympathetically when he testified of threats by "aliens" to the American way.

Before Perkins arrived, a New York City police detective had warned her about the racketeers she would encounter—dangerous men, he cautioned. The NYPD was even set to arrest one of Doak's senior officials should he enter the city.

By her second day, Perkins had established the facts and reported her findings to FDR, who laughed heartily: what a hoot that "it should be you who runs into the crooks."[11] Secretary Doak was retiring and would die rich six months later. His pack of public servants remained in office until, on March 8, Perkins fired dozens of them. Then she established IQ tests to build up an elite, uniformed border patrol corps focused on illegal entries rather than roundups of "Mexicans," and she overhauled the department's immigration functions with an eye to the general welfare.[12]

Corruption at the Labor Department had thrived in grimy offices riddled with Southern cockroaches the size of mice. After encountering them in the drawers of her big flat-topped desk, Perkins traced one source of the problem to her reception area. An elderly retainer brought in his lunch each day in a brown paper bag and ate at his desk, as he had done for twenty years, leaving crumbs. "I felt sorry about that," reminisced Perkins, "because Callus was a colored man, and at that time it was very difficult for the colored people to find any restaurants in that neighbor-hood" for midday meals.[13]

In 1933, only 27 percent of the citizens of Washington were Black. Migration from the South, bringing white flight to ever-growing suburbs, would not make the capital a majority Black city until the late 1950s, which it would remain until around 2012. During the 1930s, laws in the District of Columbia were barely less primitive than across the Potomac in Virginia. Eateries, hotels, and playgrounds were "White," whether or not so posted, even if allowances for equality were made in the city's buses and trolleys and in its libraries, as well as the baseball stadium. Such injustice awaited the arrival of Harold Ickes.

The Interior Department's neoclassical pile squatted over an entire block between Eighteenth and Nineteenth Streets and E and F. On his first day, he banished segregation throughout the building, checking his decision with no one. "White" signs were removed from washrooms and cafeterias, and before long, he was hiring Black engineers, architects, law-yers, and two of his own assistants (albeit funded privately), who handled "the economic status of Negroes." As for the rest of the city, he mostly had to bide his time.

Otherwise, Ickes arranged a receiving line to greet all of the building's twenty-five hundred white and Black employees, and this in an era when Southern whites refused to shake hands with Blacks. He also moved his desk out of the secretary's sixth-floor private office into the department's wood-paneled reception room, decorated with bison heads, in order to be in plain view of all.

Wallace in turn leapt to transform his department into what he called "a vast action agency."[14] It was the government's biggest, employing more than forty thousand, whose energy he directed toward trying to halt the slide of crop prices. Maybe that would quiet the heartland's pitchfork politics.

Like Ickes and Perkins, he was able to evade the political patronage system, which, then as today, often fills even sub-Cabinet roles with in-competents. Postmaster General (and patronage chief) Jim Farley hes-itated to compel any of these three forceful secretaries to accept his spoilsmen. He could off-load job-seeking Democrats on Commerce or on the Department of Justice, which he stacked with political appointees, or on the Post Office itself. However, Wallace was pleased to accept the smooth, brainy professor Rexford Tugwell—friendly with the Roosevelts and widely labeled the "most handsome original Brain Truster"—as an assistant secretary.

Eventually, Wallace would hang just three artifacts on the walls of his spacious second-floor office: his father's official portrait, a gently mocking cartoon of himself from the *Des Moines Register,* and a mystical "clay-colored work symbolizing the high place of corn in the Mayan civilization."[15]

On March 8, while Perkins was upending the Labor Department, Wallace and Tugwell met with FDR. They asked the president to approve a price-support system to be known as the Agriculture Adjustment Act, which again had its origins in the Hoover Administration. This would revamp the economics of U.S. agriculture into the 2020s. Government-enforced scarcity could solve overproduction by "allotting" checks to farmers, ranchers, and planters in order to reduce their output of cotton, corn, wheat, tobacco, rice, hogs, sheep, and cattle. Prices were therefore to be raised artificially to a hoped-for prewar parity with industry.

Deep down, Wallace was "actually opposed to crop restriction," recalled one of his aides, as had been his father.[16] To curtail or destroy a standing crop, let alone to cull livestock, went against human nature. So it was reassuring to know that a policy of "domestic allotment," like much else in the 1930s, was proclaimed temporary.

One sweeping emergency measure after another was underway. The most renowned in this war on hopelessness may be what FDR deemed initially the "Civilian Reclamation Corps." Perkins recalled the idea as no more than a "great brainstorm" because, she huffed, the notion was half-formed.[17] Everyone around the Cabinet table had blinked when he proposed turning gaunt, badly clothed jobless men into lumberjacks, or that is what they heard.

Although Roosevelt had not thought the concept through, he had brought off something similar in New York. The idea to draw only unmarried men between eighteen and twenty-two (later twenty-five) into so nationwide an effort came from Perkins, and her department would manage the recruiting. There would be no "dole." Tasks such as clearing firebreaks could be designated by his U.S. Forest Service, added Wallace. Ickes supported him, not least because he expected to pull the Forest Service out of the Department of Agriculture into Interior. Already, Interior controlled the national parks, including Yellowstone and Mount Rainier, where much of the work would be undertaken.

Secretary of War Dern's input gave life to what became the Civilian Conservation Corps. He was thinking about land reclamation projects in Utah, and moreover, the army knew how to pitch camps, lead men, and transport them. Its warehouses could supply boots, workwear, tents, and warm coats. Additionally, many of its reserve officers were now unemployed and eager to be mobilized.

In fact, a clever element of FDR's idea was the *civilian* in Conservation Corps. Ickes had detected the problem immediately and was already challenging the president:

"So, this will be a military training proposition?"[18]

Americans might be clamoring for rescue, yet Roosevelt already had plenty of enemies. A new organization of several hundred thousand strapping, well-disciplined, khaki-clad young men living under quasi-military authority sounded like a European fascist youth movement. Who knew how FDR might deploy such battalions if worse came to worst?

After all, around fifteen million Americans, out of a population barely a third of today's, were jobless, and Hopkins was warning that some would "starve to death."[19] To be unemployed also meant to lose one's house, and cartoonists depicted "F.R." galloping like a Rough Rider with bags of dollars to rescue homesteads besieged by foreclosing bankers. The Home Owners' Loan Act, another thrust of the Hundred Days, established a government corporation to refinance mortgages. The hitch— which reverberates today in home equity statistics, pollution levels, and still-segregated schools—was that officials imposed what became known as redlining: government maps warned away lenders from "hazardous" areas of town (i.e., inhabited by Blacks).[20]

The behind-the-scenes bank for much of this was to be the Reconstruction Finance Corporation, a quasi-independent public-private federal agency from the Hoover era. The new Administration remade it during the Hundred Days, and Congress provided the RFC with a capital base of $500 million, which it could leverage by issuing its own bonds and other securities. Financing of the federal government was being wrested from Wall Street.

All these initiatives were being conducted on dangerously uncharted terrain. In mid-March, Roosevelt—holding to his conventional belief that balanced budgets were crucial to the nation's health—cut spending across the board, which included reducing veterans' benefits by 25 percent. Nor did he fill two high-profile roles presciently created in the Coolidge era—those of assistant secretary of air in both the War and Navy Departments.

One person who believed he knew the path through these chaotic times was Lewis Douglas, thirty-nine, who had been appointed to direct the Bureau of the Budget after having served as Arizona's then-sole congressman since 1927. A tall, lean, energetic millionaire from one of the state's copper mining families, his welcoming grin and candid brown eyes gave him a distinguished appearance that stood out in the mass of some fifteen thousand people arriving to work for the New Deal.

Since he held Cabinet rank, despite not being a formal member, FDR often included him in meetings. The two conferred most mornings, along with Professor Moley, in FDR's ascetic bedroom, where Douglas noticed leg braces in a corner near the iron-posted bed and the wheelchair next to them.

Douglas represented the Democratic Party's conservative wing, which believed that salvation required austerity. He was open to spending on emergency relief, while being opposed to public works. Polite, smart, and plausible, with degrees from Amherst and MIT, he welcomed a humanizing role for government. And he was likable, no matter how much each of our four disagreed with him on policy.

Perkins never doubted Douglas's sincerity. He just wasn't discerning the possibilities she sensed around the corner. The orthodoxies of Adam Smith's eighteenth-century classical economics, such as hostility to deficit spending and the lasting faith that a nation's currency had to rest on gold, were under challenge. Few people understood economics, as the discipline exists today, and many regarded its study skeptically. Wallace dismissed economics as a "pseudo-science" and Perkins suspected that "anybody can read a book on it and know as much as the next fellow."[21] In fact, an authentic revolution was underway, and John Maynard Keynes—then at Cambridge University crafting his masterwork on the causes of prolonged unemployment—was not the next fellow.

Wallace shared Perkins's urgent curiosity. Might there be no more reason to accept such gross levels of unemployment than there was for society to tolerate diphtheria, for which a vaccine had recently been discovered? Might means of prevention exist for joblessness? Could precise analyses of business and labor come to match the findings of medical research? After all, one of the triumphs of the nineteenth century had been to overturn many of the hallowed beliefs in medicine, such as bloodletting. Conceivably, rethinking economics might now also revolutionize public policy. Terms like "pump-priming" were beginning to float around, as did arguments for boosting government outlays when private spending collapsed—pure Greek to the rest of the Cabinet, including Ickes.

Perkins was the first of Roosevelt's Cabinet to defend the New Deal's early actions before Congress. Eleanor Roosevelt accompanied her to the Hill on March 20, where the Senate and House committees responsible for labor issues were meeting jointly, and demanding details.

At one time, Perkins had assumed legislators to be patriots who deliberated like gentlemen for the good of the Republic. Her next shock was to discover she would be addressing more than a row of lawmakers. An overflowing hearing room of gawkers had gathered to behold the first female Cabinet secretary, only two weeks in office, delivering testimony. She wore a black dress and tricorne hat, as reporters would feel compelled to write for the next dozen years whenever she appeared. Newsreels were surging in 1933, and she squinted bravely into the klieg lights of the motion-picture apparatus.

To read Perkins's opening remarks is poignant: "Nothing is more destructive of the family than prolonged unemployment where a man has to sit around the house and brood." Basically, she was describing her home life until a year earlier, when Paul had to be hospitalized. Once the questioning began, she gave as good as she got, thrusting back at an overbearing committee chairman that his words just didn't make sense.[22]

Even so, Perkins's testimony lowered the heat. The CCC would have no military significance, she explained. Her department's "enrollees" (not "recruits") would carry shovels, axes, and ropes, while her colleague Mr. Ickes's Office of Education—among the countless functions within Interior—could provide courses in reading and math.

"I talked to Ickes for strength, I suppose," recalled Perkins, whether the subject during these initial months was the CCC or how to save the nation's coal industry. Mining families in Pennsylvania, she recalled, were "near starvation level," if not as degraded as those who lived in company-owned housing around tapped-out mines in Iowa.[23] The coal industry, under its ham-handed management, had been depressed even before the Crash. Then national calamity drove coal purchases far down. In late March, frantic mine owners got onto the president's calendar to plead for rescue. He then met with John L. Lewis, the giant of the United Mine Workers, and with the mine regions' anxious congressmen.

The Bureau of Mines, which mostly recorded the outcomes of deadly working conditions, was another office under Ickes. So it seemed logical to invite him to these high executive gatherings, and Ickes in turn asked whether Perkins could come.

Roosevelt told the owners that Ickes had "jurisdiction" over coal, despite no such authority being found in the statutes. Regardless, he had no time for the latest turmoil, which, Perkins observed, "was a very astonishing situation to him."[24] He therefore left it to Ickes to solve, and Ickes drew in Perkins. The two of them scheduled a hearing on April 16 with the coal barons in a small auditorium on Pennsylvania Avenue—though neither of them had ever held a hearing.

These thirty-five men represented the entire industry, except for one West Virginia field and the mines owned by the steel companies.

"Might you explain your problem and what the government should do?" asked Ickes.

The owners described coal as a commercially dead product that could never support the thousands of men who mined it, let alone the next generation that hoped to succeed to their fathers' jobs. In brief, private enterprise could no longer own or operate this $5 billion industry, and simply wanted Washington to take it over—at what it considered a fair price, to be sure, in an economy of $57 billion GDP.

"This is the damndest thing I ever heard," Ickes muttered to Perkins. "Did you ever hear of anything like that?"

"Why," she replied, "they must be out of their minds. They're crazy. Could they mean it?"

Ickes declared a lunch break during which Perkins phoned Roosevelt to say that the coal barons wanted the government to buy their industry. "The devil they do," replied FDR.[25]

Should anything like this come about, Ickes and Perkins suspected,

other big industries would plead to be absorbed: paper, shoes, and textiles, just for starters—and definitely the railroads, because the great
eastern lines all faced collapse.

After lunch, Ickes and Perkins tried persuasion.

"I think you're over-discouraged," she told the owners. "I think it's
your duty to run these mines."

By the end of the afternoon, Ickes was haranguing them from the
auditorium's platform like the coach of a losing team.

"Don't surrender," he urged. "You're as good as any other Americans."
He pledged that the government would help, without quite specifying how.

In private, at day's end, Ickes and Perkins agreed that if the mine
owners went bankrupt, too bad. America was a capitalist country, and if
a company went broke, it went broke.

Moreover, Ickes and Perkins had rapidly informed themselves about
the coal sector. Nimbler entrepreneurs were waiting in the wings, as truly
was the American way. Among such tycoons were the Guggenheims, who
had turned several failing copper companies around; mining magnate/
philanthropist Adolph Lewisohn; and the American Metal Company,
AMCO, "composed of very clever Jewish operators," in Perkins's opinion. (Her friend Henry Bruère had been on the board.)[26] Let them sort
out the industry with the United Mine Workers and put it on the road
back to success.

During the Hundred Days, Perkins had been the strongest advocate of
using public works as one way to help the unemployed, which Ickes
and Wallace endorsed. Their arguments persuaded the rest of the Cabinet.

To some extent, the demand to "economize" could be useful—it gave
Ickes and Perkins an excuse to overhaul their departments. For instance,
Interior's Office of Indian Affairs acted as a trustee for more than 330,000
Native Americans and fifty million acres of their land. Ickes knew first-
hand of the disease and hunger that this office had tolerated under Hoover.
In the name of trimming the budget, he got rid of the commissioner, a first
step toward the Indian Reorganization Act of 1934, which ended fifty
years of forced assimilation.

To the pleasant surprise of these three, Vice President Garner—shortish,
with a ruddy complexion, white hair, and piercing blue eyes under

shaggy white brows—also pushed back against budget cuts. Born in a mud-chinked log cabin, and too poor to afford college, he instead apprenticed to the law. On the Hill he had been known as the "terrible, table-thumping Democrat." Garner, who would tell his caucus to "bloody your knuckles" in legislative combat, might seem as primeval as John L. Lewis would describe him.[27]

Startlingly, at the April 4 Cabinet meeting, Garner denounced slashing "the Negro activities" that required federal help, including the capital's own Freedmen's Hospital. Perkins was amazed to see him then actually thump the table when he declared, "Mr. President. Mr. President! We promised that we would do something for the poorer kind of people. And we've got to do it quick. They are suffering!"[28]

Much about Garner has been misportrayed, as we will see. He had an expert background on fiscal and foreign affairs—even credibly handling the emperor of Japan in late 1935—and his legislative clout would be vital to the New Deal. Henry Bruère respected this plain and honest man, which was saying much, and there was room for unusual combinations between him and the Cabinet's three committed liberals.

The Uvalde, Texas, of that era had a population of 12,941, some two thousand fewer than today, largely of Mexican descent. Uvalde polled a significant Republican vote and was less part of the Old Confederacy than of the Mexican frontier. It was therefore on the edge—geographically and politically—of the South's anxieties over Anglo-Saxon supremacy. Garner was a bitter enemy of the Ku Klux Klan, and he possessed an element of humanity that came from representing a more cosmopolitan place than did most Southern politicians.

Getting to work in May, Hopkins launched programs for the "poorer kind of people." As soon as the Senate had confirmed him to run the Administration's major public relief program, he strode to a ramshackle headquarters on New York Avenue, where he cabled $5 million to state governors during his first two hours on the job.

Billions would follow, although legislators on the Hill had little affection from Hopkins. In a capital of watchful senators and congressmen, he didn't care to truck with politicians, nor did he like working with lawyers at a time when Washington was filling up with them.

All Cabinet officers agreed that a distinction had to be made between public works and Hopkins's quite different responsibilities—the program for outright emergency relief. Public works were intended to fight unemployment through very large federal construction projects. Costs could be shared with localities to build such big things as dams and tunnels, whereas emergency relief was passed out to the states to relieve the destitute as fast as possible.

Ickes would first take notice of "H. L. Hopkins" in July during a meeting with the president that Wallace also attended. The purpose was to outline progress on what had become an enormous farm relief bill, from which the Agriculture Adjustment Act would be carved, and which FDR considered a pillar of his New Deal. Like other initiatives, it was supposed to pay for itself through a web of user fees.

During these same weeks, yet one more program began to unfold, which Ickes would do much to implement: one of the president's early acts was to set aside emergency funds for the navy in the piping times of peace.

liked Ickes almost from the start," reminisced Perkins. "You could see him standing with Robin Hood's men and not with the Norman lords."[29] She recalled his lips pressed together in a determined pout as he studied Douglas's figures showing how much each department must cut to reconcile its bookkeeping. All were getting to know one another during these early weeks.

Ickes and Wallace, in their turn, discovered common qualities, as might be expected of an agriculture secretary who spoke of "the strength and quietness of grass," and a secretary of the interior who declared his "love of trees and plants." When a Cabinet meeting ended early and the weather was sunny, only those two were of the type who'd choose to "play hooky," as Ickes put it, and spend a half an hour together "lolling in the grass" on the banks of the Potomac.[30]

During 1933, Roosevelt's Cabinet initially convened on Tuesdays and Fridays at two o'clock. Within a year, he had cut the schedule back to just Friday. He held press conferences twice weekly, one always timed on Fridays at four in the Oval Office, which made it easy to wrap up the discussions in these "official family sessions."[31]

Meetings began when the president wheeled in, rarely on time. All rose as he offered cheery greetings and then, during these early days, used his strong arms and shoulders to swing himself into his chair at the head of the table. The secretary of state sat on his right, and the treasury secretary on his left. Others were seated alternately on either side of the table by seniority. Deputies might substitute if a principal couldn't attend.

According to this arrangement, Perkins, who was least in seniority, sat at the table's far end, with Wallace to her left and Ickes across from him, enabling the three to confer in whispers.

Going by protocol order, FDR would call on each department head to discuss recent events. Initially, Perkins spoke little. "I just proceeded on the assumption that this was a gentlemen's conversation on the porch of a golf club," she reflected, and there "you don't butt in with bright ideas." Nonetheless, FDR came to asking her, with "the encouraging smile of a brother," whether she had anything to say, and she always did.[32]

In their diaries and oral histories, Ickes, Perkins, and Wallace each complain about the apparent aimlessness of Cabinet meetings. FDR's Cabinet was no consultative body, even if he occasionally set out to elicit what collective wisdom it had. Chiefly, he used these meetings to address routine matters. Actual policy making was largely formulated elsewhere, and Cabinet officers—reluctant to show their cards in front of their peers—resolved serious departmental issues directly with him or through Louis Howe, who lived in the White House.

On one hand, the Cabinet was an appendage of the presidency, and it might seem that Roosevelt was just fulfilling an unwritten constitutional obligation to take it seriously. On the other, much was occurring in the interstices, and, under careful observation, arguments were expressed that could not be heard anywhere else. Moreover, the president was watching throughout—detecting evasions and sensing moods. He would question and reprimand and he might even quiz, say, Wallace about the price of cotton on the New York spot market. Those not able to answer had to follow up in writing.[33]

Major events often landed on the table, and once in a while they were about someone in the room.

In the tense two-hour meeting of Friday, May 26, for example, the question was whether Secretary of the Treasury Woodin should resign in disgrace. The Senate Banking Committee was investigating the secretive world of Wall Street, and Woodin's name had been uncovered on a list of J.P. Morgan & Co.'s "friends"—these being men assigned to receive new issues of stock at below-market prices. Should such a friend be a public official, the differential might seem akin to a bribe. Woodin had received shares at a 54 percent discount, according to files from February 1929.

A notorious foe of Wall Street, Vice President Garner simply told Woodin to quit. No matter: FDR was forgiving as Woodin sat next to him saying painfully little. Turning on him was a mite unfair, said the president, because Woodin had not been in public life when he received the discounted shares. Therefore, Woodin could not have been suborned by Morgan's. This argument made sense—which no one dared say— only if being "in public life" was deemed not to include being a director of the Federal Reserve Bank of New York.

Before the election, progressive senators had asked Ickes to lead their investigation of Wall Street. The mission looked hopeless even to him, and so he had declined. Now he rallied to Woodin's defense while denouncing the House of Morgan. After all, he knew so much about sailing close to the wind as, on these matters, did the president.

Roosevelt's gracious embrace of the things "that many of us did" prior to 1929—as in the epigraph above, with its cutoff date of 1929, the year he reentered public life—is telling. His law partner from 1924 onward, Basil O'Connor, always believed "the public [are] suckers and likely to continue so."[34] If such were the prevailing views at Roosevelt & O'Connor (a firm not dissolved until FDR entered the White House), it throws an intriguing light on how the partners approached their speculations in the Roaring Twenties.

In the event, FDR could just as well have been speaking to Ickes as to Woodin about a code of ethics, even if Ickes's financial embarrassments were not raised before the Cabinet. They just ended up being handled personally in the Oval Office by the president of the United States.

Ickes's financial difficulties were different from those of the immensely rich William Woodin. He hadn't fully covered his losses from the Crash, and he still owed Slaughter & Co. more than $113,000. The two parties had structured a payment plan. Unfortunately, this venerable Chicago business, itself maimed by the Crash, was acquired in 1931 by the Wall Street firm of Anderson & Fox. The new men wanted their money and what had become Slaughter, Anderson & Fox retained a high-profile lawyer. Rather than going to court, this amalgamated firm instructed its attorney just to tell President Roosevelt about Ickes's debt. Ickes would then have to pony up to avoid dismissal or glaring publicity.

Meanwhile a worse scandal loomed for Ickes—of a sort barely imaginable to Woodin and his gentle wife, Annie Jessup, also a philanthropist. This too would require presidential intervention.

In his unpublished memoir, Ickes reveals the affair he began at the Mayflower with "Mrs. X," who is easily sleuthed out as one Marguerite Moser Brumbaugh of Pittsburgh. He seems to have known her when he was a teenager, and she a small child. They had seen each other ten years earlier, but she had been married. Now she was a divorcée, if recently engaged.

Marguerite had phoned within a day of Anna's departure. Might the secretary of the interior find her fiancé a job? They agreed to discuss the question in Ickes's hotel room. When she arrived on Sunday, March 12, he said he was pleased to help. That settled, they kissed passionately. Tidying her makeup, she promised to return the following Sunday.

"It is funny what sex can do to a man," he writes, while conceding that he was "very reckless." To put it mildly.[35]

She dropped in to his Mayflower suite off and on, during the weeks that her fiancé was being dispatched to an Interior Department job deep in the Midwest. Thereafter, Ickes began entertaining her in his Georgetown house. Later that spring he bought her a diamond ring, and they went for country drives at night, using his official car and chauffeur so they could grope in the back seat. He got her a job at Interior too, actually in his office, and hired her female roommate as well. Troublingly, the fiancé wanted to get back to Washington. And so, before long, Ickes had placed him as well at Interior headquarters. Mistress, roommate, and mistress's fiancé were all under one official roof.

During this farce, Ickes did just one sensible thing, and only when anonymous letters disclosing the affair began to appear in Anna's mailbox, and soon thereafter at *The Washington Post,* the *Chicago Tribune,* and other papers. He called upon Louis Howe.

At least Ickes stood on firmer moral ground as a third issue worked its way into the Oval Office that spring. He was being blackmailed by a former judge from Chicago who threatened to have him disbarred over what the judge claimed to have been Ickes's corrupt handling of a trusts and estate case. The price of his silence would be the governorship of the Virgin Islands. (As interior secretary, Ickes administered U.S. territories and possessions.) Ickes refused, and so the blackmailer then brought his allegations to FDR.

None of these accusers had a clue as to what kind of ruthless men they were dealing with. Not just Ickes, but soon Roosevelt and Louis Howe. It would be years, however, before Ickes recognized that his own hard-hitting practices were child's play compared to those of the smiling, charming, beloved president.

Other than Ickes, no one involved Franklin Roosevelt in anything such as all this. Next to Ickes, at this point, Hopkins was a saint. Hopkins's immediate woes were just lack of money, a problem Roosevelt wouldn't have to sort out for three years, though Hopkins's own difficulties were already rising.

Not long after coming to Washington, Barbara Hopkins grew angry over her husband's inability to keep a cent. As Hopkins wrote to his brother, it was "worth any amount of money to have a ringside seat at the show."[36] In what today would be dicey for a high official—and was questionable even then—rich New York friends supplemented Hopkins's salary by $5,000 a year, as his seat at the show kept getting closer to the ring.

That said, by the beginning of June, two of the Cabinet's most observant members—Ickes and Perkins—believed Roosevelt's weariness to be reflecting the multitude of strains bearing upon him.

Ickes met with the president on Wednesday, June 7, a day of a record-setting 102 degrees. The Carrier Company had installed air-conditioning in several White House rooms but the cooling aggravated Roosevelt's sinuses. Everyone was overworked and irritable. Roosevelt had hoped Congress would wrap up on Saturday, yet it would not adjourn for another four stifling days. Only on Friday night could he leave by train for Buzzards Bay, Massachusetts, to set sail Down East.

As many intelligent people believed, terrible dangers still lurked. The sharpest of Brain Trusters was Adolf Berle, who had taught at Harvard Business School before Columbia Law. He remained in New York at his large Gramercy Park town house, taking "the midnight" most Tuesdays to Washington where—like Henry Bruère, the Manhattan banker/social activist—he counseled the president. FDR loved his brilliance, though the wiry Berle's gloomy New England Congregationalism made him nervous.

Perkins had also known Berle in New York, and one morning in mid-May, she greeted him chirpily at the White House.

"How are you, Mr. Berle?"

"My health is very well if that's what you mean," Berle replied. "Nothing else is good.

"I am getting my family out of the city and out into the deep country," he went on. "I advise you to do the same well before the fifteenth of June. The cities will not be safe."[37]

It was Berle's certainty that scared Perkins, who knew it was impossible to get Susanna and Paul up to her family's house in Maine until July. She immediately asked her staff and statisticians about what they saw on the horizon around June 15. Nothing worse than the usual, they replied—or so they hoped.

5

NEW FRONTIERS

Summer 1933 to the Midterm Elections, November 1934

The country will feel better and that's fine.
**Henry Luce, cofounder of Time Inc., and a
devout Republican, on Franklin Roosevelt's election**

Time magazine turned ten that March of 1933. By now it had become the nation's leading newsweekly for the upper middle class, its stories cleverly centered around people. Each of its covers depicted a single person, and to be a face on *Time* meant that its subject was recognized globally and undertaking great things.

Henry Wallace first appeared on April 10. Readers saw a black-and-white photo of him talking into a high-tech Dictaphone at his desk. The accompanying article described Wallace as taciturn, a constant experimenter, and a good Episcopalian. Just a month earlier, newsmen waiting outside the White House had not been able to identify him as he left a Cabinet meeting. Six weeks later, he was a national hero for rescuing American farmers.

On July 24, *Time*'s cover offered an unadorned photo of Harold Ickes staring with a tight wintry smile into the camera. The article emphasized his authority over the "monster" public works program and his quick rise to eminence. A photo of Anna figured in the story. *Time* described her as "tall, grey-haired and not as severe as she looks," while observing that the interior secretary had long been "known around Winnetka as 'Mrs. Ickes's husband'" because of her wealth and political success in Springfield.[1]

Perkins was on the August 14 cover, her portrait a revealingly black-and-white sketch with terribly sad eyes. The article noted that she had within herself "concentrated all the philosophy of the New Deal and most of its instinctive sympathy for the working man." In part, this meant she urged fair wages, and could easily define what was fair: "to permit a worker to call a doctor when his baby is sick without going on half rations for a month after," as *Time* summarized.[2]

As for Hopkins, he would appear the following February—his angular face, in profile, casting a lean and hungry look if ever there was one.

A long row of other suddenly famous officials would stare out from the newsstands during 1933. None of these would hold office a dozen years later when the presidency ended.

Throughout, the Roosevelt era was characterized by intense personalization, starting at the top, and it was expanded by the president's broadcasts. His smooth, compact sentences were delivered in a voice—and with an Anglicized, non-rhotic accent—that made a frightened people feel more secure. As newsreels boomed, along with pictorial journalism, key executive branch officials, not just the president, became stars.

Ickes, Wallace, and Perkins were already setting themselves apart from their Cabinet colleagues. Reporters even grouped the first two, along with Hopkins, as "dictators" of the New Deal, though surely not Perkins. For all her forceful accomplishments, who could imagine a woman "dictator"?[3]

Each of the four caught the spotlight in an era when a top official might be able quickly to complete great tasks. Fewer obstacles than today existed to trammel executive authority, providing the initiative in question enjoyed the president's confidence. One might start constructing a dam on the Cumberland River—after lining up the relevant congressmen, of course—whereas, these days, lawsuits and permitting processes would stall so ambitious a project for years. Political decisions could be dramatic. Hopkins, for instance, was indeed walking the high wire when he dispersed that $5 million in two hours. No career mandarins stood by to hold up a newly arrived minister, as in Britain and France, nor even the competent civil service of today's Washington.

Throughout, FDR benefited from the rising profiles of our four.[4] Ickes staged a popular weekly press conference much like the president's; he and Wallace each published bestselling books about the New Deal in 1934; and Perkins was a hit in the newsreels. Who, when seated in the Trans-Lux cinema, expected to stare up at a Madison Avenue matron talking with roughhewn labor leaders in a strike-deadened steel town? Fame was a means for all to do their jobs.

It was easy to acclaim a "revolution" amid the excitement of creating this FDR-driven recovery machine, not that any of our four did so. Nor was there much sign of revolution. Fiscal policies redistributed little of the nation's wealth, banks hadn't been nationalized, and certainly nothing confronted the brutalities of race. As in the early 2020s, progressives like Bronson Cutting said they had been betrayed. Instead, the ongoing priorities were to contain the economic plague, repair the worst damage, and raise structures to prevent its recurrence.

That said, relations were indeed shifting between workers and employers, creditors and debtors, farmers and wage earners, and people and the state. Would all this have come about anyway, many Americans wondered, without a Great Depression? Everyone could see that the wages of labor were inconsonant with the enormous returns going to capital. FDR himself summed up this feeling when he met with the chairman of Bethlehem Steel: Surely it wouldn't do for Mr. Schwab and his friends to take in "more million-dollar bonuses paid to the top out of stockholders' money" while their workers couldn't draw a living wage.[5]

Yet contradictions bedeviled an administration that had cut government salaries to reduce budget deficits while at the same time starting construction projects to rival Cheops. By 1934, it was not unfair to ask whether this was a far-seeing presidency, believing the country could be no stronger than its most downtrodden citizens, or was it simply a bravely led outfit with conflicting ideas and colorful personalities squaring off over bureaucratic turf?

As summer 1933 rolled in, the hard, long-term liberal core of Roosevelt's government began taking form.

The president faced few serious counterarguments to what had been achieved. No such intellectual apparatus of think tanks and scholars as thrives today existed to push back with ideas of "free enterprise," itself a recently coined slogan to be mobilized against the New Deal. Articulate opposition did not go much beyond the National Association of Manufacturers' urgent defense of child labor in textile mills, or Richard Whitney—the "Voice of Wall Street"—crying "socialism" at FDR's plans to regulate the stock market.

Nor was it easy to criticize a man so difficult to plumb as now sat in the White House. He was set on balancing the budget and might explain, in private, that he had Jewish blood in his veins, while rubbing his hands together.[6] Conversely, he would appear quite blasé each fall when one more decidedly out-of-balance budget crossed his desk.

The economy had been shrinking for forty-three consecutive months since fall 1929, and this might well not be the time to rehash the Democratic commitment to fiscal conservatism. Roosevelt was also rethinking the dollar's ties to gold. Most economists believed the dollar to be grossly overvalued in 1933, and on April 19, he issued an executive order that effectively took the country off the gold standard. In theory, the Administration could then manage the nation's currency. Even the suave Winthrop Aldrich lost his composure while testifying before a congressional committee, calling this act "more drastic than the French Revolution."[7]

Whatever the merits of FDR's decision about gold, he chose to handle the day-to-day dollar–gold ratio by himself in those morning bedroom meetings with a couple of equally uninformed aides.

Roosevelt was fascinated by the "mysteries of money," according to Tugwell. For him to shift the price of gold at random, when he knew nothing about the economics involved, let him rule the market on his terms. Commodity prices failed to rise as hoped, and Keynes famously called the results "a gold standard on booze," perhaps more correctly than he realized.[8]

The president's grasp of economics may be debatable. On one hand, he had studied the subject at Harvard, and, in the 1920s, had read such pre-Keynesian economists as William Trufant Foster. On the other, he would alarm staffers at the Federal Reserve by jauntily telling an aide that he had imposed a twenty-one-cent price increase on gold because the number was thrice the lucky number seven.[9]

On most issues, except for the navy, and occasionally on conservation, he tended to delegate freely. His technical interests went little further than rigging sailboats. So he was pleased, for instance, to give Wallace the latitude to funnel $75 million into a new surplus-commodities initiative that provided flour, rice, and lard to the hungry. It would evolve into today's Nutrition Assistance Program. True to the time, such farmers as owned land, and thus being subsidized, were, again, mostly white.

Roosevelt liked to see his people do well and to innovate, and he cared little about not grasping the particulars of any latest inspiration. OK, go do it, he said typically; and "if it doesn't work, the blood will be on your head."

Tugwell uses the word "consequence" to describe how FDR's presence forever hovered, even if he was nowhere to be seen. "Remember, Papa wants to know what you're thinking about," he would tell his Cabinet.[10]

Unlike other top officials, our four had arrived in Washington with practical, well-conceived designs for action. Perkins had laid out her plans, which included banning child labor, before agreeing to come. Ickes had blueprints for protecting the nation's forests and mountains. Wallace understood every step needed to reach the generations-old, prairie-radical dream to attain "parity" between the earnings of farmers and industrial workers.

Additionally, all four had access to long-cultivated professional networks. Hopkins, for instance, moved fast because he knew whom to call in each state to pour out the money efficiently. He had already met the right people during the 1920s, such as the directors of the Cleveland Foundation, the world's first and largest city fund. Only Farley's web of minutely categorized political allies could compare. As for remembering names, twenty years earlier it had been said of Wallace's father that he knew more farmers by their first name than any man in America. His son came a close second.

In their fusion of liberal views, experience, and hands-on executive skills, our four brought some consistency to what an increasing number of critics were calling "government by abbreviation": the AAA, TVA, FBDIC (to become the FDIC), NRA, CCC, and the CCC (Junior), which was the Commodity Credit Corporation, responsible for financing the purchase of agricultural surpluses. Many outfits had subdivisions under equally unfathomable initials.[11] Altogether, this approach to governing, believed the president, added flexibility and freshness, skirted entrenched Republican civil servants, and gave him maximum control.

The most exotic of these emergency organizations became effective on June 16, 1933, the last of the so-called Hundred Days. The National Industrial Recovery Act, and the National Recovery Administration that it spawned, attempted to revive employment by cartelizing business through codes of competition. Largely through voluntary compliance, the nation's prices, wages, and production levels were to be boxed into hundreds of sectors, from shipbuilding to publishing to selling chickens.

The NRA's enthusiasts, such as Tugwell, held this prodigy to be the mainspring of the New Deal. Industrial harmony, rather than dog-eat-dog capitalism, they believed, would lead to efficiency and, thereby, to higher employment. Similarly, the protection of workers' rights should add to such happy coherence. The worst abuses, including the hiring of children, were pressured to end, and forty-eight-hour workweeks took hold. At first, the NRA sought to embrace even more, including a $3.3 billion Public Works Administration, that sum alone having been the average size of federal budgets in the 1920s.

One of Roosevelt's more irresponsible appointments was the man selected to head the NRA. Red-faced and profane, Brigadier General Hugh Johnson (ret.) had, fifteen years earlier, helped organize industry for wartime, and, since 1927, was financier Bernard Baruch's number three man as head of research. To succeed, the NRA needed to be energized by lots of hype—which is where the garrulous, forever-in-motion, fifty-one-year-old general came in. The extent of publicity surrounding this "doer" is shown by his appearance as *Time*'s "Man of the Year" for 1933. No less than FDR himself had been "Man of the Year" in 1932, as he would be again in 1934.

In selecting Johnson, Roosevelt's acumen in reading people failed by half. Then, as rumors of Johnson's imminent appointment swirled in early June 1933, Baruch warned Frances Perkins that his "number three" would never succeed as a "number one." Unhelpfully, Baruch didn't elaborate.

Perkins added her own concerns when meeting with FDR, because Johnson had seemed too excitable during the campaign. His biometric opposite, Henry Wallace, had no faith in him at all. Regardless, Congress and newsmen expected the president to announce his nominee, and it was too late to backtrack. Yet Roosevelt had been alarmed by what he heard from Perkins. Therefore, he changed his plans for the NRA: he would cleave off half of its functions, which became the Public Works Administration.

Even before he had a chance to sign the National Industrial Recovery Act, he met on June 13 with Secretaries Ickes, Perkins, and Wallace to form a Cabinet committee that would organize the sweeping control that Congress was granting him over industry. And, if Johnson were not to run public works, an immediate replacement was needed.

Late on the morning of June 16, the day Johnson was to be anointed as "Administrator for Industrial Recovery," Roosevelt decided to place the enormous public works functions temporarily into Ickes's hands. The Interior Department already contained numerous entities, such as the Bureau of Land Reclamation. He asked Perkins to convey his ruling to Ickes. She phoned him at one thirty, just a half hour before the regular two o'clock Friday Cabinet meeting in which Johnson was to be congratulated for shouldering the entire NRA burden.

"The hell he is," Ickes responded to news of this decision to give him what became the Public Works Administration. She explained the president had only just made up his mind.

"Well, he should talk to me," growled Ickes.[12]

Just be a "temporary holder" for this massive creation, she pleaded, until the president could find an ongoing successor. As the clock ticked toward 2:00 P.M., Ickes relented.

Roosevelt invited a beaming General Johnson into the Cabinet room formally to bestow the big appointment. Then the president was struck by an idea. Far be it from him, said Roosevelt, to overburden the nation's new administrator. Therefore, it might be best to relieve the general of half his duties, those for public works. And he pointed down the table at Ickes. It was left to Perkins to mollify the infuriated Johnson before he blew up in front of the waiting reporters.

Over the next twelve years, Perkins often found herself mediating the quarrels of angry men, preventing far worse things from happening. For the time being, she needed to watch Johnson—which would prove to be an eighteen-month task in itself because, as of July 1, her partner, Mary Rumsey, found herself in his chain of command. Perkins had devised a Consumers' Advisory Board for the NRA, the first ever in Washington. Johnson had accepted Perkins's creation because Rumsey, whom he liked, agreed to serve as chairwoman. Along the way, Perkins was coming to despair, with only a handful of exceptions, of the ability of men to run anything.

Ickes was one of those few exceptions, and at this moment, he and Perkins agreed that FDR's maneuvering was "a very peculiar technique." By the next day Ickes had told FDR that he wanted to run Public Works for real. He recognized a chance for immortality that surpassed his patented dahlia.

Now Ickes would be responsible for erecting some of the world's biggest, most complicated creations, intended to outlast the century. "This job was the beginning of Ickes's great reputation," Perkins remembered.[13] He was suspicious of everybody, questioned all, and no penny passed through his fingers that could be misspent while America's infrastructure had to be remade. "I don't know what guardian angel caused Roosevelt to select Ickes for the job," wrote Wallace.[14]

In addition to his far-flung duties as secretary of the interior, Ickes now took on responsibilities that would make him one of the greatest builders in American history. In turn, Hopkins was about to become the nation's largest employer.

General Johnson was left to persuade each category of businessmen to adopt its NRA code as if they were forming trade associations. So he needed to collaborate with Ickes (now head of PWA), Perkins (because of the NRA's impact on labor conditions), and Wallace, who explained to him the "circuit flow of prosperity" between industry and agriculture: industry could not recover until the buying power of farmers was raised to prewar levels.[15]

For a time, the general was to become the personification of "Recovery," despite not being in the Cabinet and possessing few characteristics that appealed to Roosevelt. One of Johnson's aims was to stoke citizen enthusiasm for the codes. The NRA had its own postage stamp, and he created such other dramatics as the Blue Eagle, actually the Navajo thunderbird. The ubiquitous display of this totem in shop windows and on factory gates showed compliance. He staged huge parades in twenty-two cities with NRA floats and NRA bands. His all-star citizen advisory boards included men like Rumsey's younger brother, the banker Averell Harriman, who volunteered to chair the president's Emergency Re-Employment Committee for New York State.

In Manhattan, the NRA parade of September 14 remains the largest ever held in New York City. A quarter-million people marched up Fifth Avenue while nearly two million others cheered. Johnson waved imperially from a grandstand in front of the public library, along with Eleanor Roosevelt, accompanied by Louis Howe.

This hard-drinking proconsul was useful to FDR, even if the president found one of Johnson's habits—always to be in movement, even when seated—to be annoying in the extreme. Johnson was good at this hype, and Roosevelt wasn't about to make that level of vulgar noise himself. Later, Johnson rode about in a large black touring car. Newsreels showed him raising his arm in what to Perkins was an unsettlingly European salute.

That same week, smoldering resentments on the Hill could no longer be contained. Key Pittman of Nevada—lean, gray, canny, and president pro tempore of the Senate—spoke for many legislators. In a letter to FDR, he assailed Ickes, Perkins, and Wallace for "appointing Republicans instead of Democrats" to their departments. Until this problem was re-solved, he stated, there'd be a lot less cooperation between Congress and the Administration.[16] Some face-saving patronage ensued. However, there remained Hopkins, who refused to accept party hacks in major positions.

Meanwhile, it was Ickes in whom FDR was vesting immense confi-dence. During the same week as the parade and the Senate ultimatum, *The New York Times* concluded, "Secretary Ickes is considered by some the most powerful figure in the Roosevelt cabinet."[17] FDR had known him only six months, yet now Ickes personally dealt on his behalf with mayors and governors in every state.

Ickes decided who received grants or loans, and for which immensities—while usually seeking FDR's agreement. As "dictator" of Public Works, for example, he signed a contract on September 1 that gave $37.5 million to the Port Authority of New York to build the Lincoln Tunnel under the Hudson. The next day, he closed another contract to build the city's Triborough Bridge. In the Northwest, the Grand Coulee Dam on the Columbia River would a decade later be the world's largest man-made structure.

He and FDR were forming a curious bond that was to last twelve years. In late summer, Roosevelt appointed him oil administrator, which allowed Ickes to regulate production and, thereby, control the oil indus-try. Of course, an accompanying Petroleum Administrative Board sprang up. With the gushing overproduced crude of East Texas at four cents a barrel, few complaints about government interference arose from Big Oil in Houston.

Among the times Roosevelt caucused with Hopkins, Ickes, Perkins, and Wallace all together—according to Ickes's diary—was on November 6, 1933, to discuss Hopkins's latest plan for saving the downfallen. The meeting's purpose was to reach beyond the efforts of Federal Emergency

Relief to immediately help the unemployed survive the approaching winter. Maybe four million of the needy could be hired by government. Aldrich, as representative of business opinion, opposed the idea: this scheme competed unfairly with private industry.

But FDR did not routinely summon all four of his lieutenants at once lest other officials perceive them as a bloc. Alternatively, he kept using small, varying combinations. For example, Hopkins and Ickes returned before lunch the next day to discuss an executive order establishing the Civil Works Administration—a big, albeit short-term, emergency employment plan to come under Hopkins's FERA program. And he placed just Hopkins, Ickes, and Wallace on the board of the new Federal Surplus Commodities Corporation to get food to hungry families.

In the background, Roosevelt faced difficulty with a high official far closer to his own kind. He compelled the smooth, Harvard-trained lawyer, Under Secretary of the Treasury Dean Acheson—eleven years his junior at Groton and son of Connecticut's Episcopal bishop—to resign in mid-November. Acheson had been unable to win Roosevelt to his notion of sane economic policy, and this was essentially the Administration's first high-profile firing. Henry Bruère, working intermittently in Washington to bridge public and private finance, observed of the dismissal, "Everybody took it gaily and gallantly."[18]

Acheson had been poised to succeed his chief, the dying William Woodin. Instead, he returned to what was already "the most active Washington lobbyist law firm," today's Covington & Burling.[19] Ironically, he had wearied of Roosevelt's "condescension," as he called the president's first-name familiarity. At an impeccably tailored six foot one and imperially slim, with a bristling mustache, even then Acheson was the haughty Velázquez grandee he would be labeled sixteen years later as secretary of state.[20]

Another irritant for the suddenly ex-undersecretary had been the confusion arising from Roosevelt's simmering alphabet soup of new agencies, which during the New Deal would total sixty-nine, whether created by Congress or by executive order. The Treasury Department felt entangled in budget lines and, above all, by the disorders of the National Recovery organization.

Two days after Acheson left, the president opened the National Emergency Council, which itself distilled the works of a larger coordinating body created over the summer. He designated Ickes, Perkins, and Wallace to oversee this latest setup, and also Commerce Secretary Roper, already fading into history. Among FDR's lower-ranking designees was Mary Rumsey, the only woman on the council besides Perkins.

There was much for the Emergency Council to tackle, not least because FDR stated his chief concern at this juncture to be "an agrarian revolt" in the country. As the council was being organized, however, even more outfits were hatched, including the Public Works of Art Project. By now the country was taking measures never before imagined, such as levying taxes to support unemployed artists—an idea that came from Perkins, a keen student of the visual arts. FDR regarded her proposal as "partly a joke." Referring laughingly to the nearly completed Boulder Dam, he said "we can cover that all over with sculptures." She asked him to be serious. Hopkins got pulled in, "whether Hopkins or I wanted it or not," recalled his assistant, and so began the Public Works of Art Project in December 1933.[21]

The worst of the ongoing turmoil arose not from the NRA but between Ickes's Public Works Administration and Hopkins's need to ensure that millions of Americans had jobs of any sort—which could not be accomplished by building tunnels or bridges. Those required specialized skills. To resolve this difference between light and heavy public works, FDR sent Hopkins, Wallace, and Perkins to tell Ickes that about $400 million of his money would be impounded to finance Hopkins's tasks instead. Ickes heard them out and did not object, at first.

Our four lieutenants developed relationships with one another while they got their footing in Washington, as well as with the president. Perkins, who had a lifelong fascination with how people behave under stress, already knew FDR well. The other three now began to scrutinize him too. They watched him dissect and memorize documents. He read fast. Each remarked on an intellect that was at its sharpest whenever he faced a crucial move in the political game, such as corralling votes. He was similarly focused when handling navy business. They saw him thinking more generally in terms of politics over policy, so they pitched their ideas in the context of elections. Wallace's farm subsidies would help get votes in the heartland, and big-city bosses should welcome Hopkins's work-relief money.

They were less acute at noticing how he was handling them. Much of this was tactile. Perkins could be assuaged with a wink and a squeeze of the hand. Hopkins was treated like a soldier in the trenches with a long, firm grip on the arm. Ickes would gush in his diary about FDR's hand on his knee (the twist being that Ickes, brutalized as a child, otherwise hated to be touched by men, as Roosevelt would have discerned).

The president was not demonstrative toward the aloof, more somber Wallace—the type of high official who eschewed Washington parties. Instead, Wallace and his wife, Ilo, might invite Perkins, Rumsey, and General Johnson for a late summer evening boat ride to feed ducks on the Potomac. And Ickes would be asked to dinner because, Henry and Ilo worried, he was alone in the evening.

Then Wallace would retreat into his study at the Wardman Park to write in his distinctive left-handed scrawl, on departmental stationery, to his "Dear Guru"—a Russian-born painter with a following of rich disciples in New York. Wallace used code words, grandly styling himself "Galahad" or "Parsifal." When he wrote of the president, that enigmatic presence could be either the "Flaming One," should Wallace approve of FDR's latest decisions, or the "Wavering One" when he did not.

Eccentricity crossed into waste of public funds when Wallace persuaded Budget Director Douglas to finance the guru (Nicholas Roerich, aka Nikolai Konstantinovich Rerikh) and a high-living entourage for a long journey through Central Asia, starting in 1934. Wallace hoped they would collect drought-resistant grass seeds that might flourish in the Midwest.

Wallace's correspondence was a time bomb. If these silly letters should ever become public, voters would question his fitness for office. Meanwhile, the letters that swirled around Ickes were set to detonate. So far, newspapers had not dared to print the anonymous allegations about his affair with "Mrs. X," and the publishers were getting impatient.

Many people could have talked of the secrets held by Louis Howe, yet they did not, or simply feared doing so. He possessed a "sixth sense" for observing others, said Eleanor.

When Ickes went to see Howe on August 23 about what had become a whole file of anonymous letters, he knew he was confessing to FDR and, thereby, summoning the president's darker powers. Howe called in the Secret Service to put agents on the case.

Yet the letters kept coming. With Howe's guidance, Ickes called in the cruder methods of thuggish Interior Department investigators who persuaded a property manager to open the apartment of that obvious suspect, "Mrs. X's" fiancé. Carbon paper and an incriminating typewriter were removed. Within hours, the investigators and Ickes confronted the fiancé. The letters stopped, and the now unemployable man was left to linger around Washington, eventually to marry "Mrs. X," aka Marguerite Brumbaugh. Howe also excelled at keeping this type of story out of the news.

Nevertheless, still more Ickes-related trouble fell into the president's lap. On September 12, at the start of a routine meeting, FDR tossed some papers to him across the desk. They proved to include a letter to the president from the Chicago judge who was trying to blackmail Ickes. The papers also contained FDR's reply, which, according to Ickes's diary, essentially called the blackmailer's bluff: members of his official family did not behave like that. The president then asked FBI Director J. Edgar Hoover to investigate. Ickes was cleared of all charges, and the following June the judge was disbarred.

"I know you," FDR told Ickes when they were alone after the Cabinet meeting of November 15. "All of us have been in trouble some time or other." Note the "all of us"—at first glance a generous assumption of responsibility, like the "we" who had all changed our ways since 1929. In this case, to Ickes's momentary relief, FDR was not referring to the messy "Mrs. X" affair or to the Chicago blackmailer. Instead, lawyers had contacted the president about a certain unpaid brokerage account.

Ickes twice offered to resign; the president had other ideas. If Ickes could not pay, said FDR, "he would call in some friends of the Administration" to cover the debt. That likely would have been Jesse Jones, the titanic multimillionaire with an eighth-grade education, who had built Houston's skyline and now ran the Reconstruction Finance Corporation.[22] Alternatively, as actually happened, FDR might walk Ickes through a response that hammered down the brokers. The president considered himself a fine lawyer, and he knew that Slaughter, Anderson & Fox would accept an offer of around $11,000, rather than risk court costs and, it need not be said, presidential displeasure. Ickes, therefore, happily wrote a check for 9.7 percent of the debt.

Unchastened by these events, Ickes continued his high-risk adultery for a year after he confessed to Howe. FDR, who of course knew most of the story, was nonplussed. As for Anna Wilmarth Ickes, who had received several anonymous letters, she got to hear specifics about the affair from her husband during one of her rare visits to Washington, where Harold told her of his joy with Marguerite. Once home in Illinois, Anna overdosed on prescription pills—having first called her doctor, before swallowing, to assure a quick recovery.

Ickes's sexual escapades and corner-cuttings were part of the glee he took in defying the general culture. Similarly, his zeal for conservation and his hatred of bigotry in all its forms stood apart from typical beliefs of that era's upper middle class. This was a complicated life and FDR enjoyed participating in it. He got to practice law pro bono on the side, and not least, he cemented Ickes's loyalty.

Nonetheless, it took a highly unusual employer to tolerate Ickes, or, in fact, any of these four. Yet the president discerned outstanding talent—as well as distinct vulnerabilities—in each. As for Perkins, FDR already understood her at least as well as he did the others, and he was pleased that her appointment set a historic precedent. Even so, he no more grasped her full significance than did any of the other men in his administration. For, by her example, Perkins was dynamizing a generation.

Except for a few states that allowed it, women had gained the vote only thirteen years before Roosevelt entered office. Perkins exemplified what was truly new in this era more than did Eleanor, even though Eleanor had become the country's preeminent female activist and trailblazer for civil rights. People applauded the First Lady's idealism, and her stand for an anti-lynching law in an indifferent time still stirs the heart. Her concern with the downtrodden had transcended politics to become nearly mythical. That becomes apparent in the famous *New Yorker* cartoon of a deep-tunneling coal miner suddenly crying out to his mate, "For gosh sakes, here comes Mrs. Roosevelt!"

But Eleanor was not secretary of anything, and people would have scoffed had she been: she was the president's wife, and served as her husband's eyes and ears. She affected the national consciousness, over the long term—and as a passionate amateur—whereas Perkins, the born administrator, had fought her way up to ever more widely change people's lives.

Like Eleanor, Perkins discovered an intimacy with other determined women. Both had been failed by their men. Once each woman found herself not just alone, but free, she opened herself to a wider range of choice; emotionally for sure, quite possibly sexually.

Other women besides Rumsey joined Perkins's tight-knit Washington circle, such as the widowed Caroline Love O'Day, elected congresswoman-at-large from New York in 1934, and Josephine Roche, a graduate of Vassar and Columbia, with an MA in social work.

Roche had been married and divorced before coming to Washington during the 1920s to work at the Children's Bureau within the Labor Department. After her father died in 1927, leaving her 40 percent of the Rocky Mountain Fuel Company, she bought out the other shareholders, cooperated with the United Mine Workers, and grew the enterprise. Like O'Day, who had been a suffragette, she was a pioneer of women's rights, indeed Denver's first policewoman. In 1932, she had backed Roosevelt.

Two years later, FDR appointed Roche, forty-eight, assistant secretary of the treasury to focus on public health. That made her the second-highest-ranking woman in the Administration, after her Columbia classmate, Perkins—who never doubted that Roche was more suitable for the department's top job than the man who had entered office on January 1, 1934.

Treasury Secretary William Woodin had offered to resign as his health deteriorated. Because FDR declined to accept, he took a leave of absence in hopes of rest. The question of Under Secretary Acheson's replacement therefore became critical in late November 1933. The next undersecretary would become the actual, if not titular, head of the department. Time was short, as with everything in the New Deal, and one immediate possibility for the role was Henry Morgenthau, Jr., son of the party's elder statesman.

Henry Sr. had been disappointed at his boy's schooling. Young Henry had dropped out of Cornell's architecture program after three semesters, taken a leisurely break, then returned to its College of Agriculture, which, in turn, he quit within two years. Perkins had found him aimless when he had worked for her briefly in the teens. Some eighteen years later, after FDR's election, he had yearned to run the Agriculture Department, only to agree, in late April 1933, to take a lower appointment as governor of the new Farm Credit Administration.

Wallace worked with Henry Jr. at Farm Credit, later describing him as "exceedingly weak and tender physically," as well as preoccupied with various ailments.[23] Despite all, six months at Farm Credit gave Morgenthau just sufficient standing in finance. With the clock ticking, FDR moved him into Acheson's empty office as undersecretary. He was to "hold the fort as a friend of the president," recalled Perkins, until a proper secretary could be found—an issue that became imperative once Woodin insisted he needed to go by December 31.[24]

Henry Bruère was still commuting to Washington, working out of a small office at Treasury, keeping no records. He responded discreetly when FDR asked him to conduct a talent search. The natural candidate would have been Bruère himself. Instead, after much honest canvassing, he recommended Henry Morgenthau, Jr.

FDR was surprised. Yet there was no time to look further: he had long known young Henry, who passionately desired the job, and Bruère had given his OK. Roosevelt therefore submitted Morgenthau's name to the Senate. All FDR's nominees had been confirmed, so far. Suddenly, Henry Jr. outranked Perkins and everyone except Hull in the Cabinet.

Fortune magazine called Morgenthau "the most obscure Secretary of the Treasury this country has ever had."[25] However, anyone who held this role in a time of terrible depression would likely go down as a major figure—a mistaken view that is still largely held today.

Morgenthau would at least be a strong moral voice for confronting the horrors of Nazism and for aiding wartime England. As treasury secretary, however, he proved inept. Nonetheless, like Cordell Hull, he was the only other high official to serve at the Administration's heights for nearly as long as Hopkins, Ickes, Perkins, and Wallace. Sylvia Porter, a wizard financial columnist of that era who would eventually have her own *Time* cover, interpreted his inarticulateness as a sign of his basically being "ignorant and stupid."[26]

Why did Roosevelt appoint Morgenthau, besides the convenience of having him at hand? First, FDR had seen close-up how a forceful treasury secretary could overshadow presidents, as had Andrew Mellon. Second, he had gotten along rather well, the banking emergency once ended, without a full-time head of the department. And, third, FDR wanted direct, unobstructed access to the Bureau of Internal Revenue, which then, as today, was an arm of the Treasury. To appoint a strong, independent-minded chief would sooner or later have caused a blowup.

Moreover, pockets of excellence existed among that era's half-million-employee U.S. Civil Service, and several solid career men were already high enough at Treasury to keep things steady.[27]

Bruère knew what he was doing, and it is telling that he declined the country's secondmost senior Cabinet position. Perkins, who was close to him, believed he would have taken the role had FDR pressed. She also knew it would never have worked. Like Bronson Cutting, he did not want to report to Franklin Roosevelt. He grasped what shrewd politicos were beginning to detect about the president: as Edward J. Kelly, who ruled Chicago as mayor from 1933 to 1947, observed, he had never known another politician who would stay at the top and not keep his word.

Nor did Bruère feel obliged by duty to country. By late 1933, the worst of the economic plague had, it seemed, waned. Undeniably, millions remained jobless, the giant farm bill had not stemmed plunging commodity prices, nor could anyone tell whether the Recovery Act was boosting production. Even so, several of the novel emergency agencies looked helpful. For instance, the Federal Deposit Insurance Corporation protected individual savers; the Civilian Conservation Corps was putting hundreds of thousands of young men to work and sending wages to their families; and, within the Interior Department, Ickes had created the Soil Erosion Service, which would be essential to federal conservation efforts.

Still, new emergencies beset the nation and were proving equally dangerous to stressed banks. One was climate. Nineteen thirty-four proved to be the hottest year on record, and the worst drought since the Civil War now afflicted almost two-thirds of the country. The president met often with Hopkins, Wallace, and Ickes to review the devastations of grazing land and topsoil. And he mentioned to such significant listeners as the governor of Pennsylvania that Ickes was the best executive he knew.

Further emergencies arose from clashes between labor and management. The growth of unions had arrived late to America, which had the most violent strike record of any developed country. Then, in June 1933, labor organizing boomed in factories and mining towns within hours of workers hearing that the president had signed the National Recovery bill. That year, about 2.25 million people—the vast majority still men—were unionized. Most belonged to skilled craft guilds, such as the International Typographical Union, which, historically, dominated the American Federation of Labor.

However, in 1934, workers "organized, joined a union and were promptly fired," recalled Perkins.[28] Strikes became a bloody by-product of the NRA. One of the terrible things that Perkins deflected was a decision that summer by Secretary of State Hull, acting for a president vacationing at sea: he intended to send the army to crush a Pacific Coast longshoremen's strike, starting in San Francisco, long known as a strong union town.

Hull was backed by Attorney General Cummings, and Perkins barely headed them off. It was just one drama involving what her society friends called Frances's "Department for Poor People."

E ach of the four lieutenants began to see Roosevelt as a man who could envisage the future, as he did with conservation—although his handling of Treasury and the NRA was puzzling. Conservation, however, was an issue where he could be counted on to review every detail, as when he dispatched Wallace and Ickes to "Indian country" around Santa Fe during May to investigate land purchases by shady businessmen—an assignment that, in 1934, required interpreters. He got similarly into details during June, when he appointed a Cabinet committee of Ickes, Perkins, and Wallace to examine the drought's effect on the Plains states.[29]

Roosevelt could master a subject quickly, but a grasp of details does not necessarily confer an understanding. He was sharp, yet more so about people than things. Often, he flew above the clouds, although subordinates felt he just might be peering down. Because he could be so hands-off, it was Perkins's sole decision to embark, in late summer 1934, on what she recalled as one of the strangest experiences of her life. It's also one of the strangest experiences of American history.

Migrant laborers from Mexico, as well as some midwesterners fleeing the region's desolation, toiled on California's lettuce and cantaloupe farms at starvation wages. In the Imperial Valley during picking season, they were basically prisoners. Landowners had responded to a wave of initially nonviolent strikes by demanding that the army, or at least more state police, suppress the "anarchists" who went unprotected by any federal or local authority.

Wallace awakened Perkins to rural poverty, and a change of wording in Washington altered perspectives. Until speaking of "factory farming" and "factories in the field," no one had considered farmworkers to be laborers.

By now barn burnings, roadblocks, and white citizen vigilantism were breaking out and Perkins hired Pelham Davis Glassford to bring peace to the Valley. His role was simply "mediator," but he had been America's youngest general in the World War, and thereafter served as police superintendent in Washington, D.C. Glassford had quit the police over President Hoover's decision to use the army against the Bonus Marchers of July 1932 and army chief of staff Douglas MacArthur's assault on their encampment.

The brown-eyed, handsome, six-foot, four-inch West Pointer, fifty-one, had retired to a farm near Phoenix to be a painter, and his watercolors can be found at auction today. Perkins remembered Glassford's intelligence and calm when he had dealt humanely with the Bonus Marchers, and she hoped a stern military figure such as he could now stem the growing violence. She deemed the migrants to be "like children" who would take comfort in authority, and the landowners bullies who needed firm handling.[30]

Glassford drove to Southern California on a mission to establish law and order. He made his own news with the local press by parking his Ford in town squares and using his fluent Spanish to hear grievances. He was repulsed within a week by working conditions and the landowners' tactics. Then he issued a decree, written in red ink, and he ordered copies to be tacked up in scores of towns: "PROCLAMATION: I, Pelham D. Glassford, General of the United States, Representative of the U.S. Department of Labor, do hereby establish the following minimum wages to be paid in this Valley."

The numbers he invented sounded plain fair, and he phoned Perkins to say he didn't need any statisticians to help.

Glassford expanded his so-called proclamation to include requirements for clean drinking water in the fields, and expected landowners to take sick migrants to the hospital. For them to do so would avoid "an epidemic breaking out," a persuasive enough reason. He was a law unto himself when he handed down the "Glassford Wage" as if on stone tablets, and he enforced these decrees by a commanding presence. He bought a crucial year of peace until Wallace could involve the Agriculture Department, and Congress began months of hearings on agricultural labor. "I liked him," said Perkins.[31]

Her goodwill no longer extended to that other general, the NRA's Hugh Johnson, of whom she had been suspicious from the start. He could be charming, as when hacking with Mary Rumsey, his consumer adviser, at Grasslands—and also pushy when he required her to throw him one of her extravagant parties. But Perkins wondered by late summer 1934 if he even understood America's form of government, and she was alarmed when he gave her an Italian fascist tract, *The Structure of the Corporate State*. He claimed it to be an enlightening guide for resolving strikes and imposing diktats on corporations. "What have we got an Army for?" he demanded.[32]

Wallace agreed with her that Johnson should be sacked. Hopkins played both sides. He warned FDR of Johnson's eccentricities. At the same time, Perkins observed him sidling up to the general. She wasn't surprised. She recognized Harry as another man of action who, in her judgment, was similarly unconcerned about administrative procedures and "how a democracy works."[33] Yet she liked Harry and forgave his deviousness.

Before these difficulties could be resolved, Budget Director Lewis Douglas quit on August 30. The president had asked him to stay until after the election, to avoid controversy; Douglas refused. Nor did he leave his job with grace, telling reporters that FDR had no interest in balancing the books, later adding that America was becoming a "dictatorship." His letter of resignation was unpleasant. (Hopkins had seen it and couldn't wait to tell Ickes.) In response, FDR shared his opinion that Douglas's mind ran "more to dollars than humanity."[34]

Acheson had been friends with Douglas since the rich Arizonan had arrived in Washington with the Seventieth Congress in 1927. He didn't blame Douglas. Instead, he saw evidence of a president who "exuded a relish of power, and command." This is a harsh judgment, and one often misunderstood.[35] It was not meant as praise: at Groton, as well as at Harvard and Yale in those days, one learned to exercise power with discretion, rather than savoring it so blatantly.

Douglas's door-slamming departure came barely before General Johnson's forced resignation on September 24, by which time his periodic disappearances from the office were finally explained. Behavior that Perkins had glossed as "excitable" proved to be alcoholism. He'd been detoxing at the Army Medical Center while his mistress-secretary, Robbie, invented excuses for his whereabouts. Perkins was furious at Baruch for not having specified drunkenness, the one vulnerability Roosevelt did not abide.

Firings by FDR seldom entailed thunderous repudiations or expositions of failure, and Johnson could not believe he had been sacked. Once Roosevelt summoned him back to the White House to repeat the fact, he made sure Perkins was in the room as a witness. Johnson hurried to New York to complete a memoir, in which he invoked the "shining name" of Benito Mussolini. *The Blue Eagle, from Egg to Earth,* published in January, was hyped by Doubleday as the "first insider account of the New Deal."[36]

By October 1934, prospects for the following month's midterm elections looked solid. Each of our four met often with the president during the run-up. Roosevelt told Hopkins and Ickes that he regarded the two of them as part of his "inner Cabinet," which, he added, included Perkins and Wallace.[37] The president mentioned two others. One was Attorney General Cummings, which would not have surprised them. FDR needed to work hand-in-glove with Cummings on some fifty major court challenges to New Deal legislation. To this end, reporters called the AG "Roosevelt's legal yes-man." The second was Morgenthau, which amused the two confidants, to whom he was FDR's "echo" or "servant."[38]

Right before Election Day, on November 6, Ickes and Hopkins were again summoned by "the Boss," as insiders by now called Roosevelt. It was late afternoon, and they expected to discuss public works. Instead, they got an earful about Big Business being out to sabotage the Administration by planting its coldhearted sympathizers in government agencies. Roosevelt would repeat this charge in coming weeks, including to the Cabinet on December 14. According to him, the destiny of 120 million Americans was vulnerable to eighty plutocrats.

After their meeting, Ickes drove Hopkins home. Neither man could wait for the battles to come. Ickes yearned to attack the evils of concentrated wealth, among other injustices high on his enemies list, and Hopkins knew well how blood in the streets brings opportunity.

6

GETTING THE HABIT

Midterm Elections 1934 to Summer 1936 Party Conventions

I'm not going to let those Republican
sons-of-bitches have any part of our money.
President Roosevelt, smiling and waving his cigarette, to Hopkins in 1935

The Democrats' sweep of the midterm elections ratified the New Deal, and with it Franklin Roosevelt. Two months later came the swearing-in of the Seventy-Fourth Congress on January 3, 1935, the first under the Twentieth Amendment. It brought Inauguration Day forward from March to January 20 (Congress resetting its own convening day), a mark of America's accelerating tempo.

None of our four denied the mistakes being made, including plenty at the National Recovery Administration. Such were the costs of a continentally sized nation fighting for its life as a democracy, and blunders continued. FDR selected a temperamental labor lawyer, one Donald Richberg of Chicago, who fifteen years before had been a partner of Ickes's, to head the NRA after Johnson was fired. The press acclaimed this latest star adviser as an "assistant president," and he too appeared on *Time*. The label meant a brief tenure under Franklin Roosevelt.

By this point, Hopkins was cultivating friends more rarefied than any mere head of the NRA—one of these being "Mr. Wall Street," the politically astute banker Winthrop Aldrich. He, in turn, was delighted to share advice with Hopkins, to whom, for instance, he sent his paper of December 1934, *The Financing of Unemployment,* which suggested how the Chase bank might assist Hopkins's work.

The worst of the emergency had ebbed by late 1934. That year, America grew at a 10.8 percent clip, though unemployment barely crept down to 21.7 percent and the national debt expanded. Still, this offered enough breathing space for Hopkins to leave his D.C. office to make new friends.

Hopkins claimed he was born to be a country gentleman, except for not having the money. Since arriving in Washington, he had yearned to be accepted into the Virginia aristocracy. He didn't ride but was an inveterate gambler who often slipped away to nearby Maryland racetracks at Laurel and Bowie. He understood horses, which, when combined with the attraction of his official standing, opened for him the latifundia of the truly rich in both the Maryland and Virginia hunt countries.

Perkins, who always liked Harry, would invite him to Grasslands, where he charmed Rumsey as he did when visiting their house in Georgetown. Talking out of the side of his mouth in a flat, steady midwestern tone, he would earnestly press her for guidance on such matters as the plight of the underclass.

Only Ickes among the four would never visit Grasslands. He had no particular interest in Rumsey or her lavish parties, and like Wallace, he found her brother, Averell Harriman, coldly unapproachable.

Hopkins's views on the very rich were more dogmatic than Roosevelt's. He regarded most as plain undeserving, partly because he encountered few as intelligent as he. If a man had the quality to wear his riches well, as, say, did Aldrich or Harriman, that might be one thing. Otherwise, wealth was fine as long as it was properly distributed, and he intended be the one to distribute it.

Hopkins was eager to befriend Harriman, also in his early forties and now living primarily in Washington. Unlike Aldrich, Harriman was a liberal-leaning Democrat—so there was much Hopkins could offer, and vice versa. In the fall, Rumsey had encouraged her brother to join the government. Aided further by Perkins's influence, Averell became the administrative officer of the National Recovery Administration and cut his own path through the confusion. He brushed away the secrecy that had enwrapped its codes, and stifled its ballyhoo while ginning out such sincere articles as "Why the Little Fellow Needs the N.R.A."[1] Not that Harriman ever encountered little fellows.

Until then, in an era when polo was an Olympic sport, the country had known Harriman through newsreels as the six-foot, two-inch, eight-goal-ranked champion of the Sands Point, Long Island, team. To be sure, he was also a banker, entrepreneur, and corporate director. Like his sister, he threw himself completely into whatever he was doing. He always wanted to find his way to the "right people"—not socially, but whatever people could get things done on his latest interest. In government, this was assuredly becoming Harry Hopkins. The two proved a perfect match.

FDR may have been elevating and dropping professors from Columbia University and other secondary figures. Still, he maintained the original membership of his Cabinet. He was superstitious about making changes. Thus, the ineffective commerce secretary, Daniel Roper, hung around, as did the navy secretary, Claude Swanson. The latter, frail at the start, actually missed twelve weeks of Cabinet meetings in 1934 due to pleurisy, which, thereafter, only got worse. When he returned, he could barely hold his cigarette.

Given their besetting problems, it says much that not one of the four had fallen by the wayside, and that Ickes alone would come into direct conflicts with the president. For instance, he heatedly blew off a meeting with Roosevelt because he felt ill-treated over a procurement issue. So far, he had not seen FDR truly provoked.

By now, Perkins was the one most attuned to Roosevelt's thoughts, except she was distracted in mourning that winter, although she gave no sign of it while carrying out her duties.

November 17, 1934, had been Rumsey's fifty-third birthday. She had arrived at Grasslands the night before, a Friday, to ride with the Piedmont hounds in the morning. The hunt set out at 10:45 and was well underway when Rumsey's horse stumbled and then rolled over on her, breaking four ribs and fracturing her right thigh. Apparently on the mend until contracting pneumonia, she died on December 18, in Washington Emergency Hospital with Perkins at her bedside.

The next day, Wallace escorted Perkins to the funeral service at St. Thomas's. Eleanor Roosevelt sat on one side of her in the front pew and Ilo Wallace on the other. Averell Harriman was at his sister's ceremony, a sign that Hopkins was going to attend, as did his wife, Barbara. Anna Ickes represented her husband, as Eleanor did hers: both men had to put the people's business first. The press singled out such boldfaced names as Vincent Astor. Farther back, and then following in the recessional, came grooms, gardeners, and household staff from Grasslands and Sands Point.

Later that afternoon, Perkins and Eleanor, along with Averell, Rumsey's three children, and other kinfolk, accompanied the body for burial at Arden House, the presiding seat of the twenty-thousand-acre Harriman estate high on a ridge near the Hudson. For Perkins, Rumsey's death was like the loss of a spouse. Yet she felt no self-pity, given her awareness that so many others were less fortunate than she.

These least fortunate included the four-fifths of Black Americans who lived in the Old Confederacy under white supremacists, not to mention the many additional Black citizens in the half dozen other states that mandated racial segregation. The Civil War had exhausted the South economically. During Reconstruction, for instance, the town of Woonsocket, Rhode Island, held more money in its treasury than did the state of Alabama, and Reconstruction gave the South license to be maddened for a century.[2]

For instance, disease upon disease ravaged the South, notably pellagra, whose cause—a deficiency of vitamin B_3, deriving from a diet of cornmeal and salt pork—had been known for twenty years. In a case of white self-delusion, influential Southerners denounced the finding as just one more Yankee insult. Endless avoidable deaths continued.

Over the nearly sixty years since Reconstruction, the South had been restored to the Union largely on its own terms. These included the preservation of a "Southern way of life" built on states' rights, white terror, and the myth that a victorious United States had, within memory, behaved abominably to a chivalrous foe.

FDR felt perfectly at home in this culture. He described himself as an "adopted son of Georgia" because he owned a 2,200-acre farm on the rocky soil around Warm Springs where he had established his charitable foundation for polio victims. Meriwether County had seen its last lynching in 1924, the year he arrived, although respectable native-born whites in the South tended to insist such "incidents" had really occurred somewhere else, across endless county lines.

Eleanor seldom visited, nor did Perkins enjoy the area, except that they did travel there together in 1935. "We always used to feel queerly when we went South on a train and found a waiting room for colored and a waiting room for white," remembered Perkins.[3] Half the South's working population comprised women and children. Essentially, the region was a third world fragment embedded in ordinary America, having more or less the same language and bound by utterly different mores.

The border states were scarcely less lethal. In his memoir, *The New York Times*' Arthur Krock shows the degree to which racial cruelty was unremarkable, as it would be for decades to come. "Segregation incited no difficulty" in the Glasgow, Kentucky, of his youth, he insisted. After all, he could remember merely one lynching when he was a boy: he had watched "a young Negro" being strung up at night outside the town jail from which he had been dragged.[4]

Few thought ill of FDR for not alienating the once-slave South and for cultivating, when needed, appalling allies like South Carolina's Ellison D. "Cotton Ed" Smith. His purpose in the Senate, said Smith, using the slur easily, was to "keep the niggers down and the price of cotton up."[5] The dilemma posed to the North by the likes of Smith has best been explained by historian Ira Katznelson: "The men who represented the Jim Crow South constituted the pivotal bloc in the national legislature," and the 1932 election had been "an all-too-often-overlooked watershed that thrust the South into a pivotal lawmaking position."[6]

Once the New Deal arrived, men such as Smith believed that the rest of the country could finally be made to pay off its dues for the endless wrongs dealt out to a just cause not long before. The South's hatred of centralized government was now matched only by an eagerness to feed off it, provided that standard adjustments were made for race.

Since 1933, Smith had chaired the Committee on Agriculture and Forestry and, from 1940 to 1944, was dean of the Senate. Southern senators headed thirteen of the thirty-three committees, and all the most significant ones. Furthermore, the Senate was a far bigger presence in national affairs during the 1930s and '40s than it is today. In our era, any belief that the final word on matters of state is concentrated on Capitol Hill has long since been overridden by the expansion of the executive branch, the abundance of policy savants, and nonstop media attention. However, in the days when newspapers printed pages of Senate speeches, the upper chamber sat pretty much as the final council of the Republic.

Southerners held no less a sway in the House of Representatives, including overall key committees—among them banking, judiciary, appropriations, and the two for military affairs. Still, the House of that era was more like the institution we know today. It deliberated as the grand inquest of the nation, and laid issues before the Senate for a final conclusion. From 1935 to 1947, its three successive Speakers came from Tennessee, Alabama, and Texas. All held views on race similar, if quieter, to Cotton Ed's.

Roosevelt had to accommodate this chokehold by the one-party South. Cotton, for instance, was the principal U.S. agricultural export and, observed Wallace, FDR was "very, very sensitive on cotton problems." He was forever tracking its price because, Wallace added, "the Democratic party was based" on cotton.[7] However, none of Roosevelt's four lieutenants was as constricted as he by what, only a lifetime earlier, had been the slave states.

By 1935, Ickes was wearing many hats. One, newsmen asserted, was "Secretary of Negro Affairs" given his oversight of what meager government programs existed for Blacks—such as new, and segregated, public hospitals—and because of his stance on civil rights.

"Negro Americans have more confidence and knowledge of yourself than of any other member of the Cabinet," NAACP head Walter White wrote to him. As interior secretary, Ickes could appoint Blacks to federal offices in the Virgin Islands, itself a breakthrough. In Chicago, he filed suits to condemn land for "Negro slum clearance." Tenements that lacked clean water and sewer lines were replaced by public housing, all efforts coordinated with the seventy-four-year-old Jane Addams.[8]

He also cooperated with Arthur Mitchell, a Chicago Democrat who was the sole Black member of Congress, to ensure that the Civilian Conservation Corps forbade discrimination based on "race, color, or creed." As a small step to this end, Roosevelt authorized "Negro reserve officers" to be posted to several CCC camps, which were initially open to all, though under pressure from North and South alike, they later had to be segregated.

Unhelpfully, FDR's powerful aide Stephen Early was an arch-segregationist to the point of violence, as will be seen. He was ever alert to legislation, visitors, letters, or any initiative questioning "the Southern way of life" that neared the Oval Office. And he had friends on Capitol Hill. The president was perfectly comfortable employing him for twelve years.

At the beginning, in September 1933, Ickes had required Public Works contracts to contain a clause prohibiting racial bias. In all projects, such as building the U.S. Route 1 causeway through the Florida Keys, he insisted that workforces had to reflect the region's racial composition.

An example of the obstacles he confronted can be seen in the construction of the "Hoover," or the "Boulder" Dam, as he decided to rename it during the Hundred Days. To be sure, Republicans howled about the insult to the "Great Engineer," as the former president—who had laid its foundations in 1931—was also known. Ickes soon discovered that tacking a new name onto the world's largest dam was the easy part.

"I want to leave nothing undone to show that it is our purpose to avoid race discrimination," he declared while his Public Works Administration sped to complete this project in the Colorado River's largest canyon. By the time he and Hopkins accompanied the president to dedicate the dam in late September 1935, only eleven of the four thousand men toiling on the Arizona-Nevada border proved to be Black.[9]

From the day Ickes had been sworn in, he began what would be a nearly four-million-word diary. This was less a narcissistic enterprise than a chronicle of his angry fascination with how ineptly the world was governed. He depicts himself surrounded by men of insufficient skills and temperaments, save (usually) for the president. Yet in all his writings, which include observations on racial turmoil, he never explains why he was set on defending Black Americans. And Ickes did so nearly alone at the heights of idealistic New Deal Washington.

Perkins, for her part, encountered "the Negro problem," as race relations were called, from the perspective of her department: labor law simply did not apply to the South. Georgia, for instance, had no labor department. Another part of the "Southern way of life" was to keep wages low in order to lure factories and commerce from the North. As for segregation, Perkins claimed that she had never much considered it until becoming a Cabinet officer.

She was awakened when in Atlanta to give a speech.

"The Negroes were a large element in the working population of Atlanta," she remembered, "and I hadn't realized that they couldn't come into the Capitol and sit where other people sat." One of the locals, trying to be helpful, explained the situation.

"You don't seem to understand," he said reassuringly. "We treat them right down here . . . There's a place set aside for them." Nor should she worry about Blacks being excluded from a later meeting she would attend. "That's all right, too," he added. "In the Baptist Church they've got a gallery just for Negroes."[10]

When Perkins was driven to Spelman College, a teacher at that historically Black school commended her for having the simple courage to visit, leaving her baffled. She also met W. E. B. Du Bois, then teaching at the adjacent Atlanta University (today's Clark Atlanta U.) and already a figure of towering significance in American public life. "Here was a crossbreed situation, all right," she remembered of her first impression.[11] Going by his high brow and angular nose, she saw a resemblance to Winthrop Aldrich's father, the former Rhode Island senator. Du Bois's profile also reminded her of Mrs. John D. Rockefeller, Jr., who was the daughter of the elder Aldrich.

A self-invented woman of her time, Perkins spoke this way as she took comfort by knowing Aldriches, Harrimans, and Rockefellers. She references such names often in her long oral history and was also determined to maintain an upper-class life for her daughter. Just four days after Rumsey's funeral service, for instance, Susanna enjoyed a proper New York City debut, thanks to arrangements Rumsey had made over the summer.

In Washington, Perkins eventually moved in with her friend Caroline Love O'Day, the daughter and widow of oil kings, who was among the new legislators installed in early January 1935, soon ready to tackle civil rights as well as equal rights for women. Their bond became as strong as that between Perkins and Rumsey.

Perkins was no less delighted to have been "adopted," as she herself put it, by the society matrons of the Georgetown Assembly, a "very super-super" exclusive ladies' group that organized the city's cotillions. The assembly's matriarch and a dour aide visited Perkins's home to explain, woman to woman, that only Washingtonians of ancient pedigree might be members, save Perkins, who qualified by her high official status.[12]

These vanities were no more than dust on Perkins's strong spiritual core. Her Episcopal faith deepened her friendship with Henry and Ilo Wallace, who attended the same Anglo-Catholic high mass as she. All reveled in its color and ritual, usually driving together the four miles from Georgetown to St. James's near Capitol Hill, on such Sundays as she was in the city.

Wallace was also encountering "the Negro problem" firsthand. Ever since the 1930s, Black farmers have derided the Agriculture Department as the "last plantation."[13] During those years, only about one Black farmer in ten owned property in the South. New Deal policies basically excluded most of them, and the systemic consequences are felt today.

The press always called Wallace an idealist, and it made good copy to show him striving nobly at his department to fulfill his father's hopes. That said, the secretary of agriculture had been immersed in *Wallace's Farmer* since childhood, and this paper had always served its landowning readership. Furthermore, a man who spoke of the "strength and quietness of grass" was likely to be more moved by growing things than by the average man in the fields. As a result, Wallace did not grasp the consequences of his policies for the 43 percent of America's agricultural population who were wage laborers and sharecroppers.

"Domestic allotment" subsidies were based on acreage and output (as they still are), which favored large landowners. For example, "Cotton Ed" Smith would sign U.S. government contracts to retire an agreed acreage of cotton fields on "Tanglewood," his 4,500-acre family manor. In turn, under the Agriculture Adjustment Act, he received non-recourse loans— essentially payments—while Washington expected him to make good-faith efforts to let some of this money trickle down to the idled tenants who had worked those fields.

Cotton Ed himself had drafted the act's articles on cotton, and it was idealistic in the extreme to think he would not instead evict excess labor from Tanglewood. The biracial Southern Tenant Farmers Union sprang up in 1934 to resist such abuses—thereby providing convenient targets for night riders to flog and kill. More effectively still, sheer political force from Washington quelled the strikes that began in 1935.

When lawyers within the Agriculture Department moved to enforce such contracts, by challenging the use of these moneys, Wallace said he felt blindsided and fired them. The White House offered no reaction, and in his intermittently filled diary, Wallace rationalized the mess by blaming these policy contradictions on the president's "somewhat concealed approach" to decision-making.[14] As for the president's farm in Georgia, FDR removed himself from such disputes by forbidding his superintendent to grow cotton.

U nintended consequences affected numerous people besides sharecroppers, such as Shenandoah mountaineers cleared away to develop a national park. The New Deal was seen as a great cause rather than ordinary,
wearisome, detail-beset government business, and, too often, there was
little time to look deeper.

Wallace's caution about race and sharecropping arose from another
source, at least in the view of Hopkins and Ickes: he was already eyeing
the presidency for 1940. As for Hopkins, his Red Cross years had made
him more familiar with the South than were the others, and his views on
civil rights were closer to Roosevelt's: "We've got to be patient" and wait
for a new South to arise from prosperity.[15]

Yet again, like FDR, Hopkins excelled at finding unusual talents,
and two of his key men were enlightened Southerners. From 1933, his
deputy was Aubrey Williams, the same age as he, and a poor boy from
Springville, Alabama (population 903). Williams's backstory appealed to
Hopkins: progeny of a ruined, once slave-owning plantation family; a veteran of the French Foreign Legion in the World War. Williams's successor
would be another superb Alabamian, Thaddeus Holt, thirty-seven, also
from the downfallen aristocracy.

Given Ickes's example of requiring Black workers to be hired for his
projects, Hopkins likewise made some headway in getting labor unions
to desegregate. He furthermore pushed contractors to employ women—
although, when Williams insisted that women should be paid equally to
men, Hopkins warned that Labor Secretary Perkins opposed the idea
because of her traditional views of a family.

In April 1935, Congress passed the largest peacetime appropriation
in U.S. history, and the next month Hopkins was set to respond once
FDR deployed an executive order to establish the Works Progress Administration. The WPA was built on the model of Hopkins's Civil Works
initiative, which had been intended just to carry the unemployed through
the record-breaking cold of winter 1933–1934. Rapidly, the WPA became
the biggest New Deal employment/relief program of all. Nearly nine million Americans would be hired at regular wages over eight years. Still,
as Williams wrote Eleanor Roosevelt, "the negroes don't get a fair deal,"
however hard he pushed to "correct discrimination."[16]

In 1935, Hopkins appeared to be at the height of his game when he told FDR he would quit if Democratic Party operatives kept pressing him to accept patronage appointees as his state directors. He chose his people on merit, or at least on their usefulness to him personally. Anyway, his organization had thousands of lesser slots open to Democratic favoritism, which would include his sister Adah. Postmaster General / patronage dispenser Jim Farley calculated that the party had 296,500 new federal administrative jobs to use for political currency—reckoning that this meant forty votes, on average, from friends and family for every man or woman hired.[17]

Hopkins had made a halfway noble stand for good government by defending his selection of state directors. Roosevelt admired such toughness over a principle, even if he made sure that patronage slots and relief moneys were distributed lavishly to help win key races, such as a U.S. Senate seat in Kentucky.

Clashes between Hopkins and Ickes became part of New Deal lore. Tensions arose, in part, from their respective work-relief programs overlapping, which Roosevelt could have prevented, had he wanted to.

The renegade Republican Ickes derided "the Hopkins rat hole," which he saw being stuffed with a grab bag of jobs for Democrats. Before long, he was expressing fears that spending by this slinky "lawless individual" (that being Hopkins) would soon backfire on the Administration. In turn, Hopkins concluded that his life "would be a great deal easier if Ickes would play ball" and dismissed him as stubborn, self-righteous, and boring—largely because Ickes's big projects, such as the Lincoln Tunnel, were deemed to move too slowly to raise employment.[18] Annoyingly, this passage beneath the Hudson took three years to build.

These quarrels spilled into the press, to FDR's amusement. "Half my time is spent settling fights between Ickes and Wallace, and Hopkins and Ickes over extensions of their jurisdictions," he chuckled to his attorney general.[19] Whenever Ickes threatened to resign, as he did regularly, FDR would just grip the arm of "dear old Harold" and tell him not to worry.

But, on the whole during the 1930s, Hopkins and Ickes remained friends.

Ickes, who was sixteen years older and prided himself on being grumpy, wrote down a cool though upbeat assessment: "I always had a liking for him—the liking of a man who had grown up under Scotch

Presbyterian restraint for the happy-go-lucky type who can bet his last cent, even if a borrowed one, on a horse race." Indeed, he added, "we always got along well when we were together. Even during the periods when we were at each other's throats."[20]

To calm the waters that he had gleefully churned, FDR took Hopkins and Ickes on a voyage aboard the cruiser *Houston*. The party included two service aides and FDR's personal physician, all embarking from San Diego on October 2. They observed naval maneuvers, fished off Baja California, and, after passing through the Panama Canal and fishing the blue Caribbean, sailed north to anchor in Charleston Harbor on the twenty-third. Three weeks meant lots of time for Ickes and Hopkins to observe each other—and the president, too, in his favorite surroundings, aboard a U.S. warship on the high seas. Both found it remarkable how cheerfully he submitted himself to being wheeled up and down the shipboard ramps and being carried like a helpless child in and out of the fishing launch.

There was time for reading. Ickes passed along to the president Stefan Zweig's just-published *Mary, Queen of Scots,* and still there were hours for serious talk in the wardroom. Italy had invaded Ethiopia a day after they put to sea. By naval radio on October 5, FDR proclaimed an arms embargo against both nations, as required by the Neutrality Act that Congress had passed just six weeks earlier.

And all played poker. In Washington, the unbeatable pros were Vice President Garner and his fellow Texan, Jesse Jones, who also shone at bridge. Hopkins himself was pretty good, for to excel at poker entails playing one's opponents quite as much as the cards. Of the president's game, Hopkins observed that he played poorly, but thought he was swell. So Hopkins routinely beat the Boss, definitely a bad loser. That was no effective way to be a courtier, but then Hopkins was way too shrewd to try being one.

Ickes was about as adept at poker as the president. Stamp collecting was their genuine pastime. Speaking as "one philatelist to another" was part of their seagoing conversation, and on shore they would trade and study their tiny treasures.[21] Stamp collecting is a child's activity, and poker a game for mean adults with sharp elbows. These two pursuits of poker and philately nicely bracketed the characters of both FDR and Ickes: a cynical toughness, mingled with an element of endearing kindness, as might have been found in Hopkins, too.

By the end of FDR's first term, the four lieutenants faced a profoundly new political environment. Between them, Ickes's Public Works Administration and Hopkins's Works Progress Administration were consuming 38 percent of the federal budget. *Vanity Fair* identified the men as "two spenders in action" and claimed Ickes had the most enemies in Washington, which was unfair to Hopkins.[22] Spending soared elsewhere in government too. One big example was the Tennessee Valley Authority, which—vitally enabled by Ickes's loans for city power grids—brought hydroelectricity, flood control, and modern agriculture to a region not known for its driving enterprise.

Nonetheless, the president recommitted himself to balancing the budget and dreaded the mounting $33.7 billion federal debt. Tax increases were equally unprecedented. Between 1933 and 1940, federal spending would double as tax revenue tripled, which included a Wealth Tax Act in 1935, thereby raising the top federal rate to 75 percent.

Having left Washington for New York, Lewis Douglas was now vice president of the chemical conglomerate American Cyanamid. He used this role to speak before such eminent institutions as the Wharton School in Philadelphia and Winthrop Aldrich's Bankers' Club in downtown Manhattan, warning that FDR's spending would destroy America. None of our four shared Douglas's alarm. National debt was a problem they left to the president, and Ickes would always concede that "economics is out of my line."[23]

On the one hand, FDR fretted about debt. On the other, he kept being blasé. His life had been turned inside out once, in 1921, and he was open to having it turned inside out again—this time intellectually. There was much to do, and he was forever tempted to break loose from the ancient Democratic verities of steady economizing and to recast the party heretofore trapped within Jeffersonian limits.

The allure of great spending initiatives pulled Roosevelt into new realms of possibility. For instance, he hoped to replicate the TVA as a Missouri Valley Authority, a Columbia Valley Authority, and more great works. Ideas gripped him of transcontinental highways, one east to west and two or three north to south, with the government building and selling houses along the completed roads. And there must be many small federally backed hospitals throughout the nation. Fabulous opportunities for human betterment opened up before him—and marvelous political ones, too.

Once a politician is committed to big spending, he or she might as well use some of the outlay to win elections. Hopkins believed this completely as he too vowed to keep "our money" out of unworthy hands. In contrast, Ickes had become known to the nation as "Honest Harold" for his unquestioned integrity and for running the most upright department in Washington.

There's only one example of Ickes using Public Works dollars for politics. In 1935, he tried to withhold money from constructing the Triborough Bridge until New York ousted a Republican city planner whom FDR hated: Robert Moses, New York City's master builder, a man who himself lauded Ickes's skills in managing huge projects. Ickes barely escaped blame in this scandal, and *Vanity Fair* wrote that his actions arose solely from his "great affection for the president and his deepest loyalty to him."[24]

Ickes had lied on Roosevelt's behalf in trying to gloss over the Triborough Bridge affair; he wasn't going to do that again. Anyway, his eyes were fixed on a bigger political issue than bridges, as soon were the president's. Even before he entered government, Ickes had given a speech at the City Club of Chicago about taming a Supreme Court stacked with reactionaries. Now his views were hardening, as were Attorney General Cummings's. If the court's majority kept overturning progressive legislation, they believed, then the number of justices—which had been cut down from ten to nine members just after the Civil War—should be increased to achieve a friendlier bench. Here was the germ of the idea to expand the Supreme Court.

Not much later, in May 1935, the court unanimously voided the National Recovery Act. FDR appeared serene, observed Perkins. He too had become disturbed by the NRA's "neither fish nor fowl" system of cartelization.[25] Indeed, the court's ruling freed the White House to discard a blue eagle grown into an albatross.

Ickes knew the president was coming round to agree with him about the next big step. Wallace, too, was ready to join issue with the court once it invalidated his Agricultural Adjustment Act in early 1936. As for Perkins, she was more concerned about salvaging worthwhile pieces, such as pioneering labor laws, from the wreck of the NRA.

She never idealized labor leaders, whose internal quarrels splintered the effectiveness of their cause, and well she knew their bigotries against women and Blacks. FDR shared her genteel skepticism. The attitude of both toward the labor movement was a patrician one, like that of Britain's lord chancellor twenty years earlier who observed he had never encountered men stupider than those who led the mine workers, until he met the mine owners.

Throughout the 1930s, Perkins confronted nothing less than the greatest period of labor unrest in U.S. history. She might despair of union chiefs and company chairmen alike, yet her arguments resonate today: bargaining power must be equal between workers and employers for the sake of a healthy economy. Eventually, serious protections for workers to organize, bargain collectively, and to strike were achieved only with the National Labor Relations Act of July 1935, on which rests modern labor law in the United States.

Senator Robert Wagner, a formidable liberal New York Democrat, championed the bill. From experience, Perkins worried about his approach. Maybe its stipulations were too heavy-handed upon both sides. Labor leaders had their own objections about the role of government, as did Southern lawmakers. Perkins, however, finally got on board. As for the president, "he never did a thing," she recalled: "he hoped it wouldn't pass."[26]

Southern Democrats were suspicious about workers' rights. In the Senate, they were able to exclude field hands from the Labor Relations Act, as well as domestics, which—given that the rules still prevail—has largely come to mean home care workers today (mostly women, and women of color). Yet a version passed Congress, and when FDR got round to signing the bill, explains one of Perkins's biographers, he conducted a "ritual public humiliation of Frances."[27]

For the sake of Southern legislators, a reformist female secretary of labor could not be featured as driving this race-charged issue. Therefore, he refused to place the accompanying National Labor Relations Board—a quasi-judicial body only being revitalized in the early 2020s—in her department. FDR's rebuke to Perkins contained an unspoken reminder to those he held close: they should not count on him if their actions might put one of his other purely political undertakings at risk.

Nonetheless, Perkins had made her mark in the Cabinet. Men around the table avoided tangling with her. She was always prepared with overwhelming facts and figures. Ickes, however, was impatient with her bluestocking volubility and fretted when she advanced ideas or voiced objections. If it were a truly important issue, he knew that FDR would want to hear it from her one-on-one; otherwise she was wasting everyone's time as she "buzzed, buzzed, buzzed" in every meeting.[28]

In and out of Cabinet, Perkins advocated a program of government-backed pensions, aid to the jobless, and assistance for destitute mothers with children. She was also determined to prevent the firing of "over-age people [because] anybody over forty" could arbitrarily lose their job.[29] She was thinking large: Washington had never considered a *permanent* economic intervention on a scale to cover twenty-six million Americans.

To advance these initiatives, FDR had gone so far as to ask Perkins to chair a Cabinet-level Committee on Economic Security. (By 1940 it was simply known as the "Cabinet Committee.") Hopkins and Wallace were its two other principals. Morgenthau was included, contributing predictably little, and the capable AG, Homer Cummings, usually sent a deputy. Ultimately it was Perkins and Hopkins who handled the basics of what was originally styled the Economic Security Bill, drawing on Wallace to address farm labor.

Conservatives used the same arguments to resist Perkins's concept of "economic security" that Republicans would voice in 2009–2010 and again in 2020–2021 to fight expanded unemployment benefits: to compensate joblessness would dissuade people from seeking work. Then, as today, business lobbyists invoked "socialism." And, in 1935, Southern legislators could exclude maids and farmworkers from this reform as well.

Once more, Senator Wagner fought for a body of historic legislation, and on the afternoon of August 14, 1935, Roosevelt signed the renamed Social Security Act into law using a succession of pens. Photographs show Perkins in the Cabinet Room standing behind his left shoulder. At this moment of triumph, her expression is blank.

Right before the ceremony, she had received a phone call. Her husband, Paul, who was visiting the Madison Avenue flat with a nurse, had wandered off, and Perkins felt compelled to join the search.

As the ceremony droned on, Perkins knew she was too late for the Pennsylvania Railroad's 4:00 P.M. Congressional to New York. Her next hope was the Montrealer at 4:25, which she barely caught, thanks to a White House car. Only later that night did Paul turn up, walking aimlessly, miles away.

Senator Wagner's personal secretary, Maurine Mulliner, had helped to shepherd the legislation through committee. A generation later, still unrecognized for the part she had played, she would add context to that afternoon's events: "I don't think that President Roosevelt had the remotest interest in a Social Security bill or program. He was simply pacifying Frances."[30]

Three months later, Frances's daughter, Susanna, a sophomore at Bryn Mawr, suffered a nervous breakdown and was hospitalized in Philadelphia.

One of the reasons FDR endured his interior secretary's obsessive unruliness was the joy they shared as stewards of the land. "I love nature," Ickes exclaimed to a radio audience. "I love it in practically every form— flowers, birds, wild animals, running streams, gem-like lakes and towering snow-clad mountains."[31] So had T.R., and so did Franklin Roosevelt, who declared his profession on Hyde Park voting rolls as "tree farmer"—and one who could recognize the notes of every type of northeast songbird.

Unlike the Roosevelts of either Oyster Bay or Hyde Park, however, Ickes had grown up amid the environmental devastation of Altoona, Pennsylvania, home to the world's largest railroad works. He knew firsthand what could go terribly, poisonously wrong.

He had first visited Hyde Park, on its bluff overlooking the Hudson, in August 1933. This was the type of place, he told his diary, that he would dearly love to own; he didn't anticipate that would come. For now, he could outdo over a quarter of a continent what FDR was doing at Hyde Park: planting forests, preserving landscapes, and nurturing the soil.

Unsurprisingly, Ickes's view of conservation was as absolute as his other opinions. He intended to protect the nation's parks and forests "from those 'nature lovers' whose one idea is to uproot plants or else improve on God's work."[32] Then, as today, the national parks overseen by his department are dedicated to preservation, whereas the national forests and grasslands—supervised by the Department of Agriculture—lie open to commercial use, including recreation. The distinction made no difference to Ickes, who wanted to restrain hikers and timber companies alike as they pressed upon the American estate.

Predictably, as well, he instructed his National Park Service managers in the South to ignore Jim Crow discrimination—despite state laws requiring separate toilets, cabins, and picnic grounds for "colored guests."[33] To resist him, Southerners clamored states' rights, played the long game, and granted such minor concessions as removing "White" and "Colored" signs at Skyline Drive rest stops over the Shenandoah.

Civil rights apart, no public issue inspired Ickes more than did conservation, specifically, his plan to remake Interior into a Department of Conservation with sweeping control over the environment. Livid at how the nation's forests, prairies, and parks were being overrun, he compared his country with a spoiled heir. The West, he believed, was in the hands of irresponsible men. Roosevelt sympathized. It made sense, said the president, to bring the U.S. Forest Service into the Interior Department.

Roosevelt spoke of employing a million more men in the national forests, beyond those enrolled in the Civilian Conservation Corps, and of nationalizing millions of additional forest acres, too. It was a breathtaking vision that Ickes judged Agriculture Secretary Wallace incapable of implementing. FDR, having grasped Ickes's passion for the forests, employed this as a means of controlling him. He did so by forever dangling the promise of creating a Conservation Department before Ickes's eyes. To withhold final consent of transferring the Forest Service over to Interior was also a means of inflaming the quarrels between Wallace and Ickes, which he enjoyed watching.

Gradually, Ickes came to question why the president never quite signed off on the reorganization. Bronson Cutting's death that year in a Missouri plane crash offered him an early glimpse of faithlessness at the top.

Senator Cutting, a progressive Republican, only forty-seven at his end, had campaigned for FDR and backed Ickes for Interior. Later he split with the president on a single issue, albeit a sensitive one—accusing FDR of being tightfisted on veterans' affairs, which he certainly was at the start. Despite a lifelong friendship, Roosevelt—with "inordinate bitterness," observed Professor Moley—ordered Democratic operatives to oppose Cutting hard for reelection, and then to side with his opponents in accusations of ballot fraud.[34] Cutting had been returning from Santa Fe, where he gathered evidence to refute these lies. Ickes felt the death keenly, and he believed FDR's regret to be spurious.

As the clashes between Ickes and Wallace intensified, millions of tons of powdered High Plains topsoil from the eroded prairies and plains blew east on the jet stream to darken the Washington sun. On March 21, 1935, a day that seemed a judgment of God, witnesses were testifying to the Senate Public Lands Committee as to whether Ickes's Soil Erosion Service should be transferred in turn to the Agriculture Department as a "Soil Conservation Service." (It was.) Afternoon hearings were suspended as senators moved to the chamber's tall windows to stare into an outside air thick with grit. Then, come Black Sunday, April 14, the Midwest was struck by another dark blizzard. People now spoke of the "dust bowl."

ckes was dictating in his office on Saturday, August 31, around 8:45 P.M., when he learned from an aide that his wife had been in a hit-and-run car wreck on the Taos road about forty miles north of Santa Fe. He phoned long distance to St. Vincent's Hospital and then to the governor. Anna's car had been flipped into a ditch. She was dead. Then FDR called. He was to leave for Union Station at 10:40 en route to Hyde Park, accompanied by Rexford Tugwell. The president sincerely offered to stay if he could help. Ickes gratefully declined, but Roosevelt nonetheless dispatched a mutual friend, who was visiting the White House, to sit with Ickes. The widower was shaken, though did not pretend to any grief.

In Santa Fe, troops escorted Anna's body to the Chicago train. On Tuesday afternoon, Eleanor Roosevelt attended the closed-coffin funeral service at the family home in Winnetka. Harry Hopkins came, as did Ilo Wallace, Ickes's favorite person among Washington's political spouses. Perkins, along with her daughter, was in Maine at the family homestead near Newcastle. Understanding Ickes clearly enough to realize he would survive the loss, she sent an assistant secretary of labor in her place. Hundreds of others attended, including the governor of Illinois and Chicago's Mayor Kelly.

Anna Wilmarth had gotten to the point where she intended to disinherit Ickes, and actually had asked her lawyer to write a codicil omitting him from her will. According to Ickes, she had second thoughts and asked the lawyer to destroy his draft. He had not done so at the time of her death. After a meeting with Ickes in Chicago, however, he burned the codicil. Thus, Ickes remained sole beneficiary of her $800,000 estate.

This drama reverberated. A year later, Ickes's wastrel thirty-seven-year-old adopted stepson, Wilmarth Ickes, shot himself in Hubbard Woods on the anniversary of his mother's death. Ickes had to move fast to quash an incriminating suicide note. At the inquest, Winnetka's chief of police and the county coroner claimed to have searched the scene and found nothing. "They perjured themselves magnificently," Ickes reminisced.[35]

Ickes had gotten good at this, and his forcefulness on all fronts had become useful to FDR. That was particularly so since summer 1934, when Louis Howe became bedridden in his White House room—though Howe kept working and, in moments without a cigarette, reading documents under an oxygen tent.

"Honest Harold" was respected on Capitol Hill, unlike Hopkins who, with his short, dismissive laugh, did not conceal his disdain for most politicians. And it was vital at this stage for FDR to maintain his alliances in Congress, a task aided by Vice President Garner, who no one forgot had been Speaker of the House.

Dangerous impulses roamed the land: Milo Reno, leader of the militant Farmers' Holiday Association, who denounced the "Jew Deal"; in Detroit, Father Charles Coughlin, whose mesmerizing weekly broadcasts had turned against FDR for allegedly being too friendly with bankers, largely those of Hebrew persuasion; and Senator Huey Long, forty-two years old, the red-haired, doughy "Kingfish" and former governor of Louisiana.

The growing strength of Long's left-populist "Share Our Wealth" movement seemed to pose the gravest threat to FDR and the New Deal. Long could be entertaining, as when he stuck guffawing nicknames on enemies like "Lord Corn-Wallace, the ignoramus from Iowa" (for paying farmers not to produce). Long was now on the cusp of taking his supposed program nationwide: a guaranteed annual income, thirty-hour workweek, and eleven-month work year. If he formed a third party, feared Jim Farley, his five or six million supporters might win several states in 1936, perhaps tilting the national balance.

Ickes had never seen Long until a few nights before Anna's death, when he watched the spellbinder in action from the Senate gallery. By then, Ickes had halted Public Works projects in Louisiana because "Emperor" Long, as he called him, used the bullyboys of his Louisiana political machine to extract kickbacks. Besides, FDR had asked Ickes to thrash Long with insults of his own.

And the president had other ways to respond. On one hand, he co-opted his mainstream opponents' programs, as he had done with Herbert Hoover's. On the other, he just played rough. He assembled files on Father Coughlin to share with the Catholic Church's three American cardinals and the Vatican's apostolic delegate to Washington. Postmaster General Farley helped by intercepting the radio priest's mail while the Bureau of Internal Revenue scrutinized Coughlin's taxes.[36]

In Louisiana, Roosevelt redirected patronage to Long's political enemies—for once with justification—and ordered Internal Revenue to audit Long and his vicious cronies as well. "Other men's tax returns continued to fascinate Father in the thirties," recalled his son Elliott.[37] To this end, it would have been awkward if an Acheson or a Bruère or a Douglas had been running the Treasury.

Ickes returned to Washington on Friday, September 6, two days after Anna's burial. That Sunday night in Baton Rouge, Huey Long was fatally shot by a young physician acting upon obscure reasons of family honor. Long's bodyguards riddled the assassin as bullets ricocheted off the magnificent pillars of the statehouse. Surprisingly, no outcry of conspiracy sprang up.

Then as today, belief in conspiracy flourishes in this continent-wide, highly mobile nation. In the sprawling United States, with its unnumbered nationalities and faiths, one may never have encountered the people one fears and envies. But you know *they* are around. In the mid-1930s, even worse conspiracy mongering lay on the horizon.

The main challenge in 1936 still came from the Republicans: a party better funded, until recently the larger of the two, and including most of Wall Street and business. Progressive Republicans might have been split over FDR, although the bulk of the party leaned conservative and counted on the support of conservative Democrats. In fact, during 1934, such disaffected Democrats had formed and bankrolled what they called the American Liberty League to advocate for private property, free enterprise, and Roosevelt's removal. They sprinkled their leadership with Republicans to appear bipartisan.

The presidential race had begun early on January 26, 1936, when CBS broadcast coast-to-coast the vastly publicized white-tie Liberty League banquet in Washington. Among the two thousand diners at the May-flower Hotel were fourteen members of the Du Pont family (traditionally Southern Democrats), General Motors chairman Alfred P. Sloan, Win-throp Aldrich, and an unforgiving Dean Acheson. Groundwork was being laid for the conventions of the two great parties in June, and the conservative Democrats hoped to discredit Roosevelt from inside his party.

The keynote speaker was Al Smith, former governor of New York and now president of Empire State Inc., which ran its eponymous building. He too had broken sharply with Roosevelt, ostensibly over monetary policy, and he spent a full hour that evening giving FDR the hammer-and-sickle treatment. The "socialist" New Deal, said Smith, was simply a waystation to Moscow. Moreover, Roosevelt had accomplices. "In the name of all that is good and holy," Smith got around to bellowing, "who is Ickes? Who is Wallace? Who is Hopkins?

"These are the key men," he added, but where had they "blown in from?"[38] He left out Perkins. Smith and Perkins had remained friendly since Albany, and he was a gentleman.

The name to be avoided, as so often before, was Louis Howe's. He had nearly died the previous year from an attack of bronchitis and had been moved from his White House sickbed to the nearby Naval Hospital on E Street. The cash-stuffed safe he kept in his room went with him. Roosevelt had visited during Howe's final afternoon, on April 18, 1936; he died in his sleep that night. Roosevelt ordered a state funeral, and he and Eleanor accompanied the funeral train north.

Howe's larger human life was also rarely discussed. His wife, Grace, and his two children lived in Fall River, Massachusetts, where he was buried. The family had a loving relationship, though Howe seldom visited. The "little boss," as he was known in government, had turned his life over to the Roosevelts. "His influence was incalculable," reported *The New York Times*.[39]

Perkins stayed close with other New York friends besides Howe—among them were the Aldriches, although feelings grew strained after a speech of Winthrop's at the University of Virginia in June. He decried the Social Security Act as a "cruel jest" because its ruinous, road-to-bankruptcy financing was certain to push the whole nation into insecurity.[40] He said everything short of condemning Perkins.

Aldrich's charges coincided nicely with the Republican Party Convention in Cleveland from June 9 to 12. Delegates nominated "Alf" Landon, the folksy oilman governor of Kansas, for president. Second on the ticket was the bluff and hearty Frank Knox, publisher of Chicago's *Daily News* and one of T.R.'s Rough Riders up San Juan Hill.

The Democrats, of course, acclaimed the Roosevelt-Garner ticket at their convention in Philadelphia, starting on June 23—although reelection seemed far from certain. Even the Administration's friends, who for the time being still included California's progressive Republican senator Hiram Johnson, said they were "jittery" over the national debt, the rise of labor unions, the constellation of new agencies, and the president's own character.[41]

Yet there was an optimism to politics during the summer of '36 in contrast to the dread of four years earlier. Americans saw real GDP growing 12.9 percent that year, whereas it had fallen by the same degree in 1932. Furthermore, unemployment had fallen steadily—though it was still a searing 16.9 percent—and the worst of the demagogues were dead or dispersed. At Hyde Park, Roosevelt reassured family friends that their heads wouldn't be falling into baskets after all. Likely enough, he had saved them from revolution.[42]

PART II

Endurance

CREST OF THE WAVE

FDR's Campaign of 1936 to Christmas 1937

We Planned It That Way
Roosevelt-Garner campaign slogan, 1936

In 1936, the twentieth century appeared to be one of collectivism and, if civilization did not take care, of totalitarianism. The 1930s' "waves of the future"—Soviet Communism, Italian fascism, and German National Socialism—seemed only the beginnings. In the United States, however, the New Deal looked to have succeeded, and indeed to have overcome much of the despair of 1933.

More cars were being sold than ever before, except in the boom of 1928–1929. In newly big-government Washington, D.C., housing starts jumped in fall 1936 by 50 percent over the previous year. To be sure, more than nine million Americans—to include those on work relief—remained jobless, in a labor force of not quite fifty-four million. Yet an end to suffering could be seen. The Administration, for instance, declined to build a special facility to store millions of unemployment files. Surely, they wouldn't be needed much longer. Instead, it repurposed a suburban car dealership gone bust to serve as a short-term warehouse.

Neither Roosevelt nor his closest lieutenants believed that the election would be "a walkaway," remembered Perkins.[1] As late as mid-September, Wallace was alerting campaign manager Jim Farley that "in the whole middlewest the farm people aside from Catholics are Republican by ancestry" and would be hard to persuade.[2] The Republican Party looked formidable. Winthrop Aldrich, who featured in that year's bestselling *Men Who Run America,* had helped draft his party's platform and contributed to a prodigious war chest.

Above all, Franklin Roosevelt was the issue in 1936 to a degree that would not recur for a president until the election of 2020. One of his themes was America's "concentration of wealth," a problem that he said generated "inequality of opportunity." Treasury statistics showed hundreds of corporate executives to be earning more annually than everyday workers could dream of gaining in a lifetime.[3] Annual incomes of more than $100,000 towered over the $1,200 that barely half of all families could hope for.

The startling comparison made terrific campaign fodder, although today—when the average CEO makes at least 350 times as much as an average worker—such outrage might be hard to understand.

Republicans and conservative Democrats meanwhile insisted that high New Deal tax rates ruined individual incentive, although most federal revenue came from taxes on goods and services. Roosevelt was prolonging the Depression, said Richard Whitney, the "Voice of Wall Street," by imposing the alien philosophy of socialism. The head of the National Coal Association agreed and bewailed to Congress the Administration's strangling of free enterprise.[4]

The numbers that chilled Roosevelt, still firmly loyal to traditional economic principles, were those of the annual budget deficit and the mounting national debt. In 1936, the latter had crossed the terrifying red line of $30 billion, from the $22.5 billion left by Hoover. Moreover, federal spending since 1933 had itself risen from 6 to 9 percent of GDP. (Currently it stands above 20 percent.) Roosevelt believed this jump to be downright dangerous, and he cut spending by a quarter between late 1936 and into 1938—a step akin to removing around $8 trillion from two years of federal outlays today. It seemed both good and principled politics, at the time.

In every campaign, Roosevelt insisted that the only defense was to take the offense, but he was incapable of turning purple and slamming his fists as had Cousin Theodore. In public, his anger was altogether cooler, like a squire appalled to discover a hovel on a corner of his land. When furious, he usually just whistled through his teeth.

He also chose to postpone his first baldly partisan campaign speech until late September. That gained him time between the convention in June and Election Day, November 3, for supposedly nonpolitical visits to places like Nebraska's drought lands and housing projects in Bridgeport, Connecticut. Other allegedly nonpolitical tasks were also underway as his economic pump priming turned into poll priming.

While their leader stood above the fray, Democratic National Committee politicos had to marshal surrogates to speak on his behalf, and denounce a Republican platform claiming that Americans were "threatened by Government" itself.[5] Therefore, Farley had lunch with the president on July 1 to identify both the targets for attack and the people best qualified to take the offensive—no role for Brain Trusters or speechwriters.

Jesse Jones, sixty-two-year-old chairman of the Reconstruction Finance Corporation—and whose nationwide mononym of "Jesse" underscored his power—was canny, ruthless, and rectangular at six feet, three inches, with great pale hands. His presence was plainly immense, and he could have helped, except he had barely survived a fiery plane crash in June, to spend the rest of the summer fighting influenza. Nor, as a Hoover-appointed conservative Democrat, was he part of FDR's inner circle.

Vice President Garner might have contributed what Perkins called one of his "damn good speeches," but he was pointedly bass fishing on the Leona River near Uvalde, where he remained through October.[6] Known to FDR as "Old Man Commonsense," he was sensibly hedging his bets on his chief's reelection. Garner would only speak once, by radio from Uvalde, when the president insisted. Like FDR, Garner despised Wall Street, though he was angry as well that Roosevelt seemed to vilify business overall—and was also contemptuous of Hopkins's use of tax dollars for political purposes.

That left the president's "official family," which at this point seemed to include Hopkins, even if the latter would not enter the actual Cabinet until 1938.

Furthermore, the secretaries of war and navy—Dern and Swanson—were in the hospital, and Attorney General Cummings had no wish to campaign because he was eyeing a Senate-confirmed appointment to the Supreme Court. Secretary of State Hull didn't like making speeches, and made them ponderously anyway, while Commerce Secretary Roper had faded into invisibility. Treasury Secretary Morgenthau, according to Farley, was too nervous to use in any capacity. Therefore Hopkins, Ickes, Perkins, and Wallace had to carry the fight.

FDR and Farley identified Perkins as valuable in New York, where she was popular; so there, it was decreed, she should remain. She was excellent on the radio and before small groups—except that she had become gravely controversial. The American Legion had censured her as a Communist for her backing of labor unions. Then she was attacked, compelling her to write two letters for the public record declaiming her British origin and offering a dignified disclaimer that she was not a Russian-born Jew.[7] As for Wallace, it was decided he could be an effective campaigner, mostly in the Midwest. Regardless, his political standing grew during the quadrennial brawl, when he quite wrongly pigeonholed Alf Landon, with surprising vitriol, as "the same old Hoover hack."

Hopkins, in turn, needed to keep a low profile, concluded Farley, despite his having become a powerful debater. Conservative congressmen assailed him for using his Works Progress Administration essentially to bribe voters with relief aid. Farley insisted that he stop giving speeches and, as campaign manager, asked Wallace and Ickes to help keep Hopkins quiet.[8] Anyway, Hopkins, nearly always sickly, was again feeling ill these months.

That left Ickes to "take out" the Republicans, as FDR demanded. Nervousness and depression had made Ickes a poor speaker before he encountered Roosevelt. Then, within four years, he had become the Administration's leading orator, hailed as "the king's champion."[9]

Ickes had lots of advantages for such wet work. He remained a Republican. He loved attacking men by name. He enjoyed the highest standing in government among Black leaders, and his Public Works organization—unlike Hopkins's activities—was popular everywhere, including on the Hill, for its efficiently delivered results.

Ickes gave ten major speeches against the downhome Landon, whom he branded "the friend of the common millionaire." As for Frank Knox, he and Ickes had long been acquainted. They were the same age, and each lived in Chicago, had known T.R., and was a prominent progressive Republican. Still, Ickes eviscerated Knox as "the windmilling gentleman of grotesque and absurd statements," and second on a ticket that was a "marionette show" produced by the Du Ponts, Aldriches, and other "men who run America."[10] The GOP was "soaking the poor," said Ickes, while he called Landon a puppet of the Hearst newspapers, which, he claimed, had gotten Landon the nomination.[11]

Ickes titled one nationwide broadcast "Hearst Over Topeka" to evoke the mogul's 1933 movie *Gabriel Over the White House,* and through the fall, he asked, "Do the American people want it to be '*Hearst* Over the White House'?"[12]

FDR modulated much of this vitriol by reviewing Ickes's speeches in advance. The president himself was a gracefully lethal insulter, as when, at the Philadelphia convention, he denounced millionaire businessmen as ermine-lined "economic royalists." However, according to the esteemed *Boston Evening Transcript,* through Ickes the president was employing someone "so vicious as to be utterly unworthy of a Cabinet officer."[13] As Roosevelt might say, that was a peach.

Ickes was on his own, however, when he chose to speak to the NAACP's annual convention in Baltimore. Merely for him to appear aroused Southern outrage: he seemed to be challenging segregation itself. Ickes knew he was venturing onto thin ice by attending the historic Sharp Street Memorial Methodist Church, and he merely offered a bland defense of the Administration's commitment to justice for all. The young Clarence M. Mitchell, Jr.—to become one of the NAACP's most revered officers—responded. The congenial, liberal-minded president, he said, had failed to support a federal law against lynching, and needed to find the backbone to defend all Americans.

In Washington, George Dern died on August 27, long after having ceased to be aware of anything that concerned the War Department. Ickes attended the memorial service at Mount Pleasant Congregational Church the next day. FDR, along with Hopkins and Wallace, was off inspecting the sand-blown Plains states, which entailed the three of them driving along dust-ridden back roads in parched western Nebraska. Then the president's train picked them up to continue on to Dern's funeral at the Mormon Tabernacle on September 1 in Salt Lake City.

FDR elevated the assistant secretary of war, Harry Woodring, into the Cabinet. Unlike Dern, Woodring had fought in France. Nonetheless, his appointment was supposed to be temporary. He knew enough of the futility of most European wars to make him an ardent isolationist.

On the campaign trail, Alf Landon tried to exploit anxiety over U.S. ties to Europe, and he blundered by calling Roosevelt the candidate most likely to lead the country into war. Ickes responded by reminding his audiences that the munitions-making Du Ponts were "war lords for profiting" and calling the partners at J.P. Morgan & Co. war profiteers for having helped Britain to finance the World War.[14]

Little else was said about global events. Landon pressed on to a worse mistake by calling for a return to "the American way of life." Just as today, most people were actually set on achieving something better.

In the final weeks, *The New York Times* observed that no responsible Republican really believed that Roosevelt was setting out to be "a dictator after the style of Stalin or Hitler." Even so, the *Times'* editorial provoked furious retorts about the president needing to be judged from his associates—which meant by his dictatorially inclined socialist sidekicks "Wallace, Ickes, Hopkins and Miss Perkins."[15]

These charges of "socialism," whether from Republicans or conservative Democrats, made little headway. Come November 3, Roosevelt triumphantly took forty-six states out of forty-eight. He also carried with him a three-quarter majority of both Houses of Congress, and had started to cement a coalition—white Southerners, Black Northerners, big-city bosses, labor and farmers, Catholics, Jews, and other ethnic minorities—that would endure until the late 1960s.

Nonetheless, reflected Virginia's conservative Democratic senator Carter Glass, "the elections would have been much closer had my party not had a four billion, eight-hundred-million-dollar relief bill as campaign fodder."[16] Observers more sympathetic to the New Deal, and closer to Roosevelt than Senator Glass, made their own appraisals. The 1936 election was much more a personal victory for FDR than had been that of 1932, and Perkins and Senator Hiram Johnson both feared he would now be overtaken by "delusions of grandeur."[17]

Roosevelt instilled willpower and a sense of joy into people around him and into the nation itself. His roaring laugh, head thrown back, was a national image. He said he believed that the overwhelming majority of Americans had a sense of humor. Each of his four lieutenants could also find comedy in the struggle, and humor helped them to work with him.

Perkins drew an ironic amusement from observing the men around her and kept in her desk a red folder titled *Notes on the Male Mind*. "The way men take [i.e., regard] women in political life is to associate them with motherhood" was among many of her insights that critics find apt today.[18]

Wallace had less of a sense of humor than a feeling of general goodwill. In photos, he often displays an ear-to-ear grin. In person, he radiated internal preoccupation.

Hopkins found it easy to laugh at himself in a world of self-important rivals. And Ickes had a sense of humor raucous enough to be the flip side of his miseries. When he laughed, recalled Perkins, his face was sunnier than any face she had ever seen, every part of his body shaken by laughter. Moreover, he was witty, with a quick repartee—priceless when it was not aimed at you.

As for the spider king at the center, his humor was often darker. In private, recalled Perkins, he could take a fairly sharp joke on himself: nobody attempted one on him in public. He laughed naturally at something funny, even if, she added, it took him a moment to get a subtle jest.

A fine mimic, Roosevelt did imitations of the elderly Justice Louis Brandeis, whom he called "Isaiah" for the prophet, and he imitated Hull, too—even perfecting the slight lisp caused by Hull's false teeth. To mimic someone can be a way of showing power. It is like saddling a man with a nickname, such as "Henry the Morgue" for the lugubrious treasury secretary, whom, in fact, FDR chose to mimic directly. Ickes too would get a nickname, "Donald Duck": though, as with "Isaiah," it never was used to the subject's face.

And FDR found humor in the personal doings of these lieutenants. By now, he would have heard through State Department channels of Wallace's "guru," who had traveled sixteen months through Asia, getting needy enough to beg Winthrop Aldrich for a loan. Hopkins's involvements could also be hilarious, in their way, and the president raised his salary in 1936 after learning that Hopkins too had been rendered penniless by his socializing with plutocrats. And he always enjoyed tracking Ickes's indiscretions, as when he heard from a shocked Morgenthau that Ickes had propositioned the wife of a British diplomat over dinner. As for Perkins, he drove her to distraction with his joshing.[19] "That man, that man!" she would exclaim to her staff.

Throughout, FDR displayed a genius for appearing one's friend, and one determined to unite with you to save the country. It was a craft of both intimacy and towering statesmanship. Nearly simultaneously, he would employ "a prick of cruelty" that "went to the essence of a man," said Francis Biddle, his fourth attorney general (1941–1945). "It hit [a man] between the ribs into the heart of his weakness."

These thrusts were the more wounding because "one could not tease a man in private," lamented Morgenthau. And it was a degree of teasing, explained Perkins, "that would really leave its marks, its scars."[20]

Nonetheless, some examples of Roosevelt's cruelty come over as wry. For instance, Morgenthau sighed—during a long after-dinner number-crunching meeting with Hopkins, Ickes, and FDR—that he wished he had half the brains of the J.P. Morgan & Co. partner Russell Leffingwell. In a snap, Roosevelt agreed.

Felix Frankfurter, the short, sharp, lively, Viennese-born professor at Harvard Law School who adored Roosevelt, reminisced about "an innocently sadistic streak in him." Similarly, the historian Arthur M. Schlesinger, Jr., in his classic *Age of Roosevelt,* observes FDR's "thin streak of sadism," except, like Frankfurter, he does so the better to paper it over. Still, it was Roosevelt's "streak of vindictiveness," in Perkins's words, that could be startling.[21]

A habit of almost reflexive lying added to the reasons why strong, independent men of his own sort who knew him well—such as Bruère and Cutting—preferred not to work under him. And by this time Ickes had concluded Roosevelt's "word cannot be relied on." He also found him to be a man "as cold as ice inside," and knew Democrats in Congress were no longer fooling themselves about Roosevelt's pleasant personality.[22]

Harry Truman, who entered the Senate from Missouri in 1935, simply remarked of the president, "He lies." And it was always a puzzle to West Pointer Eugene Vidal—FDR's director of civil aviation from 1933 to 1937, and son-in-law of Oklahoma's blind senator—why Roosevelt lied when there was no reason to do so.[23]

Lying was a means of Roosevelt's asserting primacy. Powerful men had to sit opposite him and listen to what both knew to be untrue, or at least they would soon enough recognize that they had been lied to, as during his impending showdown with the Supreme Court. However, one could not call the beaming president across the desk a liar. The unifying factor of Franklin Roosevelt was his will to power. He could persuade himself that everything he was doing was for the best. No one, in his opinion, had more to contribute than he; no one had a greater desire to "protect the economic welfare of all the people."[24]

Even FDR had to exert a lot of effort to maintain his cheery exterior. John Boettiger, the *Chicago Tribune* newsman who married FDR's only daughter, Anna, in 1935, worked closely with his father-in-law. Boettiger—who had plenty of his own troubles, eventually hurling himself from the seventh floor of a New York hotel—remarked that Roosevelt's strongest emotion was the rage of a "cripple" toward the healthy. He may have exaggerated about "rage," but he had singled out the troubling emotion.[25]

Roosevelt's interior had much room for envying others, and for resenting them. These tended to be men of a similar background to his own. He came to detest the kind of established figures who had brushed him aside when he was the bright young assistant secretary of the navy: they had treated him as a sharp, well-married yachtsman, despite his being what was then one of the nation's four top defense officials. Then came the condescensions after the polio. Additionally, many of his contemporaries had succeeded in business where he had not, and the hostility this aroused in him is reflected in his insistence that, given a lifetime of experience with businessmen, he had learned that "they were generally very stupid."[26]

Regardless, great commanders such as Roosevelt excel at hiding their feelings. It took courage, essentially a triumph of the spirit, for him to appear so blithe.

The bitterness was more often revealed toward a group, rather than to individuals. He loathed Aldrich, for example, yet preferred to arouse a vast constituency against Wall Street's "money changers." To dwell in public on Aldrich—or, in the battles ahead, on the isolationist Charles Lindbergh—would have betrayed the obsessions of a little man, and the Reverend Peabody would have felt disappointment at his pupil's pettiness. Even so, to incur the president's disfavor all too likely placed oneself squarely in trouble.

According to Robert Jackson, his third attorney general (1940–1941), Roosevelt "had a tendency to think in terms of right and wrong instead of legal and illegal." Convinced that his motives were pure, "he found difficulty in thinking that there could be legal limitations to them."[27] His underhanded use of Internal Revenue is one example, and much of his behavior foreshadowed what became the whole culture of "When the president does it, that means that it is not illegal."[28]

This president's two-faced statements and offhand cruelties went far beyond the habits of a chief executive who chooses to manage his administration by provoking rivalries among his subordinates. Bleaker feelings were at work than those of the "quarterback," as he would describe his role, whenever he provoked able people to undercut one another.

There was nothing in the ensuing chaos "to stimulate achievement" or to confer on him "the benefit of conflicting opinions," as most historians have concluded, nor anything worth envisioning as a "management style."[29] He would not have recognized the word "management," and if it had come his way, it would have meant to him simply exercising power over others.

During a week in May 1935, for instance, he had approved two unremarkable speeches that Ickes and Wallace were to give in Philadelphia and Boston, respectively. Several days later, he summoned Vice President Garner, the Senate majority leader, the Speaker of the House, and Secretary of State Hull to an urgent meeting, largely to decry the political harm Ickes and Wallace had just inflicted by their statements.[30] He could get such a gathering to roar with mirth over men whom they knew well. Once they left his study still chuckling, they likely felt sheepish. Again, they had been put under his thumb.

Of course, when FDR saw Wallace the next day, he told him that his New England address had been "absolutely right."[31]

Ickes was "personally very fond" of Wallace. As he wrote at the time, they were the two closest colleagues in the Cabinet, despite all.[32] Yet they were increasingly at loggerheads, and at the same time Ickes's and Hopkins's responsibilities were getting entangled. Such clashes did not involve, say, Dan Roper or George Dern. It stimulated FDR to foment such conflicts among the ablest of his subordinates, and it took a special skill to spread this form of discord.

Early into the first term, he had recognized the extraordinary talents of our four. Leaving aside Perkins, he could either exert himself constantly by reining these men in, or deliberately cause abrasions. To be sure, blurring people's responsibilities left him the ultimate arbiter. If the big new administrative state had instead expanded in better order, as was surely possible, he might have been left in the role of a Japanese emperor— barely deferred to by a powerful civilian shogunate.

However, this reasonable explanation comes secondary to the fact that he loved to "watch people suffer as they wriggle to try to get out of the tight spot in which he has placed them," as Wallace finally concluded.[33] This too Ickes and Perkins would discern.

Nor was FDR the "complete softy" as he described himself in daily business.[34] He reveled in spreading this myth, which has been endlessly repeated, as by his speechwriter Robert Sherwood in the latter's Pulitzer-winning biography, *Roosevelt and Hopkins* (1948). Initially, Ickes believed it, indeed getting so exasperated over the apparently "soft" way FDR hesitated to sack a man that he told the president how he himself did it. He preferred to send a telegram: "YOU ARE HEREBY DISMISSED."

Certainly, Roosevelt could say, "If you do that again, you're going to need another job."[35] However, he would so warn a quivering thirty-year-old assistant. Predominantly, writes another admiring biographer—the businessman Conrad Black, who draws on extensive management experience—Roosevelt "discharged people in excruciating, sadistically elaborate plots, from which he derived unseemly amusement."[36] Or he might simply freeze his target out, rendering him civilly dead while still holding office, and murmuring "really, really, indeed"—nothing more—when this miserable party dared to speak.

For all FDR's deficiencies, there were many saving graces. Among these was a shining capacity to recruit talent. Moreover, until later in the 1930s, he opened himself to advice on legislative strategy from prickly John Garner, and between them they made the vice presidency more formidable than since the days of Adams, Jefferson, and Burr.

Nor should he be blamed for holding back on outright necessary firings. Such restraint was among the ways by which he preserved his notion of being a gentleman, and it was a method that kept him working in office for twelve years. If he had incessant showdowns with people like General Johnson at the NRA, the job would have killed him sooner.

Perkins found her own strength among a small circle of such female friends as Caroline O'Day—and from her faith in God. There was also a handful of men on whom she could count when things got truly rough, including Henry Bruère and, increasingly, Ickes. In 1936 and 1937, she came under attack, just to start with, from the likes of the American Coalition of Patriotic, Civil, and Fraternal Societies. After all, she was responsible for the Immigration Service during an era in which this rallying cry circulated among the "all millionaires" troops of the New York National Guard:

There's a garment strike on and it's got to be broke.
Turn out—you're Hussars of N.Y.N.G.
The strikers are gathered in Washington Square,
Their war cry of "Oi, oi Gewalt" pierces the air.

The hussars were the well-bred horsemen of the Guard's 101st Cavalry Regiment, summoned like Cossacks to crush labor turmoil ginned up by, no doubt, rootless cosmopolites.[37]

Against that backdrop, Perkins was battling the State Department over how to interpret the Immigration Act of 1924 and its nativist "national origins quota." She was also fighting a bloc of Southern legislators who opposed any liberalization, and in addition, had to confront the same sort of "patriots" who today urge reviving that 1924 codification of race hysteria. Sadly, another ordeal was beginning to mount as she sought to open the doors to the ever more numerous Jews fleeing Nazi barbarism.

On these matters, when push came to shove, she could turn to Ickes, irritated as he was at her "buzz, buzz, buzz" in Cabinet. Of course, Washington is a city of talk, and Ickes, in common with other men, habitually accused women of talking too much. In the Cabinet Room, however, the president inevitably listened to Perkins, for all her peers' eye-rolling.

It is likely that she and the Wallaces, on those Sundays they drove together to St. James's, discussed the plight of Jews in the Reich. That said, Wallace's response would have been unpredictable. He could be distant from human concerns. Another oddity was his strange humility. He embraced a strong religious faith, and was the Western Hemisphere's top agronomist, yet felt compelled to tap into men such as his "guru" Nicholas Roerich.

In contrast to this spiritually needy side of his character, Wallace's hardheaded business practicality was at last making him money. Beginning in 1934, his startup, now known as the Pioneer Hi-Bred Corn Company, grew by 28 percent a year through the rest of the Roosevelt presidency.

The private lives of Hopkins and Ickes were also changing. At midday on December 18, 1935, the two of them were examining budget numbers in the Oval Office together with FDR, as well as with Perkins and Wallace. Maybe they could scrape up an extra billion dollars for Hopkins to boost WPA spending during the coming election year. Ickes gave Hopkins a ride back to his office, and Hopkins told him of Barbara's cancer, and a recent operation on her right breast that, he explained, had involved her chest tissues. He confessed to having reassured her, falsely, that the tumor was benign, but suspected she could tell otherwise.

Ickes said little. In that era, when "cancer" in general was never discussed, what he had just heard was a display of extreme intimacy. He thought of Hopkins's three-year-old daughter by Barbara, and of the three boys from the first marriage, as well as of his frail comrade's inability to keep up health insurance.

In his diary, Ickes insists there was "never a feud" with Hopkins, despite the furies that arose from sorting out those PWA and WPA moneys. When Roosevelt inserted a mediator between the two men, it caused further confusion. "The whole trouble is with the president," wrote Ickes, "and with the president alone." Otherwise much was going well for Ickes once Anna was dead, even if he was taking double doses of Nembutal with whiskey chasers, constantly asking his doctor for "some new sleeping dope."[38]

In April 1934, eighteen months before her fatal accident, Harold and Anna were visited in Washington during spring break by Jane Dahlman, a junior at Smith and the kid sister-in-law of Anna's son Wilmarth. In fact, Harold had known the girl since she was ten. The visit was unremarkable, and Ickes had little time for guests.

Eighteen months after that, all was different when Jane Dahlman, now Smith Class of '35, wrote her "Uncle Harold," following Anna's death, for help in getting a Washington job. She came to visit from Massachusetts for two days of early fall. When Uncle Harold met her at Union Station, he was stunned by the tall sparkling woman, with flaming red hair and high cheekbones, striding down the platform. She returned for Thanksgiving, and after dinner they went to the movies. In short order he found her a job in the National Park Service and an apartment too. More movie outings followed.

On January 29, when Jane turned twenty-three, he gave her a small dinner party at his home, one of the guests being Missy LeHand. To invite LeHand, who was famously the president's right arm, meant FDR—with lifted eyebrow and slow grin—would hear all the next morning.

So far, Ickes, age of sixty-two, was still "Uncle Harold" until he arranged for Jane to be invited to a White House musicale. She asked her uncle to escort her, and bought herself a white evening gown that contrasted strikingly with her red hair. Young navy ensigns and army officers in attendance broke protocol to win her attention. Ickes admitted to his diary that he took a "malicious pleasure" when introducing Jane to Cabinet wives. She was "very good looking," Roosevelt told him the following day.[39]

At the time, Ickes was in a relationship with the heiress and divorcée Eleanor "Cissy" Patterson, fifty-five, one of the country's few women newspaper publishers. She was also chatelaine of the Patterson Mansion on Dupont Circle, with its green-liveried servants, of Dower House in Maryland, and of Cloverly Manor on Long Island, lately a residence of Vincent Astor. When Ickes stayed for long weekends at Cloverly, he would join Cissy in her private railcar, hitched to the train between the capital and Port Washington. Throughout the election year, their liaison had brought him glowing articles and editorials in her thriving, high-quality morning paper, *The Washington Herald.*

In early 1937, Ickes acquired a country place of his own twenty miles north of Washington in Olney, Maryland. Headwaters Farm was hardly rustic. He bought it from the family of a recent head of the Chesapeake and Ohio Railway, which was like buying a house today on 280 acres from a hedge fund manager. He was still courting Jane, who had fled to Europe to think things over for the summer, and whose parents were furious at what they were hearing. As Ickes and Jane drew closer, it was likely that his coverage in *The Washington Herald* would change drastically.

Roosevelt was justly confident as 1937 began. He calculated that his first term had overseen the longest period in about fifty years during which federal troops had not been dispatched somewhere to quell labor troubles in the country—blithely overlooking the deployment of two thousand soldiers and airmen against miners at Blair Mountain in 1921. As with the ringing slogan "We Planned It That Way," he was offering some big hostages to fortune.

For Ickes, Christmastime had been fun, despite his self-medication. Harry and Barbara Hopkins paid a surprise visit on Christmas Eve, and for a present, he had given FDR an album of National Park stamps. Moreover, he and the president were now speaking the same language of "moving" against anti–New Deal justices and putting the Supreme Court "in its place." For the moment, Ickes assumed, this was just talk.[40] No opportunity had arisen in the first term for FDR to make an appointment to the highest tribunal.

Inauguration Day on January 20 began with a much larger service at St. John's than in 1933. At the Capitol, Chief Justice Charles Evans Hughes again administered the oath. A temporary covering over the East Portico protected no one from gusts of horizontal rain. Hughes held the Roosevelt family Bible, this time swathed in cellophane. The Cabinet stood soaked nearby. To everybody, including Roosevelt, who had no impairment of sensation, walking over the runner of carpet on the portico felt like plodding through a soaked sponge.

Wallace and Ickes found the scene ironic. Justice Hughes was a Hoover appointee whom they regarded as abetting a bloc of four of the nine justices who were obstructing everything that they and the president were trying to achieve.

Like the Cabinet, the Supreme Court was viewed differently in those days. In a time of emergency—as the Depression refused to let go, and fascism spread through Europe—Americans clung to a schoolbook understanding of the court. It seemed to exist above the fray, providing a timeless stability. That is one big difference from our own era when public opinion of the court has plunged.

Another difference is that these nine jurists—whose number is set by federal law, not by the Constitution—tended to be appointed according to their state or region, more so than, as today, according to their predictability. Kentuckians, say, knew that they had a Solomonic figure in Washington who wore robes with a silk skullcap. Altogether, the justices seemed carved from marble, and in fact, they had moved out of the Capitol building into their own marble temple in 1935. In part because of these strong regional ties, voters did not want to see one or another justice diminished. In sum, the court looked grander than what it was—a useful group of mostly Republican-installed lawyers.

Moreover, this court was a preserver of the last generation's politico-economic orthodoxy: forty-eight largely sovereign states were engaged in commerce, and their transactions must depend on the freest of markets possible. In this view, working conditions were largely a matter for the states, even if big corporations operated as national entities. The court had upheld some state laws regulating business. In critical cases, however, it had negated attempts by Congress to administer the complexities of industrial life. Maybe the Social Security and National Labor Relations Acts would go down next.

To so shrewd an overseas observer as John Maynard Keynes, the pronouncements of the Supreme Court meant in effect that "there is no such thing as the United States."[41] Key aspects of American government did not appear at all unified, and Keynes was among those critics who believed the Administration had to alter the minds of its law lords.

For at least a year, Perkins had sensed danger as the men around her denounced the "reactionaryism" of a Court that they believed was intent on destroying the New Deal. "The only member of the Cabinet who expressed a contrary view," Ickes told his diary, "was Miss Perkins, but I suppose that was to be expected of a woman."[42] In fact, she agreed that the Supreme Court had made itself a third policy-making body of government. On the other hand, she sought workarounds, as in 1935, when every justice declared the National Recovery Act unconstitutional.

To Attorney General Cummings, the four intractable justices were "something out of the Middle Ages."[43] One, for instance, was James McReynolds of Kentucky, age seventy-five, a confirmed bachelor who abhorred Jews. He did not feel comfortable "when there is a Hebrew abroad," alluding to Justice Brandeis, during whose opinions he would read newspapers.[44]

Federal jurists are appointed for life, and at least since the summer of 1936, Cummings had been devising a bill to circumvent McReynolds and his three brethren. Should Congress approve, an additional justice would be placed on the court to match each serving one who did not retire on turning seventy. Six new Roosevelt-appointed justices could thereby take their seats. Moreover, as is forgotten in today's debates, FDR was not just "packing" the Supreme Court; he proposed to revamp the federal judiciary, with fifty new judges on the federal bench as a bonus.

Cummings, sixty-seven, looked the part of a secretive Old World minister of state. Very tall and mostly bald, he peered from under heavy brows, pince-nez halfway between mouth and eyes. In Cabinet meetings, he was friendly and cooperative, until his fury over these primitive jurists set in. "I am sure that Homer Cummings was the chief architect and proponent of the Supreme Court fight," recalled Perkins. And "he couldn't see that it would backfire."[45]

On the evening of February 4, 1937, Roosevelt summoned Cabinet officers to a special, unexplained meeting the following morning at ten o'clock. Upon arriving, they were puzzled to find the equally perplexed chairmen of the Senate and House judiciary committees in the Cabinet Room, along with the Speaker and other senior Democratic legislators. They felt awkward. Roosevelt never invited anyone from Congress to a Cabinet meeting.

Perkins sensed his love of mystery at play. When all were seated, she saw him pull his lips down over his teeth, which meant he would be evasive.

He then offered an odd explanation for what Herbert Hoover, within an hour of the announcement, would label "court-packing." Supposedly, he was worried about "the question of aged or infirm judges . . . [being] unable to perceive their own infirmities." Regrettably, he continued, they were overburdening themselves, and, through no fault of their own, delaying the execution of justice.[46] Under other circumstances, Roosevelt would have called this story a hoot.

On hearing of the scheme, and even worse, its reasoning, everyone was speechless. "A look of complete astonishment," Perkins remembered, crossed the face of Hatton Sumners, the Dallas congressman who chaired the powerful House Judiciary Committee and, until now, an unqualified FDR loyalist. When conversation resumed, Sumners insisted that he saw no reason to risk a brutal fight on the Hill. He expected two, probably three, justices to retire quite soon. Anyway, he doubted that even a friendly Congress would approve what seemed an attempt to override the court's ideological balance.

Speaking bluntly, Farley said public support didn't exist; people tended to think well of the court. "I don't know what he's doing," Wallace whispered to Ickes. Having urged a constitutional amendment to expand the court, he regarded this approach as "a little too slick."[47]

Perkins guessed that the president had not actually grasped the plan. Because "Roosevelt wasn't a good lawyer," she convinced herself, he probably had not cross-examined his attorney general, who surely was the instigator. Following Roosevelt's introduction, Cummings took over to clarify details.

Perkins gave FDR every benefit of the doubt, not that she is convincing. He never could have overlooked the months of plotting by his "legal yes-man." Nonetheless, Perkins, a protective loyalist, weighed in.

"Have you got the papers there, Homer, and may we see them?" she asked. The AG mumbled, as Roosevelt nodded. Cummings said he did not have copies, nor was there a final draft to circulate. All sighed with relief. Surely there would be a month or two to reassess such a radical misstep, and to inquire about those retirements.

The meeting over, it was followed at noon by the president sending to Congress a polished, unusually long (5,999-word) well-documented message on the "Reorganization of the Judicial Branch." It laid out his never before noticed distress on behalf of the aging justices, the document being accompanied by a bill he expected Congress to pass forthwith. Prices broke on the New York Stock Exchange.

In April, FDR could easily have compromised to achieve two additional justices, yet didn't budge.

By July, and after immense confusions coast-to-coast, the Senate buried his plan in its Judiciary Committee, which denounced the scheme as a "reckless, futile and utterly dangerous abandonment of constitutional principles."[48] In the House, Hatton Sumners, believing that he was fighting to preserve an independent judiciary, also deep-sixed the plan. Facing all this from his own party, FDR came to insist he had merely lost a battle, while winning his real objective of redirecting the court's thinking: an altogether benign outcome with which many historians agree.

Whether or not the Supreme Court tracks election returns, its decisions—at least up to our own day—usually reflect the temper of national opinion. In late March 1937, the court—supposedly cowed by FDR's reform bill—ruled 5 to 4 that the Wagner Act, which revamped labor law, was constitutional. Furthermore, the justices backed other reforms of the sort that they had recently overridden. Then in May, one of those "medieval" figures retired.

In time, FDR got to appoint eight of the nine of a suddenly emptying court. When he made his fifth appointment—Frank Murphy of Michigan, in 1939, to fill the one seat that had come to be reserved for a Roman Catholic—he joked with his Cabinet of having lost his interest in "court packing." Still, the price of the showdown, as will be seen, was damning.

This arousal of the forces of reaction drew Ickes and Hopkins closer, in their different hard-boiled ways. It wasn't unusual, however, for Ickes to get a call, as he did early in 1937 from New York's Mayor La Guardia, to ask whether he knew Hopkins was in town to dedicate one of Ickes's Public Works projects, an addition to Manhattan's Bellevue Hospital. Or at least Ickes had assumed it was his project. That said, he and Hopkins understood each other.

In the spring, Hopkins was being tormented by ulcers. And anyone could see that Ickes was also "on the ropes." Therefore, as the president insisted, they took an April fishing trip together in the Gulf of Mexico aboard a Coast Guard cutter. FDR was always at his best when lifting up people from near the edge.

Meeting in Florida, the two landlubbers bounced around at sea for ten days getting sunburned, quarreling over the weight of a tarpon Hopkins caught, and occasionally going ashore. They explored a nearly deserted Key West. That part of U.S. Route 1, known as the Overseas Highway, remained to be built, and the archipelago was impoverished by the Depression.

On the USCGC *Saranac,* they talked shop, including their belief that the president was going to create a new organization for economic planning. They expected to be part of it, along with Wallace and Perkins. They joked that Morgenthau would likely have to join. On a serious note, they wondered how to recruit the soft-spoken, iconoclastic chairman of the Federal Reserve, Marriner Eccles, whose ideas they respected. This Utah millionaire banker-conglomerator had already imposed Washington's authority over the nation's central banking system by diminishing the authority of the once godlike New York Fed.

The small, slender, dark-eyed Eccles had come into the Administration through ties to Wallace and Tugwell. He had never graduated college and it was largely through experience in business that he discerned how government spending could provide a countervailing "demand" vital to recovery.[49] He also possessed the "mathematical brain cells" Wallace admired. In fact, Eccles had testified to the Senate Finance Committee even before Roosevelt's first inauguration that big budget deficits could be sustained, with a growing national debt acceptable. It was a parallel discovery to Keynes's.

Otherwise, aboard ship, Hopkins confided in Ickes as before: he could barely live on his salary and was being drained by alimony; anyway his first marriage had been unendurable. Furthermore, the cost of one son at Yale and another at the University of Chicago was ruinous. Thankfully, there was good news too—Barbara, whom Hopkins loved dearly, was winning her fight against breast cancer.

Back in Washington, a recession approached, and by early fall, the briskly marching U.S. economy had struck a land mine. The Dow Jones fell 40 percent between August and November. An already grievous unemployment rate of 14.3 percent in summer 1937 would blow up to 19 percent a year later. Nearly one-third of the economy's hard-won gains since 1933 were lost in the century's worst downturn other than the '29

Crash and the postwar morass of 1920–1921. FDR's opponents howled as they seized upon the 1936 slogan, "We Planned It That Way."

The collapse made the Administration's successes since 1933 a mere remission in a deadly disease. The immediate decline was steeper and faster than between 1929 and 1933, thereafter becoming less intense. The term "recession" entered general usage. Yet the scary thing about such downturns is that it is hard to know while living through them how long and damaging they will be.

Many factors caused what became known as "Roosevelt's Recession," the decisive one being FDR's attempt months earlier to balance the budget for the first time since 1930. Wallace and Eccles recognized deficit spending as a tool for managing an industrial economy, and each had warned the president against drastic cuts in government outlays while the economy was still weak.

Nonetheless, FDR had hoped to round out his apparent superachievement of nearly beating the Great Depression by balancing the books. Doing so might further increase both public confidence and growth. Morgenthau was fully behind this conventional wisdom, and of course disaster followed.

For his part, Hopkins couldn't involve himself in any of this once Barbara suffered a relapse. He took her for a final holiday in Saratoga Springs, then sat at her hospital bedside for three weeks, as he was doing early on the morning of October 7, when she slipped away, age thirty-seven. At this very moment, Perkins was walking down the hallway to visit.

FDR left Hyde Park for the capital that night. He worked the next day and held separate meetings with Wallace and Perkins, among others, and conducted the regularly scheduled Friday Cabinet meeting at two o'clock. Ickes attended, and right afterward called Hopkins to insist he spend the night in Maryland.

They drove up together to the Olney estate where Ickes cooked dinner. He tried to distract Hopkins with talk of the president, and of Louis Howe, who had died the previous year. Speaking of Howe got them laughing. Hopkins had long before attached himself closely to the wizened little man, and he remarked that Howe was one of the hardest men he'd ever known, employing ruthless methods and large sums of mysterious cash from his White House safe.

Barbara's funeral came the next morning, marked by simplicity. The president and Eleanor were among hundreds of mourners at the overflowing Mount Pleasant Congregational Church. Perkins was there, with Caroline O'Day, as were Ickes and Henry and Ilo Wallace. The gist of their whispering was that the president appeared "all of fifteen years older since he was inaugurated in 1933."[50] It was hard to believe he could endure the strain of three more years.

The choice of pallbearers showed that Hopkins was not about to waste a chance to consolidate his circle. They were James Roosevelt, the president's eldest son; the presidential secretaries Marvin McIntyre and Stephen Early; the military aide to the president, Colonel E. A. "Pa" Watson; Frank C. Walker, whom the president had assigned to mediate between PWA and WPA; Hopkins's deputy Aubrey Williams; and Secretary of the Treasury Morgenthau, who imparted tone no matter what Hopkins thought of him. Barbara's brother, Commander Donald Duncan, USN, attended the funeral, though he was not a pallbearer.

The president was then driven back to the White House, along with Ickes, and the two went into an 11:45 A.M. meeting.

"She had a hard death, suffering for quite a long time," recalled Perkins, who, for weeks, had requested prayers for Barbara at St. James's, adding, "I was very tender with him."[51] Hopkins found all this comforting and she brought him to her house for several days.

In the Oval Office, the president and Ickes discussed the faltering economy that Aldrich, Richard Whitney, and the rest of Wall Street blamed entirely on the Administration: surely the prime causes were tax increases, soaring regulations, and yielding to labor unions.

However, the problem was not that simple to Keynes, who had tried, with mixed success, to convince FDR that much greater government spending was the way out of the wretched 1930s.[52]

To be fair, even the most faithful, economically savvy Democratic Congress could never have stimulated the economy to the level needed to break out of the Great Depression. To do so required a spending Congress. The Old Guard in every walk of American life would have had to accept a mindful remodeling of the country, as over its huge disparities of wealth—a very unlikely prospect.

These United States again appeared broken. In early November, Perkins told the Cabinet that the spread of hunger required a return to emergency relief. Wallace predicted a renewal of violence if farm foreclosures rose. The price of cotton fell by a third, which meant that Department of Agriculture subsidies to "Cotton Ed" Smith and his pals skyrocketed. Wallace said this attempt at stabilization could bankrupt the Treasury. Privately, he feared the Administration might "end like Hoover's."[53]

Ickes confided to his diary that the president just didn't know which way to turn, and of Roosevelt's explaining the plunge to his Cabinet as an "unconscious conspiracy" among Big Businessmen intent on compelling him to yield on taxes, regulations, and labor law.[54]

By then, Hopkins had returned to work, and he and his little girl had moved to a rented brick house with narrow stairs on N Street in Georgetown. Ickes would visit occasionally for lunch, as he did on November 25, the day before Thanksgiving. They tried to talk shop, and it is likely that Ickes mentioned he would be keynoting the annual banquet of the American Civil Liberties Union on December 8. But Hopkins was racked by a nausea and abdominal pain, which he blamed on his ulcers, and that became the story.

On December 11, he was admitted to St. Mary's Hospital in Rochester, Minnesota (now part of the adjacent Mayo Clinic), where, nine days later, two-thirds of his stomach was removed, revealing stage 3 gastric cancer. Newsmen were not told of this, nor did he tell his friends.

Meanwhile, Ickes had thrown himself into intensifying political battles. In his address to the ACLU, he vilified the "fascism" of racial bigotry at home. Then he focused on fascism overseas. He portrayed it as international Ku Klux Klanism, the only difference being that "the Kleagles and Klokards now ride bombers, tanks, battleships and submarines."[55] He pictured a worldwide struggle between the darkness and the light, assailing the worst of all tyrannies arising in central Europe.

FACING THE WORLD

A Super Island-State in the Mid-1930s

Look here, Mr. President. I'm not a
pacifist . . . I know what war is.
Frances Perkins

Nobel laureate Jane Addams, nearly seventy-five, was honored at the Willard Hotel on May 2, 1935, by the Women's International League for Peace and Freedom, of which she was a founder. Twelve hundred dinner guests heard Eleanor Roosevelt acclaim her as a pioneer. Ickes followed, lauding Addams, however improbably, as a "field marshal"; no braver defender existed of peace and constitutional rights, he thundered. Perkins attended with Caroline O'Day, the evening's toastmistress.[1]

Addams would die of cancer three weeks later, outspoken to the end. Not long before, in a speech at Swarthmore College, she had decried "the national self-righteousness of the American people," tracing this sense of being "chosen" to the Puritans.[2] The nation's self-regard didn't quite fit America's current predicament, she noted wryly. Neither did such conceit justify Washington's "tardiness" in facing violence against labor, lynch law, and barriers to the world's refugees.

Despite their nation's shortcomings, Americans still keep believing that they hold a unique place of moral leadership across the world. At the same time, they have long shown minimal interest in foreign affairs. People overseas were as puzzled in the 1930s by U.S. behavior in the world as their great-grandchildren are today.

But Roosevelt had a deeper understanding of global affairs than most of his fellow citizens, deriving from his European travels, his command of languages, and his reading of the past. Each of his four lieutenants had also encountered Europe—not to the same extent as he, though vastly more so than, say, members of the Senate Foreign Relations Committee, the purpose of which might as well have been to distance the country from foreign dealings.

Wallace's acquaintance with eastern Europe was as rare in Washington as his competent German and the Spanish he began studying when he went to Agriculture—a language he believed everyone in the United States should learn. Equally rare was his ability to discuss international economics with Keynes. Hopkins proved himself in July 1934 to be as adept at assessing Mussolini face-to-face as he was at bureaucratic infighting at home. Perkins's well-spoken French, and her trips overseas to the International Labor Organization, enabled her to gather intelligence. By 1938, for instance, she had collected enough detail from on-the-ground Q&A to furnish Roosevelt with an unmatched evaluation of France's steady weakening in the face of German armed might.

As for Ickes, he was ready by the mid-1930s to go to war against fascism, Japanese imperialism, or any dog that barked. Even so, he admitted to being unversed in foreign policy, and was baffled when Roosevelt tried to get the United States to join the World Court at The Hague. The president spoke about America needing to "throw its weight into the scale in favor of peace," only to have the Senate brush this initiative away in 1934, at what would prove to be the height of his authority.[3] Ickes did not understand why FDR seemed so stung by this rebuff, and "willing to hurt those who had brought about his defeat."[4]

Lots of Americans regretted having become entangled overseas in 1917. Perkins, for instance, admitted to a "dreadful disillusionment" with the war, and here she typified so many of her fellow citizens.[5]

An archduke could get himself shot in Bosnia, wherever that might be—and *then* see what happened. Now, during the mid-1930s, Old World statesmen were again speaking of war. Europe appeared an offshore conglomeration whose self-destructiveness would bleed the country white if the State Department were not careful.

A perceptive British correspondent had titled his book about the slaughter just past *The First World War*. Plenty of skeletons were already digging themselves out of their graves to confirm his foresight when it was published in 1920.[6] Most terribly, 1914 to 1918 had made a far bloodier war almost inescapable. Lenin became Hitler's excuse, Communism enabling him to invoke ultimate dangers and to cast himself as the brutal savior of Germany.

Doughboys had returned to ticker-tape parades, while their country withdrew behind moralist rhetoric and interest-ridden protectionism. Roosevelt had backed U.S. membership in the League of Nations as a vice presidential candidate in 1920. Twelve years later, he could argue convincingly that the nature of the league had changed. And he too had begun to share doubts about the World War. During his navy days, he had struggled against rapacious military contractors. At the 1936 Philadelphia convention, he sensibly enough denounced "war profiteering."

As it was, Americans felt overwhelmed by years of frantic excitement: fighting a war to end war in 1917 and 1918; imposing Prohibition, and thus bootlegging, on themselves in 1920; followed by a wild boom, then an unimaginable bust. A weariness with chronic emergency shaped the country's views on foreign affairs. Specifically, frustrations with the World War's outcomes surfaced in Roosevelt's Cabinet from the start.

In March 1933, at their first meeting, FDR and his Cabinet officers addressed Japanese aggression, on which he showed himself deeply informed. International affairs intrigued him, and likely more so than did the gritty problems of relief and recovery that had to be accorded top priority.

Early in the Administration as well, each of his four lieutenants felt diffident before both State Department experts and "the gold braid"— 1930s slang for the generals and admirals. This would change. Already, anyone could grasp two key phenomena remaking the world, and have reason to fear.

One was the ability of small, determined outfits to pull off the impossible, seemingly overnight. The Kaiser's government had inserted Lenin like a bacillus into Russia in April 1917 and by November the Bolsheviks—a modest faction among the Marxist Social Democrats—had seized the capital, Petrograd. Three months later, the Red Army was brought into being. Hitler had been "a human nothing," as he saw himself after the Armistice, and then, so swiftly, this Austrian corporal levered himself into the chancellorship of Germany in 1933.

The second overbearing influence was that of technology, and such technical know-how, when vividly laid out, fascinated FDR as much as did the tides of history.

No one other than science-fiction writers had conceived of atomic bombs before 1935, and it was H. G. Wells who had anticipated a uranium device a quarter century earlier in *The World Set Free* (1914). His vision followed his previous imaginings of a New York destroyed from above by German airships in *The War in the Air* (1908). Wells was thinking ahead of even his most well-informed readers, among whom was Franklin Roosevelt. Both these books are to be found in Springwood's library.

On October 21, 1937, Ickes arrived early at Missy LeHand's White House door for a scheduled meeting with the president, whom he encountered finishing lunch in the Oval Office with H. G. Wells. Ickes merely knew of him as some famous British writer. FDR brought Ickes into the conversation, which proved to be a discussion of the next world war. Wells stuck by his prediction in *The Shape of Things to Come* (1933): that war would erupt in January 1940, which, for western Europe, was off by just four months. FDR disagreed slightly. He saw it breaking in 1941, as indeed it would for the United States. All agreed that the clock was ticking.

One thing had become clear by the time of Wells's visit. The election of November 1936 had surely been the last in which Americans could avoid debating world events.

Roosevelt's presidency had begun with promises to cut spending, although that never made sense to Keynes. Why should a nation, he asked, wait for the next war to pull itself out of a depression, rather than spend its way to recovery during peace? Whether or not America would become entangled overseas, FDR's initial austerity hit the army too. In light of public opinion, it was easier to reduce the military than most programs.

Secretary of War Dern was not going to oppose FDR over budget cuts, let alone so soon after the first inauguration. The president had to face just one high-profile antagonist, the army chief of staff, General Douglas MacArthur. In July 1933, Roosevelt assigned Ickes to take the first swipe at this Caesarean figure.

During the Hundred Days, MacArthur had submitted a list of necessities totaling scores of millions of dollars for the already small 140,000-man army. Ickes called MacArthur into his office and got "a great kick," he wrote, out of informing the general that he would receive just six million bucks for coastal defense and a previously allocated six million for ammunition.[7] Instinctively, he found MacArthur—whose habits included speaking of himself in the third person—insufferable.

Perkins too was still incensed by MacArthur's abuse of the Bonus Marchers. Still, she had to be polite: he and Rumsey had been friends ever since the general had visited her family home, Arden House, when he was superintendent of nearby West Point from 1919 to 1922. Rumsey had also known his first wife, a Palm Beach socialite, from whom he was now divorced. In 1933, MacArthur was a dashing fifty-three-year-old bachelor who cultivated Washington's society hostesses, thus attending Rumsey's parties at the Georgetown house she and Perkins shared.

As for the navy, Roosevelt was hands-on, just as everyone in his official family had expected. Until 1936, his cousin, Assistant Secretary Henry Latrobe Roosevelt, could help. Early in the Administration, the president scratched his head and told his Cabinet, "You know it's a sort of a good idea to have a Roosevelt as Assistant Secretary of the Navy." Everyone laughed.[8] Theodore Roosevelt and his son Theodore Jr. had held the role too.

FDR would not fill the position of assistant secretary for aeronautics until 1941, due to his attempts at austerity. Meanwhile he monitored all aspects of navy business, which included preparing for war in the air. In April 1933, the USS *Akron*, a helium-filled rigid airship able to launch biplanes, went down in a storm off Barnegat Light. Among the seventy-three dead was the pioneering chief of the U.S. Navy's Bureau of Aeronautics. Roosevelt demanded an admiral who could fly, only to discover no flyer existed more senior than captain—and thus was let loose the aviator Ernest J. King, who would become the next war's fearsome chief of naval operations.

President Hoover had begun construction of the navy's first warship built from the keel up to be an aircraft carrier, the USS *Ranger*, which was launched in 1934—the year the new Administration began constructing two carriers of an entirely new class.

Roosevelt's early experience with the U.S. Army Air Corps also began tragically. On February 9, 1934, after a Cabinet meeting, he had rescinded by executive order the Post Office contracts held by airline companies. Questions of fraud had arisen over delivering the mail by air. Now he gave the task to the Air Corps. By April, the level of accidents had compelled him to return mail flights to private hands. Twelve army pilots had perished during the weeks in between. Among other shortcomings, they had not been trained for bad weather as had been civilian flyers. But before the president relented, Senate testimony by the former airmail pilot Charles Lindbergh had in effect cast blame on Roosevelt for the death toll and, he added, government interference was "unwarranted and contrary to American principles."[9]

Colonel Lindbergh, thirty-two, was of a type certain to stir FDR's resentment—the tall, handsome celebrity-hero son of a congressman who riveted the world with his physical bravery. He had married into a fortune, vaster than any of the Roosevelts', and the world had followed his suffering after his twenty-month-old namesake had been kidnapped and murdered. In 1934, Lindbergh was the most popular man in America, and equally famous.

That fall, Lindbergh was the obvious choice when the Treasury Department needed a technical adviser to buy planes, and Morgenthau simply mentioned to FDR that he would be hiring Lindbergh as a consultant. A quick, firm, and unexplained veto followed.[10]

Meanwhile, the very scale of the New Deal was beginning to match the challenge of military preparedness. Who would have anticipated that a promising colonel such as George C. Marshall would ever be responsible for marching city kids into the woods to clear firebreaks? He was among the officers who supervised Civilian Conservation Corps encampments, and whose skill was tested when mustering thousands of civilians—the so-called Tree Army—in peacetime.

The sheer scope of what was underway with the New Deal, the president once remarked to Ickes, could be compared only to Stalin's monstrosities, such as building the White Sea Canal, or to Hitler's construction of the *Autobahnen*. The other democracies could not boast of anything like the Tennessee Valley Authority, nor, in fact, could the tyrannies. America was meeting gigantic calamity with a mighty national response.

From those early days onward, the New Deal was contributing to rearmament. To be sure, the founding legislation for Hopkins's multibillion-dollar Works Progress Administration prohibited it from tackling military projects. Yet the WPA evolved from just hiring the unemployed for slow-motion leaf-raking, according to Hopkins's enemies, to providing authentic jobs—including for men who could smooth airport runways (for faster military planes) and deepen harbors (for ever larger warships). It also helped maintain forts and bases, such as New Jersey's ammunition-making Pica-tinny Arsenal, and Hopkins collaborated with both the army's Corps of Engineers and the navy's Bureau of Yards and Docks.

In 1938, Brigadier General George Marshall, now the army's deputy chief of staff, calculated the benefits. Hopkins's projects had basically added $250 million to War Department developments—an amount close to the average annual departmental budgets of the preceding fifteen years. As for Ickes's Public Works enterprise, the secretary would claim in 1940 that it had spent $1 billion since 1933 to help build warships, at a time when constructing a battleship cost around $50 million and took four years.[11]

All that said, when a Gallup poll had asked, in 1937, "Do you think it was a mistake for the United States to have entered the World War?" 71 percent answered yes.

Early in the Administration, it had been unclear which global dangers to anticipate. The world of the 1930s held slightly over two billion people, largely subject to empires: Africa lay under colonial rule apart from Liberia and the kingdom of Ethiopia; the French, Dutch, and British reigned over Southeast Asia; and the Russian empire, then doing busi-ness as the USSR, which Washington had finally recognized in November 1933, sprawled across eleven time zones. Outreaching all others was the British Empire and Commonwealth, whose territories were half again as large as the Soviet Union, and its population at least triple.

The term "superpower" would not be coined until 1944, when it would define the kind of great power able to project advanced military capacities most anywhere on Earth. By these lights, only one superpower existed during the 1930s: Great Britain, which held a thousand bastions worldwide and the best navy afloat. In contrast, the United States was still a super island-state.

But was Britain a bosom Anglo-Saxon partner or a disturbing rival? Right into the 1930s, deadly serious planning by sharp minds on the U.S. general staff could imagine no more probable danger to their country than that of six million British imperial troops rolling down from Canada to destroy the competitive challenge of the industrial Middle West while Japan pinned America's arms in the Far East.[12]

Such planning would have appalled Perkins, had she known the details. She revered Britain and would draw on experts from its civil service to help craft the fundamentals of Social Security. To her, the United States was forever indebted to Britain for "our own civilization, for its birth, breeding and infant protection." Such a view characterized the better sort of people along the Eastern Seaboard.

FDR saw more deeply into the British Empire than most anyone. For instance, he recognized the Foreign Office as being composed of hard, skilled negotiators—the sort of men who might have been wranglers at Cambridge (honoring in mathematics) or fellows of All Souls at Oxford. They wrote everything down and played for keeps. From the start, he shared this opinion with his Cabinet.

During 1933, for instance, Dean Acheson often substituted at Cabinet meetings for his ailing chief. In one discussion about negotiating with London over its war debt—on which Britain had defaulted—FDR basically told him "Don't."[13] It would be more prudent to delay, and to wait for British envoys to reappear with better conditions.

On the other hand, Roosevelt detected the steady decline of history's largest empire, a subject that few experts could explain and an issue about to become immensely significant. A diminished British Empire, he expounded to his Cabinet, meant that its autonomous white dominions would turn increasingly toward the United States for protection and trade. Therefore, Washington should make overtures to these already independent nations. At least one or two Cabinet members should visit Canada during 1935.

Roosevelt also suggested that such visits be made to New Zealand and to Australia, which he believed were inhabited by "cockneys," although a ten-thousand-mile voyage of this kind should wait for Washington's long summer months. The Cabinet was dumbfounded. He might as well have asked them to visit Mars. Other than his own trip to the Territory of Hawaii in July, and an inspection tour of those islands by each of the two service secretaries, no one in the room had been west of California.

He wasn't counting on the State Department. Professor Moley, who briefly served there as an assistant secretary, observed that career U.S. diplomats had "a deep-rooted sense of inferiority to the superlative technicians in the British service."[14]

From the beginning, of course, the Administration faced far graver imperial ambitions than those of Britain. In fall 1933, Perkins had already been warning her colleagues of German propaganda, and of the new National Socialist regime's U.S. sympathizers. Speaking as head of the Immigration Service, she drew on sources ranging from grassroots labor organizers to the titans of finance, and their wives. Hitler's government, she told Ickes in October 1933, had been dispatching several hundred capable men into the United States to join ethnic organizations such as the Wisconsin Federation of German-American Societies. The purpose, she argued, was to stoke anti-Jewish, Nordic chauvinist biases, and to gain political influence.

Ickes paid attention. The next morning, he called a friend in Chicago, Superior Court Judge Harry M. Fisher, president of the city's Zionist Organization. The German ambassador would soon be traveling through the Midwest: they agreed to have his activities monitored. Not that Ickes informed FDR or his Cabinet colleagues.

Throughout the 1930s, and right into the war, the Cabinet discussed every global issue affecting the United States. Occasionally FDR actually sought advice. Discussions of foreign affairs were usually more candid than those on domestic policy: rival department heads had less to conceal from one another. Nor did the Cabinet's senior member, Secretary of State Hull, lord it over his colleagues as had his predecessors.

The North Atlantic basin was still "the world" for an amazing number of practical people, including for the men and woman of this Cabinet. As for the lands beyond the Pacific Rim, they were impossibly exotic, and so too were the Middle East and Central Asia. Occasionally, *The New York Times* might carry an article that seemed torn from the pages of Kipling, such as "Afghan Rebels Gain in Fight for Kabul."[15] Of course, conflicts like those would never be a concern for the United States.

The world of the 1930s contained only a few major countries deemed "civilized," among them Italy. It had been a U.S. ally in the World War, sacrificing more than a million dead. Around two million Americans still spoke Italian at home. "We were more Italian than Italians," many would recall.[16] A source of ethnic pride to this community, Benito Mussolini had been prime minister for ten years by the time FDR was elected. Even Ickes, early on, saw him "restoring Italy," and other influential Americans, with political views as different as those of Tugwell and Thomas Lamont, believed Mussolini's corporatist blend of private ownership and government control had something to offer.

Hopkins explored the question firsthand in the summer of 1934. Despite his fiery energy, he had been in delicate health for as long as FDR had known him. By May, he looked near collapse, and the president urged him to sail to Europe. Ironically, if Hopkins accepted some make-work, he could use government funds for a holiday. He simply had to report back on the quality of personnel in various U.S. embassies.

Barbara—at least two years before her cancer—had accompanied him at his own expense, although he had to scrape for her fare. They boarded the SS *Washington* for Southampton on July 4, bearing letters of introduction from the State Department, including one to Mussolini, and one also to Hitler, whom Roosevelt was already describing as a madman. After their stay in London, the Hopkinses visited Berlin, Vienna, and Rome, and managed to enjoy two weeks of vacation in Sorrento overlooking the Bay of Naples.

These were sinister months. Hitler and Mussolini had first met in Venice, during mid-June 1934. Two weeks later, Hitler wallowed in a blood purge that slaughtered at least ninety of his disruptive "Storm Detachment" (SA) paramilitarists whom he accused, among other failings, of immorality. Then, on July 25, Austrian Nazis murdered their country's chancellor during an attempted putsch. Finally, a week later, in early August, Germany's aged president died. His passing removed the final internal obstacle to the New Reich.

In Berlin, Hopkins had wanted to be received by the Führer, who clearly had other pursuits, although Hopkins later claimed, falsely, that it was he who "refused to shake hands with a murderer."[17] He was able to see Mussolini, on Friday evening, July 20, at Rome's Palazzo Venezia.

Anyone who read a newspaper knew of the Sala del Mappamondo, the 180-foot-long hall doing duty as Mussolini's office. It offered no furniture except for a desk and three chairs placed at one extreme end. Humbled visitors therefore had to walk the hall's entire length to be greeted by Il Duce when, finally, he looked up from his state papers. Except that this time, he cordially greeted Hopkins at the door, and they strolled to the chairs together.

Mussolini, who spoke excellent English, wore a gray suit, light-blue tie, and a soft shirt. He was not the buffoon of caricature. They reviewed his public works programs, which were building bridges, roads, and canals, as well as draining swampland. Then the dictator asked to hear of Berlin and what Hopkins knew of Hitler's death squads. After all, Mussolini observed, three Italian provinces shared a 250-mile border with Austria.

This was Hopkins's first diplomatic mission. Upon sailing home from France, he reported all to FDR over lunch in the Oval Office on August 25. The following weekend he, Barbara, and their daughter were invited for the first time as a family for a weekend at Hyde Park.

The appeal of Mussolini's Italy to certain U.S. businessmen, political theoreticians, and incautious officials such as Ickes lasted for about another year. The trains ran on time, there were no strikes or lockouts, and Italy was relatively unscathed by the Depression (due to a smaller industrial base). Moreover, within living memory, Italy's Risorgimento had re-created a nation of many principalities into a single independent state.

Mussolini's posturing as a man of faith also appealed to a great proportion of Americans. His PR emphasized a reconciliation with the Vatican after more than half a century of official antagonism, and he stood as a bulwark against Godless Communism. Regrettably, columns of marching youths might force his opponents to drink castor oil, but there had been no high-profile murder since 1924, and all this was just low-grade thuggery, not Dachau.

However, this was no benign up-and-coming power. Fourteen months after Hopkins's visit, in October 1935, some two hundred thousand Italian troops swept into Ethiopia from Italy's adjacent colony of Eritrea to the north, and from Italian Somaliland to the south. Both Italy and Ethiopia belonged to the League of Nations, which ineffectually condemned Rome. Sanctions were never fully imposed, and Italy quit the league anyway. Germany had already left in November 1933.

Hopkins and Ickes were aboard the USS *Houston* on their fishing trip with the president when Italy invaded. They advised the president to return to Washington, yet instead observed close-up how unflappable FDR was at times of real crisis. They helped him to craft a statement saying that he was in constant touch with Washington by radio.

The *Houston* carried serviceable maps of that distant region, which Roosevelt scrutinized, exclaiming "Good!" whenever news arrived favoring

Ethiopia.[18] At home, Congress's antiwar sentiment obstructed a harsher response. It had just imposed the first of five Neutrality Acts, over FDR's objections. In addition to other constraints, these prevented U.S. arms sales to warring nations. To Ickes's disgust, however, Roosevelt chose not to demand sanctions. Nor, in Ickes's judgment, did he put teeth in a so-called moral embargo that might have entailed publishing the names of Americans who sailed on Italian liners, or U.S. companies trading with Italy.

Among our four—and against the backdrop of ever more violence overseas—Perkins was the second to visit Europe during this long presidency. She worried most about Germany, and for its refugees. During the first term, she tended to share her views on global matters only privately with FDR: she fretted that Cabinet colleagues might see her reaching above her place as merely the labor secretary. Nevertheless, she could pick up a lot through the International Labor Organization. Since 1934, due to her urging, it was the sole League of Nations agency to which the United States adhered.

Perkins sailed for France on July 21, 1936, with the intent of strengthening U.S. cooperation with the ILO. Her daughter, Susanna, went along. Starting in Paris, she addressed the International Federation of Business and Professional Women, a speech aired in the United States by transatlantic hookup. Days later, she and her daughter entrained on the Po-Midi for Geneva, headquarters of the league and of the ILO, which she knew to be a gold mine of information, particularly on Germany.

Once arrived, she listened to everything. Then she and Susanna continued on to the Salzburg Festival in Austria, where they spent five days in the Altstadt before circling round to London for Perkins's final conferences. Sailing from Southampton, they arrived in New York on September 1.

FDR would not return from his inspection of the drought-ravaged plains until the eleventh, and the next day, he left for a short cruise down the Potomac with Ickes and Cummings. His first opportunity to receive a detailed, uninterrupted briefing from Perkins would be at lunch on September 17. He usually ate at his Oval Office desk at one o'clock, served, as were a guest or two, on trays. For him to move to another room required help. Ickes joined them for the last fifteen minutes.

By this juncture, Hitler was violating the 1919 Treaty of Versailles in numerous ways. In March 1936, he had deployed thirty-five thousand troops into the Rhineland, a region of Germany, west of the great river, that borders France and Belgium. Versailles had intended it to serve as a demilitarized buffer zone. And, come October, Hitler and Mussolini would sign a military pact declaring the Rome-Berlin "Axis" around which Mussolini bragged Europe would rotate. In between these events, Washington that mid-September was still enjoying the tranquility of summer.

In the Oval Office, Perkins laid out what she had learned overseas, and summarized her report for Ickes once he arrived: Nazi Germany was certain to absorb Austria—a step that all of them understood would make it easier for an ever-stronger Reich to push farther east.

It was in Spain, however, that fascism had just shown its hand. "Of all our blind isolationist policies," recalled Sumner Welles, who would soon rise to undersecretary of state, "the most disastrous was our attitude on the Spanish civil war."[19]

This atrocity-ridden fratricide began in July 1936—only weeks before Perkins arrived in Europe—when a number of generals, of whom the survivor would be Francisco Franco, rebelled against the Madrid republic. The revolt was abetted by agents of Mussolini, and soon Italy intervened to back Franco's so-called Nationalist forces with troops, ships, and planes—as did Germany with its own air transports, bombers, tanks, and ships. Spain became one of the great causes of Ickes's life and involved Wallace too, try as he might to avoid the controversy.

To be sure, like each of the four, Wallace was increasingly alarmed about the spread of fascism. A year earlier, he had reviewed the problem with Albert Einstein, himself a refugee in Princeton, New Jersey, after refusing two years earlier to return to newly Nazi Germany. They had sat together at the Harvard commencement, where each received an honorary degree. Once the Nationalist junta rebelled in 1936, Wallace condemned the violence, though doing little else on the issue.

In contrast, Ickes fully supported Spain's Republican, or Loyalist, government. And he did so with a vehemence akin to Hemingway's Robert Jordan, the American guerrilla of "red, black, blinding" temper in *For Whom the Bell Tolls*. He was incensed that the democracies embargoed arms to both sides, which compelled the legitimate Spanish Republic to turn to Moscow (Soviet commissars, and General Secretary Joseph Stalin's

NKVD secret police, to follow). Ickes was among the first Americans to recognize that Spain was becoming a tryout for the next world war.

Congress had extended its first, short-term, Neutrality Act of 1935 by another act in 1936 that FDR signed with equal reluctance. It again banned exports of "arms, ammunition, and implements of war" to all belligerents, while also forbidding any grant of loans and credits. These steps further undercut the legitimate government in Madrid, and began to shape the context for America's ferocious debates, soon to come, over committing itself in Europe.

By 1937, Ickes despaired of FDR's refusal to challenge Congress over the Neutrality Act. He argued that the arms embargo was functionally one-sided. A priori, it favored any better prepared and equipped aggressor. This was "a black page in American history," he told the president.[20] No matter: the vote-counting machine was whirring behind Roosevelt's smile.

Hitler had pledged to oversee the destruction of Spain's left-leaning, anticlerical government—and the Vatican wanted to see it gone as well. FDR took some small steps to bypass the embargo, eventually to reveal to Ickes why he could not support Loyalist Spain: doing so might jeopardize the pro-Franco Catholic vote in America's biggest cities in the 1938 midterm elections.

The kaleidoscopic diplomacy underway in 1936 climaxed with a treaty signed in November between Germany and Japan proclaimed to be against Soviet Communism. And, when Italy joined this accord a year later, the three Axis powers loomed ominously on both sides of Eurasia.

Like Italy, Japan had also been associated with the United States in 1917 and 1918, except that the war had given Japan confidence to reach for empire as the nations that had once blocked its ambitions deliquesced or licked their wounds. Japan seized the great Chinese province of Manchuria in 1931 and, following a toothless condemnation by both the league and the United States, quit the organization in 1933, nine months before Germany. It spurned naval arms limitations and fortified the Caroline Islands in the Western Pacific, which Tokyo had obtained as a mandate from the league, and which now gave Japan a stronghold deep in the Caucasian imperial sphere.

Anger at Japan intensified during the long, teeth-clenched years before Pearl Harbor. Like other Western powers, the United States had a military presence in China to enforce extraterritorial privileges. Should outright war erupt between China and Japan, U.S. gunboats and marines might be caught in the middle. Moreover, Roosevelt knew the Philippines, which America had won from Spain in 1898, were impossible to defend.

"Let's get rid of the Philippines," he proposed to his Cabinet during his first year in office.[21] So much else was more important. Furthermore, America's experiment in colonialism had proved expensive, and every army officer knew the islands must be abandoned at the onset of a Pacific war. Still, pulling out was not that easy, especially once Douglas MacArthur, war hero and former chief of staff, arrived in Manila, with FDR's approval, in a role that today would be called that of a military contractor. He was to help build an army for the newly established Commonwealth, a position halfway to independence.

By 1936, Roosevelt and Hull agreed that Japan intended at least to control the Far East economically. Ickes and Perkins discerned more reasons to concur.

During March, they had been the ranking dinner guests at one of Washington's most imposing houses—the Japanese ambassador's recently built neo-Georgian mansion on Massachusetts Avenue. Of course, congressional leaders attended as well, but Cabinet officers outranked them, which gave Ickes and Perkins ample time to discover the ambassador to be as smooth as he was unconvincing when he cooed to them of peace.

Any clash with Japan would, by this point, entail a titanic showdown with its truly excellent Imperial Navy. FDR was about to commission two aircraft carriers: the USS *Yorktown* in fall 1937 and the USS *Enterprise* in spring 1938. Each had been funded by Ickes's Public Works Administration, and workers paid by the PWA were also constructing 20 destroyers and more than 130 service aircraft.

As for the Royal Navy, FDR told his Cabinet, it was ready to lay down two battleships to match the two that Japan was building, and he expected those ships to be only part of a huge $7.5 billion British rearmament program. This point was important to get across because U.S. policy was to match the rival Royal Navy in capital ship construction.

During the discussion that followed, FDR claimed he had not heard any minister in the London government say anything about world peace—a telling dig. The stubborn Dutchman, as he occasionally called himself, held no special affection for Britain, and he insisted that, had Britain dared to close the Suez Canal when Mussolini invaded Ethiopia, Spain's civil war would not now be blazing, for denying access through the canal would have doomed Italy's entire East Africa adventure—making a major commitment in Spain very unlikely.

In 1934, Congress had authorized, though not funded, the construction of two battleships. With his mind still on balancing the budget, Roosevelt had been unwilling to press Congress for more defense dollars. Each new outlay weighed on him like lead, and his vision for the navy had to proceed gradually, especially in election year 1936. With the election won, the year could end with dramatic headlines: CABINET CONSIDERS NEW BATTLESHIPS. Newsmen did not know what *kind* of battleships and tried to extract details from Perkins about relevant contracts.[22] Irrespective of U.S. decisions, Japanese yards in 1937 began secretly to lay down the heaviest capital ships ever constructed.

Claude Swanson, in his Civil War–era frock coats and winged collars, remained secretary of the navy. At the annual Cabinet dinner on January 5, 1937, Ickes and Wallace were deep in conversation in the East Room, while Swanson was talking nearby. Then, just as Eleanor and Franklin entered, Swanson pitched to the floor in a dead faint. Stewards hurried him out in an armchair. No one was ruffled, and Mrs. Swanson stayed for dinner, saying this happened often.

FDR did not mind Swanson's frailty. On the contrary. The secretary's voice had thickened over these years, and on those rare occasions when he actually questioned FDR in the Cabinet, such as over a decision to loan old naval vessels to Brazil, the commander-in-chief apparently might not hear. He recognized that Swanson just spoke for the admirals, most of whom FDR had known since they were promising shavetails during the World War, and now could handle them far better himself.

The familiar details of global affairs, such as concerned trade and immigration, still had to be conducted. In the mid-1930s, what had been seemingly routine issues were instead discussed heatedly amid rumors of war. Wallace, for instance, warned Americans in speeches during early

1937 of how the nation might be pulled again into European conflict: one belligerent or another would rip into U.S. world commerce.

To avoid war, he argued, it would be safer to expand business with Latin America and Canada. That said, to diminish involvement with Europe would require farmers to create new trade relationships with these Latin neighbors. That was a hard sell. Regardless, the nation's robust economic growth in the first half of 1937 made his proposal about turning toward Latin American markets credible.

Perkins, in turn, was focusing on immigration reform. An aide recalled that, when she spoke of reform, congressmen viewed her as "a combination of their mothers, teachers, and blue-stocking constituents."[23] Some friends might agree. During those times when they met in the Labor Department, with Perkins sitting sternly behind her large desk, Hopkins and Ickes were each reminded of the times when they had been punished as eight-year-olds.

Few issues rankled Congress more than the prospects of liberalizing immigration. Equally touchy were those State Department officials with whom she argued on behalf of Jews fleeing Nazi persecution.

The problem was not that of the quotas for German immigrants stipulated by the 1924 Immigration Act. Except for 1939, these had always been underfilled. Instead, among the obstacles she encountered was one familiar to our own era: the dread that immigrants are "likely to become a public charge."

In 1930, Herbert Hoover had issued an executive order tightening the "public charge" provision of immigration law. Perkins now challenged how the State Department's visa division and its consuls in Germany were applying that law. She explored how U.S. citizens themselves could post bonds for asylum seekers, and even pledged "that she herself is prepared to accept responsibility—if legal—to bond German refugees," wrote an astounded diplomat.

Roosevelt's "opposition to increasing immigration was well known," concludes Bat-Ami Zucker, the scholar who has best examined how these consuls put into force the Administration's restrictive policies.[24] Irrespective of diplomats—among whom were his own appointees—the president worried about opinion on the Hill. As always, he was wary of the South, whose bloc of legislators remained adamant against immigration. FDR simply kicked the problem to Cordell Hull and Under Secretary William Phillips, who tried to dodge it in their turn.

Biographers have written that Perkins was fighting this battle alone, whereas in fact she had at least two outstanding allies: Congresswoman O'Day, who served on the Immigration and Naturalization Committee, and with whom she now lived; and Ickes, who weighed in at every Cabinet debate about refugees. He, in turn, sought the advice of Judge Julian W. Mack, a former law professor of his at the University of Chicago, who, in the 1930s, was a noted presence on the federal bench—and Ickes shared what he learned with Perkins.

The judge sat on the Court of Appeals for the Second District, which includes New York, and had worked with Ickes for the NAACP. Mack knew Perkins as well because Mack had served as president of the National Conference of Social Workers. From his chambers in Manhattan, he advised them on the intricacies of immigration law, and how this applied to refugees. Mack had graduated from Harvard Law, studied further in Berlin and Leipzig, and had chaired the American Jewish Congress—no one knew this issue better.

Perkins began to weigh the possibility of bringing unescorted German-Jewish children to the United States. Regardless, as Zucker explains, "Frances Perkins's goodwill and efforts fell on deaf ears." FDR turned to refugee issues only slowly, and safely, after his reelection.[25] Even then, Perkins and Ickes received none of his support.

Judge Mack had urged Ickes, who had never met a Jew until he was sixteen, to get involved with the United Palestine Appeal, and so he did by accepting UPA invitations to speak at banquets. That is why, for instance, he was the guest of honor at a dinner in May 1936 at the Hotel Astor in New York, which raised over $1.5 million to help develop a Jewish homeland in British Mandatory Palestine. NBC carried his speech coast-to-coast.

His own clash with Nazi Germany opened a year later, soon after the *Hindenburg* disaster of May 6, 1937. This ultramodern bullet-shaped airship, measuring 804 feet stem to stern, bore two giant swastikas on its tail. While attempting to dock over Naval Air Station Lakehurst, New Jersey, it burst into flames, killing most of the passengers and crew.

No transatlantic airline service would exist until May 1939. Instead, travelers enjoyed a luxurious sixty-hour lighter-than-air crossing, thanks to Luftschiffbau Zeppelin GmbH, the German Zeppelin Company. The *Hindenburg* had made ten round trips without incident, despite the buoyancy medium for German airships being hydrogen. Then the electrically detonated catastrophe seemed to have put an end to using this flammable gas. Yet Hitler still envisioned zeppelins as one more instrument of Nazi superiority. If they were to fly safely, they would require helium, another lighter-than-air gas that doesn't combust, though more costly and less buoyant.

Since 1925, the Interior Department's Bureau of Mines had been stockpiling this by-product of natural gas, which is back in the news a century later for its defense implications. (Helium is an aerogen possessing vital properties for cooling and other computer-based uses.) In 1937, the military concern was only with zeppelins, and Washington then controlled the world's supply of the gas, extracted from southwestern fields. Furthermore, the Interior Department ran the world's only helium plant, and by law, the secretary held final authority over this product's lease and sale.

Ickes, already enraged by Germany's "race" laws and simmering over German atrocities in Spain, also remembered that, during the World War, more than fifty bombing raids by zeppelins against England had left 557 civilian dead, culminating when an armada of sixteen airships struck London. Who could guess how these behemoths—once they could use nonflammable gas—might figure in tomorrow's war in the air?

On Friday morning, May 14, 1937, FDR returned to Washington from Texas, where he had visited his son Elliott in Fort Worth after fishing for tarpon in the Gulf. He promptly met with Hopkins in the Oval Office, then lunched at his desk with Democratic donor Daisy Harriman, whom he had just appointed minister to Norway. The Cabinet convened at two o'clock as usual.

During the initial round robin, Ickes announced that Germany had asked to buy ten million cubic feet of helium in light of the *Hindenburg* disaster eight days earlier, and said he was worried that zeppelins might again be used in wartime. FDR told him to work this out with the Departments of War, Navy, and Commerce.

A few weeks later, German destroyers shelled the unfortified Spanish seaport of Almería—a month after German planes had bombed the Basque cultural capital of Guernica, killing 1,654 civilians—whereupon Ickes told newsmen that the Reich was taking civilization back to the Dark Ages. That said, U.S. lobbyists were navigating the Zeppelin Company's request past the National Munitions Control Board and the Senate

Committee on Military Affairs, which they did by using a respectable New York–based cutout business, American Zeppelin Transport, whose directors included the president of Goodyear Tire. By year's end, lobbyists had gained Hull's approval as well.

In January 1938, the German freighter *Dessau* entered the Port of Houston laden with containers ready to be filled with helium. No one less than Hermann Göring, Supreme Commander of the Luftwaffe, had conceded that Germany would limit itself to using helium for transatlantic airship operations, presumably to carry passengers. All that Luftschiffbau Zeppelin needed to resume service between Frankfurt and New York was Ickes's signature on the vital contract.

Back-to-back dramas shook the Administration during 1937: Roosevelt's court-packing plan; a failed attempt at executive branch reorganization; and then the economic collapse with its own "Black Tuesday" market crash on October 19.

Meanwhile, Japan's full-scale invasion of China began that summer, and soon something like a million Chinese and Japanese troops were grappling in and around Shanghai, wherein roughly four thousand resident Americans were protected by 1,050 U.S. Marines as part of a long-standing international force. FDR spoke caustically during August about this predicament to Admiral William Leahy, his chief of naval operations. Some twenty-five thousand Americans lived in Paris as well, said the president, without needing to be protected by marines.

Embers were drifting down on powder kegs. Americans in or out of uniform were going to get hurt, judged FDR, but he could not redeploy the marines during the middle of this mess. Moreover, he learned that they were puzzlingly stationed at the point of greatest danger. Why so, he asked Leahy, when Britain was by far the largest concession-holder in Shanghai, not to mention the biggest investor throughout China? Because the British are smart, replied the Irish-American admiral.

Swanson returned to the Cabinet Room in mid-September to offer as best he could a full-throated call for going to war now that the Japanese Imperial Army was diverted to Asia's mainland. Once Swanson had registered what everyone knew to be the opinion of Leahy and the other admirals, the Cabinet could get down to business.

Several days later, while they were reviewing the world together, FDR complained to Ickes about Secretary of State Hull being too cautious. Sidestepping this attempt to gossip, Ickes remarked that Italy, Germany, and Japan were like a plague and "neighbors had a right to quarantine themselves against a contagious disease."[26] FDR jotted down the phrase. Hopkins helped to draft the speech that the president gave in Chicago on October 5, with Ickes sitting alongside in a top hat. This was Roosevelt's most important speech to date on global affairs, in which he called for an international "quarantine" against the "epidemic of world lawlessness." He was leveling with the public in the same way that he had spoken of the economic plague.

As Roosevelt expected, U.S. blood was soon shed in China. During December, Japanese troops had pressed into Nanjing, lying 185 miles inland from Shanghai on the Yangtze, then recognized internationally as China's capital. The flat-bottomed U.S. gunboat *Panay* was anchored twenty-six miles upstream with the Stars and Stripes flying.

On Sunday afternoon, December 12, Japanese warships and bombers sank the *Panay*. Three Standard Oil tankers, floating nearby for safety, were destroyed, three Americans killed and forty-three wounded. Five days later in the Cabinet, Swanson—speaking for a united navy in his feeble old voice—demanded war. Ickes had long believed war inevitable, and he agreed that now was the time to retaliate.

Contrary to news articles a year earlier, FDR and his Cabinet had not proceeded to build battleships. This was about to change, and the president soon instructed Swanson to order naval architects to design a new class of "super battleship." From now on, until another December Sunday, in 1941, Roosevelt would seek to buy time. The great geopolitical question of the century was taking form: the rival claims of Europe and of oceanic Asia on America's future.

9

FAITH AND MAINTENANCE

January to Summer 1938

Far too much precious time has passed.
John Maynard Keynes, writing to FDR, February 1938,
urging truly large-scale government investment in the U.S. economy

One way that Roosevelt enabled each of his four closest lieutenants to soar was by encouraging their growing sure-handedness in foreign and military affairs. While skies darkened in 1938, for instance, the Nazis' *National Zeitung* editorialized: "As in all previous anti-German agitation, this time, too, the American Minister of the Interior Ickes is at the head of agitation directed against the Reich."[1]

At the same time, Hopkins was becoming the "economic and political adviser No. 1 to the White House," according to *The New York Times*. Among his other requests, FDR would call upon him to examine the potential of enlarging West Coast aircraft plants for war.[2] Similarly, the responsibilities of Perkins and Wallace swelled beyond their original remits at Labor and Agriculture.

As shrewd old Vice President Garner reflected to Perkins, "I've observed that the president runs a good deal of this government himself. He runs the State Department. He runs the War Department. He runs the Navy Department. He runs the Treasury Department. I don't know what the Attorney General ever gives him that he doesn't give the Attorney General first."[3] Garner added that FDR paid no attention to Commerce and that, at least, Farley ran the Post Office Department. That said, a huge amount of what remained at the center of an ever-expanding U.S. government was in the hands of our four.

Their roles involved them in mounting controversy. By the end of 1937, demands arose on Capitol Hill for the overreaching Hopkins, Ickes, and Perkins to resign. Wallace went unmentioned only because he was being cautious as he sought the presidency. In public, he avoided fiery subjects such as budgets, labor, and military preparation, offering anodyne remarks about the importance of maintaining the "spirit of joy" that Roosevelt had come to embody.[4]

As 1938 began, all four were established as the Administration's most enduring figures at the top. Even Rexford Tugwell, who had risen to undersecretary of agriculture and become personally close to both Franklin and Eleanor, had been hounded out of government by conservatives shrilling "Rex the Red!" Furthermore, the president's key men in Congress kept dying on the job: Speaker of the House Henry Rainey (1934), Speaker Joseph Byrns (1936), Senate Majority Leader Joseph Robinson (1937), and Speaker William Bankhead (1940). The stress of such positions in that decade was extreme. Still, each of the four lieutenants could transcend their miseries and "take it," as did their paralyzed president.

Like FDR, they all excelled at marshaling talent. For instance, many of the hotshot young lawyers dispersed through the Administration had risen with the help of Ickes and Perkins. Ickes had known Felix Frankfurter from the American Civil Liberties Union, and that Harvard professor, whom FDR would place on the Supreme Court in 1939, became a fixture of the New Deal. Ickes used him in two ways: as an occasional intermediary with FDR, and as a means to recruit sterling-credentialed young men from the law school.

As a result, Ickes became a patron of the most formidable legal duo ever to serve in American government—the so-called free-floating "law firm" of Corcoran & Cohen, which thrived within the Administration. Never again have midlevel lawyers like these appeared on the cover of *Time*, nor gained similar attention. The magazine's September 12, 1938, issue featured a color photo of puckish Thomas Corcoran, thirty-eight, standing over the shoulder of his devoted friend, the scholarly Benjamin Cohen, forty-four, of Muncie, Indiana, writing away at his desk.

Corcoran, lace-curtain Irish from Pawtucket, Rhode Island, and a holdover from the Hoover Administration, encountered Ickes in summer 1933. Like other stars from Harvard Law, Corcoran had enjoyed a short course in the higher culture while clerking for Oliver Wendell Holmes, Jr. Thereafter he liked to describe himself as a "legal entrepreneur" within the bureaucracy, who held no specific job title. He made his way into ev-

Hopkins, for his part, was fixated on putting millions of people to work, which entailed constantly dispensing money, and he was assisted in this by stellar deputies such as Aubrey Williams. He fostered the myth that he "ran his own show without any damned lawyers to complicate things."[5] Hopkins relied more on the clout of informal advisers from outside government. They included Averell Harriman, of course, and also Edward Stettinius, the thirty-eight-year-old chairman of U.S. Steel, another son of a very rich man. Their viewpoints on business were as valuable to Hopkins as the doors they opened into society. Newsmen dubbed such tycoons Hopkins's "tame millionaires."[6] No one could leverage this sort of influence better than he.

Hopkins had nearly died from his cancer operation in December 1937, although doctors claimed it a success. In fact, he would be even frailer for what remained of his life. Not that he was a Victorian deathbed figure—except when the role proved useful.

He was discharged from the Mayo Clinic's hospital in mid-January 1938, to recuperate at the New Orleans home of his recently made friend John Hertz, the Chicago entrepreneur who founded the Yellow Cab Company and Hertz-U-Drive (i.e., Hertz rental car). A month later he continued his recovery at the Ocean Drive home of another new friend, Joseph P. Kennedy, in Palm Beach.

Kennedy was one of a handful of financiers who had backed "Roosevelt Before Chicago" and thereafter stuck with him. Since 1933, he had run two alphabet agencies and also done such favors as apprenticing FDR's lanky, bespectacled, balding son Jimmy to the underside of the liquor trade. Actually, Kennedy was living mostly in New York that winter, preparing to bring his large family to England, where Roosevelt had just appointed him ambassador to the Court of St. James's.

"Kennedy is a very dangerous man," FDR told Treasury Secretary Morgenthau as the year began. "Very dangerous." He repeated it three times, asserting that he found Kennedy "too dangerous to have around here." England would just be a six-month stint, he added, which Kennedy didn't realize, yet that should be enough to clear up his "obligations" to the fella.[7]

Hopkins returned to action in late March, meeting Roosevelt in Warm Springs for four days and then following this up in the Oval Office on

erything, as did Ickes. Corcoran had been the mutual friend who
had sent from the White House to sit with Ickes on the night i
when Anna Wilmarth was killed.

In turn, Ickes knew Cohen from Chicago, of which they were
law school alumni, although Cohen had gone on to receive anot
gree from Harvard before clerking for Justice Brandeis. In 1933
Mack urged Ickes to bring Cohen into the Administration, and he
counsel to Ickes's Public Works Administration, and later a counse
Interior Department.

Five years after the duo teamed up, *Time* described the princ
Corcoran & Cohen as architects of the New Deal who drafted legi
wrote speeches, placed other lawyers throughout government, a
bied the Hill. By 1938, their prime client was the president of the
States. As for Ickes, his rage didn't surface when in cahoots wi
Gold Dust Twins," as the press had taken to calling them (after a
product). They could be fun, especially Corcoran, the more outg
the two. FDR nicknamed him "Tommy the Cork" for his effer
singing, accordion playing, and brilliance at the piano. Tommy
lightful, so long as he was not ruining your career.

Perkins's legal firepower was also impressive, one exampl
Charles E. Wyzanski, Jr., who had turned twenty-seven in summe
when he became the Labor Department's solicitor. Wyzanski too w
vard Law and had clerked for the much-quoted Judge Learned Han
while Perkins grew hardened by her disappointments, she was forev
of Wyzanski, whom FDR would make a federal judge in 1941. Du
years in between, Wyzanski had drafted the Public Works bill that e
ered Ickes. He also defended the Social Security Act before the S
Court, escaped briefly to private practice, and rode shotgun thro
for Perkins in her desperate attempts to save refugees from Nazisr

Neither Wallace nor Hopkins had lawyered up to this exten
doubted whether lawyers added much beyond the mechanics of
bling alphabet agencies such as the Securities and Exchange Commi
as Corcoran & Cohen had done in 1933 and 1934. Instead, they
hands-on operators, and Wallace already knew the Agriculture I
ment's best civil service executives from his father's time. He mad
men chiefs of his sprawling organization's score of bureaus, then
off to let them function almost independently.

April 7. Hopkins appeared with his ferocity undimmed, in his usual blue flannel suit and tan shoes.

"I believe the days of letting people live in misery, of being hungry, of moralizing about rugged individualism, are over in America," he declared. So much remained to be accomplished. After all, urged Hopkins, the levels of spending that the country needed "were nothing as compared to the government's land grants to railroads in the last century and tariffs and franchises to industry."[8] FDR kept hearing such fervor from him at a juncture when a depression within the Depression was pulling the country back under.

In 1938, Roosevelt's Cabinet had the same members as in March 1933, except for the deaths of Woodin and Dern. It "was a very human institution," recalled one of its members.[9] Throughout, FDR was set on showing himself to be the dominant figure—even debating the definition of "nematology," the scientific study of nematode worms, with Wallace, who knew the subject cold. Otherwise, he might use the Cabinet to test informed, upper-middle-class opinion. In the Q&A, Roosevelt heard what these ten decent people from around the country thought about events, ranging from sit-down strikes to the prospects of war in the Pacific.

Outside the Cabinet Room, he wanted them at his fingertips. They were the first officials to have direct phone lines from their homes to the White House (save for Ickes, a dedicated line to Olney being too expensive). You merely had to pick up the receiver in your study and the call went straight to the switchboard run by Louise "Hackey" Hachmeister and her staff of five. The president made a point of being easy to reach for Cabinet officers, aides, and legislators.

Once Hopkins returned to work, he began to attend meetings of the formal Cabinet, at the president's invitation, of course. As head of the WPA, he was not an actual member, nor did he run one of the government's ten established departments. Neither law nor custom entitled him, and the true Cabinet officers were puzzled. Hopkins was at least embarrassed, though soon fitted in.

Now Ickes had someone to commiserate with about Perkins's "buzz, buzz, buzzing." Outside the Cabinet Room, FDR laughingly told them not to refer to the secretary of labor even among themselves as "Mother

Perkins," or "Franny."[10] Wallace, unlike his two friends, never understood this banter.

Hopkins grew closer to FDR month by month, as people observed. He "had a feeling of a mistress toward President Roosevelt," recalled Frankfurter, himself labeled a White House "courtier" and worse by eminent students of this epoch.[11] Hopkins usually had no well-defined role as he moved into the position of "adviser No.1," while soothing FDR with the clever lightheartedness that included the low, salacious humor they both enjoyed. He also had an almost "feminine sensitivity" to Roosevelt's moods, recalled his friend Robert Sherwood, whom he recruited into the White House.[12] Hopkins bonded with the president's other closest admirer, Missy LeHand, and all in all appealed to FDR in ways that the other three found inexplicable.

William Bullitt, the elegant forty-seven-year-old foreign correspondent, novelist, and Philadelphia millionaire, explained why. FDR had known Bullitt since 1918 and initially appointed him ambassador to the newly recognized Soviet Union, and then to France in 1936. While in Washington, Bullitt shared his perspective with Ickes. "The President had to have someone near to him who was dependent upon him and who was pale and sick and gaunt." Bullitt added that Hopkins had even come to resemble the late "gremlin" Louis Howe, equally "cadaverous and bent and thin."[13]

In New York, that city super-planner Robert Moses held a similar opinion. Howe had been "exercising immense power from the sickroom and the shadows," emphasized Moses.[14] Now Hopkins was succeeding to the role of tortured genius. And there was more to the comparison. The financial affairs of both Howe and Hopkins were a mess, which in both cases FDR found comical.

No one, of course, could have pictured Louis Howe as president— whereas Roosevelt is often said to have pushed Hopkins to succeed him, though Perkins didn't believe a word of it. Already in spring 1937 FDR had poked Morgenthau, while cruising down the Potomac, by mentioning the possibility. "Now I have somebody who has a good voice on the radio, is popular with the people and thinks the way I do," said the president to an official far more senior than Hopkins, who, as a Jew, would never be considered.[15]

Still, Hopkins's popularity with "the people" is questionable, and he wasn't admired on the Hill. Moreover, FDR did not realize until 1938 that Hopkins's New York divorce, nearly a decade earlier, had exposed him as a confessed adulterer. "The people" might disapprove. On the other hand, FDR concluded, Hopkins was recently widowed, with a small child. Sympathy might prevail. As for Hopkins, if there was a way up, he was going to take it on whatever terms.

No one ever called Hopkins aloof—a description usually applied to Wallace, whose interest in the presidency was also clear. FDR heard from Missy LeHand and Grace Tully that the secretary of agriculture cold-shouldered them when visiting the Oval Office. Still, Wallace was not being unkind. He was just unaware. More troublingly, Wallace had held back during FDR's fight over the Supreme Court, and did not even register as a Democrat until 1936.

FDR's deft handling of each of these four had become second nature. A lesser president would never have tolerated Ickes's years of impudence. Instead, FDR could turn Ickes's anger into play, often addressing him as a boy. After Roosevelt scolded him, he would tell him he had been spanked. Or he forgivingly would ask Ickes to come along on a trip to hold the presidential hand. And there was FDR's physical touching of this formerly abused child, as when telling Ickes that he could not take sides between him and Wallace because he loved them both.

Alternatively, Roosevelt addressed him as a spouse, responding, in handwriting, to one furious letter of resignation: "We—you & I, were married 'for better, for worse,' and it's too late to get a divorce & too late for you to get out of the home—anyway, I need you! Nuff said."[16] Who could desert "Papa," as the president called himself to his official family, after receiving that?

Several factors made Ickes un-dismissible. For one, he tended to contradict FDR on the right issues, as the president himself realized. In 1938, those included trading with Nazi Germany, Jewish immigration, and civil rights. And it was hard to blame Ickes for his fierce impatience over how best to manage conservation. Stewardship of the land and opposition to injustice were the Reverend Peabody's doctrines at Groton, no matter how disrespectfully conveyed by Ickes, former class president of Englewood High.

Amid these dramas, FDR genuinely brought fun into his official family, and everyone had gotten the irony in June 1937 when he invited several Cabinet officers to join his real family at the Delaware wedding of Franklin D. Roosevelt, Jr., his third son, to twenty-one-year-old Ethel du Pont. The bride's father was a director of E.I. du Pont de Nemours and Company, the great family chemical firm, and had attended the infamous 1936 dinner hosted by the Liberty League, which had by now nearly evaporated. For the moment, this happy union bridged the political and economic chasm, and the party at Owl's Nest, the well-guarded Tudor Revival family estate, seemed to consume a substantial slice of the Du Pont fortune.

Never would Hopkins or Perkins have missed this spectacle. The Wallaces also came; Ickes stayed away. Unlike FDR, he took to heart the talks they had held about the reactionary "Sixty Families" who supposedly ran America. And, not least, FDR had told him that the new in-laws were dodging taxes.

In fact, this marriage would be among the more tragic of the nineteen entered into by the five Roosevelt children.

Henry and Mrs. Morgenthau had driven up to northern Delaware, as shown by a photo of their car stopped at the Du Ponts' gatehouse. Not that he made time for Perkins, even at such a festive gathering, which is how he behaved in Cabinet meetings too. "Morgenthau never paid any attention to anybody," she recalled. During the eleven years they sat together, she rarely saw a gleam of recognition.

Vice President Garner just found Morgenthau "servile." Hopkins put him to use for his own needs, as would Ickes, who judged Morgenthau to be "somewhat stupid."[17] In fact, Morgenthau was a simple, kindly soul whose truculence came out only when forced to see that he was in a job vastly over his head.

"He was lightly regarded by most of his colleagues in the administration," summarizes historian Alan Brinkley, "who watched his consistently inept performance in Cabinet meetings and other public forums."[18]

FDR—who could talk steadily for an hour—enjoyed gossiping unreservedly with Morgenthau, although the president might "go down his throat" in a sudden fury, as he rarely did with others. Mostly, their Monday lunches dealt with people. "Do you think that Jesse Jones is old enough now that we can trust him?" the president had asked in 1937.[19] Besides Morgenthau, Jones was one of the few others to serve at the top through most of the Administration. His power as head of that giant funding mechanism, the Reconstruction Finance Corporation, was nearly as vast as it was autonomous. Among the trappings of his private success, he owned the *Houston Chronicle*. All this strength and independence worried FDR. However, Jesse, as everyone called him, could be tapped discreetly for cash when needed.

"Jesse," said Perkins, was "a man of extraordinary ability—astute and quick." She added that "he knew how to make two dollars grow where one had grown before." And Roosevelt would mock him on that point, with a smile, saying for instance, before a dozen people, "Jesse always wants to make a profit. He can't bear it if there isn't a profit even when it isn't his money." Jesse would utter a dutiful hollow laugh.[20]

He wasn't part of Roosevelt's poker coterie, who preferred small, gentlemanly stakes. He played in games so stiff as to run to five hundred or a thousand dollars an evening, while the U.S. median family income was barely $1,200, if that. Among those across the table was Hopkins: how he covered his losses was anyone's guess.

Roosevelt's love of gossiping with Morgenthau even extended to the Reverend Peabody's family. One episode reveals how deep FDR's bitterness went behind the charming exterior. In this case, Morgenthau wanted to hire Robert Minturn Sedgwick, thirty-seven, as his special assistant. FDR knew Sedgwick, a son-in-law of Peabody who had taught for a year at Groton and had hoped one day to step into the headmaster's shoes.

During one of the usual Monday lunches, Morgenthau chirpily described Sedgwick's record as "excellent," and it was familiar to Roosevelt: a champion boxer at Harvard, leaving to be an Army officer on the Western Front, then back as star right tackle of the 1920 team. Sedgwick was also financially astute. He worked at the Boston firm of Scudder, Stevens & Clark, which pioneered the investment counsel industry. But this résumé of successes had almost been compiled to stoke FDR's resentments, and he offered various reasons against hiring the son-in-law. The only (unmentioned) explanation that made any sense to Morgenthau was that Sedgwick's uncle, who edited Boston's *Atlantic Monthly,* had criticized Jimmy Roosevelt's shady business practices in that city.

Roosevelt's bitterness did not extend to such categories as Jews or Italians—and this at a time when such upper-class prejudices were common. It was more against personal types, especially a broad-gauged high achiever of his own class, such as Sedgwick. A similar object of his malice was Winthrop Aldrich: very rich, academically impressive, a renowned sportsman, supremely successful in business, and a member of those eighteen exclusive clubs to boot.

At this juncture, Aldrich was also a formidably influential political figure as he took issue with Federal Reserve chairman Marriner Eccles. For a nation to go deeper into debt in order to grow, Aldrich insisted before Congress and in dozens of business conclaves, did not compute. He also warned of inflation, as would Republicans a lifetime later who similarly opposed greater spending for social programs. The Administration needed to attain the "confidence" of business, averred this elegant front for the House of Rockefeller, and, well, *he* did not feel that confidence.[21]

For a century Americans had enjoyed paternal ties with China—via Protestant missions, the outreach of universities including Yale and Harvard, and such great foundations as Rockefeller and Carnegie. Grandfather Delano's clipper ships had plied a flourishing trade. Come December 1937, Japan's sinking of the *Panay* had made what people called an "Asiatic war" appear imminent. Besides, Americans were disgusted that month to learn of the savagery unleashed by the Japanese Imperial Army on Nanjing. News of rapes, mutilations, and some three hundred thousand dead were so terrible in their details that Roosevelt would not read them in Cabinet out of respect for Miss Perkins.

The fulcrum of Western power in mainland East Asia was the British crown colony of Singapore, which harbored the world's largest naval base. In Washington, FDR speculated around the Cabinet table as to what various ways the U.S. and Royal Navies might cooperate to fence off Japan, though nothing came of this. Meanwhile, the Nationalist government of General Chiang Kai-shek was in retreat from its Nanjing capital. Ickes had just read the immensely influential new book, *Red Star Over China,* in which journalist Edgar Snow recounted the months he had spent in the barren reaches of Shaanxi Province with Mao Zedong's apparently indestructible Red Army. Ickes, who shared books with FDR, handed this one to him with a certain emphasis.

In addition to the Japanese invasion, exposed in shocking newsreels, China was enduring civil war. Mao's forces had proved as effective against Japan as in fighting Chiang. The president told Ickes he had gotten similar information to Snow's in a letter from a captain of U.S. Marines embedded with the newly created Eighth Route Army, a coalition of Communist and Nationalist troops.[22] Yes, surely more had to be learned about China as a warrior nation. And far more had to be learned about Nazi Germany, which was revealing the extent of its rearmament.

That January of 1938, Ickes addressed, for the third consecutive year, the annual meeting of what had been renamed the United Jewish Appeal. This time the banquet was nearby, at the Mayflower Hotel. Wallace had recently appeared before the National Conference for Palestine, and New York's Rabbi Stephen Wise, a prominent Zionist, was trying to cultivate FDR by lauding his "deep understanding of Israel's needs."[23] Like Ickes and Wallace, however, FDR knew little of British-run Mandatory Palestine, starting with who was already living there.

Whatever the topic, Ickes by then was in demand when people wanted to hear about foreign affairs. The BBC had asked Roosevelt to open a series of twelve speeches on the subject, to be radioed throughout the British Empire. It was presumptuous to expect the president of the United States to undertake anything like this, and so the task was passed on to Ickes. He readily agreed to deliver an address on February 22, 1938, at the CBS studio in Washington, which would be carried by telephone to New York and then by shortwave to London, whence the BBC would relay his words to its stations around the globe.

This would be the first time that a Cabinet officer had spoken to Europe over the air. Two days before Ickes's speech, Hitler staged a three-hour harangue in the Reichstag in which he threatened Austria's independence and blamed the Jews for the war in Spain.

The title of Ickes's speech, which he wrote with Benjamin Cohen, posed a question: "Democracy or What?" To be sure, the State Department had to see a draft. Policy did need to be coordinated. Ickes's pages were returned filleted with red ink. Didn't Ickes know he was addressing the world, not pitching to Chicago aldermen? In a fury, he once more confronted FDR, who tweaked some lines and gave him a Depression-weary "just go ahead with what you wrote." Ickes was amazed, and equally so that the BBC would permit his criticism of Prime Minister Neville Chamberlain's irresolute government.

One way or another, the speech was front-page news, and the by now unfriendly Hearst papers—their mastheads emblazoned with "AMERICA

FIRST"—accused Ickes of Communism. He had not attacked Hitler or Nazism directly, but Hearst's sympathies nonetheless lay with Germany. Yet for the moment, Ickes was praised in Cissy Patterson's *Washington Herald*. The ghastly answer to his question, ". . . or What?" was becoming clearer by the day.

Despite mounting worries over Nazism, the helium contract awaited by Luftwaffe Supreme Commander Göring moved forward. He had agreed to allow U.S. inspectors to verify compliance: the gas would be put to no military use. President Roosevelt and his interior secretary signed the deal on Friday, March 10. Two days later, the Wehrmacht rolled into Austria—having a Jewish population of about 192,000—to form a "Greater Germany" that, together, also included 30,000–35,000 Roma.

At the next Friday's Cabinet meeting, FDR conducted his usual round robin among the official family, until he came to Ickes. The interior secretary explained he was compelled to reconsider what he and the president had signed a week earlier: Germany's aggression shed new light. The chill was palpable.

According to Ickes, Roosevelt and Hull said the Administration had a moral obligation to honor a contract. When Hull steepled his long slender fingers and began to speak of duplicity, FDR moved quickly to avert an eruption. The matter could wait. He would just tell the press that international troubles had caused a delay. The president was buying time, to leave the following Tuesday for ten days in Warm Springs. The interval let Ickes share his concerns with Judge Mack and other friends.

On April 2, Ickes addressed a dinner in Chicago to honor the *Daily Jewish Courier*, without mentioning this growing quarrel. CBS carried his speech over the system's 110 affiliates. FDR had asked him to "make Cordell happy" by not being explicit about "Nazis" and "Hitler." Instead, Ickes excoriated "the political monster that hunts by day and prowls by night," an adequately oblique description of the Reich and its Führer.[24]

Off and on that month, he and FDR discussed the problem of helium, while Ickes explained why sales to Germany now violated U.S. law. Anyway, he argued, the president would get credit for canceling the deal. That was unclear.

Lobbyists from American Zeppelin Transport were petitioning the White House, and the president had to weigh German-American opinion in such states as Wisconsin, where 40 percent of citizens claimed

German ancestry. It was a small matter to question Hermann Göring's "word of honor." However, to challenge "the good faith of the German government," as Berlin alleged, was luring the Administration onto sensitive diplomatic terrain.[25]

The impasse over helium continued, amid a multitude of other issues. One favorite technique of FDR's, when faced by a stalemate, was to get everyone around the table to seek a compromise, which is just what he did on the morning of May 11 in the Oval Office. He wanted the sale to proceed, as did Secretary Hull, who was not invited. Instead, FDR included Chief of Naval Operations Leahy and Army Chief of Staff Malin Craig.

The president spoke for all save Ickes: given that there was no real military value to helium, why not sell to Germany? Ickes disagreed and, by law, the sale could not be closed without the interior secretary's approval. If there was no military significance, Ickes inquired archly, why was Admiral Leahy including dirigibles and helium in his budget, and planning to train naval officers on zeppelins in Germany?

The president countered, according to Ickes's diary, that the helium wouldn't be shipped without "a guarantee from Hitler that it would not be used for military purposes."

"Who would take Hitler's word?" inquired Ickes.

FDR was by now losing patience. He therefore had invited a fourth man to the meeting, Solicitor General Robert Jackson (attorney general in 1940, and a justice of the Supreme Court in '41). Already, Jackson regarded Ickes as "the center of a great deal of difficulty."[26]

"Well, Mr. President," said Jackson, "I don't see that you can do anything about helium unless you do something about your Secretary of the Interior first."

The president's only recourse, he advised, would be to fire and replace Ickes. At which moment, Roosevelt ended the meeting, and the White House issued a press release, which basically said "the President is powerless to make any decision."[27]

Two days later, on May 13, the battle was rejoined in the Cabinet. Ickes wouldn't budge. He had rallied Morgenthau and Perkins, though neither opened their mouths. Finally, Hull gave up, grumbling that further discussion was pointless. FDR acted in his most natural character. Throwing back his head, he laughed heartily, and declared the situation absurd.

Later, he told newsmen he'd reconsider the helium problem sometime in the future. That said, Germany was not finished. The president heard from his ambassador in Berlin that Göring would retaliate against U.S. efforts on behalf of Jews and other "requests for favors from the German Government."[28]

As for Ickes, he was getting ready to slip off to Ireland on the eighteenth and had to finalize the details of obtaining a false passport to get him through the press mobs that besieged every outgoing and incoming liner. Two weeks earlier he had told the president he was to be married.

Perkins, meanwhile, had been facing the growth and muscle flexing of the labor unions. Unionization had surged after summer 1935 as activists—building upon the terrors of unemployment—began to organize such mass-production industries as steel, textiles, mining, and automobiles. Labor was becoming the equal in weight of corporations and now of government.

She was also doing much else for FDR. He asked regularly for her perceptions of men whom he was supposed to trust. Such important figures tended to open up to Perkins, leaving her forever startled by how businessmen, in particular, confessed "the sins, misdemeanors, and wrong things they had done in their lives." She kept confidences, except those that she disclosed to FDR.

As for her seat in the Cabinet, Perkins could be ambivalent. She didn't believe that Roosevelt was remaking the world, and she regularly questioned his "brilliant ideas," such as enlarging the Supreme Court. In her opinion, "even the average Sunday-school superintendent had a better conception of organizing and executing a program" than he.[29] Perkins was herself a superb administrator, though her verdict does, perhaps, bite too sharply. Mostly, Roosevelt was an enthusiast, and Perkins believed that the more frequently men get excited about something, the more certain they are to make fools of themselves.

Unlike FDR, who she claimed knew little about unions, she recognized the labor leaders as smart and tough, and advised him that John L. Lewis, president of the United Mine Workers, was "quick as a cat." She equally found Lewis pigheaded and besotted by his own genius, except still a man who would never make a deal to his personal advantage.[30] Ickes, who would get to know Lewis all too well during the war, conceded that "his strength is almost overpowering." He described Lewis, at age fifty-seven, with blazing blue eyes and flowing brown hair, as a "great, huge bull of a man who gives the impression that nothing can stop him short of his objective."[31]

Lewis had also assembled the Congress of Industrial Organizations, an aggressive federation of unions organizing itself across entire industries, such as rubber manufacturing, rather than around a trade or craft, as in the past. Owing largely to him, strikes were multiplying by 1936. Industrial relations grew even worse two years later, when the CIO tore away from the long-established American Federation of Labor. Yet both factions claimed that employers were ignoring their right to bargain collectively.

In 1934, Perkins had helped avert disaster during the West Coast waterfront strike, when Hull and the attorney general had intended to call out the army. Come 1936, she faced something alarmingly novel. The recently formed United Rubber Workers, part of Lewis's CIO, stopped production in Akron, Ohio, tire plants—and told its brotherhood to remain in their workplaces around the clock, rather than just to man picket lines.

"Roosevelt was as much surprised and bewildered by the new technique as anyone else," wrote Perkins in her memoir about this ominous phenomenon. Privately, in her oral history, she would elaborate on how he also "had one of his bright ideas that used to come to him at times": he wanted personally to sort out labor grievances—a step she firmly discouraged.[32]

Strikes then rolled across the steel industry. These upheavals involved abrasions of ethnicity as well as of class because the workforce included the kind of men whom Perkins matter-of-factly called "bohunks" (i.e., immigrants from Bohemia, Hungary, and elsewhere in eastern Europe, and the origin of "honky"). Now the Smiths and Jablowskys alike were demanding that employers recognize the Steel Workers' Organizing Committee, another branch of the CIO—and they did so against a backdrop of violence that included ten workers shot dead by police outside a large Republic Steel plant in South Chicago. As for equivalence, no corporate directors were being killed, and Ickes labeled the massacre domestic fascism.

Perkins summoned the head of the industry's biggest corporation, Edward Stettinius of U.S. Steel, to a secret midmorning tête-à-tête in her

New York City club, the Cosmopolitan, on Park Avenue. They set about crafting the formula for a historic collective bargaining agreement, committing to a standard pay scale and an eight-hour day.

Before running U.S. Steel, Stettinius had been an assistant to Alfred P. Sloan, chairman of General Motors, rising to be vice president of GM, the largest industrial enterprise in the world. (Stettinius's father, a Morgan partner, had been a GM director.) What *Time* called the "Automobile War of 1937" escalated when two thousand workers occupied a GM plant in Flint, Michigan.

However, prosperous readers of the *Detroit Free Press* in Grosse Pointe had honest reasons to be scared. The tactic of sit-down strikes had originated in Europe, to be brought home by activists like Walter Reuther, the thirty-year-old West Virginia redhead who built the United Automobile Workers. He spoke Russian fluently, having worked two years in the Gorky Automobile Factory. In fact Reuther was such a quiet, patriotic man that neither Henry Ford nor Republican Party minions could tar him a Communist.

The men whom Lewis and Reuther were mobilizing had an average age of twenty-eight. Detroit hired no one over forty, nor employed workers after forty-five. Walter Chrysler, Henry Ford, and Sloan had unwittingly created a labor force composed of men at their peak of energy and daring.

Sloan and his executives would not meet with the UAW, which puzzled Roosevelt. He anticipated the police "killing a lot of people" over a crime he believed no worse than trespassing, which is how he regarded a factory sit-down strike.[33] Here too, the outcome came to the edge of disaster. Throughout the GM strike, Perkins was juggling the phones with Michigan governor Frank Murphy. Murphy finally ordered fifteen hundred National Guardsmen in—except this time to protect workers from police and company goons.

As even Ickes acknowledged, Perkins briefed the Cabinet with "great flair" over an uninterrupted thirty minutes, except for a few questions from the president. Finally, she had gotten Sloan to consider negotiating with the UAW—even if, as Sloan wrote in his own memoir, "its agents forcibly held possession of our properties."[34] He'd engage in a Washington peace parley, Perkins told the president. And then Sloan called her at home, while she had friends for dinner, to say he had changed his mind.

She replied he could burn in hell—a staple of Perkins lore—and then asked calmly, while her daughter and guests listened, "Are you a grown man, Mr. Sloan? Or are you a neurotic adolescent?"[35] He exploded and, revealing his long-suppressed Brooklyn accent, declared that he was worth $70 million and couldn't be talked to like that. She hung up, with a certain sympathy that this dandily turned-out industrialist was "a fellow creature in what I regarded as a humiliating and disgusting position." Nor did she share the details with Roosevelt. Had she done so, she knew, "he would have loved it in the wrong way." She expected that "he would have just thought it was killingly funny and felt more than ever that Alfred Sloan was a low comedy figure, which he thought anyhow."[36]

As often before, Perkins was on her own. "The president doesn't know anything about what I'm saying," she told newsmen. Except in this instance FDR backed her straight up. Sloan worked out of GM's New York headquarters on Broadway. When he offered to return to Washington if the president himself requested it, Roosevelt snapped, "A representative of the President did ask him to come down."[37] GM finally got to the bargaining table, turning Sloan's negotiations over to a face-saving vice president.

Other industries such as meatpacking and coal would be hit by work stoppages, and not even Perkins could face every heavyweight opponent by herself.

In secret, three unlikely men helped her to calm the nation's most dangerous strikes: Jim Farley, Jesse Jones, and Thomas Lamont of J.P. Morgan & Co. She called on them repeatedly to intervene, almost silently, when she felt cornered.

To receive a phone call from Thomas Lamont's office at 23 Wall Street would make any businessman jump to attention at his desk, only able to stutter at Mr. Lamont's polite inquiry about when, for example, production might be resumed at Consolidated Widget. Should the call be from Jesse, he would be thinking fast of how he could oblige this behemoth. If from Farley, this businessman would be grateful for the string-pulling Farley promised to deliver for his next contract if only he placated those hotheads who were occupying one or another of Consolidated Widget's factories.

In 1934, Perkins had first called upon Lamont to explain to the presidents of the American-Hawaiian Steamship Company and other shipping lines that it was truly wise to settle. As for Jesse, so many corporations were indebted to him that Perkins couldn't recall how often he assisted her. Certainly, he played decisive roles at Akron with Goodyear and Firestone, and later with Big Steel. At GM, Farley naturally did the politicking, while Lamont, Perkins reveals, "worked at it through the financing operations."[38]

Perkins could generally handle the labor leaders, and she was increasingly helped by Ickes. Hopkins added his voice, in May 1938 in Scranton, Pennsylvania, when speaking to union organizers. "Every time you turn around you step on a lobbyist in Washington," he asserted. So businessmen shouldn't object when government helped "people at the bottom."[39] Backed by her friends and allies, Perkins was enabling an anxious middle class to see Big Labor as another form of corporation—not a Communist conspiracy—that was helping millions of Americans to lift themselves up in an unquestionably capitalist order.

Altogether, the country began to benefit from the "union premium" that roughly continues today, albeit in a political economy that is more anti-labor than at any time since the Wagner Act passed. Still, for a lifetime, union workers have earned about 20 percent more than their nonunion fellows in similar jobs, with the greatest benefit over these decades having accrued to the least educated. Moreover, nonunion members have prospered as well when labor and management negotiated as equals. Perkins anticipated all this, and Thomas Lamont was inclined to agree.[40]

No member of the Cabinet was more committed to economic planning than Henry Wallace, and in peacetime, no one in U.S. history had been "granted remotely so much power to carry out that planning," wrote a Washington newsman.[41] The Agricultural Act of 1938 alone, signed by FDR in February, regulated what was still around 30 percent of the economy, and contained 128 clauses that essentially specified new powers for Wallace. In the Cabinet, however, he by now rarely spoke about agricultural issues, unless asked directly. Instead, he voiced intelligent insights on economics, domestic politics, and foreign affairs.

Still, as always, Wallace appeared odd and bashful. On the one hand, he was a solid midwestern scientist and entrepreneur. On the other, people might feel uneasy around him because, with his multiplex mind, Wallace could seem not to be in the same room. He was often oblivious to the simplest human amenities, even among friends.

Yet, for someone ridiculed as a mystic, he could master immense bodies of data, and he ran a study group in 1938 that included the best government statisticians, economists, and researchers, such as the Federal Reserve's E. A. Goldenweiser. Perkins took their efforts very seriously. They had all read Keynes's *General Theory* and were seeking a path to recovery. Wallace was also more laissez-faire than how he's still caricatured as a New Deal planner. Government, he argued, should leave as much as possible to private enterprise, to the extent private enterprise refrained from destroying itself.

In March 1938, the already tarnished Old Guard of Wall Street, as moneymen called the ruling elite of the New York Stock Exchange, was indeed self-destructing. "The end of the age of the gentleman" had come, sighed these eminences, once Richard Whitney, recently president of the exchange, delivered his world up to Franklin Roosevelt when exposed as an embezzler.[42]

The worst that Wallace or even Ickes could have imagined about the "economic royalists" proved miserably correct. More contemptibly still, much of the money Whitney had stolen had been drained from the pension fund for maids, stewards, and other employees of the New York Yacht Club. Not least, the House of Morgan had to testify carefully before the SEC, because Thomas Lamont had helped to keep Whitney afloat, albeit suspecting his securities were being unlawfully employed.

The name partner of Richard Whitney & Co. turned out to be a wretched investor. No one was better positioned than he to assess the value of a blue-chip stock, yet Whitney had sunk into ruin by squandering every solid dollar he could get on flimflam, such as a dubious Florida resort. He too became one of the "suckers," as Basil O'Connor, previously of Roosevelt & O'Connor, had generalized about the investing public.

Pressure from Washington compelled the Big Board to adopt long-obstructed reforms, unimaginable before the Depression. A young technocrat from St. Louis quickly became the NYSE president, eventually to be followed by the forty-year-old head of Trinity College, in Hartford, Connecticut. Whitney got five-to-ten for grand larceny, and on April 12, he was sent up the river.

While one of the Reverend Peabody's most distinguished graduates was doing time in Sing Sing, another was trying to pull the nation out of a major bust. Yet the White House ignored this heaven-sent scandal and even Ickes had to zip his lips. Roosevelt felt no bitterness toward a man who was down, and Peabody was watching.

Two days after Whitney entered prison, FDR reversed himself on austerity. At noon on April 14, he delivered a relief bill to Congress, requesting nearly $5 billion of outlays, lending, and credit expansion. He had no explicit Keynesian hope: the economic collapse of fall 1937 simply persisted, and the nation was again in crisis. The press summarized that night's fireside chat as a "War on Recession."[43] The CIO rallied immediately to announce that jobs would go on evaporating without huge payouts on public works.

Roosevelt had been inching toward renewed spending for several months. On February 1, he had received a letter from Keynes describing the recession as "partly due to 'an error of optimism'" (no need to mention FDR) and urging "large scale investment."[44] Even so, Roosevelt remained more of a Micawber than a high roller. What Keynes was saying about pump priming might have helped in 1933, when the well was dry, but what about now? Hadn't the real emergency passed?

No, it definitely had not. Ultimately, a formidable bloc coalesced, as an acute student of this episode relates: "Hopkins, Ickes, Perkins, and Wallace, aided by Marriner Eccles of the Federal Reserve, urged vigorous resumption of government spending."[45]

One advantage of accepting Keynes is that he provides an intellectual confidence for doing what seems counterintuitive. None in this lineup except Wallace and Eccles cared about multipliers or counter-cyclical theories—nor, of course, did the president. Regardless, something had to be tried.

Higher spending was required not only to relieve near-1933 levels of unemployment, but also to strengthen the navy. Sensibly, Wallace had told FDR during an Oval Office lunch in mid-January just to go ahead and build ships without any claim that this was to provide jobs. Roosevelt took off the wraps. Support existed on the Hill after the *Panay* incident, and naval construction was an inherently defensive step for America, then a super island-state. So on the twenty-eighth, he had asked Congress to dedicate a billion dollars to develop a "two-ocean Navy." God willing, it should be achievable by 1946 or '47.

On April 16, right after FDR had sent Congress a bill for a huge degree of relief spending, he had another, unusually long two-hour lunch with Wallace in which they reviewed the altered fiscal terrain. All was friendly, but the president knew that Wallace had no interest in joining him that night when he and Hopkins, along with three aides and Jimmy Roosevelt, would drive up to Ickes's estate for dinner, poker, and a bottle of 152-year-old Scotch.

Two weeks later, Hopkins and Ickes testified back-to-back before the Senate Appropriations Committee. They outlined big new WPA and Public Works programs, and also spoke of enlarging the Civilian Conservation Corps. Wallace followed, to make his own case for more cash to support wheat and cotton prices.

During May, Congress appropriated the largest peacetime naval outlay in history. A month later, it opened its purse even wider once Roosevelt had signed the multibillion-dollar Emergency Relief Appropriation Act of June 21.

Summer had fallen on Washington, and so he did the signing in shirtsleeves at Hyde Park. Then he rocked back in the swivel chair of his tiny office, next to Springwood's dining room, to field questions for a handful of reporters. No, he would not predict the date when the business upturn might start. Nor would he say if he agreed with what they called the "Hopkins school" of thought, which believed that this immense scale of government largesse might now be a permanent feature of American life.[46]

Anyway, all such predictions—whether by Roosevelt, Hopkins, the three other lieutenants, or informed critics in the press—were very soon to be passed by events.

TURNING POINTS

Reforms of Summer 1938 to a
New Congress, January 1939

ROOSEVELT, MINUS LUCKY CHAIN, VOTES AND GLUES EAR TO RADIO
The Washington Post, November 1938

Precious time was indeed being wasted, as Keynes had warned earlier in the year. People had experienced the ups and downs of previous business cycles, yet alarm was growing that perhaps downswings in the modern era would just be terrifyingly bigger.

Might "emergency" in fact be the normal state of affairs, newsmen wondered, when they heard Hopkins speak of the "classes of permanent unemployed"?[1] Relief programs on the scale of his WPA helped relieve hunger when the economy plunged in 1937. Even so, reports from insiders remained pessimistic. Wallace, and Eccles of the Federal Reserve—the two most original minds in the Administration—anticipated little if any prospect for recovery until 1941.

Time was also being squandered in FDR's quarrels with Congress. The showdown over court-packing had been the worst, and one tragedy of the court project was the price to be paid in trust. For instance, he had promised to appoint Senate Majority Leader Joe Robinson of Arkansas to be the first new justice on an expanded Supreme Court. He went so far as to invoke God when repeating this pledge in an argument with Hugh Johnson, who had become a syndicated columnist. Still, he had revealed to Morgenthau that he had no such intention. Legislators of both parties had caught on to this cheerful man's deceptions.

Winthrop Aldrich, addressing the U.S. Chamber of Commerce in May 1938, called for a "breathing spell" in New Deal reforms.[2] Capitol Hill paid attention, as did the mostly Republican members of the

Chamber, which has long identified itself as the country's largest lobbying organization. Opinion polling from Gallup and Henry Luce's *Fortune* magazine showed that a steady 40 percent or so of Americans were convinced that recovery was being delayed by Roosevelt's hostility to business. Lewis Douglas reappeared to emphasize these points at the Senate Office Building.

The former budget director, grown bored at American Cyanamid, was returning to the political stage. Among his first steps was to accept a lunch invitation on the Hill from Senators Carter Glass of Virginia, "Cotton Ed" Smith of South Carolina, and other Democratic reactionaries. Douglas's message was, for the most part, the same as in 1934: extravagant New Deal spending was worsening the Depression.

By 1938, however, Republicans and conservative Democrats alike were feeling hopeful. The president's legislative defeats, and his inability to raise the country even from the depression within the Depression, might force him to compromise with the likes of the Chamber and men such as Aldrich.

National security was at stake—although, in 1938, when Congresswoman O'Day so claimed, this term did not mean any armed global presence. Nothing like that existed, or was contemplated. Instead, the concept entailed the nation's well-being at home, which rested on citizens' stable and secure family lives. It was a quality that could be measured, unlike today's amorphous usage. In the later 1930s, O'Day assessed "security" as wages to get by on; good enough to save children from toiling in factories, mines, and fields.

To this end, there had come two progressive triumphs during the first week of summer 1938. First was the Emergency Relief Appropriation milestone. Four days thereafter came the second: Roosevelt signed the Fair Labor Standards Act, which established minimum wages and maximum hours for industrial workers. It changed the American workplace.

In 1938, everything came together for labor—expanding membership, plus winning the wages and hours legislation. On this issue, unlike her quest for the Social Security Act, Perkins had FDR's support—if only because he was cornered, having pledged during the 1936 campaign to fight starvation wages and grueling hours.

And they faced the same arguments heard today. Manufacturers feared a "possible wedge for socialization of industry," and warned that next to be introduced would be what in the 2020s is called a universal basic income (i.e., a monthly check of some amount to every American).[3] Moreover, as others cry today, Alfred P. Sloan insisted that a minimum wage would worsen unemployment. The logic that higher pay would bring larger employment, by generating spending, did not enter into the argument.

Southern politicians, for their part, argued that an initial 25-cent minimum (about $5.10 today) would destroy their people's competitiveness with the North. Furthermore, as had happened with Social Security, they expected the Administration to buckle on race. Ultimately, the Fair Labor Act covered only one worker in five. And now, in the 2020s, battles are again being fought over who should be brought under a federal minimum wage statute.

At least this legislation prohibited most hiring of children. Still, Perkins found herself condemned by an unholy alliance of the National Association of Manufacturers and the Roman Catholic Church. They denounced her for toppling the sacred autonomy of the family, because, they claimed, only parents should make decisions about their children.

Nevertheless, by summer 1938, the machinery was already in place to implement the vast changes FDR had just signed into law. And it was mostly in the hands of our four. However, he knew that the country's two most dire problems, as he listed them, were far from being solved: reducing unemployment and achieving a more equitable distribution of income. He did not raise the problem of economic growth.[4]

During these months, FDR could discern Wallace's ambitions for the presidency in 1940, and he had already stoked Hopkins's. One afternoon, alone with Ickes in the Oval Office, he listened for the umpteenth time while Ickes lambasted Wallace for his obstruction of a Conservation Department. "As a matter of fact," the president interrupted, "unless we have an economic recovery before 1940 no one can be elected."[5] By this, of course, he meant no Democrat—and the clock was ticking.

Roosevelt warmly received Ickes's news in early May that he would soon marry "the beautiful Jane," as FDR called her. Age should be of no concern, he advised the prospective groom. After all, his father was almost sixty when he married the much younger Sara Delano. (He had actually been fifty-two.) Jane was also the sort of tall, upper-crust horsewoman and tennis player whom Roosevelt admired. He agreed that the wedding must be secret, probably overseas.

As a Cabinet officer, Ickes was already famous. Still, for curmudgeonly Harold Ickes to marry Smith College's Jane Dahlman took him into the realm of celebrity, and the event was certain to cause a media frenzy. So Ickes would have to travel incognito. To this end, FDR asked Hull to join them for a half hour to discuss passports. Hull produced blank forms and the necessary visas, Ickes choosing to use the name of a deceased cousin.[6]

The wedding would take place in Ireland, where Jane's uncle, John Cudahy—a Democratic donor from a meatpacking fortune, not a career diplomat—was serving as U.S. minister, after a tour as ambassador to Poland. Jane sailed for England on the *Queen Mary* a month ahead, spent time in London, then stayed with her uncle in Dublin to plan the event, from which he tried hard to dissuade her.

On May 19, Ickes boarded the *Normandie* for Southampton. After five days, its arrival was delayed by fog. He barely caught the boat train to Dublin via Liverpool, then screeched into Adelaide Street Presbyterian Church on the twenty-fourth at 9 A.M. as the service began. Jane was waiting with the wedding license in her purse. Three guests from the legation served as witnesses, and Ickes described himself as "lawyer" in the marriage register. "I had no idea it was one of President Roosevelt's Cabinet," the astounded pastor later told the world press.[7]

The newlyweds made a fast getaway to Cork, after a cheery cablegram to FDR.

The next day they took an overnight cattle boat to Wales, under the name "Mr. and Mrs. Woods," hopping the morning train from Fishguard to London—where scores of newsmen and photographers were waiting for them at Waterloo Station. "How long had they known each other?" ("Fifteen years.") "Who knew about their wedding?" ("Only Mr. Roosevelt.") "What about selling helium to Germany, Mr. Secretary?" ("I'm not discussing it.")

Ickes announced that they would stay at the Grosvenor House, a premier hotel, for a few days before honeymooning in France. The fuming uncle had refused to attend the wedding. Once *The New York Times* caught up with events, it diligently reported that twenty-five-year-old Mrs. Ickes was sister to the widow of Ickes's stepson.

Ickes dismissed Ambassador Joseph Kennedy as a stock swindler unqualified for the post he had been holding since March. At these of all times, he believed, America should have sent one of its best. Nonetheless, Mr. Kennedy had to receive any Cabinet officer visiting London—this being Ickes's first time—and so, two days later, he invited the couple to dinner, a concert, and a nightclub, the latter boring Jane.

Kennedy's spectacle for the spring social season, later that week, was another story. Jane was dazzling in a new gown and Chinese coat. They met Prime Minister and Mrs. Chamberlain, the home secretary, Winston Churchill, Virginia-born Lady Astor, herself also a member of Parliament, and the ambassador's twenty-one-year-old son, Jack. Other eminent American visitors were Mr. and Mrs. John D. Rockefeller, Jr., of Standard Oil, with whom Ickes had become friends because of their donations to the national parks. He wrote that Churchill appeared "a dumpy-looking person," with a very alert expression.[8]

Chamberlain voiced his approval of Ickes's decision on helium, as, the following day, did the foreign secretary, Lord Halifax. Ickes and Jane also lunched in the House of Commons with the leader of the Labour opposition, Clement Attlee. Every political leader they met expected that Hitler's irredentist demands on Czechoslovakia would result in war—and insisted that America must rescind its latest Neutrality Act.

At week's end the couple flew to Paris on Imperial Airways, where Bill Bullitt was waiting at Le Bourget to drive them the thirty-five miles to his château in the ten-thousand-acre forest of Chantilly. The next day they settled into a small hotel on rue Saint-Honoré. Bullitt, whom Ickes liked, had become so flawlessly French that the Ministry of Foreign Affairs half-jokingly said he should be their ambassador to Washington. Bullitt too expected war over Czechoslovakia but had confidence in France, while suspecting that Britain might desert the continent's democracies.

Ickes and Jane attended another magnificent embassy dinner on June 8, which Bullitt gave for the president of France's senate. The country's principal ministers and military commanders appeared, as did, unfortunately, Jane's uncle. Ambassador Cudahy, also a friend of Bullitt's, had just visited Prague. Jane ignored him, yet he buttonholed Ickes. He wanted Ickes to convince Roosevelt that the Czechs would fight, and that they'd call on their ally, France.

Mr. and Mrs. Ickes sailed from Le Havre aboard the *Ile de France,* docking in New York on June 21. Newsmen, photographers, and columnists pounced once they left quarantine. Movietone cameras rolled. The press adored Jane. She was poised and witty in her responses. "I have thanked God more than once that I had not married a flapper or flibbertigibbet," wrote Ickes in his diary.[9] However, inspectors discovered he had lowballed his customs declaration. They allowed him to rewrite the document without being fined, though records were kept. As things had a way of doing, these passed into FDR's hands.

Meanwhile, up the Hudson that morning, the president was signing the Emergency Relief Act, which he promptly did after a ten o'clock meeting with Ambassador Kennedy, who had returned to attend the graduation of his eldest son, Joseph P. Kennedy, Jr., from Harvard.

The newlyweds headed straight to Maryland, where, two days later, Harry Hopkins drove up for dinner. Beaming congratulations, he said the obvious: Ickes had married far above his station. Hopkins also informed Ickes of developments in the Cabinet. Wallace, he reported, had been trying to turn the absent Ickes out of office over a spurious charge of having leaked Cabinet secrets earlier that year—and, added Hopkins, Wallace had rallied Hull to his side.

Ickes, however, sensed Roosevelt's hand behind the latest friction. "The president would bait Ickes and Ickes would give him back much worse," Perkins recalled. Ickes could even startle himself by how harshly he had come to "speak to a president of the United States."[10] That said, they knew each other's habits. Three days later, that Sunday, Ickes and Jane lunched with FDR, Missy LeHand, and Grace Tully in the president's study. Roosevelt got to kiss the bride. After hearing their impressions of the political climate overseas, FDR shared his suspicions of Joe Kennedy's disloyalty. Yet Ickes was startled to learn that he intended to retain Kennedy in London for "a couple of years."[11]

Among the dinner guests at the Paris embassy on June 8 had been Secretary Perkins, landed a day earlier from London after attending British ministerial meetings, with more to follow at the *ministère du travail*. Perkins had known Bill Bullitt for ages and understood France nearly as well.

At the embassy, Perkins had met Jane for the first time, and compared notes with Ickes on British politicians. After her consultations in Paris, she planned to take several weeks' holiday of the sort she enjoyed—wandering about doing research. In the Cabinet, Roosevelt had been raising ever more questions about the fate of Europe, "often to the detriment of his interest in domestic affairs," she observed—and, perhaps, she could ferret out the answers.[12]

Perkins was staying on the rue de Vaugiraud with her New York friend Anne Morgan, daughter of the original lord of finance, J. P. Morgan, and sister of J. P. Morgan, Jr. She and Anne had known each other since the teens, when Anne, a progressive, had volunteered as a tenement inspector. Since the war, Anne had mostly lived as a philanthropist in France—rehabilitating Picardy's war-devastated farms and villages, and earning the Legion of Honor, along with her life's partner, Dr. Anne Murray Dike.

Morgan invited Perkins to join her on Sunday at Blérancourt, a war-wrecked château seventy-five miles north of the capital, which she had partially restored and turned into the Franco-American Museum.

Perkins ended up addressing sixty people seated at lunch in Blérancourt's garden, shaded by chestnut trees. The museum's president was there, of course: Philippe Pétain, eighty-two, Marshal of France, hero of Verdun, and savior of his country. Perkins heard him acclaimed as one of the two most trusted men in France. They were able to talk at length, and Perkins admitted to being skeptical of France's political cohesion. She had heard angry outbursts in cafés over the still-blistering Stavisky financial scandal of four years earlier, as well as rage over a recent conscription law that extended military service to two full years. Pétain replied carefully, clearly expecting his words to pass from her lips—as a minister of state—to her president.

First, Pétain seized the opportunity to express his admiration for Roosevelt, which came from the heart. At that moment, he could regard himself as a lesser version of FDR, whom he saw as a strongman, beloved by America's common folk, and a savior of the Republic from its dissolute elites. Pétain was also charming, with welcoming blue eyes, and a passionate reader of French drama. Like FDR, he had a sense of theater, united with a disdain for much of his nation's leadership.

Next, he assured Miss Perkins that Britain was overstating the threat of Hitler, that the Maginot Line's network of concrete-and-steel defenses along the German frontier was impregnable, and France's military stronger than ever. "He tried to lay it on thick," she recalled, about the inherent fighting strength of French farm boys as matched against goose-stepping machine-like Germans.[13] But then Pétain was from a peasant family, and as a commander, his caution with soldiers' lives had made him worshiped by the *poilus* on the Western Front.

Perkins already knew the other man alleged to be the most trusted in France. This was General Aldebert de Chambrun, a descendant of Lafayette, who, by a controversial tradition, could lay claim to U.S. citizenship. She was already friends with his wife, the former Clara Longworth of Cincinnati, a noted Shakespeare scholar. Perkins had gotten the New York bar to allow their son René to practice law in the city. She took Chambrun very seriously, and like Pétain, he believed France invincible.

That summer, she traveled through many towns and villages, chatting with everyone from a cobbler in Orange, to recruits loafing outside their barracks in Annecy, to women washing clothes on the banks of the Garonne. She saw herself as a social scientist who asked such open-ended questions as "Wouldn't it be nice if you had a central water supply?" which had a way of eliciting opinions about government. She was startled by their hatred for the *gratin* in Paris, and by their certainty that France's army was hollow.

Of course, she visited other flossy friends, including the Duchesse de La Rochefoucauld and the Prince de Broglie, both of whom she knew through Anne Morgan. She gauged their opinions as well, although, in her oral history, she drops such a landslide of aristocratic names that she gets these grandees confused.

She even uncovered discrepancies in the country's use of steel—an industry she had come to know well. Understanding how U.S. mills tracked every ton they produced, she discovered, oddly enough, that France was not importing American steel to the extent allowed by trade quotas. What she had been hearing about the state of France's weaponry, and the scale of its fortifications, might therefore be untrue. France itself neither produced sufficient steel, nor imported enough from Britain, the other big producer.

Basically, Perkins concluded, "if anybody gave France a good push with a fist, she'd go all to pieces and fall."

Later she shared her discoveries with Ambassador Bullitt, who remarked, "That's perfectly ridiculous, Frances."[14] What he told her, he added, was exactly what he reported to FDR: *Of course* Frenchmen grumbled. At the same time, every expert recognized France to be at the zenith of its strength.

While sailing home, she compiled her findings for the president.

Roosevelt saw her for two hours in the Oval Office on the afternoon of August 15, in the company of a vice admiral whom he trusted, from the fleet's Scouting Force. FDR always picked up on everything. The question was how he acted on what he heard.

Roosevelt knew France like an old shoe, and from studying his atlases, he knew the country's geography down to its small river valleys. "No diplomats go there," he told her when she described exploring the Nouvelle-Aquitaine region of southwest France, which he also knew to be a bastion of the long-entrenched Radical-Socialist party.

As for the admiral, who had served in Geneva on an arms-control delegation and as an aide to FDR, he said nothing. Instead, the president explained that Bill Bullitt was telling him the exact opposite about the national fabric of France and the condition of its army. By five o'clock, Roosevelt asked Perkins to report everything to Secretary of State Hull.

"Do I dare?" she remembered asking.

"Go ahead," FDR replied, Cordell would be open-minded.

She called upon State several days later. Hull was, as always, polite and, as ever steepling his fingers, replied, "Our information from every quarter is entirely contrary to that, Miss Perkins, and the Department has many sources."[15] This was a moment she remembered because, two summers later, Hull had the grace to apologize for not having understood.

FDR once remarked that, when he heard experts on international affairs claim war to be imminent, he could rest easy; he worried when they sounded confident of peace. The U.S. diplomats of his youth, whom he had met in Europe, had mostly been accredited to monarchies. Now, he felt, such men—with their court dress and rich wives—were presuming to educate him about the world. For instance, he grew impatient with prevailing views on Britain. "The trouble with England," he believed, "is that they're twenty-five years behind"—still unmatched as a true global power, while unaware that time was not on the side of aging empires.[16]

The president saw Hopkins and Wallace the day after Perkins. In fact, Wallace would be his weekend guest at Hyde Park and, by this point, was arguing that Germany intended "to take a bite at a time."[17] These bites, he believed, would soon include Latin America, which Wallace had previously deemed safe.

Tommy Corcoran passed to Ickes a bit more of FDR's thinking on Germany—or at least the president's conclusions about voters' opinions of Germany: he was going to back off on the sale of helium. Should FDR proceed at this point, Corcoran explained, it would offend the Jewish vote come November. Ickes didn't say that the Jewish electorate had not been mobilized by chance. In any case, Berlin would now have to return to using hydrogen for its airships, including the *Graf Zeppelin II.*

By 1938, Americans recognized that both Japan and Germany were driven by philosophies of divine preeminence and racial supremacy. The Nazis had proclaimed "segregation of the races" since Hitler's first months as chancellor, when Nazi race law began to mirror legislation in the United States on white supremacy.[18] Ickes had compared fascism with "the Southern way of life" in his December 1937 address to the ACLU, and Roosevelt would imply something similar in a speech in Georgia in March.

Nonetheless, Ickes, as well as his three colleagues, had to deal warily with what Perkins called the South's "touchiness about its special privileges."[19]

Ickes lamented in his diary that it was pointless to bang his head against the wall of segregation. Even so, Southern politicians suspected his every move on behalf of Blacks was intended to mix the races. After all, nearly his first order of business in March 1933 had been to hire Romanian-born New Yorker and Harvard Law graduate Nathan Margold as the Interior Department's solicitor. At age thirty-three, Margold was already a lightning rod to segregationists. The year before, he had launched an NAACP legal campaign known as the Margold Plan to flood the Southern states with litigation to assert Black equality. Then, suddenly, this Margold was atop the pyramid in Washington.

To have appointed him was a jab at the South. Even so, segregation persisted on Ickes's doorstep. For instance, Mississippi senator Theodore "The Man" Bilbo—former governor and a paunchy, five-foot, two-inch Klansman—sat on the committee responsible for overseeing the segregated capital. Ickes might take NAACP executive director Walter White to lunch in one of Washington's better restaurants and itch to be challenged for violating Jim Crow. To his disappointment, this never came about, less from his official stature than the fact that White was so pale-skinned as to pass for Caucasian.

Perkins trod carefully indeed. In 1935, she had noticed a rope segregating employees in the new Labor Department building and promptly had it removed. But washrooms and other facilities remained separate, as they had been since 1913, when the Virginia-born President Wilson segregated the federal workforce, reassigning Blacks to menial roles.

Of course, she had known of segregation before being exposed to it in Atlanta in 1934. She had just "never heard there was anything wrong with segregation if it was decently done."[20] Such would have been the prevailing view in New York. In those days before television, the South was a strange, remote land. Then again, she had the gumption, early in the Administration, to promise Black executives of the Urban League that there would be no discrimination in the Civilian Conservation Corps. Moreover, she had dared to ask, "Are not colored people also consumers?"[21] Even so, she could only go so far.

Unlike Ickes, people scrutinized her as the first woman in a presidential Cabinet. Had she been truly outspoken on race, it would have appeared sentimental and unbecoming. She already had one enormous civil rights battle on her hands, which was to extend labor's right to organize. To do much more than integrate a department's cafeteria, she believed, wasn't about to accelerate change in the South.

As might be assumed, Hopkins moved more carefully still. To be sure, by 1938 his Works Progress Administration could boast of employing nearly a half million Blacks. On the other hand, by then he was installing himself as "adviser No. 1" in a White House containing three entrenched, long-trusted presidential aides from the South. Obtaining justice for Blacks was the least of their cares, and Hopkins was not going to make waves.

Nor would he have had much time. By this juncture, he was more than ever circulating in what columnist Arthur Krock observed were "very luxurious households on Long Island, in Washington and—yes, actually—the foxhunting country of Virginia."[22] And indeed, Krock could have added, households in newly magnificent Beverly Hills and Santa Barbara too.

For Wallace, it was important to achieve the Brotherhood of Man, despite his compromises with landowners for the sake of raising the price of cotton. Except no redress for sharecroppers and tenants was to be seen before 1937. Even then, the Administration's reformist planning barely touched the cotton regions.

Wallace might sit on the broad veranda of Tanglewood with "Cotton Ed" after a plantation breakfast, having the detachment to just gaze at the landscape. He understood that the South's denials of humanity were an evil that might well cost America its soul. No one in public life spoke more eloquently than Wallace about the nation's original sin and how this afflicted the entire country, not just the South, as when "a mob wrecks a Negro's home in Detroit [and] police run down citizens of Harlem."[23]

Yet it would be ten years before he released these passions, and in 1938, he still believed that time, long drawn-out time, would overcome racial tyranny. He also pictured himself as Roosevelt's successor, which he could only achieve as a Democrat. The contradictions ensured that "his struggle with himself was painful and tragic," recalled Rexford Tugwell, his former undersecretary.[24]

Even if Wallace had adopted such enlightened views in 1938, FDR would not have let him loose on the subject of race, as he did Ickes. Politically aware people still regarded Wallace as a faithful Republican. For Roosevelt to have permitted two *Republican* Cabinet officers to attack the South would have been incendiary. Republicans were hated for more reasons than "catering to the Negro," as Cotton Ed saw it.[25] New York banking, decades of tariffs working against the agricultural South, and the dark mythology of Reconstruction led the list. Overall, from FDR's point of view, Ickes was delivering just the right amount of official concern about race.

Anomalies swelled as government expanded. Ickes, for instance, had desegregated Interior: Each department also took its own approach. Equal rights were seen as low grade in the gentlemanly State, War, and Navy Departments. Integration would not be brought about at Commerce until 1948, when President Truman appointed a midwesterner who found existing arrangements abhorrent. Nor was desegregation instated at Treasury, despite Henry Morgenthau, a man without prejudice, mocking Wallace, behind his back, as "Cotton Henry" for the secretary of agriculture's appeasement of the South.[26]

Before FDR appointed him to the Cabinet, Henry Wallace had lost the family newsweekly, his startup had struggled, and an "emptiness at the core of his personality" made him remote. Yet suddenly he was a hero. So too was Harold Ickes, the tormented small-time lawyer who described himself as a "failure."

Frances Perkins hesitated to join FDR's Cabinet. An anguished personal life made her dread the inquiries of newsmen and politicians. She knew Harry Hopkins since he had arrived as a twenty-something social worker in New York's slums. She introduced him to Governor Roosevelt and then brought the sleeplessly ambitious Hopkins into New Deal Washington.

Master and commander. Yet FDR was as wounded as each of the lieutenants he chose. He stands beneath a battleship's sixteen-inch guns with wife Eleanor, daughter Anna, son Jimmy, and redoubtable "Mama," Sara Delano Roosevelt.

Roosevelt's original Cabinet, placed according to seniority: Wallace and Ickes back row left, with Perkins on the right. Secretary of State Hull sits on FDR's right, and Treasury Secretary Woodin to the president's left. All except our four would be gone from the heights of power by 1945.

Einstein and Henry Wallace receiving honorary degrees at Harvard's 1935 commencement. University president James Conant sits in the middle. *The New York Times* wrote of Wallace's "freakish" intellect. FDR preferred to call him a "philosopher."

Pictures and newsreels of "Madame Perkins" in factories and union halls riveted Americans. "It's time to treat ourselves to some civilization," she said of the New Deal.

Cabinet officers were deemed the president's "official family" and to be statesmen—with Hopkins soon regarded as the de facto "Secretary of Public Welfare." Each of our four could look the part, even the tweedy Wallace and disheveled Hopkins.

FDR with Ickes and Wallace. Roosevelt worked to divide them and wreck their friendship, though each recognized this. Below, Hopkins and Ickes, before Hopkins's health truly derailed. "We always got along well when we were together," Ickes reminisced, "even during the periods when we were at each other's throats."

Ickes had long wanted to expand the Supreme Court: it was a preserver of political-economic orthodoxy, with four of its nine justices being "medieval." Roosevelt might have succeeded in 1937, but he undercut himself.

Perkins was immersed in defense policy even before the war. Kept secret was her role in providing FDR with the keenest insights of anyone on Europe's crumbling balance of power.

Harold and Jane Ickes in May 1938, home from a European honeymoon, with political insights for FDR. The president adored "the beautiful Jane" and was amused by the Ickeses' forty-year age difference.

Ickes's decision that contralto Marian Anderson would sing at the Lincoln Memorial on Easter Sunday 1939—after she was spurned elsewhere in segregated Washington—could not be reversed. "Genius knows no color line," he avowed when introducing her.

A meeting of capacious minds. FDR chose Wallace as his running mate in 1940 because, he told Perkins, who had lobbied for Wallace, he liked "the way Henry thinks." *Used with permission of Department of Special Collections and Archives, The University of Iowa Libraries.*

By 1940, Hopkins sat in FDR's formal Cabinet but had few friends on Capitol Hill. His hearings a year earlier to be commerce secretary had been vicious. He told senators he could not recall having registered to vote as a socialist, yet, if he had, it was because of idealism.

Critics by 1941 derided the Administration's chaos—much of it induced by FDR—as "the Washington War." Here Perkins quarrels with FBI director J. Edgar Hoover, whether over fingerprinting or his spying on labor unions. Below, she confronts labor leader John L. Lewis of the CIO. Perkins proved indispensable to victory in war, as in peace.

Roosevelt and Hopkins. Harry had become FDR's "Number 1" defense adviser and expediter even before Pearl Harbor, December 1941. Hopkins lived in the White House, shared a doctor with FDR, and handled all.

Hopkins as FDR's eyes and ears, flying to London, 1941, to meet Prime Minister Churchill. Hopkins played go-between. FDR and Churchill were never friends, contrary to myth. Like Hopkins, FDR expected Churchill to be ousted after Germany's surrender.

Hopkins at war. Above, he inspects troops in North Africa, January 1943, with Major General George Patton (in the middle). In November, he flew to Tehran with FDR to meet Stalin—where an interpreter stands between them—having first encountered the *Vozhd* in Moscow in 1941. Stalin was a far more intelligent psychopath than Hitler. Neither Roosevelt nor Hopkins knew what they faced.

Ickes at war. He held sixteen posts, including energy czar. Victory was impossible without his six billion barrels of American oil. Below he's in Hollywood at a bond drive. Katharine Hepburn was a friend of Jane's, and Jane opened doors to a younger generation, including to another friend, Anna, FDR's daughter. Anna became a secret source of information within the White House.

Wallace may have done most to shape the world, through science. The startup he founded in 1926 to commercialize hybrid seed corn is today's colossus Pioneer, and the Wallace Global Fund carries on his ideals. But, like FDR and Hopkins, he was deceived by the Soviet Union. Below in 1944 he visits Kolyma, Siberia. Hearty NKVD guards disguised as "miners" have replaced Stalin's slave laborers at this "Auschwitz without gas chambers."

Used with permission of Department of Special Collections and Archives, The University of Iowa Libraries.

FDR's Cabinet in its final year, 1944. The titanic Jesse Jones sits to the left of Vice President Wallace; Treasury Secretary Morgenthau is on FDR's left. What Perkins called the "coffin-shaped" table had arrived in summer 1941. *Harry S. Truman Presidential Library*

Perkins at the top of her game. She was tireless and claimed never to be sick, nor in need of a nap. In peace and war, she saved the men around her from awful mistakes.

FDR, Harry Truman, and Wallace, who was VP until January 1945. FDR looks weary, and Truman anxious. Wallace had campaigned nobly for their election. He and FDR now spoke about the fun they'd have when living near each other in upstate New York once the fourth term ended in 1949.

Harry Hopkins at ease in the Mediterranean after flying to the Yalta conference with FDR, February 1945. Anna Roosevelt despised Hopkins, and talks instead to John Gilbert Winant, U.S. ambassador to Britain. "Gil" was Perkins's friend, and Perkins intended him to succeed her. Like much else, that hope ended once FDR fell to a stroke on April 12—to be listed as a casualty of war.

might have been thought to have a certain priority in national affairs. We are also expected to overlook the Southerners gathered around FDR who were ready to act, had he taken the initiative. It need not have been Yankees who took the lead.

Most Americans in 1937 and 1938, according to Gallup polls, wanted Congress to make lynching a federal crime, and this majority included white Americans in the South. In 1937 alone, legislators brought fifty-nine anti-lynching bills to the Hill. Of course, furious Southern politicians insisted that the North's urban violence killed more people than did vigilantism, and also that the North itself was responsible for lynching. After all, low prices for cotton drove unemployed Blacks into crime, and such crimes included "insults to white people," as documented in the *Congressional Record*.[29]

That hardened Texan, Vice President John Garner, disagreed, as he sat in the Cabinet Room beneath its portrait of Woodrow Wilson. "I am in favor of an anti-lynching law," he declared as 1937 began and, he emphasized, "some measure of justice should be accorded to the Negroes." Virginia's Claude Swanson recoiled while the rest of the Cabinet concurred, including Daniel Roper, who carried much weight in South Carolina.

Crucially, Garner restated his convictions at the end of January. In effect, he had always been the "Vice President in Charge of Congress," and no VP in memory exercised more influence on federal legislation. At this moment, the former Speaker of the House—known to be the shrewdest political strategist of his generation—was "vehement" that there must be such a law.[30]

Only Garner's political protégé Jesse Jones rivaled him as a more formidable opponent of lynching, and Jesse's huge funding agency, the Reconstruction Finance Corporation (RFC), held thousands of loans, notably including every Southern congressional district. Notwithstanding, there was no direction from the top.

No record exists of FDR's response, if any, to Garner, while Cummings said the Justice Department was pursuing something similar to the Lindbergh Law of 1932 that federalized kidnapping. Ickes knew that the correct approach was the Constitution's equal protection clause. Yet at this juncture, in late January 1937, FDR and Cummings were about to spring their court-packing surprise on the country.

Cordell Hull was absent when Garner made his first pronouncement,

Woodrow Wilson had segregated the whole federal workforce by fia
During his twelve years in office, FDR issued 3,728 executive order
including administrative regulations barring discrimination in the WPA–
and, once war arrived, in defense industries. Nonetheless, no such orde
returned government departments overall to life before Wilson. FDR
most consistent supporting votes remained those of the South, and th
South pervaded the New Deal.

It was trickier for FDR to maintain a distance from the anti-lynchin
bills that pressed upon Congress during 1937 and 1938. High-visibilit
atrocities kept raking the nation's conscience. The decade's first bill ha
been introduced in 1934 by Senator Wagner. Like those that followed, i
was intended to apply federal law to the sheriffs, mayors, and other loca
authorities who abetted lynching. In this version, federal courts coul
impose heavy fines, with the proceeds going to the victims' families.

Eleanor championed civil rights well beyond the anti-lynching bills
This was convenient for the president: when called upon, he had a way o
disavowing "the missus" while benefiting from the many hopeful people
who believed that he shared her convictions, which he did, to an extent,
having deplored lynching in a 1934 message to Congress.

Eleanor explained FDR's thinking to Walter White in March 1936.
"The president," she wrote, "feels that lynching is a question of the states,
rallying good citizens, and creating public opinion so that the localities
themselves will wipe it out." If Northerners attempted to suppress lynching, she continued, that would be "antagonistic," and the president had
actually told her that "it is unconstitutional apparently for the Federal
Government to step in to the lynching situation." She advised White "to
talk to the more prominent members of the Senate."[27]

Yet to publicly back an anti-lynching bill, as FDR famously told
White, would mean that Southern Democrats "will block every bill I ask
Congress to pass to keep America from collapsing."[28] This presumes that
Southern whites would ruin themselves rather than compromise. And he
may well have been right. We only need to recall how racists acted against
their own interests, in the 1960s, by shutting down an entire Virginia
school system, or draining municipal swimming pools, rather than obey
court orders.

Nonetheless, politicians' excuses invite us to think twice, and the rescue of 12 percent of the country's population from night-riding terror

and Tennessee ranked seventh among the nation's worst offenders. Still, Hull had spent decades working with Garner in Congress and was attuned to civilized opinion in Europe's democracies. Plus, Tennessee had a courageous governor who offered enormous rewards to convict lynchers and was popular among his fellow World War veterans. Rallying the secretary of state, with his unsurpassed respect in Congress, was likely.

Additionally, there was the campaign cash. South Carolina financier Bernard Baruch, then white-haired at sixty-eight and forever stereotyped as "elderly," was among FDR's few cheerleaders on Wall Street. Still, the president was suspicious of Baruch, though he accepted him as a practical idealist who by and large jumped at FDR's requests. He had long funded around fifteen Southern senators—so heavily that insiders called them the "Baruch string"—who had included Swanson when he represented Virginia.

Altogether, and state by state, FDR had at his disposal a daunting combination of Southerners to crush the region's prime instrument of terror and could have done so in tandem with such enlightened Southern organizations as Women for the Prevention of Lynching. Republicans were available to be mustered as needed; they had called for the equal opportunity of "colored" citizens in their 1936 platform. The president did not have to invite Republicans for tea: lynching by now revolted their wives and children, and they could not avoid hearing of it at home.

None of these Southerners regarded segregation as a problem, nor did most people in the North. Mobs inflicting medieval torture—as Luce's new, all-photographic *Life* magazine showed the nation two weeks after the Duck Hill, Mississippi, blowtorch atrocities of April 13—were something else.

Today, only the misguided insist that "opposition to the legislation was so strong that it never had a chance."[31] The problem was that Roosevelt always had other priorities. The tragedy of his attempt to expand the courts—doomed by his untruths and overreach—was the opportunity that it had lost for an anti-lynching bill. Still, a safe majority to pass the bill seemed to exist for much of 1937.

No one ever questioned Garner's word, but, finding ever less reason to trust Roosevelt's, he began to pull back and, ultimately, did not use his position as presiding officer of the Senate to invoke cloture against filibustering by the likes of Cotton Ed and Theodore Bilbo—with whom, as Garner's former constituents expected, he chose to side.

Moreover, FDR was thinking of the 1940 election. "I'll just bet this man goes on for a third term," Perkins had concluded after he won in 1936.[32] For that, Roosevelt would require the Southern bloc.

Yet Vice President Garner kept up his opposition to lynching, and was set on achieving some measure of justice after others had moved on. When again he raised the issue with FDR, during January 1940 in the Oval Office, he would provide the president a pathway through the Senate.

To be a national figure is not the same as being able to wield national power, although an overwhelming electoral victory can cloud a president's judgment on that point. Such triumphs as Roosevelt enjoyed in 1936 tend to carry the victors away, if equally we think of Lyndon Johnson and Richard Nixon. Two years later, when *The New York Times* wrote of "New Deal 'revenge' politics," Roosevelt was feeling little restraint and busily settling scores.[33]

Already in May 1937, it was "time to attack," he had instructed Morgenthau. "You have got more material than anybody else in Washington to lead this attack," he stressed. Such material, to be certain, reached into the Bureau of Internal Revenue.[34] Roosevelt intended to retaliate against rich businessmen and also against "reactionary" Democrats in Congress who had obstructed him over the Supreme Court and other New Deal measures.

First up for retribution was business. Roosevelt aimed to set examples. For several years, he had tried to do so by having his Justice Department prosecute former Treasury Secretary Andrew Mellon for tax fraud, to find nothing would stick. Then Mellon died, inconveniently, at age eighty-two in 1937. That year, the president told Morgenthau he wanted a high-profile U.S. Senate investigation of tax evaders. Possibly it should be led by up-and-coming Thomas Dewey, a thirty-five-year-old prosecutor in New York City, who was getting headlines as a crime buster.

Senate leaders replied they were overwhelmed already. FDR solved that problem, albeit without Dewey, by leaking information to incite public demand. "He's having a grand time doing it," Morgenthau informed Treasury's chief counsel.[35]

The president loved getting into personal details, and one characteristic of his vindictiveness was to prey upon the small fry. For instance, while breezing through case files with Morgenthau and Attorney General Cummings, he randomly pulled one out, pounded on his desk, and demanded, "Why don't you attack this fellow? Why don't you call him a son of a bitch?" As Roosevelt read the file out—concerning one Edward M. Smith, a Los Angeles manufacturer—he "worked himself into a fervor," Morgenthau told Treasury colleagues, and ordered Cummings to take the man to trial.[36]

Congress's new Joint Committee on Tax Evasion and Avoidance held hearings throughout 1937. It named sixty-seven prominent men, including Alfred P. Sloan, whose business deductions included his 246-foot yacht, *Rene,* and its crew of forty. Just six of the malefactors were Democrats.

Before long, the Administration's would-be purge of conservative Democratic legislators during summer 1938 got even more ink. Month after month, the ruling party was turning on itself, as was the Communist Party in newsreels of the Moscow show trials. Today, with somewhat less ruthlessness than was manifest in the Soviet Union, "to primary" an incumbent means to aggressively challenge the renomination of someone deemed insufficiently partisan. But in 1938, skeptical observers of what befell Roosevelt's opponents saw other than political principles at issue.

This dose of revenge had long been planned. Eighteen months earlier, FDR had confided to Morgenthau that he intended to use the primaries to bring down a dozen officeholders whom he adjudged turncoats. Come June 1938, he explained in a fireside chat that he would call upon his party to uphold progressive principles in the run-up to the midterm elections. Of course, as president, he added, there'd be no interference from the Oval Office with the renominations of long-term fellow Democrats.

Within days of his broadcast, there unfolded the coast-to-coast drama that reporters styled "the purge." Hopkins summarized his own motivations, and his boss's ostensible ones: "I don't want to vote in the same party primary, or for the same candidates, as any man whose fundamental political views are opposed to mine."[37]

It sounded noble, except that Susan Dunn, the leading scholar of this frantic episode, tells us how FDR burned with resentment—even against women's magazines that had opposed him on such legislation as the Fair Labor Standards Act. And "federal money rained down" on his preferred primary challengers.[38] Moreover, Hopkins and Tommy Corcoran ran what they called an "elimination committee" to dispatch enemies from California, Florida, Georgia, Iowa, Kentucky, Maryland, New York, and Oregon.

People chuckled uneasily that "purge" and "elimination" sounded like echoes from the cellars of the Lubyanka, headquarters of Soviet dictator Joseph Stalin's secret police. Jim Farley, still postmaster general as well as national committee chairman, wisely dismissed these efforts as awakening bitterness within the party and being "too silly for words."[39] Knowing that a president could not compel local apparatchiks to fall into line, as did Stalin, he warned FDR of a debacle.

The purge was never discussed in the Cabinet, nor could Perkins, taking her words from Moscow, envision any of its intended victims as "an enemy of the people."[40] She too knew the purge would fail. She believed it arose from FDR's humiliation over the court bill, and hoped, once in heaven, that he could find a way to explain his behavior to Saint Peter.

After they start, purges rarely limit themselves to big shots. As with Mr. Edward M. Smith of Los Angeles, the president also liked to uncover bit players, provided he could do so surreptitiously—his confidence buoyed by his knowing the dull details of so many things. Firing an obscure person from a barely identifiable job was no exception. On one hand, these preoccupations seem, from outside, wastes of time. On the other, their very arbitrariness is a reminder of a ruler's power and reach.

For instance, at the start of 1938, FDR instructed Morgenthau to drop the collector of customs in District No. 17, Statesboro, Georgia. Granted, Roosevelt told a protesting Morgenthau, the man was "honest and capable," and popular too. Then he said this political appointee was "not our kind," which could have meant anything, though it had assuredly nothing to do with lynching.[41]

There were similar examples, as with a customs collector in Florida, another state swept by the purge. In each case, the functionary's friends and patrons learned that a superior being was somewhere at work: *Your man is suddenly out and there is nothing you can do about it.*

Executing the purge was largely Hopkins's doing, backed by Corcoran, whom Perkins blamed—along with FDR—as the higher instigators. Little made sense. Hopkins had become so confusingly close to FDR by mid-1938 that he presumed *he* could endorse a candidate, as in Iowa, to oppose the sitting senator, a friend of Wallace's whom Wallace, as well as Baruch, was funding.

"Tommy makes me so nervous that I can't take it," Perkins shuddered, even in 1954.[42] It was always a shock for a man in FDR's disfavor to realize that such a sunny, can-do, musical person like Tommy was employed as a political assassin. That said, by 1941, when Tommy's moment to be purged came, he would discover FDR to be far smoother than he.

Because Ickes always behaved ferociously toward opponents, reporters assumed that he was doing the eliminating as well. In fact, he had doubts, even if he involved himself in two or three primaries and attended Hopkins's early committee meetings. His Public Works Administration also kept raining dollars at a helpful time.

Ickes might gleefully dispose of Democratic troublemakers on the Hill, and he did not mind the idea of a predominantly liberal Democratic Party. Except a purge like this could not protect the nation's forests. Nor would backing one pro-lynching Senate candidate against another—as the janissaries of the elimination committee were doing in Georgia, Florida, and South Carolina—bring an end to this drumroll of atrocities. Additionally, the Southerners whom FDR was seeking to eliminate—such as Cotton Ed Smith, who had rebelled over court reform and the Fair Labor bill—were as keen as Ickes on fighting Germany.

Ultimately, only one of the purge's intended victims went down—no Southerner, but a New York City congressman—although underlings, such as customs collectors, disappeared unnoticed into the shadows.

The eliminators may have known how to handle top people on the Hill and in the Administration. They failed more deeply to grasp how America's democracy functions. You might adore FDR and believe the New Deal had given you a job, except a job didn't mean that the senator who shook your hand on Confederate Heroes Day should be turned out of office on the word of some unknown fixer from Washington. Roosevelt had essentially ventured into foreign territory—a good way of thinking, for instance, of South Carolina in 1938—where charm and dollars did not work. Nor would this be the last time.

Despite all, Roosevelt's Cabinet was characterized by goodwill. "Can I sell you a few German munitions this morning?" joked Morgenthau before turning to business with Ickes in a routine phone call. "Or a little helium?"[43] (In the transcript, Ickes confined himself to "Umph.") And everyone was dreaming of an economic recovery, which, in late summer '38, seemed excitingly imminent. The numbers peaked in December, only to fall steeply. Wallace, Eccles, and others had hoped that emergency investment might be able to jolt the Depression into retreat. That money had not been enough.

On November 8, the midterm congressional elections were held against a backdrop of war. Britain and France had capitulated to Hitler over his demands for the Czech Sudetenland, and informed observers expected this cave-in to incite more ultimatums. Nevertheless, Americans voted on kitchen table issues: 19 percent joblessness, high taxes, no end in sight. The president cast his ballot at noon in Hyde Park, without wearing the special watch chain that he used as a good luck charm. He later followed the returns on radio with Hopkins.

The Democrats lost eighty seats in the House and eleven in the Senate. This vast unexpected reversal solidified a coalition of Republicans and conservative Democrats powerful enough to bring the New Deal to a halt. Virtually no one targeted by the purge had suffered a whit, and now FDR would have to work with his intended victims in the new Seventy-Fifth Congress, convening on January 3, 1939.

Roosevelt liked to rehash events with his Cabinet, as he did on the Friday of this election week, Hopkins, as usual, attending. And, as usual, few of FDR's remarks in the Cabinet, as elsewhere, lacked heroic optimism. Election results, in his opinion, could be seen in a different light.

The Democratic majority was still larger than at any time since the Civil War, except for the two years now ending. Maybe so, but a skeptic like Arthur Krock could take his own view. The outcome was a signal, he wrote, that voters wanted aggressive liberals—as he named Ickes and Hopkins—to be ejected for "moderate Democratic leaders."[44]

Two days after the election, Nazi Germany let loose a hurricane of violence, *Kristallnacht,* Night of the Broken Glass, throughout the Reich. The Federal Council of Churches immediately asked Ickes to respond to the concentration camp internment of some thirty thousand Jewish men, the hundreds of murders, and the vandalizing of synagogues and shops. Ickes would do so on the fourteenth in a forty-five-minute CBS broadcast to be heard live in Europe: Ben Cohen helped write the speech. It was

FDR who insisted they remove references to Germany, Hitler, Göring, and Dr. Goebbels, the sinister propaganda minister.

This was among at least three occasions in which Ickes complied with FDR's "request" to cut denunciations of Hitler and Nazism from his speeches. Nevertheless, his broadcast made its point with its condemnation of barbaric "fascist" persecutions of the Jews. For good measure, he belittled Charles Lindbergh's acceptance in October of a diamond-encrusted swastika medallion from the hands of a certain bloated central European air minister.

These were angry days at home too. The new House Special Committee to Investigate Un-American Activities was probing threats that it deemed worse than Nazism. Those were the ones inflicted domestically by socialism, immigration, labor unions, and Blacks. To this end, the hulking, cigar-smoking chairman Martin Dies of eastern Texas issued a press release that listed the most dangerous people in the world. To be sure, he included Hitler, and of course Stalin, then—in careful order—Perkins, Ickes, and Hopkins. Clearly, all these autocrats were inciting race hatred, an accusation that appeared in every newspaper the day Ickes went on the air.

Needless to say, FDR found the charges hilarious: Ickes did not, and was set to obliterate Dies, likely enough by using Interior Department investigators and wiretaps. By now, there were rumors about how far Ickes might go, as there had been about Louis Howe. FDR held him back. And Hopkins could not afford to be his usual insouciant self about inquisitors' antics on the Hill. Roosevelt was set to bring him into the actual Cabinet, and that required Senate confirmation. Hopkins had so much to explain to Congress that his enemies could hardly wait.

No one had resigned from Roosevelt's Cabinet until the president announced, with very sincere regret, the departures of Attorney General Cummings and Commerce Secretary Roper.

Then, on the morning before Christmas 1938, he revealed Roper's successor to be Harry Hopkins—and, in a flash, used a recess appointment to enable Hopkins to be sworn in at eleven o'clock. Fifty-four people attended a quickly planned ceremony in the president's second-floor study. Ickes, accompanied by Jane, was the only Cabinet member to appear. Perkins and Wallace had gone home for Christmas.

The Commerce Department usually speaks for business, except that

Hopkins's own interests in private enterprise, from what anyone could tell, never went much beyond playing poker with tycoons. Ten days earlier, the president had explained his choice to Ickes: "Harry does get along with the economic royalists. There is something debonair and easygoing about him that makes him personally attractive."[45] *The New York Times* cited other supporters of Hopkins, who insisted that he had befriended many company chairmen "at Southern resorts and at Northern racetracks," for all his career in social work.[46] Maybe this was enough to satisfy the corporate sector.

The next day, on Christmas, Hopkins and his six-year-old daughter joined the Roosevelts for a morning service at St. Thomas's church, and then for a holiday lunch. At 8 A.M. on the twenty-sixth, he began work at his cavernous office, in the building named today after one of his predecessors, Herbert C. Hoover.

FDR was also working through Christmas week in Washington, as was Ickes. The president ended the year by watching a short, powerful documentary, *Inside Nazi Germany*, recognized today by the National Film Registry. It depicts the Reich's massive rearmament, marching legions, brutal antisemitism, and a wildly hopeful populace living for the State and its Führer. The implicit question from the film's producer, Time Inc., was whether America was up to facing this juggernaut.

SPARK TO FLAME

"Munich" in Autumn 1938 to
War in Europe, September 1939

Don't think I am not watching everything with an eagle eye.
President Roosevelt to Harold Ickes, September 1939

In the Washington of the late 1930s, Franklin Roosevelt and Henry Wallace remained savvier about foreign affairs than most commentators of their day or ours. They spoke other languages, knew history, and grasped the geographic fundamentals. In 1938, they understood the details surrounding Czechoslovakia's vulnerability to conquest despite its defense treaty with France, which was aligned with Britain, and they could gauge the consequences. For starters, U.S. cotton exports would be damaged by any loss of access to Czech mills.

In those days, the United States possessed no central intelligence organization, and reports from service attachés were all too often pedestrian. FDR was influenced by what he heard from Wallace, as he had been by Perkins's observations of France. At the time, Wallace was receiving on-the-spot insights from his sister, Mary Bruggmann, who remained in Prague with her husband, Charles, the Swiss ambassador. Wallace was proving useful in other ways too, as by urging rearmament. His well-informed zeal might help should there ever be a need to rally the country for war. Experts credited Wallace with the best voice on radio, after Roosevelt's, and the 1936 campaign had shown him to be a fighter.

Wallace was already writing to columnists to emphasize the dangers posed to America by Hitler's gun-backed diplomatic triumphs—and also insisting to FDR that this was no time to dwell on quarrels over class. America, he said, needed "a national consciousness of unity" to bring together labor and business against foreign perils. Only then, and if the economy could resume growing, would the country be able to achieve an "integrated plan for national defense."[1]

All four lieutenants were in the thick of these deliberations. Roosevelt explained to Ickes that the small democratic nations of Europe were a tripwire. Should these fall to Hitler, who strutted on every newsreel as the patron of alienated groups of German-speakers outside the Reich, the Nazis could easily turn on larger prey.[2] And most of the countries adjoining Germany were weak.

FDR sought guidance from his Cabinet that September, which was rare. Ickes and Hopkins discussed with him the pluses and minuses of whether to mediate between Germany and the nations it was threatening. Wallace advised him bluntly that it would be like "delivering a sermon to a mad dog."[3]

The president also reviewed with his Cabinet the tactics that Britain and France might use in war, although he emphasized that America shouldn't get entangled. Presumably, the Royal Navy would trap the Kriegsmarine in northern ports while Britain, France, and the Soviet Union hammered Germany from the air.

On Monday, September 26, 1938, listening to Hitler's threats broadcast live from Berlin's Sportspalast, Roosevelt remarked to his cousin Daisy Suckley how the huge crowds were making "noises like animals."[4] The next afternoon he called a special Cabinet meeting and had a radio placed on the table for his official family to hear the sixty-nine-year-old prime minister, Chamberlain, deliver an evening address to the empire from 10 Downing Street.

Chamberlain recounted his efforts with "Herr Hitler" in Berchtesgaden and Bad Godesberg to avert war. Appeals to the Führer's better nature had apparently failed. Hitler only stiffened his demands, to insist that Czechoslovakia's strongly fortified Sudeten borderland be handed over by October 1. To those in the Cabinet Room, Chamberlain's tired, reedy voice sounded without hope. He spoke disbelievingly of civilians in England trying on gas masks because of quarrels "in a faraway country."

FDR spent most of that Tuesday with Hull and Welles in the Oval Office, and he also saw Jane's uncle, Ambassador Cudahy, back home to report on the gathering storm. Driven by the furies of his temperament, Ickes could sympathize with other difficult people. He brought Cudahy out to dinner in Olney with Jane and, to make a foursome, invited Cissy

Patterson to drive over from Dupont Circle. No record exists of either guest visiting again.

FDR suspected that Chamberlain was set on buying peace at any price, as proved right three days later, when Britain and France compelled Czechoslovakia to accept Hitler's diktat as laid out to them at Munich.

Poland opportunistically snatched Czech land near the Olza River; even so, Roosevelt's irritation focused on Britain. He told Ickes of having warned the British ambassador that he was willing to help, but "would do nothing if Great Britain cringed like a coward."[5] However, he conceded to Ickes, Germany and Italy possessed an overwhelming preponderance of airpower—about which he was much mistaken.

Looking back, Perkins identified Munich as one of the dividing lines of Roosevelt's presidency. The "terror" being felt in Britain, she recalled, "naturally communicated to us, and quite directly to Roosevelt."[6] London was the world's largest city, with a population of nine million inhabiting 611 square miles. In 1938 and '39, people imagined a second world war in terms similar to how they would envision war between the U.S. and Soviet superpowers in the coming thermonuclear age. In the late 1930s, weapons of mass destruction—bombs of mustard and phosgene gases— were expected to wipe out whole cities, leaving civilian casualties in the hundreds of thousands. Yet still deterrence failed.

Amid these tensions, FDR sent Hopkins to the West Coast to survey— very quietly—the production capacity of aviation manufacturers, notably Douglas Aircraft, Lockheed, and Boeing. Hopkins kept few records, as was his habit on sensitive matters. Once home, he briefed the president, and then recapped his findings over dinner with Ickes and Jane in the Maryland countryside on October 5.

Hopkins found exceptional military men to assist him in these defense matters—and also to be useful to him personally. He first met Briga- dier General George Marshall, the army's new deputy chief of staff, in mid-November 1938 at a twelve-person White House conference. People in the room discerned a preternatural authority in Marshall that made his low-key presence daunting, to all except the commander in chief.

FDR outlined a plan to build ten thousand planes for the Army Air Corps, predecessor to the U.S. Air Force, by using WPA money to con- struct factories. Thus, at this juncture, aviation was set to be transformed.

A year earlier, Marshall had been the commander at Vancouver Barracks in Washington State, when three Soviet transpolar aviators landed in front of him out of the blue early one Sunday morning: "a most interesting experience for the U.S. Army," he called it.[7] In fact, from a military perspective, the event captured the sudden range, as well as menace, of airpower. All one had to do was to rotate the globe ninety degrees and the short polar distance between North America and Eurasia leapt out.

Right at the beginning of 1939, Roosevelt announced plans to train twenty thousand college students a year as pilots to "meet the aeronautical crisis" caused by dangers overseas. Hopkins's former deputy, Aubrey Williams, was to handle the finances.[8] In his State of the Union address on January 4, the president spoke of war having been averted, which is how the Munich Agreement was seen. Yet, he warned, peace was not assured, and the nation had to get its house in order.

He also asked for $300 million to build planes, and an explicit rearmament program soon began. Before month's end, however, it was Ickes rather than the president whom Hitler singled out for attack. Goebbels had first denounced him for ruining the spirit of the Christmas season, after a blistering speech Ickes had delivered to the Zionist Society of Cleveland. Then the Führer himself unmasked Ickes as the main puppet of Jewish interests.

The expression "policing the world" entered American politics, at first to be used mockingly.[9] Why even think of enforcing peace in Europe and Asia when the country remained stuck in the Great Depression? At the same time, another epic concern was taking form. Prosperity, for most of the decades to come, would not be the nation's priority. Wealth became secondary to a "security" of the political-military sort that could never be fully established, one forever seeming so easy to lose.

Newspaper photos taken the day after Christmas 1938 showed an emaciated yet chipper Hopkins behind his Commerce Department desk, his shirt collar clearly too large. Ickes still believed him to be suffering from ulcers. One kept quiet about cancer in those days, because people might react as if one were a "cripple." The invincible disease ate and deformed those it afflicted, and such terrible news was usually concealed even from friends.

Hopkins had been suspicious when Roosevelt first spoke of sending him to Commerce. The appointment had nothing to do with the president wanting "to give Hopkins breathing space from the turbulence of the WPA," as has been claimed—an interpretation that imputes to FDR an unusual tenderness. In fact, Hopkins confided to Ickes that he suspected he was just being used as a "stalking horse" for FDR's maneuvering with Congress.[10]

Besides, everyone knew that any attempt to confirm Hopkins would inflame the Senate. Still, he was willing to play along. More so than the three others, he could ride with FDR's moods. That December, he told Morgenthau, he had just received "a public beating" from Roosevelt, over what he wasn't sure.[11]

Hopkins's stature would not change, except in protocol, if he formally joined the Cabinet. Nevertheless, senators were all too anxious lest he use Commerce as a springboard—just as FDR possibly intended. Ten years earlier, Herbert Hoover had leapt from Commerce to the presidency, also having never held elective office.

Hopkins was already pale and drawn when, beginning on the morning of January 10, the Senate subjected him to a brutal cross-examination. He looked sicker by the day while California Republican Hiram Johnson and other former friends of Roosevelt unbottled their fury at the New Deal, and at him. Had he registered as a Socialist in New York City in summer 1914? Hopkins could not recall. Oh? Well, if so, "it was because of the idealism of a young man," Hopkins murmured.[12] Leaving all that aside, the numerous survivors of Hopkins's "purge" had their own questions.

Finally, FDR told Vice President Garner, as presiding officer of the Senate, to "call off the dogs" for the party's sake—though it was late in the day for any favors from Garner.[13] Their relationship, always odd, had soured.

Disputes over court-packing, sit-down strikes, and more recently lynching were only part of the problem. Garner was thirteen years older than FDR, and a veteran of thirty years in the House when the Administration opened. He had sassed his president from the start. This startled observers, although, initially, their banter was something of a show. The president responded with what he called "teasing." Except that, as time went on, Roosevelt's teasing cut deep enough for him to ask Ickes if he'd gone too far. *Yes.*

Garner simply claimed to have no influence on Hopkins's tormentors—rubbish, of course. Nonetheless, after several days, the agony stopped, as if Garner had turned off a faucet. Enough had been enough. The Senate of that era deferred to a president's choice, even if the choice was Hopkins. He was confirmed on the twenty-third by a party vote of 58 to 27, although eleven Democrats—conservatives and liberals alike—abstained.

Hopkins threw himself into a big new project, one that Wallace admired. He proposed to "go after business with hammer and tongs in South America" in order to get customers for U.S. producers.[14] He brought stellar deputies into Commerce and hired the best publicity man available to handle the press. He also drew on the department's Business Advisory Council, which he had helped the ineffectual Daniel Roper to assemble earlier in the 1930s. Its off-site meetings at the Mayflower Hotel were chaired by Averell Harriman, who had testified for Hopkins during the ordeal of confirmation.

In February, Hopkins explored his prospects for a 1940 presidential run. It would have to be as a native Iowan, even though he hadn't lived in Iowa for twenty-seven years and was using a Manhattan hotel as his voting address. Among other worries, he needed to consider that running as a New Yorker might spotlight his louche involvements in café society. Just the previous October, the socialite Mary Donovan Hale had jumped from her apartment on the sixteenth floor of the Hampshire House. It was nobody's Goddamned business whether or not they were engaged, according to Hopkins, and the story vanished from the press.[15]

Harriman accompanied the presidential aspirant to Iowa, where he leased a 388-acre stock farm and rejoined the Methodist Church. The railroad scion lent his presence, and his name as an eminent man of affairs helped to offset anxieties that Hopkins might be a Socialist. Des Moines executives were impressed. Then Hopkins became ill, and left to recover at the South Carolina estate of another rich friend, Bernard Baruch.

Perkins, for one, never believed that Roosevelt endorsed any of Hopkins's higher ambitions. For one reason, Hopkins was always taking ill, just as he did now. Nonetheless, he was utterly convinced of FDR's support, and when his life drew to a close, he hoped that people would remember him for having come so close to the prize.

Perkins had another candidate for 1940—Henry Wallace, in his case an authentic Hawkeye, who, she concluded, "had in him the makings of presidential timber."[16] But in early 1939 she was consumed by the gravest professional crisis of her life. On January 24, an impeachment resolution was filed against her, as would happen to no other member of this Cabinet.

Perkins's alleged high crime was to have undercut immigration law by delaying attempts to deport the Australian-born Harry Bridges, head of the International Longshoremen's and Warehousemen's Union (ILWU). Both the Judiciary and the Un-American Activities committees denounced him as a Communist. She knew well enough that Bridges espoused some kind of Marxism. She also believed him to be among the most stabilizing influences in the West Coast maritime industry.

In 1935, FDR had instructed Perkins to have Bridges investigated. Now he told her—as well as Ickes, poised to counterattack—that surely no legal justification existed to deport Bridges. Ultimately, Roosevelt, Ickes, and Perkins were thinking alike.

Perkins succeeded—barely, she would admit—in not weeping under the public interrogations.

Her ordeal on the Hill would last through winter. She relied on the strength of Caroline O'Day, she prayed for her enemies, and visited St. James's each morning. She relied too, not for the first time, on Ickes, whom Dies also denounced as a "Red"—although he was on firmer ground when describing Ickes's savage response as "a fit of uncontrollable rage" that made the interior secretary unsuitable for any Cabinet.[17] Years later, Perkins remembered undergoing one of the few mystical experiences of her life: when entering the House, "My Lord walked beside me into the jaws of death."[18]

Ironically, the same congressmen who hounded her for not throwing Bridges out of the country turned to denouncing her for not allowing Leon Trotsky—the Russian revolutionary, political theorist, and mortal enemy of Stalin—*into* the United States from exile in Mexico to testify about Communism. FDR found the contradiction sidesplitting.

As it turned out, Bridges would continue to lead the ILWU for nearly forty years, and the House Judiciary Committee found no grounds to impeach Perkins. Other than offering a legal opinion, however, FDR had been unhelpful. She dealt with a smiling, admiring man who lauded her work—yet, as she recalled, he offered not even "a sympathetic word."[19] There were few political gains for him in this fracas.

During her congressional testimony, however, Perkins pushed back by declaring that America needed to accept the world's most imperiled people, current approaches being shameful.

Nearly a year earlier, after Hitler had annexed Austria, the Administration indefinitely extended some fifteen thousand visas for German and Austrian citizens already in America, and also relaxed the "public charge" clause. Perkins, as head of the Immigration Service, and Congresswoman O'Day had rallied influential New York friends to pressure FDR into this decision. Ickes at the same time undertook larger questions of refugee resettlement, and Morgenthau held long, rambling conversations with the president about how the United States might help to finance the placing of eighty thousand Jews a year among various other nations such as South Africa or—Mussolini willing—recently conquered Ethiopia.

Conservatives on the Hill opposed the president's idea of America itself accepting twenty thousand Jewish refugees annually. Germany's immigration quota only came to be filled in mid-1939, and many legislators held views similar to those heard in Congress today: immigrants take jobs from deserving Americans, go on welfare, and—to get themselves more largesse—become liberal Democrats. The narrative of the time was that every Jew who arrived had surely been radicalized by oppression and was set to embrace the New Deal.

Ickes by 1939 was patrolling an ever-larger bureaucratic terrain. His department's Office of Insular Affairs had been formed in 1934 to include responsibility for Alaska and Hawaii, and soon for Puerto Rico. He then took charge of the Philippines from the War Department in July 1939. He had long been demanding that America provide a home for refugees from Nazism, and he acted. Amid much else, he proposed Alaska as a haven for Jewish refugees from Germany, and he and Perkins pressed this hope into the early months of the war.

Still, Roosevelt's habit of stirring up discord did not stop even over this searing issue. For instance, he implied that he alone among his officials supported helping the Jews. "Particularly Ickes," he claimed to an influential friend, "objected on account of the immigration laws."[20] Of course, the opposite was true.

When it came to Ickes's Alaskan Development Bill, hope collapsed once FDR urged a limit of only ten thousand immigrants with a maximum of 10 percent Jews, a number he later reduced. Objections had come from Alaska's territorial delegate, from a representative of the American Legion, and from Seattle's Chamber of Commerce. All imagined an influx of Jews, with many likely to head south. Such objections were enough to make Roosevelt cave.

Ickes also proposed the Virgin Islands as a sanctuary—another territory under his authority. Regardless, elements in Congress dreaded it would be a refuge for subversives and wards of the state. Ickes and Perkins rushed to find any safe haven, and Morgenthau did try to help. With equal fervor, Perkins and O'Day, who had standing on the issue from her seat on the House Immigration and Naturalization Committee, joined forces. They backed identical bipartisan bills (the German Refugee Children's Bill) sponsored by their friends Senator Wagner and Representative Edith Nourse Rogers, Republican of Massachusetts. Maybe, thought Perkins, at least twenty thousand children, as specified in the bill, could be rescued from the "bizarre types of cruelty being visited upon the Jews."[21]

Such top Republicans as Herbert Hoover, Dutchess County congressman Hamilton Fish, and former presidential candidate Alf Landon endorsed the Wagner-Rogers legislation. So did labor leader John L. Lewis, who thunderously punctured the ludicrous arguments that admitting these children would add to unemployment.

Roosevelt offered no support. He left the question to Congress, which included senators like Pat McCarran, Democrat of Nevada and soon chair of the Judiciary Committee, whom a British diplomat reported to be "anti-socialist, anti-Russian, anti-Communist and anti-Jewish."[22]

Nor did Jewish leaders, who feared an antisemitic backlash, present a united front. Ickes might extoll the settling of Palestine, but he failed to understand Jewish anxieties when he exhorted his audiences to support his fight to open U.S. borders as well. Neither did he comprehend what it was like to be Jewish in 1939 America. For instance, he urged FDR to appoint Ben Cohen to be undersecretary of the treasury when the slot opened that year. Roosevelt agreed that Cohen was a good man, before questioning the wisdom of appointing a Jew to go under Morgenthau. Ickes was perplexed. Why?

To be sure, FDR recognized a looming humanitarian disaster, although few could imagine that it would lead to extermination. His ideas for settlement also included Palestine, where, he told the British ambassador, there was plenty of land, although Arab inhabitants might have to be shipped to "adjoining Arab countries."[23] It's the first instance of the squire of Hyde Park—as pundits needled him—addressing the removal of foreign populations, notably Palestinians and, later, Poles and Germans.

The Arab Revolt was ending in Palestine during spring 1939, and the British had hanged 108 rebels while killing another 3,382 who had been fighting for their freedom and their land. That having been accomplished, the Foreign Office replied that it would be immoral to transfer residents of Palestine to distant places: and why wasn't America offering its own territory? Nonetheless, Britain did offer to help. Its own immigration quota to America of 65,721 was more than twice the size of Germany's, and only 5 percent of this quota had been used in 1938. London proposed to turn over the remaining number of slots to Jewish refugees, not that Roosevelt was persuaded.

He intended to go for a third term, as Perkins had been among the first to recognize, and he did not need one more fight, however humane.

The Communist Party USA, established in 1919, was never an independent political organization, and its true believers were in thrall to Moscow, with covert Soviet subsidies extending into the 1980s. Hopkins, moreover, observed that the party contained a "high proportion of distinctly unsympathetic Jews," a point FDR endorsed.

Already Perkins was tracking Communist Party operatives through the labyrinths of labor union politics. She believed that she could sense them from years of "having contact with Commies" in New York social movements.[24]

She did not worry about Bridges, nor such a salt-of-the-earth type as the founding president of the National Maritime Union, whom she concluded was a mere Communist dupe. And, backed by Ickes, she ignored FBI Director Hoover's anger when she placed labor leader Walter Reuther on a defense factory inspection board.

Instead, she was alarmed by smoother people "operating in the Communist field" who kept to the shadows. They surfaced in such pivotal unions as the Radio Operators of America, and she found them altogether too agreeable for their purported jobs. She knew the behavior of authentic union men, who never "tattle-taled," as she put it, on their brothers. Meanwhile she traced activists in one union or factory who, after a time, would submerge, only to turn up a year or two later playing labor politics under another name.[25]

Her own departmental headquarters in Washington had two unions, one affiliated with the traditional AFL and the other with the upstart CIO. Ironically, the latter saw fit to call a strike, occupying her outer office for nearly three days. She waited them out behind her desk, while her personal staff kept order until the activists wore down. And here too she kept noticing the most improbable characters working undercover as Communist Party agitators while gravitating to sensitive roles in government. One she believed to be the woman who led the CIO local at the Labor Department.

Alger Hiss, a lean mandarin from Harvard Law School whom Moscow code-named ALES, served at Agriculture until 1936, when he segued to State. Somehow, the State Department's entire Division of Eastern European Affairs was abolished in 1937, and its library dismantled. "Here, if ever," recalled diplomat George Kennan, "was a point at which there was indeed the smell of Soviet influence, or strongly pro-Soviet influence, somewhere in the higher reaches of government."[26]

Two weeks after Perkins's impeachment ordeal ended on the Hill, *The Saturday Evening Post* began serializing defector Walter Krivitsky's memoir, *In Stalin's Secret Service*. Eventually, his body would be found, complete with an unconvincing suicide note, in a locked hotel room near the Capitol. General Krivitsky's death paralleled the mysterious fate of the trade unionist and CPUSA agent Juliet Poyntz, who vanished from a New York City street after *deviating* from the party.

The Soviet Union was itself a ghastly hybrid of seventeenth-century quasi-Oriental despotism and nineteenth-century messianic radicalism. No one in Washington understood what was happening within it, though they could see newsreels. "It just doesn't make sense," FDR said of Stalin's 1937–1938 show trials, in which eminent Bolsheviks confessed to treason, and were promptly liquidated.

The terror that descended in 1937 would also behead the Soviet Union's army and navy by executing three Red Army marshals out of five, some two hundred corps and division commanders, plus dozens of admirals. Ickes believed "Stalin had become mad with bloodlust."[27] Even so, these victims were a fraction of perhaps twenty million innocents killed by the man whom his shivering subordinates called "*Vozhd*" (roughly Supreme Leader)—including the 3.9 million murdered by starvation during the Holodomor in Ukraine.

Nazidom had penetrated the United States too, as Ickes and Perkins had recognized in 1933, except it was usually less insidious than Stalin's Communist International. Much, in fact, was aboveboard—as instanced by the blowhards of the Führer-inspired Amerikadeutscher Volksbund, which claimed two hundred thousand members. The Bund appears at the end of the documentary *Inside Nazi Germany*, like an alarm bell. Its jackbooted enthusiasts are shown marching and heiling through mid-Manhattan, flaunting swastikas as if at a torchlight parade in Nuremberg.

Perkins had been mystified at the ferocity of the Un-American Activities Committee, and doubted that its anger arose solely from her defense of Bridges. To be sure, Congressman Dies hounded the Bund as he did Communist agents. Nonetheless, she observed him and other primitives on the Hill, such as Senator McCarran, amplifying Bund propaganda that Jews controlled America.

Yet government vigilance was random. Years earlier, FDR had wanted every Civilian Conservation Corps enrollee to be fingerprinted, for reasons unexplained. Perkins had stifled that idea. Now he was growing concerned about the international scene and, in December 1938, instructed Cabinet officers to make sure that foreign visitors to their departments should first be screened by the State Department.

Fingerprinting at the time was discriminatory, and it had a disgraceful air. For example, the FBI, as Director Hoover noted in a memorandum early in 1939, routinely fingerprinted laborers who were indicted, though rarely businessmen. As Perkins had told Hoover himself, the procedure in any event violated the sacredness of individual privacy.

Yet now Roosevelt insisted that all employees of every department lay down their oily fingers.

"I am in favor of fingerprinting all these aliens who come into the United States," he told the Cabinet. "All opposed say 'Nay.'"

"Nay," said Perkins loud and clear.

She was echoed by Ickes, and only then by Wallace, who said that the idea sounded like Germany. This was too much for Garner, who insisted that every American should be fingerprinted, for no honest man or woman would object.

Leaning over, Wallace whispered to Perkins, "He means to say you're not an honest woman."

"I haven't been for a good many years," she replied.[28]

Facing this impasse, FDR made a workaday joke and agreed to postpone the decision.

Even so, ever more reasons existed to worry about internal security as the German threat intensified once Hitler dismembered the rest of Czechoslovakia on March 15. Mary Wallace Bruggmann and her family had been in Prague when the Nazis roared in at dawn, and she reported events to her brother. By evening the Führer's personal banner, with its gold-bordered swastika, was flying over Hradschin Castle, the state residence of Czechoslovakia's president.

In Washington, on that day of Czechoslovakia's fall, FDR went about his business. He met with Wallace and the Agriculture Department's administrators and endured a visit from the National Labor Relations Board. At four thirty he received Congresswoman O'Day. Unlike Perkins, she was an actual pacifist and for a year had been pushing a "standard of ethics" to prevent belligerent nations from air bombardment of civilians and cities.[29] FDR had to suffer her visit, too. Roosevelt's usual way to divert such tendentious callers would have been to occupy forty-three of the forty-five minutes allotted to O'Day with a monologue of stories, likely about sailing, or good old times in New York. This tactic never worked with her.

So he had to hear her out. Also on the fifteenth, he acted quickly to order all U.S. mail in transit to Czechoslovakia to be diverted immediately to the embassy in Paris. No one had thought of that, but FDR knew what he was dealing with in Berlin. Some of that mail likely contained material useful to the Gestapo and, once opened, would compromise the recipients.

Once the Cabinet convened two days later, on Friday, the president grew angry when discussing Hitler's assault. Germany was now poised to attack Poland from the south as well as the west. Sixteen days later, on March 31, Britain pledged to defend Poland, and France concurred. In Washington, the men, and a few women, who had so greatly been preoccupied with pulling their country out of the Depression, watched Europe sliding into the abyss.

The last fascist offensive of the Spanish Civil War occurred in the final week of that same month. Madrid surrendered to the mutinous professional army of Generalissimo Franco on March 29. Ickes nonetheless stuck with his cause. He chaired the Spanish Refugee League Campaign Committee, to which schoolchildren contributed dimes and for which Caroline O'Day gave much more from her oil fortune. Nathan Margold of the Interior Department had signed petitions for the Lawyers Committee on American Relations with Spain, as did Ickes. Neither man hesitated to attach his government title.

Ilo Wallace also donated to the Refugee League, although Henry barely responded to the cause, claiming later to have opposed arms shipments to either side. As it turned out, this was less a matter of principle than of his being as politically cautious as the president. In contrast, Morgenthau backed Ickes when the Cabinet debated Spain, and Ickes also involved Felix Frankfurter, whom Roosevelt had placed on the Supreme Court in January, in the Loyalist cause.

For Ickes, the fight over Spain never ended. He used legal muscle to ensure that the dictatorship in Madrid would receive no U.S. government loans, nor would it be granted the diplomatic recognition promptly extended by Britain and France. Having got Hopkins and Morgenthau to agree, he enjoyed hearing FDR admit, to the entire Cabinet, that the U.S. arms embargo had been a dreadful mistake.

The triumph of fascism looked inevitable when, in April, Mussolini overran Albania, proclaiming it part of the Italian empire. Yet, as this predation continued, Washington to all intents and purposes had no secretaries of war and of the navy.

Newsmen wrote of "little Henry Woodring," who was short to begin with, and who also kept shrinking as secretary of war. A formidable bloc of opinion agreed. To Ickes, he was as a "midget General MacArthur." Hopkins chimed in that FDR had made "a terrible appointment." Perkins found him "very vain," and Wallace calmly dismissed him as "a pleasant politician who didn't see the big issues."[30] Nonetheless, Woodring was a useful Democrat from Republican Kansas, so FDR kept him on.

In turn, the aging Claude Swanson at the Navy Department simply could not be seen. His assistant secretary was now Charles Edison, son of the late inventor, nearly deaf, and a businessman who knew nothing of the navy or the sea. Yet he repeatedly had to substitute for Swanson at serious meetings. To be sure, FDR would continue to be his own navy secretary—and, slightly less obviously, his own secretary of war and of state and of the treasury too, and his own attorney general besides. Few believed that his approach to governance worked, and now the bell was tolling.

Roosevelt and Ickes lunched in the Oval Office on March 21, after which the president held a press conference at four o'clock. Two hours later, he left with his physician, his press aide Stephen Early, and the genial, newly promoted Brigadier General Edwin "Pa" Watson for the twenty-mile drive north to Ickes's place in the country. Morgenthau drove up directly from his big Georgian house on Thirty-First Street. Wallace, as usual, had no interest in these gatherings, and little patience for the jovial Watson—now the White House appointments secretary—whom he believed FDR had "deliberately picked because he wasn't too bright."[31]

Hopkins, in turn, was resting at home under doctor's orders.

At Olney, it usually took just a few minutes to unwind over drinks before turning to dinner, more drinks, and poker. Ickes used the chance to recap what he and FDR had discussed at lunch—the government's re-organization bill, which Congress would finally approve on April 3, and the pusillanimity of the British and French foreign ministries.

With Watson shuffling the cards, FDR told a story about how Frank-furter had recently come over to the White House for cocktails, although first Frankfurter had stopped to see Garner in his hideaway back of the Senate chamber, around 4 P.M. Garner had taken out his customary bot-tle of whiskey and seized the opportunity to ply Frankfurter until nearly seven o'clock, at which point the justice unsteadily appeared in the pres-ident's study.

The president, known for foisting perfectly horrible dry martinis upon his guests, offered one to Frankfurter—a man known for speaking quickly in a slight Viennese accent. But not that evening. Before long, Roosevelt had everyone in stitches as he mimicked Felix's slooooow, caaaareful *Wie-nerische* enunciation. His listeners howled at the pitiless cartoon of this eminent figure being helped home by the Secret Service.

By now FDR could easily behave like one of the boys, though no one stretched the familiarity. White House logs show that he and his crew returned at two thirty in the morning.

No stories exist of any of the four actually being drunk, even Hopkins, who was given to drinking heavily. Wallace did not mind alcohol; he just said he couldn't abide the taste. In this respect, each was reliably clear-headed. After all, they were responsible for running most of a colossally expanding government.

Still, there was levity. Wallace recalled being tweaked by Hopkins's "many stories of the highlife at Palm Beach"—a resort Wallace said he was happy never to have visited.[32] Hopkins by now was imitating FDR's habit of teasing, though with Hopkins it was good-natured ribbing. According to one account, he told Wallace of having observed Winthrop Aldrich gambling for large stakes at the Everglades Club with a lady definitely not the fifty-one-year-old Harriett Alexander Aldrich. You see, Hopkins explained, his trips to Palm Beach were essential, because he could then scout out the deep-pocketed sources whom FDR might tax for his next big relief program.

Between Roosevelt and Wallace there was a meeting of intellects, and Wallace would send over clippings from *The Economist* or the galley proofs of his latest book, such as those of *Whose Constitution? An Inquiry Into the General Welfare,* which FDR annotated.[33] Both men possessed extraordinary memories, and much of the interest they shared about nature rested on science. In early spring 1939, for example, Wallace gave Roosevelt 150 kernels apiece of fifteen kinds of corn to plant at Hyde Park—specifically during the first week of May, as he calculated it.

Wallace told his diary that Roosevelt was an expert on climate, as well as on geography—and to read that opinion from him is startling. In this instance, Wallace had developed his hybrids for the weather of lower New York State, and their thicker stalks could resist the high winds of Roosevelt's Hudson Valley fields better than the conventional corn being grown. The president was fascinated.

FDR treated the remote, brilliant Wallace differently from the other men with whom he worked so closely. He snapped at Farley that Wallace was "not a mystic" but "a philosopher. He's got ideas. He thinks right."[34] He evinced no petulant moods with Wallace, nor did he hang a nickname on him. He would no more have slapped Wallace on the knee than he would have General George C. Marshall.

In contrast, Roosevelt liked to call Morgenthau *"Kulak"* every week or two and shared this fact as a matter of conversation with a baffled Wallace. Why in the world designate the treasury secretary as a rich Russian peasant? "Because Henry didn't like it," beamed his host. However much Wallace was fond of FDR, he thought him "strange."[35] And for Wallace to call a man strange, even on paper, meant that he was genuinely odd.

Of course, all four lieutenants were strange. Wallace even questioned Ickes's "mental state" after Ickes dispatched a salvo of furious letters, including a vicious single-spaced twenty-eight pager, to Gifford Pinchot, the well-born forester and politician.[36] Ickes blamed everyone, from the Weyerhaeuser timberland company to the Sierra Club, for the U.S. Forest Service not being placed in his hands.

His rage climaxed in the year after April 1939, once Congress passed the Reorganization Act—the watered-down version of a law FDR had long sought. The limits Congress placed on presidential hopes of reworking administrative functions reflected the distrust that both political parties had come to feel for him. In Ickes's view, however, this legislation was a breakthrough because it finally enabled FDR to establish a Department of Conservation, should he be willing.

The man-years being consumed by the Forest Service transfer quarrel look ridiculous at that moment when civilization faced collapse. Still, in Ickes's mind, the service was the missing link in the Conservation Department of his dreams.

For Ickes, the one great hero of his life was Theodore Roosevelt, who had established at least 150 national forests. Now another Roosevelt was blocking his path to a true Conservation Department. Moreover, if only he could take command of the Forest Service, he would have gained even more purchase on the president's attention. Franklin Roosevelt, the self-designated "tree farmer," loved forests nearly as much as the sea. Wallace, in turn, never forgot that his own grandfather had championed the Forest Reserve Act even before T.R.'s day: and why should the forests now pass to Ickes?

Yet Wallace was friendly enough to empathize: "Ickes felt he had an absolute commitment from President Roosevelt for the transfer at the very time that Roosevelt was indicating to me that nothing of this sort was being contemplated." Wallace also realized FDR was doing "that kind of thing almost for fun—as if it were to keep in practice."[37]

One of the delights of power is that subordinates and stakeholders are compelled to painfully work out what the ruler truly intends—and for this the Forest Service transfer drama remains Exhibit A. Ickes then sank into gloom. Without his becoming the secretary of conservation, he wrote to himself, he was a failure. Never in Washington had he been so sad.

All he had accomplished—which had been a lot—faded into insignificance. Just for openers, he had run a scandal-free stewardship of the vast national lands year after year. By 1939 he was dramatically expanding the parks to embrace Jackson Hole, Olympic, Kings Canyon, and more. Yet endless pages of Ickes's diary lament how Roosevelt has double-crossed him once again. As spring blossomed in 1940, he grew angrier than ever.

He boycotted Cabinet meetings, shunned FDR's invitations for drinks and poker, and found himself too busy to have lunch together—only to be cornered once FDR shifted lunch plans to accommodate him. Of course, nothing got resolved, and Ickes's talk of resignation became a drumbeat. Insiders scoffed, but he wasn't bluffing, as the president could tell. Ickes savored intense relationships, and his threats to storm out of the official family were just another example of how he loved to live on the edge.

On it went. In May, the president promised truly to "make a Department of Conservation," and, he added, Ickes needn't kiss him for doing so. However, FDR still kept the Forest Service out of reach. Given Ickes's horror of compromise, this was torture.

Whatever the Interior Department might be called, it was running much of the District of Columbia, including parks, memorials, and government buildings, plus the White House compound. Yet Congress believed that *it* controlled the District, and *it* possessed oversight committees to do so.

Congress interfered relentlessly in the District, and, in 1939, the Dies Committee tried to fire Howard University's Black president, whom it accused, naturally, of Communism. Ickes managed to defuse the row, once Margold found him a technicality. Even though the university was maintained by federal funds, with Ickes essentially chairman of the board, Howard was not a government institution. A far graver issue arose when the university's School of Music concert series invited Black contralto Marian Anderson to sing, and then lost its theater to fire.

The city's board of education, under the thumb of Congress, forbade using an auditorium: her concert might, after all, be attended by Blacks and whites together. Then the all-white Daughters of the American Revolution refused to allow a Black to perform at Constitution Hall, which it still owns. Faced by all this, Ickes arranged for a free program center-ing on the Lincoln Memorial—after checking with the president, because Eleanor's resignation in protest from the DAR had turned Anderson's concert into a national drama. Roosevelt is often said to have given his blessing. In fact, that came when Ickes left him no choice.

On April 9, 1939, a cool and clear Easter Sunday afternoon, Ickes introduced Anderson and her pianist to a crowd of at least seventy-five thousand, who packed the Mall as far as the Washington Monument. "Genius draws no color line," he declared in a four-minute speech, possi-bly the best he ever made. Then Caroline O'Day walked Anderson to the microphone. Millions listened on the radio.

O'Day and Perkins had helped acquire sponsorships for the concert from rich friends. Various distinguished figures in and out of government had also been asked to lend their names. Hopkins did what he could, though he had been sick and hoped to be recovering at Warm Springs with the president that same day.

Ickes began smoking out those people who had not replied. One of them was Wallace, whom he telegraphed twice to create a paper trail. Still he got no answer. Wallace might attend a gathering in Manhattan's Carne-gie Hall to denounce racial and religious hatred—except that event, sev-eral months before, had been an easy call, largely concerning Germany's persecution of the Jews. Even the *New Yorker Staats-Zeitung* endorsed it.

Segregation was a different story, leaving Wallace to equivocate. To him, the South was assimilating slowly to superior forms of agriculture and nutrition, and looked to be a culture open to higher ideas. Yet the Anderson concert outright defied the Southern way of life: being held in a segregated city, it posed a problem for a newfound Democrat inching toward the presidency.

Wallace eventually fobbed Ickes off with the excuse that he never lent his name to events. As for Roosevelt, he was indeed conveniently in Georgia that Sunday afternoon. Eleanor, who was on one of her many travels around the country, had a nobler reason for staying away: she did not want to divert attention from Marian Anderson.

Thereafter, Ickes was set to open Washington's public playgrounds, golf courses, gardens, and swimming pools to Blacks. That said, he needed to contend with the shrewd and ruthless chairman of the District Com-mittee, Theodore "The Man" Bilbo of Mississippi, who was not a mere segregationist. Bilbo wanted to ship every Black citizen to Africa, as explained in his self-published book, *Take Your Choice: Separation or Mongrelization*. (Available today on Amazon.)

Initially, Ickes could ignore Bilbo and his friends, and he made a start at Haines Point, the peninsular recreation area near today's Jefferson Memorial—only to discover that freedom of access proved trickier than staging an alfresco gala. Of course he longed to respond violently as soon as jeering, booing gangs of whites began hurling stones at Black families, and he could have used thugs he had recruited into the U.S. Park Police to make his point. But having witnessed the bloodcurdling Chicago race riot of 1919, he knew where this might lead. Even the most powerful of Cabinet secretaries could only go so far.

The Negro has made the most distinctive contribution to American music," said the four-page White House program for the evening of June 8, 1939, the day when Marian Anderson sang "Ave Maria" for King George VI and his consort, Elizabeth.[38] Her performance topped a state dinner on the first full day of Their Majesties' unprecedented visit to Washington, New York City, and finally Hyde Park.

That morning, the president and his Cabinet had greeted the surprisingly small royal party of fourteen at Union Station. The weather was already scorching. After prolonged ceremonies, Ickes escaped to the Interior Department, where Jane waited for him in the cool of his huge blue-carpeted office. The two were bidden to a large garden party at the British embassy but decided to bolt. Seven months pregnant, Jane needed rest, and Harold was set on not bowing and scraping with the herd. Instead, he drove up Connecticut Avenue to the air-cooled Kennedy-Warren apartment of Texas congressman Lyndon Johnson, thirty-one. Together, they "kept the wheels of progress greased," as New Dealers described their afternoon lubrications.

Later, at the White House, Anderson's appearance made the entire week "magnificent" for Mr. and Mrs. Ickes. She sang in the East Room, where Jane sat next to an attentive Harry Hopkins amid stifling heat.

A cruise downriver to Mount Vernon occupied the next day. The distinguished visitors, the Roosevelts, the Cabinet, and anyone who could get an invitation boarded the USS *Potomac*, a converted Coast Guard cutter commonly designated as the presidential yacht. The English wore thick woolen morning coats and silk hats; the Americans cotton suits and straw boaters. Hopkins and Ickes stayed by themselves and talked shop as the *Potomac* steamed past Alexandria. They agreed to block commodity credits to Franco's Spain and to telegraph their decision to "Jesse," as the Administration's titanic banker was simply known.

Once back ashore in Washington, they attended a tea party that Eleanor had arranged on the White House lawn. The king and queen wanted to know more about the inner workings of America. Only our four had been invited from the Cabinet.

The royal party and the Roosevelts left by midnight on two separate trains for New York.

FDR's original invitation to King George had argued that a visit would benefit Anglo-American relations. As it happened, little of this trip appeared to be geopolitically significant. No fleets were reviewed, nor troops inspected. Instead, George and Elizabeth visited the "Court of Peace" at the New York World's Fair.

To the surprise of most Americans, including the Roosevelts, the royal couple possessed the demeanor of plain people who had suddenly—with Edward VIII's abdication in 1936—found themselves at the apex of history's largest empire. To such savvy U.S. officials as FDR's closest lieutenants, George VI appeared more of a worthy, heavily burdened civil servant than he did the King-Emperor and "Kaiser-i-Hind" (Emperor of India), which glowed among his sixty to seventy royal titles.

An event as magical as the king and queen of England on American soil fascinated people, even the millions in the Midwest who had little regard for things British—a category including Ickes and Wallace, who suspected that London might make peace with Hitler, allowing him in exchange a free hand in South America. Yet even those two could recognize how the visit helped to rebuild Franklin Roosevelt. The president appeared more than the equal of kings. George and Elizabeth not only stayed overnight at his house in Hyde Park, they partook of that fabled all-American picnic of hot dogs and beer, joined by gardeners and cooks. FDR's defeats were, for a time, put aside.

All in all, the visit went radiantly at a moment when observers on both sides of the Atlantic were awaiting catastrophe, and it offered a Hollywood-like distraction while the United States rearmed.

That summer, the *Graf Zeppelin II* indeed revealed a military purpose. Churchill writes of it floating up and down the British east coast in August to pick up secret radar frequencies. (No plane could lift the heavy load of instruments tended by more than two dozen analysts.) Equally ominous, as August approached, Europe's democracies had not yet reached an entente with Nazi Germany's mortal enemy, the Soviet Union.

For the moment, the U.S. Navy consumed most of the country's rearmament spending, as became clear when Swanson finally died on the morning of July 7, aged seventy-seven. Washington went into convulsive mourning. It was "a great big state funeral, a horrible affair," remembered Perkins. Roosevelt declared Swanson's passing "a great loss" to the nation, and this spectacle, too, reflected an increasing sense of dangerous times.[39]

That was because Swanson embodied the rise of America's preeminence at sea. An unparalleled peacetime expansion had been going on from the depth of the Depression in 1933: 197 warships completed or underway, including aircraft carriers and 8 battleships. To be sure, Swanson reported to the ultimate navy president (who would have been happier with 197,000 warships). FDR immediately replaced the fallen hero with Charles Edison, Swanson's deputy.

The cost of the overall army and navy buildup during the Great Depression came to more than $6 billion, and Franklin Roosevelt was happy to avoid the limelight on this one. Nonetheless, Republicans would soon denounce him for neglect.

In summer 1939 came what looked like an authentic loss to the country. Hopkins was still trying to form a presidential base in Iowa. When he appeared in the Cabinet on July 14, however, he looked pallid and told Ickes he felt sick. He had been operated on in May for a throat infection and was rarely in his office. He "began to get sicker and sicker," recalled Perkins. "Averell Harriman was helping him out," she added, but Hopkins was not going to be the whirlwind commerce secretary everyone had expected.[40]

He became nearly unreachable until ultimately returning to the Mayo Clinic in mid-August. The White House physician finally told Ickes that Hopkins's intestinal agonies had come from cancer. At this time, FDR doubted that Hopkins would ever be able to work again.

The economy was sputtering, and so, by August 2 and 3, FDR had

back-to-back lunches with Wallace and then Eccles, from whom he heard
nothing positive. Late on the morning of the seventh, he left on his special
train for Hyde Park to spend four days handling minor appointments,
conducting two small press conferences, and writing to his mother in
Paris. He was then driven to lower Manhattan to board the heavy cruiser
Tuscaloosa for Campobello Island and fishing.

FDR's leadership had a monarchical detachment. He did not need to
be crouched over the White House ticker while war loomed in Europe.
It made no difference where he might be. He was in charge, receiving by
plane or ship the most important paperwork, such as bills to be signed
or vetoed. He possessed a quick eye for details: subordinates could never
anticipate which ones he might check.

On August 23, he was sailing from Halifax, Nova Scotia, to Sandy
Hook, New Jersey, when the world learned of the ten-year Hitler-Stalin
nonaggression treaty signed in Moscow, Germans calling it the *Teufels-
freundschaft,* "Devils' friendship." Secretary of State Hull and Under Secretary Welles met the president the following afternoon at Union Station.
They spoke for twenty minutes in his train car, then regrouped at the
White House that evening. The Cabinet was scheduled to convene the
next day, the usual Friday at 2 P.M.

By then, FDR had been weighing every possibility. Here too, blame
seemed to rest upon England for not first aligning with Stalin before he
sidled up to Hitler.

A German attack on Poland now looked certain, and in the Cabinet
meeting, Roosevelt anticipated the worst. In case of war, he explained,
marines were to occupy the engine rooms of German vessels in U.S. ports.
That would avert crews sabotaging their own ships, which had occurred
when Congress declared war in 1917. And war matériel should be rushed
into Canada or shipped beyond the three-mile limit before he was compelled by law to declare neutrality.

Exactly a week later the Cabinet reconvened—on Friday, September
1, sixteen hours after German tanks had blitzed into Poland while the
Luftwaffe began to raze Warsaw. Early that morning, Roosevelt's first
pronouncement had been an appeal to the belligerents to refrain from
"bombardment from the air of civilian populations or of unfortified cities."[41]

Perkins was in Maine, where she listened to the news on a car radio, before catching the 11 P.M. sleeper out of Boston. Only Ickes and Wallace were at their end of the table. Hopkins was bedridden at the Minnesota clinic but expected to be home after the weekend. He did not realize he was dying.

What each of the four was thinking can pretty well be assessed, and their thoughts closely matched Roosevelt's. Hitler assuredly despised the democracies and those who led them, yet they were incredulous that even this most depraved of dictators would choose to gamble on a war of annihilation.

LINE OF FIRE

War in September 1939 to Attack
in Western Europe, May 1940

Here is to Sara and Eleanor Roosevelt. One of them borned him, and
the other married him, and both of them advertised him.
Frances Perkins, March 4, 1940. Her toast for that year's
Cabinet dinner honoring FDR (which she decided not to give).

The war that opened with an order to British officers to sharpen their
swords would end in a heave of nuclear ash—from a bomb that had
been brought into existence only sixty-one years after the invention
of a device as simple as the ammunition clip. The world was being remade, as factories rolled out B-17 Flying Fortresses faster than Model Ts
had so recently been clanged together.

The First World War had been the generals' war, in which the hec-
atombs of the Western Front were the acceptable price of winning one
more shattered village or leveled wood. The Second would be the politicians', as radio and the lost illusions of 1914–1918 enabled them to lean
over the shoulders of their uniformed experts. The clout of home front
administrators became far greater as well.

Britain and France declared war on Sunday, September 3. That evening, FDR assured his nation of America's neutrality. The Marine Corps
boarding parties he had envisioned the previous week would have to
wait. America itself was not at war. Then he summoned the Cabinet for a
special meeting that Monday afternoon.

By law, he told his official family, a statement of neutrality had to be
issued, though he sought delay. There was much to consider, including
how to reorganize the Administration for war. Maybe he could use the
1918 statute, never repealed, that had created the Council of National

Defense. This body had consisted ex officio of the secretaries of war and navy—and also of interior, agriculture, commerce, and labor. Twenty-one years later, that meant Ickes, Wallace, Hopkins, Perkins, and two fading nonentities.

However, said FDR, he would likely wish to add representatives from business and the unions. His Cabinet meetings were never interrupted, yet at this point an usher entered to hand Ickes a message. Jane had delivered a baby boy, all was well, and the doctor from Johns Hopkins Hospital waited on the phone. Ickes sent a note up the table asking to be excused, and the president, who knew the situation, gave a smiling nod. That evening, Ickes phoned FDR from Baltimore to share the excitement. The president congratulated him and then burst into a diatribe about Wallace's unhelpful attitude after Ickes had left.

Apparently, Wallace had advised against proclaiming a state of emergency, even though doing so multiplies a president's authority. For example, the Communications Act of 1934 contains a provision—still valid today—that allows a president to suspend broadcasting overall by decreeing an "emergency." FDR had just announced one, notwithstanding Wallace's advice. Except this took the form of a limited emergency. He had already stretched the elastic when it came to Congress regarding him as trustworthy.

On the same day that the Cabinet met, September 4, Europe was being consumed by war. Everyone at the table, as Perkins remembered, believed the conflict would spread on a yet greater scale. In New Delhi, the viceroy had made the immediate decision, together with London, to bring all of giant India into the fight. By Sunday evening (Greenwich Mean Time), New Zealand and Australia had acted on their own constitutionally given right to declare war on Germany. South Africa, another co-equal dominion, had to vote out its own government before committing itself on the sixth.

Washington observed with fascination. Canada, which Roosevelt had pledged only a year earlier to defend, was saying nothing. And so, on Tuesday the fifth, Secretary of State Hull telephoned Ottawa to ask if, perhaps, Britain's declaration of war meant Canada too was at war. "No," answered the prime minister. Canada finally entered on the tenth. As this sequence shows, no one in the U.S. capital understood how the British Empire and Commonwealth functioned.

On September 17, the Red Army, faithful partner of Hitler, attacked Poland from the east. Stalin cut a new Soviet-German border to run through that obliterated nation and shipped a half million Poles into the Gulag, an acronym for Stalin's vast "archipelago" of so-called corrective labor camps.[1] The Kremlin's official myth, to this day, remains that its rapprochement with Nazism bought Stalin time to prepare for war, an argument conclusively debunked. Instead, the partnership enabled Stalin to divide the spoils, while giving him a free hand also to occupy Estonia, Latvia, and Lithuania.

Perkins had already detected two perilous aspects of this collusion: America would inevitably be pulled into the war, as Roosevelt believed; and U.S. labor unions, in turn, were ever more endangered by Communist penetration. For Americans, the Crash, the Depression, and now another European inferno looked to be a pattern of eternal emergency. Couldn't the country keep its distance from this one, many of them hoped?

As in domestic politics, FDR had an uncanny sense of timing. He told Ickes at lunch in mid-September that Germany would either have gained ascendancy over Britain and France by June 1940 or have to risk falling apart internally. He expected the Low Countries to be invaded—and so he made a grand, secretly conveyed offer to Queen Wilhelmina of the Netherlands that November. She and her children could be "members of our own family" should they need refuge in America.[2]

Earlier in the year, FDR had explained to senators of the Military Affairs Committee that he approved of selling weaponry to Britain and France in order for the United States to have breathing room to rearm. Inevitably, his reasoning leaked out and whatever he said was reported as "American frontiers are on the Rhine." Such an expansive vision infuriated the large number of people set against European entanglements. FDR used the familiar excuse of politicians to insist he had been misquoted. As it turned out, he was only twenty-one years early: when candidate John F. Kennedy asserted the same six words in 1960, no one thought it amiss. In both cases, the remark played well with Europe's democracies.[3]

Nonetheless, by fall 1939, Secretary of War Woodring—virulently opposed to any such military dealings—had been undercutting his chief's efforts for many months. And so, when FDR judged it time enough, he had asked Morgenthau to head a special coordinating committee to short-circuit Woodring and ship over patrol aircraft, fighter planes, and munitions to Britain and France. In fact, Morgenthau was already pressing FDR to do so. As a result, Ickes grew quite well disposed to Morgenthau, with whom he was cooperating on questions of Spain and refugees. In turn, Morgenthau that fall was pushing FDR to name Ickes secretary of war. By now, Wallace had grown similarly tolerant of Morgenthau, despite finding him "a little slow in catching what was going on."[4]

All very well, except that Harry Dexter White, a key assistant to Morgenthau, and soon the liaison between the Treasury and State Departments on all foreign policy matters, was a Soviet agent, with his own nearby NKVD handler. And, as we'll see, so were more figures high in the Administration.[5]

Still, Roosevelt was trying to awaken the country to the fact that it was part of the world though much of the press and public were suspicious. In late 1939, newsmen looked back to find a name for the tumultuous era covered by his presidency, which, after two terms, was likely coming to an end. *Time* suggested "Age of Distrust."[6] Americans did not trust their social system, the economy, Washington, or any of the belligerents overseas. Lots of the mistrust had been sown by the president himself and by Hopkins, his "adviser No. 1," just to recall purging and court-packing.

Toward Asia, the U.S. stood in fall 1939 much as it had for two years: wait, avoid fighting Japan, yet support China, which had not collapsed as feared at the time of the "rape of Nanjing." Gallup polls showed that nearly three-quarters of Americans favored embargoing war-making materials to Japan, but the U.S. ambassador in Tokyo warned FDR that cutting off steel exports, and the American oil on which Japan relied for 80 percent of its consumption, risked triggering war.

As for Germany, Professor Moley, now a columnist for *Newsweek,* snickered at Ickes and Wallace imagining Nazi assaults on the Americas, as well as at FDR's wanting to "police the world." Ohio's first-term senator, Robert Taft, son of the twenty-seventh president and already seeking the GOP's 1940 nomination, echoed Moley. He assured the nation that it was as unlikely that a German army would invade America as it was that an American army would invade Germany.

That said, in war it is nearly always the defeated of the last struggle who do the deepest and hardest thinking. It is they who keep themselves open to radical ideas, determined to do better next time. They have no lulling memories of success. This is what the world faced from Germany, at a time when domestic politics constricted Roosevelt's room for maneuvering against it.

Harry Hopkins was not part of the grave anxieties of these months. Doctors at the Mayo Clinic had pulled him back from the edge of death, and in late September, they transferred him to the Naval Hospital in Washington before he would be allowed to return home in mid-October, still under strict medical care. Ickes phoned him right away, to hear Hopkins explain that he was confined to bed and unable to see anyone, albeit insisting he was better.

Nonetheless, Hopkins's influence was making itself felt. On September 1, George Marshall became chief of staff of the army and its air corps, still, altogether, made up of fewer than two hundred thousand men. Marshall's biographer credits the general's "strange friendship" with Harry Hopkins for his leap in rank from one star to four.[7] It was a friendship of opposites. Hopkins was genuinely awed by Marshall, fifty-nine, who had risen slowly through the ranks—a calming, pared-down citizen-soldier. In turn, Marshall was intrigued by Hopkins's speedy ascent, bureaucratic techniques, and adaptability, a quality that flag officers prize in wartime.

Promptly, Marshall let it be known that only a quarter of his men were equipped to fight, and, as he testified to Congress, time was running out.

Upon the outbreak of war in Europe, most of the Americans who cared expected Britain and its empire, along with France, to cope with the Hitler menace. Britain, too, had a small regular army, but one with a tradition of expanding fast, being backstopped by the dominions and enormous colonial levies, and of a quality that had made Germany's general staff call it "the perfect thing apart."[8] Additionally, the Royal Navy was the world's largest, and generally rated the best. It immediately imposed a blockade on Germany, as in the last war, just as FDR expected.

Wallace and Ickes also exhorted outright rearmament, though Wallace at least recognized the constraints imposed by a faltering economy. During these months, he would examine why America remained stuck in the Depression and press his findings on FDR.

The reasons, he argued, were these: The continued pace of laborsaving technological change had created high unemployment; little expansion was likely in mature industries such as automobiles and radio; the big coal and rail sectors offered poor returns on capital; and an overhang existed from the 1920s real estate glut. All was now worsened by dwindling foreign investment and lost overseas markets.[9]

Yet Wallace's first two conclusions were topsy-turvy, although shared by thinkers like Eccles. Even Keynes, who was passing into journalistic folklore, had little sense of U.S. industrial power and could not imagine the dynamism about to unfold. The House of Morgan he knew well. Yet he did not factor into his equations such grease-under-the-thumbnails tycoons as Henry Ford or aviation pioneer Glenn Martin, let alone the unknown shipbuilders about to expand production fourteen-fold in just four years.

Neither did Wallace have reason to anticipate government spending on a Keynesian scale, large enough to finally stimulate heavy industry. Always lukewarm about borrowing, FDR had found one thing on which he could agree with Vice President Garner: they were baffled by this "doctrine that the deeper in debt we get, the richer we will be."[10]

Roosevelt still yearned for balanced budgets, despite the experience of his eponymous recession, and his efforts were typified in 1939 by what Wallace labeled the president's "autumnal custom." The fiscal year of that era ran from July 1 to June 30. At budget time, FDR would cut his departments' arduously prepared spending plans line by line, a task he enjoyed.

"I cut out $500 million; no, I think it was $600 million" from Agriculture, he told Wallace that fall. When Wallace turned pale, he added that Wallace should cheer up because next he was going "to operate on Harold."[11]

Roosevelt's pseudo budget-cutting ritual reveals the administrative chaos our four had to face. Each year, once Congress had passed the federal budget, Roosevelt would then thunder to Wallace, or one of the others, something like, "Tell Jesse not to be a Hebrew, and tell him I said so"—meaning banker Jesse Jones, head of the RFC, had to find more cash.[12] In truth, little or nothing was being cut. The president was just subtracting money from one year to account for it in another, and "doing a lot of strange monkey business which I didn't think brought him a thing," said Wallace.[13]

Soon the national debt would surpass $45 billion—which seemed to confirm the dread of Aldrich, Senator Glass, and others at FDR's recklessness. That sum was 40 percent of national production (compared with today's debt level of more than 100 percent), and Wallace expected public outrage over this impossible number to bring trouble at the polls in November 1940.

From his sickbed, Hopkins gamely tried to participate in FDR's autumnal amusements. He remained desperately ill, although Ickes was finally able to visit, stopping at Hopkins's house on the way home one day in early December. Hopkins was still confined to bed save for all but two hours a day. At least he had time to plow through his Commerce Department budget, he joked, except that he was having the "customary difficulty with Morgenthau" at this time of year—meaning the Treasury worked with the president on budget cuts.[14]

To a credulous press, Hopkins was even now suffering "a bout of stomach ulcers."[15] Nor were newsmen more penetrating about the life of Henry Wallace, who arrived for his own, grimmer, visit a week later.

Over the years, reporters had come to picture Wallace as a crank. Lean and fit at fifty-two, Wallace clung to crazy behaviors. He trained in the seldom-used Senate gym, rather than getting his exercise in the steam room, as did most legislators; and he climbed Pikes Peak, which for twenty-five years had boasted a perfectly good road to the top, up which Wallace might have driven. In winter, he kept the temperature of his office at a steady 68 degrees. His diet largely comprised fish, vegetables, and nuts, and he was unbeatable at paddleball—while disdaining golf and the Nineteenth Hole.

Moreover, he lived in a different intellectual world. His favorite poet was Robert Frost, and he studied languages and equations for fun. Little of this endeared him to newsmen who made their living by chronicling Washington's merry-go-round of personalities. They had little desire to ask Wallace about cross models or Indo-European linguistic structures.

When Wallace came over to Georgetown, he was on a mission and, as usual, had little time for Harry's mordant wit. What was the latest diagnosis, he asked the bedridden patient? Hopkins described the chronic weakness, cramping, and diarrhea. He added that he was on yet another special diet, this one devised by his Naval Hospital physician—and, at the time, according to medical biographer Steven Lomazow, the hospital would have been state-of-the-art on intestinal diseases.[16]

Yet Hopkins was basically starving to death. Thankfully, he had added sixteen pounds since coming home, though this was due to his being fed three times a week through his rectum. And still he remained gaunt, at 143 pounds. Worryingly, he exhibited edema of the legs; and his eyesight was failing while his upper intestinal tract could not absorb proteins or vitamins.

At this point, he cooperated enough with Wallace to read a Department of Agriculture yearbook on nutrition, *Food and Life* (1939). Wallace's help in keeping him alive seems to have been crucial, beginning with the insight that Hopkins could assimilate protein from vegetables and cheese. Ever after, Hopkins was sustained by specially made nutrients, which he carried in a satchel along with medicines.

It is doubtful that this complex blend of nutrients originated with Naval Hospital physicians, or that they kept producing them year after year. More likely, Wallace mobilized scientists within his now 146,000-employee department. By no coincidence, and with the right nutrients, Hopkins rebounded quickly after Wallace's visit. Come mid-January, he was able to take short walks in Georgetown and, by February, was back at the Cabinet Room table.

During the late 1930s, "isolationist" was a term applied pejoratively by critics to people intent on keeping "the war hounds of Europe" at bay—and the enlarged government that would follow, too.[17] All four lieutenants decried "isolationism," as they understood it. Perkins did so fervently. She was among those upper-class New Yorkers convinced that it was America's duty "to defend the poor old mother who might be in trouble."[18]

In contrast, Roosevelt deployed a nuanced view. Of course, it was in America's interest to help defend Britain's democracy, but it is naive to think that he entertained any special affinity for Britain. To call him an "Anglo-Saxon" reflects the same misconceptions held in London at the time.[19] Weren't all Americans really Englishmen who had changed their accents? Far from it: he was an heir of Manhattan's earliest Dutch settlers, and "Anglo-Saxon" was a strange way to describe someone named "Delano Roosevelt."

FDR's views of Britain were closer to those of Wallace, who was wary about London's efforts to get its "chestnuts pulled out of the fire," and both men were alert to the attempt of "Tory England"—a dismissive term for Britain's class-ridden elites—to manipulate the United States.[20] To be sure, Roosevelt was "pro-British." He was also pro-French, and *very* pro-Dutch. Other men around him were entirely less accepting of Britain.

One was Tommy Corcoran, whom newsmen, during the long months of Hopkins's absence, began to label FDR's chief adviser. Centuries of brutal Saxon oppression in Ireland, wrote Tommy in an unpublished memoir, made George VI's state visit to Washington repellent. Similarly, FDR's former law partner, Basil O'Connor—as well as O'Connor's brother, a conservative New York congressman—were patriotic Irishmen with long unforgiving memories, though perhaps not as long as that of thin, gray Peter Goelet Gerry of Rhode Island. This aristocratic Democratic senator, whom FDR had known since they were children, declared his opposition to aiding Britain: after all, his family angrily "remembered the redcoats."[21]

Additional skeptics weighed in. FDR valued the opinions of Adolf Berle, the former Brain Truster whom he had appointed an assistant secretary of state. During an Oval Office meeting, Berle reminded him that America had been "virtually an adjunct to the British war machine" during the World War. It should not happen again, he cautioned, and Roosevelt concurred.[22] Yet they recognized that the immediate problem was to counter America's antiwar movement of the time, to be known as "isolationism."

They agreed that a world-class rabble-rousing agitator of their own had to be tossed into the ring. Their opponents had several, including Idaho's renowned orator, Senator William Borah, and, at the grubby extreme, the radio priest Father Coughlin. In his heavy, choppy way, Berle then voiced what Roosevelt was thinking: "Ickes seems to be the best bet, and the demagogue style is right down his alley."

Berle by now believed Ickes to be a "pure psychoneurotic." Certainly, Ickes did not need encouraging.[23] Ten months earlier, he had ridiculed Charles Lindbergh as the "Knight of the German Eagle" for accepting that swastika-bedecked medal from Göring's fattened hand—and for seeing no reason, as an American hero, to return it three weeks later after *Kristallnacht*. Since then, Lindbergh had become yet more outspoken—and even more deeply alarmed at Englishmen and Jews than by the Reich.

Lindbergh and FDR had met only once, for thirty minutes the previous April. Of course, Lindbergh liked the president, while still recognizing FDR's likability as being dangerous. After his child's kidnapping, and ghoulish attention from the press and public, Lindbergh had moved his family to an isolated, feudal corner of England, and then to a small island off the rocky north coast of Brittany, on the edge of France. Foremost, he was a flyer and technologist whose loyalties were international, which kept him on excellent terms with fellow aviators in Berlin.

He was a highly intelligent man with a simple mind, which qualified him to be a close working colleague of Nobel laureate surgeon Alexis Carrel, who nursed his own repellent opinions about eugenics. Lindbergh, a colonel in the air corps until resigning his commission in April 1941, was still immensely popular, and he approached the perils of high politics with the same certitudes that had enabled him to fly solo across the Atlantic. In 1939, he provided a fabulous name around which FDR's opponents could rally.

The Neutrality Act obstructed Roosevelt's efforts to get war matériel to the democracies once they declared war on the Axis. Fortunately, Congress redrafted the act, which he signed at noon on November 4, 1939. It lifted the outright arms embargo upon warring states, thereby allowing munitions to be exported openly to Britain and France. Nonetheless, legislators still hesitated to place much authority in FDR's hands, and by no means dropped the act entirely, as he had hoped.

Time was wasted through November trying to figure out what the revised Neutrality Act meant. Then, on the thirtieth, Stalin invaded the republic of Finland. His pact with Hitler had given him a free hand over this nation too. Aping its Nazi ally, the USSR declared war by bombing Helsinki at dawn. Wallace was anxious. One of his sisters, Ruth, lived with her family in Helsinki, where—on the latest front line—her husband was Sweden's ambassador.

The Cabinet, still without Hopkins, met as scheduled the next afternoon. All agreed that Stalin was "more than out-Hitlering Hitler."[24] The most perceptive people at the table—Ickes, Perkins, and Wallace— witnessed FDR acting with a rare purposefulness. Provoked by what he called "the rape of Finland," he ordered an embargo on the USSR, whether legal or not. Wallace, in turn, began to work with executives of the Farm Bureau and the Grange to organize food shipments.

Roosevelt also turned to internal security. He warned Cabinet officers that their phones were likely tapped, though by whom he did not specify: Nazis, Communists, or both. Then he revisited the prospects of finger-printing, which, he insisted, had become a defense necessity. Why not fingerprint munitions workers? Again, Perkins objected. What, the president asked her, if he made his case over the radio and told Americans he himself had been fingerprinted? Once more Perkins disagreed, and Ickes supported her, as did Wallace. Others at the table stayed mum.

Doubts were growing within the official family, as on Capitol Hill, about Roosevelt's sense of civil liberties.

He reopened this dispute in Cabinet on December 22, coming as close as was gentlemanly possible to ordering Perkins immediately to fingerprint every alien seeking to enter the country. When she balked, he suggested that a better argument might be to stress how fingerprinting prevented crime. This didn't convince Perkins, either, who knew from her early days at Labor that it was pernicious to group aliens with criminals. After the meeting, she asked Ickes what she should do. *Do not give in,* he said.

The term "counter-intelligence" surfaced during these months—a capability that America so far lacked. As Roosevelt knew, government departments barely cooperated to shield confidential information from foreign eyes. He directed the FBI to ferret out spies, but the bureau's expertise lay in pursuing crooks.

At this point, Roosevelt—as did Ickes, Perkins, and Wallace—seriously feared Nazi infiltration. Berlin's tentacles, for instance, could by now be seen reaching into the Bund, and penetrating extremist groups of which, as today, there was no shortage. Ickes identified about 150, including the Christian Mobilizers, the Silver Shirt Legion, the Christian Front, the Knights of the White Camelia—and of course the Klan. Even mainstream patriot organizations seemed to be vulnerable. Agnes Peter of Tudor Place, whose family was known deferentially as the "Original Proprietors of the City of Washington," passed it on to Wallace that the Colonial Dames were encountering Nazi overtures.

Unexplained funds were also rumored to be nourishing such influential midwestern papers as *The Gazette,* in Cedar Rapids, Iowa, and dark money was penetrating Congress.

In January 1940, Senator Borah, seventy-five years old and the ranking

Republican on the Foreign Relations Committee, died suddenly after a fall. He had become an ally of Ickes's in fighting corporate monopolies, and Jane had beguiled him at the state dinner for the British monarchs. Yet Borah hated all Anglo-American connections. A civilized opponent of global meddling, he had sympathized with Germany after Versailles. However, by the late 1930s, he spoke more consistently for the Reich than any other senator did for any other nation, while comparing Hitler favorably to Charlemagne. He fought FDR's spending on the navy, as he had any lifting of the arms embargo on Britain and France. This pattern of action still puzzles writers today.[25]

Borah had lived off his salary in conspicuous simplicity. He had no investments, nor did he gamble, and his obituary in *The New York Times* reported that he died relatively poor for a senator. Ten days later, the *Times* reversed itself. Nearly $200,000 in government bonds (about the income of 180 median American households) had turned up in a safe deposit box. Nobody knows how he got this, though Oklahoma's former senator Thomas Gore, who stayed on in Washington, believed he knew. His blindness enabled him to elicit many confidences, and, Gore told family, it was from "the Nazis. To keep us out of war."[26]

Already in 1938, Ickes had been the first top official to back Roosevelt for an unprecedented third term. He disdained Hopkins's "nurturing his own sickly and absurd boom" for the presidency. In any event, Hopkins's chances were derailed by illness and by Iowa's Democratic Party grandees in early 1940. They decided to back Wallace for the nomination, but only in the event that FDR declined to run.

Roosevelt had brushed off sallies about whether he was pursuing a third term, and he didn't seem to mind other Democrats competing for the nomination, although he warned Perkins, among others, that a Roman Catholic—meaning party chairman Jim Farley—would be un-electable. Then there was Wallace. However, by the end of 1939, Wallace had detected that Roosevelt was determined to stay in office.

If ever a sign existed that FDR had it in for you, it would be his earnest assertion that you would make a far better president than he. Wallace was therefore cautious about displaying his ambitions: to be seen hungering for the Oval Office, he knew, meant "getting it in the neck."[27]

The smooth, erudite Democratic chairman of the Bronx, Edward J. Flynn, one of the preeminent big-city bosses, examined the question of a third term. Overlooking Perkins, he concluded that the New Deal's three major pillars—Hopkins, Ickes, and Wallace—were largely responsible for pushing the idea. They were doing so, he believed, because each knew that any Democrat who took office other than Roosevelt, let alone a Republican, would fire them all.

Vice President Garner, lacking any interest in remaining VP, declared his own candidacy in December 1939, although, as FDR told his close supporter, Senator Burton K. Wheeler of Montana, "I love Jack Garner personally, but he could not get the nigger vote."[28] (Garner himself did not use that slur, nor did decent people, including any of our four.) Nevertheless, polls placed Garner as the leading Democratic prospect, should Roosevelt retire.

By this juncture, ill feeling between Garner and Roosevelt went deep, despite that "love." Earlier, in 1937, an argument over sit-down strikes had erupted in the Oval Office in which the two men showered foul language on each other. Since then, relations had been caustic. FDR taunted Garner, as by deriding congressmen as "all Uriah Heeps"—Garner having been one for thirty years—and by ridiculing his success in business. Maybe, Roosevelt suggested, Garner might chisel out an extra 5 percent return on his investments. Hopkins found such remarks "priceless."[29]

Garner went about his duties, one of them being to meet the president in the Oval Office at noon on January 2, 1940, the day before Congress convened. He brought along the House and Senate leadership: Speaker William Bankhead of Alabama, Senate Majority Leader Alben Barkley of Kentucky, and another Texas protégé, House Majority Leader Sam Rayburn. They were to discuss legislation, and a certain bill was again before Congress.

"We ought to pass the anti-lynching bill at this session," urged Garner.

"But down in your state and elsewhere in the South they say that the anti-lynching bill is unconstitutional," replied Roosevelt.

Garner, the shrewdest of all legislative strategists, was ready, and whatever he promised was certain to occur on Capitol Hill.

"Well the court would not have time to pass on it until after the election," he answered. "I can talk to [Texas senator] Tom Connally and line him up and you can get other southern Democrats to support the bill.

It would pass the House easily, and I think we could put it through the Senate by a two to one vote."[30]

Given Garner's longstanding views, it is misguided to see this dialogue as a ploy for the Democratic nomination. Of course, Garner had the November election in mind. One did not converse with FDR on a serious issue without finding a political element, or having calculated the electoral consequences.

At stake was the loyalty of Blacks in northern cities—a loyalty Republicans were toiling to reclaim. However, Democrats hoped again to win the Black vote as in 1936, whether or not FDR was on the ballot. For them to federalize the crime of lynching would make that certain. Yet, if Democrats on the Hill succeeded in passing the anti-lynching bill, Garner might reap the credit, which could benefit his run for the presidency.

For FDR, this meeting was one more hoot. He had to share the fun right away, as he did that evening with Tommy Corcoran while they worked on the annual budget message, and Tommy informed his other patron, a puzzled Harold Ickes, the next day at lunch.

Sometime later, Roosevelt confided the story to Farley, while Missy LeHand listened. "I have the grandest joke for you," Farley recalled being told, and Roosevelt "laughed till tears came down his eyes." As he had done with Tommy, the president guffawed about the absurdity of "old Jack" lining up the South against lynching. "Don't you love it?"[31]

Roosevelt could only think of Garner's electoral aims; absent the president's backing, Garner's plan went nowhere. The anti-lynching bill again passed the House, eight days after this visit, and then returned to the Senate. There, Tom Connally instead threatened a filibuster, and the bill lingered in the upper chamber until it died in October. The Anti-Lynching Act, which makes lynching a federal hate crime, would not arrive until 2022.

Roosevelt prided himself on being from Georgia just as much as from New York, according to Wallace, and believed he understood his Southern neighbors.[32] Ickes had none of this sympathy toward the South and joined with Wallace, who was worried enough about the GOP reconstituting itself as "the party of Lincoln" to discuss "the Negro problem" with FDR after the Cabinet met on January 26.

The Republicans, they explained, were providing "key Negroes" jobs in the Republican National Committee. Roosevelt knew this—which should have been no surprise—and he put forward a solution: It would be a good time to give Negroes some District judgeships.[33] Lynching, however, was no longer before the Cabinet.

Prime Minister Chamberlain called the months preceding April 1940 the "twilight war" because a false peace shadowed western Europe. No cities in the west had yet turned into Wellsian infernos, and the great fortifications were upholding the status quo—the Maginot Line, the 390-mile-long German Siegfried Line that lay opposite it, and the largest and strongest fortress in the world, Belgium's Eben-Emael. The armies of Britain, France, and Germany squared off, yet held their fire.

About 70 percent of Americans wanted to keep out of the war, according to polling after the first month of hostilities, even if Britain and France faced defeat. By January 1940, Roosevelt's annual message to Congress seemed divided: America would remain neutral, though the war was very much its business, and the army and navy would be strengthened.

For Ickes, the new year should have been the happiest of times. He was at his country home with Jane and their child, yet he was wrenched between his ambitions. He learned from Tommy that Roosevelt was considering him for secretary of war. To have the chance of pummeling Germany and Japan, however, meant sacrificing his dream of creating a Conservation Department.

On New Year's Day, a shiny black seven-passenger Packard drove up the mile-long private road of the Ickes residence. Its only passenger was the president's mother, Sara, paying a call on Jane and hoping to see four-month-old Harold Jr. Mrs. James Roosevelt was candid about her affections. She never much liked Harold Sr., but she approved of Jane's pedigree and warmed to her good nature.

So flattering a visit to his splendid estate gratified Ickes for only a minute. Already he felt that FDR had crushed his spirit by having removed him from the Public Works Administration. It mattered little to Ickes that, in October, the president had appointed him to chair the National Defense Power Committee, which oversaw the country's biggest energy projects. The Forest Service—well defended by timber interests and old-school foresters alike—remained out of reach.

Ickes's nerves had never been worse, nor had he slept less. He doubted whether he could go on, and his "clam-up days" (Perkins's phrase), when he spoke to virtually no one, became more frequent. It was only a minor annoyance that Cissy Patterson's now-expanded *Times-Herald*, the capital's best-selling paper, was eviscerating his every public utterance.

Still, one delight was Hopkins's return to the Cabinet on January 26 for the first time since summer. He looked pale and weak, though he insisted that he felt better. Anyway, he asked, as the secretary of commerce, wasn't there lots to do about employment and production?

Ickes usually kept quiet during debates over the economy and conditions indeed were perplexing for anyone. The previous quarter's forecasts had been dismal, yet signs of recovery were sufficient to cheer Roosevelt until Wallace pricked his balloon: "The advance in business is just as sound as the war, Mr. President."[34] Wallace, who had immersed himself in Keynes's writings, recognized that economic vigor would last only as long as did the Administration's unprecedented peacetime outlays.

Hopkins and Ickes meanwhile returned to old habits when Perkins embarked on her longest, most stern lecture to date, concerning unemployment. Twenty minutes lumbered by, then thirty.

"We're having an advanced course," whispered Hopkins.

"No," Ickes whispered back, "this is a full semester."

When Perkins brought up "frictional" unemployment—deriving from the time lag between workers moving from one job to the next—the president seemed tickled.

As the meeting closed, Ickes shared his irritation with Wallace as both men headed out the door. "She lectures to us just like we were in a seminar."

"We're all different," replied Wallace, speaking as if he were a parent.[35]

It was an annoying response, but Ickes's latest outburst over the Forest Service, which remained in Wallace's grip, refocused itself on the president. On February 7, he sent FDR a formal letter of resignation via Missy LeHand. "I cannot be true to myself," he reiterated, without heading a Department of Conservation.[36] It has been an honor, Mr. President, and good-bye.

When Missy gave Roosevelt the letter, he hit the ceiling, snapping at her to call Harold immediately. Roosevelt thundered that Ickes was making his life miserable.

Ickes was among the few who were allowed to glimpse Roosevelt's own powers of volcanic rage. When the president "let go," as he called it, rooms echoed with "Goddamned this" and "Goddammed that." Yet once more the lava cooled, and Roosevelt pledged to get Ickes the Forest Service.

Hours later, there followed that penciled note from the president about the two of them being "married," for better or worse, and it being too late for a divorce. On other occasions, he had written to Ickes as if to a child: "My dear Harold, will you ever grow up?"

"You can't believe a Goddam thing he says," Ickes concluded around this time, yet simultaneously it was he who ensured Roosevelt's name was being entered in every state primary during that winter and spring.[37]

If New Deal liberalism was to last much beyond 1940, Ickes recognized, the subject of what had set Perkins to buzzing was a vital one. She still headed the Economic Security Committee—the "Cabinet Committee"—and worked with Wallace to examine why joblessness remained so disturbingly stuck at 14.5 percent. There was nothing amusing each week in the Cabinet Room when Roosevelt asked Hopkins to report on *The New York Times*' Weekly Business Index, the era's definitive measuring stick of such progress as had been made since 1929.

"All of the orthodox methods of meeting unemployment have been tried," Perkins told Wallace, with unexpected brevity, and still the CIO leaders were pressuring her to "do something."

Perkins had asked John L. Lewis and his friends what they proposed, to learn they also had nothing to offer. Exasperated, she wondered if FDR's presidency had brought this squeeze on itself by overemphasizing the problem. What was "normal" unemployment anyway? Regardless, nine million Americans remained jobless after seven years of the New Deal. Maybe more heretical measures should be tried, she argued to Wallace—such as going further to induce industry to expand production.

The certain way to concentrate Roosevelt's mind on an economic problem was to discuss it in political terms, which is what Wallace had been doing all through winter and spring.

By March 1940, Thomas Dewey, who had been elected district attorney of New York County two years earlier, was the GOP's front-running candidate for November. "Mr. President," Wallace said soon after, during lunch in the Oval Office, "both you and Dewey need to go further."[38] He implied that the two men's policies were indistinguishable, which opened

Roosevelt to being regarded as what today is called a deficit hawk—in brief, another tightfisted Republican.

Hopkins had also come to recognize that "the President's periodic concern for the [balanced] budget had resulted again and again in our making a half-hearted recovery."[39] By now Wallace and Hopkins were in agreement: throughout these years, the Treasury had been "just as re-actionary as under Mellon." Hopkins went further. He told Wallace that Morgenthau's bailiwick was worse because Hoover's treasury secretary at least knew what he was doing.[40]

The world of 1940 was too dangerous for a vacillating fiscal pol-icy, yet FDR kept wreaking havoc on the U.S. economy. Fortunately, the country was now at a point where his appalling shibboleths could be concealed by going all out on defense spending. Of course, none of his lieutenants phrased it this way, no matter what they thought.

In any event, a Depression-stunted U.S. leadership embarked in ear-nest that spring on immense military expenditures.

Wallace still had to attend to his duties at the Agriculture Department, and the president set him to work with Ickes on a problem of public graz-ing lands. Neither secretary would be the first to call the other. In April, when still nothing had moved forward on the Forest Service, Ickes again boycotted the Cabinet, spreading word that he was in no mood to see the president. On the other hand, it might be interesting to be secretary of war.

In early 1940, Franklin Roosevelt was becoming a world statesman. He used these months to seek peace in Europe, to build up U.S. airpower, and, before the Finns were forced to accept Soviet terms in March, to explore ways he could help them repel waves of badly led Red Army divisions in the bleak frozen borderlands.

If Congress refused to lend money to help Finland buy munitions, Roo-sevelt told his Cabinet, then the Administration should circumvent the Hill by selling arms to Sweden, which could transship matériel across the Gulf of Bothnia, perhaps to Turku, a city on Finland's southwest coast. Aiding the Finns would encourage other small nations—Denmark, the Netherlands, and Norway—to withstand the predator states. He did not add that Wallace's Swedish brother-in-law would have to facilitate such a plan.

Schemes such as this rankled former Speaker Garner, who knew less of the larger world but much about the Constitution. Roosevelt talked more boldly when Garner was not in the Cabinet Room. Should he attend, however, FDR would glare at him across the table when discussing military aid, and speak of Pontius Pilate's evading responsibility. Roosevelt might then pointedly pretend to wash his hands.

By this time, FDR felt the need for direct sources of intelligence more than ever. America still possessed no espionage service, and he disdained the "cookie pushers" at State, despite having been responsible for the department over nearly eight years. Jane's uncle was one useful source, and since January he had served as ambassador to Belgium, which held a pivotal geostrategic role. Its impregnable fortress of Eben-Emael—a mile in circumference and honeycombed with an internal railroad and thirty miles of corridors—dominated the vital nexus of Germany, Holland, and Belgium.

Wallace, in turn, shared insights with FDR on the west European standoff, received from his other brother-in-law, Charles Bruggmann, Switzerland's ambassador (technically "minister") in Washington since October. Bern afforded unique information: selected bankers and businessmen in Europe's capitals doubled as its Strategic Intelligence Service agents.

In late February 1940, Roosevelt dispatched Under Secretary of State Sumner Welles to explore any chance of reconciliation. Until now, Cordell Hull had spoken only favorably of Welles. But FDR had contrived this mission so narrowly that Hull learned of it just hours before Welles was to depart, and in the Cabinet, Perkins could tell by his face that Hull grieved over the slight.

At forty-eight, Welles was tall, slender, correctly tailored, and a forbidding career officer, fluent in five languages. His country seat, Oxon Hill, today embraces a suburban Washington town and his house on Massachusetts Avenue is the Cosmos Club. However, Wallace recognized that "behind this impressive exterior, there was inside the soul of a rather frightened small boy."[41] FDR knew Welles infinitely better. He had already discerned the psychosexual wounds and drawn him close.

In London Welles saw George VI—whose demeanor was now grim—and also Chamberlain. He met too with Churchill, sixty-five, who had joined Chamberlain's cabinet in a position equivalent to, though grander than, secretary of the navy. On March 2, Welles spent ninety minutes talking quietly with Hitler in Berlin's monstrous new chancellery, which looked like a factory building planted on the Wilhelmstrasse. Welles could report only what was tragically plain: every decision had already been made, precisely the dire news Roosevelt expected.

The weeks before Hitler made his next move sparked a jumble of ideas. For example, FDR conveyed a message to Bern via Wallace. "If the Germans should invade so much as one foot of Swiss soil," he asserted, Switzerland should fight, and he described to Wallace how best it could defend various mountain passes. Wallace asked, "Then what?" Of course, FDR admitted, America, given isolationist opinion, could do nothing at all.[42]

While Hitler planned and plotted, Wallace mused about how Roosevelt might actually perform in case of war. It was difficult to understand a man so ruthlessly self-centered as FDR, yet one who held an endless interest in other people. Wallace discussed the subject with Iowa senator Guy Gillette, who, having been targeted recently by Hopkins's elimination committee, was no fan of FDR. Despite all, Gillette thought Roosevelt would make "an unusually good 'war President,'" and so did Wallace.[43]

Wallace also asked Tugwell, who now chaired New York's City Planning Commission and still dined occasionally with the Roosevelts. Tugwell, who resented never having been brought into the Cabinet, was skeptical. When Wallace extolled FDR's amazing energy and described him as "a veritable Peter Pan," Tugwell replied that Peter Pans weren't known to be capable in global affairs. Nor, Tugwell added, did he "think the Japanese will be deterred by Peter Pans."[44]

Decidedly, there was a childish side to Roosevelt. He saw himself in the middle of excitements, like Peter Pan. "To die must be a very great adventure," says Peter. That is the feeling of a brave teenager, just as FDR's enthusiasm was accompanied by a childlike possessiveness. "Mah navy," he would say, as the admirals stared at the ceiling. There was also the juvenile cruelty.

That said, his lieutenants were discovering that the characteristics they had long deemed odd could also be those of a potentially daunting warlord. A commander needs to be feared, not by everyone perhaps, but by those many elements who must be compelled to agree with him.

Always, a commander of this rank casts a mystique, often enough mingling with his subordinates and fighting men, yet more than ready to act ruthlessly. FDR had shown himself to be fearless like his predecessor Ulysses Grant—to recall the icy courage displayed in Miami after the assassination attempt. And any wartime commander lives with tragedy on the scale of Cold Harbor. When things go wrong, he smiles and moves on. He is likely to be unpredictable and always capable of the fastest improvisation. He also finds it easy to delegate large swaths of authority, while, perhaps, acting at the edge of morality.

The four lieutenants came to see other attributes in a new light. Wallace most valued uplift. "I could come," he remembered, "and always go away with fresh energy, and fresh insight."[45] Perkins, in turn, thought Roosevelt's flexibility perfect for command. Both identified his masterly sense of geographic space, as did Ickes, who had never encountered anyone who knew geography so well. FDR grasped how distance and "broad ecological facts" of geography might overcome particular problems. They recognized him to be a visual person with his joy for stamp collecting, naval prints, and maps. Plus, there was always his disconcerting ability to read faces. All in all, they credited the sharpness of those visual qualities to the loss of his freedom, years before, to be the athlete he was.

And, again, Roosevelt's humor, when it was good-hearted, could prove essential to the cohesion of a small unit, such as our four. But, inevitably, there was always purpose to such levity.

For example, Perkins had sometime earlier modernized her Bureau of Labor Statistics. The pricing lists it compiled of manufactured goods turned out to be decades old, including the price of ladies' high-button shoes, last a fashion necessity in the late Victorian era. Perkins made the mistake of sharing this find with her chief. For the rest of his presidency, through the Depression and the World War, she could not mention "labor statistics" without his booming reply, "Oh, well, how much do ladies' high-button shoes cost now, Frances?"[46]

Of course, to hear this joke for the hundredth time while, say, one was trying to discuss wage rates in a munitions plant had its own degree of annoyance. And the very repetition of a joke is a more or less gentle reminder of who's in charge. In this case, it also served as a genial dismissal of the overly studious.

Whatever was happening on land, a naval war was surely underway, which included the sinking of the battleship *Royal Oak* by a U-boat within the main British base of Scapa Flow. Otherwise, Germany made no further attack after the Polish campaign until Tuesday, April 9, 1940, when it pounced on neutral Norway and Denmark.

Daisy Harriman's midnight telegram from Oslo to the watch officer at State was the first alert. Nearly simultaneously, the British asked Washington to assume their diplomatic interests in Norway. At 1 P.M., the president left Hyde Park for Washington. A press conference, and three days of foreign and domestic policy meetings ensued before the Cabinet convened on Friday, right after he had lunched with Wallace.

Ickes was still staging his boycott. All others in the Cabinet Room were appalled at the details filtering out of Europe. The attacks had succeeded with staggering speed. German soldiers in disguise, speaking Norwegian or Danish, had sprung out of nowhere, to be followed quickly by infantry divisions and warships. Sweden was now encircled given Germany's alliance with Moscow and Russia's hammering of Finland. That night the president had dinner as well with Wallace, Hopkins joining them to examine these latest disasters.

None had imagined such swiftness and stealth, nor had anyone in Washington thought about war like this. The rest of the country was equally shocked. The Aldriches, for instance, were in Colorado Springs to enter their son in prep school. Winthrop felt compelled to cut short his trip, telling reporters, as he left for New York, that the crisis at least should not affect Wall Street. Loans to Denmark and Norway had been made through the Export-Import Bank, a New Deal credit agency designed to boost American jobs.

The president felt no need to remain in Washington, leaving on the eighteenth for eleven days in Warm Springs, with whistle-stops in Virginia, the Carolinas, and then through Georgia. The pressure in government circles was palpably less when he left town. Not that Ickes cared if he never saw Roosevelt again, as he wrote in his diary—though, of course, Ickes did see him again. It was for lunch in the Oval Office on May 8, by which time Neville Chamberlain's government faced collapse for its inept responses to Hitler.

The same afternoon, Roosevelt wrote to Ambassador Cudahy in

Brussels about Hitler's latest threats to the Dutch and Belgian govern-ments. "Of course, my hope, being of the Netherlands on my Father's side and Belgium on my Mother's side, is that both nations will resist the rumored ultimatum to the bitter end."[47] The next night, at close to eleven o'clock, and after a long dinner with Vincent Astor, FDR was alerted to reports from Cudahy. German forces were storming across the border in a massive offensive against the neutral Low Countries. Only Berlin fully understood what had been unleashed at dawn on Friday, May 10.

The Cabinet met as usual that afternoon at two, Hopkins speaking flu-ently on war production. An usher interrupted at three fifteen with word that Chamberlain had resigned, to be replaced by Churchill, whom FDR acknowledged was probably England's best man. All this world-rending news at least brought harmony to the official family. Ickes became agree-able, and Vice President Garner—though still more opposed than ever to a third term—now welcomed arms shipments for Britain and France.

Mystery only compounded the disasters. How could the keystone of democratic defense, Eben-Emael, with a thousand defenders, itself too solid to bomb, have fallen within three hours, effectively turning the flank of France's Maginot Line?

Dark visions of some supersecret weapon haunted all national lead-erships in these modern times. From Berlin, Goebbels heralded a deadly machine and *The New York Times* conjectured about a war-winning in-vention or an anesthetizing gas. Instead, eighty storm troopers in skull-tight helmets and archaic/futuristic leather jerkins had staged a Valkyrie descent by glider. Once landed on Eben-Emael's roof, they burst the seams of this colossus with hollow chemical charges never before used in war.

Germany seemed to have united science fiction with its fearsome Prus-sian regimentation, and within weeks, given its alliance with Stalin, ruler of 180 million people, totalitarianism would stretch from the western coast of Europe to the Pacific. If Britain fell next, what then of still poorly armed America?

However, all things considered, the Depression had been contained, and the Republic was both more confident and more unified than it had been in 1933. For sixty years, America had been moving toward huge, agglomerated institutions—U.S. Steel, GM, GE, and Alcoa, just to start.

All had withstood a crushing decade, as had entrepreneurs such as spirited Henry Kaiser, whose empire was driving the industrialization of the American West.

If it was given the right leadership, the country was poised to attain immense material objectives by bringing together Big Government with Big Business and Big Labor. This was the orthodoxy of a New Deal great power, and the contest ahead might as well have been made for the United States.

PART III

Hope

DEVOTEES OF FORCE

Blitzkrieg of May 1940 to
FDR's Inauguration, January 1941

You have to lead men in war by requiring more
from the individual than he thinks he can do.
General George C. Marshall, U.S. Army Chief of Staff, June 1940

ot long after the worst of all wars ended, *Scientific American* would describe the surge of energy reshaping the nation as an "acceleration of history." But an alternative start date might be assigned to that late spring of 1940, when many Americans abruptly stopped thinking of their country as an island. After the fall of France, and having seen the merciless tempo of blitzkrieg ("lightning war"), the aerial bombardment of London compelled Americans to imagine the same fate overtaking Washington, New York, San Francisco . . .

At home, the dread reaching out from Europe amplified the New Deal practices of urgency, action, and improvisation. "War," after all, had been the New Deal's favorite metaphor, and Americans in 1940 were facing a real one. If the New Deal years had been squeezed by time, such pressure was multiplied by the deadly-swift Germans, and before long Japan. "National security" now took on the meaning we know today.

By this juncture, most people had come to regard government as the patron of much that was worthwhile. "Distress unemployment"—that is, the situation when all of a family's resources have been exhausted— was no longer life-threatening. Life expectancy, in fact, rose during the Depression. Nor did banks regularly fall like dominoes.

By 1940, our four had been waging a seven-year "war on poverty" throughout a fraught and wearying peace. The vital task of defusing the menacing violence of the early 1930s had been achieved, and they remained at the top—despite having gathered more enemies and carried more personal burdens than anyone else high in government, except Franklin Roosevelt himself. Each evinced some facet of their president: Ickes's anger, Hopkins's invalidism, Wallace's remoteness, Perkins's deep loneliness.

"Efficient businesslike management" in the face of war, however, was not among this Administration's qualities, at least as judged by major newspapers, if mostly owned by Republicans. In 1917 and 1918, President Wilson had recruited "dollar-a-year" men from Big Business to oversee war production, and pressures were mounting for Roosevelt to muster such talents as well. Perkins and Ickes were skeptical, whereas Hopkins already had taken the matter in hand with his advisory boards and his ties to Harriman, Stettinius, Nelson Rockefeller, and others of the very rich.

By now, all four of FDR's key lieutenants had entered the national imagination. In 1940, one could read of Hopkins in *The New York Times* as well as in the tabloids. "Honest Harold," in turn, held a role unknown in the U.S. political system: it was what Europeans call a minister without portfolio, a role that can enable a senior official to get into anything. Troubling to many on both sides of the aisle, Ickes was both a minister without portfolio and a minister *with* portfolios. It was an enormous remit, only starting with the Interior Department.[1]

Wallace, for his part, remained preoccupied with national recovery. Industrial activity was improving in the second quarter of 1940, which Commerce Secretary Hopkins told him was due to demand for steel. Why wait for a war, with its need for massive government spending, to haul the economy out of the Depression, Keynes had asked? Lo and behold, the mailed fist of "military Keynesianism" began to pound, and bigger deficits were mysteriously boosting growth.

Nonetheless, lots of Americans feared that the costs of defense might permanently ruin a still Depression-burdened economy. FDR, for one, did not see deficits as stabilizing: deficits meant more borrowing, and thus deeper debt, and—as this thinking would have it—a slippery path to ruin.

And how might FDR organize his Administration for war? The question was as puzzling as Keynesian economics to Congressmen, voters, and to most of his Cabinet. "The President [has] no intention whatever of creating any involved, complicated machine for national defense or emergency measures," announced White House press secretary Stephen Early.[2] That remained to be seen.

Just three days before Germany had struck France and the Low Countries on May 10, 1940, FDR and Wallace spent forty-five minutes in the Oval Office discussing military preparedness. The only army America needed, insisted the president, was "just a sufficient force of men to send a good expeditionary force to Brazil—or some similar country—in case of invasion."[3] The Republic would be shielded by its airpower and navy, and he expected Congress to soon pass the Two-Ocean Navy Act, which, the press reported, might include thirty-five battleships. He reiterated this argument when Sumner Welles, an authentic expert on Latin America, joined them for a final fifteen minutes.

Such thinking was upended within seventy-two hours. Germany's latest assault showed the apparently unstoppable power of operations combining armor, dive-bombers, and commandos. From Brussels, Cudahy reported that Hitler was about to seize control over one of the historic routes into France, last used in 1914. But the instinct in Washington was to look first to protecting its own hemisphere.

Since 1933, FDR had adopted a "Good Neighbor" policy toward Latin America, a part of the world that fascinated him and that, during sea voyages in 1934 and 1936, he was the first president to visit. Special relations should flourish, many people hoped, because Latin American governments were themselves nominally republics, not European monarchies. Once Hitler appeared likely to unify Europe, Latin America—for a time—gained priority.

Distinguished men were already specializing in that continent. These included Welles, of course, and Wallace, but also the thirty-two-year-old Republican Nelson Rockefeller, grandson of Standard Oil's founder and Aldrich's nephew, whom Hopkins brought into government to coordinate Latin American policy. German radio broadcasts outnumbered those in English ten to one in most of these nations, and Wallace was alert to Nazi inroads, as increasingly were Hopkins and Ickes.

Within weeks of Germany's western offensive, Hopkins asked Wallace to help him create a government-backed Inter-American Trading Corporation to manage strategic materials. Wallace found his friend's foreign policy instincts "excellent" at this point: both expected the struggle to spill across the Atlantic. On his own initiative, Wallace directed certain businessmen in Mexico, Brazil, and Argentina to work with the

FBI, employing a secret payroll crafted by J. Edgar Hoover.[4] Such moves seemed necessary, in part, because the Berlin Institute of Inter-American Affairs was welcoming all too many Latin influencers to Germany.

Threats to these neighboring republics stirred popular attention. Those who read maps suddenly realized that northeastern Brazil was only sixteen hundred miles by air from southwestern Senegal, a French colony that Germany just might occupy. In East Hampton, New York, the Maidstone Club turned a dinner dance into a joyously patriotic "All Americas Ball." Three hundred guests in native costumes of some sort enjoyed a Cuban bar, Mexican nightclub, and tropical Brazilian room. More seriously, Rockefeller had gotten to work in the Commerce Department— with a staff of seventy-five and a $3.4 million emergency budget.

That said, it was in Europe where civilization was at stake. Each day brought more chilling news. The Germans broke deeper into the west, General Erwin Rommel shouting from the head of his panzers that he was "through the Maginot Line."[5] Actually, he had come around it from the north, the French and British still not understanding what was hitting them. The Royal Air Force was ordered to strike the rail lines, as if this were 1914, even as German tanks—inspired by new doctrines—raced to the Channel by road.

On Thursday, May 16, 1940, at 1 P.M., Roosevelt displayed his finest hour since 1933. Slowly, stiffly, and leaning on the arm of an aide, he walked in his hidden braces, resting his weight on a cane, up a long ramp from the well of the House of Representatives to the rostrum. He told a rapidly summoned joint session of Congress that America required impregnable defenses against a "lightning war." Using short, sharp sentences, he warned that midwestern cities such as St. Louis and Omaha were no longer distant from attack but within reach of Axis bombers, perhaps racing in at two or three hundred miles per hour from Greenland or the Caribbean. Everyone knew what the Luftwaffe had done to Warsaw and, just two days earlier, to Rotterdam. He asked applauding legislators to enact a $1.2 billion program to make U.S. defenses impregnable, and to join in producing at least fifty thousand warplanes a year.

This sounded inconceivable: two years earlier, output had been ninety a month. Yet he sensed the potential of a soon-to-be thriving industrialized continent, and Hopkins was contributing better insights than those of any expert. Lindbergh derided this number as "fantasy."

A day later, Roosevelt and Ickes examined the war before entering a Cabinet meeting. Barely were all gathered when word came that the Netherlands had fallen. "Fortress Holland" had felt safe behind its dikes, sections of which the Dutch had been prepared to blast if attacked, greeting invaders by an inrushing sea. But no one in the Hague had imagined paratroopers and hydroplanes.

Churchill delivered his first broadcast to the empire as prime minister on Sunday, May 19, and those Americans who listened were as riveted as his fellow subjects. At that very moment, the 390,000-man British Expeditionary Force was falling back to the Channel. Nonetheless, he asserted that they and the French Army, backed by the RAF, would stabilize "the Western Front," as in 1914.

The president and Ickes met one-on-one throughout these weeks, a persistent topic being how to replace the two service secretaries, Woodring and Edison. It would not have necessarily been a step up for Ickes to move to the War Department, and he did not push. Roosevelt had made some stunningly irresponsible appointments since 1933, but to designate Ickes as secretary of war was one he avoided. Looking back, Ickes suspected that Hopkins had blocked his path, though that is unlikely. FDR could foresee the outcome of having Ickes in a role where he could appeal loudly to patriotism and vengeance while forgetting that the war secretary was subordinate to the president of the United States.

All sorts of contingencies pressed upon Roosevelt's mind. Should England fall, what would become of the Royal Navy? Would the Kriegsmarine absorb it, to rule the Atlantic?

Before the May 24 Cabinet meeting, Ickes and Hopkins put their heads together. Hopkins remarked that he had no idea what the president had actually concluded about the war. That was curious because Hopkins had been living at the White House since the tenth, when FDR had asked him to stay over after working through the day of Hitler's latest invasion. The arrangement would last three and a half years, his daughter Diana, now eight, who was being mothered by Eleanor, living there too.

As Ickes and Hopkins took their seats in the Cabinet Room, they saw Jesse Jones had been invited, as would become routine. The president then lectured his Cabinet about Europe for an hour straight; all knew this was his way of developing ideas. Soon he moved on to the country's hysteria over aliens. Even the governor of Georgia was busily hunting them down, although, so far as he could tell, few aliens inhabited Georgia.

Perkins did not engage this time. She instead used the opportunity to review labor problems. After one long breath, according to Ickes, she "started out on a twenty- or-twenty-five-minute discourse."[6]

After that session, Hopkins would go a step further, phoning Ickes several days later. If Woodring and Edison were to be pried loose, maybe this was a good time to get rid of Frances, too—Hopkins intending to use her position for one of his more recent friends.

Concurrently, the president had asked Wallace to investigate the economic consequences "if England and France were completely wiped out." On May 28, Wallace followed up with Hopkins at the White House, where he found him in bed on the second floor.[7] Hopkins had moved into Louis Howe's old rooms, confessing he had pushed himself too hard.

They mostly reviewed Nazi designs on the hemisphere, and when Wallace actually asked whether FDR would run for reelection, Hopkins could only reply that he had heard nothing. War in Europe seemed to have eclipsed everything. Fittingly, both men still worried about FDR's continuing hopes for balancing the budget. He had already cut back money for pilot training. "If the international situation is as grave as the president thinks it is half the time," said Hopkins, "we ought to be approaching the problem in a much bigger way."[8]

Ickes was of course suspicious of what lay behind Hopkins's new address. It seemed more than ever that Hopkins was becoming another Louis Howe, without Howe's devotion and political acumen. The generous "Pa" Watson had suggested to Ickes that the president felt sorry for Harry and was comforted by knowing that "a Howe or a Hopkins" was sleeping nearby.[9]

FDR and Ickes continued to examine the war. Ickes wanted to intervene, by any way possible. He no more sympathized with FDR's arguments about "buying time" when handling Germany than he did with the president's hopes to "buy time" with Japan. Most of all, Ickes concluded it was Hitler who was benefiting from any "buying of time."

In mid-May, Churchill had asked the president for some fifty mothballed, four-stacked destroyers laid up from the World War, plus airplanes and other munitions. At least these could help keep the English Channel uncrossable. But he went rebuffed. Ickes objected, telling his diary he felt "depressed," and then demanding reasons for this decision. Roosevelt explained that the vessels were obsolete, lacked antiaircraft guns, and probably could do little against invasion.

Ickes wasn't convinced. To persuade the president, he knew that he needed to make the issue "purely political," and said so: should Britain be invaded, the American people will ask "why were we not told that the British needed help to defend the Channel"—and voters would then "blame someone other than themselves." Ickes documented his opinions in a letter, though closing with upbeat advice: "We Americans are like the householder who refuses to lend or sell his fire extinguishers to help put out the fire that is right next door, although that house is all ablaze and the wind is blowing from that direction."[10] A tepid "Memorandum for H. L. I." arrived four hours later.

Ickes concluded that his chief's actual reason for not transferring the warships was that it might require Congress's approval. He therefore asked Ben Cohen to reexamine this law, and, in mid-July, submitted Cohen's twelve-page opinion to Robert Jackson, attorney general since January 1940.

Meanwhile, FDR explained to Ickes, Britain was quietly receiving the latest U.S. military aircraft, and he was shipping machine guns and artillery to France. Ickes could see how thin a line the president was walking, between stripping the U.S. armory and trying to bolster what remained of America's defensive frontier in western Europe.[11]

"The Blitzkrieg doesn't wait," cabled Cudahy, speaking from experience.[12] The British had pulled off a miraculous nine-day evacuation of one-third of a million men from Dunkirk's shell-pocked beaches by June 4, but the bulk of France's army still had to retreat along a hard-pressed sixty-mile front. With Paris about to fall, a German assault team disguised as Dutch and French refugees entered the disintegrating capital to target France's domestic intelligence directorate. On Sunday, June 9, they removed its complete files in boxcars. It was another example of fine-structure warfare that the democracies had yet to learn.

A week later, France sought an armistice—having lost more lives over six weeks than had the United States in combat during World War I. And by this time, Italy was also in the war on Hitler's side. Only the British Empire kept fighting.

The rush of events, not to mention FDR's eagerness to leave for a long weekend with Hopkins at Hyde Park, meant the Cabinet convened that Thursday the twentieth. Hopkins looked unusually well as he sat down, kidding Vice President Garner about their having stayed up late playing poker, and how he had lost heavily, as anyone would to Garner.

Earlier in the day, Roosevelt had shaken Washington by nominating Henry Stimson to be secretary of war. At seventy-two, he had been not only Herbert Hoover's secretary of state but, from 1911 to 1913, William Taft's secretary of war. Stimson had always worked with Republicans, going back to Theodore Roosevelt. The jolt was intensified by FDR nominating Frank Knox to Navy on the same day. It was difficult for sensible members of the GOP to paint Roosevelt as an archenemy of the Constitution when such Republican statesmen had joined his official family.

Ickes cheered these appointments and happily made way for Stimson, who had the stature of a Republican that Ickes knew he lacked. (Ickes never allowed himself to be considered a Democrat.) Moreover, he admired Stimson, who had served in France during World War I—as had Knox—and who embodied old ties to Theodore Roosevelt. Additionally, the new secretary's law firm of Winthrop, Stimson, Putnam & Roberts was representing Spain's former Loyalist government in a complex case involving silver assets in U.S. custody. This notwithstanding, FDR's choice of these two "pro-Ally foreign policy" sympathizers infuriated antiwar Democrats.[13] And Republican leaders felt betrayed by such "turncoats" on the eve of their party's convention.

The 1940 campaigns were gearing up against the background of global disaster, and especially of what Hopkins would term "the stupefying disappointment" of France's surrender on June 22.[14] The shock was all the greater for the speed and originality of German victory over an army deemed to be the commanding physical force in Europe. Nor did the lightning stop. Some days before, the president had told Hopkins and Wallace—as well as Ickes, in a separate Oval Office meeting—that he thought Japan was ready to reach an understanding. Yet suddenly—with their metropoles occupied—French Indochina and the Dutch East Indies were marooned. Perhaps the Indian subcontinent and Malaya would follow. Compromises with Japan became unlikely.

oosevelt told no one whether he intended to break George Washington's two-term precedent. He possessed ample reason not to run that November—including the boredom he confided to Missy LeHand.

Among his dreams upon leaving government was to reorganize a railroad, and he had asked Morgenthau to find him such a busted corporation within the Internal Revenue's Receivership Department—and to bring him every file. For a man born in 1882, this desire combined playing with toys and a visible ongoing power over massive objects of steel and steam. Morgenthau had seldom seen him so excited about an idea.[15]

Other possibilities included writing history or memoirs, although a memoir from him would have been consumed by politics, with personal utterances limited to asides about yachting. He might contribute to *Collier's* magazine, and he was setting his own precedent by building a presidential library at Hyde Park—which an infirm Harry Hopkins, newsmen reported, was slated to direct. To be fifty-eight, in such days, was aging, and maybe he would return full-time to helping the disabled. Or he could work on his stamp collection, acquiring as many stamps as possible before the nations issuing them disappeared under the Third Reich.

Ultimately, Roosevelt was not going to shut himself away on his mother's estate while Europe warred and America rearmed. He must live with disaster, never having truly defeated paralysis: now he faced one more catastrophe. Not least, to be a warlord would be "a very great adventure."

By 1940, the great-man notion of political leadership had swept through the industrial or quasi-industrial nations—not only in the worst of the dictatorships, but also in Portugal, Greece, and, for a while, even in Britain, where the philosopher R. G. Collingwood had raged against the propagandized indispensability of Neville Chamberlain. Practical Democrats regarded the first political master of the radio as himself irreplaceable—and FDR was their great man. No one in the party had grown enough to compare. A vacuum—largely of his own creation—was pulling at him, and the people around him whom he trusted.

A sign of Roosevelt's ascendancy over the nation is that most Americans patiently accepted his refusal—right into mid-July—even to say whether or not he would run.

At their convention, in Philadelphia from June 24 to 28, Republicans nominated the forty-eight-year-old Wendell Willkie, a Democrat until two years earlier who, at any other time, would have presented a dangerously liberal figure to Republican Party traditionalists. Suddenly, not that long after the era of Herbert Hoover, there arose a respected, serious alternative to FDR.

Willkie was a superb, politically active corporation lawyer and CEO from Elwood, Indiana, which *Time* reported to be one of those unassuming little places with ordinances against Blacks being within its precincts after sundown. Now he was a New Yorker, running Commonwealth & Southern, the country's biggest utilities holding company. He was large, shaggy, wide-grinning, and perpetually youthful. Churchill would compare him to a Newfoundland—the big, sweet-tempered working breed that shakes on everyone when wet.

This blue-eyed Hoosier had never held electoral office, but won the nomination because the Republican platform of 1940 had gone far to co-opt the New Deal. Hopkins explained the phenomenon to newsmen, in his flat steady midwestern way. "The Republicans don't oppose any of it publicly," he said, sitting on his desk lighting a cigarette. "They don't dare."[16] But should they win, he added, they would wreck the New Deal. He knew of what he spoke. Just that week, the Securities and Exchange Commission had decreed that investment advisers must act as trusted fiduciaries to their clients. Wall Street furiously resisted the decision.

Such Republican internationalists as Henry Luce and Thomas Lamont, as well as Lewis Douglas, who headed "Democrats for Willkie," backed the nomination. Unlike Landon in 1936, Willkie and Roosevelt evinced striking similarities. Each was skillful, globally oriented, and just about never pinned down. Franklin aside, there had been no presidential candidate so dynamic since T.R.

On the day of Willkie's nomination, FDR told the Cabinet he was convinced Willkie at heart was a totalitarian. Having said that, he appointed Ickes to crush him, asking Ickes to work with Attorney General Jackson, who was previously assistant general counsel at Internal Revenue and then head of the Justice Department's Tax Division. There should be no waiting, as in '36. The counterattack must start now.[17]

Perkins recognized this talk of a Willkie dictatorship to be absurd. Through friends in Manhattan, she knew both the gregarious Willkie and his mistress, the *New York Herald Tribune*'s book review editor, Irita Van Doren, and she liked them both.

That did not protect her from Manhattan's district attorney, Thomas Dewey, who had been the runner-up in Philadelphia. If Republicans had acquiesced to the New Deal, then Dewey never got the message. He singled out Perkins and Hopkins as "symbols of incompetence, disunity, and class hatred," all of which meant *socialism*—calling upon Roosevelt to fire them in the seven short months the president had left.[18]

The Democratic National Convention, from July 15 to 18, followed the Republican one. Wallace visited with Hopkins in his White House bedroom a week before. Hopkins revealed he was now certain the president would seek reelection, though admitting that Roosevelt had not told him so. They chuckled over Ickes's being sore after having gone out on a limb to argue for a third term—declaring that a "counter-revolution" would result were Roosevelt not elected. Yet the president was still refusing to enlighten anyone.[19]

Hopkins added that he knew of no plans to manage the incumbent's nomination. As for a running mate, he mused, Roosevelt probably wanted Cordell Hull, even though Hull was convinced the party would lose, or maybe James Francis "Jimmy" Byrnes, senator from South Carolina. But who really knew? After all, because of FDR's silence, Jim Farley, Garner, maybe Jesse, and several others were bidding flat out. As for attending the convention himself, Hopkins doubted whether his health permitted it.

Two days later, on July 11, Wallace boarded the streamlined Capitol Limited for the Windy City. He needed to appear early because, as an Iowa delegate, he was to serve on the Resolutions Committee.

Whom should Wallace see huddled with two political aides in a nearby compartment but Harry Hopkins? They had a friendly breakfast and discussed the political bigotries of Roman Catholics, among other topics, before arriving at the Harrison Street station and going to separate hotels. Wallace sought Hopkins out on the convention's first day, sensing it prudent to involve him when calling the White House. FDR was supervising every step, even while playing solitaire in his study, and they asked him to clarify the party's stance on foreign policy.

Conventioneers were mystified by just what Hopkins was doing in his two-bedroom suite at the Blackstone. All they knew was that he had the only telephone line in Chicago that ran through the White House switchboard, and that he could be found conspiring at night with big-city bosses at various clubs around the Loop and at the fabled Chez Paree.

Whatever his authority, Hopkins's own style of operating was increasingly like Roosevelt's. There was the same duplicity, of course, and the anonymous emissaries, but also a similar preference to making suggestions over issuing orders. As with FDR, what Hopkins said facetiously was often more important than what he might say straight. And what he left unsaid lost nothing in its effectiveness.

Perkins loved the history and hoopla of these quadrennial events. She recalled having gone to Chicago "to be generally useful," staying at the Blackstone with Susanna.[20] She visited Henry and Ilo Wallace in their out-of-the-way hotel and encountered Ickes milling around with various politicos, among the crowd of thirty thousand, at the Chicago Stadium. The huge indoor arena served as the convention hall, and as Ickes warned her, was packed with "all the lowdown crooks, all the low-lived creatures" in the city.[21]

FDR was set on being drafted rather than show his hand. Once Hopkins had helped engineer a first-ballot nomination, the choice of a running mate seemed to have been left to the delegates, which was when things turned sour.

"Everybody's selling everybody else down the river," Ickes complained to Perkins as the convention spun out of control. At this point, she phoned FDR: "The situation's very bad, very unpleasant, everybody's unhappy."

He refused her appeal to come to Chicago, explaining that he wanted to avoid having to make promises to all the city bosses, and suggested that she ask Eleanor to come instead, which indeed she did. Yet Perkins had worried him.

"Everybody would like to know who you want for vice president, but you haven't declared yourself," she continued.[22]

"Well, what do you think?" he asked.

Since early spring, Perkins had been reminding FDR of Wallace's intellect and loyalty, and now she was working both the Oval Office and the convention for Wallace.

"Well, you know I've thought for some time that Wallace would be the best possible man if you want him," she replied.

For Perkins, what followed sounds like an eye-rolling disconnect of a conversation: FDR pitched the idea to her as if it were his own.

"Well, don't you think Henry Wallace would be pretty good, Frances?

He's a man of great ability. And he's learning about politics. He's got lots of qualities. Don't you think he'd be good, Frances?"[23]

Well, yes.

Roosevelt asked her again what she thought of his idea, which she once more assured him was splendid. Then, she recalled, he reviewed his decision two or three times before telling her to inform Hopkins, but not by phone: "His wires are probably tapped."[24] To reach Hopkins's door, she needed to bustle through hallways of newsmen, clamoring to know what she was about.

"Oh nothing," she said, while raising the most boring of irrelevant subjects. "Just a little routine about the equal rights for women amendment."[25] Interest fizzled, and she got through.

"Yes, I've got an absolutely fool-proof wire right to the White House," Hopkins assured her.[26]

Still, he took nothing on faith, even from Perkins, and phoned the president to check: "Frances said . . ."

Hopkins then informed Wallace, and relayed the news to waiting delegates, who "turned ugly on Wallace," she remembered. Many detested the agriculture secretary for his peculiarities or his liberalism, and for having long been a Republican. Also, Perkins concluded, much of the bad feeling was "a kind of distracted ugliness" against Roosevelt, whom none dared attack directly.[27]

Once Roosevelt selected Wallace, he made it plain to the convention that he would refuse to run without him. At no other time would he have given such an ultimatum, not even in 1944 when he chose Harry Truman. If the delegates defied him, he appeared ready to leave them to the tender mercies of the Republicans, whose war chest was nearly three times as large.

The arena erupted in boos and catcalls as Wallace's nomination was pushed through. "I can never forget his face," recalled Perkins, and his "sense of terrible suffering, without understanding."[28] Sitting on the podium not far from Eleanor and holding Ilo's hand, he had to take it.

Until well into the twentieth century, vice presidents were rarely chosen with an eye to their possible succession. Yet FDR, as so often, was thinking ahead. "If I should be bumped off," he told Farley, or "hit with a bomb," he wanted a man who could step in fast.[29] And, with rare candor, he also spoke to Farley of his health. Where it came to a paralytic, who knew? But there is a better reason for why he selected Wallace. He liked the workings of Wallace's mind. A match had developed between the great user of other people's skills and, with Wallace, an exceptionally talented man, though ill-adapted to using the political skills required.

FDR's praise of Wallace as a "practical idealist" baffled Ickes, and once everyone had returned to Washington, FDR patiently explained his choice to "Honest Harold," several times. Regardless, Ickes insisted to FDR that Wallace was the weakest of candidates and would make a perfectly terrible president, although he had grunted something to Perkins about Henry at least being a loyal New Deal liberal. Wallace, for his part, heard Hopkins say he "was working for me at the Convention," though who could tell?[30]

Wallace and Hopkins visited Hyde Park during the first week in August to coordinate the coming campaign. Roosevelt also showed Wallace the spot in a hemlock enclosure where he wished to be buried.

Wallace believed, as did Hull, that Democrats were consigned to defeat in 1940, had it not been for the shock of France's collapse. Roosevelt could win if voters believed him to be the best choice to keep the country out of war. For his part, Willkie spoke sincerely of Wallace as a "fine gentleman" and an "eminent public servant," and said that he wished to avoid quarreling over personalities during the campaign. Ickes then went for his throat. He implied Willkie was a demagogue and, starting mildly, unveiled this man who pretended to be a self-made, small-town midwesterner as in fact "a simple, barefoot Wall Street lawyer."[31]

"If the President is going to pose as being too deeply immersed in the duties of his office to electioneer," scolded *The New York Times,* he should not permit a Cabinet officer "on the public payroll to make personally abusive speeches on his behalf."[32] The worst, from both sides, was yet to come.

The National Association of Manufacturers, for instance, distributed a pamphlet labeling Hopkins, Ickes, and Perkins as Communist sympathizers. September's vitriol was offset only by Perkins's traditional Labor Day address, which she always broadcast from station WFFI in Boston. Speaking as a humanitarian, she extolled New Deal advances in labor law, and urged that Social Security and the Wage-Hour Act be expanded to cover factory farms, like those in California's Imperial Valley.

That month, Hopkins's deteriorating health compelled him to leave the Commerce Department, and he returned with his daughter to New York. Now jobless, he still took an apartment in the Essex House on Central Park South, although he appeared to be living on his last cent. He tracked the campaign, but insiders agreed that his political life was finished.

Wallace then embarked on a seven-thousand-mile, thirteen-state swing to brand Republicans "the party of appeasement." His hometown paper, the *Des Moines Register,* actually headlined, NAZIS PREFER GOP.[33] Even Ickes was impressed by Wallace's ferocity. Republicans struck back, and the two parties fought over whom the Führer genuinely preferred and which campaign's propaganda most resembled Goebbels's.

In October, the president arose from his duties and, smoothly as ever, excelled at gentlemanly mockery. Except there would be no debates, Ickes declared: the chief executive had little time to divert his attention from the war; he needed to monitor global events, such as the now-raging Battle of Britain, in which the duel between the Luftwaffe and Royal Air Force seemed about to settle England's fate.

As for Wallace, he never stilled the doubts of many who found him too eccentric for the second-highest office. Republicans tried to make this point once letters to his guru from 1933 and '34 fell into their hands. Wallace at first claimed that they were forgeries, which was untrue. Roosevelt had to intervene, deterring publication by having his opponents realize that he had people "down the line" set to expose Willkie's not having lived with his frail, devoted wife, Edith, for years.[34] Finally, as FDR had done with Ickes's own letters from those same years, he let Wallace appreciate the fact that he retained photostats.

Perkins kept working to lower the heat, as she so often did. She reminded the country that August had been the twentieth anniversary of women's suffrage. Women, she said, needed to exert their political clout, and she was followed on NBC by uplifting words from Representative O'Day. Jane Ickes also worked for civility when she joined Eleanor on a visit to Charleston, West Virginia, with other Administration wives. Mrs. Roosevelt addressed "a mostly feminine audience at the state capitol," reported the town's *Gazette,* "on topics of interest to women."[35]

Jane, twenty-eight, wore a sailor hat with a fitted dress and matching jacket.

For all that, the campaign grew uglier in its final days. Democrats were fighting hard to separate Black voters permanently from the "party of Lincoln"—which, in 1940, championed both a square deal "for citizens of Negro descent" and an immediate end to segregation within U.S. government offices. Trouble occurred in New York on the night of October 28, a week before Election Day.

Starting at 10 P.M., FDR had aroused twenty-two thousand cheering admirers in Madison Square Garden. Soon after eleven, a motorcade drove him fifteen blocks to West Thirty-Sixth Street, where his special train waited beneath Pennsylvania Station. Uniformed New York City police still secured the platform after he boarded, but big, fat-jowled Stephen Early, the press secretary following the main party, dashed up. When Patrolman James Sloan challenged him for his credentials, Early kneed the Black officer in the groin and barged through.

The Colored Division of New York's Republican State Committee denounced the attack as "a graphic illustration of the New Deal's interest in the colored man."[36] Heavyweight boxing champion Joe Louis—the "Brown Bomber," stumping his home state of Missouri for Willkie—reminded Black audiences that Roosevelt did not "give us an anti-lynching law," whereas Republicans were demanding federal legislation to curb the terror.[37] His words rang louder because, days earlier, a Democratic bloc had once more stifled such a bill before the Senate. Louis then flew to New York, where he visited the injured Sloan in his apartment on West 110th Street. In short order, it looked as if Roosevelt might lose Chicago—which had many activist Black voters—and thereby Illinois.

This was not a mere political spat to be handled by aides or speechwriters, nor would FDR touch it. Hopkins tracked Ickes down by phone in Wilkes-Barre, Pennsylvania, just before he was about to remind its Central Labor Council that the New Deal–leaning Willkie was a "rich man's Roosevelt." The two friends discussed a response. Ickes wanted Early to resign and didn't mind Thomas Dewey preparing an arrest warrant. But how about starting with an apology?

Stephen Early got out something vague and shifty before voting day, November 5, and the aftermath of this white-on-Black violence was predictable.

Roosevelt won thirty-eight of the forty-eight states, and the popular vote by ten points. Again, he had brought together the bib overalls and the cities, including so many Blacks of the Great Migration. He accepted congratulations that night in Hyde Park, lucky watch chain gleaming, with his eighty-six-year-old mother and Hopkins standing nearby.

The election over, the issue of assault was dropped fast by Republicans and Democrats alike. Patrolman Sloan, who had been decorated for valor before the outrage, returned to duty that December, but was demoted to clerk in the Information Bureau at police headquarters. At the White House, Stephen Early remained powerful and well trusted in FDR's outer office. He stayed alert to civil rights "agitators," and upheld the pretexts that kept Black journalists out of press conferences.

On Thursday, November 7, FDR and Vice President Elect Wallace returned separately to a capital city reverberating with the likelihood of war. The Democrats still held Congress, but there were fewer of them, and the cross-party conservative bloc was larger. Roosevelt and Wallace also had to reckon with activists who opposed intervention, including the America First Committee, founded in August, which was eager to accuse them of being "devotees of force."

For the time being, Ickes had set aside long-held doubts about the British Empire, as had Wallace. Ickes was also backing the American Committee for the Defense of British Homes, which collected and shipped to England personal revolvers, .30-06 deer rifles, and family shotguns for a last-ditch resistance to Nazi invasion. Moreover, Ben Cohen's well-reasoned legal opinion had proved convincing. Attorney General Jackson was persuaded that the destroyers for which Churchill had pleaded could be released without involving Congress.

The president had therefore been able to issue an executive order on September 2 allowing Britain to obtain ships and munitions in exchange for U.S. base rights in eight British possessions arching from Newfoundland to then-British Guiana. Two weeks after that, he supported bipartisan legislation to impose the first peacetime draft in the Republic's 164-year history. Young men were inducted for twelve months of service, starting in October.

Roosevelt returned to the capital as a different kind of president. No longer was he talking of a nation being one-third ill-housed and ill-fed, but rather of how the country might survive in an epoch of lethal overseas threats to "national security." He was once more the young idolater, as from 1913 to 1921, of the U.S. Navy.

Ickes phoned to congratulate the vice president elect and, after the necessary pleasantries, they discussed "the danger of an attempted *coup d'état*" by rich irreconcilables in league with factions in the U.S. Army. They agreed the government had to be vigilant. This wasn't paranoia. Gore Vidal, fifteen-year-old son of FDR's former head of civil aviation, and future man of letters, would recall that he "listened several times to Air Force generals discuss . . . the ease with which the White House could be seized, the Congress sent home, and the nation kept out of the war that the Jew Franklin D. Rosenfeld was trying to start against Hitler."[38]

In the event, no insurrectionists appeared, and the hallways of Congress remained open to all, even during the war.

Ickes and Wallace also wondered about Hopkins, who they assumed was going to be rusticated to Hyde Park as a librarian. Yet once more Ickes saw "the inevitable Harry Hopkins" surfacing everywhere. Ostensibly he resided on Central Park, yet again he was haunting the White House. And just what was he living on?

Toward year's end, only three of Roosevelt's original New Deal Cabinet officers remained: Hull, Ickes, and Perkins. Jones had replaced Hopkins at Commerce that September; Wallace's former deputy ran Agriculture; and Jim Farley had quit as postmaster-patronage-dispenser after his feckless run for the presidency. The Administration was also on its third attorney general.

Once he added Stimson and Knox, Roosevelt felt no need to strengthen his Cabinet further—as, say, by dispatching Hull to neutral Stockholm. Morgenthau hung tight at Treasury. It would have been difficult to replace him, even if FDR had been inclined to substitute a distinguished financier. Morgenthau was established as the Cabinet's only Jew, and an alternative would have had to be drawn from a very select circle.

Roosevelt and his original Cabinet had failed since 1933 to break the back of double-digit unemployment, which, at the beginning of 1940, was stuck at slightly under 15 percent. Only by summer was an authentic turnaround to be discerned.

One indicator that FDR tracked closely was cotton textiles. In June

1940, he had asked Wallace and Hopkins to work out whether this sector's upswing might prove to be permanent: their findings delighted him. Perkins, too, was hopeful. By fall, she predicted defense spending would add six to eight million new jobs, which could boost demand for consumer goods of all kinds, including textiles, and therefore deliver two to three million additional openings.

That said, Perkins wanted to leave office. Indeed, yearning to FDR for "a proper place in life."[39] By this time, her husband, Paul Wilson, had been transferred to a North Carolina psychiatric facility far less expensive than the Haven. Her daughter, Susanna, aged twenty-four, seemed in good health after her own hospitalization and had married a well-off society photographer who made a specialty of Navajo portraits.

For several years, Perkins had found serenity in monthly visits to All Saints Convent near Baltimore, and her relationship with Caroline O'Day appeared enduring. There was so much else she wanted to do. (The presidency of Mt. Holyoke College seemed one possibility.) She was also weary of being cast as a "classic type of soft-minded liberal," as the anti-Roosevelt *Saturday Evening Post* described her in 1940.[40] Her peers in government often characterized her the same way. To believe this depiction, one must ignore her recent campaign to expel racketeers, Communists, and fascist "fifth columnists" from the American labor movement.

Soon after the election, she visited FDR in his study, where he was working on his stamp collection. Politely, of course, he laughed off her request to resign. Over Thanksgiving, *The New York Times* wrote she was "going," but rumors often swirled of Perkins being dropped out of sheer woman's inability to bear up. Roosevelt was genuinely irked that he needed to deny the latest speculation publicly. Finally, his "absolute no" to Perkins's petition was delivered by Eleanor, who explained that the president could not possibly start working with some new man as secretary of labor: "You do understand each other."

So she stayed, and took it. Meanwhile, she was preparing her department for war. "You have to be able to foresee, to project your mind into a situation that never has been," she instructed her staff.[41]

I f this indeed was America's direst moment short of war, there was much to be done in the ten weeks between election and inauguration. Urgency was underlined that fall as the Tripartite Pact, or Axis Alliance, bound Germany, Italy, and Japan to declare war on whatever nation attacked any one of them.

New Deal institutions, for instance, looked overdue for reorganizing, and one change FDR imposed that year was to remove the Immigration and Naturalization Service from the Labor Department. To believe he "stripped" it from Perkins is another myth of this presidency that echoes her gloating critics of the time.[42]

Actually, she had long wanted INS gone. It had not made sense since the 1920s to place immigration and labor under the same roof. But she did question whether the Justice Department was the right place for INS to end up, especially after the president's executive order stated that Justice could assure a "more effective control over aliens." Sharp entry limits soon followed to "curb spying," and the barriers to immigration kept rising as the country moved closer to war.[43]

In December, the annual Who's Who issue of *The American Hebrew* honored Ickes and Wallace for their commitment to saving Europe's persecuted Jews. Yet Ickes seethed. Early that month, the State Department blocked his attempt to make the U.S. Virgin Islands a sanctuary for some two thousand refugees. He had responded by calling a press conference to declare that "even a few lives saved from firing squads and concentration camps are worthwhile." And how were all the spies and subversives among these huddled masses to get to the mainland anyway, he asked? Should they swim, he would take responsibility.

On the eighteenth, he received a letter from FDR directing him to back off. The Virgin Islands had enough "social and economic problem[s]."[44] The United States opened its borders to somewhere between 180,000 and 220,000 European refugees between 1933 and 1945. But Ickes recognized that many more lives could be saved if the 132 million people of the sparsely populated American domain had truly opened their gates. "The right of asylum for political refugees, of which this country used to be so proud," he asserted, "has been allowed to die."[45]

Wallace stayed aloof from this quarrel, and was also looking beyond the urgencies of war. Greater than kings and warriors, wrote Swift, is the man who has made two blades of grass grow where one grew before. Those lines might as well be carved on Wallace's tombstone.

Three weeks after the election, Henry and Ilo Wallace headed south in their Plymouth on a six-week road trip to Mexico. He wanted to perfect his Spanish. Roosevelt had asked him to combine language study with bilateral security, by serving as ambassador extraordinaire at the December 1 inauguration of Mexico's president. After departing Laredo, Wallace's two-car caravan kept wandering off the Pan-American Highway as the vice president elect aroused sensations by strolling around to talk farming with *campesinos* and *haciendados* alike.

Wallace further explored the Mexican countryside, once he had completed his goodwill visit. Corn was the principal food of the masses, but he was appalled to calculate that it required two hundred hours of labor to harvest the bushels yielded in Iowa by ten. This he could change. The Wallaces flew home on January 2, as Nazi propagandists warned the new Camacho government against being pulled into a futile war by Washington. That said, what Wallace was about to initiate with the Rockefeller Foundation would revolutionize the world's food supply.

Britain faced hunger as well, and possibly worse. Much of its war effort was fraying after the first full year of conflict. The island lived by trade, but U-boats were cutting its lifelines. The Bank of England's hard-currency reserves for buying outside the empire were fast dwindling. Mass Luftwaffe attacks against cities, picturesque towns, and industrial targets had already killed 23,422 civilians, and a German invasion by sea still loomed. Churchill admitted Britain's desperate condition in a ten-page typewritten letter to Roosevelt in December.

The president needed "refueling" before the inauguration, as Hopkins put it, and so accompanied FDR on December 4 aboard the USS *Tuscaloosa* out of Miami. Several days before they left, Ickes had lunched with the president, whom he described as looking "terribly tired." Hopkins he had already consigned to the "invalid class."[46]

FDR received Churchill's letter, by seaplane with other documents, on the morning of the ninth while at anchor off Antigua. He returned to the White House a week later amid a midafternoon rain. But he was suntanned and zestful and immediately entered a two-and-a-half-hour meeting with Hull. They were joined by Norman Davis, a former diplomat-banker now heading the Red Cross, who, after Versailles, had expertly restructured economic ties among Europe's so recent belligerents.

Roosevelt introduced his latest idea at a press conference the next day. "Suppose my neighbor's home catches fire, and I have a length of garden hose four or five hundred feet away," he asked reporters on December 17. "If he can take my garden hose and connect it up with his hydrant, I may help him to put out his fire. Now, what do I do?"[47]

Ickes, of course had an answer, and would soon deliver it in what scholars consider one of the great speeches of the twentieth century. "We must give the British everything we have, and by everything, I mean everything needed to beat the life out of our common enemy."[48] But for the moment he held his tongue.

Now it was Roosevelt who publicly criticized the Nazi regime. In his fireside chat of December 29, he urged his countrymen to become the "Arsenal of Democracy," a phrase being used in official circles and put into the speech by Hopkins. His annual budget message to Congress on January 3 then called for a mounting supply of warships, planes, tanks, and guns to confront a world at war. On the afternoon of the sixth, he delivered his State of the Union address. He stood before Congress to ask with great solemnity for all aid short of war to Britain, while he portrayed a future world founded on freedom of speech, freedom of worship, freedom from want, and freedom from fear.

By tradition, the Cabinet attended his address. Newsmen reported Ickes's absence as due to a slight indisposition, but it might have been a "clam-up day."

That morning, Hopkins had boarded a Yankee Clipper floatplane at New York's LaGuardia Field marine terminal. It was a Pan American Airways flight bound for Lisbon, refueling at Bermuda and the Azores, bearing six passengers and 1,165 pounds of mail. He was flying to London, but the Neutrality Act still prohibited direct travel to airports of warring states, and so he switched to a British-based transport in Portugal.

Hopkins flew as a private citizen with no title or salary. More tellingly, he was the "personal representative of the President of the United States" who would determine how widely America should open the gates to its arsenal. The day after he arrived in London, Congress received a sweeping bill drawn to afford the president a blank check to lend or lease war matériel to whatever nation he chose.

Inauguration Day finally came on January 20, with a biting northerly wind. Wallace was sworn in first, as is customary. Ickes and Perkins witnessed with the rest of the Cabinet. Wallace chose the outgoing John Garner to administer the oath, as a capstone to Garner's thirty-eight years in

Washington. Perkins had called on him earlier, in private, to say farewell. Then Chief Justice Hughes swore in Roosevelt, who was cheered by a shivering crowd of more than seventy-five thousand spilling out of Capitol Plaza. Right after delivering his serviceable thirteen-hundred-word Inaugural Address, FDR leaned over and whispered to Garner, "I'll miss you, Jack," and Garner slipped off for Union Station and Uvalde—not that Garner had voted for him.[49]

America makes it a practice to bring opposites together swiftly and fruitfully, as with Roosevelt and Garner. This quality would be vital during the war, akin to Hollywood films with bomber crews of farm boy Smiths and city-bred Jablowskys.

Shortly before the inauguration, Roosevelt and Ickes had been conspiring once more in the Oval Office. The habit of command is dangerously easy to acquire, and this time they were plotting the presidential race for *1944*. Opponents had lambasted FDR for adding another term to his presidency. If a third, why not a fourth, and a fifth? But no one truly expected him to run again. The purpose of that day's lunch was to discuss building up someone to succeed him, for which Ickes advised there was no time to lose.

Ickes suggested one distinguished figure whom FDR nixed, leaving him puzzled. "The trouble with Bob [Jackson, the attorney general] is that he is too much of a gentleman," FDR explained. "You and I are not."[50] Roosevelt knew that dishonesty and bare knuckles would be required to take a reluctant country into war, and once at war, the fight would be to the death.[51]

14

ELEVENTH HOUR

Inauguration 1941 to Pearl Harbor, December 7

> If we learned anything from the Depression, we will not allow ourselves
> to run around in new circles of futile discussion and debate, always
> postponing the day of decision.
> **Franklin Roosevelt**

For a lifetime, the United States has enjoyed vast technological superiority in every fight, engaging Koreans, Chinese, Vietnamese, Iraqis,
and Afghans with tragic certitudes of easy victory. To oppose the
Third Reich, however, meant sending one's sons, brothers, husbands,
and daughters against the world's supreme military power, while further
entailing a march into the unknown. What unimaginable weapons did
German scientists have in store, and where might Nazi commandos strike
next? Could fifth columnists truly awaken "racial enmities" in American
cities, as the president warned?[1]

Moreover, the Soviet Union was ostensibly neutral but, as Ickes and Wallace each told Stalin's nonplussed, always-smiling Ambassador Umansky,
"neutral on the side of Germany."[2] Moscow shipped millions of tons of timber, nickel, manganese, iron ore, wheat from Soviet Ukraine, and rubber for
tires into the Reich—and, of course, oil. All this meant that Stalin, whom the
Kremlin today elevates to heroic stature, was fueling the bombing of London.

Although the Royal Navy kept the continent under blockade, the long-
range Battle of the Atlantic was being lost in 1941 as U-boats sank British
merchantmen twice as fast as shipyards built them. From the Nile to the
frontier of Tunis, Britain's Western Desert Force was desperately facing
General Rommel's thrusts toward the Iraqi oil fields. Indian and British
troops might liberate Ethiopia from Italy that spring; yet, in England

itself, the Blitz went on targeting population centers, to kill 60,595 men, women, and children by war's end.[3]

On February 7, Secretary Hull told the Cabinet that Britain would fall within ninety days. His sources anticipated tens of thousands of English-speaking paratroopers in disguise descending on the Home Counties, while assault troopships unloaded Wehrmacht divisions from Ramsgate to Portsmouth.

The Germans by then had occupied most of France, leaving a fragment of its south to function as a rump state, with a capital in Vichy headed by the aged Marshal Philippe Pétain, his country's recent ambassador to clerical-fascist Spain. Washington had not broken off relations with France, which Roosevelt justified as an effort to modify Vichy collaboration.

Ickes ever more vocally took the opposite approach from his president on the future of America's oldest ally. He became a member of France Forever, the relief committee of General Charles de Gaulle's London-based Free French resistance, once the committee was organized in New York. Exiled too in London were the governments of the Netherlands, Norway, Poland, Czechoslovakia, Belgium, Luxembourg, and Greece.

Bill Bullitt and Daisy Harriman had returned from their diplomatic posts in 1940. Both would, early the next year, endorse Lend-Lease in the nation's now hugely active debate. Jane's uncle, John Cudahy, chose to speak for America First.

Also coming home, via Spain and Portugal in January 1941, was Anne Morgan, whose charitable foundation had been sopped up by Vichy. Disembarking on a New York pier, she urged the public to send food to occupied France, perhaps through Marseille, although her brother, J. P. Morgan, Jr., there to greet her, intruded on the message. "Get out of the way, you devils!" he roared, scattering newsmen and photographers with his cane. The New Deal, if anything, had intensified feelings of gigantic entitlement—driven by bitterness—among more than a few of his class.[4]

Americans expected Britain, as the world's political-military superpower, to be a bulwark against totalitarianism. They were coming to see the empire as an outer fortress, somehow worth aiding, while the United States hurried to build battleships and bombers. And they discovered an upside to these immense outlays. "We were by no means on an economic picnic," recalled Perkins of the swelling economy, but unemployment in 1941 fell below 5 percent, and consumer spending returned to the levels of 1929.[5]

Roosevelt assembled what he privately called his "war cabinet," which echoed Churchill, whose small, authentic war cabinet included tough anti-fascist—and anti-Communist—Labour Party leaders. FDR's model, which for public consumption he preferred to see identified as the "inner defense council," was a four-man war cabinet without a war, and mostly for show.

It comprised the elder statesman Henry Stimson, who delegated heavily to staff, and Knox, whose Navy Department was controlled by the commander in chief. The presence of a third member, Cordell Hull, might be reassuring to Southern war hawks, except that Roosevelt utterly bypassed him on European issues. Then there was Morgenthau, whom the president valued because he "has tried to carry out my plans in every respect"—by which he meant asking "how high" when told to jump.[6]

Along the way, ever-greater responsibilities were being piled on Roosevelt's four lieutenants. Henry Wallace was applying his "freakish" intellect, to recall *The New York Times*' adjective, while becoming the most powerful of America's vice presidents, at least into 1943. Already, it was natural for Roosevelt to ask him to see the MIT engineer Vannevar Bush, who headed Washington's Carnegie Institution for Science, to discuss how two or three pounds of uranium-235 might produce a chain reaction. Wallace knew the basics. He followed the work of Einstein's younger colleagues, such as Enrico Fermi, and he was aware, too, of the Kaiser Wilhelm Institute's ambitions on these matters.

Of course, Wallace understood his stature as vice president depended solely on a chief executive whom he considered as "unpredictable as a small boy."[7] Wallace also kept perspective by reminding himself that no professor of American history could name all the vice presidents of the United States.

As for Hopkins's capacities, Perkins said, with genuine surprise, "none of us supposed he had developed an extraordinary talent" to design, finance, and oversee the underpinnings of America's imminent global preeminence.[8]

Too little has been known about how Hopkins worked his magic during the war years. His reputation was polished dazzlingly from the start by the important men for whom he did the most, beginning with Averell

Harriman, George Marshall, Robert Sherwood, and, in time, Churchill and Stalin. Myths therefore arise, such as comparing Hopkins to "people that were not as gifted like Harold Ickes and Henry Wallace," or spreading Sherwood's myth that he was the second-most-powerful man in government. This would have been true only if weapons, oil, morale, and so much else had not been required to win the war, and if we overlook how the nation came to change its mind about confronting the Axis in the first place.[9]

Throughout, newsmen wrote of Hopkins as "Roosevelt's closest friend," though Perkins took a deeper look. "For a period of time, but with certain limitations, Harry was a friend" of a man to whom anyone could get just so close and no closer.[10]

Hopkins, at fifty-one, had a supreme ability to insinuate himself onto the ground floor of whatever venture would turn out big: emergency relief early in the Depression; the need to put millions of Americans to work during a decade of joblessness; and, ultimately, serving history's greatest wartime alliance. Always, he intuited FDR's needs, connected the dots, ignored proprieties, and fulfilled his chief's objectives.

Hopkins's presence rested on three sources, other than his being the president's confidant. One derived from extraordinary abilities that mirrored FDR's own. A second was his longtime habit of cultivating the rich, which now became systematic. He "specialized in bringing first one type of business man and then another type of business man into government," recalled Wallace.[11] Usually, these weren't mere corporate executives. Beginning around 1939, it was a "general campaign of Harry's to make himself solid with a certain element among the very wealthy, and he did it very skillfully."[12] Nelson Rockefeller, who had led Rockefeller Center Inc., and whom Hopkins would elevate to assistant secretary of state, was just the youngest and most dynamic of this circle. Averell Harriman was among these businessmen—which barely describes him—and Hopkins had just spent Thanksgiving with Harriman and his wife, Marie, the gallerist, in New York. Thanks to Hopkins, Harriman was on the staff of the recently established Defense Advisory Commission. Another friend of Hopkins's, Edward Stettinius, now forty, had quit his $100,000-a-year job as chairman of U.S. Steel to take charge, without pay, of this commission's industrial materials section.

With friends such as these, who owed him a steady flow of favors, Hopkins's source of income should not have been a mystery.

"When Harry was Secretary of Commerce," Ickes explained to Wallace, several of Hopkins's friends, including Harriman, began "to get together an annual purse for Harry." Ickes knew this as fact, because one of those friends was John Hertz, the auto entrepreneur and owner of a Kentucky Derby winner, with whom Ickes had been acquainted since they were scrappy twenty-year-olds in Chicago. Hertz had told him that the subsidy was "about $25,000 a year so Harry could support his two families and pay his hospital bills."[13]

Ickes elaborated that Bernard Baruch, another devotee of the track and tireless reader of *The Racing Form,* had added to "Hopkins's purse." This detail made sense to Wallace. He knew Baruch had recently given Hopkins and Stephen Early fully paid life memberships in the Jefferson Islands Club, an exclusive Maryland resort favored by Southern Democrats—an offer Wallace had received, and spurned.

A third source of Hopkins's authority was illness. From 1941 onward, he was always the sickest man in the room. If he could overcome such agonies, how could your own small sacrifices possibly compare? Right through summer 1945, newsmen, politicians, diplomats, and an array of world leaders hung on any word of Hopkins's condition. Recently, physicians writing in the *Journal of Medical Biography* have rediagnosed his "mysterious syndrome."[14] Except for new clinical details, it was much as Wallace had discerned. Hopkins's intestines were starving him, his symptoms including weight loss, abdominal pain, diarrhea, malabsorption of nutrients, impaired vision, and loss of balance. No one at the time asked how much of it was consciously or unconsciously self-inflicted, nor has anyone since.

Much of Hopkins's suffering was unnecessary. Ickes would lay out the pattern, echoed by the president's physician: Harry could keep away from hard drinking for long periods, up to the point where doctors said he was better; then he would start downing whiskey and wine. Or, as Admiral Ross McIntire put it, "When he thinks he's restored to health he goes out on the town—and from there to the Mayo Clinic."[15]

Repeatedly, everyone had to bow to Hopkins's miseries, and between intervals of dying, he radiated an enjoyment of his very public ordeals. Novelist and music critic Marcia Davenport saw Hopkins before he left for London in January. "He was like a walking corpse, bone-pale, emaciated, bent and stooped."[16] Nonetheless, during the hour before his Yankee

Clipper cast off, he had been feisty enough to spar with reporters while sipping black coffee in the customs room of LaGuardia Field. In doing so, he offered a characteristic exaggeration—something about having met Churchill in London during 1928 (not that Churchill remembered, and no clue of such an encounter exists in the Churchill Archives).

Three days later, after finally landing outside London, Hopkins arrived at night at Waterloo Station aboard a blacked-out train amid the banshee wails of air-raid sirens and the thunder of detonating five-hundred-pound bombs. The discreet security provided at Claridge's hotel by lean, well-armed watchers in crisp dark suits, and also the stomach agonies that he endured in his suite, are all portrayed rivetingly in Jerome Weidman's historical novel *Before You Go*.

The next day he lunched with Churchill for three hours at Downing Street. "This was the opening of new horizons," declared his friend and biographer Sherwood.[17]

For the next five weeks, Hopkins appeared everywhere with Churchill: at Number 10, on trains to Manchester and Birmingham, at Dover and Portsmouth, giving a poignant speech in freezing mid-January Glasgow, and weekending at the prime ministerial getaways of Chequers Court and Ditchley. He met with the Board of Admiralty, visited the King and Queen at Buckingham Palace, and stumbled through East End rubble. To boost the nation's morale, Churchill presented Hopkins far and wide as the personal representative of President Roosevelt, the best friend that Britain has ever had.

Hopkins suffered throughout from fever and chills, and from the diarrhea he tried to stave off with opiates. Churchill himself was close to indestructible for a man who worked tirelessly, lived indulgently, and had taken little exercise since giving up polo at fifty. Ignoring strict British food rationing, he was fed like a fighting cock—to the general good. While possessing a generous heart—toward white people—it rarely occurred to him that individuals in his circle were more destructible.

Intimacy with Churchill meant eating heartily and drinking wine, port, whiskey, and champagne—a festival that started early. Heavy meals were certain to bring agony upon Hopkins, and even when left to his own devices, he freely consumed bottles of wine and Scotch.

Whatever his suffering, Hopkins could not escape a sense of history being made, and he sent handwritten accounts to FDR of how Britain would be able to endure. He insisted that America must supply merchant vessels, patrol ships, .50-caliber machine guns, bombers, rifles with fifty million rounds of ammunition—and this was just going to be the beginning. Twenty-four years of Hopkins's life had gone to marshaling immense resources against disaster. The question of Britain just presented a yet higher magnitude of assessment and triage.

Roosevelt glowed as he recounted to his Cabinet how effectively Harry had joined forces with Churchill to establish a pipeline for everything from weapons to trucks to food. He was pleased with himself for his selection of an envoy. Who would have thought Harry could get on swimmingly with Churchill, grandson of a duke, and less so, yet still OK, with Anthony Eden, forty-four, the glamorous, brave, patrician foreign secretary who exemplified worldly expertise, and was the closest of Churchill's political allies?

This wasn't puzzling to Ickes. He told his diary that Churchill was so desperate for America's help that, had Roosevelt sent a man with the bubonic plague as his personal representative, Churchill would have hugged him. Nor should anyone wonder why FDR had dispatched Hopkins rather than, say, a savvy diplomat such as Welles or Bullitt.

For Hopkins was expendable. Had Congress defeated the Lend-Lease aid bill, or if Britain indeed had fallen to invaders, it would have been stickier for FDR to turn his back on a mission that had been led by an undersecretary of state or a recent ambassador to France. By using Hopkins—an unsalaried private citizen—Roosevelt, as always, was giving himself maximum room for maneuver.

During these crucial weeks, FDR also called upon Wendell Willkie as an envoy to London. Willkie was such a "thoroughly enjoyable fellow," according to Wallace, that even Roosevelt, who never forgot a slight, had to appreciate his warmth of character.[18] In contrast to Hopkins's prime task of large-scale assessment and reporting, the gregarious Willkie's fortnight in the British Isles turned out largely to be a goodwill trip. Men from Iowa and Indiana had the democratic confidence to feel at home anywhere.

Until Hopkins called on him at the Dorchester hotel, Willkie had never met the figure whom FDR had described, at their send-off meeting in the Oval Office, as "the half-man around me."[19] Thereafter, Hopkins wrote FDR that Willkie's whirlwind presence was of real use. However, neither of these men, at this point or in subsequent trips for Roosevelt, was doing anything along the lines of "taking America into the world," as has been argued.[20] Roosevelt was infinitely savvier about foreign involvements than these two envoys.

Joseph Kennedy, a tireless advocate of appeasing the Reich, had left his embassy in October 1940. Churchill loathed him for truckling to the Nazis, and Kennedy actually suspected that there was "a 50/50 shot" that Churchill would have him killed in a mishap skillfully ascribed to Hitler. He had mentioned one lethal scenario to Senator Hiram Johnson. For "defeatist Joe Kennedy," as Ickes called him, and the ranking minority member of the Foreign Relations Committee to entertain such possibilities exemplifies the furies of this moment.[21]

In January 1941, Kennedy spent five hours waffling before the House Committee on Foreign Affairs. It was hard to tell whether or not he backed Lend-Lease, also known as the British Aid Bill. Willkie returned a month later to offer more persuasive support, testifying as the titular head of the Republican Party. "I think there would be less chance of getting in [the war] if you help the British than if you don't," he told the Senate Foreign Relations Committee on February 11.[22] This was to be the Administration's key justification for upholding Britain.

Hopkins, who returned to Washington on February 17, was unwelcome on the Hill. "I'd be of no use to you," he told FDR when they discussed whether he too should speak up for British aid. "People would never pay attention to my views, except to vote the other way."[23]

Roosevelt rarely hesitated to use the FBI and Internal Revenue against his enemies, even those in Congress. They included his own Representative in Dutchess County, the anti-involvement Republican Hamilton Fish. Nor, as previously, would he pass over the small fry. Early in 1941, J. Edgar Hoover ordered his agents to blackball any applicants to the bureau who had been associated on campus with America First. He was unlikely to have taken such a decision unbeckoned. The twenty-seven-year-old Gerald R. Ford was among those excluded when graduating Yale Law in June. Disappointed, he volunteered for the navy.[24]

One did not need to speak against Lend-Lease, or what the truly isolationist *Chicago Tribune* called a "dictator bill," to be caught up in this vindictiveness. Winthrop Aldrich headed the British War Relief Society, and he appealed to friends and politicians for aid. Nonetheless, FDR bundled his dislikes, telling Eleanor that Aldrich would be "the first to welcome Hitler with open arms" in New York.[25]

Lend-Lease finally got through Congress, and on March 11, Roosevelt signed what was formally titled "An Act to Promote the Defense of the United States." It waived the terms of "cash-and-carry" to thereafter underwrite Britain's survival. The return in kind, to be sure, would be the defeat of the common enemy. Nonetheless, Washington extracted concessions over industrial patents and imperial protectionism. Ill feelings boiled up in both capitals.

The same day that Lend-Lease became law, headlines shouted that U-boats altogether had sunk twenty-nine merchant ships over the previous week, most due to a wolfpack's ambushing of a big convoy two hundred miles southwest of Iceland. Hitler declared that no amount of aid could save Britain.

Why, then, asked a good number of Americans, should the United States throw its industrial strength behind the losers? Others already yearned for all-out war. "It is amazing how warlike Southerners are," Wallace reflected. In Texas, the Rangers were practicing shooting down German paratroopers—who, presumably, might leap over from Mexico. He found it laughable, except that "so many unexpected events keep happening these days."[26]

A week after Roosevelt signed the Lend-Lease bill into law, and following a quick midafternoon meeting with Perkins, he left with Hopkins and Ickes on a Florida fishing trip. Those two had not seen each other for months, but they slipped easily into their old caustic banter.

Since the election, Ickes had lined up a lawsuit against Alcoa, alleging monopolistic practices, and had joined with Perkins in leading a hush-hush sub-Cabinet committee to counter German propaganda. He was also fulfilling FDR's hopes by savaging America First and denouncing Lindbergh, as well as the aviator's wife, Anne Morrow, as being "Nazi tools." Not content with that, he ignited another firestorm by accusing every adherent of America First of treason.[27]

Other vacationers on the president's ten-car, air-cooled train to Florida were Attorney General Jackson and FDR's usual staffers: Stephen Early, Pa Watson, and Ross T. McIntire, the White House physician, all of whom stayed up late over cards. It was Roosevelt who woke at sunrise to inspect the new naval air station in Jacksonville, the train then rolling on to Fort Lauderdale, where the cutter *Potomac* waited to sail the following morning.

More than ever, Roosevelt needed "refueling." He suffered from multiple infirmities besides paralysis, including flu, throat infections, frequent bronchitis, and likely melanoma.[28] Additionally, sinus pressure required treatments so primitive that this must have felt as if nails were being driven up his nose. Notations for "doctor's office" blacken his own calendar. He looked increasingly drawn and gray, with fatigue pockets under his eyes, and in late winter 1941 his words might ramble. Then he would rebound, as he always did at sea.

After the *Potomac* embarked from Fort Lauderdale, there followed eleven days of generally miserable cruising in rough waters. FDR didn't mind. Never seasick, he enjoyed himself trolling successfully off the fantail. Antiaircraft guns were now riveted aft of the anchor windlass, and an escorting destroyer hovered half a league away. Hopkins mostly lay in bed, rising only for cocktails and dinner in the wardroom. Ickes's feelings were hurt by seeing close-up the intimacy between Hopkins and Roosevelt, and his sense of exclusion only deepened when he overheard them murmur of how to apportion $7 billion of Lend-Lease.

The president returned to Washington with his still-queasy shipmates early on April 1. Aides took him straight up to his study for a meeting with Vice President Wallace.

Right after the fishing trip, Roosevelt announced that Hopkins would direct Lend-Lease, returning him to the government payroll at $10,000 per year. Opposition to the bill in Congress would have been even fiercer had legislators anticipated who would be filling that new position.

In government, as in the military and corporations, just to be an adviser or staffer rarely bestows sufficient power for any length of time. It is divisional command or profit-and-loss responsibility that carries weight, and Hopkins made Lend-Lease his general operating base for the next four years. He immediately turned daily management over to Stettinius and sent Harriman off to London to align the pipeline's other end. He himself had more important things to do.

With all this underway, Ickes told Jane they had no reason to worry further about the war. Harry would be running everything.

In early May, six weeks after the fishing trip, a *Time* magazine correspondent observed that "FDR looked as bad as a man can look and still be about."[29] Eight years of leading the country through the Great Depression would have wrecked anyone's health, and, each time Roosevelt exhausted himself, it took longer for him to bounce back. At this point, he nearly died from a radical deficiency in his level of hemoglobin.

That crisis launched Dr. McIntire into what turned out to be a four-year cover-up until FDR died. He began by passing off Roosevelt's severe unexplained bleeding from somewhere in the lower GI tract as a "slight gastrointestinal upset." Ickes noted that FDR was bedridden during the middle weeks of May, atypically seeing no one. Ickes would not have been told of the first of at least nine transfusions FDR received during 1941.[30]

Smoking was the universal anodyne that millions found soothing. Hopkins smoked four packs a day, FDR rather fewer, from the tin of Camels in his study. Nonetheless, Hopkins also seemed to possess an endless resilience, and the arsenal of democracy that he had unlocked—vitally including dried fruit from California, midwestern grain, other foodstuffs, farm equipment, and oil—kept Britain in the war.

Roosevelt remained a commander of voracious energy, able to express his vitality to those around him. Before long he returned to action. That spring, and then through the summer, he imposed ever-firmer measures against Germany, such as extending naval patrols of the 159-ship Atlantic Fleet farther eastward. Simultaneously, he took a step or two back, as by declining to seize a German vessel—as his Cabinet had expected him to do by way of retaliation—when a U-boat sank the U.S. freighter SS *Robin Moor* on May 21.

Perkins realized that the country was "standing on the rim of a world holocaust" and saw the president readying his Cabinet "to get a gun someday"—by which she meant preparing them for total war.[31]

That spring, the Wehrmacht stormed into Yugoslavia and Greece, and in May, Hitler gave his last in-depth interview to an American. It was to none other than John Cudahy, who is among those obscure characters in history solely remembered for being found everywhere crucial. His initial exploit had been as an army captain in the 1918–1919 anti-Bolshevik U.S. intervention in Siberia. The final one, before he was killed in a riding accident, at age fifty-five, was to appear at the Berghof, Hitler's aerie in the Bavarian Alps near Berchtesgaden, as a special correspondent for *Life*.

Cudahy was taken aback by Hitler's unhealthy pallor, and, he wrote, the Führer's "melancholy fragility reminded me of Harry Hopkins."[32] Through an interpreter, Hitler assured Cudahy that he held no designs on the Western Hemisphere. Then he cited Roosevelt's 1939 statement about America's frontier being on the Rhine. Had anyone in the Reich ever referred to Germany's frontier being on the Mississippi? No. He also intimated that America was risking war by convoying British freighters.

On May 27, Roosevelt proclaimed an unlimited national emergency—speaking in the East Room to governors of the Pan-American Union while Hopkins lay in his upstairs sickroom listening to a radio. Much of the nation listened as well, and the decree rested tremendous power in the president's hands, which most Republicans doubted he would ever relinquish. For instance, he could limit profits on capital and prioritize defense work in factories. Within twenty-four hours he appointed Ickes petroleum coordinator for national defense. Among much else, this allowed Ickes to control oil exports.

Henry Wallace became crucial to readying the country to face the worst, which he expected to be war with Germany, the most dangerous foe. Neither Stimson nor Hull could have done this, nor Ickes, who everyone knew never feared a fight, let alone Hopkins, nor FDR himself—who, Ickes concluded, had so far "not aroused the country."[33]

Wallace fit well as vice president. There was no grinding of teeth over thwarted ambitions for the Oval Office, and accustomed as he was to the mockeries of newsmen, he could jokingly describe himself as a "practical mystic." All through 1941, his speeches, interviews, and writings made military intervention respectable at a time when many citizens still saw the prospect of war as playing into the hands of Jews, Wall Street, the British Empire, and other "globalists" of this era. Wallace spoke with the passion of a man of the soil from the isolationist heartland, who imparted moral authority to the sacrifices that the crusade to come would exact.

Henry Wallace of Iowa looked as if he would rather be breeding corn than sitting on war committees, yet he was arguing that America's separation from Europe endangered the Republic. Nazi criminality, he avowed, was not just a geopolitical threat from the Old World. America's essence as a nation was at stake. Freedom must be defended overseas because our own democracy could so easily be broken too.

People at home knew that Wallace was sentimentally patriotic for the realm between the Alleghenies and the Rockies, although he seemed to have doubts about the coasts. Rising high had not joined him to the East. Knowing every verse of the Bible, he scattered them over his homilies. The well-informed, such as editors of the influential *St. Louis Post-Dispatch,* also knew that Wallace scorned British imperialism. Yet here he was backing Britain. All this carried weight across the Midwest, and any deep shift in midwestern opinion would to some degree pull the whole nation with it. Wallace appeared to have changed his mind about the world, and when good citizens listened—say in Waynesville, Ohio—they might want to do so too.

Of course, the well-armed Republic must confront evil, but this broad-gauged man equally envisioned an America that did even greater things to better the world. In early January, weeks after returning from his south-of-the-border road trip, he urged the Rockefeller Foundation to embark on a corn-breeding experiment in Mexico, an initiative that would become life-altering for its nearly twenty million citizens. In time, the high-yielding varieties of cereal grains he pioneered would set the Green Revolution underway across the world, keeping hundreds of millions from starvation.

However, Wallace's views often displayed a thinness of human connection, as when he advised the foundation to send agronomists to Mexico—and not physicians. Public health programs would lower the country's mortality rates, leading to "population crowding on the means of subsistence."[34] He deployed a long, cold perspective on Mexico's ratio of people to resources.

Ickes muttered about Wallace's ringing calls for intervention. For the time being, he and Wallace were at odds over lesser matters. At other times, he might embrace the quirky plant grower as a champion of liberalism. Moreover, Ilo Wallace—a protégé of Frances Perkins in Washington social circles, "very graceful and cordial, always beautifully dressed"—had become one of Ickes's favorite people in Washington.[35] When the Wallaces came to visit at Olney, Henry would knowingly inspect Ickes's shafts of wheat and the girth of his cattle. At such moments, the interior secretary seemed content.

Organizing the government for war, or any other issue, was not Roosevelt's strong suit. Indeed, Perkins sniffed at what she came to call "those wartime fantasies that the President rigged up." And Wallace was equally skeptical whenever he found Roosevelt and Hopkins "trying to cook up one of their typical over-all reorganizations." Nonetheless, the myth prevails that all this rigmarole was some type of managerial "strategy," whose infighting was a "precondition to victory."[36]

Many notable dollar-a-year men were arriving in the capital. That said, our four remained the biggest targets for the Administration's opponents, who sought long-visible officials to blame for 1941's grave delays in military preparedness. The Women's National Republican Club, among other civic groups, insisted that "you cannot unite America behind Mme. Perkins," nor "Harold Ickes or that amiable and ailing man, Harry Hopkins."[37] Wallace went unmentioned because vice presidents cannot be fired.

War may be the health of the state, in the classic phrase, but a democratic state is unlikely to be a tight ship under any circumstance. Whenever FDR created a new agency or office, it seemed to spawn half a dozen others overnight. In July 1941, moreover, FDR established an Economic Defense Board, at whose chair he placed Henry Wallace. It was intended to buy strategic materials abroad, and its transactions seemed to be duplicating State Department responsibilities. In August, he also put Wallace atop a Supply Priorities and Allocation Board to liaise between alphabet agencies and the White House. Hopkins of course had a seat at every table, but rarely showed up, saying he hadn't time for "bullshit."[38]

Ickes predicted that few among the influx of "publicity saints," a term of the day, would last. Since 1933, he had seen quite a few of FDR's "crushes" wax and wane. Most such infatuations ended unhappily—as, say, with William Knudsen. He was a self-made Danish immigrant on leave from the presidency of General Motors, and one of the two men awkwardly running the Office of Production Management, until OPM was disbanded.

Despite these sudden attachments, FDR preferred stayers, whenever possible, in the highest ranks of government. He knew the administrative axiom that to hire a man makes a dozen enemies among those passed over, and that to fire him creates a dozen more enemies among his friends. Amid the tumult, people could see that our four would remain on the heights.

Other familiar faces were returning, such as Dean Acheson, who became an assistant secretary of state to handle congressional relations. Surprisingly, he proved adept, given his volatile temper and a demeanor that even Jane Ickes found "snobbish." In just as amazing an example of FDR's forbearance, Acheson was followed back into government by his friend Lewis Douglas, who eventually unclogged the bottlenecks of the War Shipping Administration.

White House personnel had already been upgraded in 1939 by the Reorganization Act, which allowed Roosevelt to hire six confidential assistants to create the Executive Office of the President. Until May 1941, Missy LeHand functioned, additionally, as a de facto chief of staff. Yet, horrifically, she was crippled that month by a series of strokes. At only forty-five, the tragedy of Missy's paralysis, which extended to her voice muscles, was worse than an amputation for Roosevelt, who felt an affection for Missy that he held for very few.

She and Ickes had become friends, and he sensed longer-term consequences: she had kept Roosevelt steady as president, and, suddenly, she could help FDR no more.

All this upheaval of new offices, and of people coming and going in the shadow of war, was compounded by labor unrest. The percentage of workers on strike was nearly as high as during 1937, except that now work stoppages were constricting national defense. A furious public found the secretary of labor easiest to blame.

Two years earlier, the Supreme Court had ruled sit-down strikes illegal. Still, picket lines at factory gates were plenty effective. Strikes broke out at Allis-Chalmers near Milwaukee, among the machinists of Bay Area shipyards, at North American Aviation, and at the violently anti-union Ford Motor Company's giant River Rouge plant in Dearborn.

Workers' pay was not keeping up with corporate profits, among other inequities. And in the background, Perkins had further to confront Communist sabotage, springing from the Hitler-Stalin pact—notably at Allis-Chalmers and on the assembly line at Bendix in South Bend, Indiana. Gears could literally be jammed. Yet here, too, she urged her senior colleagues to be calm. She knew, if no one else did, that the military police had placed officers in work clothes "in every factory that had any kind of important arms contract."[39] That said, graver labor problems were looming, and in 1941, a pattern began of recurring strikes in the nation's coal mines.

As war approached, Perkins and Ickes had been the first top officials to prepare their departments for the worst, without awaiting White House orders. In fall 1939, Perkins had begun to expand her Bureau of Labor Statistics. Ickes, in turn, had created a defense resources committee at Interior to stockpile strategic minerals, open huge tracts of land for bombing ranges, and redirect the tremendous power output of the great western dams toward arms production. In addition, he was urging Native Americans to enlist and enlarging the Alaska Railroad.

By November, he also was appointed solid fuels coordinator. Altogether, he dominated every usable form of energy in the country: hydroelectric, oil, gas, coal, coke. And by now he had created his own directorate for forestry resources that also covered the Territory of Alaska, where Interior and the War Department were frantically prepositioning military supplies against an expected attack from Japan.

At four o'clock Sunday morning, June 22, 1941, proudly modern Germany, relying on two hundred times more horses than tanks, blitzed three million men into the lands Stalin had occupied since 1939, then pushed ever farther east. Nothing was heard from the White House for two days, until Roosevelt stated matter-of-factly at his regular Tuesday afternoon press conference that, yes, the Soviet Union would likely qualify for Lend-Lease. But that seemed moot. He met with Chief of Staff Marshall and Chief of Naval Operations Harold Stark on Wednesday morning and lunched on Thursday with Marine Corps Commandant Thomas Holcomb. All insisted the Red Army would collapse in four or five weeks. Stimson and Knox gave it three.

At least Perkins saw Bolshevik subversion in defense plants—now that Moscow no longer backed its Nazi ally—cease overnight once the Communist Party USA fell into line behind Stalin.

Germany seemed to be multiplying its strength beyond measure. Furthermore, Soviet Russia—now fighting in its west—had signed a neutrality pact with Tokyo in April, intended to protect its eastern reaches. With a neutralized, preoccupied Russia across the Sea of Japan, Tokyo's militarists were thereby much freer to thrust south—to the Philippines, the Dutch East Indies, Indochina, and Australia. Altogether, after June 22, Americans were looking down a much shorter gun barrel across the

Pacific. Still, Roosevelt was determined to postpone the day of decision as long as possible.

"I simply have not got enough navy to go round," he explained to Ickes, who wanted to lash out simultaneously over both oceans.[40] Instead, Roosevelt tried to apply the new instrument of economic warfare against Tokyo. Cordell Hull had to make the case personally to Chase Manhattan Bank for the need to restrict credits, although he could only do so to an underling: Chairman Aldrich was unavailable for the secretary of state, a clear sign of the New Deal having changed only so much in American life.

Then as today, sanctions were a natural tool for a business democracy, except that trying to fine-tune economic warfare always proves more difficult than politicians, journalists, and church organizations expect.

While the clock ticked through 1941, America was walking closer to the edge than decision-makers realized. Few grasped how close a "best-case scenario" of containing Japan at its most vulnerable points came to Tokyo's own "worst case" of Western supremacy and domestic economic collapse.

Japan still depended on the United States for 80 percent of its oil, and Ickes decided to squeeze this chokepoint. Why postpone the day of decision?

During mid-June, a Japanese tanker lying in South Philadelphia ready to be pumped full gave him the palpable excuse of there being inadequate oil supplies for the Eastern Seaboard. Nor did he just impose a halt: there rapidly followed a de facto oil embargo. No one on the White House staff had ever seen FDR so angry as when he heard of this—nearly too furious to speak. An exchange of nine letters ensued between Ickes and Roosevelt, just four blocks apart, as the president accused the secretary of being so ignorant as to risk provoking Japan into grabbing the oil wells of the Dutch East Indies.

Declaring himself happy to resign, the unrepentant Ickes rebuked his chief for not taking much more drastic action against Germany too. From this point on, the flow of oil and gasoline to Japan was steadily curtailed, and Ickes's original decision proved too popular for it to be reversed, or for him to be fired.[41] And, within weeks, he was echoed by Wallace, who saw reason to caution the president against taking an "appeasing stand."[42]

More prudently deployed sanctions against Japan were falling away under the conflicting pressures of "too many policies within one administration," concludes Jonathan Utley in *Going to War with Japan: 1937–1941*. The U.S. approach to Tokyo was "plagued by chaos," and Roosevelt, who in any event liked this disorder too much, was running out of time.[43]

As in our more recent past, Washington barely considered the lack of self-awareness among aggressors who, when resisted, feel livid at being unjustly threatened.

That summer, FDR returned Hopkins to London, this time as a government official. He flew out of Canada in mid-July on a B-24 Liberator bomber among twenty-one aircraft being ferried overseas for Lend-Lease. In England, he attended a meeting of Churchill's war cabinet, joined bilateral military staff talks, delivered an inspiring speech over the BBC, and also met with the Soviet ambassador. On the twenty-eighth, he braved the Arctic cold to take a perilous twenty-one-hour flight in an unheated Catalina floatplane. It soared from Invergordon in Scotland around the German-occupied north coast of Norway to Archangel, the Russian White Sea port.

Once the Russians flew him to Moscow, which was under air attack—the Wehrmacht pressing only two hundred miles to the west—he met with Stalin for a total of six hours.[44] In the Kremlin, Hopkins's conscious proletarian airs as the "harness maker's son" fell flat. Excluding Minister of Foreign Affairs Vyacheslav Molotov, who came from the haute bourgeoisie, every Politburo member had fought his way up from far grittier origins.

No matter: Hopkins had to assess Soviet Russia's ability to survive. He judged that it would, which was the first step to four years of Stalin receiving oceans of lifesaving Lend-Lease aid of every form—TNT, rifles, boots, and uranium, too. No conditions were asked, with consequences to be seen. A deeply experienced military attaché at the American embassy had doubts about forfeiting all this U.S. leverage. Brooking no disagreement, as usual, Hopkins had him replaced by another colonel, now known as an NKVD asset.[45]

Hopkins was fitting together the economic framework of world war, while knowing nothing of the Soviet system of slavery, nor of its predatory appetites, let alone the degree to which the NKVD and other Soviet "organs" had penetrated the Administration. His highly classified reports to FDR about Stalin would be in the hands of the *Vozhd* within weeks of his return.

Pale and tired, at times inaudible, he fell desperately ill on the thirty-hour return flight to Scotland and required lifesaving blood transfusions in the sickbay of the HMS *Prince of Wales* after deplaning, so heroically, in rough seas at Scapa Flow on August 2. (Consciously or not, he had left his satchel of medicines and nutrients at Spaso House, the U.S. embassy residence in Moscow.)

Another reason for Hopkins's visit to London had been to convey an invitation from Roosevelt. The first of what would be eleven wartime conferences between FDR and Churchill occurred clandestinely between August 9 and 12 aboard ship in Newfoundland's wilderness-encircled Placentia Bay. Hopkins crossed the Atlantic along with Harriman and Joseph Kennedy's replacement as ambassador in London. That was the spiritual John Gilbert Winant, one of Perkins's favorite people, as well as of Ickes's, and a pioneer chairman of the Social Security Board. All sailed with Churchill and his top advisers on the war-scarred battleship known to its swabbies as "The POW."

Ickes, meanwhile, had launched the first shipment of gasoline to Russia, sent in steel drums during early August aboard a Soviet freighter on the 5,508-mile run out of Los Angeles to Vladivostok. He expected more Russian tankers to dock in L.A. soon and promised Roosevelt to additionally launch fuel shipments from East Coast ports on the more perilous route to Archangel—as Stalin had demanded. The Soviets would get two and a half million barrels of fuel by year's end. Due to Hopkins's Lend-Lease plans, Ickes also rushed to hand over scarce U.S. tankers to the Soviet Union, a major oil producer that still needed Lend-Lease to supply it with cracking machinery to refine aircraft fuel.

Also, he threw himself into constructing the world's mightiest pipelines from southwestern oil fields to East Coast ports—beginning to do so with Jesse, whom he assessed as a "law unto himself," and therefore helpful, for the moment.[46]

By this time, Ickes was on the edge of a breakdown, and Jane pulled him away for two isolated summer weeks in a five-room log cabin on Mount Storm King in Washington State's Olympic National Park. Even so, newspapers filtered in from the ranger station, so he could read of the annihilationist siege of Leningrad by Hitler's Army Group North. And equally grave, he learned of Hopkins's appointment as special assistant to the president.

The outcome of Roosevelt's meeting with Churchill, with whom he had been exchanging calls and cables since the war began, was "very, very lucky," Perkins reflected.[47] She claimed to have met Churchill through mutual friends before the First World War, and FDR had therefore been pumping her for insights before he sailed into Placentia Bay.

"Frances, you know Churchill pretty well, don't you? What kind of a fellow do you think he is? Will he keep his word?"

Perkins was worried about how FDR would react to a man more blue-blooded than he, a veteran of forty years in Parliament who led a quarter of the world, possessed far more experience of war, whose self-composed speeches FDR envied, and whom he had met glancingly in London, during July 1918, only to feel snubbed. Worse yet, Churchill in 1937 had decried Roosevelt's "ruthless war on private enterprise."[48] Yet this encounter "somewhere at sea" turned out to be successful, even if much was symbolic, such as the Atlantic Charter.

This document was basically a 374-word U.S.-proposed press release. The British Empire would adhere to little of it for another twenty years, such as calls for the self-determination of nations and equal terms of trade. And, always, the pivotal fifth clause—the very one that reflects the clout of Ickes, Perkins, and Wallace in the thinking of this Administration, even on grand strategy—is overlooked. Though FDR would soon backtrack on this aspect of war aims, so as not to alarm conservatives, the fifth clause proclaims "improved labor standards, economic advancement and social security" worldwide.[49]

Nonetheless, many Americans remained indifferent. They had what Perkins called "a kind of 'where is Europe?' state of mind." Some interest existed along the East Coast, she discerned, but otherwise feelings of insularity persisted.[50] The House of Representatives reflected public opinion on August 12, 1941, when it famously voted only 203 to 202 to extend 1940's Selective Service Act, the alternative to which would have been discharging tens of thousands of conscripts who were beginning to call themselves "GIs."

By this time—two weeks after Hopkins returned—Germany's Army Group Center of nearly two million men had encircled Soviet forces in the Battle of Kyiv and rammed through Smolensk, the key to Moscow. The Cabinet met on August 21 around a new, coffin-shaped table—five feet wide in the middle and tapering to three feet at either end. That seemed symbolic too. Roosevelt now sat at the middle, with his back to the tall French windows. Otherwise, everyone kept their places by seniority, as they listened to him enthuse about his recent days at sea.

Perkins watched him acutely. Beyond his excitement, she sensed that the tone of the Cabinet meetings had become grimmer, and the president more distracted. It was she, most of all, who recognized FDR's despair over the death of "Mama" in September, so soon after Missy's terrible strokes. His mother, Sara, was the only continuing intimate in his life since his days at Groton. For a year, he wore a black mourning band on his left sleeve.

Late that September, Harriman followed up on Hopkins's venture to Moscow. He arrived with an Anglo-American delegation to establish, under Lend-Lease, the deliveries of everything from tanks and trucks to telephones and tin. Yet warfare was entering the atomic age.

At 11:30 A.M. on October 9, 1941, Roosevelt met in his study with Wallace and Vannevar Bush. Wallace, as FDR would have expected, crisply summarized what the physicists and engineers had to offer; Professor Bush confirmed the facts. Whereupon the president, within fifteen minutes, authorized the unprecedentedly expensive and secretive crash program to build the first atomic bomb. His visitors were nearly out the door when, already thinking ahead, he asked, What about the "after-war control" of this horror they were creating?[51]

The same day, he requested authority from Congress to arm U.S. merchant ships. "We were, of course, very close to the edge of what can't be done, either legally or practically," said Perkins, yet here she credited FDR's inventive mind with finding the means to do what was needed.

Certainly, the U.S. Navy—once FDR had pushed its patrols farther east into northern waters—was already in an undeclared war with U-boats. Lives were being lost, including one hundred of the ship's company of the destroyer USS *Reuben James,* torpedoed at dusk off the coast of Iceland on October 31 while escorting a forty-two-ship convoy.[52] Three hundred and thirty-one American merchant mariners also were lost in the cold Atlantic during 1941.

Roosevelt was seeking a casus belli, while each of his lieutenants worried that this might not be ignited before Soviet Russia collapsed or Britain was overrun. Yet his sense of timing had been influenced by what he so enjoyed calling his "Navy years." He recalled seeing in 1917 how fast the United States could clear the decks to recover the European balance.

A week after the *Reuben James,* senators approved FDR's request to amend the Neutrality Act by arming merchantmen. It was November 7, and Stalin had decided to go ahead with Moscow's annual Great Socialist Revolution parade. When the battle-hardened Wehrmacht had invaded, its generals expected to be the ones parading in Red Square that day. Still, they were forty miles away, and the State Department learned of a secret German requisition order. It had been issued a month earlier to France's Vichy government, requiring two hundred thousand heavy sheepskin coats for frontline officers.[53] What Russians called "General Winter" was closing in early on the vast, frozen, windswept plains.

At the White House, FDR placed a lot on the Cabinet Room table as, unknowingly, they all approached Pearl Harbor. Forty-seven percent of draftees were being rejected mostly for poor teeth and venereal disease, and he demanded that something be done; eight hundred marines were still stationed perilously in Shanghai, and he wanted them out; and U.S. factories, he scolded, were being converted at a snail's pace to war production. Speed was essential. Meanwhile, Hopkins—back at the Naval Hospital since November 5—lay in bed, calling around Washington to snap out orders of his own.

In a Cabinet meeting on November 17, Roosevelt went around the table asking each member whether public opinion might support a decision to intervene if the Imperial Japanese Navy attacked the British island stronghold of Singapore, as seemed likely. This was more of a judgment check than a vote. Nonetheless, for once he really wanted their thoughts. All answered "yes," provided he first explained everything to the country. At this moment, Perkins believed, Cabinet members saw themselves as "all one band of brothers."[54]

The president followed up with Ickes over lunch four days later. He asked Ickes's opinion about whether Japan was playing poker because Tokyo had sent senior diplomats to Washington, ostensibly to relieve tensions—or if it had a gun up its sleeve. Certain that Japan would soon attack, Ickes urged the president to strike first at a place of America's choosing—but, Ickes told his diary that night, FDR had concluded Japan was too distant to reach and preferred to let negotiations play out.

Hopkins discharged himself from the hospital on Wednesday, December 3, in time for supper with the president in his study. They were joined by the nineteen-year-old daughter of Lucy Mercer Rutherfurd, Roosevelt's lover from his "Navy days," whom FDR was now seeing in secret. Two days later, there convened the last Cabinet meeting before Pearl Harbor.

Hull, wrapped in gloom, sat next to the president, having concluded that negotiations with Japan had become pointless. To Perkins, it seemed what she was hearing from Navy Secretary Knox had to be based on secret intelligence. An excitable man who talked impulsively, he spluttered that the Japanese battle fleet had left home waters. The president nodded, scowled, and cut Knox off before he could elaborate. In fact, U.S. code breakers had been decrypting Japan's diplomatic cables for eight months.

"Most of us looked as though our eyes would pop," as Perkins recalled of the ensuing discussion.[55] Yet all in the room had complete faith in the navy. The following day, the Navy Department would release its *Annual Report* for the previous fiscal year: "The United States Navy is second to none," stated the first paragraph.[56]

Perkins and Wallace left for New York once Roosevelt dismissed the Cabinet. Ickes was driven to his Olney estate, where he and Jane would host a large luncheon party on the seventh, while Hopkins remained in the White House with Roosevelt, who had invited Vincent Astor to dinner on Saturday.

That bright Sunday dawn in Hawaii would instill a fear that has endured into our own lifetimes: one moment's inattention and the unparryable blow might fall. The country's leaders were coming to expect anything. Nothing could be certain, nothing secure.

NEW EXTREMES

Attack at Pearl Harbor to November 1942 Midterm Elections

There will be plenty of headaches, but there's plenty of aspirin.
Harry Hopkins, November 1942

White House operators logged Frank Knox's call at 1:47 P.M., putting the navy secretary through to the upstairs study where Franklin Roosevelt was surveying his stamp collection. Hopkins, like FDR wearing a scruffy sweater, lounged on a nearby couch. Sandwich trays had just been cleared away. There was nothing "immediate" or "instant," as is often said, in Roosevelt's response to the Japanese attack.[1]

A full eighteen minutes passed before the president phoned Cordell Hull to tell him war had come. Up till then, he had sat thoughtfully, offering some intermittent words to Hopkins.

Roosevelt needed time to reflect, but he was also displaying steadiness, starting with how he treated his special assistant. Calmness is a supreme manifestation of authority. Had he rushed into action, it would have indicated—to his many enemies—plain panic over warnings that had been missed.

His valet helped him change into a dark sack suit before Knox and Secretary of War Stimson arrived at 3:05. Hull, General Marshall, and Admiral Stark entered one by one during the next few minutes. Press Secretary Stephen Early meantime summoned Cabinet officers to convene that evening.

Ickes proved easy to find at his Maryland estate. Perkins was located at the Cosmopolitan Club in New York, she and Wallace having spent the previous evening with Latin American diplomats. The two regrouped within an hour at LaGuardia Field to board a government plane.

Because the Secret Service has long been within the Treasury Department, Morgenthau phoned at 6:33 to urge that troops be deployed around the White House grounds. "Well, wait just a second," interjected FDR.[2] Additional Secret Service men would do, and he instructed they be posted at every hundred feet along the black iron fence.

All ten of the Cabinet, plus Hopkins and Wallace, gathered at 8:40 sharp to form a semicircle around the president at his study desk, near the door opening into his bedroom. Ushers had already arranged extra chairs. It is significant that Roosevelt called the conference in his study, rather than in the solemnity of the Cabinet Room, or the stateliness of the Oval Office. By remaining in the family quarters, he was asserting a personal primacy and his intention to lead the fight.

At first, he did not even look up. Then, once all were seated, he spent nearly an hour telling them of America's losses: eight battleships wrecked or on the harbor bottom, the mounting death toll, and how Berlin had goaded Japan to attack. He read aloud a draft declaration of war, and wrote down changes suggested by Ickes, then by Wallace. The Cabinet was not totally surprised, having been told at the Friday, December 5, meeting that the Japanese fleet was at sea.

Ten leaders of the House and Senate had assembled downstairs in the East Room. They were invited up at 9:30, entering the study to find the Cabinet still seated and the president behind his desk flanked by Wallace and Hopkins. More chairs were arranged for, notably, Sam Rayburn, by now Speaker of the House, and his fellow Texas war hawk Senator Tom Connally, chairman of the Foreign Relations Committee. They observed FDR's calmness as well as how pale and ill Hopkins looked.

Newsmen were waiting on the North Portico around eleven o'clock as this host of leading figures began to spill out of the executive mansion. Connally, in a tearful rage, stomped off to his car, then halted and turned around. He exclaimed that Frank Knox was a damned fool for having told him that nothing like this could happen.

Connally's denunciation of the navy secretary went patriotically unreported, but there was plenty of blame to go around, and the exact number of dead—2,403—would not be known for months. Sailors entombed alive in capsized vessels were still dying.

Hull urged the president to present Congress with a long, detailed argument; because, he explained, America was entering mankind's most important war in five hundred years. Instead, Roosevelt delivered a six-and-a-half-minute speech the following day at 12:30 P.M., which is remarkable for its measured disdain for the enemy. Slowly as ever, he walked stiffly to the House rostrum, pitching his body forward, using his cane and leaning on the arm of his son, Captain James Roosevelt, USMC, in blues.

The Cabinet sat on his right, the black-robed Supreme Court to his left; behind them the Senate and the House. For once, the legislators had not blustered over who sat where in a joint session. Ilo Wallace and Jane Ickes watched together from the press gallery.

Roosevelt spoke like an eminent, case-hardened judge somberly imposing the death sentence on a murderer. He reminded his listeners of civilized society's moral and material superiority. Before pronouncing the verdict, he had scratched out "world history" in his draft to substitute "infamy," much as he had crystallized the decisive moment a year earlier by keenly replacing Ickes's "fire extinguisher" with the plainer "hose."

He made no mention of Germany, nor of its lackey, Mussolini's Italy. Reports from Europe indicated that both Axis powers would declare war on the United States, which they did three days later. Wallace affixed his signature on behalf of the Senate before he left the Hill. The president did so on the final war resolution less than an hour later, at 4:10 P.M. in the Oval Office, relaxed and confident toward assembled legislators.

Nearly a year earlier, the U.S. service chiefs had crafted war plans giving top priority to victory in Europe. These had just been coordinated with the British high command in November.

The nation's businesslike routines continued uninterrupted, and their very dependability would contribute much to victory.

On the night of December 7, for instance, a three-man arbitration panel sided with the United Mine Workers against U.S. Steel, thereby curtailing strikes in the coal pits that had menaced military preparedness. Come Monday morning, in the hours before Congress declared war, Ickes conducted a previously scheduled meeting of his rapidly renamed Petroleum War Council, which compelled cooperation between Standard Oil, Gulf, and the industry's other giants on everything from refining to laying pipelines to synthesizing rubber.

Meanwhile, far-reaching decisions were being made around the world. "I beg you," Joseph Stalin wrote in response to a telegram from

Chiang Kai-shek, "not to insist that Soviet Russia at once declare war against Japan."[3] The Red Army was barely holding back three distinct German field army groups and could not divert its strength to the east. Russia stayed neutral toward Japan, as it would until August 1945, while Britain declared war on the same day as the United States—as did Canada.

Churchill arrived in Washington on the twenty-third with an eighty-man delegation of service officers, diplomats, and administrators. The two parties examined every strategic and policy issue of the war, established a combined chiefs of staff organization, and reaffirmed their strategy of "Europe-first."[4] Japan's fate largely fell to the United States—and to General Douglas MacArthur, whom FDR had summoned back into service the previous summer to command U.S. Army Forces in the Far East. By then MacArthur had retreated with some seventy-six thousand American and Filipino soldiers into the Bataan Peninsula.

In early January, the city of Moscow, heart of the Eastern Front, was holding—just as Hopkins had predicted in October when the onslaught was getting so close. Germany's advance on the capital now ground to a halt. The Grand Alliance of the British Empire, the United States, and the Soviet Union began to take form.

A mong the many things inconceivable at the outset of Roosevelt's Administration in 1933 would have been to imagine *The New York Times* labeling Harry Hopkins, nearly a decade later, as "war lieutenant." The *Times* showed Hopkins to be an intimate of FDR's unrivaled since the death of the "gnome-like secretary, Louis McHenry Howe." It also described a new inner circle, akin in its function to the original Brain Trust. This body supposedly included Hopkins, of course, General Marshall, and Admiral Stark (soon to be replaced), the two service secretaries, and Vice President Wallace. "Secretary Ickes and Miss Perkins," the paper added, "now merely do their jobs"—the *Times* once more running an article titled "Perkins Resignation Rumored."[5]

Reporters failed to grasp what the military chiefs came to accept. For America, this was to be a war of logistics, as well as one of production, of oil and machines, and of applying the full weight of an open society against tyranny.[6] The mere "jobs" held by Ickes and Perkins affected every facet of the effort in what became "Roosevelt's private war," as lamented

Republican Arthur Vandenberg, ranking member of the Senate Foreign Relations Committee.[7]

The first big wartime conference began formally on Christmas Eve day in what is today the Marriner S. Eccles Federal Reserve Building on Constitution Avenue. On the twenty-sixth, shortly before noon, Churchill addressed a joint meeting of Congress, extending his fingers in a "V for victory" sign as he left the chamber.

Early in the conference, Wallace deployed his total recall of numbers, and his authority as chair of the new Board of Economic Warfare, to collaborate with Churchill's Minister of Supply, Lord Beaverbrook. They came up with the astounding U.S. production targets that Roosevelt was about to unveil to Congress: 60,000 planes in 1942, then 125,000 in 1943, plus 75,000 tanks and ten million tons of shipping.

Hopkins found his way into these details too, such as determining how to rush out a thousand heavy bombers per month. To be sure, he preferred to work at the highest level. "Here is the redraft which the President did last night," he told Admiral Stark about proposals for the newly designated Southwest Pacific Theater, "and which he would like the Joint Chiefs to chew over." In such ways, Hopkins let it be known that everyone was under Roosevelt's eagle eye.[8]

Geography and history were among the "freakish" aspects of Wallace's intellect that intrigued Roosevelt, and both men shared a fascination with the world's deserts. To Wallace, the next step was clear. The direct, cross-Channel assault on the Third Reich being urged by General Marshall seemed premature. Alternatively, he concluded, the Axis might be attacked in the Mediterranean, opening with strikes against German and Italian forces in North Africa. FDR already had this in mind.

Wallace gave him a copy of *The Dangerous Sea: The Mediterranean and Its Future* (1937) for Christmas. It's a vividly insightful book, also to be found at Springwood, and inscribed to "the leader who had the vision to protect this chosen land while there was still time." Wallace included a note urging a Mediterranean strategy. FDR's reply of January 9, 1942, indicates that the busy president had at least skimmed *The Dangerous Sea,* while FDR, Churchill, and the brass were indeed weighing a landing in North Africa.

Eventually, Churchill packed up from the Rose Room, and the White House was distinctly quieter once he and his entourage left town on

Wednesday evening, January 14. Hopkins, who had been struggling to walk, returned to the Naval Hospital that Friday after lunch with FDR. He stayed for two weeks of blood transfusions and injections of liver extract for B$_{12}$ deficiency and wrote friends of "doing his usual tour" in the sick house. When he was finally discharged, FDR shared the good news with Churchill.[9]

Ickes observed these comings and goings while slowly forming a happier existence. By now he and Jane had a seven-month-old daughter, their second child, and he was finding it possible to stay off of his whiskey-drug combinations for weeks at a time. Total war suited him, and he basked in telling his fellow citizens, two days after Christmas, that he was restricting their buying of auto tires to save rubber. Before long, rationing began to bite.

Perkins, in turn, prided herself on never being ill—"like everyone else," she might as well have told herself. Ever since war had broken out in Europe, she braced herself for the worst. Besides expanding her Bureau of Labor Statistics, she had prepared for the moment when she would be pulled into decisions about retooling factories, mobilizing labor, cutting back nonessential industries, and having to adjust the laws governing wages and hours. She enlarged Labor's cadre of arbitrators, the Conciliation Service, in the hope of keeping the peace in mines and factories. She also tripled the staff of the Children's Bureau, knowing it would be needed in any upheaval.

As in the 1930s, Perkins was able to head off a number of truly awful things. Just to begin with, she had deflected Secretary of War Stimson from ordering the army to take over coal mines being picketed by the United Mine Workers the previous fall—the very labor issue that had been resolved with U.S. Steel on the day of Pearl Harbor. Ickes had sat back and watched this conflict unfold over a Cabinet meeting. In these situations, Perkins recalled, "Harold Ickes was a realist. He always agreed with me."[10] To him, Stimson appeared obtuse, and then almost in tears, when FDR sided with Perkins.

At least she felt "jolly glad" that her social legislation had passed Congress before the war, which naturally began to impose other priorities.[11] That said, the New Deal had done much to prepare the country for war.

First had been the quiet military buildup, most apparent with the navy, while Ickes's and Hopkins's recovery programs were strengthening other aspects of defense. Furthermore, the Civilian Conservation Corps had ended up serving as a training ground for commanders such as George Marshall as well as a de facto academy for high-initiative noncommissioned officers, whose training and experience conferred a unique battlefield flexibility on the army. Plus, for nearly a decade, Hopkins and Ickes, and to some extent Perkins and Wallace, had worked more closely with the armed services than had any other senior official except the president. They knew these entities' language, culture, and needs.

Second, the New Deal's qualities of innovation and resilience passed into the war machine, priming the country for the tremendous military outlays of 1940–1941. Huge public-private company structures were by now familiar, with can-do executives prepared to run sprawling organizations such as the Defense Plant Corporation and other novel crossbred subsidiaries of the RFC.

Finally, and despite all, the New Deal had given the country reason to expect that its children were in the hands of capable, familiar people. Far stronger confidence existed in government than when America went to war in 1917.

Right after Pearl Harbor, Americans had barely heard of soon-to-be-famous generals and admirals such as George Marshall, Ernest King, and Henry "Hap" Arnold—and what they may have known of Douglas MacArthur was troubling. In contrast, the public knew of the high-profile, hands-on operators in Washington who—criticisms aside—had long been accomplishing gigantic tasks, such as building the Grand Coulee Dam and establishing Social Security.

And this would be a war of societies, more than of generals.

Nonetheless, one big New Deal feature was utterly contrary to the war effort: the indulgence of "action" for its own sake. Half the battle during the 1930s had been to put people to work, whether usefully or not, and one of FDR's famous rules was to consider "energy more efficient than efficiency."[12] In war, such thinking can lead to the Charge of the Light Brigade.

Ultimately some of the worst of the New Deal's administrative habits would bedevil the Washington of 1941–1945: ceaseless reorganizations, shooting-star appointees (each with his own *Time* magazine cover), and bitter, pointlessly fomented intrigues.

One way for a ruler to keep subordinates aware of his or her fundamental power is to yank one of them very visibly away from favor.
Roosevelt was easy to reach by phone. Around one hundred legislators
and senior officials could count on having their calls put through, until
one day a man might find himself ignored. Others would begin to notice.
If one was fortunate, the grand old friendship might resume months later,
as if there had been no interruption.

Beginning in early January 1942, Roosevelt rendered Ickes civilly dead
for what turned out to be eleven months. Ickes's calls were not accepted;
there were no lunches and meetings à deux, nor trips together. The president looked through him at Cabinet meetings. There were three reasons.

First, Roosevelt had a war to fight and no energy for their psychodra-
mas, to use a term of the day. Second, Roosevelt was taking cold, ripened
vengeance against Ickes for having defied him the previous summer, when
the interior secretary had pushed the oil embargo against Japan. During
a Cabinet meeting of January 16, he handed authority for petroleum
exports to Wallace and what was now his Board of Economic Warfare.
When doing so, he told everyone—as Ickes sat in his appointed chair—
that, should artists ever portray events of this war, "there ought to be
a picture of Harold stripped to his underwear, saying 'they have taken
everything away from me.'"[13] A third occasion for this banishment surely
stemmed from Ickes's newly autonomous life. There were the new children, and his beautiful, supportive wife. His speechless "clam-up" days
were fewer, and he seemed ever in the national spotlight. ("Mr. Ickes"
springs joyfully through a satirical song from that year's film *Yankee
Doodle Dandy*.)

Whatever the cause of this rupture, Wallace could not understand
Ickes's distress at being shunned. So what? He told Ickes that neither of
them "had any kick coming" from their work for their chief.[14] Of course,
Wallace had developed heartfelt ties of his own with the boss. "I used
to have dreams that I would be walking with Franklin Roosevelt," he
recalled, and remembered feeling "very happy when I found Roosevelt
could walk."[15]

Wallace had the keenest insights of the four into Roosevelt's strange
mosaic of strengths and weaknesses. Indeed, he had been right about FDR
proving to be an "unusually good" war president, one reason being that,

all in all, FDR had been a fine, agile peacetime leader. Only Perkins's insights were similarly acute, as, of course, had been Missy LeHand's, who from May 1942 onward lived as a neglected invalid with her sister in their working-class hometown of Somerville, Massachusetts.

"In the world today," FDR told a press conference, as if to underscore his dexterity, "things change every twenty-four hours," and America, in December 1941, had truly entered the first war in history to be utterly discontinuous with the past. A desperate search for alternatives to the mutual destruction of 1914–1918 helped assure that almost everything was new: bombers, aircraft carriers, paratroop formations, armored divisions, the ocean-wide objectives of marine warfare, and the strategic deployment of commandos.[16]

The shock of Pearl Harbor was likely greater than that of 9/11 for us: there was nothing for the country to compare it to. Then the Philippines, Hong Kong, the Dutch East Indies, and finally Burma went down within five months. Thailand and French Indochina became satellites. A masterstroke of Japanese special warfare took Singapore, one of the most heavily defended places on Earth, in February. And the rich possibilities of Australia and India were now in Japan's crosshairs.

Among the defeats had been the sinking of the HMS *Prince of Wales* and the HMS *Repulse* by Japanese air attack off the Malayan coast. It was catastrophic proof that battleships no longer ruled the seas, and even Roosevelt and Churchill, two highly imaginative former naval administrators, had never anticipated this technological revolution.

Yet the true course of a war may not be reflected by the alarming loss of terrain on the big maps of a situation room. The United States experienced nothing irreversible during these dreadful times. Defeat in the Philippines was searing to those Americans who knew about it—except that the islands were not a crucial asset, as FDR understood.

Losses in Asia by Britain, France, and the Netherlands to "little yellow men," as Churchill dismissed the enemy, were another story.[17] It was the death knell of empires. FDR could restrain his grief because he only cared, to a degree, for the colonial claims of his ancestral homeland. In the spring of 1942, he wrote consolingly to Queen Wilhelmina, in her London exile, to explain why he could barely help the Dutch East Indies. Beating Germany had to come first, and he feared that Hitler might pull Soviet Russia to its knees over the summer. This understood, he pledged that "the Netherlands Indies must be restored—and something inside me tells me they will be."[18]

Otherwise, the man at the center pondered with White House aides whether he should deliver broadcasts in French, and in Spanish, or perhaps in German too, so that people overseas could hear the sound of his voice.

In the Pacific, the U.S. Navy finally handed Japan its first major defeat during June 3 to 6 at the Battle of Midway, and did so with aircraft carriers, now recognized as the most important ships afloat. Given U.S. industrial strength—and how it would be marshaled at the top, as by Ickes—the downfall of Japan was surely a matter of time.

After December 7, 1941, Americans expected to lead the fight, although Churchill no more conceived of George VI's immense, historic realms taking second place to the United States than he would ten years later—when, for the first time during peace, he would return to the premiership. Friction between Washington and London was inevitable, and Hopkins's uncanny abilities in lowering the heat proved vital.

Another reason one listened to Harry in 1942 was he seemed to have just made the crucial difference: he had helped to convey a lavish amount of aid to Britain, when America was still neutral; and then he applied the same urgency to aiding Soviet Russia when the Red Army was on the edge of defeat—when such help, if any, could have moved at a snail's pace due to justified suspicions of Bolshevism.

Whatever FDR and Hopkins were accomplishing in 1941 and 1942, however, was not intended to prepare the country to impose a postwar "Pax Americana" across the planet.[19] Very few people dreamed of any global primacy, and it was Wallace's resonant voice that offered a bracing alternative to the more inflated of these global notions.

An April 1941 editorial in *Life* magazine by its publisher Henry Luce had coined the term "the American Century." Basically, Luce was urging U.S. political-military preeminence after the war, to be backed at gunpoint. Wallace's response of May 1942 was the most influential speech he ever gave, and received far more attention.

"Some have spoken of the 'American Century,'" Wallace said at a banquet for the Free World Association, before proclaiming "the century of the common man." He talked of standing against the devil and all his angels to exert Christian "social justice"—which, for Americans themselves, entailed healthcare for workers and federal backing of education.[20] The New Deal had to be spread through the world because all men are made in the image of God: to the Middle East, India, and Africa. So motivated, he argued, the American people would fight with relentless fury: "The Götterdämmerung has come for Oden and his crew."

Columnist Walter Lippmann—the cerebral journalist-as-part-time-statesman—assured Wallace that this speech, and Paramount's Oscar-nominated short *The Price of Victory,* which is based on it, were the "most moving and effective thing[s] produced by us during the war."[21] The psychological warfare people translated it into twenty languages, distributing it everywhere to show what America stood for.

Of course, nothing like that was possible with Luce's editorial. Moreover, Wallace had skirted the pridefulness of Luce's "American Century." As secretary of agriculture, after all, he had encountered worse poverty in the Mississippi Delta, the Great Smokies, and Appalachia than anything seen among the peasantry of Europe.

As for Britain, Wallace's views on the first global superpower were closer to those of Franklin Roosevelt's than has been understood. Beginning in 1942, FDR frequently spoke to the men around him of the likelihood of a world that contained little room for Britain and its empire. He portrayed England as an "old, tired power." It lagged behind the United States, Russia, and even China; soon it would be overshadowed by Australia, New Zealand, the Scandinavian countries, "and possibly Holland."[22]

Nor should one see the ties between Roosevelt and Churchill as "an Epic Friendship."[23] A man whom Missy LeHand and Perkins believed incapable of that emotion, and forever bearing great depths of resentment, was unlikely to make an exception for this ducal hero.

Roosevelt and Churchill had little in common besides the war, although both were energized by whatever was huge, such as hydroelectric power, whether on the Zambezi or the Columbia, and also by maps. In contrast to Roosevelt's loneliness, Churchill had a gift for friendship and felt sincere affections across parties and types. First elected to Parliament in 1900, he was a fount of stories, memories, and insights. Nevertheless, Churchill's enthusiasms could wear thin. The harmonious wartime correspondence between the two may give an impression of intimacy and candor. Yet each man knew that history was looking over his shoulder, and both were composing for the record. The "special relationship" that they supposedly personified was, from the start, much less than it seemed.

As for India—the jewel in Britain's imperial crown—Roosevelt and Vice President Wallace wanted it to be independent. So did Ickes, who believed it "inconsistent" to support Britain while it oppressed India.[24]

FDR told congressional leaders how horribly "the British had made a botch of things in India" and discussed with his Cabinet the nonviolent protests being led by Gandhi to "Quit India"—a problem so bad that he threatened, with a chuckle, to hand it to Ickes's Office of Indian Affairs. For his part, Churchill insisted that the Atlantic Charter's call for self-determination did not apply beyond Europe or to people who were not white. In September 1942, he ordered that Gandhi be jailed—about which, wrote a White House aide, the president "wanted something done."[25]

U.S. interests were at stake. Britain's "botch of things" would bring death by famine to somewhere between 2.1 and 3 million Bengalis in 1943, while London held back from diverting ships and food needed elsewhere. Wallace insisted that Britain's heavy-handed imperialism was undercutting all of Asia's opposition to Japan, which duplicitously avowed its anticolonialist principles. Of course, Americans themselves were on thin ice when deploring Britain's subjugation of nonwhite peoples, and Wallace's ideals overall were far from being applied at home.

In Washington, racism was ubiquitous, but not universal. Most "good white Christians" held opinions such as those of Secretary of War Stimson, who believed Blacks "lacked the moral and mental qualifications" to handle modern weaponry, or of the president, who concluded that "the Negro is inferior in combat"—presuming himself an expert because of what he had observed of Senegalese troops on World War I's Western Front. Ensconced outside the Oval Office, Stephen Early was as vocal about "Goddamned Jews" as he was violent toward Negroes.[26]

Ickes was among a handful of officials at the top convinced that Black Americans made equally good fighting men. As for Europe's Jews, he knew where the responsibility lay for "the right of asylum having been allowed to die." He faulted his own Administration, not Congress.

Throughout her husband's presidency, Eleanor Roosevelt was the nation's preeminent voice of humanitarian concerns, whether those might be Blacks, Jews, or Japanese Americans. Yet, when expedient, she used her pulpit to rationalize some of the Administration's worst failings, which had included explaining away in her newspaper column Stephen Early's assault on Patrolman Sloan.

Prospects for "political refugees," which then largely meant Jews, were near hopeless by 1942, and made worse by unfounded imputations of espionage. Here as well Eleanor championed the oppressed, although she might also rationalize her husband's inaction. She tried to reassure one Jewish advocate: "He [FDR] feels that if a few of the people are turned down you should not become discouraged, because sometimes things are discovered in an investigation which make it necessary to refuse and these investigations have to be made."[27]

August to October 1942 proved to be the Holocaust's deadliest months: 1.32 million Jews were exterminated, as were Roma, Jehovah's Witnesses, and others "unpure." By then Washington had incontrovertible evidence.

On October 7, after being approached by Rabbi Wise, Secretary Ickes revived hopes about the Virgin Islands becoming a refuge, and he wrote to FDR urging that the territory might help save even just a thousand Jewish children. The president's written reply asked him to speak to the State Department "in regard to the Jewish children"—which meant slamming the gates.[28]

There was no more "context" here—beyond FDR's personal political convenience—than in his obstruction of the anti-lynching bill.

Ironically, Secretary Morgenthau, a man more tender to minorities than most of his Cabinet colleagues, was the first top official to encounter another tragedy of this Administration. It was in the Treasury Department, just days after Pearl Harbor, that the decision-making began that would lead to Roosevelt's February 19 executive order imprisoning Americans of Japanese ancestry, most of whom were citizens.

Japanese-Americans lived mostly in the westernmost states, where resentment at their successes in farming and small business had been gathering for at least thirty years. During 1941, racist hatreds had intensified from Los Angeles to Seattle, fed by government civil defense programs highlighting "fifth columnists." Treasury was at the forefront of what ensued because of its responsibility for monitoring Japanese assets in the United States.

On the night of December 11, Henry Morgenthau had arranged a multiparty call in his office with Secret Service and Customs agents in San Francisco. J. Edgar Hoover, director of the FBI, as well as Treasury's general counsel, sat near the secretary's desk, bare except for a silver ashtray prominently engraved, FDR TO HM JR. XMAS 1939. It was impossible, said the department's operatives in California, to separate U.S. businesses owned by interests in Japan from those belonging to immigrants who often listed property in the names of their native-born children. Anyway, "a Japanese is always a Japanese," declared one functionary.[29] Prospects for sabotage were real, added Treasury's general counsel, and this was no time to think of civil liberties.

"No one except Harold Ickes and myself could want to go further [in protecting the nation]," responded Morgenthau, "but when it comes to suddenly mopping up a hundred and fifty thousand Japanese and putting them behind barbed wire," he needed "some time to catch my breath."[30]

Wallace and Perkins never mention the subject in their thousands of pages of oral history and memoirs. Hopkins was too careful to express an opinion, though he inquired about how best to sell off the internees' property to hurry their removal into camps. Ickes held his fire, although he had become known as "Conscience to the Administration" for his liberalism, in contrast to what *Time* called the president's "natural laissez-faire attitude" to civil rights.[31]

Ickes would have risked causing terrible disunity in Washington had he opposed Roosevelt and Stimson publicly on internment so soon after Pearl Harbor. Moreover, California's progressive senator Hiram Johnson, now seventy-six and Ickes's longest political ally, was a ringleader of these arrests, along with Navy Secretary Knox, who was desperate to escape blame for December 7 by fingering what Roosevelt described as "potential fifth columnists."[32]

The "mopping up" of what turned out to be 125,284 people was no radical departure from the scale of the New Deal. Yet the FBI's Hoover opposed internment. He saw no probable cause. Even so, neither Ickes nor Hoover could prevent Roosevelt from yielding to race-baiting political demands.

In March, FDR set up a quintessential New Deal type of alphabet agency, the War Relocation Authority (WRA), to manage the imprisonments. Ickes deemed its work "stupid and cruel," and its key enablers—

Stimson and one of his two assistant secretaries, John J. McCloy—of backing "fancy-named concentration camps."[33] At a Cabinet meeting on June 5, he pilloried the Relocation Authority for settling families on parched, remote Indian reservations. When Roosevelt asked if he preferred the Interior Department to handle the whole "relocation" project, Ickes backed off.

Hopkins went with the flow. He surveyed the camps and reported that they were basically echoes of small-town America, with churches, hospitals, and Main Streets. Vice President Wallace merely advised WRA officials on how to navigate the Senate. Many imprisoned young men—American-born Nisei—were clamoring to enlist in the army, and WRA did not dare to allow this without guidance from the Hill.[34] Wallace, as presiding officer of the Senate, helpfully told these officials which senators to approach to enable such patriots to fight for their country—proving that, once passion takes hold, irony is vaporized.

On April 4, Hopkins flew to London with General Marshall. It was the war's lowest ebb and, one way or another, FDR wanted U.S. forces to grapple with the Wehrmacht before year's end. The two emissaries cast off from Pan Am's flying boat base in Baltimore on the way to Britain via Bermuda and Ireland.

Also aboard was a navy doctor whom the White House physician had assigned to care for Hopkins, and whose orders Harry of course ignored. He observed that Hopkins disposed of medicine "in the bathroom in preference to taking it."[35]

The hardest-fought strategic decision of the war lay between Britain, Russia, and the United States as to where the two democracies would strike in 1942. Stalin demanded the opening of a second front in the west while the U.S. Army favored a straight cross-Channel drive on to Berlin through France. The British, in turn, dreaded a repeat of World War I's generation-winnowing horror in the trenches and pressed for an offensive in the Mediterranean.

The impasse risked splintering the three-way Grand Alliance before it was fully built. Hopkins became critical to diplomatizing the acrimony, as in London during July. But it was FDR's decision to side with the British, and an assault on North Africa took shape. America had not staged a combat landing since Cuba in 1898.

Hopkins returned from his latest mission to be married in the president's study on July 30. In his seminal biography, *Roosevelt and Hopkins*, Robert Sherwood avoids addressing Hopkins's relationships with women. Throughout, Hopkins's personal life had been colorful, and it came as no surprise when, for instance, he brought film star Paulette Goddard—still Mrs. Charles Chaplin—to spend a weekend at Hyde Park during early May. However, the third wife of Harry Hopkins, fifty-two, was Mrs. Louise G. Macy, thirty-six, a divorcée and former Paris editor of the Hearst-owned fashion magazine *Harper's Bazaar*.

They had met through a former fashion model whom Hopkins had probably dated. Early in 1942, "Louie" interviewed with him for a Washington job, albeit over breakfast at the St. Regis in New York. Since then, he had decided to take (relatively) better care of himself, rapidly gaining ten pounds by wedding day.

General Marshall was quick on the uptake. His career had always benefited from strong patrons—John J. Pershing, Newton Baker—and now, even though he was chief of staff, he had a patron in Hopkins. Hearing the news, he wrote to Louise, describing her fiancé as "one of the most imprudent people regarding his health that I have ever known." He asked her to help curb Harry's "indiscretions" (i.e., drinking and personal destructiveness) and gushed of him as "self-sacrificing in the extreme."[36]

The wedding was to be simple, wrote *The New York Times*, and only for close family. The ten-minute ceremony was modest to a point: Hopkins in his usual blue suit and the president wheeled into his study wearing a white linen one. But "close family" turned out to include Marshall, Admiral King (who cared nothing about Hopkins), Sherwood, Stephen Early, Judge Samuel Roseman (recently appointed presidential counselor), and other White House aides.

Contrary to legend, there was no "one-hundred-person luncheon." Nor, as historians write, was Roosevelt the best man; *The New York Times* reported it to be Hopkins's son David.[37] Only later would Louise receive the diamond tiara that Bonaparte had given Josephine, a wedding present from Lord Beaverbrook. Bernard Baruch's war ration–defying wedding party blowout of caviar, steak, and champagne for scores of the select at the Carleton Hotel could wait until December.

Neither Ickes, Perkins, nor Wallace witnessed the nuptials. FDR had excluded Ickes from White House circles; the Wallaces went to few social events; and Perkins was caring for Caroline O'Day, who was in ill health. No one felt amiss at being left out. They knew Harry. The newlyweds would reside at the White House, wrote the *Times*.

A convulsion, such as brought about by Pearl Harbor, tends to revamp government departments and to install new organizations, as had occurred during the Hundred Days (and after 9/11 in our own time). With the arrival of war, the alphabet agencies of 1940–1941 were retitled, recast, or replaced altogether.

On June 30, the last day of the fiscal year, a hefty overnight mail pouch arrived at Hyde Park. It was Roosevelt's habit to review such documents while lying in bed. But it was difficult for him to find peace. Nightmares tormented him, recalled his cousin Daisy Suckley, who often slept over in a nearby bedroom, and wrote in her diary of hearing him "calling for help in blood curdling sounds."[38] The Secret Service didn't rush in; they told her they were accustomed to his shrieking.

That morning, Hopkins entered the president's bedroom to assist with the paperwork. One draft executive order put Ickes in charge of the fishing industry, which gave FDR second thoughts. He joked that Ickes might do something so hurtful as to confiscate fishing boats from Gloucestermen. Hopkins grew serious. Actually, he replied, Ickes would more likely spark a clash with the navy. Nonetheless, Ickes became fishing coordinator. It was another big job: civilians, fighting men, and their allies were consuming six billion pounds of American seafood annually.

Then, on Thursday morning, once back in Washington, he signed what he remarked with a chuckle was the biggest appropriations bill in the history of the world—$43 billion for the army.

FDR no longer looked to the government's big, established departments to handle every wartime responsibility, so he layered emergency agencies atop most of them. Perkins, for instance, had to endure a novel War Manpower Commission being housed in her department, directed by a handsome former governor of Indiana whom she considered "very lightweight."[39]

Ultimately, these agencies were bypass mechanisms for their creator. As before, it was easier for Roosevelt to appoint new people to new organizations rather than, say, to seek congressional approval to carve out an additional assistant secretaryship at the Commerce Department. Similar to 1933–1934, he also hoped that new "action agencies" might add dynamism, and once more he found it politically useful to staff them with significant figures drawn from around the country.

Nevertheless, this second incarnation of emergency outfits was different. A specially created agency, if given authority over a sensitive matter such as civil defense or propaganda, could be shut down once victory arrived, and he asked Wallace to remind nervous chairmen on the Hill of this fact. Also, the men he was appointing to run the agencies were even more grateful to him for, supposedly, giving them a voice in conducting the war. Of course, he was also distributing the blame for mistakes as widely as possible.

Businessmen, most of them Republicans, fitted well into policy making. They knew how to adapt machinery to new designs, to build and expand factories, and to manage supply chains, as did William Knudsen, who enabled GM to manufacture gun barrels despite army artillerists' claiming the task to be impossible. When everything occurred in sequence, Perkins noted, the rhythms, relationships, and techniques of these new government-corporate processes were as beautiful as a ballet. Success, however, required the long-standing departments such as Labor to staff, house, advise, and sustain the wartime pop-ups.

Perkins played a vital role during the war, not least her importance in sustaining those new alphabet agencies, for better or worse. To believe she was pushed into "handling sideshow skirmishes" is the opposite of what occurred, let alone that she suddenly, for reasons unexplained, "lost her nerve" and became "dispirited."[40]

Some of this misremembering arises from cuts to the Labor Department head count—at least as shown on organization charts—as her people were reassigned to the new agencies. However, Perkins swiftly co-opted the allegedly streamlined functions of these sister organizations—such as the Manpower Commission—into her own department's regular operations.[41] Doing so required keeping a sharp eye on the momentary stars whom FDR brought in to advise and direct, such as Sidney Hillman, head of the Amalgamated Clothing Workers Union. In practice, Labor Department employees might be reassigned to work for him, whereas Perkins made sure that key personnel reported first to her.

Additionally, much of the Labor Department's work was being done indirectly for the army and navy. In the case of recruitment, just for one example, the armed services would furnish the Selective Service System with the number of men they needed in uniform, and the call-ups in turn had to be coordinated with the War Production Board so as not to undercut the labor force in mines, shops, and on farms. In most cases, the key analyses and decisions landed in Perkins's office. This was hard, Perkins reflected, while adding that she spent "hundreds of hours straightening out Roosevelt's administrative messes."[42]

Ickes, for his part, dealt with the new arrangements as he pleased. Even when banished from the Oval Office, he remained FDR's brawny reserve player, always available to tackle big challenges, from coal and oil production to labor unions. Even fish. He held about sixteen major jobs during the war, and in 1942 he had just been designated high commissioner of the Philippines. Lots of planning was needed for the day General MacArthur kept his promise to return, bringing independence with him.

New kinds of lawyers were also coming to Washington, notably the brilliant Tennessean Abraham Fortas, whom Ickes got appointed in June, at age thirty-two, to be undersecretary of the Interior. ("He is a Hebrew, isn't he?" FDR had inquired before approving.)[43] Ickes drew upon both Fortas and establishment figures such as Assistant Secretary of War John J. McCloy—down from Wall Street's Cravath, de Gersdorff—whom Ickes called on to help sort out bureaucratic problems after Tommy Corcoran got purged.

For years, Tommy had sparkled like a brilliant adolescent, believing he possessed entrée to the great man's very heart. Still, there was room for only a single "No. 1 adviser," which meant the days of "that little Jesuit," as Hopkins called him, were numbered.[44] Moreover, Tommy became uncomfortably assertive for his chief's liking. He had expected a top appointment after the 1940 election, even a seat on the Supreme Court. Nothing came in 1941. And by then it was plain that Tommy was placing all too many of his own loyalists throughout the Administration.

Increasingly, Tommy's function had become to "handle all the dirty work" for FDR, recalled one of those acolytes, and his methods, added Wallace, were by now "altogether too extreme," which implied work even too edgy for Ickes or Hopkins.[45] At least thirty-five senators also wanted Tommy gone.

For FDR to purge Tommy, and do so with exquisite humiliation, did not mean that Tommy's kind of backdoor activities had ended.[46] Tax audits and FBI surveillance—with Hopkins on call for "hitting them right between the eyes"—would have been routine as FDR turned to his latest iteration of "New Deal 'revenge' politics." Even Ickes, by spring 1942, felt free to go directly to Morgenthau when, for instance, he wanted Internal Revenue to hand over Congressman Martin Dies's tax returns.[47] It was another matter for the White House to be involved, during May 1942, in implicating the very liberal senator David Walsh, a Massachusetts Democrat, for patronizing a male brothel in Brooklyn catering to navy personnel.

By this point in his life, FDR was too sophisticated to care one way or another about sexual preference, but it was dangerous to make him an outright enemy. And Walsh had done so repeatedly: opposing court expansion, backing Farley for president in 1940, then fighting for "complete neutrality" while chairing the Committee on Naval Affairs, and—the last straw—suggesting that Roosevelt himself was culpable for Pearl Harbor.[48]

"You wouldn't think they would go that far," Wallace recalled about Walsh's fate.[49] As we'll see, it was not to be the last time such a sex sting reached out from the Oval Office.

Then Ickes got involved through his intimate ally Drew Pearson—Cissy Patterson's former son-in-law and the country's most widely syndicated columnist—who told him of other incidents with Walsh. Ickes was merciless: he met with Attorney General Francis Biddle to urge prosecution and rid the Administration of Walsh's criticisms.

"The way matters of this sort were handled in the Army," Roosevelt told Senate Majority Leader Alben Barkley, "was for a fellow officer to take a loaded revolver to the man and leave it with him." Barkley, however, was unenthused about asking Walsh to shoot himself.[50] Given what Wallace knew about this incident, he urged Barkley as leader to defend Walsh on the floor of the Senate. In the end, because this was a Senate affair in the 1940s, the scandal could be contained, at least for a time.

When needs must, FDR was perfectly able to get along with opponents, such as Wendell Willkie, whom he always enjoyed mimicking. ("Resvaaar of goodwill" for "reservoir" was part of the repertoire.) In late August, he dispatched Willkie on a global mission of friendship. Once back, Willkie's party reined him in.

That spring, Willkie had become chairman of Twentieth Century–Fox, and studio financing has always come from New York. Therefore, at one remove, Winthrop Aldrich was paying Willkie's $100,000 salary—and so Aldrich reminded him. Willkie might speak of "one world," only to hew the Republican line as November approached. He turned to condemning Roosevelt for having crushed free enterprise beneath unconscionable taxes and regulations.

The cost of living had rocketed 11 percent between September 1941 and September 1942, and the budget director viewed inflation as the country's biggest danger since Pearl Harbor. Additionally, voters were angry at the apparently arbitrary rationing of items from sugar to shoes, and they felt chilled by the war's long casualty lists, with no conclusive victory.

The national myth credited America with having won the First World War in only nineteen months. Now, nearly a year after Pearl Harbor, Japanese soldiers occupied Alaskan islands, and U-boats were torpedoing American freighters off Miami. Roosevelt and Hopkins believed a ground offensive against Axis forces to be crucial politically and awaited the landings in North Africa as Election Day approached. General Marshall explained that these required minimal moonlight, and the only opportunities, going by maritime tables, were early in October or early November.

The sheer complexity of Operation Torch meant October was too early, and, come Election Day, November 3, the Democrats were trounced. They held the Solid South, of course, while elsewhere losing eight Senate seats and forty-six in the House, plus nine governorships. It was a miracle that the Democrats had held the House and Senate, given the astoundingly low turnout, only 33.9 percent—which had clearly favored Republicans. Naturally, FDR still showed himself in high spirits the following day.

"The U.S.A. Goes Republican," *Time* may have crowed, yet it is difficult to see a repudiation of the New Deal, or of "big government," in so indifferent an electorate, as is frequently claimed.[51] The pendulum was swinging in 1942 and a weary nation turned its back on the party in power after a decade and a half of bad times. Nonetheless, the GOP of Landon, Willkie, and increasingly of Thomas Dewey, now governor-elect of New York, once again showed itself to be accommodating to the world of the New Deal—despite widespread anger among the party's followers.

16

WASHINGTON WARS

Operation Torch, November 1942,
to the Coal Strikes, November 1943

What does the State Department know
about postwar planning anyway?
Frances Perkins to Henry Wallace

In August 1942, FDR had circulated a ban against all department and agency heads taking their fights into the press, and against name-calling, too. By the time a chief executive gets to this point, his control of an organization may seem in jeopardy. Chaos penetrated government functions from food rationing to price controls. Therefore, as inflation kept climbing in October, he set up a hugely publicized Office of Economic Stabilization with blanket authority over the civilian economy. Everyone hoped this OES alphabet agency might also stem the infighting.

By 1943, Washington basically had two lines of government, one civilian and one military, with the Joint Chiefs, under the president's command, waging the war capably. Military production delays had been resolved by mid-1942, and the intricate U.S.-British assault upon the Vichy-controlled *département* of Algeria and the protectorate of Morocco, on the moonless night of November 8, 1942, demonstrated precision and Allied cooperation.

A week later, Operation Torch segued into a military occupation. Yet, just four days after that, there followed the angriest Cabinet meeting anyone had seen. A furious FDR rebuked Hull and Morgenthau for allowing their people to interfere with operation commander Lieutenant General Dwight Eisenhower's civil affairs duties in North Africa. Then he turned on Wallace, for letting his Board of Economic Warfare intrude on top of this. But, as the meeting ended, he admitted to Francis Biddle, the attorney general since summer 1941, that his wrath was really aimed at the "power hungry" Ickes.[1]

Newsmen dubbed the capital's battlefield din the "Washington War." The origins of this disorder once again largely "came back to the president," as Ickes had observed. At the very next Cabinet meeting, Biddle was amazed to hear Ickes being named petroleum administrator for war, which granted the interior secretary even vaster power.

Altogether, the third year of the war crisis, as the press called 1943, saw the worst fights of what reporters also styled America's "war within the war."

Following the 1942 election, the insular, bashful Wallace insisted to FDR that he wanted nothing to do with coordinating the overall war effort. Yet FDR pushed him to be a hands-on administrator, a uniquely formidable role for a vice president. When FDR asked him to tackle postwar planning, he added that Wallace must not get caught by the State Department. Cordell, the "old dear," would be jealous, although, added FDR, Hull had done nothing to "clean up" an institution "composed of men who were like trained seals."[2] Of course, Hull got wind of Wallace's planning, which fueled what, by mid-1943, became the war's biggest bureaucratic crack-up.

Reporters speculated for a while that Roosevelt was grooming Wallace as his successor in 1945. After all, Wallace had a big, far-reaching executive headquarters from which to operate. His Board of Economic Warfare had a worldwide remit. Behind the scenes, he also served on the Top Policy Committee, where in 1942 he had helped organize the Manhattan Project, which set out to build an atomic bomb. One timely contribution was to prevent the army from interning Columbia University's Enrico Fermi, the Italian-born Nobel laureate for physics, as an enemy alien.

However, on Capitol Hill, where he sat as president of the Senate, Wallace was never one of the boys. Harry Truman, who was fighting Washington wars of his own as chair of the Committee to Investigate the National Defense Program, told him so directly—and blamed much of Wallace's unpopularity on his having shut down John Garner's open bar, which, as vice president, he had inherited.

Yet Congress presented the Administration with bigger worries. The legislators sworn in on January 3, 1943, reflected an even larger cross-party conservative base, many of whom believed that the election proved that voters were sick of Congress's subservience to FDR. Therefore, one priority was to push back.

Within hours of the Seventy-Eighth Congress convening, Caroline O'Day died at her New York home after a long illness that had prevented her from seeking a fifth term. Perkins arrived alone on January 6 for the funeral service at Sunbright, O'Day's estate in Rye. Neither Hopkins nor Wallace attended, as they had for Mary Rumsey eight years earlier. Nor, given the difficulties of wartime, was Eleanor among the fifty mourners, despite having been close to O'Day for twenty years. Perkins endured the loss of a second "private friend." Another stage of her loneliness began, made worse by her troubled daughter, Susanna, now divorced and dependent.

At one time, O'Day had been a pacifist, until Hitler's storming of France and the Low Countries shattered her convictions. By this January, there were more corpses piling up in distant Russia than she could have imagined: the Nazi ring that encircled Leningrad was finally penetrated on the sixteenth, during an 872-day siege in which nearly a million civilians perished, mostly from hunger; and, in the icy ruins of Stalingrad, a great industrial port city, Soviet forces were finishing off what remained of Hitler's Sixth Army. The price was nearly a half million Russian dead, including at least 13,500 "cowards" and "panic-mongers" shot by the NKVD.

During these weeks, FDR observed to an aide that "Stalin is pursuing a policy of attrition the same as I am doing in the Southwest Pacific"—where Allied forces, predominantly sixteen thousand U.S. Marines supported by heavy naval guns, virtually exterminated the thirty-one thousand Japanese defenders of Guadalcanal by February 9.[3]

Roosevelt had no idea what he was so airily talking about. The bestiality and scale of the Stalingrad carnage alone included the *Vozhd*'s wastage of scores of thousands of lives as his generals lined up bodies to throw against a supremely skilled foe. He was conducting the war with the same mercilessness as had destroyed millions of his peacetime subjects.

On January 14, 1943, Roosevelt and Hopkins flew to the colonial French Moroccan port city of Casablanca for a ten-day summit with Churchill and the combined Anglo-American chiefs of staff. Wallace had only been informed of the trip forty-eight hours ahead and, even then, received few specifics. By the time of the conference, Rommel's Afrika Korps was about to be pincered by British forces advancing west out of Libya and Eisenhower's GIs pushing east into Tunisia.

At Casablanca, the president was able to size up Lieutenant General Eisenhower, fifty-two, and Hopkins inspected troops with Major General George Patton. In the conference itself, Roosevelt called for "unconditional surrender" and the Allies laid out the next phases of attack, including the invasion of Sicily and a night-and-day joint bomber offensive over Germany.

Across the Strait of Gibraltar, clerical-fascist Spain remained neutral. As for Morocco, this was French territory, and Germany by now had occupied all of France. It was in Casablanca that Roosevelt first met the six-foot, five-inch General Charles de Gaulle, who was heroically rallying Free France. In a suburban villa one evening, they argued—in French—about the makeup of a legitimate French government. They parted, with FDR convinced that the towering, physically heroic, and already world-famous resistance leader was "a very dangerous threat to us."[4] Ickes—who had thrown his heartfelt public support entirely behind de Gaulle—found FDR's emotions hard to understand.

The president returned to Washington on the evening of January 31, tanned, enthused, and seemingly well. The next afternoon, he met in the Oval Office with Wallace and the top three leaders of Congress (all Democrats, and often designated with the VP as the "big four"). That night, he screened the just-released Warner Bros. film *Casablanca* and, within days, reviewed the conference with his Cabinet.

Hopkins at this point was speaking "as though he were directing the war," noticed Morgenthau; and, even as vice president, Wallace admitted to himself that he avoided issues "where Harry Hopkins' finger was in the pie."[5] Nevertheless, the president had a personal request.

Perhaps it would be timely for his vice president to fly to Moscow to examine military affairs with Stalin, who had not attended Casablanca. The Marshal of the Soviet Union, as he was to glorify himself in March, had been unwilling to leave Russian soil at the height of battle, and there was much to resolve. No second front had opened in western Europe, and Stalin was accusing his allies of abandoning the Red Army to the Wehrmacht's full murderous might.

Wallace was already being tutored in Russian, as well as giving sym-

pathetic speeches about the great Soviet ally. The "security of her frontiers" after the war, he had declared, needed to be as firm as those of the
democracies.[6]

Yet Wallace appraised the world somewhat differently. It seemed more
important first to shore up U.S. ties throughout the Western Hemisphere.
Surely, Pan-Americanism must serve as "the vertebral column" for the
postwar United Nations Organization that the president was creating.[7]
So, instead, Wallace left in mid-March to tour seven Latin American republics, not to return for six weeks. He was already distancing himself
from crucial decisions.

Throughout, Wallace kept assessing the qualities of his chief. He observed, for instance, that "the President was very good at logistics," and in
White House conferences, he had seen him address problems of how best
to concentrate ships, guns, and troops upon a specific place.[8] He listened
carefully to Roosevelt's flow of reminiscences and watched for moments
when the president might tip his hand. He learned how the storytelling
could reflect moods and intentions as well as be a means by which the
president could narrate himself into cheerfulness.

Perkins agreed. To her, Roosevelt "suffered more intellectually and
spiritually" than other men, because of his diverse and understanding
mind.[9] She admired his courage and powers of improvisation—all the
more so in wartime—except that unlike Wallace, she questioned his intellect. She granted he had flashes of brilliance, and she spotted his ability
to discern patterns between wide-ranging problems. Yet it was a gift, she
reckoned, that came and went.[10]

She never realized how much Roosevelt enjoyed playing the insouciant Edwardian gentleman. He liked to make even the grimmest of difficulties look easy. He kept hooting about her Bureau of Labor Statistics
("High-button shoes, Frances!"), though he made sure that the bureau's
brilliant director, Isador Lubin, whom Perkins had hired from the Brookings Institution in 1933, was reassigned to the White House early in the
war as "special statistical adviser to the president."[11]

With such apparent casualness, the president fostered an atmosphere
in which one could speak out. He was ever devious about statistics, for
instance, yet Lubin had no qualms about opposing a request to fix inflation numbers. Always, he was unsurpassed at giving the impression of
having real concern. It was when someone was truly hurt, such as when a

son was killed or mutilated in combat, as befell Hopkins and Ickes, that he was able to display authentic warmth.

Throughout, the strain of war had to be crushing upon anyone at the top. Even the ebullient Churchill lay near death with severe pneumonia and heart fibrillations in 1943—and the prime minister had not been in office for ten years. In Casablanca, FDR had run a fever. In fact, he had returned exhausted. Today, the sharpest diagnosis by a medical biographer identifies Casablanca as a "definite turning point in his health."[12]

Except, to look back, such apparent "turning points" had twisted their way through events off and on since 1933. Ten years later, Britain's Foreign Office, as well as its Secret Intelligence Service, were tracking his condition. Reports to London documented periods of shocking weariness, trembling hands, and sudden losses of color; they further recounted how, the following day, he might be seen racing his bright-blue Ford Phaeton along the narrow roads of Hyde Park.[13]

He was able to conceal one grave illness after another, partly because wartime security allowed him to become ever more remote. Save for Hopkins and a handful of aides, few people were likely to know his whereabouts. Like the Caliph in *One Thousand and One Nights,* he moved secretly through the land, to appear suddenly in a California shipyard, at a turbine factory in Wisconsin, or aboard his special train's U.S. Car No. 1 on a Chicago rail siding.

For much of 1943, victory over Germany still did not look inevitable, let alone that the Reich would disintegrate "unconditionally." U-boats had sunk eight million tons of U.S. shipping the year before and early in 1943 were torpedoing 30 percent of U.S. tonnage annually, or from 2 to 2.5 percent per month. Ickes had been monitoring the whereabouts of every tanker, fearing that they could be "swept from the seas," making Britain's defeat "inevitable."[14]

Wallace assisted those experts working with Isador Lubin to calculate the trade-offs between air patrols, ship losses, and the number of destroyer escorts required—each destroyer consuming three thousand gallons of oil an hour. Only by May 24, after new tactics and technologies were adopted, did the sinking of twenty-six U-boats within three weeks indicate victory in the long and terrible Battle of the Atlantic.

Churchill was in the White House that day, having returned with 160 aides and officials—utterly determined to head off U.S. plans for a cross-Channel invasion of Normandy. "A submarine a day keeps the famine away," he chirped over lunch to Wallace, who believed that U-boats in their terrifying wolfpacks had been the Reich's last realistic hope.[15]

Meanwhile, Washington's "war within the war" intensified: three days later, Roosevelt issued an executive order creating the ultimate super-agency, the Office of War Mobilization (OWM), in hopes of bringing every vexatious domestic problem under one controlling hand.

"Czar" is a revealing term when applied to U.S. administrative positions. Reporters had coined it in 1933 for one or another luminary of the New Deal. No other advanced country uses "czar" in the American way—except, recently, Britain, which readily adopts American slang. In the 1930s and '40s, this alien word highlighted the unprecedented and often arbitrary power accumulating in the capital.

In 1943, FDR appointed a czar to rule over all previous czars. It was South Carolina's James F. Byrnes, sixty-one, with his slight frame and perpetually furrowed brow, who had known FDR since the "Navy days" of World War I, and had served successively in the Senate (1931–1941), and then briefly on the Supreme Court. It is an example of Roosevelt's political genius that he could get Byrnes to leave the court in order to serve, at pleasure, as a super-administrator in the White House—initially as director of economic stabilization. Before long, newspapers went beyond just labeling Byrnes a "czar" to deem him the "Deputy President of the United States."[16]

The whole time, Byrnes and his staff (which included the brilliant Benjamin Cohen as general counsel) were quartered in the East Wing, where Hopkins also had his office. Early on, when Hopkins strolled over to say hello, Byrnes looked up to reply, very pleasantly, "There's just one suggestion I want to make to you, Harry. Keep the hell out of my business."[17] Ickes heard all the details because Cohen often came to Olney for the night, talking late with Ickes and Jane.

Naturally, Byrnes expected to attend Cabinet meetings, as did other directors of big wartime alphabet agencies. The tight-knit conclaves of the 1930s swelled into a "mob," in Perkins's view, and press leaks rose geometrically. "No business whatever was done," Wallace added wearily. FDR responded by quietly summoning the "real Cabinet," composed of his original ten, in addition to Hopkins—when the special assistant had time—and Wallace. This sowed a bitterness of its own among heads of the new agencies.

Meetings of the "real Cabinet" were much as they had been. At the least, they were useful for "just trying it on the dog," slang for raising ideas. However, Perkins was often ignored while the men talked of war. And here her true contributions need special emphasis, given how her war years have gone slighted in contrast to the more publicized efforts of Hopkins, Ickes, and Wallace.

Just to start, the social programs that sprang from her department were heavily supporting the more than sixteen million women in the nation's workforce by Labor Day 1943, with the number rising fast. Women were suddenly tackling most everything: "We have women helping design our planes in the Engineering Departments, building them on the production line, [and] operating almost every conceivable type of machinery, from rivet guns to giant stamp presses," the aviation pioneer Glenn L. Martin told a reporter.[18]

By private persuasion and public advocacy, Perkins was adding a forceful voice—as a Cabinet officer—to open entire sectors to women, such as the machine tool industry (wherein it was discovered that women could lift and haul weights of some forty pounds). And her speeches urged more women to fill the gaps left open by men fighting overseas.

It had barely occurred to the men around the Cabinet table that women, too, had to support dependents. Initially, Perkins opposed recruiting mothers of young children into the wartime workforce, whereas Eleanor championed a campaign for daycare centers. But Perkins rallied to this cause as well. Her department's Women's Bureau, its Children's Bureau, and even the Wage and Hour Division upheld this enormous segment of the nation's work effort. The government's one-off wartime gesture of establishing federally backed childcare centers—many of them, alas, segregated or limited to areas of "war impact"—is only the best-known of such initiatives.

Otherwise, Perkins's child services staff worked with the army and navy to set up hospitals, hire obstetricians, and care for the wives and offspring of enlisted men. After all, given armed forces that would peak at 12.4 million, she calculated that there'd be some 350,000 births annually in military families, excluding those of officers. And during 1943, she had to fight Congress to get every penny for these needs.

At the same time, she was breaking down prejudice against employing women over the age of forty-five. Their country needed them, she urged Congress. Agreed, they were too elderly for war plants, yet they could staff canteens while younger women entered factories and shipyards. By this point, unlike in the 1930s, she was pushing equal pay for equal work.

"After you get used to them, they're all right," satisfied employers kept telling her.

"I have never found out what it is they have to get used to," she said in a speech to the Women's Trade Union League.[19]

Always, Perkins maintained her essential task of heading off terrible things. One was Roosevelt's idea of a "Women's Land Army," in which city women were to be conscripted for farmwork to make up for lost rural labor. The idea, which she considered "ridiculous," originated in a fleeting program from World War I, and had taken hold in Britain. She asked him to think it through: to begin, how might this actually work once sullen young "land girls" drafted from Chicago or Detroit showed up at the door of an Iowa farmer?[20]

At a grander level, Perkins was contributing to high politics. During 1940, she worked closely with her friend John "Gil" Winant, once a Republican governor of New Hampshire, who at that point was directing the International Labor Organization; together, they helped to relocate the ILO from Geneva to Montreal to escape German influence. By 1943, in part through this body, she was launching her own postwar programs, about which she testified on the Hill. She also spoke at such forums as *The New York Times*' symposium, "Our Future World," of the need to promote "New Deals" overseas.

Throughout, Perkins had to cooperate with Byrnes, because she found herself on so many of what she called the alphabet agencies' "wretched boards." He called her "Miss Frances," in his polite Southern way, and she found him lovely, as when over dinner, with endless stories of his own, and an excellent mind. Still, this was politics, she concluded, and he was a politician with "little experience as an operator." Moreover, he sought the spotlight, for he was eyeing the presidency. She took a different view of public service: "Prestige really doesn't mean much of anything outside of Washington."[21]

Morgenthau still largely ignored Perkins in the Cabinet. He also had travails of his own. As FDR told him, with sinister candor, he always needed "a couple of whipping boys," and assuredly, Henry Jr. was among them.[22] In contrast, Jesse Jones, secretary of commerce, who sat next to Perkins in the "real Cabinet," had to be handled warily.

Jesse had become—Morgenthau or not—the country's war financier. When appointed to Commerce in 1940, he had maneuvered FDR into allowing him to remain as head of the Federal Loan Agency, created a year earlier to include not only Jesse's colossal loan shop, the Reconstruction Finance Corporation and all of its subagencies, but also the Federal Deposit Insurance Corporation, and much more. And, since 1940, he had also been running the Defense Plant Corporation, the source of nearly all capital investment for war facilities and equipment, with massive loans outstanding in forty-six states.

Jesse's interests on the Hill were managed by Texas senator Tom Connally, and the upper chamber accommodated these arrangements at Jesse's confirmation. After all, most everyone in Congress was in his debt, and so, too, was the president.

Jesse had recently placed his own vast holdings into the Houston Endowment, a private foundation he had created to benefit the city: untold millions remained in his pocket. A year earlier he had rescued FDR's second son, Elliott, from a particularly messy $280,000 debt in Fort Worth—merely one of the favors requested by the president. Another favor, that very year, was the grossly inappropriate purchase by the Reconstruction Finance Corporation of 741 acres next to Hyde Park to prevent the land from being sold to a Black spiritual leader.

Once politicians have built institutions of a certain size, such as the gargantuan RFC, they are likely to find other uses for them, and Roosevelt interested himself as deeply in the corporation's business as he did in his opponents' taxes. Wallace concluded that Jesse was keeping a file of every loan and purchase that the president had personally requested. Moreover, he believed, Jesse first required the president to initial the authorizations for such unusual transactions.

Another reason for FDR's caution in handling Jesse was the Texan's closeness to Southern senators. By 1943, according to *Time*, throughout the country there was "only one man whose power is greater: Franklin

Roosevelt's."[23] Privately, the president derided this nominal subordinate as "Jesus H. Jones," though he could not move against him, for the moment.

Since spring 1942, Wallace had been clashing with Jesse over the scope and financing of Wallace's Board of Economic Warfare. At the same time, Hull had united with Jesse to denounce this board as having become a duplicate State Department. Nonetheless, Wallace recorded in his diary, "the president agreed to back me up 100%."[24]

Skeptical about this statistic, Ickes reminded Wallace that FDR never stuck to anything a "hundred percent." Nonetheless, Ickes pledged solidarity in any showdown with Jesse and State, though Wallace told him not to worry: the seriousness of the times would smooth over these differences. Of course he was wrong. Nor could Byrnes—treading carefully with his sights on November 1944—prevent a detonation.

Trouble escalated once Wallace accused Jesse of delaying shipments of quinine to marines dying of malaria in the Pacific. Nerves were raw—not least because the childless Jones had a nephew, whom he regarded as a son, captured by the Germans in North Africa. Additionally, Wallace had sent a letter to FDR that appeared to remind the president of those initialed chits in Jesse's hands.

Roosevelt came down hard in mid-July, although largely by dissolving Wallace's board. A new Office of Economic Warfare emerged, which would mutate into a Foreign Economic Administration, then to be subsumed into the State Department, the last place FDR had wanted to place these functions.

Once again, the president wrote to all department and agency heads about their quarrels: if they took their disputes to the press, they had better first resign. Of course, Arthur Krock, Cissy Patterson, columnist Drew Pearson, and every journalist in the capital chronicled the outburst.

Wallace seemed the one person in town unable to realize that he himself had been scuttled. Within the White House, Sherwood saw this drama unfold and would write that Wallace's public blasts at Jones had destroyed his chances of staying on the ticket in 1944. Looking back, Wallace tended to agree.

Roosevelt's decision to side against Wallace threw Ickes into a rage. He called Wallace after reading the next morning's newspapers, declaring his loyalty to be foremost to the nation, and only secondarily to "the

Boss." Messes like this, he shouted down the phone line, were damaging the war effort. He had also come to view Jesse as the spearhead of a bipartisan corporate fascism, into which FDR was playing all unaware. Wallace agreed. Then Ickes fell quiet, "feeling very blue," as Wallace told his diary, and closed the conversation by moaning that the peace was already lost.[25]

Wallace wasn't bitter toward FDR for stripping away the extraordinary powers attached to this vice presidency. He was being done a favor, he explained to Perkins, by being pulled from the firing line. He now had more time to deliver speeches and to engage with Vannevar Bush and other top scientists about war secrets, including technical deficiencies in the navy, nuclear research, and German rocketry.

That summer also witnessed the downfall of Under Secretary of State Sumner Welles, of whom Hull was determined to be rid, as was former ambassador Bill Bullitt, who coveted his job. Among their means of ruining him were press leaks, including both to Krock at the *Times* and to Cissy, which implied that Welles was a security risk. Rumors of Welles's being "a sex pervert with [a] predilection for Negro men" had been circulating since an incident in summer 1940, and Roosevelt had dispatched J. Edgar Hoover to investigate.[26] The rumors proved true, which supposedly made Welles blackmailable. Yet the president had shown a rare loyalty by retaining him.

Up to a point, during that era, enlightened people could overlook a friend in high politics being gay, despite recognizing how intolerable his life of sin was to most of the country. He might as well secretly be an atheist, with whom one could be on fine terms—until his failings became inescapably known.

In August, FDR reluctantly dropped Welles from the department. He pitched his decision as a way to ending factionalism, though the press wrote of his "appeasement of Southern Democrats" set on ousting Welles on Hull's behalf.[27]

Two things quickly followed. First, FDR elevated Hopkins's ill-tutored protégé, Edward Stettinius, who had been running Lend-Lease, to succeed Welles as undersecretary of state—not the desperately ambitious Bullitt, whom the president blamed for the "unchristian" behavior. Second, and within a fortnight, Bullitt's longtime private secretary and friend, Carmel Offie, was picked up in Lafayette Park by the city police for, as J. Edgar

Hoover phrased it in his report to FDR, "being a pervert." Scholars write that this may have been a coincidence.[28]

Once FDR had ended Bullitt's hopes for higher office, his former ambassador joined de Gaulle's Free French Forces in North Africa. Nonetheless, he left behind useful insights, warning FDR that Harry Hopkins was "a babe in the woods" in foreign affairs, and that notions of friendly cooperation with Stalin after the war were ludicrous.[29]

The *Congressional Directory*, which serves as a working handbook for the government machine, listed a slew of titles for Hopkins in 1943: everyone knew him to be the president's liaison with allied governments, therefore commanding a next-to-final say over all munitions, money, and other outpourings of aid overseas.

Among his titles, Hopkins chaired the president's Soviet Protocol Committee, which thrived from October 1941 into mid-1945. Basically, it placed U.S. factories, production, technology, and intellectual property at Stalin's disposal. It interpreted Lend-Lease—only toward the Soviet Union—to place all transfer of goods free of conditions. As it turned out, when more items were needed beyond this massive transfer, Stalin's agents simply stole them under what Moscow called "Super Lend Lease."[30]

Roosevelt had stated to his Cabinet that the Soviet Union would get priority for war materials over any other country, including Britain.[31] And, in contrast to Britain, Stalin paid nothing for Lend-Lease goods, other than token fees in 1942, ultimately receiving (legally) roughly three times more in value. Congress exercised no oversight, and a career could end if one questioned Hopkins about such generosity, as had that of the U.S. military attaché in Moscow at the start.

To enable this flow, the Army Air Forces closed what had been the world's busiest airport—today's Newark Liberty International—to commercial aviation and dedicated it to Soviet use, with Soviet security, as it did Great Falls Army Air Base in Montana. Spirited out as well were diplomatically sealed suitcases, initially dozens, and then tons. These contained classified State Department and military documents, stolen blueprints, and details of the Manhattan Project.

The FBI, concludes historian Ellen Schrecker, was a classic "New Deal agency in that it shared the Roosevelt administration's commitment to big government." Yet even as the Bureau expanded, it never in that century developed the expertise to contend with Moscow—certainly not at this moment.[32] Moreover, what Director Hoover's special agents did uncover during 1943 was handled strangely at the White House.

Hopkins believed he knew how best to manage Stalin and indeed all-around relations with the Soviet Union. Above all, he wanted nothing to affect the overflowing shipments of Lend-Lease. "Every effort must be made to obtain her friendship," he wrote in one strategic assessment.[33] Therefore, when Hoover told him in May that an FBI listening device had detected Soviet espionage in San Francisco, which linked to the Manhattan Project at Los Alamos, Hopkins quietly alerted Moscow's embassy. "If we can only convince them to trust us . . ." was to echo across Washington for decades.

As in this episode, the urgencies of war have a way of making one's allies appear to be enduring "friends" for people at the top of a democracy. And a friend should be given the benefit of the doubt. Roosevelt and Hopkins did so toward Stalin in mid-1943 when Radio Berlin revealed that thousands of Polish prisoners of war had been shot point-blank in the neck, a number to total 21,892—as shown by eleven graves of neatly stacked corpses lying in and near the Katyn Forest around Smolensk.

Two years earlier, after the Nazi-Soviet carve-up of Poland, Stalin had signed the death warrants, along with his NKVD chief Lavrenty Beria, whom he would soon charmingly introduce to Roosevelt as "our Himmler," referencing the Reichsführer of the SS. Cleverly, Stalin turned the tables to condemn Germany for "this monstrous crime against the Polish officers," and then Hopkins too denounced Poland's London-based government-in-exile for daring to pin the Katyn Massacre on Moscow.[34]

Military necessity imposes terrible compromises, and the Red Army was proving decisive on the Eastern Front. On one hand, the democracies could not have defeated Germany without the Red Army. On the other, concludes Russian historian B. V. Sokolov, "without these Western shipments under lend-lease the Soviet Union not only would not have been able to win the Great Patriotic War, it would not have been able to oppose the German invaders."[35] Still, Roosevelt and Hopkins were never going to cross Stalin.

Similarly, under the "necessity of military operations"—i.e., a deter-

mination to take the speediest path to eliminating Hitler—the Administration avoided any prospect of attacking the Nazis' extermination
apparatus, such as bombing the rail lines to Auschwitz. Hopkins's latest
biographer concludes, "The record is bereft of any evidence that [Hop-
kins] became involved" in the question.[36] Plenty of records survive of his
ties to other politically infused military questions, yet on this decision we
can find only silence.

From the president's Map Room, Hopkins controlled the most sensitive communications. He also served as the gatekeeper who could exclude
anyone except the "Boss" from these loops, even Admiral William Leahy,
whom FDR had appointed, in June 1942, chief of staff to the commander
in chief (basically the president's prime military adviser).

In practice, Hopkins was by now writing FDR's cables to Churchill,
with whom, since early 1941, he had achieved an intimacy of the kind he
had established with Roosevelt. No U.S. official, other than a president,
had ever dealt with London as did Hopkins, to whom the prime minister
was "Winston." Yet, by late 1942, Hopkins anticipated that Churchill
would be ousted once peace arrived. He shared this opinion freely around
Washington, dismissing Churchill as a "hopeless imperialist." Wallace
agreed, much though both enjoyed Churchill's company.

At the White House lunch on May 24, during that third U.S.-British
wartime conference, Wallace had grown tired of Churchill's speechifying
about the indivisibility of America and Britain, and of how these two
great civilizations must be unified—starting with a global postwar armed
alliance—in order to ensure that "the English-speaking people" would
run the world.

"And so you believe in the pure Anglo-Saxon race, or Anglo-Saxondom
über alles?" asked Wallace.[37] Churchill replied that his vision had nothing
to do with race; rather he was speaking of common ideals.

Six weeks later, FDR offered his own opinion of Churchill's tenure
at 10 Downing Street, as reported to London by the British air attaché,
Roald Dahl, justly popular in Washington social circles (and to be one
of the great British writers of the postwar decades). Eleanor had invited
Dahl to Hyde Park for the July 4 weekend, and FDR would have known
him to be, in fact, an intelligence officer with good lines to Churchill.

"What do you think of Churchill as a postwar premier?" asked one of
the twenty or so guests on Springwood's terrace that evening.

"I think I would give him two years after the war has finished," FDR replied casually, while drinking a Tom Collins with three tots of gin.[38]

By then Cissy Patterson's *Times-Herald*, and other anti-Administration papers, were ridiculing what was surely Roosevelt's own determination to stay in office well after the war had finished.

Back in Washington on July 9, Roosevelt convened his Cabinet on Friday. A horde of outsiders, as Perkins considered them, crammed into the room. Therefore, he could not share even a hint that 150,000 U.S. and British troops, supported by overwhelming numbers of ships and planes, would invade Sicily within fifteen hours.

He called this the "beginning of the end" of Hitler's New Europe. In fact, the Third Reich was really meeting its end on the Eastern Front, where two and a half million Red Army soldiers were—at a massively lopsided cost of lives—mauling nearly a million German combatants at the Battle of Kursk, 260 miles northeast of Kyiv. Before returning to Hyde Park on the night of the sixteenth, the president spent two hours in the Oval Office alone with Ickes, reviewing it all.

Less than a month later, Churchill was again at Hyde Park, scheduled to regroup days later with Roosevelt and Hopkins in Quebec City for a week's conference with their combined chiefs of staff and, for purposes of courtesy, Canada's premier. Events were quickening: Mussolini would be deposed by the Fascist Grand Council on September 8, to be followed a month later by Italy's declaration of war on Germany. In Quebec's Citadel, Roosevelt and Churchill pledged to cooperate after the war on the atomic bomb. More importantly, Roosevelt, as did Hopkins, believed Churchill had finally committed himself to the idea of a cross-Channel invasion of Normandy.

Yet, Hopkins confided to Wallace, every time an agreement seemed to have been reached with the British, they "kicked over the traces"—as was about to occur in their endless obstruction of the head-on attack to be known as "Overlord." Neither Wallace nor Secretary of State Hull was at Quebec, although Wallace had urged Hopkins to keep pressuring Churchill. Simultaneously, the vice president was urging Vannevar Bush—deep into the Manhattan Project—to limit the information being shared with British scientists. Both found London "too acquisitive."[39]

Hopkins returned to Washington tormented by diarrhea. His weight plummeted. He had been relatively well early in the summer. Then, at

Quebec, he was drinking hard, only to find himself back in the Naval Hospital for transfusions and injections, with Roosevelt, Churchill, Marshall, and the press once more gravely concerned.

In John O'Hara's short story "Imagine Kissing Pete," a renter in wartime New York pays his landlord $20 for a price-controlled house, but then also $80 for the un-price-controlled radio—a total of $100 for monthly rent. Millions of Americans were making their own arrangements in the heated, tightly regulated wartime economy, and, along the way, were bit by bit undermining the statist attitudes that had evolved since 1933.

Perkins, however, did not believe that war had brought an end to liberal reform. Looking back, she reflected that Roosevelt had said in 1943 "some fool thing, like Dr. New Deal is dead and Dr. Win-the-War is with us."[40]

Wallace agreed with her and believed FDR was wooing conservatives out of necessity. To be sure, Congress abolished programs such as the Civilian Conservation Corps and the WPA in 1943, but these were no longer needed, given the huge demands for young military manpower. As for conservatives on the Hill who still railed against Frances Perkins, Harold Ickes, and Harry Hopkins—and who launched another impeachment motion against Perkins that year—well, that too seemed from another era.[41] Instead, new kinds of reform emerged, such as the president's executive order on Fair Employment Practice to prevent discrimination in defense industries.

Ickes, for one, realized that Jim Crow could best be attacked through the urgencies of war production: "If anyone feels he can't work on courteous terms with a Negro," he said of the enormous number of people now doing business with the government, "I would be very glad to accept his resignation." Still, in 1943, he was attempting to enforce equal employment against the backdrop of deadly race riots in Detroit, Los Angeles, Birmingham, and New York—with Washington primed to explode.

Unlike Ickes, Perkins sought workarounds when facing brick walls, as she had done in the 1930s. She used her department's Employment Service (now technically under the inept War Manpower Commission) to cut off government business from employers who ignored fair practices. She did make exceptions. For example, it was OK for staffers to overlook a segregated factory floor, as in race-crazed Baltimore that summer, if the alternative meant violence.

As for Wallace, he became a rallying point in 1943 for partisans who acclaimed him an uncompromising "New Dealer," as if this were 1933. He could thrill them by, for instance, denouncing the "American fascists" who ran General Motors, U.S. Steel, and other corporate giants—except that the country's hundred largest companies had become responsible for 70 percent of war production.[42] Public outrage compelled him to backtrack, yet ever more people suspected he was out of touch.

To Wallace, however, a "leftist" truly meant Harold Ickes, around whom he saw other "leftists" gathering. But apart from problems of civil rights, Ickes was showing himself able to compromise with the biggest of businesses. The world was at stake. Journalists being fascinated by this switch, Ickes thereby kept getting more press than any other of the four.

First, as petroleum administrator for war, he recruited several of the country's top oilmen, such as W. Alton Jones, who ran the Cities Service oil and gas conglomerate (today's CITGO) to help him manage his end of the war program. Second, while Ickes ferociously cut civilian use of gasoline, he cooperated easily with enterprises such as Sun Oil to boost quantities of this war-winning commodity. Third, he worked behind the scenes with John D. Rockefeller, Jr., with whom he remained friendly because of the Rockefellers' ongoing donations to the national parks. Should an oil company executive balk at Ickes's demands, Mr. Rockefeller would give the fellow a call.

As always, Ickes made it personal. For instance, he threatened to revoke the prized "X" ration cards of senators caught driving to a bash in northwest Washington hosted by socialite Evalyn Walsh McLean and her best friend Cissy Patterson. On a cheerier note, he heroized J. Howard Pew, oligarch of Sun Oil (Sunoco) and rock-ribbed benefactor of the Republican Party, as a farsighted patriot: Pew's immense new catalytic plant on the Delaware River produced 100-octane gasoline as a superfuel for fighter planes and bombers.

Victory depended on which side kept pumping the most oil into the fight. Oil shipped from California was filling the bunkers of destroyers in the Southwest Pacific, while tankers from the East Coast fueled the mechanized divisions advancing northward in Italy. Ickes worked hand-in-glove with the Texas Company (Texaco) to construct 2,753 miles of

24-inch pipeline from Longview, Texas, to Norris City in the Illinois Basin, and thence to Camden, New Jersey. All of this was completed in August, and augmented by a smaller pipeline, in conjunction with seventy thousand railroad tank cars and countless oil trucks. In parallel, he was partnering with Standard Oil of New Jersey to achieve breakthroughs in the vital production of synthetic rubber.

Big—very big—government was framing the war effort by marshaling public opinion, making two-thirds of the investments in plants and facilities, and paying the bills. Private corporations were its means. So were entrepreneurs such as Henry Kaiser, an ally of Ickes's since the days of building the Boulder Dam and the daring innovator who licked the cargo problem in '43 by mass-producing Liberty ships. Ultimately, the army, navy, and air forces never lacked oil of the right kind, in the right locations.

By war's end, the United States would have supplied six of the seven billion barrels that all U.S. and allied forces had consumed to defeat the Axis: one of the great industrial achievements in history.

To succeed, Ickes had to get the War Production people to allocate steel for the pipelines, as well as the Office of Defense Transportation to allot barges for shipping oil. To develop rubber entailed either tangling with Jesse or the new Office of Economic Warfare, as well as keeping FDR's hands out of the problem. (The president insisted that he was "an expert about rubber.")[43] All this was part of the "Washington war" too, except Ickes now described himself as a "super bureaucrat," for whom these battles were not easy, just routine.

Nor had he abandoned his favorite fights. He supported the Izaak Walton League's anti–stream pollution bill to prevent new army bases from fouling rivers, fought Congress over what he believed were attempts to lowball the population numbers of Native Americans, and, thinking as a conservationist, he spoke of the day when it might be possible to squeeze enough oil from low-grade shale. Also looking ahead, and reverting to type, he warned the country against becoming the "futile dupes of big business" once victory arrived.[44]

Oil may have won the war, but coal provided more energy to the nation than other fossil fuels and hydroelectric power combined—steel mills and railroads alone consuming 20 percent of the supply. MINE AMERICA'S COAL, exhorted the Norman Rockwell war poster, WE'LL MAKE IT HOT

FOR THE ENEMY! However, an unemployment rate below 2 percent (assuring tight labor markets), rising corporate profits, runaway inflation, and stalled labor contract negotiations made 1943 a perfect year for John L. Lewis's 534,000 United Mine Workers to go on strike.

The threat of work stoppages in such critical industries as coal—and under urgencies of war—gave labor immense leverage to negotiate. When this failed, an enraged public called what followed "war strikes." Perkins would document some 3,700 strikes of all sorts for 1943—two-thirds of which impacted coal production. Most of Congress and the press saw them as a threat equal to any on the battlefield.

The man whom Perkins amiably called "John" had come to loathe the president. John L. Lewis accused him of dictatorial ambitions and campaigned vigorously for Willkie in 1940. Lewis was himself an inspired mimic, capable of flawlessly imitating FDR, and Perkins too. She, at least, did not mind.

Yet the strikes that peaked in 1943 didn't reflect Lewis's "personal vendetta against FDR."[45] There were reasons for the UMW to act. Coal producers, who a decade earlier had pleaded to be nationalized, were now resisting a two-dollar-a-day wage increase and other adjustments, notably on safety: the industry's bloody record remained worse than even the dismal one of Britain's mines. More than ever, the outcome of strikes was coming to depend on Washington's decision-makers.

Mine owners refused to budge and offered no counterproposals, not believing Lewis would dare call a nationwide strike as negotiations failed that spring. Perkins was drawn in through the National War Labor Board, which she despised as "the greatest pain in the neck." And Ickes got involved because, in April, FDR had expanded his remit to become fuels administrator for war, with even greater authority, such as to ration coal to industries and homes.

Unlike Perkins, Ickes barely knew Lewis and, with contracts set to expire on May 1, Lewis let it be known that he had no time to waste with the NWLB or other alphabet agencies, or with "Deputy President" Byrnes, who knew nothing about labor anyway. He would deal directly with the president, or maybe with Perkins. He might have engaged with Wallace, a fellow Iowan with whom he shared friends back home, but that spring the vice president was distracted by more purely Washington wars.

Again, Secretary of War Stimson wanted the army to seize the mines, and again Perkins reminded him of the miners' refrain, "You can't dig coal with bayonets." Nor, she added, would it be a pretty sight to have a soldier standing behind each miner at the pit face. And how many regiments might this take?

The deadlock became serious enough for Hopkins to get involved—except by then, "Harry had found the labor men a bore," recalled Perkins. He also accepted the hard-line views of the Army Service Forces' Lt. General Brehon Somervell, who had run WPA's operations in New York from 1936 to 1940. As far as Harry was concerned, the miners were "pretty dumb."[46] Like Byrnes, he could not conceive of anyone acting other than from self-interest and therefore expected Lewis to cut a quick, face-saving deal with the president. Hopkins also believed, as did the commander in chief himself, that the miners could just be ordered back to work.

General Somervell was poised to send in troops, and, by the last days of April, the country expected Lewis to be arrested.

For heaven's sake, Perkins told Hopkins, block any such order. The miners would never listen to any president, and they would scoff at threats to send in the army, or to draft them into uniform. Roosevelt tried speaking to them directly, and was set to deliver an ultimatum. In coal country, he was being ignored.

Strikes were already spreading even before the Saturday, May 1, deadline. Within hours of FDR's having sent a needlessly threatening telegram to Lewis, remembered Perkins, she called, secretly, on the president. She made him swear, or so she reminisced, "to keep his mouth shut" as she laid out an idea of her own: let the interior secretary take over the mines.

"Have you checked with Harold?" he asked, always intrigued by new ideas.

"No," she answered, misleadingly, "and don't say one word to Harold because if you do it'll never work."[47] In fact, she had already broached this idea with Ickes.

First, she had to get Lewis to agree to an Interior Department takeover in the name of the United States government. He was willing, given what he knew of Ickes, whereas Perkins was certain that "the United Mine

Workers [would] behave much worse" should Stimson deploy soldiers into coal country. Yet she still had to convince Harold.

"Can you do it?" she asked.

"Well, Frances, I've been thinking about it ever since that day we held that crazy hearing in the first month of the New Deal. Sure we can do it. I know how to do it now. Can I trust Lewis?"

"You can absolutely trust him to the death," she answered. "I've never had him fail me."[48]

Ickes had asked her to get the president to call him. He was not going to make the first move on something this explosive. She returned to FDR to lay out the sequence of steps: he called Ickes soon before May 1. On that morning, Ickes quietly arrived in FDR's bedroom where the president signed an executive order at 10 A.M. All U.S. coal mining had basically come to a halt, except in parts of the western states. Then, suddenly, the White House announced, with enormous fanfare, that Ickes, as custodian for the government, would be in charge of the mines.

Whereupon Ickes immediately did three things: the Stars and Stripes was hoisted over 3,300 pits; he assembled an organization to operate what had been seized; and he sent his own telegram, shared with the press, inviting Lewis to participate in operating the mines.

Nonetheless, FDR proceeded with a forceful speech to the nation, drafted by Hopkins and Sherwood, on Sunday, May 2, at 10 P.M., and ordered the miners back to work. It was a needless irritant. Lewis had agreed with Ickes an hour earlier that the miners would return, and they brushed off this Oval Office excoriation. The decision had already been made by the UMW, and by Ickes.

He asked Perkins to say nothing more in public about the strike. He'd take it from here, and she was delighted to agree. That accomplished, Ickes took lunch on Monday with generals from Free France, who were visiting on behalf of de Gaulle, and they all discussed the future of Europe.

The mine owners were "left holding the bag," recalled Perkins.[49] The property was still theirs, to be sure, but it was Ickes who would be deciding questions of work safety and profit.

It would take months of truces and showdowns for these upheavals to come to their end—with political skirmishes in the "Washington war" that included a decision by the War Labor Board that, for a while, "blew Harold Ickes' delicate work skyhigh," according to *Time*.[50] Then Congress weighed in by imposing a heavy-handed War Labor Disputes Act, which FDR vetoed on the advice of Ickes and Perkins—only to have that veto swiftly overridden.

Two more shutdowns followed, and further seizures were imposed on the mines in November.

John L. Lewis was another figure whom FDR told aides that he hoped would kill himself. Already Lewis was being investigated by Internal Revenue and the FBI. However, at this point, the president "put aside his hatred of Lewis," explains one of Ickes's biographers.[51]

At the end of his rope, the president finally gave Ickes authority to negotiate contracts directly with the United Mine Workers. Ickes thereby could circumvent the War Labor Board, and, should the worse really come to worst, he was empowered to call in the army. After no more than ninety minutes of discussion, Ickes and Lewis signed what became the industry's first agreement of national scope. Ickes had always respected the miners, reminding Wallace at a Cabinet meeting that they were as important to victory as soldiers.[52]

"Well, one thing I've learned," FDR said cheerily to Perkins toward year's end, was that "mine workers won't work because the president of the United States tells them to."[53]

She did not say "I told you so," although she may have put that to Hopkins. She just remarked that the coal miners were patriots in their own way—having nearly depleted the UMW treasury to buy war bonds—but they simply did not recognize Franklin Roosevelt as some kind of ultimate mine boss.

HARD POUNDING

Stalin in Tehran, November 1943,
to D-Day, June 1944

This is very interesting. I had no idea England was broke. I will go over
there and have a couple of talks and take over the British Empire.
FDR to Treasury Secretary Morgenthau, summer 1944

The Great Depression darkened not only the 1930s but shadowed the
war years of 1941–1945 and the full decade thereafter, as Americans
continued to dread its return. Effects would linger into our own day,
because so many people who lived through the 1930s would forever regard the U.S. economy as fragile.[1]

Toward the end of 1943, as victory began coming into sight, the MIT
economist Paul Samuelson anticipated that peace could only bring "the
greatest period of unemployment and industrial dislocation which any economy has ever faced." Industrialist Henry Kaiser even warned Vice President
Wallace that America faced a return of unemployment "so high as to risk
bloody revolution," and such opinions reached into the White House.[2]

Many informed people believed the military-induced recovery to be a
mere interruption of the 1930s collapse. How could it be otherwise when,
before long, ten million or more fighting men were to be demobilized,
presumably into unemployment, with concurrent job losses among the
twenty million workers who had been supplying the troops?

Ickes offered his own doom-ridden perspective to Wallace in late '43.
He combined his disgust at the Washington wars with despair over the
economy's future: the domestic situation was "never in such a mess as it
is in right now." He overrode Wallace's mild objection that, at least, FDR's
foreign policy had succeeded. What about having abandoned Loyalist
Spain and truckled to Vichy France?[3]

Indeed, the fear of being unable to attain a just and enduring peace was the second concern beginning to grip Americans. What was this Communist behemoth on the other side of the globe, the land to which, since 1941, their country had been providing billions of dollars in aid—thousands of bombers, trucks, and guns, millions of tons of food, and entire factories—and which, in turn, was ripping the heart out of the Wehrmacht? Nor were Soviet intentions the only worry: America might "have more trouble in the Post War World with the English than with the Russians," Roosevelt told his Cabinet in late 1943.[4]

Nonetheless, he rhapsodized during these months about the world to come. He envisioned a United Nations Organization, to be sure, and an abundance of other innovations: Tennessee Valley Authorities for Europe and Africa; trusted, multinational "Free Ports of Information" to assure truthful news worldwide; and a re-created Hanseatic League for free trade around the Baltic. The Sahara should be irrigated, China electrified, and tourism developed in the West Indies so the islands could produce, as he told administrative assistant Jonathan Daniels, more than "sugar and niggers."

"He was like a boy playing trains with the world," Daniels concluded.[5] Hopkins, Ickes, Perkins, and Wallace were—once more, as in 1933—the only officials at the top who were unfolding well-considered plans for a radically new environment. In this case, it was for a postwar order. Again, they were thinking expansively—though usually with more specificity than their chief—and they were set for action both internationally and at home.

Just to look overseas: one of Hopkins's victory visions was to convey surplus industrial equipment to "under-privileged countries." Ickes, in his role of petroleum administrator, was working to break British oil monopolies in the Middle East, as the Administration had begun to do in 1943, with what the State Department's Adolf Berle frankly called $5 million in bribes to the still-not-very-rich Saudi royal house. Perkins was busy reestablishing the International Labor Organization—telling both FDR and Churchill directly that humane labor standards had to be written into any peace treaty to protect "primitive peoples far off from the centers of civilization."

Henry Wallace, in turn, was laying out the specifics underlying his "Century of the Common Man," such as how to end famine in China. As before, he was also able to speak of economics nearly as an equal with Keynes, who glided in and out of Washington for His Majesty's Treasury, and they conferred on Lend-Lease, monetary policy, and trade arrangements.[6]

Such planning for a new world in the making was coming from nowhere else at the Administration's heights—surely not from Hull, nor Stimson or Knox, and nothing from "deputy president" James Byrnes. Morgenthau presided over the July 1944 Bretton Woods monetary conference of forty-four nations—which recognized the dollar as the centerpiece of international exchange—but did little more.

FDR's other powerful quadrumvirate—the military team of Leahy, Marshall, Chief of Naval Operations King, and General Henry "Hap" Arnold, commanding army air forces—was focused on winning the war, which Admiral Leahy simply defined as turning Japan "into Carthage."

In contrast to these plans, Stalin continued to demand a here-and-now "real Second Front" to draw down the Nazis' ninety-eight divisions in the East, both sides ordered to "Stand to the Death." His allies' success in North Africa, and then their slow-moving thrust into Italy, were no substitutes. Ickes and Wallace had no direct role in military planning. This gave them the latitude to be similarly impatient. Each rallied public support for the Soviet ally, as when celebrating November 7, 1943—the twenty-sixth anniversary of the Bolshevik revolution, as well as (nearly) the tenth year of restored U.S. relations with Moscow.

The following night, Ickes, joined by the Soviet ambassador, addressed a crowd of twenty-two thousand that filled Madison Square Garden. The future of civilization, he insisted, depended on U.S. ties to the Soviet Union, and he denounced the "newspaper axis"—including Cissy Patterson's *Times-Herald,* her cousin Robert McCormick's *Chicago Tribune,* and the entire Hearst conglomerate—for their equal hatred of Roosevelt and of Stalin. If Communism had its faults, he expounded, well, so did capitalism.

Within days, both *Pravda* and *Izvestia*—editorializing on behalf of "Soviet public opinion"—had praised his speech.[7] The adjutant general of the U.S. Army also attended that night, and the National Council of American-Soviet Friendship, which organized the event, read, to wide applause, a congratulatory telegram from Wallace. Altogether, the highest U.S. officials were marching onto slippery moral ground, Roosevelt and Hopkins included.

Ickes, at least, stood on firmer terrain when, on November 11, the twenty-fifth anniversary of Armistice Day, he sent his own congratulatory telegram to the representatives of Free France. He was delighted that, in Algiers, General de Gaulle was moving closer to dominating the French Committee of National Liberation—despite Roosevelt's opposition.

In fact, the president had just been ruminating to Wallace about the future of France. Few in the Old World seemed to understand our country, he said, let alone its goodwill. Why, in his library at Springwood, he had more than a hundred books about the new American republic written by Europeans early in the nineteenth century—implying he had read them all, which was possible. None of the books, he concluded, had lasted, except for de Tocqueville's.

That Armistice Day morning, Roosevelt laid a wreath before the white marble Tomb of the Unknown Soldier in a cold, windy Arlington National Cemetery. Then the line of dark limousines crossed back over the Potomac. At an eleven thirty Oval Office meeting with Wallace and the congressional leaders, he told them all he was going away for a while, that very night. They knew enough to assume it was to confer somewhere in Africa with Stalin and Churchill.

Later, Franklin and Eleanor dined with Harry and Louise Hopkins before the two men secretly left the White House at nine thirty, joined by Admiral Leahy and various aides, including son-in-law Major John Boettiger. Cars sped them to the Marine Corps base at Quantico, Virginia, where they boarded the presidential yacht to sail downriver for an early morning rendezvous with the year-old battleship *Iowa* at the confluence of the Potomac and Chesapeake Bay. Admiral King and Generals Marshall and Arnold had already boarded so that they, the president, and his "war lieutenant" Hopkins could conduct planning sessions during the five-day voyage to Algeria, the first stop on the journey to meet Stalin in Tehran. No diplomatic advisers would accompany this trip, certainly not Hull.[8] From what Wallace observed, it was the latest sign of the president's having "an ancient score to settle" with the Department of State.[9]

Presidents often have a divided impulse between wishing to appear tremendously powerful and trying to show that, in reality, all their power furnishes them with only a minimal grip on the doings around them.

Sometimes this show of looking simultaneously omnipotent and helpless can be amusing, as when FDR complained for his whole twelve years in office about the terrible food served up from the White House kitchen. Other times the contradiction amounts to tragedy, as it did when President Lyndon Johnson would lament, falsely, of having so little control over his generals in Vietnam. FDR's pretention that he was a marginal figure to the State Department bordered on the catastrophic.

Throughout, it was convenient for him to ridicule State, which he could have transformed to his liking at almost any time. Each of our four listened to his derisions of the department year after year, with Hopkins echoing him by dismissing its employees as "pansies." With his basic decency, Wallace at least reminded FDR that America's diplomats—meaning 701 Foreign Service officers, two of whom were women—included devoted public servants, although many had nothing to commend them save wealth.

In the event, the *Iowa* berthed in the Great Harbor of Oran soon after dawn on November 20, where General Eisenhower met the president and his subordinates. The military chiefs went on ahead while Eisenhower flew Roosevelt and Hopkins to his headquarters in Tunis, where they toured the recent battlefields and saw the ruins of the authentic Carthage. Then Eisenhower escorted the presidential party to Cairo for Roosevelt's five days of meetings with Churchill and the Combined Chiefs of Staff, as well as with Chiang Kai-shek, the embodiment of U.S. hopes for a Christian, democratic China.

Roosevelt, without the benefit of any adviser on Asian matters, claimed to know most everything about China, given his grandfather's experience in the China trade. However, he in fact was ignorant of even a basic problem, which was the ruinous inflation undercutting Chiang's Nationalist regime. As to Soviet Russia, he anticipated that he would "educate" its decision-makers—whoever they might be—by his ability to "get at," or charm, Marshal Stalin.[10]

Finally, the voyagers departed at dawn on the twenty-seventh, having been joined by Averell Harriman, whom Hopkins had persuaded the president to nominate in October as ambassador to the USSR. From Cairo, they flew six and a half hours more, to Tehran. Stalin had insisted that his "colleagues" in the Politburo forbade him to venture farther from the Motherland than Soviet-occupied northern Iran. Of course, another highly visible tactic of command is for a ruler to compel others to come to him, not least when they have to travel ten times as far.

It was a punishing journey for Roosevelt. In Tehran, he, and therefore Hopkins, chose to stay at the grand czarist-era Soviet embassy, rather than at the even grander British one over the garden wall, or with the seventy other Americans at the distant, shabby U.S. legation. To be sure, Roosevelt "was bugged like no other American president in history," according to a CIA retrospective.[11] Yet he believed, as did Hopkins, that their sheer goodwill left little to hide.

At this juncture, Roosevelt and Hopkins might have considered imposing political conditions on the torrent of Lend-Lease supplies flowing to the Soviet Union—an unquestioned total of $11.3 billion shipped to Stalin from 1941 to 1945, in contrast to an obsessively scrutinized $4.34 billion extended to Britain. Instead, they committed to "give and give and give, with no expectation of any return, with no thought of a quid pro quo."[12]

FDR had identified Hitler early on as a madman: Stalin, sixty-five, was equally a psychopath, but neither Hopkins nor Roosevelt had any idea they were confronting something other than a god-awful brutal tyrant. Nor was Harriman, at this point, about to stray from Hopkins's benign perspective, although he knew more of Russia. In 1926, he had invested over $4 million into a manganese concession, encountering Leon Trotsky and other Soviet leaders, and since 1931 had been drawing annual payments, which had run out only that July.[13]

Roosevelt tended to subscribe to the prevailing doctrine of the enlightened, as voiced by columnist Walter Lippmann: the future lay in the "movement of opinion within the mass of the Russian people who are now much waked up and very conscious of their strength." Pressed on by vox populi, one could believe, Roosevelt and Stalin might develop a noble friendship, or at least close personal ties. The alternative, as Roosevelt encouraged his vice president to warn publicly, might be "World War Three."[14]

Stalin had a brilliant grasp of intrigue and the deepest uses of terror, as well as a wry humor, which convinced Hopkins of his "sense of proportion," as he explained to FDR.[15] The *Vozhd* was a cobbler's son and former seminarian from Georgia, with a thick accent: Either he couldn't shake it, or he chose to keep it as part of the menace he exercised over his Russian subordinates.

Stalin never wasted a word nor raised his guttural voice as he sat quietly at wartime conference tables in his finely tailored field marshal's uniform, stuffing his pipe with reliably supplied Virginia tobacco. He seemed deeply knowledgeable of whatever subject was being negotiated. Also, he was a tireless reader who possessed a large library of extensively annotated works of history, biography, European literature, and, to be sure, all the canonical texts of Marxism.

Stalin would say little until late in a discussion, then calmly offer an agreeable point or two. Should a request have to be refused, he did so with apparent regret, occasionally warming the atmosphere with a slight smile. He was, of course, disheartened not to be more helpful because, alas, he was subject to the pressure from those stern "colleagues" in the Politburo.

A more helpful way to conceptualize the *Vozhd* is to recall an observation from one of his favored killers in the 1930s purges, Nikita Khrushchev, who would come to head the Communist Party shortly after Stalin's death. "We never knew when entering Stalin's presence," he reminisced about the Kremlin's courtiers, "if we would come out alive."[16]

By the end of 1943, Stalin had come to personify the soul of Russia for his subjects. Months earlier, Bullitt had tried to portray Stalin to Roosevelt as a cruel, totalitarian dictator driven by imperialism. And Bullitt was the most knowledgeable person in government about the Soviet Union, ever since he had negotiated with Lenin himself in 1919. Yet he received an odd reply: "Harry says he's not," the president wrote back, "and that he doesn't want anything but security for his country."[17]

FDR would not return to the White House until Friday, December 17, having sailed home from Dakar, where he had been transferred gaily from a smaller vessel to the giant *Iowa* in a specially rigged boatswain's chair. By then he had wrapped up a second conference in Cairo, visited U.S. troops in Sicily, and again scrutinized Eisenhower, who he concluded was a fine politician. That was a supreme accolade, which led to his choosing Eisenhower to command Overlord, the cross-Channel invasion of France that he had just promised Stalin for May 1944.

The Cabinet and senior legislators awaited the president in the Diplomatic Reception Room, and after their greetings, he headed straight to work in the Oval Office. He had lunch with Hull—as he would on Saturday with Stimson and on Sunday with Ickes. A later encounter would come with Perkins, to whom he boasted of having talked with Stalin like "brothers," and of his "elegance of manner."[18]

Stalin, of course, cared nothing of what Roosevelt thought of him personally, providing he was deceived.

At each of these White House one-on-ones, the president relived his accomplishments. Dealing with Churchill had been difficult, he said, given the prime minister's relentless opposition to Overlord. In fact, Churchill's disagreement had, by this point, turned into "sabotage," concludes the best analysis of the problem, Nigel Hamilton's *War and Peace* (2019).[19] Nevertheless, the president could tell each of the three Cabinet officers that Churchill had been compelled to accede to the invasion (no need to credit Harry's arm-twisting).

Moreover, Stalin had confirmed that he would declare war on Japan after Nazism had been crushed. Only the date was to be decided. On a relatively minor topic, Roosevelt noted, he had told Churchill, Chiang, and Stalin alike of his resolve not to allow France, once peace arrived, to return to its colonial holdings in Indochina, a cluster of subjugated nations that were to become terribly familiar to another generation of Americans as Cambodia, Laos, and Vietnam.

Additionally, during that first Friday home, he met with his Cabinet as routinely scheduled, at 2 P.M. It was the "real Cabinet," not "the mob," and the meeting went long. He gave them a review of his time abroad, after offering a travelogue of vivid personalities and astonishing sights, such as having flown over Jerusalem and Baghdad, during his 17,442-mile odyssey by land, sea, and air. He spoke, too, of dividing Germany, of offering Stalin access to a port in the Persian Gulf, and of his idea of reforesting Iran—a land, after decades under British oppression, with the worst poverty he had ever seen.

Before long, his demeanor changed. He had returned on the cusp of a nationwide railroad strike and, while at sea, had already summoned the labor bosses and rail executives to the White House for a Sunday afternoon conference. If the Administration bungled this latest industrial crisis, he fumed, there would be repercussions at the polls come November.

Growing testier, he called Washington a "squirrel cage." Worse yet, it was one in which he could smell Southern Democrats, like South Carolina's "Cotton Ed" Smith, trying to form a new party. The problem was connected to the latest fight over the "Soldier Vote." In theory, men and women in uniform had been able to cast absentee ballots in the 1942 elections, although less than 1 percent managed to do so. With November 1944 in sight, demands arose for new legislation to enable an authentic Soldier Vote. However, half a dozen states had no provision for absentee voting and anyway, voting absentee might evade the poll tax in the eight states that required it.

Worse yet, to Southern Democrats, absentee balloting might open the door to Black suffrage. They were uniting with Republicans equally intent on keeping new citizens away from the ballot. Gallup indicated that the Soldier Vote could swing the election for Roosevelt. The ensuing debates led another Democrat, Senator Joseph Guffey of Pennsylvania, to intro- duce a resolution to abolish the Electoral College, wherein lay the power of the South.

The combination of labor upheaval, with a possible split in his own party, so enraged the president that he declared the best thing to happen would be for German bombs to fall on the United States. Maybe that would wake people up. End of meeting.[20]

The next morning, he returned to discussing his travels once Wallace arrived in the Oval Office with the three leaders of Congress. Wallace's diary adds telling details. The subject of Palestine had, Roosevelt was relieved to say, been avoided with Churchill. Then he shared his idea of a customs union for all of a liberated Europe—"Europe" apparently not to include Lithuania, Latvia, and Estonia. FDR had basically accepted Stalin's view: these once-independent democracies were to be absorbed into the Soviet Union, after "liberation" by the Red Army, with maybe some plebiscites to allow the Democratic Party to save face with such ethnic voters.

Wallace was alert to the Baltic republics. Bullitt had told him earlier in the year that it would be "utterly cock-eyed" to believe that Stalin would ever stage legitimate elections anywhere. He had given the same warning to Roosevelt: the NKVD would first cleanse any of these nations of their leading citizens.[21] And so too of Poland, homeland of some five million American voters. FDR reported nothing to his Cabinet of just what had been discussed with Stalin on that topic.

By January 4, 1944, the Soviet murder machine was grinding back over Poland as the Red Army smashed across what had been its frontier before the "Devils' Friendship." Come October it pressed into East Prussia, the Reich's farthest eastern redoubt, with a cry of "Blood for our Blood."

Harry Hopkins reached the peak of his influence during this passage through the larger Middle East. One reason was his capacity to ameliorate Churchill. Roosevelt, in trying to create a rapport with Stalin during his four days in Tehran, had "teased Churchill about his Britishness," he boasted to Perkins.[22] Additionally, in hopes of gaining trust, FDR had excluded Churchill from his first encounter with Stalin, while initiating talk not only about India's independence but of its development "somewhat on the Soviet line." In Washington, around the same time, Vice President Wallace was advising British diplomats that their kingdom's standing with America after the war all depended on its treatment of their four hundred million subjects in India.

Once back in the White House, FDR had scoffed to his aide Jonathan Daniels that "Churchill is acting now as if he is afraid of always getting hit."[23]

Historians describe Hopkins at this point as the de facto secretary of state—which in a sense he was. But mandarins at the Foreign Office, drawing on its centuries of memory, actually regarded him as something greater, and styled him "Secretary of the Grand Alliance," in analogy to Baron von Gentz, the "Secretary of Europe," who moved on equal terms with sovereigns and statesmen during the wars with Bonaparte.[24]

At both Cairo and Tehran, Hopkins indeed spoke to Churchill as an equal, making it clear that the prime minister had no alternative but to accede to U.S. plans for a "real Second Front." Nonetheless, for reasons both geopolitical and personal, he had to maneuver delicately with the weary yet still provocable Churchill. The British superpower was having to confront an entirely novel form of global preeminence looming across the Atlantic, and after their first meeting in Placentia Bay, Roosevelt had barely extended himself to Churchill.

Cheery follow-up cables from FDR early on, such as "It is fun to be in the same decade with you," sound mechanical from such a charmer, and for the president to speak repeatedly of "Winnie" back in his Cabinet was dismissive. A more telling sign of FDR's cold sense of primacy has been overlooked.

Among other achievements, Churchill was a historian, and *Marlbor-*

ough: His Life and Times (1933–1938), the four-volume biography of his warrior-statesman forebear, the seventeenth-century John Churchill, had been a bestseller of the previous decade. It remains a solid account of another epoch in which Europe's fate hung in the balance, and it is just the type of book that, at one time, Roosevelt would have devoured. That said, he never mentioned a scintilla about this fascinating literary accomplishment to Churchill.

Had Roosevelt spoken of *Marlborough*—perhaps after asking Wallace to gin up a summary—he would have put Churchill under his spell forever. FDR had no trouble, during these burdensome years, of discussing Thackeray with personal secretary Bill Hassett. Given that Roosevelt envied Churchill's speechwriting abilities, as Perkins tells us, he surely envied his standing in the world of literature.

"The president couldn't accomplish what Harry could," Perkins observed. One example was to shoulder what, to FDR, was the burden of having to finesse the prime minister.[25] And by now Hopkins tended to be as measured as was his boss. His brusque manner and darting eyes were less noticeable. In fact, he had become like a mathematician who studies the conditions in which a given order necessarily appears, and who can then reduce a twenty-page proof to two lines.

Large tasks often collapse upon themselves out of their sheer complexity, but Hopkins was a wizard at simplifying these challenges before they got out of control—and then persuading people at the top to see the essentials. Additionally, he knew all the secrets; his presence was morbidly dramatic; and one would think twice about ignoring his crisp summaries, for fear of getting trapped in the weeds.

Yet even the Hopkins Touch could fail with Churchill, who kept running off on a hundred tangents: wanting to attack Germany through the Arctic, or the Balkans, or by penetrating the Dardanelles. Ultimately, in early 1944, while Hopkins was deathly ill, Churchill succeeded in pressing his allies into a disastrous amphibious landing at Anzio, on the western Italian coast behind German lines south of Rome.

Otherwise, Hopkins could dismiss with a "So what?" the tirades of generals and admirals, and, like the Boss, could play very rough. Over the years, he had become close to FBI Director J. Edgar Hoover, through nightclubbing and the track: if someone seriously crossed him amid the Washington wars, Harry might forward an observation or two to the Bureau.[26]

His widely known sufferings amplified such skills and ruthlessness. Churchill writes of Hopkins not as a man who was ill but rather as one who sacrifices and demands too much of himself—a very different perspective.

Hopkins had his detractors, and his supposed friend Stephen Early remarked, "The trouble is to find a clean spot on Harry anywhere."[27] Yet in his better moments, Hopkins personified the ideal of a son of the heartland rising high to fight, until the edge of death, for a better world.

While in the Middle East, Hopkins had once more visibly exhausted himself, while further destroying his gastrointestinal tract with alcohol and, for him, a cripplingly affluent diet. He then developed influenza around New Year's, his weight drained to 126 pounds, and by January 5 he was back in the Naval Hospital, by then relocated to the flat meadowlands north of Bethesda. Churchill pressed for a prognosis in letters to FDR marked TOP SECRET.

Hopkins was so ill that physicians feared a return of his gastric cancer, and recommended a laparotomy, which he had first undergone in 1937. But he needed strength before any operation. And so, on the early morning of February 12, he boarded the Silver Meteor to Miami, clinging to his medicine satchel and accompanied by a nurse. He received two injections a day of B_{12} and longed to rest in the sun.

Hopkins always had close, loving relationships with his children: the three boys by Ethel Gross and his daughter with Barbara Duncan. That night, the president's telegram reached him in Jacksonville, Florida, saying that Hopkins's youngest son, Stephen, eighteen and a marine private, had been killed in action at Kwajalein, in the Marshall Islands, and buried at sea. Later, Admiral King would offer more details: on his first day of combat, Stephen had been shot through the head by a sniper while rushing forward with a box of ammunition.

Later, Ickes also reached Hopkins. They talked of the country's sacrifices. Just three days before Stephen's "bad luck," as the marines call it, the secretary had spoken to a class of new marine officers at Quantico. His theme to these second lieutenants had been "liberty," and standing at ease before him was his own son Raymond, thirty-one, who had quit as an assistant U.S. attorney in Chicago and was now set to deploy, like Stephen, to the Pacific.

Hopkins would finally arrive at the Mayo Clinic in mid-March, whence, on the twenty-fifth, he scrawled a bleak note to Wallace: "Things have not gone as well for me as I hoped." Four days later he underwent surgery, as always displaying a careless courage, as if he, too, were Peter Pan: "OK, boys," he said before going under, "open me up; you might find the secret to a fourth term."[28]

There was no cancer, though arduous weeks of recuperation followed. General Marshall acclaimed Harry's "cold nerve and great courage" and, on May 7, flew—together with Louise, working in the capital as a nurse—to Rochester, Minnesota, to meet him on his discharge.[29] They escorted Hopkins to the Greenbrier, the eleven-thousand-acre resort in the mountains of White Sulphur Springs, West Virginia, which the army had requisitioned as a hospital.

Hopkins would endure more setbacks before he returned to Washington on July 4, after an absence of six months. Throughout, whether at the Mayo Clinic or the Greenbrier, he had never missed an issue of the specially delivered *Daily Racing Form.*

Writing in his diary on the second anniversary of Pearl Harbor, the young journalist Allen Drury, who would author that definitive novel of midcentury Washington, *Advise and Consent,* chronicled a frightening realization: he was shaken by how much America's democracy "is founded upon good will—sheer human liking and ability to get along together."[30] The State of the Union message, which Roosevelt had merely sent up to the Hill on January 11, 1944, offered more than enough material to further erode such spirits.

He proposed, for instance, a "Second Bill of Rights." These additional eight were to guarantee the people's "security," i.e., economic well-being. They included rights to housing, a decent job, medical care, social insurance, higher education, and also freedom from the weight of corporate monopolies (a "right" that only today is being reframed to protect consumers from the anti-competitive practices of mighty enterprises).

At this point, the country was enjoying its greatest ever industrial expansion, while also living through the only decade in the twentieth century to experience a downward redistribution of wealth. Even so, on the same day that Roosevelt submitted his constitutionally mandated message, Winthrop Aldrich warned Chase Bank stockholders of a "false and fleeting prosperity" in the face of what soon could be a $250 billion national debt.[31] Washington was spending about two dollars for each one it raised—except in 1943, when it had spent three.

That said, each of FDR's four lieutenants during 1944 was advancing plans for the domestic postwar landscape, as they were for the globe. Perkins introduced a four-point program to enable the country to "get rolling after the war," which entailed extending Social Security to include longer-term benefits for the temporarily unemployed and their dependents. Ickes used speeches, radio talks, and congressional testimony, as well as writings in *The Nation* and *The New Republic,* to champion programs such as covering all student costs for higher education. And Wallace kept offering what he called "idealistic speeches," including ones promoting a domestic Lend-Lease program to guarantee suitable jobs for every American, along with a way to prevent hospital patients from having to "buy health at monopoly prices."

Finally, by summer, Hopkins weighed in with a detailed "prosperity plan" to keep boosting the economy. He urged an expanded Social Security system, to be sure, and also a higher minimum wage, slum clearance projects, and government-built housing. Then, to everyone's astonishment, he urged corporate tax cuts, which might spur growth.[32]

To argue today that "almost no real New Dealers remained" in the Administration by the end of 1943 shows how the significance of each of the four, let alone the degree to which they were sharing ideas among themselves, and with their president, has been misconstrued.[33]

Perkins fought hard for one pillar of that Second Bill of Rights, supported alike by Ickes and Wallace. She believed, as did Ickes's friend, the big, feisty industrialist Henry Kaiser, that the greatest fear among Americans—which endures today—was to get sick and incur doctors' bills taking years to pay off.[34] Millions of demobilized troops, she thought, would reemphasize the problem, putting their families, of course, in equal peril.

Then as today, there was no magic to providing low-cost, population-wide health services. Nonetheless, Perkins's hope of universal coverage, which FDR was echoing as the right to "enjoy good health," would be blocked from the start—as being the linchpin of *socialism*—by physicians' groups, insurance providers, and conservative politicians, relentlessly into the 2020s.

Few employers during the war years, when labor unions were experiencing phenomenal growth, were so enlightened about employee benefits as Henry Kaiser, whose legacy is Kaiser Permanente, the giant integrated healthcare consortium. To complicate matters, these unions had learned to play off one alphabet agency against another, and 156 of those often-overlapping executive branch agencies, boards, offices, and the like would be spawned before peace arrived.

Roosevelt's organization charts, which he and Hopkins "kept trying to cook up," as Wallace had put it, only contributed to the disorder. Still, one fiasco for which Perkins did not blame the president was the impending nationwide rail strike of late December '43. After all, she reminisced, the situation had collapsed right down on him the day he returned from Tehran—though its subsequent handling, in her eyes, was a train wreck.

The railroad brotherhoods had rejected a four-cents-per-hour raise proposed by one alphabet agency, while another, the Office of Defense Transportation, warned that a rail strike could be as damaging as anything inflicted by foes abroad. As with the miners, FDR believed the union leaders to be "rotten" and he appealed directly to the rail workers' patriotism to stay on the job. He proved no more successful. Thus, on December 28, headlines of ARMY SEIZES RAILROADS ON PRESIDENT'S ORDER pushed aside news of Flying Fortresses and Liberators bombing the German emplacements in northern France for rocket guns, the *Vergeltungswaffen-1*, "Vengeance Weapon 1."[35]

However, the army didn't need to fix bayonets, as Secretary of War Stimson, by now an obviously old man with tired eyes, had expected. Ickes and Perkins had gone far during the coal strikes to establish a model by which government could manage such disruption. So, instead, some two hundred army officers were set to work as temporary executives to manage the books and write checks to the employees and vendors of the Pennsylvania Railroad and other formidable entities.

Nonetheless, the clash with the rail workers led Perkins to tell Wallace, at the Cabinet meeting of January 21, 1944, that this time-wasting upheaval had been utterly avoidable: war mobilizer / deputy president Byrnes had "mishandled the strike in a terrific way."[36] Even the railroad CEOs could not make sense of what had happened. They ended up with more profit than they had ever expected when negotiating originally with the unions. In short order, the brotherhoods won an hourly raise of nine to eleven cents, plus "fringe benefits" (a new term from the War Labor

Board), and other great corporations such as the Southern Pacific and New York Central reverted to their happy owners.

Throughout, Perkins again was helping to lower the heat, and this at a time when John L. Lewis was declaring "free enterprise" to be a competition between employers to find out how little a worker needed to eat. She used various tactics to spread calm over the nation, such as calculating the time lost to industrial accidents, which she discovered was equivalent to that needed to build forty-five battleships—and then letting the country know that 90 percent of those on-the-job injuries were preventable. Perhaps work stoppages were not being driven just by greed and treason. Without her, the reaction against labor's growing strength would have been far worse.

In his January 1944 State of the Union message, Roosevelt had also called for legislation to conscript every able-bodied man (between 18 and 65) and woman (18 to 50) into "national service" for the war's duration. One reason, he said, was to "prevent strikes" and the threat of strikes. Bizarrely, he justified this notion of compulsory labor by adding that such national service laws existed in the British Empire and Commonwealth—though he had no clue, just for starters, of how labor needs were being managed in the coal fields of Wales and the Midlands.

However, he had done at least part of his homework. Republicans simultaneously introduced a bill to enact his request, though denying any coordination. Under this labor conscription system, government would have the power to direct any person to perform any service in any place in the country.

At this point, Perkins stepped in with foursquare opposition to such overreach. It may have been her most important contribution of the war. She, and that other allegedly rabid New Dealer, Harold Ickes, favored using economic incentives to get people into the right jobs, while Republican statesman Henry Stimson extolled government fiat. Troublingly, Roosevelt's advocacy of national service would only intensify into 1945 as strikes decreased and victory approached.

Perkins recognized that no one backing the president's plan—certainly not Stimson—had any idea of what went on within a factory or on a farm. To fend off this dangerous thrust, she had to attend every meeting of the War Manpower Commission, which "always teetered on disaster," as she remembered, at the very edge of an "opera bouffe."[37] As with Ickes, her admiration for Stimson dimmed as FDR allowed him to extoll what was being called the National Service Bill.

"A system of anarchy" was gripping America, the secretary of war testified in his fading old voice to the Senate Military Affairs Committee. Only national service could cure the "disease" of picket lines and strikes. "Every hour counts," he insisted: wasted time was being paid for in lives.[38]

On that last point Stimson was in some ways correct. Yet the principal cost lay in the Washington wars, and in other distractions such as this bill. FDR's fomenting of local conflicts now combined with that authoritarian notion to allow time, far too much precious time, to pass uselessly.

Ickes by this point knew everything that occurred within the White House. The president's daughter, Anna Boettiger, had come to visit for Christmas and, until her father's death, would stay in the Lincoln bedroom suite previously occupied by Howe and then Hopkins. She too provided FDR the companionship he needed. Now thirty-seven, she had become best friends with Jane Ickes, thirty, and spent frequent weekends in Olney. She served as a conduit for Ickes, recognizing his loyalty, his goodwill, and his growing distrust of Hopkins—which she shared. To this end, she disclosed whom her father was seeing in secret and what he was truly thinking, and even handed over such sensitive documents as Ickes had never seen, including several about Japanese American internment.

Predictably, Ickes got drawn into the conflict over the National Service Bill, again alongside Perkins. His speech on liberty to the marine officers at Quantico had, at this juncture, surely been aimed at Roosevelt. He pointedly stressed the right to be "free of compulsory labor" and from "irresponsible and ambitious" government authority.[39]

Except Ickes was grappling with a hundred other struggles—including what FDR gleefully called the making of "sheep eyes" on Britain's dominance of the Middle East. That entailed Ickes having to direct another RFC subsidiary, the Petroleum Reserves Corporation, its very name redolent of the New Deal, to construct a pipeline across Saudi Arabia and to build a refinery for petroleum war products near Dhahran. Nonetheless, Ickes could never resist a fight over civil liberty.

However, he felt that his latest crusade must be on behalf of those U.S. internees whom, in every instance, he called "Japanese Americans."

Roosevelt, after being criticized endlessly by his secretary of the interior on this issue, had simply appointed him, in February 1944, to direct the War Relocation Authority. Ickes accepted reluctantly. Interior was already involved anyway. Internment camps were on federal land. He was further conversant on these issues because, as secretary, he was responsible for the governance of Hawaii, which had been under martial law since Pearl Harbor. More than a third of its population was of Japanese ancestry.

As WRA director, however, he pushed for Japanese-Americans to be released, labeling his opponents as wanting a "lynching party." Nor, when several hundred internees rioted at the Tule Lake Segregation Center, in California, was he about to "crush" what Roosevelt, in his naval parlance, styled a "mutiny." Along with Wallace, he talked FDR down from that idea at the tetchy December 17 Cabinet meeting, right after Tehran.[40]

Simultaneously, Ickes was fighting to uphold the government's Fair Employment promises to Blacks. Here too he faced resistance, led by Senator Richard Russell, key opponent of anti-lynching bills and the Georgia Democrat whose name today graces the most venerable of the upper chamber's three office buildings. Overall, Ickes despaired of the Administration's indirection, as he told the president face-to-face in the Cabinet on March 3.[41]

Ickes quickly left the room once that meeting ended. Wallace lingered to talk privately with Roosevelt, as one or two Cabinet officers usually did when something personally important had to be raised. Here Wallace took the opportunity to argue as well against the hesitancies he detected, particularly what he feared might be FDR's willingness to accept Churchill's latest attempt to scuttle Overlord, or at least to delay it into 1945. Then he turned to what was really on his mind—visiting Moscow, as Roosevelt had proposed just a year earlier.

FDR demurred, advising him that to appear in the Kremlin might work against Wallace in the coming election campaign, given his already full-throated support of the USSR. In fact, he did not want Wallace in the mix of negotiations with Stalin.

Instead, what about visiting China—perhaps flying along the reaches of the Russian frontier, then curving down through Central Asia? After all, he added expertly, the Alaska-Siberian daytime temperature would average a near perfect 63 degrees around June 15. Roosevelt loved to plan other people's trips.

The formal Cabinet, as had convened that Friday, largely remained what it had been in the 1930s, a "very human institution." Four hours later, its members regrouped along with their spouses—Perkins, as always, attending alone—to hold their annual dinner for the president. Perkins chose to sit next to Ickes. For the first time, she spoke to him of her husband, revealing that Paul was no longer institutionalized continuously; she hoped to see him at home,

FDR commemorated his original March 4 inauguration yearly, which he paid for himself. This was the last. Other events followed over the weekend.

The next morning, on the actual day, an Episcopal service was held for more than two hundred worshippers in the East Room. The Reverend Peabody, now eighty-seven, led the prayers, including one "For Our Enemies" from the *Book of Common Prayer*. It was also the last time that the headmaster and student would see each other. The White House Correspondents' Association had arranged for its own annual dinner to coincide with March 4, the president, as usual, attending. He sat with his son-in-law and military aide, Major John Boettiger, roaring with laughter at the gags of comedian Bob Hope.

A smaller, briefer gathering took place in the Oval Office before they dashed off to the Hotel Statler. Roosevelt's tailor, Samuel Scogna, arrived, likely to have the honor of personally delivering carefully altered suit jackets. Roosevelt had endured a severely persistent bronchial infection since returning from Tehran in mid-December, which affected his weight, all in his torso.

By the end of March, he had a fever of 104. His own visits to the Naval Hospital had been more frequent, for which he used a long list of aliases to conceal his appointments and medical records. At this point, as he began his last year of life, he was diagnosed with "acute congestive heart failure." At least equally grave, he was suffering from complex partial seizures, with symptoms of dropping muscles of the jaw, glassy eyes, and fainting.

The Cabinet would not reconvene until Friday, April 7. This time, both Perkins and Wallace remained behind, and it was Wallace who recalled never having seen FDR look worse. Even so, the humor persisted: "What do you think of my sending Henry to Chungking?" he boomed to Perkins.

That destination, which was today's Chongqing, the wartime capital of Nationalist China, just plain shocked her. Yet she kept quiet, although beginning to suspect the worst—that Roosevelt wanted to get Wallace out of the country during the buildup to the Democratic Convention in mid-July. At least since late 1943, newsmen and politicos had been speculating that, should FDR go for a fourth term, his running mate would be a more conservative Democrat, such as ex-justice James F. Byrnes.

It is doubtful whether Roosevelt was acting so single-mindedly, and Wallace knew FDR would wait until the last moment to decide. Nor did Wallace plan to shore up his own position. "Roosevelt wouldn't tolerate that kind of thing," he recalled. "A man who went out to get delegates would inevitably get his throat cut."[42]

Moreover, real needs existed for the second-highest U.S. official to confer with Generalissimo Chiang Kai-shek, given the complexities of aid and military cooperation. There were heartfelt personal interests, too, behind FDR's urging such a journey.

By Roosevelt's design, it would include Central Asia, the Gobi Desert, and also Outer Mongolia, where no U.S. official had ventured for seventeen years. Looking back, Wallace would conclude that, most of all, Roosevelt had visualized himself in Wallace's shoes and had hoped Wallace would see things he himself could never experience.

More practically, they each believed, as Wallace had just written in *Survey Graphic* magazine, that Siberia and China would furnish tomorrow's greatest frontiers. Helping to develop the resources of eastern Asia, particularly Siberia, might be needed as an offset to postwar unemployment, while serving to win Stalin's favor.

The late afternoon Cabinet Room conversation of April 7 ended when the president told Perkins and Wallace that he would be going away for a while, to a house with no phone where he could sit in the sun and fish. No one, other than the Secret Service, Admiral Leahy, and a few aides such as Bill Hassett—with whom he always traveled—needed to know more. This little party arrived two days later, on the morning of Easter Sunday, at a railhead five miles distant from Bernard Baruch's nearly seventeen-thousand-acre South Carolina barony, "Hobcaw," where Roosevelt intended to rest in near isolation.

He had ever more to conceal in his personal affairs, whether declining health or secret liaisons with the just-widowed Lucy Rutherfurd. At the same time, he was "juggling"—a description he enjoyed—problems of industrial shutdowns, a threatened split in his party, the imminent opening of "a real Second Front" in Normandy, and his gearing up for the fourth presidential campaign.

One of Bob Hope's jokes at the correspondents' dinner on March 4 had everyone in stitches, if some uneasily. "The Republicans want to carry the South in the next election," he remarked. "They are going to run Rhett Butler."[43] Behind the fun, he had spotlighted questions about the vice presidency, as well as the power of the South.

The austere, often awkward, former Republican Henry Wallace was Rhett Butler's antithesis, and, in real life, had by now gone far to antagonize the Southern bloc. He was becoming outspoken on race, as by opposing the poll tax, though unlike Ickes he was still willing to trim his sails. For instance, he did so in a speech on "equality" in the postwar world. Roosevelt asked him to make clear that he meant *economic* equality, suggesting—as Wallace understood the correction—that to imply *social* equality might offend Southern senators.[44] He obliged.

In addition, the big-city bosses who had reviled him at the Chicago convention in 1940 had only grown more opposed. As for corporate bosses, they were enraged, for some reason, by his definition of "an American fascist as one who . . . puts money and power ahead of human beings."

Yet since 1940, Wallace had become pretty quick on his political feet. After inspecting the White Motor Company's plant in Cleveland, for example, he climbed on a truck to address several thousand workers, many of them women. Here too he envisioned the postwar world, observing that women would soon have more leisure time given the marvels of electronic household appliances. "So," he declared, "when you go back to your homes . . ." Loud boos and hisses erupted from the women. Stunned, he had swiftly added, "If you want to," and they cheered.[45]

In short order, Wallace supported the Equal Rights Amendment, first proposed by the National Woman's Party in 1923. Perkins disagreed with him on that, fearing such legislation would undercut the special, state-level labor laws for women, ones for which she had fought, as in New York. Still, she and Wallace could discuss everything, whether economics or the ERA, as they often did over Sunday breakfast with Ilo after Holy Communion at St. James's.

No doubt, Wallace had become a far more adept and popular politician than FDR could have imagined four years earlier. *The Washington Post* acclaimed him the "New Deal Symbol" for having picked up the banner of reform that "Dr. Win-the-War" Roosevelt had discarded. Another of the capital's leading papers, *The Washington Star,* called Wallace "the President's right-hand man," given Hopkins's absence.[46]

Indeed, the vice president had again been drawn deep into executive responsibilities, including being updated on the Manhattan Project. He dealt that spring with its overall director, Major General Leslie Groves, not just the scientists, who handed him the most interesting document he had ever read, leading him to conclude that the war would end in eighteen months, as it did. He was also by far the top choice among Democratic voters to join FDR on a national ticket.

On the other hand, Roosevelt had plenty of reasons to feel ambivalent toward Wallace's renomination, including what Wallace recognized as his chief's "extreme vindictiveness" toward anyone in his orbit who appeared to be building up a rivalrous strength.[47]

At this juncture, Perkins descended on Wallace's office in the Senate, specifically to warn him about his pending trip.

"Henry, I think somebody will sell you down the river while your back's turned. Out of sight is out of mind, very easily. I wouldn't go one step from this place if I were you. I'd stay right here with my eye on everybody, and in plain sight—so that *nobody* would forget you."

"Oh, that's all right," replied Wallace, never a man to go out of his way to see enemies. "I've talked to the President about it, and the President assured me it's all right."

Perkins interpreted the "it" to mean renomination, and then Wallace laughed and told her of being eager to leave the country during the pre-convention maneuverings.[48]

Hearing of the imminent trip, Ickes was perplexed. He did not fly, having been compelled to do so but three or four times since summer 1933 when visiting Hyde Park. That Wallace would even want to soar around the far reaches of the earth at any time of year just confirmed the man's total strangeness.

FDR returned to the White House on May 7, looking tan, and also thinner (from prescriptions for digitalis and laxatives). He received Wallace and the congressional leaders the next day, and Ickes several days later. On May 18, Roosevelt left for Hyde Park after dinner, to spend another week resting. The planning for D-Day was going well under Eisenhower's overall command, although the British were haunted by memories of their army's 564,715 dead in France and Flanders just twenty-five years before.

Early on Friday evening, Wallace and Ilo held a small dinner at their apartment for the army air force crew who would fly the vice president— accompanied by three experts on these regions—to the East. He embarked at dawn in a C-54 Skymaster cargo plane, taking the Great Circle route over Alaska to Velkal in the Soviet Chukotka Peninsula, not to return for fifty-one days. Throughout, Wallace would practically be out of touch, receiving no political news. As it turned out, nearly four of these weeks were to be spent in Soviet Asia. That also left him in the dark on D-Day, June 6.

Wallace and his little traveling party were honored that night at a banquet in the Siberian city of Krasnoyarsk. An aide entered, then whispered to the highest-ranking Soviet official at the table, Serghei Goglidze, who was wearing a bulky, wide-lapelled suit. Goglidze stood to offer a toast.

"Vice President Wallace, it is my pleasure to tell you"—his voice broke with emotion—"that this morning our American and British Allies opened the Second Front in Western Europe."

All pushed aside their chairs to stand and drink multiple toasts of 105-proof vodka, dinner being forgotten.

In fact, NKVD Colonel-General Goglidze headed State Security Far East, and was chief executioner of the Gulag. He was masquerading as a regional civil administrator, part of a *maskirovka* ("disguise") operation at which the Soviet Union—soon to be America's deadliest ever of enemies—would excel for decades.

LONG SHADOWS

*Operation Overlord, Summer 1944,
to FDR's Death, April 1945*

Elated as I am, personally, for the President's victory, the four years
ahead are going to be the most difficult ones this country has ever faced.
Harry Hopkins to Henry Wallace, a week after FDR's election to a fourth term

O n the night of June 5, 1944, 156,151 Allied assault troops set out
across 120 miles of rough Channel waters to open what Hitler called
the war's decisive battle. Nearly five months later, after Paris had
been liberated in August, the millionth GI would walk through the counting machine on the docks at Southampton.

D-Day underscored Roosevelt's qualities as commander in chief, just
as Wallace had anticipated before America entered combat. His uncanny
selection of talent was pivotal to delivering success—initially the foursome of Leahy, Marshall, King, and Arnold, to be sure, and then of Eisenhower to lead the "Crusade in Europe."

The war showed Roosevelt's ability to excel at organizing those things
he cared to organize, so different from the disorder he fostered on the
home front. He loved to quote Clemenceau's "War is too important to be
left to the generals," although he never trifled with his military chiefs and
combatant commanders. The stakes were rather different from the fun of
his divvying up budgets between PWA and WPA.

He kept in place what he called his "war team," to include the service
secretaries. He gave this reason for elevating Frank Knox's deputy, James
Forrestal, fifty-two, to the Cabinet as secretary of the navy, once Knox
died from heart attacks on April 28.[1] FDR eulogized Knox, although
Ickes concluded the president no more lamented Knox's passing than
might a woman who had lost a servant. The lean, coiled Forrestal was of

a different type and had been an FDR favorite since arriving in 1940 as one of the president's six administrative assistants.

This five foot nine World War I naval aviator, boxer, Princeton drop-out, and banker now became the Administration's first strong, energetic, and farseeing Cabinet secretary for either of the armed services. Here too, FDR's instinct for talent—when he wished to seek it—is clear. So is his weariness. He had long directed the navy personally, albeit since 1942 with Admiral King, to the extent that he called it "Ernie King's navy." Yet a tired president could no longer oversee the sailors hands-on.

Forrestal had already bonded with Ickes for two reasons. During the war's last eighteen months, Forrestal kept working against segregation in the navy—and thereafter, as the nation's first secretary of defense, would break it throughout the armed forces. And he collaborated with Ickes to crack open Britain's political-military-economic dominance of the Middle East, with an eye to securing oil in the postwar world. At this point, Wallace liked Forrestal, too, believing him to have "more brains than the typical man from Wall Street in Washington." Yet in the Cabinet, Wallace also recognized him (a suicide in 1949) as being "curiously twisted by something."[2]

As with Ickes and Perkins, the vice president was not part of FDR's "war team" ex officio, though he too contributed much to victory, and aspects of Wallace's Far East odyssey did prove useful. Just one example: when in Chongqing, he was "instrumental," reported the U.S. ambassador, to enabling an American observer group to enter Communist-held Yan'an Province.[3] Besides intelligence gathering, the group's weather reporting aided the B-29 Superfortress bombing of Japan, which began that June. On the other hand, his weeks in Soviet Asia reflected a tragic, if widely shared, wishfulness toward Moscow.

The NKVD's Serghei Goglidze was Wallace's guide throughout the Soviet part of the journey, including through Kolyma on the East Siberian Sea. It would be years before Wallace learned the identity of this "very gentle and understanding" man. But then Wallace was no more naive about Stalinist Russia than Roosevelt, Hopkins, and Ickes.[4]

Right before D-Day, Wallace had spoken, in Russian, at the opera house in Irkutsk, a largish city along the Trans-Siberian railroad, about the necessity of U.S.-Soviet cooperation.[5] Stalin allowed his words to be broadcast, there being no "mass opinion" in the Soviet Union, as too many in Washington believed. It was Kolyma that typified Soviet Russia, and, at Kolyma, Wallace encountered strapping young NKVD chekists posing as "settlers." Starved slave laborers had been hidden away, watchtowers removed, and barracks painted.

Behind this façade, Kolyma was an arctic extermination center: "Auschwitz without gas chambers," a rare survivor would report. By 1944, its 160 camps and subcamps overflowed with Lend-Lease tractors, bulldozers, field telephones, machine guns, barbed wire—underscoring how Hopkins's Protocol Committee was blindly agreeing to every Soviet demand, not to mention the thefts.[6] On the whole, Wallace was dazzled by Stalin's care of the land and his commitment to public works.

After taking all this in, Wallace and his three experts flew out of Ulaanbaatar on July 4, stopping at Chita—another lethal, well-disguised outpost of the Gulag—then to soar over the Pacific dateline. They landed in Fairbanks on the fifth, where, by phone from Washington, Wallace received his first news in weeks. After speaking in Seattle on Sunday the ninth, he bounced through thunderstorms to arrive in Washington the next day, when he would brief the president.

By this point, Stalin's Operation Bagration—launched on June 23 by more than 2.4 million troops, and named for the Georgian-born prince and "God of the Army" against Bonaparte—was tearing open the Eastern Front. At Tehran, the *Vozhd* had promised an attack to support his allies' D-Day assault. Despite this seventeen-day delay—which allowed Hitler to transfer a full SS panzer corps to Normandy—Roosevelt and Hopkins regarded Bagration as evidence of his trustworthiness.

Perkins did not share this faith in the USSR. She was facing Communist-inspired attacks over her labor statistics—from within government and without—while tracking ongoing Soviet-directed attempts to move favored people up the ladder within the unions. During a small dinner at her home that spring, she also cautioned Wallace about these grim discoveries.

Politicians tirelessly acclaim loyalty, largely because their calling is so full of betrayal. For all the dozen years of his presidency, however, FDR never once doubted the loyalty of any of his four lieutenants. And he would have sensed such fidelity when drawing them close in 1933, Wallace being no exception.

While still in Alaska, Wallace received a call from the White House aide whom *Time* described as "roly-poly Samuel Rosenman, the president's speechwriter and confidant," while adding that Rosenman was "now filling much of Harry Hopkins' old role."[7] Rosenman, who also lived at the Wardman Park, asked if Wallace might meet with him and Ickes before coming by the Oval Office to tell the Boss about that 27,000-mile trip. To this end, after red-eyeing it back to Washington, Wallace had the two of them over for a late lunch at his residence. Once seated, looking over Rock Creek's forests, Ickes extolled Wallace as the only other true liberal left in town—before suggesting that Wallace not join the ticket. Rosenman, who never did anything independently of FDR, just beat around the bush.

Lunch having barely been eaten, Wallace replied that he wouldn't talk politics until seeing the president, and showed them the door. Unknown to him, a car waited downstairs to whisk Ickes and Rosenman to the White House, where they spent nearly an hour reporting to FDR in his bedroom, slipping out five minutes before Wallace arrived for his four thirty appointment in the adjacent study.

Obviously, Wallace spoke of Russia and China, yet Roosevelt's mind was on the convention, to open ten days later at the Chicago Stadium. He could not bear the thought of Wallace's name being put before the delegates, said the president, only to be rejected. How would Ilo feel? This might all be a repeat of July 1940.

Unlike Ickes and Hopkins—and certainly FDR—Wallace had a full life outside politics, much of it in science. His former startup, Pioneer Hi-Bred, was on its way to becoming one of the world's two largest seed corporations, which would generate a fortune for his family dwarfing that of the Aldriches and Astors, let alone of the Roosevelts. It is doubtful that Wallace was "obstinate" about joining the ticket, or that he was "digging in his heels."[8] More believably, he replied that the president should by all means replace him if he had a stronger candidate.

Roosevelt said he would not hear of such a thing, according to Wallace's diary. Instead, he invited his vice president for lunch the next day—which, as it turned out, was the day Roosevelt announced, to nobody's surprise, that he would seek a fourth term.

Ickes had been focused solely on a winning ticket, but now began to regret having played go-between. He also had a Tuesday lunch—with the director of the budget, to whom he offered a confession: Jane had told him that he "was a fool to get into a mess like this" and would get what he deserved, by abetting Roosevelt's ouster of the VP.[9]

At the same moment, as they lunched off trays in the Oval Office, FDR was warning his vice president that many people thought him a Communist; to which Wallace unfolded polling results far more supportive of him than those of 1940. For all this, nothing was resolved, except FDR invited him back for another lunch on Thursday. It was after this third visit to the White House that he gripped Wallace's hand, to pull him down—ear next to his mouth, a thoroughly unusual act between them—and half-whispered, "Henry, I hope it'll be the same old team."[10] Wallace went away convinced of his chief's support.

The convention opened in blazing hot weather the following Wednesday, July 19. Perkins was working with the Resolutions Committee, and Ickes was also there, as a delegate-at-large for Illinois. By then he realized he had been misled about Wallace's backing. Clearly, he jotted to himself, Wallace was "the idol of labor and the Negroes, to say nothing of the Jews"—and so he told the Illinois delegation, in secret caucus. Thereafter he sent a strident telegram to FDR: in sum, Henry Wallace is the strongest man at this convention, which the corrupt city bosses are taking over. Then he leapt into Wallace's corner. Hopkins was scarcely involved, being mostly prostrate in Georgetown.

Wallace gave a spellbinding speech on July 20 to second Roosevelt's nomination, albeit demanding "the poll tax must go!"—a matter from which FDR had retreated, dismissing the tax purely as a "state issue."[11] Perkins was certain that Wallace would be renominated. And, beyond doubt, he would have been, except that FDR, acting through intermediaries, tilted the weight of his influence against Wallace throughout the convention.[12]

Looking back, Wallace blamed what became a framework of lies on Roosevelt's being "in a very bad physical condition."[13] Perkins agreed, thinking her president too weary that summer to have resisted the party bosses and the conservatives, North and South. As for herself, she honestly couldn't wait to pack her bags, no matter who won the election.

Harry Truman was the champion of the "stop-Wallace forces," and, as every wavering state delegation soon learned, of the White House too. Therefore, a Roosevelt-Truman ticket would confront what the Republicans had already decided would be theirs of Thomas Dewey and Ohio's handsome if vacuous conservative governor, John Bricker. (Willkie had been drubbed in the primaries.)

With nothing to be gained once the convention adjourned on July 21, Ickes sent another telegram to FDR, this one scorching, that asserted Wallace to be a far stronger figure than Truman, the convention's choice. The president would reply patiently in a letter.

Ickes didn't mind Truman personally, and Blacks and labor could also swallow the unexpected nominee. Still, he questioned Truman's views on race, given Southern backing for this homespun product of a border state, and was convinced that Wallace was more progressive and deserving. Perkins wrote her own supportive letter, but she had sense enough to just send it to Wallace, rather than to blast FDR.

Unlike Wallace, that remote presiding officer, Truman, of Missouri, was popular in the Senate. Wallace would show his boredom by slumping down behind the vice president's desk when awaiting a roll call. Whether in "bad physical condition" or not, FDR had instead chosen someone who would be far more suitable once he required the advice and consent of the Senate on whatever treaties might end the war. Roosevelt had personal reasons, too.

Truman seemed a less complicated soul. Personally, he was more distanced from FDR than the insular, globally oriented, intellectual vice president. For an exhausted man, enough had been enough of the highbrow intimacy FDR had developed with Wallace, a relationship in which the president so often felt compelled to exercise one-upmanship: should Wallace campaign in Spanish, for instance, Roosevelt had to tell him of his doing so in French along the Canadian border. Nor did Truman have a serious national constituency, such as had formed around "the fightingest New Dealer in high position," to quote *The New Republic,* and Wallace was finding what that accolade cost.

Once Wallace had returned to the capital, Hopkins assured his friend that rumors of his trying to oust him from the ticket were untrue, although Wallace thought he was protesting too much.[14] Wallace felt no bitterness toward Roosevelt, actually telling the Senate majority leader, Kentucky's famed orator Alben Barkley, that he was happy with how things stood. He felt freer and more his own man.

"Harry, we are both Masons," Wallace told Truman kindly enough once they regrouped in the Senate Office Building.[15] He saw good instincts in Truman, whom he judged set on doing the right thing, yet also a man of limited background who'd likely get caught in the webs of his own making.

The closest Roosevelt had gotten to the Chicago Stadium was when his special train stopped secretly at the Fifty-First Street rail yard on the Saturday night before the convention. He was able to collude in his armored Pullman car with the DNC chairman and Mayor Kelly, then to rumble on to San Diego—whence he was to sail on the twenty-second for Honolulu to confer with his Pacific commanders. After D-Day, most Americans felt that the war would soon be over, as shown by a sudden drop in the Treasury's sale of war bonds—an assessment that Roosevelt did not share for a moment.

A huge welcome of ships and warplanes met FDR's heavy cruiser, the USS *Baltimore,* after it entered the Hawaiian Sea Frontier. Hopkins was too ill for such a voyage, nor did FDR include Marshall, King, and Arnold. From July 26 to 29, it was he alone who arbitrated the winning strategy of the Pacific war, that between Admiral Chester Nimitz, commander of the Pacific Fleet, and General MacArthur, leader of the Army's counterattack against Japan. He hadn't seen MacArthur for years and regarded him as "some boy," meaning a problem child.[16]

Still, FDR embraced the brilliant, vainglorious general in their Diamondhead meeting rooms as "my great friend," although everyone was his "great friend"—from the King of England to Charles de Gaulle, whom FDR had most reluctantly welcomed to the White House earlier that month for a diplomatically useful tour d'horizon. MacArthur had a dominating presence of command and an imperial confidence that only he understood the "oriental mind." Yet FDR easily handled him with the same soothing and flattery he had spread for nearly a dozen years over Harold Ickes.

Ickes himself was running his own vast part of the war, leaving aside these purely military matters. Among much else, he was responsible for governing the Territory of Hawaii, over which, that July, he kept hammering Secretary of War Stimson for needlessly keeping the islands under martial law. Ickes accused him of "perpetuating bad government," with letters copied to FDR.

He further added to the president's mail pouch by demanding "a determination with respect to revocation of the order excluding Japanese

Americans from the West Coast." And he hit his chief that month with the reasons: imprisonment without trial was unconstitutional; it was no more a military necessity than martial law in Hawaii; and psychological damage was being wrought on Japanese-American children who were "becoming a hopelessly maladjusted generation."[17] Of course, he knew that FDR would evade the issue until after the election.

For a decade, strangely intimate ties had existed between Ickes and FDR, among them being Ickes's close friendship with Missy LeHand. He was one of the few friends from her previous life to visit in Somerville, saddened that she could not speak except to utter "yes," and indicate "no." Then, on the morning of July 31, Ickes was among the first to learn of her death, at age forty-seven. FDR got the news while on the *Baltimore* as it zigzagged north from Hawaii to evade Japanese submarines.

Roosevelt had not seen Missy since she had moved home from Washington in May 1942, despite his promises, even if he paid all her medical bills, occasionally phoned and wrote, and sent mementos. In one of Ickes's own letters to Missy—remembering how she had steadied Roosevelt while in the White House—he said soberly, "I think some things would have gone differently if you had been here."[18]

The president returned from his five-week voyage at 6 A.M. Eastern War Time on August 17, after a leisurely four-day trip from Seattle. Minutes before his train pulled into its secret wartime station beneath the Bureau of Engraving, he would have passed the Pentagon on the Virginia side of the Potomac. This colossal structure, which broke ground in 1941, asserted to the world that the United States would never return to the so-recent days of a 140,000-man army, just as its scale and rapid construction declared the nation's economic might.

In 1944, however, Americans worried that reconverting the economy to peace would prove more difficult than gearing it up for war. To prepare, Congress had passed a quintessential New Deal measure in June that offered sweeping benefits to veterans. The GI Bill was imaginative, large-spending, focused on what today is called "human capital," and all too structured in a way that discriminated against 1.2 million Black veterans.[19] Yet in these same months, Perkins was hearing talk within the Manpower Commission that millions of servicemen might just have to stay in uniform: discharging them into a jobless peacetime economy risked all sorts of instability.

And what of working women, such as those at the White Motor Company, who might not want to return to the kitchen? Surveys by Perkins's Women's Bureau showed that three-fourths of them hoped to keep their jobs, although the burst of female employment hardly reached into white-collar roles, let alone into higher government office. The Federation of Business and Professional Women's Clubs emphasized that women lacked virtually any voice in directing and planning the war. The War Production Board, for instance, had 146 senior officials, of whom one was female; the Office of Price Administration had 69, with again a single exception.

Such numbers underscore Perkins's extraordinary personal achievement, and in 1944 at Catholic University she could offer hope to other women. Yes, the female labor force of eighteen million would be reduced sharply with victory. (The Women's Bureau classified seven million as "new women workers" since 1940.) Even so, she expected cuts to be largely voluntary: young women would return to school, and older ones choose to raise families full-time. Still, that left women "who must work to support themselves or their dependents"—women, Perkins could have added, such as she.

Women had long been teachers, nurses, and social workers. Tomorrow, she declared, they'd be working also in the electrical industry, in plastics, at drafting boards, as chemists and engineers—as well as in such familiar trades as textiles. Then she made more news: "If we plan with care, we should be able to work out a program that will provide jobs for the men now fighting our battles as well as for women working today who will need jobs in the postwar period."[20]

Perkins discerned a healthier national attitude than in 1919, after the last war. Americans, she believed, had become more open to the new— such as to the idea of women working as chemical engineers. Around the same time, she also addressed the National Council of Negro Women, pledging to extend the Social Security system to agricultural and domestic workers. Here as well the country must think anew.

She was among the few people in or out of government to express such confidence in the postwar economy. In contrast, the Bureau of the Budget that summer expected a quick return to a catastrophic jobless rate of 14 percent once war came to its end. Wallace, as during the 1930s, agreed with her forecasts. Each did the calculations that today seem obvious: pent-up demand from the Depression and wartime rationing would combine with savings from the current boom to deliver full employment at that era's high wages.

Wallace was able to share these speculations with the president during an amiable lunch in the White House garden ten days after FDR's return from the West Coast. They had not seen each other for nearly two months—since right before the convention—yet FDR, in high spirits and looking well, brushed off any lingering unpleasantness. Wallace, he said, was just four years ahead of his time—and of course he had taken no role in displacing his own vice president from the ticket.

At that instant, given a lie so outrageous, Wallace decided that he could never trust him. A belated resolve. Still, why argue with this beaming, cordial performance? There was much to be discussed. For starters, inflation was up 25 percent since early 1941, and had to be addressed in the reelection campaign, which was getting off to a fast start.

Marriner Eccles, with whom Perkins and Wallace had worked so closely on economic problems, had lost his enthusiasm altogether for Roosevelt after Chicago. Not that he wanted Dewey to win; he just no longer regarded the president as a liberal. Eccles, for once, may have been wrong. As the campaign gathered steam, FDR would express a stunning vision for the economy, much as he had done, out of the blue, for warplanes in 1940.

He regarded himself as a master at business. Similarly, he believed he knew most everything worth knowing about agriculture, or at least more about agriculture "in every part of the country than [has] any other president," as he once told Wallace. Altogether, he felt pretty sure that things would work out. So in October, he would predict an American future of "60,000,000 productive jobs," secured, moreover, by his Economic Bill of Rights.

Wallace had no idea from where Roosevelt got that daring number, and let it be known he was skeptical. Then, two days after FDR made this assertion, Wallace received a wire: "I promise to make good on this prediction."[21] (He would be proved right, in 1947.)

Less presciently, Roosevelt was determined to have Congress pass his National Service Bill and had extracted implied endorsements from General Marshall and Admiral King.

Roosevelt compared the importance of his proposal to that of the Selective Service Act in 1940, and *The New York Times* agreed. Clearly, "everybody" wouldn't be drafted, its editors explained. Instead, local boards would determine the call-ups and decide who should be matched with each critical labor need. For instance, nurses—who were then exclusively women—might have to be drafted. The president himself had just laid out a "most urgent immediate requirement" while the army demanded ten thousand more.[22]

Naturally, what such a form of conscription meant for Blacks was never considered. Of all the citizens who served on the nation's 640 military draft boards, just twenty-four had been Black, less than half of 1 percent. Instead, "discrimination," when discussing national service, was held to be against soldiers in the field. All civilians, that bill's proponents argued, would be obliged to accept the same legal obligations as men and women in uniform.[23]

In parallel, despite the military's grave nursing shortage, a report from the surgeon general indicated that only 217 Blacks had been accepted in the Army Nurse Corps, and none by the Navy Nurse Corps. The National Association of Colored Graduate Nurses asked if the president might take this discrepancy into account, and if—in his earnest call for nurses—he was aware of the many women (being Black) eager to serve. Ickes, at least, was fully appraised of such authentic discrimination, while he continued to fight both against the National Service Act and for every form of civil liberty.

Just as did Perkins, he saw a larger danger in the bill. Labor conscription meant a government whip hand over the unions. Besides, a National Service Act might very well be upheld by the courts. And who was to say that the compulsion of a government-directed workforce would end with the war? Nonetheless, during the last fourteen months of his life, national service became, in domestic affairs, the sole idée fixe Roosevelt ever held during this longest of presidencies.

Meanwhile, Britain, which he emphasized to be his model for national service, was still tense in the throes of a death struggle. At home, Churchill's support was falling. Yet in facing the world, he was as tenacious as when saving his country in 1940–1941—and now he wanted another summit. Roosevelt acceded, coyly telling Wallace during their lunch that he felt compelled to see a "distinguished Englishman" in Canada. So he did two weeks later, again in Quebec, from September 11 to 16.

The gathering was unneeded. Far worse, it enabled the capital's "war within" to combine with the Administration's deep penetration by

Soviet intelligence—to enduringly grave effect in Europe. Historian Sean McMeekin, deploying extensive new research in Russian archives, calls it the "Soviet High Tide in Washington."[24] Of course, no one from State accompanied the president, nor did Hopkins, although the Combined Chiefs of Staff conferred.

His lone civilian adviser, Morgenthau, was joined by Harry Dexter White. The easily manipulable treasury secretary carried a document, to be known as the Morgenthau Plan, that proposed to extinguish Germany's industries, flood its mines, and basically return a conquered enemy to the pastoral eighteenth century. By definition, this would entail starving millions of Germans, precisely how many millions having been debated between Morgenthau and an outraged Secretary of War Stimson, supported by Ickes, with Hopkins sinuously in the middle. "As many as seven Soviet agents," Meekin shows, "had a hand in drafting this document." And Stalin's objectives are clear: to establish the "legal principle that the war's victors could loot German industrial assets for restitution or reparation," of which slave labor was to be a part.

At Quebec, British and Canadian diarists noted Roosevelt's sagging shoulders, glassy eyes, and suit jackets a size too large. Exhausted and ill, he went along with the Treasury Department's concoction. But back in Washington, an idea this macabre couldn't stand the scrutiny of leaks and counterleaks to *The Washington Post* and *New York Times*. Hopkins did some quick second-guessing to help scuttle the plan, with the elections six weeks away.

Still, Berlin's propagandists exploited the dystopian blueprint to energize a fight to the death on the Western Front, as already in the East.

Roosevelt squared off that fall against the forty-two-year-old Governor Dewey, a candidate similar to General George McClellan, whom the Democrats had run in 1864—the last presidential election held in wartime—McClellan also having been a small, very intelligent man whose vanity got in the way.

Dewey zeroed in on "tired war leaders" and charged Roosevelt with pitching himself as indispensable. In truth, said Dewey, Roosevelt was only "indispensable to Harry Hopkins, to Madame Perkins, to Harold Ickes," and, he added, to the head of the American Communist Party.

He banked on the country having had its fill of these three overexposed celebrities as well as of a president who wanted to hold office for sixteen years. Throughout, as Sherwood observed, Republicans erupted in "hoots and catcalls whenever Hopkins or Ickes or Frances Perkins was mentioned."[25] (Even to Republicans, Wallace was presumed to be out.)

Additionally, Dewey targeted the Administration's "domestic blunders." Instead, "the snap and efficiency of youth will prevail" in a Dewey presidency, wrote columnist Raymond Moley, in contrast to the disorder among those feuding, aging mandarins.[26]

Roosevelt knew that Union soldiers had given Lincoln the crucial margin over McClellan in 1864—and that the Soldier Vote might be decisive eighty years later. Then as today, expanded access to voting favored Democrats, and Republicans were working hard to make voting for Roosevelt as difficult as possible. The debating points from Southern Democrats, and many Republicans, might as well have come from the 2020s: at issue was "an assault on the fundamental idea that states, not the federal government, should decide how to run their own elections."[27]

Ickes knew how to exploit this fracas. He would turn matter-of-fact statements by Southern senators about absentee voting against the Republicans—such as those assertions heard from Louisiana's John Overton on the Senate floor: "Down in the Solid South, we are bound to maintain white supremacy."[28]

FDR didn't veto the Soldier Voting Act of 1944, which allowed poll tax states to retain their discrimination, but he did say that the final legislative compromise was too confusing. And so it proved. Only 25 percent of eligible voters in uniform were able to cast their absentee ballots.[29]

Roosevelt wasn't at all certain he would win in any case, as he said to his cousin Daisy Suckley, going by what he was seeing from Gallup.

Right after Chicago, he announced that the war was too serious for him to engage in an active campaign. Priority had to be given to his constitutional duties as commander in chief. Basically, this indicated that Americans would soon hear lots more from his famous lieutenants.

No matter how exhausted FDR might be, he would perk right up when turning on the radio to listen to an Ickes political speech. Ickes by now was seventy, his hair white, portrayed by newsmen as having grown surprisingly mild, his voice less acerbic. Wallace, too, was said to be aging, at fifty-six, no matter his famous athleticism. Allen Drury, covering the Senate for United Press International, wrote of his shaggy arc of silver-graying hair and a "sainted other-worldliness" having become more pronounced.[30] The press could not have been more wrong about either of them.

Days after the Chicago convention, Ickes, for once, had risen above his disappointments to tell Wallace that their only recourse was to fight the harder for Roosevelt's reelection. Dewey, he was convinced, had all the makings of a "fascist dictator," and he promised to share with Wallace his hoards of political intelligence.[31] Wallace agreed on all counts, replying that he would speak everywhere for FDR, and focus on the vital issue of assuring full employment after the war.

That said, he explained he would not appear under the auspices of the Democratic National Committee, which he believed corrupt. Instead, he would buy his own train tickets, handle all costs, and ask the state parties to arrange his events. At their late August lunch, Wallace told Roosevelt the same thing—though the president must already have known. One purpose of their sitting together was to recap the weeks that Wallace had already spent barnstorming through New England and the South, for which the candidate seemed grateful.

In short order, Ickes reprised his role as "King's Champion," or more accurately chief mudslinger, talking most days with Anna Boettiger to hash out ideas he hesitated to discuss directly with FDR. On the trail, he unloaded such outrageous statements as calling Dewey "an enemy of the Negro." Hadn't the governor just endorsed the states' rights Soldier Voting Act supported by the white supremacists? Next, suggested Ickes, Dewey might want to impose lynch law nationwide.[32] In Milwaukee, he charged the entire Dewey campaign with bringing joy to the hearts of Nazis and to all their followers (presumably Republicans) in the United States.

On this theme of Nazis, the "sainted" Wallace announced in Des Moines that a Dewey victory "will inevitably give hope to the wrong elements in Germany and Japan." An indignant *New York Times* quickly drew the parallel to his shocking statement of 1940, that to elect Willkie "would cause Hitler to rejoice."[33] Vice presidential nominee Harry Truman wasn't remotely as aggressive: he merely condemned rivalry between the army and navy (on which all could agree) while comparing Dewey, a mite unfairly, to President Warren Harding.

Ickes and Wallace were a formidable tag team, whether alone or when together in Harlem's Golden Gate Ballroom. Each could take a higher road, too. Wallace spoke of FDR having built a bridge to a better world, and Ickes emphasized the commissioning of Blacks as service officers, for the first time, as well as the 1.5 million jobs that had been opened for Negroes under Fair Employment rules. Each could also speak, as both had been doing for years, against "intolerance," a euphemism of the day for raw antisemitism: Ickes as co-chairman of the Washington chapter of the Emergency Committee to Save the Jewish People of Europe, and Wallace loyally telling the National Conference for Palestine of Roosevelt's hope for a free and democratic Jewish commonwealth.

Of course, the Republicans struck back. Alfred P. Sloan said the New Deal would soon be dead in any event, and cynics might have thought he meant Roosevelt.[34] Dewey echoed FDR's target of sixty million jobs, with the authoritative Winthrop Aldrich to support him. Yet the candidate fell to Roosevelt's masterly ability to hit the right spot and to go charmingly low. The president turned his eighteen-pound Scotch terrier, Fala, into a comrade in arms. Never did he call Dewey a remarkably little man (not that he actually was). He just threw the spotlight on tiny Fala, which, said FDR, resented libelous statements by the Republicans.

On November 7, the day of Roosevelt's fourth decisive victory, Wallace sent a cheery note from the campaign trail to Hopkins, who had been working full-time at the White House, again making himself central to foreign policy. These weeks had been a wonderful experience, Wallace confided, and he found it more fun to campaign for someone else than for himself, a generosity that baffled Hopkins.

Having voted at Hyde Park, the president returned victoriously to Washington on Friday morning, the tenth, and all four lieutenants attended the Friday 2 P.M. Cabinet meeting. High on FDR's agenda was an expanding Ku Klux Klan.

Ickes thought he looked haggard, yet put worries aside once the president thanked him for having given the most devastatingly effective speeches of the campaign. Wallace observed more closely, this being his first Cabinet meeting since the Chicago convention. That night, judging from the lack of acuity he witnessed, he wrote in his diary that FDR's intellect was certain to fade.

Two days later, at noon, a White House operator called the Ickes residence: Mr. Roosevelt would like to speak with Jane. Might he come for tea, accompanied only by Miss Suckley? He had not visited Olney since inviting himself and Hopkins up in March 1943 for poker and dinner. Jane immediately had to phone Dean and Mary Acheson, at their farm in nearby Silver Spring, to cancel plans for supper. Ickes had come to regard the elegant assistant secretary of state as a "good friend"—and his key source of State Department information—although Jane always found him snooty. She enjoyed telling the Achesons that Mr. Roosevelt was about to arrive.

Drawing room conversation that warm Indian summer afternoon, while Daisy sat silent, was a flow of animation and fun, marred only briefly by the president's bitter observation that he hated Dewey and was going to keep hating him. Otherwise, Ickes poured Scotch, FDR held Jane's hand, and all was like old times. The president returned to the White House after an hour, to spend forty-five minutes with his doctors.

The U.S. First Army had smashed its way into Germany during mid-September and, six weeks later, General MacArthur returned, as promised, to the Philippines. Yet the worst fighting in both parts of the world lay ahead. At home, the shockingly sudden deaths of former governor Al Smith, seventy, on October 4, and, four days later, of Wendell Willkie, fifty-two, both from heart attacks, cast a pall of their own over campaign hoopla. Nonetheless, despite total war and the closest race of his presidency, Roosevelt had time for the latest installment of "New Deal Revenge Politics," which, between April and late November, showed itself as the largest sedition trial in American history, held in the capital's U.S. District Court.

Except possibly to Hopkins, indicting twenty-nine right-wing crackpots and isolationists—this time entirely small fry—made no sense to our four. Ickes pointedly argued to Attorney General Biddle that the Justice Department had better things to do, like prosecuting the lynching in Mississippi of two fourteen-year-olds for "attempted rape." Still, the charges levied in Washington were grave: plotting the violent overthrow of the government of the United States. The president had compelled a very reluctant Biddle to take everyone to court, which launched the "Brown Scare" (referencing Nazi Brownshirts). What became a circus ended in a mistrial the week after Thanksgiving.[35]

"I'm a Republican, not a Nazi!" cried one of the pathetic defendants,

whom the judge compelled to undergo a mental examination.[36] Overlooked during these months of the Great Sedition Trial were the Soviet
agents burrowing within the Manhattan Project, at high levels of State
and Treasury, and around Hopkins. Moscow had at least six times more
agents deployed in the United States, about whom the Administration was
oblivious, than in the Third Reich.[37]

Ickes was just as wishful about the Soviet ally as were Roosevelt,
Hopkins, and Wallace—except he was driven by a misguided belief that
Russia had solved the problems of racial and religious equality. Maybe
America had something to learn.

After winning reelection, the president finally revoked his West Coast
General Exclusion Order against Japanese-Americans, not that Ickes—
with his own superb ties to the press—gave him much choice. Ickes had
also succeeded in getting martial law lifted in Hawaii, albeit not until two
weeks before the election, when Roosevelt no longer worried about that
controversy.

During July 1944, Ickes had even made headway on immigration,
using his role as head of the War Relocation Authority to help save 984
refugees, mostly Jews from eighteen different countries. They were the
first witnesses to Nazi atrocities to be brought as a single group to America, and he dispatched his personal troubleshooter "to hold their hand."
That was thirty-three-year-old, Brooklyn-born Ruth Gruber, who held a
doctorate in literature from Cologne. He gave her the rank of an army
general to exercise authority as she escorted them on a troopship from
the Italian war zone to New York.

"Mr. Secretary," she said when first hearing of this possibility, "it's
what we've been fighting for all these years. To open doors. Save lives."

"It came up in a Cabinet meeting," he replied wearily, leaning back
in his chair.[38] Having found their way into Naples, these men, women,
and children had become a problem for the military, who sought to have
them moved out.

Ickes and Gruber were stunned that the magical number of "one thou-
sand Jews" had been allowed entry, although these miraculously escaped
people were to be interned upstate, behind barbed wire at Fort Ontario, in
Oswego. Nonetheless, this event was a breakthrough and a result of Henry
Morgenthau's singular contribution to this twelve-year presidency. In 1944,
FDR condemned before Congress Hitler's "insane desire to wipe out the

Jewish race," but it was Morgenthau who had pressured him to form a dedicated agency that January to rescue what remained of European Jewry.[39]

The War Refugee Board helped to save about two hundred thousand Jewish lives, and twenty thousand non-Jewish ones, by war's end—granted, only to be sent to other "free ports" overseas, but showing that rescue was possible. The Oswego refugees were all that Congress and FDR dared to accept in an election year. Moreover, the president and his State Department "never wanted [the Board] to come into existence in the first place," concludes Rafael Medoff in his definitive study of U.S. refugee policy and the Holocaust.

Ultimately, Ruth Gruber herself was appalled to read FDR's secret instructions to Attorney General Biddle, that the Oswego refugees—from five months to eighty years in age—"should in fact be returned to Europe as soon as a favorable opportunity arises."[40]

Within the Cabinet itself, Roosevelt had two immediate postelection objectives.

First, he wanted to retain Wallace in his official family. Wallace had been diminished since his heady months before Chicago, and FDR envisioned him in the role of a "Mr. Outside" in world affairs, in contrast to their previous intimacy. He could help craft the peace. Wallace was popular with millions of voters, and far more of a world figure than anyone in government other than Roosevelt. He was multilingual, in a day when English was no lingua franca; he possessed world-changing scientific expertise; and when the time came, he might help rally the country for the peace treaties, as he had rallied it for war. And who else could do that? Certainly not Harry Truman or, by now, an exhausted president.

Second, FDR wanted to dispose of Commerce Secretary Jesse Jones, whom Wallace would describe, with little exaggeration, as wielding "greater power for a longer period than any human being in the history of the United States."[41] Therefore, at their garden lunch in late August, he had offered Wallace any job in the Administration except for secretary of state. After all, "dear Cordell," as FDR often referred to him, would be essential to working those treaties through the Senate. Given Wallace's interests and qualifications, only three roles truly remained: Commerce, Interior, and Labor. Surely, FDR could have anticipated Wallace's response to those possibilities. He wasn't going to accept jobs belonging to "my old friends in the Cabinet," Ickes and Perkins.

Over the table, the president and Wallace had agreed it would be "poetic justice" for the outgoing VP to replace Jesse, who—abetted by Roosevelt, of course—had undercut Wallace during the summer of 1943.

On November 30, Wallace telegrammed the president: "My interest in poetic justice is stronger than ever."[42]

Three days earlier, Hull had resigned claiming ill health, which had long been true, although the Morgenthau Plan debacle was a last straw. He was replaced within hours by his deputy: the tall, handsome, white-haired Edward Stettinius, now forty-four. This was equivalent to Harry Hopkins becoming secretary of state, without the bother of another confirmation battle. Harry's peers agreed about that, and about Stettinius. To Wallace, Stettinius was a country gentleman, a "fairly good administrator [although] not an intellectual heavy weight." Perkins saw him as "an awfully nice man and a good fellow, but no world beater." Ickes regarded him as "a failure in every job he has held," though, clearly, useful to Harry.[43]

Roosevelt acted on Wallace's telegram about replacing Jesse. He deployed Perkins, as so often when seeking to know the true thoughts of the men around him. "He talked to me about a place for Wallace," she remembered, and, when she called on him, Wallace laughed with her about the Chicago convention—"first rate Henry," she felt. That said, Wallace believed that Jesse possessed enough compromising material on FDR to avoid getting sacked. The president calculated differently.

"Frankly, if I can't have State, I would like Commerce," Wallace told Perkins, as he had told FDR.

"Well, all right. Shall I tell that to the president?"

"Yes, that's all right."

Perkins recalled going straight back to FDR, to be surprised to hear his anger over "Jesus H. Jones," who he insisted was not "on the level."[44] She disagreed, urging that Jesse was "a good and very powerful man"— the last three words being a gentle reminder. Hoping to calm these waters as well, she remembered drafting talking points for the president to use in handling what had to be an extremely delicate situation.

Roosevelt spent his last New Year's Eve with Eleanor at the White House, joined by Henry and Elinor Morgenthau for supper and to watch *Thirty Seconds Over Tokyo*. It was MGM's version of the Doolittle bombing raid, that gleam of hope during the terrible days of spring 1942.

Tokyo would not finally be incinerated until March 1945, under Major General Curtis LeMay's air attacks, the deadliest in history.

The president was getting ready to meet with Stalin and Churchill in the Crimea, among the most difficult places on Earth for a paraplegic to reach from Washington. As with the gathering in faraway Tehran, Stalin basically told FDR and Hopkins to take it or stay home.

Roosevelt spent forty-five minutes on January 2 with Secretary Stettinius, Under Secretary Joseph Grew, and Acheson to discuss what lay ahead. Thereafter, he took a two-hour lunch with Ickes to get perspective. Unhelpfully, Ickes offered his conciliatory views of Moscow, as he did on the eighth during another of his long lunches with FDR—who wasn't giving such time to Stettinius, or Stimson, or unfortunately, to James Forrestal, the only Cabinet officer who could have offered well-argued insights about Stalin's slave empire.

Roosevelt was preoccupied these weeks with his National Service Bill. He had just sent Congress a tedious eight-thousand-word State of the Union message, to be read by the Clerk of the House, once more pushing for this labor act. But senators were no longer bowing to him and had grown weary of dealing with his liaison, their sinuous former colleague Jimmy Byrnes. "Hardly anyone in Congress trusts Franklin Roosevelt with the enormous power envisaged in national service," the UPI's Drury put in his diary.[45]

In his own diary, Wallace observed that FDR seemed to have become a different person under the burdens of war, and likely of disease. He saw the president at noon on Friday, January 19, before the 2 P.M. Cabinet meeting. FDR proclaimed himself delighted that Henry and Ilo were staying in Washington, although heartbroken over his own vice president not having been renominated in Chicago. Wallace further told his diary that he couldn't even think "bullshit." Regardless, both men again had business to discuss: FDR was now set to oust Jesse.

Jesse sensed that something was up. Just the day before, he had sent Roosevelt a letter concerning ownership of the sensitive 741 acres, which, at the president's request, the Reconstruction Finance Corporation (i.e., Jesse) had bought in 1942 solely to protect Roosevelt's Springwood home.

Cynical about politics as Wallace and Perkins had become, each was open-mouthed to see FDR chatting gaily across the Cabinet table with Jesse about all that they'd be accomplishing in the coming year. Hopkins, too, was in this mix.

Perkins had warned him that, if this titan were to be fired, Harry needed to tread carefully on FDR's behalf, and be "gentlemanly."

"I don't care whether Jones's feelings are hurt or not," snapped Hopkins.

"Well, now don't talk like that, Harry. You know it's important not to." And as she elaborated in her oral history, "I called Harry twice to remind him of this."[46]

On Saturday, January 20, the inauguration wrapped up quickly around noon on the South Portico of the White House rather than on Capitol Hill. Officially, this was due to the war, although, as Wallace saw from twelve feet away, the president's whole body shook as he tightly grasped the side of the lectern to deliver a mere 558 words, probably the last speech he would give standing. Surely, this was the only inauguration at which no one was seen to smile.

That morning, Roosevelt had sent a curtly humiliating letter of dismissal to Jones's residence at the Shoreham Hotel, which was waiting for the commerce secretary when he returned from these ceremonies. It thanked him for his service and advised him to "speak to Ed Stettinius" should he want an ambassadorship or something. "He hit the ceiling," remembered Perkins.[47]

She got an anxious call from Hopkins, who at last sensed danger. After scolding Harry—"You've hurt the old man's feelings, and made an enemy"—she immediately telephoned Jesse to apologize for "this brutal thing," the thoughtless handling of which arose surely from a mistake between Hopkins and the president.

"So you knew that I was to be out?" he asked icily.

"Well, I heard of it, vaguely, but I was sure it was all to be made clear," she quickstepped—bringing on a long conversation.

The next morning, she attended church with Henry and Ilo; afterward they had breakfast. She stayed clear of this drama, instead speaking with Ilo of how frail the president had looked: could he really endure another term? Perkins remarked that she, for one, wanted to be gone from Washington as soon as possible. She had cleared out her office, and been firm with Mr. Roosevelt. But, she continued, he "cried" when asking her to stay, at least until her friend Gil Winant, still in London, could step into her shoes. That she seemed to have named her successor indicates, once again, her clout during the war. Nonetheless, she told the Wallaces, there was nothing more that she could do here in the capital, because of her "family difficulties."[48]

Except there certainly was. Jesse had demanded a meeting with the president, who had no choice but to see him—which led to a disagreeable half hour early Sunday afternoon. That evening, Jesse released two letters to the press: FDR's original and his own reply, which, newsmen agreed, was "a masterpiece of sarcasm."[49]

Hopkins was not around to mollify Jesse—if he had been able to. At nearly the same moment that Roosevelt and Jones met, he was boarding the president's plane for London, his first stop in a ten-day diplomatic tour. It included Paris and Rome, and this was the first time that he'd give high-profile press conferences on foreign policy, as if, indeed, he were "assistant president." Perkins was left to clean up a mess for which Harry was much responsible.

Knowing that she must face Jesse, and the sooner the better, she went to the Shoreham late that afternoon as newsmen clamored outside. She not only admired him, she was close to his gentle wife, Mary, who sobbed in the background throughout the visit.

"I've saved the President from many, many troubles and I've fished him out of all kinds of hot water," Jesse told her, with a chilling calm. It wasn't just the Hyde Park property deal, of course. He knew of other activities, large and small. Just one, for instance, involved Morgenthau, who oversaw Roosevelt's investments and taxes. Merely as a matter of routine, the treasury secretary had advised FDR to withdraw securities from Lazard Frères, an international bank, about to be scrutinized by federal authorities.[50]

Perkins's long, personal, and soothing intervention surely staved off, at a critical moment, this ferocious mogul from going public with far more than a sarcastic letter. She bought time, and within three months Jesse's revelations wouldn't matter.

On inauguration morning, the president asked Perkins to pray for him. Amid all the confusions of politics and war's end, she had guessed that he would soon be slipping overseas. One more task remained before he left. Right after brushing off Jesse on Sunday, he submitted Wallace's nomination to the Senate. These ninety-six men, for their various reasons, mostly held Jesse in awe. Thereby, Roosevelt "had chosen to deliberately do the one thing that would antagonize them more than anything else,"

judged the UPI's Drury.[51] That accomplished, Roosevelt and daughter
Anna sailed two days later from Newport News, Virginia, aboard the
heavy cruiser *Quincy,* passing through the submarine net-gate at Hampton Roads at 9:36 A.M. to join a task force of destroyers setting course
for Malta.

Hopkins, Stettinius, Harriman, the Combined Chiefs, as well as Churchill and his own advisers awaited the president and his shipborne party
in the Grand Harbor of Valletta on the morning of February 2. Though
Hopkins was already stricken by diarrhea and severe abdominal pain, this
had done nothing to cut his drinking. Shortly before midnight, the two
350-man delegations flew out in a wave of twenty planes, under substantial fighter escort, for the Soviet Union.

Roosevelt, just turned sixty-three, arrived at Yalta bundled in a wheelchair, despite the mild climate afforded by the sheltering mountains to
the north. His big frame looked frail; he had just two months to live.
U.S. service officers sought to explain away the photographs in which he
wanly appeared: he was having trouble with his dentures, they claimed,
which affected his speech and caved his face in.[52]

Hopkins grew worse, pinned mostly in bed, though his room remained
"a center of activity, with members of all three delegations stopping by
to seek his advice," writes one historian. Another, rather throwing up his
hands, writes that "little is known . . . of these bedroom conversations."[53]
Of course, all was known to Stalin about the motley U.S. delegation that included hangers-on like Jimmy Byrnes and party boss Ed Flynn of the Bronx,
plus Stephen Early, as well as Soviet agent Alger Hiss from State and even
Carmel Offie, who, after his arrest in Lafayette Park for immoral activities,
had somehow landed at the Office of Strategic Services, precursor to the CIA.

The NKVD protocol here was identical to that in Tehran: precise
transcripts of everything heard by microphone were ready for Stalin at
8 A.M. daily. He had long penetrated his allies' secrets: here, he was more
intrigued by how these men interacted, with special reference to the intonation, length of pauses, and tone of each American—all yielded by the
write-ups.[54]

At Yalta, the principals addressed those nations and regions that
would erupt over the years ahead: the division of Germany; Iran, Greece,
Turkey and the Balkans, the Middle East, then-French Indochina, and
Korea; and also swaths of what are known today as the Bloodlands—the

conquered and reconquered terrain between the Baltic and the Black Sea, in which Hitler and Stalin from 1933 to 1945 slaughtered no fewer than fourteen million innocents.[55] However, much about that terrible landscape was by now moot. That very week, the Red Army was establishing bridgeheads forty-three miles from Berlin, while Russia's allies in the west were still 370 miles away.

Yalta culminated a series of U.S. blunders and concessions, including a fecklessness that had exposed the Republic to grievous, far-reaching Soviet espionage. Moreover—and by now for several years—Roosevelt was assuming that "Stalin can be handled," that the *Vozhd* basically viewed the world as did he. Hopkins, of course, concurred.[56]

Just the previous summer, Roosevelt had swallowed Stalin's insulting excuses for refusing to even let the western allies assist the Warsaw uprising of Poland's Home Army, while Stalin's divisions stopped six miles away—the Nazis then free to crush the resistance, while killing 150,000 to 200,000 men, women, and children. Ultimately, by 1945, Roosevelt and Hopkins had thrown aside all leverage over Stalin, which they had never thought of in the first place—although this was considerable, just starting with Lend-Lease.[57]

After Yalta, the president would repeat gloomily to those around him, "It was the best I could do," and, by this point, he was probably right. To begin, that entailed accepting Soviet promises of allowing democratic elections in Poland.

"We really believed in our hearts that this was the dawn of the new day we had all been praying for," Hopkins would tell Robert Sherwood. Soon after the conference dispersed, he claimed that he was too sick for the eight-day transatlantic crossing, insisting to FDR that he must disembark the *Quincy* at Algiers to fly home—although the president required him to stay aboard for speechwriting and companionship. Nonetheless, Hopkins left—flying to Washington, then on to the Mayo Clinic.

Being "special assistant to the president" was still a new and vague position in Washington, and Hopkins always supposed he could be dropped at any moment. That time came at Algiers when he showed himself no longer able to "take it." His curt, cold departure from the *Quincy* had all the elements of a sacking. At best Hopkins was civilly dead, and he would never see the president again. Averell Harriman, much of whose public prominence was owed to Hopkins, knew how the relationship ended and could be harsh in his reminiscence of FDR, as a man who "always enjoyed other people's discomforts."

The president returned from his five-week trip early in the morning of February 27, thirty-five pounds below normal weight. Ickes described him as "a sitting ghost."[58] Still, the Washington wars had been kept raging in his absence.

On February 18, Henry Stimson had given an ugly speech to push FDR's labor-draft legislation, dignified as the National Service Bill. Lives were being blasted away on the battlefields, Stimson charged, while the Senate Military Affairs Committee listened to the voices of "special interests." Those, of course, would largely be of the unions, which confronted the president, the military, and the very largest corporations to oppose this authoritarian overreach. Equally vicious were Wallace's confirmation hearings, with senators showing little "faith and trust in the President of the United States," wrote Drury.[59]

Roosevelt himself descended on Capitol Hill, at 12:30 P.M. on March 1, mostly to invoke the Yalta conference before a joint session of Congress. In a fifty-minute address, he also alluded to the fallout of the Morgenthau Plan by insisting that the Allies had no intention to starve or enslave Germany. However, he spoke, gray and exhausted, from behind a desk in the well of the House, brushing away a thirteenth microphone, and explaining why he wasn't standing: ten pounds of steel were on his legs. Only now, in his last weeks of life, did he refer to his being "crippled." But never would he admit to being worn out by serving as president over a dozen years of unrelenting crisis.

He rambled and, in telling of a "solution reached on Poland," downright deceived his audience. The press noted Ickes and Perkins in the front row, among the rest of the Cabinet, watching soberly.

The Senate gathered right after and, following two more hours of debate, confirmed Wallace as secretary of commerce, 56 to 32—though shearing off the role of virtually all the immense financial power that Jesse had held in the name of emergency. Wallace merely remarked that he had never wanted to be a banker anyhow. Ickes and Perkins attended his swearing in the same day.

During March, the president held three Cabinet meetings, in which Perkins kept telling him that, given the latest coal dispute, he was not to think of using the army. But he dwelled on the evils of "war strikes." On the eighth, in his second-floor study, FDR pressed Vice President Truman and the Democratic leaders of Congress hard for his National Service Bill as one solution—a prospect he revisited on the morning of the fourteenth with Ickes.

Addressing Congress on the first of March, Roosevelt had roused applause by declaring that the marines had Iwo Jima well in hand. By then the bloodiest battle of the Pacific war had been raging for nine days. And on the eighth, a sniper shot Ickes's son Raymond—leading his platoon—through the back, the bullet piercing a lung and exiting his left armpit. When Ickes saw FDR two days later, he had no idea if Raymond would live, so he was taking lots more Seconal than usual, washed down with whiskey. But FDR was made to lift up the people closest to him, as he did here.

The president saw Perkins as well, to whom he whispered of his plans for a state visit to England after delivering the opening address for the United Nations conference in San Francisco, come April 25. As for Wallace, they met alone for the last time on March 19, with Wallace remembering that he had told the president to be his own man in the fourth term and not let people like Hopkins run things.

Roosevelt left for his last visit to Hyde Park on the twenty-fourth, returning five days later to Washington for just seven hours before continuing on in his special train to Warm Springs, in search of rest. Churchill was already sending long telegrams about Stalin's behaving contrary to the alleged understandings so recently achieved at Yalta. But the president responded tepidly, in these final days, in notes mostly composed by aides. Then, in Washington, the Senate unequivocally killed his compulsory labor bill at the start of April.

On April 12, Cabinet officers received no explanation when each was summoned to the White House. Roosevelt had died from a stroke in Warm Springs at 3:35 P.M., Central War Time, eighty minutes before. Perkins was among the few who had not heard the news flashes before entering the Cabinet Room. She saw Harry Truman over by one of the large French windows, gazing out at the garden, and chirpily inquired, "Well, this is a queer hour for a Cabinet meeting. What's up?"[60] She did remember having thought it odd that, when she had walked in, he was standing right next to the president's leather chair.

EPILOGUE

During a one-minute ceremony, at 7:08 P.M., Chief Justice Harlan Stone swore in Harry S Truman beneath Wilson's Cabinet Room portrait. Department heads stood mostly behind Truman, with Secretary of State Stettinius—next in line of succession—being the closest, and Perkins at the far left edge of what would be the official photograph.

She, as well as Ickes and Wallace, would each claim to have anticipated Roosevelt's death. So too would aides and politicians in a flood of memoirs. All were misremembering. Truman's calendar as vice president shows that no officials had been courting him, as might have been expected of an imminent chief executive, over the eighty-two days since the inauguration. Each of our four was stunned when he died, as was Truman, and so too the country.

Roosevelt's body arrived at Union Station from Warm Springs on Saturday morning, April 14. Hopkins appeared in time for that afternoon's funeral services in the East Room because Isador Lubin of the White House staff, helped by Army nurses, had rushed to bring him back from the Mayo Clinic. As nearly 400 mourners gathered, only Perkins, among the other three, spoke with Hopkins. He looked to be dying, with sunken eye sockets, and was too weak to board the seventeen-car funeral train that left before midnight for Hyde Park carrying the flag-draped casket, family members, the Cabinet and Supreme Court, and senior aides such as Rosenman and Daniels.

Military records listed Franklin D. Roosevelt, Commander in Chief, as a war casualty, among that day's fallen, who included Sergeant Paul Shimmer, the millionth GI to have landed in France, killed by a shell while leading his men against a fortified Bavarian hill. The Reich had just six weeks to last, while, in the Pacific, Iwo Jima had been taken. That victory prepared the way to invade Okinawa, one of Japan's six main Home Islands.

It was a cool, bright Sunday morning along the Hudson Valley when Roosevelt was buried at eleven o'clock, on April 15, in the hemlock hedge enclosure that he had shown Wallace in August 1940. He had once shown it to Perkins, too, who told him how silly he was to talk of such planning.

Harold and Jane Ickes, Henry and Ilo Wallace, and Frances Perkins, who came alone, stood together near the grave site—Wallace on one side of her, Ickes on the other. After the brief Episcopalian rite, the grave was covered, the flag handed to Mrs. Roosevelt, and Cabinet members followed the family from the garden. Wallace held Perkins's hand, and she would remember Ickes's sobs while they walked, tears streaming down his face. "Oh God, if this could only have been prevented," he moaned. He had drunk more whiskey than ever before, on the night Roosevelt died, and realized how grievously depressed he was.

Perkins had crossed herself before turning away, saying, "God rest his soul"—the customary wish when Episcopalians bury their dead, which she had expressed at the grave of her father, her mother, at those of Mary Rumsey and Caroline O'Day. But Wallace would never forget hearing her words. It was how she said them: "God-rest-his-soul." There was nothing ritualistic about it.

Wallace understood that she had judged Roosevelt's soul as a tortured one, restless and uncertain of its direction. She asked God to calm it. As for Wallace, he felt more alone than ever. "We'll continue to miss Roosevelt for the rest of our lives," he told her.

The journey south that night, observed Justice Robert Jackson, showed how "the loyalties of politicians shift quickly."[1] Men were jostling between train cars to meet and plot. Wallace was seen in deep conversation with another of Roosevelt's appointees, Justice William O. Douglas, forty-six, the most committed civil libertarian ever to sit on the court, and a likely Democratic candidate for 1948, should Truman stumble. As for Ickes, he was overheard speaking unguardedly about a sudden vacuum of leadership in the Oval Office—which got back to the new president. Perkins, as often before, was adding calm. She sat with an anxious Bess Truman to advise her that no one expected her to be another Eleanor.

In Washington, Hopkins lay bedridden at home, for which he was missing rental payments. Still, he was in the swing.

Sherwood visited, and, speaking of the fallen president, Hopkins declaimed, "We have had it too easy all this time, because we knew he was there. Now we've got to find a way to do things by ourselves."[2] He began to receive hosts of people in his sickroom: Stephen Early, Felix Frankfurter, lawyer Morris Ernst, Sam Rosenman, Colonel James Roosevelt, Lord Halifax, Aubrey Williams, every member of the Joint Chiefs of Staff, and, of course, Secretary of State Stettinius. Bernard Baruch appeared too, despite having fallen out badly with Hopkins, who he believed was blocking him from any responsible wartime role.

Perkins also visited him, during April and May, though not Ickes or Wallace. Hopkins believed each was blaming him for not being president— especially Wallace, who had missed the succession by months. He was wrong. Wallace, like Ickes, just no longer cared to trundle over for an audience.

In his first hour as president, Truman had asked all the Cabinet members to remain. Yet Perkins hoped to leave, and Ickes felt ambivalent about serving a man whom he suspected of answering to party hacks. Wallace, however, discovered he could work easily with Truman.

Government now seemed to function better. Truman, for instance, ran taut, crisp Cabinet meetings, and Wallace realized he could collaborate too with Stettinius, though seeing him as "definitely a Hopkins protégé." He was amazed at the absence of rivalry with State, given the Commerce Department's duties overseas. "There was plenty of that," Wallace reflected, when he ran the Economic Warfare Board.[3] Except now the Oval Office wasn't inciting wars on the home front.

Bureaucratic life became easier for Perkins too. She warned Truman not to repeat the "great mistake" Roosevelt had made in his last eighteen months: do not, as president, grapple personally with labor troubles. Leave them to experts. She felt he understood.

Germany surrendered unconditionally on May 7, by which time the Red Army had taken Berlin as well as the rest of central and eastern Europe, including Vienna. Truman soon called in Hopkins. Was he physically able to mediate worsening tensions with Stalin? The skin on Hopkins's face was a cold dead white, yet he came alive to fly to Moscow with his wife, Louise, as well as with Harriman, to attend five meetings in the Kremlin, from May 26 to June 7.

By Hopkins's account, Stalin again guaranteed a democratic Poland. Of course, in reality, Poland was doomed, as was every land occupied by a tyrant for whom problems of nationalism were merely those of enough cattle cars to ship entire races of people into the Gulag. Nonetheless, Hopkins returned to Washington, once more dying, to be extolled by the press for his heroic diplomacy.

Ickes believed this trip to be "crazy," though only because it presumed Hopkins once more indispensable. Otherwise, Ickes remained obtuse about Soviet totalitarianism, and for a while longer, he would scoff at suspicions of Russia as mere "Goebbelese."[4]

Inevitably, Truman sought his own people for the Cabinet. On July 1, Perkins, now sixty-three, was finally allowed to leave. "Frances has taken a terrible beating throughout the years," reflected Ickes.[5] Morgenthau departed too, despite trying to hang on. Hopkins had already decided to retire from public life, and the next day he resigned formally as chairman of the President's Soviet Protocol Committee, of the Munitions Board, and innumerable other posts. Stettinius was then out on the third.

Several times during 1945, Truman told the press that he wanted Ickes and Wallace to carry on. At this juncture, it would have been difficult to remove either in any event. To large liberal constituencies, each embodied the New Deal.

Still needing an income, Perkins therefore became a Civil Service commissioner, yet she was appalled by her replacement at Labor. In her oral history, she recalls Truman remarking that the next labor secretary needed to be "a strong man," though, for political reasons, it would not be her friend, that formidable Republican, John Gilbert Winant. Instead, Truman appointed a forgettable onetime Democratic senator, ignorant of labor policy. His odd habits included bringing a beloved Pekinese daily to the office—to be fed, walked, and chauffeured home by department staff. The results of appointing this "great strong man" were predictable. "Will they never learn?" Perkins wondered. Ickes, as now had become routine, shared her views completely.[6]

Jimmy Byrnes, a friend of Truman's since the Senate, took over at State, though knowing less of foreign affairs than even Stettinius. Therefore, it was Byrnes who accompanied Truman and the Joint Chiefs to the final summit of the Grand Alliance, in Potsdam, an intact, well-gardened suburb ten miles from a flattened Berlin. The conference, from July 17 to August 7, began a day after the first-ever test of an atomic bomb, in Alamogordo, and overlapped with Churchill's ouster as prime minister.

Among our four, only Hopkins and Wallace knew about that era's deepest of secrets, the Manhattan Project. Ickes could guess: something gigantic was swallowing natural resources from the Smoky Mountains to the Columbia River Valley, and he had heard from the War Department that the army was working on a new form of energy. Perkins had her own guesses, given that some 600,000 people had been diverted from the U.S. workforce. She knew thousands of them to be hard at work on something top secret in eastern Tennessee, where in fact uranium was being enriched in the hidden city of Oak Ridge. Versed in metallurgy, she also recognized that various strange government research programs were underway.

Regardless, there had never been a hint in the Cabinet of the project, and none of the four knew of its success until Hiroshima on August 6, Japan's surrender to follow after Nagasaki was bombed on the ninth. Ickes then wrote that Roosevelt's "personal decision to spend $2 billion on what could have been a will-of-the-wisp" underscored his greatness.[7]

Much as Roosevelt and Hopkins had anticipated, Churchill that summer had lost Britain's first general election since 1935, to be succeeded by the Labour Party's Clement Attlee. Arriving as foreign secretary was Ernest Bevin, the harsh, barely educated union organizer who, as minister of labor, had spent 1940 to 1945 mobilizing his country's workforce for total war. He was the workingman's John Bull, and the Labour Party's Churchill. Hopkins and Perkins already knew this daunting figure well, and Eleanor had been impressed when she met him in London in October 1942.

Very quickly, Bevin began to execute a foreign policy that was the antithesis of earlier attempts by Roosevelt and Hopkins, and indeed by Churchill, to placate Stalin. What ensued undercuts an enduring myth of FDR's presidency—i.e., had Roosevelt lived, as Harriman put it, "the cold war wouldn't have developed the way it did, because Stalin would have tried to get along with Roosevelt." That was an unlikely outcome.[8]

First, Marxist-Leninist teachings informed every aspect of Stalin's life, and he was set to make dangerous use of a prostrate western Europe. Second, Bevin was prepared to lead the British Empire—and, to a large extent, the Americans—into showdowns with Soviet Russia, whether over Iran, Greece, or Berlin, while reviling Stalinism to foreign minister Molotov as "Hitler theory." Men might speak, in the better drawing rooms of the Northeast coast, of "the American Century," but their enthusiasms weren't being echoed in Chicago, Louisville, Salt Lake City, or Seattle. As the Iron Curtain descended, the United States had far less political-military agency upon these perilous events than is believed.

Bevin's towering leadership also proved significant that fall as Ickes and Perkins each continued to help lay out U.S. policy overseas—well before the Truman Doctrine and the Marshall Plan became policy during 1947 and 1948.

Ickes had calmed his nerves sufficiently in late September to board the president's generously loaned C-57 for a flight to London. He encountered Bevin, who, he wrote, was "a roughly hewn man who gave evidence of real strength," and one who reminded him of John L. Lewis, another ferocious anti-Communist union boss.[9] Ickes's views on Russia began to harden, and for him to cooperate with Bevin was significant. Truman had given Ickes authority to negotiate and sign a petroleum agreement with Britain—at a time when the empire still dominated the Middle East.

Ickes would leave London for Paris and then Frankfurt, where he conferred with General Eisenhower at Supreme Headquarters Allied Expeditionary Force (SHAEF) about tackling the desperate fuel shortages of a vulnerable, just-liberated Europe. The crux of Ickes's journey, in its focus on energy and maneuverings with Bevin, was to take America further into the Middle East. Cassandras in the Senate anticipated the rest. For Washington to involve itself with the Saudi monarch, and those sheiks and shahs of other mysterious lands, was "a reckless venture in imperialism fraught with international complications, dangers and hazards."[10]

Perkins was also shaping foreign affairs at a juncture when, as Eisenhower would reflect, "there seemed to be little thought to our continuing security . . . piled high with threats to our victory."[11] While secretary of labor, she had promised to attend the first postwar International Labor Organization conference, to be held in Paris during October and November 1945. Though she had left her department, Truman still allowed her to go. She was the conference's star. Coordinating too with Bevin, she helped to revive Western Europe's democratic labor movement in the face of Soviet plotting—and also well before the new Administration began improvising a muddled approach toward Moscow, to be known as "containment."

At home, America entered the worst period of labor strikes in its history, beginning three weeks after Japan's surrender: initially elevator and tugboat operators, then steel, automobile, meatpacking, coal mining, rail, and electrical equipment manufacturing unions. The economy was getting stronger, but the costs of housing, food, and transportation were skyrocketing while wages stagnated or fell with the return of millions of soldiers from the war.

Notionally, such upheavals had become Harry Hopkins's concern. In late summer, New York's mayor La Guardia had appointed him to be the impartial chairman for the city's clothing industry, with offices at Garment Union headquarters, and a big $25,000 salary. Yet Hopkins still relied on Harriman, who leased a six-story house for him on Fifth Avenue. Little time remained for Hopkins to enjoy the views of Central Park. By October, he was unable to do any real work. Barely fifty-five, he lingered in New York's Memorial Hospital through Christmas and into January 1946, while medical bills rose and he again worried about money. His debts included $10,000 owed once more to Ethel Gross, his first wife.

Hopkins's funeral on February 1, at St. Bartholomew's Episcopal Church on Park Avenue, was spectacular. Lord Halifax represented the British Empire among the thousand mourners, who included Nelson Rockefeller, Forrestal, Baruch, J. Edgar Hoover, Frankfurter, Morgenthau, Fleet Admirals Ernest King and William Leahy, as well as Elliott Roosevelt for the family. (General Marshall was in China, and Harriman in Moscow.) Several of his pallbearers, such as Baruch, had come to loathe Hopkins, as did Elliott. Only Perkins, of the other two, was there.

The same day, Ickes was busy testifying before the Senate. He charged that a recent treasurer of the Democratic National Committee—and staunch supporter of Truman's, who Wallace agreed was "the least pleasant smelling" of the president's cronies—had pledged to raise several hundred thousand dollars. Except a quid pro quo would have required the federal government to relinquish its rights to California's offshore oil. It was amazing Ickes had lasted at Interior as long as he did, given his hectoring of Truman, who, in turn, spoke to newsmen of "shitass Ix."[12] On February 13, Truman told him to leave within forty-eight hours.

Ickes became a columnist for the *New York Post* Syndicate at $50,000 a year, using his perch to write furiously about civil rights. He demanded an FBI investigation that July of the Moore's Ford, Georgia, lynching of two young Black couples, and his writings compelled legislation to redress the loss of Japanese-American property—resulting in the Evacuation Claims Act of 1948. As for those 984 refugees behind barbed wire in Oswego, they had remained interned when the war ended, and Ickes had refused to sign a letter, produced by the Departments of Justice and State, authorizing them to be deported. They were not to be freed until December 1945, at which point Ickes—summing up years of struggle for Jewish immigration—had told Ruth Gruber, "We won."[13]

Wallace was the last of our four to depart, during mid-September 1946. In a speech at Madison Square Garden, he called on America to eliminate racism, and also to sever ties to "British imperialistic policy in the Near East." At that moment, Secretary of State Byrnes was at a Council of Foreign Ministers' meeting in London: he demanded that President Truman choose between him and Wallace. Truman had read and approved Wallace's speech but gave in.

Yielding to a subordinate's ultimatum would have been inconceivable under Roosevelt. With Wallace's exit coming a half year after Ickes's, the firing appeared to symbolize the end of an era for American liberalism.

In Allen Drury's *Advise and Consent,* as the funeral cortege approaches Union Station, the senior senator from Indiana tries to assess the dominant personality and forceful career of the unnamed president—a charming, theatrical, double-crossing titan, and clearly FDR. In the final analysis, he asks himself, was this a good man? The senator realizes that it will take generations to say with certainty.

Great leaders, surely in a democracy, have to possess some kind of remarkable allure, but he or she does not have to be nice. Franklin Roosevelt was a hero in the simplest sense: he aroused devotion in order to confront the worst dangers of peace and war, though he also had a heroic capacity to cause harm. He sincerely appealed to the "common sense of decency" in American life. Often, he was instrumental in turning the nation's policy against the destructiveness of poverty, and indeed, in a society of plenty, against the moral unacceptability of want.

That said, he rarely took such steps if they undercut a ruthlessly self-centered drive for power. Many of the characteristics, such as his deviousness, that enabled him to be a great servant of his country were also the least attractive part of his disposition.

Each of our four came to realize this dismaying fact and, at least midway through their common adventure, each recognized that anyone who trusted Roosevelt was a fool. As for his intelligence, it was tellingly Wallace who grasped its full impressive strength. And Wallace adored his chief's "lovely character" nearly to the end. Yet he recognized "you never knew when he would turn off that side and become the most unscrupulous opportunist in the world."[14] There was just as much to dislike as there was to admire. Explicitly, Ickes, Perkins, and Wallace looked back after April 1945 with a sense of having been taken in. As for Hopkins, he rationalized his affection for Roosevelt by knowing that he had gotten as close as possible to an even greater fixer.

None of them could determine whether FDR was stunningly brave—which was the most likely explanation—or simply not quite grown up in his belief that nothing could stop him. There was no "inner well of serenity" to Roosevelt's soul, as historians have long argued—except when he faced death or national disaster, to recall the attempt on his life in Miami and the thunderbolt of Pearl Harbor.[15] But it can be easy for us to be deceived by that polished exterior. The public never saw him being furious, as it had Cousin Theodore, forever wound-up about *something*. As for communicating warmth, all four knew that "he more or less turned it on automatically."[16]

In a world of emergencies, Roosevelt still had the Greek quality of ultimately not going too far, despite an authoritarian tendency that, at the end, displayed itself in his idée fixe for compulsory national labor. And he would pass along a still limited presidency, certainly compared to our day of chief executives who exercise the highest power of taking the country into wars with basically no involvement of Congress.

Roosevelt had a boundless interest in the deficiencies of those around him. To succeed, he needed to mask his many resentments and cruelties, while relying on a foursome of equally wounded lieutenants whose deep human vulnerabilities proved central to his pursuits. The New Deal and World War II chewed up scores of eminent men, yet these four vital hands-on operators at the very top were aboard for the ever-extending duration.

Surely this fractious "team" of four was the single most important to ever have shaped their country's history, perhaps even embodying a "collective leadership," as writes the eminent Roosevelt scholar Susan Dunn.[17] That raises the question, when examining an achievement so vast, as to how much of FDR's greatness is due to them. The best way to answer is by posing another question. During the 1930s, and throughout history's most destructive war, who would have stood in for any of these four? Together, they were able to translate American energy into an expanding sphere of possibilities in ways that Roosevelt could not. Yet it was he who gathered his fellow wounded to bear up without dismay the ruins of a falling world.

No one of comparable weight would ever hold any of their positions again: no one of the stature of Henry Wallace has ever appeared at Agriculture, nor of Ickes at Interior, nor of Perkins at Labor—nor has there been anything like a "Secretary of Welfare," as FDR envisioned that role, to equal Hopkins. Today, vice presidents have a bigger hand in government than even did Wallace from 1941 to 1943, except none have been so influential in national politics. And no foreign policy / defense official has ever worked closer with a president than did Hopkins.

Wallace had more of his beliefs enacted into the New Deal than did the others. Perkins, in contrast, channeled the novel clout of the labor unions, but she didn't create the unions in the way Wallace created the agricultural settlement that governs a weighty part of the U.S. economy today ("a program that pays farmers not to farm").[18] Her achievements with Social Security and the rights of workers—where groundwork already existed—were of a different sort, though they are still firmly part of our lives. She kept the New Deal alive during the war, and pushed it into the future, believing with Keynes that "anything we can actually do, we can afford."[19]

Hopkins, in turn, was pivotal to creating a government unafraid to pump out money to its citizens in dire emergency. Until the New Deal, it was a radical notion to assume that citizens might be as endangered in peace as in war. As for Ickes, he was the strongest of the era's liberal reformers on every front: land stewardship, Wall Street, Big Business, racial justice. On his readiness for war, he was the fighter whom his own hero, Theodore Roosevelt, would have understood best. Always describing himself as a progressive Republican, he was yet pleased to be labeled "a New Dealer."

To Ickes, being a New Dealer meant fighting for the highest order of individualism, one in which any American could thrive without restrictions of health, education, race, religion, or by having his or her destiny impaired by the privileges of others. He wrote in his diary that history would approve.

Perkins never allowed herself to be so pigeonholed. She claimed to have no idea what "a New Dealer" might be, other than an official who shared a general humanitarian impulse.[20] Hopkins and Wallace also elided such a provocative tag.

Ickes died in February 1952 amid a failing undeclared war in Korea, a self-destructive reaction on Capitol Hill to Soviet espionage—which by then had largely been uncovered—and a nationwide steel strike that dragged in Truman and the Supreme Court. Nonetheless, Ickes's final column, a week before he died, was a benediction upon "these United States"—an old, proud way to refer to the Republic. He wrote of "an apple crisp and sweet," a land full of opportunity and hope, for all its faults.[21]

On another Sunday afternoon in April, this one in 1952, Marian Anderson returned to the steps of the Lincoln Memorial. She sang Bach's "Come Sweet Death" in tribute to Harold Ickes. Jane and their small son and daughter were there, as was the interior secretary of the day, and a throng of more than ten thousand. Truman was expected, though he didn't return from a weekend cruise down the Potomac.

Only in September 1952 did Henry Wallace acknowledge publicly his naivete about Stalinism. Still, he treated lightly the fact that his quixotic presidential campaign in 1948 on the Progressive Party ticket—against Truman, Governor Dewey, and the Southern racist States' Rights spin off of the Democratic Party that FDR had foreseen—was influenced heavily by Communists, in whom he benignly trusted. Writing of the war years, Wallace admitted to having "not the slightest idea there were many slave labor camps in Siberia in 1944 and that of these the most notorious was Magadan"—gateway to the Kolyma region—of which he had spoken so glowingly.[22]

Two months after that confession, Dwight Eisenhower was elected president. NATO's recent supreme commander would write that, during the war, "the President made light of my fears" of Soviet ambitions and that he had come to regard Roosevelt as "almost an egomaniac" in his "belief in his own wisdom."[23]

However, it is Eisenhower's perspective on the domestic accomplishments of Roosevelt's presidency that echoes today. "Ike," as Roosevelt always called him, understood that millions of Americans had emerged from the World War determined to keep their pieces of the New Deal, and of what Truman rebranded the "Fair Deal" to signal that there'd be no going back to the America before FDR. Eisenhower built on enough of those policies for fellow Republicans to denounce his "dime store New Deal" while voicing their party's default position of the 1930s—and of the 2020s: a president was "undermining the American work ethic."[24]

Perkins left her part-time duties on the Civil Service Commission in 1952 when Paul Wilson died. For the first time in years, with help from attendants, she had been able to care for him at home, a small house of her own in Washington. As always, she was deeply comforted by her faith, reflecting of her husband's torments that "they were truly past man's understanding."[25] She still had to work, however, and through the decade, did so as a university lecturer, mostly at Cornell's School of Industrial and Labor Relations in Ithaca, New York. She often saw Henry Wallace, who, faded from politics though backing Eisenhower's reelection in 1956, lived on a farm in South Salem, fifty miles from Hyde Park.

In the early 1960s, they taught an undergraduate seminar together at Cornell, inspired by a shared conviction, as Perkins stated it, that a Christian society should have "a pattern of social cooperation and social justice expressed in legal, economic, and social relationships."[26]

By then, Wallace's struggling startup, Hi-Bred Corn Company, had turned into a global colossus. The family fortune that resulted became the basis for world-changing philanthropy when, in 1959, Wallace used shares to start the Wallace Genetic Foundation, his son Robert in time launching the Wallace Global Fund for sustainable development. At the turn of the century, DuPont would buy what is today's Corteva Agriscience for $9.1 billion.

FDR recognized that Wallace was "no mystic," but a genius who was turning out to be a mega-entrepreneur, and any builder on such a scale must be an exceptional improviser, as indeed were each of the four, and above all their chief.

Perkins and Wallace died within six months of each other in 1965—a time when Jane Ickes was marching, that late winter, with Dr. Martin Luther King, Jr., in Selma and funding Planned Parenthood.

Perkins's bestselling book, *The Roosevelt I Knew,* had been published nearly twenty years earlier, and it provided some modest financial stability for her later years. She would save what she really knew of Roosevelt for her oral history. Nevertheless, her memoir examines "twelve years of constant crisis," and closes with a nearly audible sigh of relief, in late 1946. "Thank goodness that's all over," she seems to be saying. Amazingly, America had pulled through.

Except the age of extremity was just beginning. Within a year of FDR's death, the world's greatest war was followed by history's least plausible peace. Once the Soviet Union collapsed a generation later, it would fall to us to confront a new array of fears: fanatic terror, disease, military failures, war in Europe, more dark hours of national life. Yet an inspiring definition of victory is to find oneself able to face even greater challenges. And that is the strength which these five left to us a long lifetime ago.

ACKNOWLEDGMENTS

I'm grateful to executive editor Elisabeth Dyssegaard for having acquired *Unlikely Heroes,* for her editorial skill, and for marshaling her expert team at St. Martin's Press. A wise friend, Will Lippincott, of Aevitas Creative, introduced us and guided our thinking. Encouragement has been supplied by Angela, to whom this book is dedicated, and by her mom. I'm thankful too for the tasks at which we've been set, as reminded by the Reverend Timothy A. R. Cole.

David Webster—student of the American presidency, former White House Fellow, and corporate lawyer—read the entire manuscript. So did Timothy Dickinson, who, uniquely, has guided writers as well as institutional investors since his days with *Harper's, Paris Review,* and select advisory firms. Bob Coulam, author of the enduring *Illusions of Choice,* is another lifelong friend who weighed in.

Acute insights on world affairs came from Ambassadors Marc Wall and Eunice Reddick—my fellow classmates at Columbia University—and from Maximilian Weiner, author Meena Ahamed, and from the American Enterprise Institute's Leon Aron, who is among the country's foremost analysts of Russia. Like Leon, I'm a disciple of Michael Mandelbaum's, professor emeritus at SAIS, and I've welcomed Michael's guidance since the days of brown-bag seminars at Harvard's Program for Science and International Affairs.

Washington, D.C., where I live, has its own flourishing book world. In no small part, that's due to playwright John B. Henry and his Stone Hill Foundation, and to John Hauge, who, in 2010, organized an extraordinary book club that came to shape the lives of its brethren. I've benefited from every minute of knowing him, Antoine van Agtmael, Liaquat Ahamed, Bruce Bartels, Arturo Brillembourg, Bobby Haft, Michael Helfer, Dani Levinas, Randy Quarrels, and Jeff Weiss.

At the National Museum of the U.S. Army—which is backed by the

Army Historical Foundation—the AHF's Lt. General Roger Schultz (USA-Ret.) and chief historian Matthew Seelinger have expertly fielded questions about the U.S. armed forces.

My longtime friends Jim Strock, author of *Serve to Lead,* and Christopher Gray introduced me respectively to two of the world's leading historians: Richard Norton Smith and Wm. Roger Louis. I'm humbled that those scholars have taken an interest in my work.

Other supportive friends have been Tim Carrington, Mike and Donna Carey, and the literary critic Laure Berger, as well as Hannah, Jade, and Kemi of *notre quartier.* A day job in business has allowed me to work with visionaries of technology, including Michel Biezunski, founder of Infoloom, and also with entrepreneurs Greg Duncan, John Park, and Janet Janjigian.

Finally, I'm grateful for the inspiration of my father, a soldier of Orange.

At age twenty-five, Onno Leebaert spent the afternoon of November 3, 1941, with President Roosevelt at Hyde Park. The president wanted to hear directly of conditions in the Nazi-occupied "homeland," from which my father had escaped. FDR meanwhile practiced his Dutch while, in Springwood's library, he displayed children's books, written in Dutch, that he had read a half century before. America would not enter all-out combat for another thirty-five days, but Roosevelt offered complete assurance that Holland would be liberated.

Always, among young people, he felt free to drop his insouciance, tall tales, and manipulations. That afternoon, FDR had a question: "What will you be doing when this is all over?" After all, Roosevelt continually felt the future to be bright. To him, no task was impossible, including the rescue of democracy, and then the saving of civilization.

NOTES

ON SOURCES

Frances Perkins and Henry Wallace produced formidable oral histories of 5,566 and 5,520 pages each, and Wallace added documents as well as material from his intermittent diary to his. Harold Ickes, in turn, began a diary once he entered office. It grew to roughly four million words, 800,000 of which have been published in three volumes. He was "the peer of another narcissistic bureaucrat, Samuel Pepys," concluded political journalist Richard H. Rovere, referencing England's famed seventeenth-century diarist. Harry Hopkins died too soon for an oral history, and he didn't keep a diary. Moreover, he hesitated to put revealing matters on paper. Still, his friend Robert Sherwood's magisterial biography drew on their intimacy, on the notes and scrapbooks Hopkins assembled, and on some 224,000 pages of records that became the Hopkins Papers. Therefore, readers of *Unlikely Heroes* can see many events from two, three, and sometimes four perspectives. These multiple viewpoints, supported by archives, enhance the accuracy of the principals' reminiscences and journals. It's a helpful approach, particularly when FDR's most trusted, longest-serving paladins are observing the president himself.

INTRODUCTION
1. "Mr. Hopkins's Opportunity," *New York Times,* January 25, 1939, 16.
2. Frances Perkins Oral History, Columbia University Libraries Oral History Research Office, pt. 4, session 1, p. 487.
3. "Vice President and 'Good Neighbor,'" *New York Times,* January 26, 1941, 2.
4. Raymond Moley, *After Seven Years* (New York: Harper & Brothers, 1939), 101.
5. Arthur M. Schlesinger, Jr., *The Coming of the New Deal* (Boston: Houghton Mifflin, 1959), 549.
6. Grace Tully, *F.D.R., My Boss* (New York: Scribner's, 1949), 172–73.
7. H. W. Brands, *Traitor to His Class: The Privileged Life and Radical Presidency of Franklin Delano Roosevelt* (New York: Doubleday, 2008), 294.
8. Rexford Tugwell, *Roosevelt's Revolution: The First Year, a Personal Perspective* (New York: Macmillan, 1977), 129.
9. Frances Perkins, *The Roosevelt I Knew* (New York: Viking, 1946), 140.

CHAPTER 1: STEPPING FORWARD
1. FDR was able to simultaneously translate one of Hitler's broadcasts into English, which would qualify as ILR 4 in today's State Department assessments. Sumner Welles attests to FDR's Spanish in *The Time for Decision*

(New York: Harper, 1944), 192. FDR's excellent French can be heard at FDR Audio Recordings, Franklin D. Roosevelt Presidential Library.

2. Historians have been describing Howe with variations on "dwarfish" since the label was affixed by James MacGregor Burns, in *Roosevelt: The Lion and the Fox* (New York: Harcourt Brace, 1956), 44. Howe probably stood five feet, three inches—to judge from photos of him next to Roosevelt—but no record of his height exists, even on his Secret Service identification card.

3. Samuel L. Rosenman, *Working with Roosevelt* (London: Rupert Hart Davis, 1952), 111; Geoffrey C. Ward, "The Lost Mencken," *American Heritage,* December 1989, which can be read here: https://www.americanheritage.com/lost-mencken; Ted Morgan, *FDR: A Biography* (New York: Simon & Schuster, 1985), 375, on Wilson.

4. Frances Perkins Oral History, Columbia University Libraries Oral History Research Office, pt. 7, session 1, p. 315. Perkins emphasizes that she heard FDR say "mean at heart" directly and that he had "a good deal of self-knowledge." He preferred to think of himself as having been "an awfully mean cuss" just in his early years. See Arthur M. Schlesinger, Jr., *The Crisis of the Old Order* (Boston: Houghton Mifflin, 1957), 339.

5. "Roosevelt Inaugurated Governor; Call for Cooperation," *New York Times,* January 1, 1929, 1.

6. Frank Freidel, *Franklin D. Roosevelt: The Ordeal* (Boston: Little, Brown, 1954), 100.

7. On McDuffie's handicap, see undated handwritten document titled "Legs" in Elizabeth and Irvin McDuffie Papers, Box 10, Archives Research Center, Woodruff Library, Atlanta University Center.

8. "Republican Party Platform of 1928," American Presidency Project, https://www.presidency.ucsb.edu/documents/republican-party-platform-1928.

9. "Miss Perkins Takes the Oath of Office," *New York Times,* January 15, 1929, 3.

10. "I'm a domestic person at heart" sums up her yearning for a family and traditional homelife. "I like to dust." (Though she didn't cook.) Perkins OH, pt. 3, session 1, p. 561.

11. Perkins OH, pt. 2, session 1, pp. 64–66.

12. Hopkins would state "shock the Methodists" to Ickes on their October 1935 fishing trip, but he was more likely trying to shock Ickes; see Robert E. Sherwood, *Roosevelt and Hopkins: An Intimate History* (New York: Harper, 1948), 29, citing Dr. Jacob Goldberg, secretary of the Association.

13. "I did not care" and "friendlessness" are from Harold L. Ickes, "Unpublished Personal Memoirs," Harold L. Ickes Papers, Library of Congress, 76, 93.

14. See the *A.D.S. Golden Year Dahlia Record,* September 18–20, 1964, on Ickes.

15. Harold Ickes, *The Autobiography of a Curmudgeon* (New York: Reynal & Hitchcock, 1943), 312.

16. "I don't talk to her [Ilo] about things of this sort," Wallace wrote in his diary when having to decide in 1944 whether or not to stay in Washington for the

third term. See Henry Wallace Oral History, Columbia University Libraries Oral History Research Office, 3390.

17. Arthur M. Schlesinger, Jr., *The Coming of the New Deal* (Boston: Houghton Mifflin, 1959), 34.

18. "1929: Born 'n Bred in a Briar Patch: Market Crash Rocks Class Temporarily," *Harvard Crimson,* June 15, 1954, 1.

19. Hutchins recalled this incident to Timothy Dickinson in 1973 at the Center for the Study of Democratic Institutions. The author has benefited from a half dozen interviews, each for more than ninety minutes, during 2019 to 2022 with Mr. Dickinson. They focused on his own encounters with figures who participated in the events explored in this book. During the 1960s and '70s, Mr. Dickinson was a researcher for historian Barbara Tuchman, an editor at *Paris Review* and *Harper's Magazine,* and a civil rights activist. (In fact, due to the pump-and-dump Radio Pool, RCA reached a dizzying $505 before crashing to $10. The New Deal would outlaw this practice.)

20. Republican Party Platform of 1928.

21. A portrayal of Rumsey claiming "she was not extravagant" misunderstands her parties of endless champagne, her limousines, and a truly Gilded Age life, her daughter's debutante ball being just one example. See Adam Cohen, *Nothing to Fear: FDR's Inner Circle and the Hundred Days That Created Modern America* (New York: Penguin, 2009), 201.

CHAPTER 2: ECONOMIC PLAGUE

1. Edwin G. Nourse et al., *America's Capacity to Produce* (Washington, DC: Institute of Economics, Brookings Institution, 1934), 33.

2. Frances Perkins Oral History, Columbia University Libraries Oral History Research Office, pt. 4, session 1, p. 302.

3. The myth of "laissez-faire" under Hoover originated in the writings of New Dealers such as Rexford Tugwell, but then was set in stone by historians who idealized the New Deal such as Arthur M. Schlesinger, Jr., and Henry Steele Commager. The myth that "Mr. Hoover [was] passive in the face of the Depression" continues today. See David Leonhardt, "A Better Economy Under Democrats," *New York Times,* Sunday Review, February 7, 2021, 2.

4. In 1930, 4.2 percent of GDP was spent on infrastructure; in 2016, it was 2.5 percent. American Society of Civil Engineers, "Changing the Infrastructure Equation," March 2019. Such denunciations began what some remember today, as at Stanford University's Hoover Institution, as Hoover's "crusade against collectivism." Note this podcast with historian George Nash: https://www.hoover.org/research/herbert-hoovers-life-and-his-crusade-against-collectivism.

5. Perkins OH, pt. 3, session 1, p. 439.

6. NPR *Morning Edition,* January 14, 2021, interview with Deborah Berkowitz, National Employment Law Project, concerning the meatpacking industry; on "Jablowsky," see Perkins OH, pt. 3, session 1, p. 223.

7. Perkins OH, pt. 3, session 1, p. 243.

8. Perkins OH, pt. 3, session 1, p. 88.

9. Perkins OH, pt. 3, session 1, p. 216.

10. "Whitney Points Out Stock Market Lessons," *New York Times*, June 11, 1930, 3.

11. June Hopkins, *Harry Hopkins: Sudden Hero, Brash Reformer* (New York: St. Martin's Press, 1999), 153.

12. For "character destroying," see John T. Flynn, *Country Squire in the White House* (New York: Doubleday, 1940), 40.

13. Perkins OH, pt. 3, session 1, pp. 254–55.

14. "Crossbreeding Increases Yield," *New York Times*, March 9, 1930, 44.

15. Anna Wilmarth Ickes, *Mesa Land* (Boston: Houghton Mifflin, 1933). It was well received in the *New Mexico Historical Review,* January 1934, 105.

16. Perkins, OH, pt. 2, session 1, pp. 86–87.

17. John Culver and John Hyde, *American Dreamer: A Life of Henry A. Wallace* (New York: W. W. Norton, 2000), 95.

18. Perkins OH, pt. 3, session 1, p. 332.

19. Kathryn Smith, *The Gatekeeper: Missy LeHand, FDR, and the Untold Story of the Partnership That Defined a Presidency* (New York: Simon & Schuster, 2016), 104.

20. Perkins OH, pt. 2, session 1, p. 548.

21. Kirstin Downey, *The Woman Behind the New Deal* (New York: Doubleday, 2009), 111.

22. George McJimsey, *Harry Hopkins: Ally of the Poor* (Cambridge, MA: Harvard University Press, 1987), 43.

23. Perkins OH, pt. 4, session 1, p. 469.

24. Chicago's population in 1931 was 3.37 million, whereas today it's 2.7 million. The Lawyers Committee for Better Housing estimates Chicago evictions for 2018 at 23,000 annually. See www.lcbh.org/news/more-23000-eviction-filings -year-chicago-open-new-door-housing-problems.

25. Edmund Wilson, *The American Earthquake* (New York: Doubleday, 1957), 462.

26. Culver and Hyde, *American Dreamer,* 99.

27. Halvdan Koht, Nobel Prize Award ceremony speech, December 10, 1931, https://www.nobelprize.org/prizes/peace/1931/ceremony-speech/.

28. Matthew Josephson, *Sidney Hillman: Statesman of American Labor* (Garden City, NY: Doubleday, 1952), 354.

29. Barron H. Lerner, "New York City's Tuberculosis Control Efforts: The Historical Limitations of the 'War on Consumption,'" *American Journal of Public Health* 83, no. 5 (May 1993): 169.

30. Forrest C. Pogue, *George C. Marshall: Education of a General: 1880–1939* (New York: Viking, 1963), 100.

31. William D. Hassett, *Off the Record with FDR: 1942–1945* (New Brunswick, NJ: Rutgers University Press, 1958), 101, diary entry for August 15, 1942.

32. As a boy, FDR had bought many of these books himself; as an adult, he often browsed through them in this library. See John Gunther, *Roosevelt in Retrospect: A Profile in History* (New York: Harper, 1950), 75.

33. Henry Wallace Oral History, Columbia University Libraries Oral History Research Office, 3200, recalling his first meeting with FDR.

CHAPTER 3: SURGE TO POWER

1. Studs Terkel, *Hard Times: An Oral History of the Great Depression* (New York: Random House, 1970), 145.

2. June Hopkins, *Harry Hopkins: Sudden Hero, Brash Reformer* (New York: St. Martin's Press, 1999), 159.

3. *The Public Papers and Addresses of Franklin D. Roosevelt, 1928–1932* (New York: Random House, 1938), 756–70; *Sioux City Journal,* September 30, 1932, pp. 1, 7, 8.

4. Philip A. Grant, "The Presidential Election of 1932 in Iowa," *Annals of Iowa* (Winter 1979): 546.

5. Henry H. Adams, *Harry Hopkins: A Biography* (New York: Putnam, 1977), 48.

6. Franklin D. Roosevelt Library, Master Speech File, 1898–1945. Cheyenne, Wyoming, Extemporaneous Remarks, September 16, 1932.

7. Charles Michaelson, *The Ghost Talks* (New York: Putnam, 1944), 11.

8. Author's interviews with Timothy Dickinson. He recalled discussing this phenomenon with his friend Richard L. Dougherty when the latter was press secretary for George McGovern's presidential campaign.

9. "Little General Staff" is Raymond Moley, *After Seven Years* (New York: Harper & Brothers, 1939), 21. The origin of "brain trust," and its facetious connotation, is John F. Weston, Commissary General of the Army, who resented the General Staff. See the entry for "Brain Trust" in *Stevenson's Book of Quotations* (London: Cassell, 1964).

10. H. W. Brands, *Traitor to His Class: The Privileged Life and Radical Presidency of Franklin Delano Roosevelt* (New York: Doubleday, 2008), 289. For instance, when they presumed to instruct FDR on the basics of social insurance, they discovered he already knew the subject, having been briefed for years by Perkins. Brands also writes that FDR "knew more about the world abroad than any president before him," 439. But see any biography of Herbert Hoover.

11. A leading scholar of FDR's presidency has concisely laid out this argument. See Eric Rauchway, "The New Deal Was on the Ballot in 1932," *Modern American History* 2 (2019): 201.

12. Frances Perkins Oral History, Columbia University Libraries Oral History Research Office, pt. 7, session 1, p. 492.

13. One of the friends with whom Mrs. Tuchman reminisced years later was Timothy Dickinson, who helped research her book *The Proud Tower* (1966), as he conveyed to the author.

14. Perkins OH, "repulsive" is in pt. 4, session 1, p. 455. To be "initially repulsed by his physical appearance" was still the common reaction, even by someone as decent as Aubrey Williams, Hopkins's deputy. See John Salmond, *A Southern Rebel: The Life and Times of Aubrey Willis Williams* (Chapel Hill: University of North Carolina Press, 1983), 69.

15. Lawrence W. Levine, "The 'Diary' of Hiram Johnson," *American Heritage,* August 1969, 111. He is referencing a January 29, 1929, letter by Johnson, in the Hiram Johnson Papers, University of California, Berkeley.

16. John Culver and John Hyde, *American Dreamer: A Life of Henry A. Wallace* (New

York: W. W. Norton, 2000), 7. That said, there was nothing "faddishly scientific" about Wallace, as one FDR biographer asserts. Wallace was among the world's great agronomists. See Conrad Black, *Franklin Delano Roosevelt: Champion of Freedom* (New York: PublicAffairs, 2003), 336. Nor was Wallace, at this time, "wealthy" with "credibility as an agribusinessman," let alone a "successful agribusinessman," as another biographer asserts. See Robert Dallek, *Franklin D. Roosevelt: A Political Life* (New York: Random House, 2017), 130, 145.

17. Adams, *Harry Hopkins,* 48.

18. Louis Howe, "The Winner," *Saturday Evening Post,* February 25, 1933.

19. "Two Wounded by Shots at Roosevelt Meeting," *Miami Herald,* February 16, 1933, 1.

20. "Attack on Garner," *New York Times,* July 29, 1939, 2. It is mistaken to dismiss Garner as an "undistinguished Speaker" who "served at the bidding of publisher William Randolph Hearst," as does David Levering Lewis in *The Improbable Wendell Willkie* (New York: W. W. Norton, 2018), 67. Hearst had started his slide to bankruptcy and was equally a pawn of Garner's. Garner wanted greater stature beyond the South; Hearst needed Garner as a major politician. As for Garner's speakership, it was but one term.

21. Hopkins and Perkins, in Perkins OH, pt. 7, session 1, p. 557.

22. Perkins OH, pt. 2, session 1, p. 679.

23. Perkins's letter to FDR on "grave personal difficulties" is shown in transcript at Perkins OH, pt. 3, session 1, p. 519.

24. Perkins OH, pt. 3, session 1, pp. 369–72, on encountering Ickes.

25. Perkins OH, pt. 3, session 1, p. 570.

26. Moley, *After Seven Years,* 127.

27. Ibid., 129.

28. Perkins OH, pt. 3, session 1, p. 570.

29. "Miss Perkins Ready for Cabinet Duties," *New York Times,* February 24, 1933, 2. Unlike the other appointees, Perkins's appointment was greeted by a flood of "human interest" stories, such as one about her Irish terrier, Balto, getting lost before he could accompany her to Washington.

30. John Morton Blum, ed., *Public Philosopher: Selected Letters of Walter Lippmann* (New York: Ticknor & Fields, 1985), 469, Walter Lippmann to Bernard Berenson, July 11, 1945.

31. First Inaugural Address of Franklin D. Roosevelt, March 4, 1933, https://avalon.law.yale.edu/20th_century/froos1.asp.

32. James A. Farley, *Jim Farley's Story: The Roosevelt Years* (New York: McGraw-Hill, 1948), 39.

33. Arthur M. Schlesinger, Jr., *The Coming of the New Deal* (Boston: Houghton Mifflin, 1959), 140, describes Cutting as "sensitive," which, in 1957, was still a well-known euphemism for being gay.

CHAPTER 4: ACTION NOW

1. Arthur M. Schlesinger, Jr., *The Crisis of the Old Order* (Boston: Houghton Mifflin, 1957), 8; Frank Freidel, *Franklin Roosevelt: A Rendezvous with Destiny* (New York: Little, Brown, 1990), 99.

2. FDRL, President's Personal File, FDR to William Hearst, April 1, 1933.

3. Henry Wallace Oral History, Columbia University Libraries Oral History Research Office, 3620.

4. On referencing Bonaparte, with whom he otherwise found it repellent to be compared, see Ted Morgan, *FDR: A Biography* (New York: Simon & Schuster, 1985), 416.

5. "New Cabinet Circle of Simple Tastes," *New York Times,* March 4, 1933, 4; "Mrs. Ickes Departs," *Washington Herald,* March 7, 1933, 3.

6. Hopkins had come to Washington with a colleague from Albany, and they had briefed FDR together. On "inroads" and "Mrs. Roosevelt," see Frances Perkins Oral History, Columbia University Libraries Oral History Research Office, pt. 7, session 1, pp. 542, 544.

7. June Hopkins, *Harry Hopkins: Sudden Hero, Brash Reformer* (New York: St. Martin's Press, 1999), 160; Plutarch, *Caesar,* 11: "I would rather be first here [a squalid barbarian village] than second in Rome."

8. FDRL, MSF, Box 28, Chicago, Campaign Address, October 14, 1936.

9. Perkins OH, pt. 4, session 1, p. 208.

10. Perkins OH, pt. 4, session 1, p. 214.

11. Perkins OH, pt. 4, session 1, p. 249.

12. Department of Labor, *Annual Report of the Secretary of Labor* (Washington, DC: Government Printing Office, 1940), 8.

13. Perkins OH, pt. 4, session 1, p. 271.

14. John Culver and John Hyde, *American Dreamer: A Life of Henry A. Wallace* (New York: W. W. Norton, 2000), 113.

15. Ibid., 112.

16. C. B. Baldwin, who became Wallace's assistant in 1933 and served until 1945. Interviewed in Studs Terkel, *Hard Times: An Oral History of the Great Depression* (New York: Random House, 1970), 255.

17. Perkins OH, pt. 4, session 1, p. 95.

18. Perkins OH, pt. 4, session 1, p. 98.

19. Hopkins, *Sudden Hero,* 167.

20. Derrell Bradford, "The Left Defends the Legacy of Redlining," *Washington Post,* June 14, 2021, 19.

21. Perkins OH, pt. 4, session 1, p. 467.

22. "Miss Perkins Firm in Job Bill Defense," *New York Times,* March 24, 1933, 10.

23. Perkins OH, pt. 5, session 1, p. 29.

24. On inviting Perkins, see Harold Ickes, *The Secret Diary of Harold L. Ickes,* vol. 1, *The First Thousand Days, 1933–1936* (New York: Simon & Schuster, 1953), 10; Perkins OH, pt. 5, session 1, p. 277.

25. Perkins OH, pt. 5, session 1, pp. 282–92.

26. Ickes, *The First Thousand Days,* 295, February 17, 1935.

27. As cited in a profile of one of Garner's successors as Speaker, Sam Rayburn. See https://greatest-ever.livejournal.com/4680.html.

28. Ickes, *The First Thousand Days,* 16, April 14, 1933.

29. Perkins OH, pt. 3, session 1, p. 177.

30. "Custodian of Our Vast Public Domain," *New York Times,* June 4, 1933, 7; Ickes, *The First Thousand Days,* 40, May 19, 1933.

31. James A. Farley, *Jim Farley's Story: The Roosevelt Years* (New York: McGraw-Hill, 1948), 54.

32. Perkins OH, pt. 4, session 1, p. 327.

33. An example of a seismic issue mentioned only in the Cabinet is Attorney General Cummings's hinting during the second half of 1936 what he had in store for the Supreme Court. See Perkins OH, pt. 7, session 1, pp. 111–18; on FDR's follow-up demands, see Henry A. Wallace Collection, University of Iowa Libraries, HAW letter to FDR concerning wheat prices, November 3, 1937.

34. Beatrice Bishop Berle and Travis Beal Jacobs, eds., *Navigating the Rapids, 1918–1971: From the Papers of Adolf A. Berle* (New York: Harcourt Brace Jovanovich, 1973), 55. Memorandum, August 5, 1932.

35. Harold L. Ickes, "Unpublished Personal Memoirs," Harold L. Ickes Papers, Library of Congress, 255.

36. Henry H. Adams, *Harry Hopkins: A Biography* (New York: Putnam, 1977), 66.

37. Perkins OH, pt. 4, session 1, pp. 461–63.

CHAPTER 5: NEW FRONTIERS

1. "The Cabinet," *Time,* July 24, 1933.

2. "Labor: Truce at a Crisis," *Time,* August 14, 1933.

3. "A New 'Dictator' in Roosevelt's List," *New York Times,* September 10, 1933, 2.

4. It is misremembering to write that FDR didn't want these lieutenants "to have or develop independent reputations or constituencies," as does biographer H. W. Brands in *Traitor to His Class: The Privileged Life and Radical Presidency of Franklin Delano Roosevelt* (New York: Doubleday, 2008), 294. First, each already had a "constituency" when appointed; second, FDR was explicitly pleased about their "independent reputations," which he did much to foster.

5. James A. Farley, *Jim Farley's Story: The Roosevelt Years* (New York: McGraw-Hill, 1938), 42.

6. Wallace observes the claim to Jewish blood, and the hand rubbing, in Henry Wallace Oral History, Columbia University Libraries Oral History Research Office, 198.

7. Arthur M. Schlesinger, Jr., *The Coming of the New Deal* (Boston: Houghton Mifflin, 1959), 202.

8. Frank Freidel, *Franklin Roosevelt: A Rendezvous with Destiny* (New York: Little, Brown, 1990), 133. By fall 1933, debtors could repay their obligations in paper dollars, which had a progressively smaller value, but creditors were steadily diminished.

9. Historian Eric Rauchway argues powerfully for FDR's expertise in *The Money Makers* (New York: Basic, 2015). Alternatively, David Kennedy, a future treasury secretary, was then at the Federal Reserve and got such stories about the superstitious president. See his interview in Studs Terkel, *Hard Times: An Oral History of the Great Depression* (New York: Random House, 1970), 275.

10. Frances Perkins Oral History, Columbia University Libraries Oral History Research Office, pt. 7, session 1, p. 861; Ickes also chronicles this curious warning.

11. "Government by Abbreviation," *New York Times,* November 29, 1933, 1.

12. Perkins OH, pt. 2, session 1, pp. 157–58.

13. Perkins OH, pt. 5, session 1, p. 171.

14. Henry A. Wallace, *New Frontiers: A Study of the Mind of America and the Way That Lies Ahead* (New York: Reynal & Hitchcock, 1934), 350. Also see Wallace OH, 351.

15. "New Sense of Duty Guiding President, His Chief Aides Say," *New York Times,* May 22, 1933, 1.

16. "Patronage Revolt Faces Roosevelt," *New York Times,* September 13, 1933, 1.

17. "A New 'Dictator' in Roosevelt's List," *New York Times,* September 10, 1933, 2.

18. Bruère Oral History, Columbia University Libraries, Columbia Center for Oral History, 160.

19. On Covington and Burling, see John T. Flynn, *Country Squire in the White House* (New York: Doubleday, 1940), 83.

20. On Acheson being described in 1949 as a "Velazquez grandee," see my portrait of him in *Grand Improvisation: America Confronts the British Superpower, 1945–1957* (New York: Farrar, Straus & Giroux, 2018), 163–67.

21. Harold Ickes, *The Secret Diary of Harold L. Ickes,* vol. 1, *The First Thousand Days, 1933–1936* (New York: Simon & Schuster, 1953), 110, October 19, 1933, on "agrarian revolt; Perkins OH, pt. 5, session 1, p. 522, on sculptures; Jacob Baker, oral history, Archives of American Art, Smithsonian Institution, September 25, 1963.

22. "I know you" and "friends" are from Ickes, *The First Thousand Days*, 122, November 14, 1933.

23. Wallace OH, 163.

24. Perkins OH, pt. 4, session 1, pp. 553–55.

25. A draft biographical article was sent to Morgenthau by *Fortune* associate editor Wilder Hobson, March 24, 1934. This is the opening line of the article, which infuriated Morgenthau. See the FDRL, Diaries of Henry Morgenthau, Jr. (Morgenthau diaries), volume 1, 78.

26. Sylvia Porter, in her column, as cited in entry "Sylvia Porter," *Current Biography* (Hackensack, NJ: Grey House Publishing, 1992). The impression that Morgenthau was "underrated," as Arthur M. Schlesinger, Jr., argued in 1959—when the former treasury secretary was still alive—is dated, yet endures. Moreover, Schlesinger's belief that FDR "kept Wallace at arm's length" is simply wrong, as can be seen by examining twelve years of the president's daily calendar. See Schlesinger, *Coming of the New Deal*, 538.

27. That was Daniel W. Bell, who was initially assistant to the secretary of the treasury and who became undersecretary in 1940.

28. Perkins OH, pt. 5, session 1, p. 234.

29. Ickes, *The First Thousand Days,* 165, May 11, 1934, on "Indian country."

30. Perkins OH, pt. 4, session 1, pp. 400–439, is exciting.

31. Glassford's "Proclamation" can be seen at pt. 4, session 1, p. 414; Perkins says further of Glassford that "he was the type of man the Greeks used to call sanguine."

32. Perkins OH, pt. 5, session 1, p. 302.

33. Perkins OH, pt. 5, session 1, p. 535.

34. Robert Browder and Thomas Smith, *Independent: A Biography of Lewis W. Douglas* (New York: Knopf, 1986), 153; Perkins OH, pt. 5, session 1, p. 535.

35. "Relish of power" is used admiringly as a chapter title in Conrad Black, *Franklin Delano Roosevelt: Champion of Freedom* (New York: PublicAffairs, 2003), 268.

36. Hugh Johnson, *The Blue Eagle, from Egg to Earth* (Garden City, NY: Doubleday, 1935), 113.

37. Ickes, *The First Thousand Days*, 201, October 2, 1934.

38. Kathryn Smith, *The Gatekeeper: Missy LeHand, FDR, and the Untold Story of the Partnership That Defined a Presidency* (New York: Simon & Schuster, 2016), 124; Ickes, *The First Thousand Days*, 224, November 15, 1934.

CHAPTER 6: GETTING THE HABIT

1. Hearings Before the Committee on Ways and Means, House of Representatives, 74th Cong., May 20–24, 1935 (Washington, DC: Government Printing Office, 1935), 37.

2. Herbert Agar, *The United States: The Presidents, the Parties & the Constitution* (London: Eyre & Spottiswoode, 1950), 443.

3. Frances Perkins Oral History, Columbia University Libraries Oral History Research Office, pt. 8, session 1, p. 338.

4. Arthur Krock, *Memoirs* (New York: Funk & Wagnalls, 1968), 16.

5. "The Nation: Curtains for Cotton Ed," *Time,* August 7, 1944.

6. Ira Katznelson, *Fear Itself: The New Deal and the Origins of Our Time* (New York: Liveright, 2013), 21, 149.

7. Unlike FDR, none of our four were responsible for the party's future—two of them being Republicans—nor were any of them seeking national office, at least not yet. Wallace consistently reported to FDR on developments concerning cotton, and, for instance, refers to FDR's "interest in cotton" in his letter of September 27, 1937, Henry A. Wallace Collection, University of Iowa Libraries. Wallace speaks in his oral history of FDR's sensitivity to cotton, and of his price tracking. Wallace concluded the entire party itself rested on cotton. See Henry Wallace Oral History, Columbia University Libraries Oral History Research Office, 404–7.

8. Ickes Papers (LOC), Letter from Walter White to Ickes, March 11, 1936, Container 246; On slum clearance, see Harold Ickes, *The Secret Diary of Harold L. Ickes,* vol. 1, *The First Thousand Days, 1933–1936* (New York: Simon & Schuster, 1953), 211, October 16, 1934.

9. Jeanne Clarke, *Roosevelt's Warrior: Harold L. Ickes and the New Deal* (Baltimore: Johns Hopkins University Press, 1998), 98.

10. Perkins OH, pt. 5, session 1, p. 467.

11. Perkins OH, pt. 5, session 1, p. 470.

12. Perkins OH, pt. 5, session 1, p. 456.

13. Alan Rappeport and Ana Swanson, "Biden Administration Ramps Up Debt-Relief Efforts for Black Farmers," *New York Times,* March 26, 2021, 12.

14. John Culver and John Hyde, *American Dreamer: A Life of Henry A. Wallace* (New York: W. W. Norton, 2000), 153.

15. Frank Freidel, *Franklin Roosevelt: A Rendezvous with Destiny* (New York: Little, Brown, 1990), 145.

16. John Salmond, *A Southern Rebel: The Life and Times of Aubrey Willis Williams* (Chapel Hill: University of North Carolina Press, 1983). See chapter 1 ("Boyhood in Birmingham") and chapter 2 ("'Over There'—and Other Places"), in which the author addresses Williams's romantic background. He is citing undated correspondence from 1934, FERA Records, Old Subject File, interracial relations.

17. "Our New Spoils System," *Atlantic Monthly,* February 1936, 190.

18. Ickes, *The First Thousand Days,* 434, 487, December 16 and September 8, 1935; Ted Morgan, *FDR: A Biography* (New York: Simon & Schuster, 1985), 417, for Hopkins.

19. Robert H. Jackson, *That Man: An Insider's Portrait of Franklin D. Roosevelt* (New York: Oxford University Press, 2003), 61.

20. Harold Ickes, "My Twelve Years With F.D.R.," *Saturday Evening Post,* July 24, 1948, 22.

21. Ickes, *The First Thousand Days,* 16, April 4, 1933.

22. Raymond Gram Swing, "Rude and Honest Ickes," *Vanity Fair,* April 1935, 15–16.

23. Harold Ickes, *The Secret Diary of Harold L. Ickes,* vol. 2, *The Inside Struggle, 1936–1939* (New York: Simon & Schuster, 1954), 112, April 3, 1937.

24. Swing, "Rude and Honest Ickes."

25. Perkins OH, pt. 7, session 1, p. 102.

26. Perkins OH, pt. 7, session 1, p. 147.

27. Kirstin Downey, *The Woman Behind the New Deal* (New York: Doubleday, 2009), 222.

28. Ickes, *The Inside Struggle,* 212, September 19, 1937.

29. Perkins OH, pt. 4, session 1, p. 278.

30. Downey, *The Woman Behind the New Deal,* 244. Perkins also worked closely with Wagner's professional assistant, lawyer Simon H. Rifkind, and elaborates on his role in OH, pt. 7, session 1, p. 141.

31. Harold L. Ickes Historical Marker, https://explorepahistory.com/hmarker.php ?markerId=1-A-342.

32. "Custodian of Our Vast Public Domain," *New York Times,* June 4, 1933, 7.

33. Susan Shumaker, "Untold Stories from America's National Parks," *Segregation in the National Parks,* 2009, PBS.org, transcript, p. 29, https://www.pbs.org /nationalparks/media/pdfs/tnp-abi-untold-stories-pt-01-segregation.pdf.

34. Raymond Moley, *After Seven Years* (New York: Harper & Brothers, 1939), 126.

35. Ickes, "Unpublished Personal Memoirs," 344.

36. Morgenthau Diaries, May 23, 1935, Vol. 5, Part 3, 133.

37. Burton Folsom, Jr., "FDR and the IRS," Hillsdale College, https://www.hillsdale .edu/educational-outreach/free-market-forum/2006-archive/fdr-and-the-irs/.

38. "Smith's Address Attacking the Roosevelt Regime," *New York Times,* October 2, 1936, 4.

39. "Louis M'H. Howe, Roosevelt Friend, Dies," *New York Times,* April 19, 1936, 1.

40. "Social Act Perils Security of All," *New York Times,* July 11, 1936, 1.

41. Lawrence W. Levine, "The 'Diary' of Hiram Johnson," *American Heritage,* August 1969, 112.

42. Moley, *After Seven Years,* 389.

CHAPTER 7: CREST OF THE WAVE

1. Frances Perkins Oral History, Columbia University Libraries Oral History Research Office, pt. 1, session 1, p. 1.

2. Henry A. Wallace Collection, University of Iowa Libraries, letter HAW to James A. Farley, September 15, 1936, 2.

3. "Salaries of 18,000 Over $15,000," *New York Times,* January 8, 1936, 13.

4. Hearings Before the Committee on Military Affairs, House of Representatives, 74th Cong., 1st Sess. (1935). (Statement of John D. Battle, executive secretary of the National Coal Association [excerpts]). The coal industry believed it was being undercut by the Administration's entry into the power business through the TVA.

5. The 1936 Republican Party platform begins, "America is in peril." See American Presidency Project, https://www.presidency.ucsb.edu/documents /republican-party-platform-1936.

6. Perkins OH, pt. 7, session 1, p. 734.

7. "Miss Perkins Gives Reply to 'Whispers,'" *New York Times,* April 5, 1936, 43.

8. Wallace Collection, letter HAW to Farley, August 25, 1936, on persuading Hopkins. Hopkins was furious about Farley's attempt to exclude him, and took two steps: he lunched with Morgenthau, to get him on his side and, right after, met with FDR to complain about Farley. See Morgenthau Diaries, MemCon of August 24, 1936, Vol. 30, 251.

9. W. Scott Nobles, "Harold L. Ickes: New Deal Hatchet Man," *Western Speech,* Summer 1958, 242. Nobles is citing his interview with Thomas Corcoran of January 28, 1955.

10. Ibid., 364.

11. "Ickes Denounces 'Cry of Soak Poor,'" *New York Times,* January 5, 1936, 39.

12. "Landon's Angels," *Star Press* (Muncie, Indiana), October 19, 1936, 2.

13. Nobles, "New Deal Hatchet Man," 383, citing *Boston Evening Transcript,* August 5, 1936.

14. Ibid., 392.

15. "A Reasoned Choice," *New York Times,* October 1, 1936, 24; "Fear of Socialism," *New York Times,* October 11, 1936, 11E.

16. Rixey Smith, *Carter Glass: A Biography* (London: Longmans Green, 1939), 99.

17. Lawrence W. Levine, "The 'Diary' of Hiram Johnson," *American Heritage,* August 1969, 114.

18. David Brooks, *The Road to Character* (New York: Random House, 2015), 34.

19. Morgenthau told FDR of Ickes attending a Cissy Patterson dinner party at which Ickes wandered into the garden with a woman and tried to "date her up," by phoning and asking to come to her home to see her. Morgenthau

Diaries, November 27, 1934, Vol. 2, 61; FDR, to be sure, would then tell Ickes of stories Morgenthau had been spreading. See Harold Ickes, *The Secret Diary of Harold L. Ickes,* vol. 1, *The First Thousand Days 1933–1936* (New York: Simon & Schuster, 1953), 269, January 11, 1935.

20. Arthur M. Schlesinger, Jr., *The Coming of the New Deal* (Boston: Houghton Mifflin, 1959), 537, quoting Biddle; John Morton Blum, ed., *From the Morgenthau Diaries: Years of Crisis, 1928–1938* (Boston: Houghton Mifflin, 1959), 236; Perkins OH, pt. 7, session 1, p. 316.

21. Recorded in talks with Harlan B. Phillips, *Felix Frankfurter Reminisces* (New York: Reynal, 1960), 283; Schlesinger, *The Coming of the New Deal,* 537; Perkins OH, pt. 7, session 1, p. 315.

22. Ickes, *The First Thousand Days,* 606, May 29, 1936.

23. See Carl M. Cannon, "Presidential Lies," *The Atlantic,* January/February 2007; "Interview with Gore Vidal on 'the Great Depression,'" Washington University Film and Media Archive, https://www.youtube.com/watch?v=E76ArLbSABA.

24. FDRL, Master Speech File, 1898–1945, April 14, 1938, Fireside Chat 12.

25. Dickinson interviews. He recalls the Democratic Party operative Russell Hemenway, who knew Boettiger well, emphasizing Boettiger's judgment on FDR. Dickinson and Hemenway discussed this at a meeting of the National Committee for an Effective Congress during 1975.

26. Raymond Moley, *After Seven Years* (New York: Harper & Brothers, 1939), 337.

27. Robert H. Jackson, *That Man: An Insider's Portrait of Franklin D. Roosevelt* (New York: Oxford University Press, 2003), 75.

28. Transcript of David Frost's interview with Richard Nixon, https://teachingamericanhistory.org/library/document/transcript-of-david-frosts-interview-with-richard-nixon/.

29. Freidel, *A Rendezvous with Destiny,* 274. Arthur M. Schlesinger, Jr., perceived managerial structures in this mishmash that he labeled a "competitive theory of administration." See William Doyle, "Franklin D. Roosevelt: The Creative Executive," archive.nytimes.com/www.nytimes.com/books/first/d/doyle-oval.html. Another historian, Doris Kearns Goodwin, also believes that FDR had an effective "style" to elicit "conflicting opinions" from the infighting. See Doris Kearns Goodwin, *No Ordinary Time: Franklin & Eleanor Roosevelt: The Home Front in World War II* (New York: Simon & Schuster, 1994), 24.

30. James A. Farley, *Jim Farley's Story: The Roosevelt Years* (New York: McGraw-Hill, 1948), 52.

31. Henry Wallace Oral History, Columbia University Libraries Oral History Research Office, 405.

32. Ickes, *The First Thousand Days,* 523, January 23, 1936.

33. Wallace OH, 3596.

34. FDR to Sherwood, in Robert E. Sherwood, *Roosevelt and Hopkins: An Intimate History* (New York: Harper, 1948), 72.

35. Katie Louchheim, ed., *The Making of the New Deal: The Insiders Speak* (Cambridge, MA: Harvard University Press, 1983), 286. Her interview of James Rowe.

36. Conrad Black, *Franklin Delano Roosevelt: Champion of Freedom* (New York: PublicAffairs, 2003), 561.

37. Renata Adler, "A Reporter at Large: The Guard," quoted in *The New Yorker,* October 3, 1970, 43, It was a poem written for the Guard's Squadron A in 1925.

38. "Feud" and "trouble with president" are Ickes, *Thousand Days,* 656, August 6, 1936; Harold Ickes, *The Secret Diary of Harold L. Ickes,* vol. 2, *The Inside Struggle, 1936–1939* (New York: Simon & Schuster, 1954), 13, December 10, 1936, is "sleeping dope."

39. Ickes, *The First Thousand Days,* 528, January 29, 1936.

40. Ibid., 705, about the Cabinet meeting of November 6, 1936; Ickes, *The Inside Struggle,* 32, January 3, 1937.

41. Wallace Collection, University of Iowa, Abstract of Conversation with Mr. John Maynard Keynes, pp. 1–3. Reel 67 (undated).

42. Perkins OH, pt. 7, session 1, p. 65; Ickes, *The Inside Struggle,* 65, February 6, 1937.

43. Perkins OH pt. 7, session 1, p. 65.

44. James E. Bond, *I Dissent: The Legacy of Justice James Clark McReynolds* (Fairfax, VA: George Mason University Press, 1992), 54.

45. Perkins OH, pt. 9, session 1, p. 68.

46. "Roosevelt Asks Power to Reform Courts" and "Aim to Pack Court Declares Hoover," *New York Times,* February 6, 1937, 1.

47. John Culver and John Hyde, *American Dreamer: A Life of Henry A. Wallace* (New York: W. W. Norton, 2000), 172.

48. *Congressional Record–Senate,* p. 2607, https://www.govinfo.gov/content/pkg /GPO-CRECB-1937-pt3-v81/pdf/GPO-CRECB-1937-pt3-v81–4.pdf.

49. On "brain cells," only Wallace talked like this: Wallace OH, 198.

50. Ickes, *The Inside Struggle,* 246, November 8, 1937, at Barbara Hopkins's funeral.

51. Perkins OH, pt. 7, session 1, pp. 524, 539.

52. Wallace Collection, Conversation with Mr. John Maynard Keynes.

53. Jerry Pytlak, "Cotton Economy in Depression," *New International 5,* no. 8 (August 1939): 247–50; Alan Brinkley, *The End of Reform: New Deal Liberalism in Recession and War* (New York: Vintage, 1996), 30.

54. Ickes, *The Inside Struggle,* 241, November 6, 1937.

55. "Drive for Fascism Charged by Ickes," *New York Times,* December 9, 1937, 2.

CHAPTER 8: FACING THE WORLD

1. "1,200 Pay Tribute to Jane Addams," *New York Times,* May 3, 1935, 7.

2. "Jane Addams Hits National Boasting," *New York Times,* October 23, 1932, 11.

3. Message of President Roosevelt to the Senate, January 16, 1935, in *Peace and War: United States Foreign Policy, 1931–1941* (Washington, DC: U.S. Government Printing Office, 1943), 246–47.

4. Harold Ickes, *The Secret Diary of Harold L. Ickes,* vol. 2, *The Inside Struggle, 1936–1939* (New York: Simon & Schuster, 1954), 287, February 2, 1935.

5. Frances Perkins Oral History, Columbia University Libraries Oral History Research Office, pt. 1, session 7, p. 756.

6. Charles Repington, *The First World War, 1914–1918* (London: Constable, 1920), 112.

7. Harold Ickes, *The Secret Diary of Harold L. Ickes,* vol. 1, *The First Thousand Days, 1933–1936* (New York: Simon & Schuster, 1953), 70, July 27, 1933.

8. Perkins OH, pt. 7, session 1, p. 638.

9. "Lindbergh Assails Air Mail Measure," *New York Times,* March 17, 1934, 1.

10. Morgenthau Diaries, November 28, 1934, Vol. 2, 196.

11. "Ickes Upholds PWA," *New York Times,* August 22, 1940, 14.

12. Thaddeus Holt, "Joint Plan Red," *Quarterly Journal of Military History,* Autumn 1988, 48–56; see also Thaddeus Holt, *Naval Warfare in the Twentieth Century* (London: Croom Helm, 1977), 169–70. (Holt is the eldest son of the Hopkins deputy with the same name.)

13. Ickes, *The First Thousand Days,* 106, October 13, 1933.

14. Raymond Moley, *After Seven Years* (New York: Harper & Brothers, 1939), p. 131.

15. "Afghan Rebels Gain in Fight for Kabul," *New York Times,* January 17, 1929, 12.

16. Paul Pisicano interview in Studs Terkel, *"The Good War": An Oral History of World War II* (New York: MJF Books, 1984), 140.

17. David L. Roll, *The Hopkins Touch: Harry Hopkins and the Forging of the Alliance to Defeat Hitler* (New York: Oxford University Press, 2013), 39.

18. Robert E. Sherwood, *Roosevelt and Hopkins: An Intimate History* (New York: Harper, 1948), 79.

19. Sumner Welles, *The Time for Decision* (New York: Harper, 1944), 57.

20. Ickes, *The Inside Struggle,* 388, May 7, 1938.

21. Morgenthau Diaries, May 1, 1934, Vol. 2, 41.

22. "Cabinet Considers New Battleships," *New York Times,* December 19, 1936, 11.

23. "Frances Perkins's Career Memorialized," *New York Times,* May 15, 1965, p. 46, quoting Charles E. Wyzanski.

24. Bat-Ami Zucker, "Frances Perkins and the German-Jewish Refugees, 1933–1940," *American Jewish History,* March 2001, 4, 9. Also see Bat-Ami Zucker, *In Search of Refuge: Jews and US Consuls in Nazi Germany 1933–1941* (Chicago: Vallentine Mitchel, 2001).

25. Bat-Ami Zucker offered additional views of Perkins at the March 2015 conference, "Allied Powers' Response to the Holocaust," Menachem Begin Heritage Center, https://www.youtube.com/watch?v=0I83VnUmS3g; Richard Breitman and Allan J. Lichtman, *FDR and the Jews* (Cambridge, MA: Harvard University Press, 2013), 4.

26. Ickes, *The Inside Struggle,* October 9, 1937.

CHAPTER 9: FAITH AND MAINTENANCE

1. *National Zeitung,* November 17, 1938.

2. Arthur Krock, "The Ubiquity and Influence of Mr. Hopkins," *New York Times,* October 18, 1938, 24.

3. Frances Perkins Oral History, Columbia University Libraries Oral History Research Office, pt. 7, session 1, p. 659.

4. "Wallace Opposes Scaring Capital," *New York Times,* January 4, 1938, 15.

5. Rexford Tugwell, *Roosevelt's Revolution: The First Year, a Personal Perspective* (New York: Macmillan, 1977), 112. Tugwell is quoting Hopkins. Of course, Hopkins's organizations required lawyers, and one who passed muster recalled being told, "The first time you tell me I can't do what I want to do, you're fired," cited in Gilbert Gall, *Pursuing Justice: Lee Pressman, the New Deal, and the CIO* (New York: State University of New York Press, 1999), 32.

6. Robert E. Sherwood, *Roosevelt and Hopkins: An Intimate History* (New York: Harper, 1948), 110–11.

7. Morgenthau Diaries, December 8, 1937, Vol. 101, 69. FDR explained he would have Kennedy "watched hourly" in London.

8. "Hopkins Believes in Spending More," *New York Times,* October 25, 1938, 7.

9. Robert H. Jackson, *That Man: An Insider's Portrait of Franklin D. Roosevelt* (New York: Oxford University Press, 2003), 30.

10. Harold Ickes, *The Secret Diary of Harold L. Ickes,* vol. 2, *The Inside Struggle, 1936–1939* (New York: Simon & Schuster, 1954), 128, May 2, 1937.

11. Harlan B. Phillips, *Felix Frankfurter Reminisces* (New York: Reynal, 1960), 182; David M. Kennedy, *Freedom From Fear: The American People in Depression and War, 1929–1945* (New York: Oxford University Press, 1999), 124, calls Frankfurter "unctuously insinuating"; Ted Morgan, *FDR: A Biography* (New York: Simon & Schuster, 1985), 362, describes Frankfurter as FDR's "two-faced admirer," 362.

12. On what Perkins calls "the low side" of humor that Hopkins and FDR shared, see her OH, pt. 7, session 1, p. 548; and Sherwood, *Roosevelt and Hopkins,* 2.

13. Harold Ickes. *The Secret Diary of Harold L. Ickes,* vol. 3, *The Lowering Clouds, 1939–1941* (New York: Simon & Schuster, 1955), 616, September 20, 1940.

14. Conrad Black, *Franklin Delano Roosevelt: Champion of Freedom* (New York: PublicAffairs, 2003), 176.

15. Morgenthau Diaries, May 24, 1937, Vol. 69, 208. Morgenthau observes he was being baited by FDR.

16. FDR's strange relationship with Ickes is distilled in this sentence, which was spotlighted in a fine essay. See Nelson Lichtenstein, "Born for the New Deal," a review of T. H. Watkins's *Righteous Pilgrim,* in *New York Times,* December 9, 1990, Section 7, 1.

17. In fact, John Garner called Morgenthau "the most servile." See John Gunther, *Roosevelt in Retrospect: A Profile in History* (New York: Harper, 1950), 132; Harold Ickes, *The Secret Diary of Harold L. Ickes,* vol. 1, *The First Thousand Days, 1933–1936* (New York: Simon & Schuster, 1953), 239, December 7, 1934.

18. Alan Brinkley, The *End of Reform: New Deal Liberalism in Recession and War* (New York: Vintage, 1996), 26.

19. Morgenthau Diaries, January 4, 1937, Vol. 51, 16.

20. Perkins OH, pt. 7, session 1, pp. 623, 629.

21. "Aldrich Asks 'Breathing Spell,'" *New York Times,* May 3, 1938, 1.

22. The marine was Evans F. Carlson, whom FDR knew well as the former executive officer of the marine detachment at Warm Springs.

23. "Fight Any Closing of Palestine Door," *New York Times*, February 7, 1937, 42.

24. Ickes, *The Inside Struggle*, 348, March 30, 1938; "Fascism Our Foe," *New York Times*, April 4, 1938, 2.

25. *Foreign Relations of the United States 1938*, volume 2 (Washington, DC: Government Printing Office, 1955) 457–58, 459–60.

26. Ickes, *The Inside Struggle*, 392, May 12, 1938; Jackson, *That Man*, 30.

27. "Ickes Halts Helium Gas Sale," *New York Times*, May 12, 1938, 9. According to the Helium Act, such a sale would have required the unanimous approval of all six members of the Munitions Control Board, of which Ickes was one, and he therefore had veto power.

28. *FRUS 1938*, 2:461–62.

29. Perkins OH, pt. 9, session 1, p. 564.

30. Frances Perkins, *The Roosevelt I Knew* (New York: Viking, 1946), 325, on "Not knowing much"; on "personal advantage," see Perkins OH, pt. 7, session 1, p. 404.

31. Ickes, *The Inside Struggle*, 92, March 15, 1937.

32. Perkins, *The Roosevelt I Knew*, 319; Perkins OH, pt. 6, session 1, p. 44.

33. Ibid., 322.

34. Ickes, *The Inside Struggle*, 55, January 24, 1937; Alfred P. Sloan, Jr., *My Years With General Motors* (New York: Doubleday, 1963), 393.

35. Perkins OH, pt. 6, session 1, p. 205.

36. Perkins OH, pt. 6, session 1, pp. 208, 209.

37. "Labor: Washington v. Detroit," *Time*, February 8, 1937.

38. Perkins OH, pt. 7, session 1, p. 506.

39. "Hopkins Predicts Swift Union Gains," *New York Times*, May 18, 1938, 14.

40. Henry Farber, Daniel Herbst, et al., "Unions and Inequality Over the Twentieth Century: New Evidence from Survey Data," National Bureau of Economic Research, Working Paper 24587, April 2021. And such evidence accumulates by the year. See "Mandatory Anti-Union Meetings Are Under Scrutiny," *New York Times*, April 8, 2022, B4.

41. "Wallace Weighs Our Changing Farm Problem," *New York Times*, November 27, 1938, 139.

42. Louis Auchincloss, *The Embezzler* (Boston: Houghton Mifflin, 1966), 12. The novel is based on the Whitney epic, and Auchincloss, a Grotonian, was a partner in a white-shoe firm—New York's Hawkins Delafield & Wood—who would hear much of the story firsthand.

43. "War on Recession," *New York Times*, April 15, 1938, 1.

44. Henry A. Wallace Collection, University of Iowa Libraries, Conversation with Mr. John Maynard Keynes.

45. Jean Edward Smith, *FDR* (New York: Random House, 2007), 397.

46. "Roosevelt Signs $3,753,000,000 Bill to Speed Recovery," *New York Times*, June 22, 1938, 1.

CHAPTER 10: TURNING POINTS

1. "Hopkins Predicts 20 Year WPA," *New York Times*, September 18, 1938, 9.

2. "Aldrich Asks 'Breathing Spell,'" *New York Times*, May 3, 1938, 1.

3. "Wage-Hour Outlook," *New York Times,* June 19, 1938, 3.

4. Morgenthau Diaries, "January 16, 1939, Vol. 160, 84–85. This is a MemCon of their Monday lunch.

5. Harold Ickes, *The Secret Diary of Harold L. Ickes,* vol. 2, *The Inside Struggle, 1936–1939* (New York: Simon & Schuster, 1954), 360, April 10, 1938.

6. Ickes would absolve FDR and Hull from handling a false passport. He stuck with a story that a friend had allowed him to use his name for a week. See Ickes's letter of April 19, 1943, to the *New York Post:* https://www.amazon.com/Harold-L-Ickes-Letter-Signed/dp/B00JAN5EQS.

7. "Ickes in London on Wedding Trip," *New York Times,* May 27, 1938, 3.

8. Ickes, *The Inside Struggle,* 406, June 26, 1938.

9. Ibid., 410.

10. Frances Perkins Oral History, Columbia University Libraries Oral History Research Office, pt. 7, session 1, p. 379; Harold Ickes, *The Secret Diary of Harold L. Ickes,* vol. 1, *The First Thousand Days, 1933–1936* (New York: Simon & Schuster, 1953), 425, August 27, 1935.

11. Ickes, *The Inside Struggle,* 415, July 3,1938.

12. Perkins OH, pt. 7, session 1, p. 321.

13. On Perkins and Pétain, see Perkins OH, pt. 7, session 1, pp. 345–60.

14. Perkins OH, pt. 7, session 1, p. 360.

15. Perkins reports her insights on France to FDR, and then to Hull: pt. 7, session 1, pp. 373–76.

16. Morgenthau Diaries, "Possible Control of Japanese Credits," December 17, 1937, Vol. 103, 59 (on not doing economic sanctions, for instance).

17. Henry A. Wallace Collection, University of Iowa Libraries, letter HAW to Hugh Johnson, September 22, 1938.

18. "Nazis Gather Race Data," *New York Times,* May 5, 1933, 9, quoting the public health director of Dortmund.

19. Perkins OH, pt. 7, session 1, p. 313.

20. Perkins OH, pt. 8, session 1, p. 338.

21. "Urban League Officials Confer With Labor Secretary," *Chicago Defender,* April 29, 1933, 1, and editorial, "The Week," *Chicago Defender,* August 5, 1933.

22. "In the Nation," *New York Times,* October 18, 1938, 3.

23. Henry Wallace, NBC, September 13, 1948, radio address. See https://www.blackpast.org/african-american-history/1948-henry-wallace-radio-address/.

24. Rexford Tugwell, *Roosevelt's Revolution: The First Year, a Personal Perspective* (New York: Macmillan, 1977), 133.

25. "Negro Issue Raised," *New York Times,* August 23, 1938, 5; Northerners "catering to the Negro," or to the "Negro vote," were commonly denounced by other Southern legislators too, like Josiah Bailey (D-NC); see "Congress: Black's White," *Time,* January 24, 1938.

26. Morgenthau Diaries, phone transcript with Farley, February 9, 1939, Vol. 164, 181.

27. Eleanor's complete letter of March 19, 1936, can be read here: Library of Congress, Manuscript/Mixed Material, Letter, Eleanor Roosevelt to Walter White, https://www.loc.gov/item/mcc.015/.

28. "Eleanor Roosevelt's Battle to End Lynching," Paul M. Sparrow, https://fdr
    .blogs.archives.gov/2016/02/12/eleanor-roosevelts-battle-to-end-lynching/. This
    is an excellent, concise analysis by the former director of the FDR Presidential
    Library.
29. David Robertson, *Sly and Able: A Political Biography of James Byrnes* (New
    York: W. W. Norton, 1994), 283.
30. Ickes, *The Inside Struggle*, 20, December 20, 1936, and 61, January 30,
    1937. In the latter entry, Ickes emphasizes Garner's uncompromising
    fervor—the vice president demanded an anti-lynching law in "no
    unmistakable language."
31. "Never had a chance" is the mistaken conclusion of the distinguished
    biographer William E. Leuchtenburg, in "Franklin D. Roosevelt: The American
    Franchise," featured by the University of Virginia's Miller Center, https://
    millercenter.org/president/fdroosevelt/the-american-franchise.
32. Perkins OH, pt. 7, session 1, p. 379.
33. "Farley Seen in Growing Rebellion Against New Deal 'Revenge' Politics," *New
    York Times,* June 1, 1938, 4.
34. Morgenthau Diaries, Morgenthau meeting with Oliphant et al., May 17, 1937,
    Vol. 68, 237.
35. Morgenthau Diaries, "Re President's Remark's on Income Tax Evasion," May
    21, 1937, Vol. 69, 255, 259.
36. Morgenthau Diaries, May 24, 1937, Vol. 69, 255–60. Cummings, as if arguing
    for the defendant, replied that Mr. Smith had already agreed with Internal
    Revenue to pay the full taxes he owed, plus penalty and interest. Nonetheless,
    Smith was sentenced in June to eighteen months over his 1929 and 1930
    delinquencies, and the six hundred employees of his Emsco Industries, as
    Cummings warned would happen, became jobless.
37. "National Affairs: The Janizariat," *Time,* September 12, 1938.
38. Susan Dunn, *Roosevelt's Purge: How FDR Fought to Change the Democratic
    Party* (Cambridge MA: Harvard University Press, 2012), 173.
39. Morgenthau Diaries, phone transcript with Farley, February 9, 1939, Vol. 164,
    181.
40. Perkins OH, pt. 7, session 1, p. 313.
41. Morgenthau Diaries, Confidential memorandum from FDR to Morgenthau,
    January 31, 1938, Vol. 108, 188.
42. Perkins OH, pt. 7, session 1, p. 319.
43. Morgenthau Diaries, transcript, April 13, 1939, Vol. 178, 334.
44. Arthur Krock, "Taxpayers Revolt," *New York Times,* November 10, 1938, 1.
45. Ickes, *The Inside Struggle*, December 18, 1938, 526.
46. "Hopkins Sworn In," *New York Times,* December 25, 1938, 1.

CHAPTER 11: SPARK TO FLAME

1. Henry A. Wallace Collection, University of Iowa Libraries, HAW to FDR,
   December 3, 1938.
2. FDR understood the vulnerabilities of those small democracies. It was no
   coincidence that the Netherlands and Belgium each hastened to pacify restive

German-speaking communities by, in turn, adding Frisian and Luxembourgish as an official language in 1937 and 1938, respectively.

3. Henry Wallace Oral History, Columbia University Libraries Oral History Research Office, 515 oral history, which includes his letter of April 13, 1939, to FDR.

4. Geoffrey C. Ward, ed., *Closest Companion: The Unknown Story of the Intimate Friendship Between Franklin Roosevelt and Margaret Suckley* (New York: Houghton Mifflin, 1995), 125.

5. Harold Ickes, *The Secret Diary of Harold L. Ickes*, vol. 2, *The Inside Struggle, 1936–1939* (New York: Simon & Schuster, 1954), 474, September 24, 1938. Whether or not FDR's account is true about his popping off to Britain's ambassador, Sir Ronald Charles Lindsay would have agreed with him. Such was Lindsay's opinion too.

6. Frances Perkins Oral History, Columbia University Libraries Oral History Research Office, pt. 7, session 1, p. 312.

7. Forrest C. Pogue, *George C. Marshall: Education of a General, 1880–1939* (New York: Viking, 1963), 307.

8. "Roosevelt Orders Air Pilot Training," *New York Times,* December 28, 1938, 1.

9. Raymond Moley, *After Seven Years* (New York: Harper & Brothers, 1939), 70.

10. There is no evidence of a kindly FDR appointing Harry to Commerce "to give Hopkins breathing space," as claimed by Goodwin in *No Ordinary Time,* 31. All believed Hopkins was being thrown into the fire. Among other evidence, see Ickes, *The Inside Struggle,* 527, December 18, 1938, wherein Hopkins says "he realized he was merely being used as a stalking horse" by FDR.

11. Morgenthau Diaries, phone transcript with Hopkins, November 21, 1938, Vol. 152, 36.

12. "Hopkins Concedes It was His Error to Talk Politics," *New York Times,* January 12, 1938, 1.

13. Ickes, *The Inside Struggle,* 557, January 15, 1939.

14. Morgenthau Diaries, MemCon, December 28, 1938, Vol. 158, 133.

15. Henry H. Adams, *Harry Hopkins: A Biography* (New York: Putnam, 1977), 137, citing Hopkins's reaction to press inquiries.

16. Perkins OH, pt. 7, session 1, p. 388.

17. "Dies Urges Ickes to Quit," *New York Times,* November 25, 1938, 3.

18. Perkins OH, pt. 6, session 1, p. 518.

19. Arthur M. Schlesinger, Jr., *The Coming of the New Deal* (Boston: Houghton Mifflin, 1959), 583, quotes Perkins saying of FDR, "It is my final testimony that he never let me down," but Schlesinger is citing her 1946 bestselling memoir, not her long-private oral history.

20. Richard Breitman and Allan J. Lichtman, *FDR and the Jews* (Cambridge, MA: Harvard University Press, 2013), 104.

21. Perkins OH, pt. 7, session 1, p. 364.

22. Derek Leebaert, *The Fifty-Year Wound: The True Price of America's Cold War Victory* (New York: Little, Brown, 2002), 76.

23. Breitman and Lichtman, *FDR and the Jews,* 117.

24. Ted Morgan, *FDR: A Biography* (New York: Simon & Schuster, 1985), 639; Perkins OH, pt. 7, session 1, p. 279.

25. Perkins OH, pt. 7, session 1, pp. 286, 287.

26. Leebaert, *The Fifty-Year Wound,* 109, on domestic subversion.

27. Ickes, *The Inside Struggle,* 330, March 4, 1938.

28. Wallace OH, 766, referencing the Cabinet meeting of January 26, 1940.

29. "Rep. Caroline O'Day Urges Standard of Ethics to Make Mass Killings in War as Wrong as Individual Murder," *Washington Post,* January 27, 1938, 13.

30. Ickes, *The Inside Struggle,* 135, May 9, 1937; 127, May 2, 1937; Perkins OH, pt. 7, session 1, p. 644.

31. Wallace OH, 431.

32. Wallace OH, 347.

33. On presidential edits, see Wallace Collection, HAW letter to FDR, December 30, 1936. FDR annotated the drafts of Ickes's books as well. Each man would have been startled by historians who write, "None of his associates ever knew him to read a book," as reported in David M. Kennedy, *Freedom From Fear: The American People in Depression and War, 1929–1945* (New York: Oxford University Press, 1999), 112.

34. James A. Farley, *Jim Farley's Story: The Roosevelt Years* (New York: McGraw-Hill, 1948), 293.

35. Wallace OH, 674. "Kulak" was also what students of agriculture at Cornell were called, but Wallace was unaware.

36. John Culver and John Hyde, *American Dreamer: A Life of Henry A. Wallace* (New York: W. W. Norton, 2000), 204. FDR chose not to resist timber and conservation interests on behalf of Ickes. See Richard Polenberg, "The Great Conservation Contest," *Forest History* 10, no. 4 (January 1967): 18.

37. Wallace OH, 326, 1428.

38. FDR June 12, 1939, telegram to King George, http://docs.fdrlibrary.marist.edu /psf/box38/t343y01.html.

39. Perkins OH, pt. 7, session 1, p. 639.

40. Perkins OH, pt. 7, session 1, p. 526.

41. Appeal of President Roosevelt, September 1, 1939, https://avalon.law.yale.edu /wwii/ylbk325.asp#:~:text=%22I%20am%20therefore%20addressing%20 this,cities%2C%20upon%20the%20understanding%20that.

CHAPTER 12: LINE OF FIRE

1. Sean McMeekin, *Stalin's War: A New History of World War II* (New York: Basic Books, 2021), 405–406, on number of Poles.

2. FDRL, PSF, Hull to the Hague, Netherlands file, November 11, 1939.

3. Frank Freidel, *Franklin Roosevelt: A Rendezvous with Destiny* (New York: Little, Brown, 1990), 311; Derek Leebaert, *The Fifty-Year Wound: The True Price of America's Cold War Victory* (New York: Little, Brown, 2002), 294, about John F. Kennedy declaring "American frontiers are on the Rhine."

4. Henry Wallace Oral History, Columbia University Libraries Oral History Research Office, 474. Only with Perkins, of the four, did Morgenthau's relationship remain sour.

5. See the portrayal of Harry Dexter White as "Stalin's Man at the Treasury" in McMeekin, *Stalin's War,* 379.

6. "The Presidency: Decade's End," *Time,* January 8, 1940. For instance, Virginia senator Carter Glass argued that FDR's urgent request for Congress to drop the Neutrality Act was but another power grab.

7. Forrest C. Pogue, *George C. Marshall: Ordeal and Hope, 1939–1942* (New York: Viking, 1965), 24.

8. Sir Edward Spears, *Liaison 1914: A Narrative of the Great Retreat* (London: Eyre & Spottiswood, 1930), 163. Spears is quoting Germany's General Staff prior to World War I, which acclaimed Britain's army as "a perfect thing apart" for its long service contracts and worldwide experience, among other qualities.

9. Morgenthau Diaries, Meeting of Fiscal and Monetary Board, June 6, 1939, Vol. 194, 396, which included Eccles; Wallace OH, 538, and includes a copy of a letter from Wallace to FDR, May 19, 1939.

10. Morgenthau Diaries, Garner letter to Morgenthau, December 29, 1938, Vol. 158, 156.

11. Harold Ickes, *The Secret Diary of Harold L. Ickes*, vol. 2, *The Inside Struggle, 1936–1939* (New York: Simon & Schuster, 1954), 67, February 6, 1937.

12. Wallace OH, 401.

13. Wallace OH, 500.

14. Wallace OH, 635.

15. "Hopkins: Right Hand Man," *New York Times,* August 11, 1940, 85.

16. Author's telephone interview with Steven Lomazow, MD, September 14, 2021.

17. "Think Borah Left Little," *New York Times,* January 21, 1940, 37. Such was easy for reporters to assume; Borah was a notorious skinflint.

18. Frances Perkins Oral History, Columbia University Libraries Oral History Research Office, pt. 7, session 1, p. 836.

19. Among other writings, Roosevelt is unhelpfully called "a lifelong Anglophile" in Nicholas Wapshott, *The Sphinx: Franklin Roosevelt, the Isolationists, and the Road to World War II* (New York: W. W. Norton, 2015), 101.

20. Wallace OH, 1342.

21. "You see, you haven't got what I have—a memory of the red coats," Senator Gerry told Felix Frankfurter, a fervent supporter of Britain, in 1940, at a Norwegian embassy dinner. See Harlan B. Phillips, *Felix Frankfurter Reminisces* (New York: Reynal, 1960), 276.

22. Beatrice Bishop Berle and Travis Beal Jacobs, eds., *Navigating the Rapids, 1918–1971: From the Papers of Adolf A. Berle* (New York: Harcourt Brace Jovanovich, 1973), 258, 342. Berle had been in army intelligence during World War I and knew of what he spoke.

23. Ibid., 258, September 29, 1939.

24. Ickes, *The Inside Struggle*, 75, February 16, 1937.

25. Nicholas Wapshott, *The Sphinx: Franklin Roosevelt, the Isolationists, and the Road to World War II* (New York: W. W. Norton, 2015), 123, observes, "Borah's response to Hitler's illicit territorial acquisitions is hard to credit." Except all evidence points to the senator being paid by Berlin.

26. "Think Borah Left Little," *New York Times,* January 21, 1940, 37; "Borah Box Yields $200,000," *New York Times,* February 1, 1940, 16. Gore Vidal writing of his grandfather's conclusion is in "Theodore Roosevelt: An American Sissy," *New York Review of Books*, August 13, 1981.

27. John Culver and John Hyde, *American Dreamer: A Life of Henry A. Wallace* (New York: W. W. Norton, 2000), 193.

28. Senator Burton Wheeler, "Memo on conference at the White House with the President, August 4, 1939," Special Collections, Montana State University, 2. I am grateful to the distinguished author Rafael Medoff for sharing a copy of the original. It is in this memo that FDR also talks of his being of "Dutch stock" and of knowing his ancestors, who had "no Jewish blood" in their veins.

29. Wallace OH, 974, 784, 848. He is discussing Cabinet meetings of February and March 1940.

30. Harold Ickes, *The Secret Diary of Harold L. Ickes,* vol. 3, *The Lowering Clouds, 1939–1941* (New York: Simon & Schuster, 1955), 107, January 21, 1940.

31. James A. Farley, *Jim Farley's Story: The Roosevelt Years* (New York: McGraw-Hill, 1948), 220.

32. Wallace OH, 407.

33. Ickes, *The Inside Struggle,* 766.

34. Wallace OH, 656.

35. Wallace OH, 763, using diary notes of January 26, 1940.

36. Ickes, *The Lowering Clouds*, 127, February 11, 1940.

37. Jeanne Clarke, *Roosevelt's Warrior: Harold L. Ickes and the New Deal* (Baltimore: Johns Hopkins University Press, 1998), 309; Wallace OH, 2893. He inserts a record of a conversation with Ickes on December 8, 1943.

38. Wallace OH, 860.

39. Wallace OH, 1113.

40. Wallace OH, 858, referencing a meeting with Eccles and Hopkins, February 13, 1940.

41. Wallace OH, 1587.

42. Wallace OH, 1025, referencing his lunch before Cabinet with FDR.

43. Wallace OH, 990.

44. Wallace OH, 812.

45. Wallace OH, 1427.

46. Perkins OH, pt. 7, session 1, p. 692.

47. Susan Dunn, *1940: FDR, Willkie, Lindbergh, Hitler—the Election and the Storm* (New Haven, CT: Yale University Press, 2013), 37. Professor Dunn is referencing FDR's letter to Cudahy, May 8, 1940.

CHAPTER 13: DEVOTEES OF FORCE

1. Perkins discloses in her oral history that FDR envisioned the Interior Department "to be like the Home Office in England," which is a sweepingly powerful department with responsibilities that include internal security and immigration; Frances Perkins Oral History, Columbia University Libraries Oral History Research Office, pt. 1, session 1, p. 865.

2. "Industrial Heads Only as Advisers," *New York Times,* May 23, 1940, 11.

3. Henry Wallace Oral History, Columbia University Libraries Oral History Research Office, 1078.

4. Wallace OH, 1164, on the FBI.

5. B. H. Liddell-Hart, ed., *The Rommel Papers* (New York: Harcourt, Brace, 1953), 20.

6. Harold Ickes, *The Secret Diary of Harold L. Ickes,* vol. 3, *The Lowering Clouds, 1939–1941* (New York: Simon & Schuster, 1955), 180, May 26, 1940.

7. Wallace OH, 1099. FDR had given Wallace this task at the May 17, 1940, Cabinet meeting.

8. Wallace OH, 1113.

9. Ickes Papers (LOC), diary, 7271, December 6, 1942.

10. The seminal August 2, 1940, correspondence between Ickes and FDR concerning destroyers can be seen at FDRL, PSF, Interior, Harold Ickes file, August–December 1940.

11. Mark Skinner Watson, *Chief of Staff: Prewar Plans and Preparations* (Washington, DC: War Department, Center of Military History, U.S. Army, 1991), 310–15, addressing "Aid to Britain Versus Rearming America."

12. "Cudahy Sees Issue," *New York Times,* October 28, 1940, 20.

13. Ickes, *The Lowering Clouds,* 214, June 23, 1940; "Capital Surprised," *New York Times,* June 21, 1940, 1.

14. Charles de Gaulle, *The Complete War Memoirs of Charles de Gaulle, 1940–1946* (New York: Simon & Schuster, 1964), 760. This is how Hopkins would explain Washington's reaction, when he spoke with General de Gaulle.

15. Morgenthau Diaries, January 27, 1938, Vol. 107, 134.

16. "Hopkins: Right Hand Man," *New York Times,* August 11, 1940, 85.

17. Perkins and Wallace document this exchange during the Friday, June 28, 1940, Cabinet meeting in their oral histories, as does Jim Farley in *Jim Farley's Story: The Roosevelt Years* (New York: McGraw-Hill, 1948), 244. They observe that the president told Ickes to "go to it," while wanting cooperative senators and congressmen to start attacking Willkie on Monday.

18. "Dewey Asks End of 'War' at Home," *New York Times,* June 9, 1940, 6.

19. "Third Term Vital," *New York Times,* May 19, 1940, 41.

20. Perkins OH, pt. 7, session 1, p. 420.

21. Perkins OH, pt. 7, session 1, p. 431.

22. Perkins OH, pt. 7, session 1, p. 460.

23. Perkins OH, pt. 7, session 1, pp. 462–63.

24. Perkins OH, pt. 7, session 1, p. 464.

25. Perkins OH, pt. 7, session 1, p. 465.

26. Perkins OH, pt. 7, session 1, p. 559.

27. Perkins OH, pt. 7, session 1, pp. 467–68.

28. Perkins OH, pt. 7, session 1, pp. 476–77.

29. Farley, *Jim Farley's Story,* 293–94.

30. John Culver and John Hyde, *American Dreamer: A Life of Henry A. Wallace* (New York: W. W. Norton, 2000), 223; Edward J. Flynn, *You're the Boss: The Practice of American Politics* (Springfield, OH: Collier, 1962), 157–59.

31. Ickes, *The Lowering Clouds*, 396, December 26, 1940. Ickes acknowledges he got the phrase from columnist John Carter.

32. "Campaign Mud," *New York Times,* August 21, 1940, 18.

33. Culver and Hyde, *American Dreamer,* 235.

34. Thomas Mallon, "Books: The Electric Man," *New Yorker,* September 17, 2018, 62. Democratic threats deterred publication.

35. "Women Share Interest During President's Visit," *Charleston Gazette,* September 4, 1940, 7.

36. "'Kneed' Policeman Gives Interview," *New York Times,* October 31, 1940, 25; Grace Tully's ghostwritten memoir asserts that Stephen Early was "shoved violently" and merely "raised an arm and a leg to protect himself." Such was Early's defense. See Grace Tully, *F.D.R., My Boss* (New York: Scribner's, 1949), 153.

37. "Louis Urges Willkie," *New York Times,* October 31, 1940, 18.

38. Ickes, *The Lowering Clouds*, 363, November 9, 1940; Gore Vidal, "West Point and the Third Loyalty," *New York Review of Books*, October 18, 1973.

39. Perkins OH, pt. 7, session 1, p. 826.

40. "Madame Secretary: A Study in Bewilderment," *Saturday Evening Post,* July 27, 1940.

41. Perkins OH, pt. 7, session 1, p. 759.

42. Kirstin Downey, *The Woman Behind the New Deal* (New York: Doubleday, 2009), 324. This biographer writes that Perkins was "stripped" of the immigration service.

43. *The Public Papers and Addresses of Franklin D. Roosevelt, 1940 Volume* (New York: Macmillan, 1941), 223; "Border Spy Curbs," *New York Times,* November 10, 1940, 1.

44. FDRL, Office File 3186, as cited in Rafael Medoff, *The Jews Should Keep Quiet: Franklin D. Roosevelt, Rabbi Stephen S. Wise, and the Holocaust* (Lincoln: University of Nebraska Press, 2019), 94.

45. "Delays War Haven in Virgin Islands," *New York Times,* December 13, 1940, 11.

46. Ickes, *The Lowering Clouds*, November 23, 1940, 374–75.

47. Roosevelt Press Conference, December 17, 1940, http://docs.FDRLibrary .marist.edu/odllpc2.html.

48. Harold Ickes, "What Is an American?," May 18, 1941, delivered in New York's Central Park. See William Safire, ed., *Lend Me Your Ears: Great Speeches in History* (New York: W. W. Norton, 2004), 65–73.

49. "Garner Bows Out," *New York Times,* January 21, 1941, 6.

50. Ickes, *The Lowering Clouds*, 378, December 1, 1940.

51. The dishonesty, for starters, would be to approve $1 billion worth of strategic exports to Russia "without reference to Congress, and without the knowledge of the public." See Sean McMeekin, *Stalin's War: A New History of World War II* (New York: Basic Books, 2021), 31.

CHAPTER 14: ELEVENTH HOUR

1. Kenneth S. Davis, *FDR: The War President, 1940–1943* (New York: Random House, 2000), 83.

2. Henry Wallace Oral History, Columbia University Libraries Oral History Research Office, 1087, from diary notes of May 13, 1940.

3. William L. Shirer, *Berlin Diary:The Journal of a Foreign Correspondent: 1934–1941* (New York: Knopf, 1941), 760.

4. "Anne Morgan Back," *New York Times,* January 8, 1941, 8.

5. Frances Perkins Oral History, Columbia University Libraries Oral History Research Office, pt. 7, session 1, p. 668.

6. James A. Farley, *Jim Farley's Story: The Roosevelt Years* (New York: McGraw-Hill, 1948), 115. Morgenthau was also useful for handling petty corruption, which he recounts in his diary. For instance, FDR ordered him to redirect all government advertising in the Seattle region to the *Seattle Post-Intelligencer* after son-in-law John Boettiger became publisher in 1936. See Morgenthau Diaries, memorandum, morning staff meeting, June 15, 1938, Vol. 128, 476.

7. Wallace OH, 3200.

8. Perkins OH, pt. 7, session 1, p. 623.

9. On "most gifted," see History News Network, "FDR's Alter Ego: Interview With Historian David L. Roll," June 10, 2013, 18. Throughout *Roosevelt and Hopkins,* Sherwood presents Hopkins as the Administration's "most powerful man," after FDR, of course.

10. Perkins OH, pt. 7, session 1, p. 562.

11. Wallace OH, 1161, from diary notes of June 17, 1940.

12. Wallace OH, 3583.

13. Wallace OH, 2890, conversation with Ickes, December 8, 1943. Wallace observes that *The Saturday Evening Post* of April 19 and 26, 1941, as well as *Look* magazine, have also shed light on Hopkins's sources of outside income.

14. See Theodore N. Pappas, "The Life, Times, and Health of Harry Hopkins: Presidential Adviser," *Journal of Medical Biography,* June 2016.

15. Ickes Papers (LOC), diary, 10, 125, November, 14, 1945. Admiral McIntire is in Robert E. Sherwood, *Roosevelt and Hopkins: An Intimate History* (New York: Harper, 1948), 6.

16. David Levering Lewis, *The Improbable Wendell Willkie* (New York: W. W. Norton, 2018), 179.

17. Sherwood, *Roosevelt and Hopkins,* 242.

18. Wallace OH, 2365.

19. Lewis, *Improbable Wendell Willkie,* 187.

20. Exaggerations have arisen about Welles's trip, as well as about his influence, along with that of Hopkins and others, regarding their "taking America into the world." For a corrective, see Conrad Black, "Roosevelt and His Diplomatic Pawns," *National Interest,* September 2013, in which Black, a biographer of FDR, reviews Michael Fullilove's *Rendezvous with Destiny: How Franklin D. Roosevelt and Five Extraordinary Men Took America into the War and into the World* (2013).

21. Ickes's slur for Kennedy is in Harold Ickes, *The Secret Diary of Harold L. Ickes,* vol. 3, *The Lowering Clouds, 1939–1941* (New York: Simon & Schuster, 1955), 370, November 17, 1940; Lawrence W. Levine, "The 'Diary' of Hiram

Johnson," *American Heritage,* August 1969, citing Johnson's letter to his son, February 17, 1940.

22. "Willkie Says Tide Turns," *New York Times,* February 22, 1941, 7.

23. Sherwood, *Roosevelt and Hopkins,* 230.

24. "Those in Congress" would include Senator Arthur Vandenberg, the Michigan Republican. See his superb biography by Hendrik Meijer, *Arthur Vandenberg: The Man in the Middle of the American Century* (Chicago: University of Chicago Press, 2017), 139, on opening a Michigan FBI office to cover Vandenberg; Richard Norton Smith kindly shared a draft chapter of his forthcoming Gerald Ford biography, referencing Ford and the FBI.

25. Doris Kearns Goodwin, *No Ordinary Time. Franklin & Eleanor Roosevelt: The Home Front in World War II* (New York: Simon & Schuster, 1994), 99, from the Lash Papers, FDRL.

26. Wallace OH, 1201, including diary notes on "Texans and War," July 2, 1940.

27. "Ickes Denounces 'Appeasers,'" *New York Times,* December 18, 1940, 30; "Lindbergh Called Nazi Tool by Ickes," *New York Times,* July 15, 1941, 13.

28. Steven Lomazow and Eric Fettmann, *FDR's Deadly Secret* (New York: Public Affairs, 2009), 5, 6, 12, on malignant melanoma.

29. "The Presidency: A Week in Bed," *Time,* May 19, 1941.

30. See "FDR's Weight Chart and 1941 Bloodwork," which documents the abrupt rises in hemoglobin levels: https://www.scribd.com/document/20430562/FDR-s -Weight-Chart-and-1941-Bloodwork, Steven Lomazow, MD.

31. Perkins OH, pt. 7, session 1, pp. 839, 844.

32. John Cudahy, *The Armies March* (New York: Scribner's, 1941), 168.

33. Ickes, *The Lowering Clouds,* 526, May 30, 1941.

34. Wallace OH, 1292. In the short term, he reasons coldly, it wouldn't help Mexico to have healthier citizens who couldn't eat.

35. Perkins OH, pt. 7, session 1, p. 434.

36. Perkins, pt. 8, session 1, p. 323; Wallace OH, 3596, using diary notes from December 7, 1944; Davis, *FDR: War President,* 303, on FDR's bureaucratic game-playing having something to do with "strategy." For the mistaken belief that such behavior was a "precondition of victory," see the review of James Lacey's *The Washington War: FDR's Inner Circle and the Politics of Power That Won World War II* (2019) by H. W. Brands in "Bureaucratic Battle and Political Skirmishes," *Washington Post,* June 14, 2019, Book World.

37. "Assails Roosevelt Aides," *New York Times,* May 21, 1941, 10.

38. Katie Louchheim, ed., *The Making of the New Deal: The Insiders Speak* (Cambridge, MA: Harvard University Press, 1983), 191. Her interview of Arthur Goldschmidt, who worked for Hopkins and then for Ickes.

39. Perkins OH, pt. 7, session 1, p. 290.

40. "How Roosevelt Attacked Japan at Pearl Harbor," National Archives, https:// www.archives.gov/publications/prologue/1996/fall/butow.html.

41. Dean Acheson, who chaired the joint Treasury-State-Justice Foreign Funds Control Committee, followed up on Ickes's freelancing. The episode is reported jauntily in Edward C. Green and Helena Meyer-Knapp, "Uncommon Impact," *Groton School Quarterly,* Winter 2020, 25. However, Acheson's accounts of his

role—as in this instance—are often exaggerated and must be used cautiously. See Derek Leebaert, *Grand Improvisation: America Confronts the British Superpower, 1945–1957* (New York: Farrar, Straus & Giroux, 2018), 97–102. For instance, Acheson's tale in *Present at the Creation* (1969) of his supposedly vital role in launching the Marshall Plan overlooks that of his friendly rival, Secretary of the Treasury George Snyder, the Administration's most powerful figure other than the president.

42. Wallace to Roosevelt, August 29, 1941, FDRL, as cited in Joseph Lelyveld, *His Final Battle: The Last Months of Franklin Roosevelt* (New York: Knopf, 2016), 160.

43. Jonathan Utley, *Going to War With Japan: 1937–1941* (New York: Fordham University Press, 2005), 118.

44. The myth of "the German army rumbling in the distance" comes from Goodwin, among other writers. See Goodwin, *No Ordinary Time,* 258.

45. Sean McMeekin, *Stalin's War: A New History of World War II* (New York: Basic Books, 2021), 360. This is the replacement of Colonel Ivan Eaton by his already controversial predecessor, Colonel Raymond Faymonville.

46. Ickes, *The Lowering Clouds,* 631, October 18, 1941.

47. Perkins OH, pt. 8, session 1, p. 22.

48. FDR to Perkins is in her OH, pt. 8, session 1, p. 20. Churchill's claim of FDR's "ruthless assault," which Willkie deployed in the 1940 campaign, is in the fascinating account by Lawrence B. Glickman, *Free Enterprise: An American History* (New Haven, CT: Yale University Press, 2019), 84.

49. The Atlantic Charter document can be seen at https://avalon.law.yale.edu/wwii /atlantic.asp; an eightieth anniversary review essay emphasizes grand strategy and the "freedom of peoples," but not the pivotal clause five, emblematic of the New Deal. See Paul Kennedy, "Joined With Single Purpose," *Wall Street Journal,* August 28–29, 2021.

50. Perkins OH, pt. 8, session 1, pp. 153–55.

51. Wallace OH, 1402, citing meeting of October 9, 1941.

52. Casualties are often reported incorrectly, even from official sources. The National Archives says 115 men were lost on the *Reuben James,* and historians repeat. See https://www.archives.gov/exhibits/a_people_at_war/prelude_to_war /uss_reuben_james.html. This number is used by Robert Dallek and David M. Kennedy, among others, with Goodwin eliding "over a hundred" (282). However, the U.S. Naval Institute lists the *names* of each of the dead, which total precisely 100. See the ship's log at https://www.ibiblio.org/hyperwar/USN /ships/logs/DD/dd245-cas.html. The discrepancy seems to have started with Sherwood (1948).

53. Ambassador Douglas MacArthur II, "An American Diplomat in Vichy France," oral history, Association for Diplomatic Studies and Training, Washington, DC, 1986.

54. Perkins OH, pt. 7, session 1, p. 832.

55. Perkins OH, pt. 8, session 1, p. 40.

56. *Annual Report of the Secretary of the Navy for the Fiscal Year 1941* (Washington, DC: U.S. Government Printing Office, 1941), 1.

CHAPTER 15: NEW EXTREMES

1. H. W. Brands, *Traitor to His Class: The Privileged Life and Radical Presidency of Franklin Delano Roosevelt* (New York: Doubleday, 2008), 631 on "immediately." A rare account of FDR's tempered delay exists from 1950, in John Gunther, *Roosevelt in Retrospect: A Profile in History* (New York: Harper, 1950), 319.

2. Morgenthau Diaries, December 7, 1941, Vol. 470, 19–20, phone transcript.

3. Morgenthau Diaries, "Telegram to General Chiang Kai-shek from Stalin," December 12, 1941, Vol. 472, 133.

4. Joint History Office, *World War II Inter-Allied Conferences* (Washington, DC: U.S. Government Printing Office, 2003). See Proceedings of the American-British Joint Chiefs of Staff Conferences, December 24, 1941, "List of Papers." "Defense of the British Isles" was Subject One, with "Enemy Attack on West Coast of North America" being a close second.

5. "The Men Around the President," *New York Times,* March 29, 1942, 8; "Perkins Resignation Rumored," *New York Times,* February 18, 1942, 15. The "mere jobs" argument would enter conventional wisdom in part due to Henry H. Adams's *Harry Hopkins: A Biography* (New York: Putnam, 1977), 363.

6. Admiral King, a 1946 report to the secretary of the navy: http://strategicgrowthmanagement.com/military-logistic-quotes.

7. Hendrik Meijer, *Arthur Vandenberg: The Man in the Middle of the American Century* (Chicago: University of Chicago Press, 2017), 217.

8. Joint History Office, *World War II.* See JCS, R&RA Section, Annex 1 to JCCSs-6, December 30, 1941, Hopkins to Admiral Harold Stark, CNO.

9. David L. Roll, *The Hopkins Touch: Harry Hopkins and the Forging of the Alliance to Defeat Hitler* (New York: Oxford University Press, 2013), 193, citing Hopkins's correspondence to Barry Lowman, January 22, 1942.

10. Frances Perkins Oral History, Columbia University Libraries Oral History Research Office, pt. 8, session 1, p. 29.

11. Perkins OH, pt. 8, session 1, p. 146.

12. Doris Kearns Goodwin, *No Ordinary Time. Franklin & Eleanor Roosevelt: The Home Front in World War II* (New York: Simon & Schuster, 1994), 318.

13. Ickes Papers (LOC), diary, 6,242, January 18, 1942.

14. Henry Wallace Oral History, Columbia University Libraries Oral History Research Office, 2994, referencing diary notes of December 8, 1943.

15. Wallace OH, 3656.

16. "President Derides Giving Away Navy," *New York Times,* January 18, 1941, 1.

17. After two years of fighting, nearly a third of the country did not even know the Philippines had fallen. See Sir Gerald Campbell, *Of True Experience* (London: Hutchinson, 1948), 149; on racist views, see the Kemper Lecture 1998 by William Roger Louis, "Churchill and the Liquidation of the British Empire," www.nationalchurchillmuseum.org/kemper-lecture-roger.html.

18. FDRL, PSF, Netherlands file, April 6, 1942.

19. The Quincy Institute's Stephen Wertheim discerns a "plan of global military

superiority" unfolding in "How military superiority made America less safe," *Vox*, December 29, 2020. But he exaggerates the importance of Luce's speech and the influence of largely Northeastern policy-making elites. Only in 1957, recalled Richard Nixon, did the United States take over "the foreign policy leadership of the free world." See Derek Leebaert, *Grand Improvisation: America Confronts the British Superpower, 1945–1957* (New York: Farrar, Straus & Giroux, 2018), 481.

20. "Century of the Common Man" address, formally titled "The Price of Free World Victory": www.americanrhetoric.com/speeches /henrywallacefreeworldassoc.htm.

21. John Morton Blum, ed., *Public Philosopher: Selected Letters of Walter Lippmann* (New York: Ticknor & Fields, 1985), 431, Lippmann to Wallace, November 26, 1942.

22. Wallace OH, 1649, using diary notes of June 15, 1942. Even to allow how FDR might, for some reason, have wanted to humor Wallace on this matter in 1942, his opinions reflect those he had already shared with his Cabinet during the 1930s.

23. For example, *Franklin and Winston: An Intimate Portrait of an Epic Friendship* (2004) is the title of a romanticized study by Jon Meacham. This account helped set in stone notions of "their friendship" and of a "sentimentality" even, held by FDR. See Nicholas Wapshott, *The Sphinx: Franklin Roosevelt, the Isolationists, and the Road to World War II* (New York: W. W. Norton, 2015), 287.

24. Ickes Papers (LOC), diary, 6522, April 11, 1942.

25. Wallace OH, 1647; "something done" is in administrative assistant Jonathan Daniels, *White House Witness, 1942–1945* (New York: Doubleday, 1975), 131, February 17, 1943; handing the problem to Ickes is from Ickes Papers (LOC), diary, 7070, November 21, 1941.

26. Daniels, *White House Witness*, 215. FDR elaborated with the nonsense that the Negro's deficiencies are to be seen less in Russian-type offensives than in action such as to be found on beachheads; on Stephen Early's own bigotry, see Ted Morgan, *FDR: A Biography* (New York: Simon & Schuster, 1985), 445.

27. Richard Breitman and Allan J. Lichtman, *FDR and the Jews* (Cambridge, MA: Harvard University Press, 2013), 177, referencing Eleanor Roosevelt Papers, at the FDRL: ER to MacDonald of the President's Advisory Committee on Political Refugees, March 2, 1941.

28. FDRL, PPF, Ickes to FDR, October 7, 1942, and FDR to Ickes, October 10, 1942.

29. Morgenthau Diaries, phone transcript, December 11, 1941, Vol. 471, Part I, 65.

30. Morgenthau Diaries, Vol. 472, Part II, 242.

31. "The Cabinet: Nobody's Sweetheart," *Time,* September 15, 1941.

32. Knox on fifth column—and FDR's original, as citied in Ruth Gruber, *Haven: The Dramatic Story of 1,000 World War II Refugees* (New York: Three Rivers Press, 2000), 11.

33. T. H. Watkins, *Righteous Pilgrim: The Life and Times of Harold L. Ickes, 1874–1952* (New York: Henry Holt, 1990), 792.

34. Wallace OH, 1919, includes diary notes on "Japanese in the U.S." from October 28, 1942.

35. Robert E. Sherwood, *Roosevelt and Hopkins: An Intimate History* (New York: Harper, 1948), 532, account by Commander Fulton, the naval doctor, as he submitted it to Sherwood.

36. Larry I. Bland and Sharon Ritenour Stevens, eds., *Papers of George C. Marshall,* vol. 3, *The Right Man for the Job* (Baltimore: Johns Hopkins University Press, 1991), 266.

37. Goodwin, *No Ordinary Time,* 100, on an enormous "luncheon"; Joseph Lelyveld, *His Final Battle: The Last Months of Franklin Roosevelt* (New York: Knopf, 2016), 219, identifies FDR as the best man, as does Roll, *Hopkins Touch,* 219, among many other historians.

38. Geoffrey C. Ward, ed., *Closest Companion: The Unknown Story of the Intimate Friendship Between Franklin Roosevelt and Margaret Suckley* (New York: Houghton Mifflin, 1995), 246, diary note of October 4, 1943.

39. Perkins OH, pt. 7, session, 1, pp. 395, 852.

40. Kirstin Downey, *The Woman Behind the New Deal* (New York: Doubleday, 2009), 326; Maury Klein, *A Call to Arms: Mobilizing America for World War II* (New York: Bloomsbury, 2013), 336.

41. Perkins OH, pt. 8, session 1, p. 87.

42. Perkins OH, pt. 8, session 1, p. 226.

43. Ickes Papers (LOC), diary, 6661, May 31, 1942. Ickes replied to FDR with the answer he knew would work: Yes, but "one of the quiet, unobtrusive types."

44. T. H. Watkins, *Righteous Pilgrim: The Life and Times of Harold L. Ickes, 1874–1952* (New York: Henry Holt, 1990), 681.

45. Katie Louchheim, ed., *The Making of the New Deal: The Insiders Speak* (Cambridge, MA: Harvard University Press, 1983), 67, her interview of Joseph L. Rauh, re "dirty work"; Wallace OH, 900, referencing diary notes of March 31, 1940.

46. The humiliation was that FDR invited Corcoran to bring his new wife, Peggy Dowd, for an Oval Office visit. She bought a new dress. Corcoran and bride were then kept waiting for two hours, until Hopkins emerged to say FDR was too busy to receive them as scheduled.

47. Morgenthau Diaries, March 19, 1942, Vol. 509, 55–58. Morgenthau acted within two hours of Ickes's request to hand over Dies's tax returns.

48. "'America First,' Urges Walsh in A.I.L. Speech," *Harvard Crimson,* November 16, 1939, 1.

49. Wallace OH, 1537. Wallace was close to the scandal because his personal lawyer, Morris Ernst, served as counsel to the liberal *New York Post,* which broke the story. Ernst was also a confidant of the president and of FBI Director J. Edgar Hoover.

50. Wallace OH, 1536, concerning a "big four" meeting in the White House, May 5, 1942.

51. "The U.S.A. Goes Republican," *Time,* November 16, 1942.

CHAPTER 16: WASHINGTON WARS

1. FDR displayed his fury at the Cabinet meeting of November 20, 1942. Leaks to columnist Arthur Krock, likely by Secretary Hull, intensified FDR's lingering

anger. "The Nation," *New York Times,* December 4, 1942, 24. Wallace observed FDR and Biddle afterward.

2. Henry Wallace Oral History, Columbia University Libraries Oral History Research Office, 1648, with diary notes from June 15, 1942, of FDR complaining that Cordell "had not done a thing" to "clean up the State Department." FDR ranting about "trained seals" is at 1491, April 8, 1942.

3. William D. Hassett, *Off the Record with FDR 1942–1945* (New Brunswick, NJ: Rutgers University Press, 1958), 148–49, diary entry December 22, 1942.

4. FDR's argument with Charles de Gaulle is in Charles de Gaulle, *The Complete War Memoirs of Charles de Gaulle, 1940–1946* (New York: Simon & Schuster, 1964), 391–92; see Robert Dallek, *Franklin Roosevelt and American Foreign Policy, 1932–1945* (New York: Oxford University Press, 1979), 406, on "very dangerous."

5. Morgenthau Presidential Diaries, December 4, 1942, Vol. 5, 1204; Wallace OH, 1280.

6. Wallace OH, 2055, after Cabinet meeting, January 11, 1942; "Russian-American Issues Brought Into Open," *New York Times,* March 14, 1943, 63.

7. "Foreign News: Mr. Wallace Goes South," *Time,* April 5, 1943.

8. Wallace OH, 3657, on logistics.

9. Frances Perkins Oral History, Columbia University Libraries Oral History Research Office, pt. 7, session 1, p. 565.

10. Perkins OH, pt. 7, session 1, p. 362.

11. Wallace OH, 1535, concerning White House meeting with Wallace and Hill leaders, May 5, 1942.

12. Steven Lomazow and Eric Fettmann, *FDR's Deadly Secret* (New York: PublicAffairs, 2009), 90.

13. Morgenthau Diaries, May 24, 1937, Vol. 69, 208, on FDR appearing too weary; intelligence reports were sent routinely to London by British observers such as Roald Dahl and William Stephenson.

14. Ickes Papers (LOC), diary, 6647, April 19, 1942.

15. Wallace OH, 2774, with diary notes of May 24, 1943.

16. "Commander in Chief for the Home Front," *New York Times,* June 6, 1943, 11.

17. Robert E. Sherwood, *Roosevelt and Hopkins: An Intimate History* (New York: Harper, 1948), 634.

18. La Verne Bradley, "Women at Work," *National Geographic,* August 1944, 23.

19. "Women Cautioned About War Jobs," *New York Times,* December 13, 1942, 5.

20. Perkins OH, pt. 8, session 1, p. 105.

21. Perkins OH, pt. 8, session 1, p. 322; Perkins OH, pt. 7, session 1, p. 870.

22. Morgenthau Presidential Diaries, September 7, 1942, Vol. 5, 1169. In this case, the abuse was over Morgenthau's shortfall in a drive for war bonds, and FDR blamed his impatience on pressure he was getting from Wallace and Perkins to boost the U.S. rate of savings.

23. "The Cabinet—Emperor Jones," *Time,* January 13, 1941, as cited in Steven

Fenberg, *Unprecedented Power: Jesse Jones, Capitalism, and the Common Good* (College Station: Texas A&M University Press, 2011), 377.

24. Wallace OH, 1491, with diary notes of April 8, 1942.

25. Wallace OH, 2583, with diary notes of July 16, 1943; Ickes's version of this exchange is in Ickes Papers (LOC), diary, 7994, July 20, 1943.

26. Jonathan Daniels, *White House Witness, 1942–1945* (New York: Doubleday, 1975), 192.

27. "Capital Convinced Welles Resigned," *New York Times,* August 26, 1943, 3.

28. Among the best essays written on FDR and his times is Frank Costigliola, "Broken Circle: The Isolation of Franklin D. Roosevelt in World War II," *Diplomatic History*, October 2008, 677–718. Here Professor Costigliola draws on the William Bullitt Papers, MemCon with the President, July 27, 1943. J. Edgar Hoover's involvement is at 712–13, citing D. M. Ladd to the director, September 9, 1943, Carmel Offie FBI file.

29. Will Brownell and Richard Billings, *So Close to Greatness: A Biography of William C. Bullitt* (New York: Macmillan, 1988), 291.

30. On "Super Lend Lease" and Soviet espionage, see Derek Leebaert, *The Fifty-Year Wound: The True Price of America's Cold War Victory* (New York: Little, Brown, 2002), 107–10.

31. Ickes Papers (LOC), diary, 6474, about the Cabinet meetings of March 20 and 29, 1942.

32. Leebaert, *Fifty-Year Wound*, 111. Later FBI performance during the Cold War is addressed in chapters 8, 9, and 10.

33. Hopkins on strategic assessment is in David L. Roll, *The Hopkins Touch: Harry Hopkins and the Forging of the Alliance to Defeat Hitler* (New York: Oxford University Press, 2013), 294.

34. Stalin to Churchill, April 21, 1943, in David Reynolds and Vladimir Pechatnov, *The Kremlin Letters: Stalin's Wartime Correspondence with Churchill and Roosevelt* (New Haven, CT: Yale University Press, 2018), 237.

35. Albert Weeks, *Russia's Life-Saver: Lend-Lease Aid to the U.S.S.R. in World War II* (Lanham, Maryland: Lexington Books, 2004), 9.

36. Roll, *The Hopkins Touch*, 281.

37. Wallace OH, 2475, 2477, with diary notes of May 22 and 24, 1943.

38. Wallace OH, 2561, Wallace recounting his conversation with the observant Roald Dahl, who was a guest, and who reported all to British intelligence.

39. Wallace OH, 2477, with diary notes of May 24, 1943.

40. Perkins OH, pt. 8, session 1, p. 146.

41. Alan Brinkley, *The End of Reform: New Deal Liberalism in Recession and War* (New York: Vintage, 1996), 141.

42. "Wallace Cast in Role of New Deal 'Martyr,'" *New York Times,* September 5, 1943, 3, for the shift in the amount of national production from 30 to 70 percent between 1940 and 1943.

43. Ickes Papers (LOC), diary, 6269, documenting the Cabinet meeting of January 23, 1942.

44. Harold Ickes, *The Autobiography of a Curmudgeon* (New York: Reynal & Hitchcock, 1943), 340.

45. Michael Rogin, "The President, the cousin he was having an affair with, the cousin he was married to, and her girlfriend," *London Review of Books,* September 21, 1995. Rogin is addressing Goodwin's *No Ordinary Time,* among other books, which, he says, treats "the wartime mining strikes as Lewis's personal vendetta against FDR." Perkins never perceived any "vendetta"; she understood the reasons behind the UMW's outrage.

46. Perkins OH, pt. 7, session 1, p. 800.

47. Perkins OH, pt. 8, session 1, p. 252. In his diary, Ickes documents several prior conversations with Perkins during April 1943 about his taking over the mines.

48. Perkins OH, pt. 8, session 1, pp. 468, 461; pt.5, session, 1, p. 288. Ickes's parallel account is in his diary for May 9, 1943, 7719–731.

49. Perkins OH, pt. 8, session 1, p. 460. After calling in Ickes to oversee the mines, Roosevelt did not have "the Army operate them," as biographer Robert Dallek states in *A Political Life,* 516.

50. "Labor: Strike II," *Time,* June 14, 1943.

51. T. H. Watkins, *Righteous Pilgrim: The Life and Times of Harold L. Ickes, 1874–1952* (New York: Henry Holt, 1990), 758; Doris Kearns Goodwin, *No Ordinary Time. Franklin & Eleanor Roosevelt: The Home Front in World War II* (New York: Simon & Schuster, 1994), 441, on "suicide."

52. Wallace OH, with diary notes of April 7, 1944.

53. Perkins OH, pt. 8, session 1, p. 470.

CHAPTER 17: HARD POUNDING

1. The last congressional hearings to address prospects of the Depression's return were in 1955, following the nation's dread in 1949 of what was expected to be the world's biggest economic calamity of all. See Derek Leebaert, *Grand Improvisation: America Confronts the British Superpower, 1945–1957* (New York: Farrar, Straus & Giroux, 2018), chapter 9.

2. Henry Wallace Oral History, Columbia University Libraries Oral History Research Office, 2839, with diary notes of November 4, 1943, titled "Post War Planning"; FDR aide Jonathan Daniels writes of planning defenses against the inevitable dislocation and riots "which will probably follow demobilization." See Jonathan Daniels, *White House Witness, 1942–1945* (New York: Doubleday, 1975), 130.

3. Wallace OH, 2893.

4. Biddle and Ickes each chronicled their opinions regarding the tumultuous December 17, 1943, Cabinet meeting. It is referenced in Frank Freidel, *Franklin Roosevelt: A Rendezvous with Destiny* (New York: Little, Brown, 1990), 652, n. 43.

5. Daniels, *White House Witness,* 180. Daniels recounts this quote about "sugar" for July 29, 1943; "playing trains" is at March 11, 1944, 222.

6. Frances Perkins Oral History, Columbia University Libraries Oral History Research Office, pt. 8, session 1, p. 596; Harry Hopkins, "What Peace Will Bring Us," *American Magazine,* January 1944. Ickes discovered that this popular magazine paid Hopkins more to write articles than it did him— causing further ill feeling.

7. "Pravda Acclaims Friendship," *New York Times,* November 18, 1943, 3.

8. Charles E. Bohlen was the sole State Department representative but attended only as an interpreter.

9. Wallace OH, 3192, with diary notes on "score," of March 11, 1944.

10. David Reynolds and Vladimir Pechatnov, *The Kremlin Letters: Stalin's Wartime Correspondence with Churchill and Roosevelt* (New Haven, CT: Yale University Press, 2018), 13, on FDR's eagerness to "educate" Stalin and company.

11. Gary Kern, "How 'Uncle Joe' Bugged FDR," *Studies in Intelligence* 47, no. 1 (2003), Central Intelligence Agency.

12. Robert Dallek, *Franklin Roosevelt and American Foreign Policy, 1932–1945* (New York: Oxford University Press, 1979), 295. Dallek is quoting Harriman in Moscow during October 1941, who at this point was basically an echo of Hopkins.

13. V. O. Pechatnov, "Averell Harriman's Mission to Moscow," *Harriman Review,* July 2003, 1–3.

14. John Morton Blum, ed., *Public Philosopher: Selected Letters of Walter Lippmann* (New York: Ticknor & Fields, 1985), 446, September 7, 1943, Lippmann to Jessie Allen Paige; Wallace OH, 2406, with diary notes of March 4, 1943; the warning that FDR encouraged Wallace to deliver is reported in "Vice President Wallace's Address," *New York Times,* March 9, 1943, 4.

15. Joseph P. Lash, *Roosevelt and Churchill: 1939–1941* (New York: W. W. Norton, 1976), 17.

16. Nikita Khrushchev Speech to the 20th Party Congress, *New York Times,* March 18, 1956, 2 (section 4).

17. Will Brownell and Richard Billings, *So Close to Greatness: A Biography of William C. Bullitt* (New York: Macmillan, 1988), 293, from the Bullitt Papers.

18. Frances Perkins, *The Roosevelt I Knew* (New York: Viking, 1946), 85. Her account of FDR's combination of naivete and cockiness regarding Stalin at Tehran is consistent with events, contrary to Joseph Lelyveld, *His Final Battle: The Last Months of Franklin Roosevelt* (New York: Knopf, 2016), 48, who dismisses Perkins's report. Having been in the White House, Sherwood is explicit: Hopkins concluded that "Stalin's power was not so absolute as he had at first imagined," Roosevelt believing this too (345).

19. Nigel Hamilton, *War and Peace: FDR's Final Odyssey, D-Day to Yalta, 1943–1945* (New York: HMH, 2019), 30, 43.

20. Wallace OH, 2918–22, includes diary notes from the furious "squirrel cage" Cabinet meeting of December 17, 1943.

21. Brownell and Billings, *Close to Greatness,* 291.

22. Perkins, *The Roosevelt I Knew,* 84.

23. "Soviet line" is from the Hopkins Papers, as referenced in Sean McMeekin, *Stalin's War: A New History of World War II* (New York: Basic Books, 2021), 497; Daniels, *White House Witness,* 222.

24. Timothy Dickinson recalling his tutorials with historian A. J. P. Taylor, Magdalen College, Oxford.

25. Perkins OH, pt. 7, session 1, p. 535.

26. George McJimsey, *Harry Hopkins: Ally of the Poor* (Cambridge, MA: Harvard University Press, 1987), 196.

27. Daniels, *White House Witness*, 209.

28. Wallace OH, 3235; David L. Roll, *The Hopkins Touch: Harry Hopkins and the Forging of the Alliance to Defeat Hitler* (New York: Oxford University Press, 2013), 336, from the Robert Hopkins Papers.

29. McJimsey, *Harry Hopkins: Ally of the Poor,* 313–14.

30. Allen Drury, *Senate Journal 1943–1945* (New York: McGraw-Hill, 1963), 17, entry of December 7, 1943.

31. "Aldrich Sees Peril," *New York Times,* January 12, 1944, 1.

32. During 1944, the press chronicled how our four were laying out plans to shape postwar America: "Miss Perkins Tells Peace Labor Plan," *New York Times,* September 5, 1944, 6; Wallace on "monopoly prices" is in "Wallace Assails Medicine Cartel," *New York Times,* December 12, 1943, 4; and Hopkins's initiative is in "Hopkins Proposes a Prosperity Plan," *New York Times,* October 3, 1944, 24.

33. Alan Brinkley, *The End of Reform: New Deal Liberalism in Recession and War* (New York: Vintage, 1996), 145.

34. "Hospital Costs Are the Real US Healthcare Scandal," *Financial Times,* July 28, 2021, 4.

35. Geoffrey C. Ward, ed., *Closest Companion: The Unknown Story of the Intimate Friendship Between Franklin Roosevelt and Margaret Suckley* (New York: Houghton Mifflin, 1995), 264, diary entry for December 27, 1943. Press headlines are those of the *New York Times,* December 28, 1943.

36. Wallace OH, 3032, with diary notes for January 21, 1944.

37. Perkins OH, pt. 8, session 1, p. 126.

38. Henry L. Stimson, "The Case for National Service," January 19, 1944, https:// archives-manuscripts.dartmouth.edu/repositories/2/archival_objects/364704.

39. "For Post War Freedom," *New York Times,* February 10, 1944, 3.

40. T. H. Watkins, *Righteous Pilgrim: The Life and Times of Harold L. Ickes, 1874–1952* (New York: Henry Holt, 1990), 795; Kevin Leonard, *Battle for Los Angeles: Racial Ideology and World War II* (Albuquerque: University of New Mexico Press, 2006), 234.

41. Morgenthau Presidential Diaries, March 3, 1944, Vol. 5, 2301, emphasizing "people have just been drafted left and right" in new call-ups because of a presidential order that FDR said he never issued.

42. Wallace OH, 3091.

43. "Hope for America," Library of Congress, https://www.loc.gov/exhibits/hope -for-america/from-my-house-to-the-white-house.html.

44. Wallace OH, 1941, with diary notes of November 5, 1942. Wallace wrote: "Apparently the president is very sensitive to what the Southern Senators feel."

45. Osler Peterson, "Henry Wallace, A Divided Mind," *The Atlantic,* August 1948, 26.

46. The front-page articles on Wallace are, respectively, *Washington Post,* January 23, 1944, and *Washington Star,* May 22, 1944. On FDR and Wallace, it is absurd to state "Roosevelt did not like him anyway," as concludes Jay

Winick—while offering zero evidence—in *1944: FDR and the Year That Changed the World* (New York: Simon & Schuster, 2015), 476.

47. "Wallace Top Choice for Vice President," *New York Times,* March 5, 1944, 8; Wallace OH, 3661.

48. Perkins OH, pt 8, session 1, pp. 503–4.

CHAPTER 18: LONG SHADOWS

1. "Stettinius Appointment," *New York Times,* November 29, 1944, 16.

2. Henry Wallace Oral History, Columbia University Libraries Oral History Research Office, 1191, 3478.

3. *FRUS, 1944, China,* vol. 6, C. E. Gauss to State, June 10, 1944, 3465, https://history.state.gov/historicaldocuments/frus1944v06/d215.

4. Henry A. Wallace, *Soviet-Asia Mission* (New York: Reynal & Hitchcock, 1946), 82.

5. Wallace by now had been tutored for two years in Russian and was near-fluent. He had not "started studying Russian in preparation for his journey." One does not learn Russian so quickly, contrary to Joseph Lelyveld, *His Final Battle: The Last Months of Franklin Roosevelt* (New York: Knopf, 2016), 152.

6. Vadim J. Birstein, "Three Days in 'Auschwitz Without Gas Chambers': Henry A. Wallace's Visit to Magadan in 1944," CWIHP e-Dossier No. 34, referencing George Zoltan Bien, https://www.wilsoncenter.org/publication/three-days-auschwitz-without-gas-chambers-henry-wallaces-visit-to-magadan-1944.

7. "Democrats: The Struggle," *Time,* July 24, 1944.

8. Nigel Hamilton, *War and Peace: FDR's Final Odyssey, D-Day to Yalta, 1943–1945* (New York: HMH, 2019), 289.

9. Wallace OH, 3207, with diary notes of August 2, 1944, when Ickes told him of having had lunch with budget director Harold Smith.

10. Wallace OH, 3408.

11. For FDR's retreat on the poll tax, see Bruce Ackerman and Jennifer Nou, "Canonizing the Civil Rights Revolution: The People and the Poll Tax," *Northwestern University Law Review* 103, no. 1 (2009): 72.

12. Wallace's renomination "without doubt" was the consensus opinion among a cross-section of journalists including Drew Pearson, Frank Kent, and Marquis Childs, as well as publisher Mark Ethridge of the *Louisville Courier Journal,* let alone of Senate Majority Leader Alben Barkley.

13. Wallace OH, 3118.

14. Wallace OH, 2477, with diary notes of May 24, 1943.

15. Wallace OH, 3443, with diary notes of August 3, 1944.

16. Wallace OH, 1761, diary notes of August 20, 1942, on "some boy."

17. Commission on Wartime Relocation and Internment of Civilians, University of Washington Libraries, microfilm A737, Box 3.

18. Ickes's letter is cited in Sam Roberts, "How Marguerite LeHand Shaped the Franklin D. Roosevelt White House," *New York Times,* October 23, 2016, 24. An example of FDR's grave unsteadiness at this juncture was his push for the "Great Sedition Trial," over the objections of Attorney General Biddle.

19. See this excellent overview: Erin Blakemore, "How the GI Bill's Promise Was

Denied to a Million Black WWII Veterans," June 21, 2019, https://www.history
.com/news/gi-bill-black-wwii-veterans-benefits.

20. "Predicts New Jobs for Many Women," *New York Times,* February 18, 1944, 12;
"Miss Perkins Tells Peace Labor Plan," *New York Times,* September 5, 1944, 9.

21. FDRL, PSF, FDR to Wallace, November 1, 1944.

22. "Roosevelt Calls for Service Act," *New York Times,* January 7, 1945, 10; "War-
Nurse Needs Rise," *New York Times,* December 8, 1944, 8.

23. Editorial, "National War Service," *New York Times,* April 22, 1944, 13.

24. Sean McMeekin, *Stalin's War: A New History of World War II* (New York:
Basic Books, 2021), 578–79, and all chapter 31.

25. Robert E. Sherwood, *Roosevelt and Hopkins: An Intimate History* (New York:
Harper, 1948), 823.

26. Richard Norton Smith, *Thomas E. Dewey and His Times* (New York: Simon &
Schuster, 1982), 399, quoting Moley.

27. Editorial, "Joe Manchin's Voting 'Compromise,'" *Wall Street Journal,* June 23,
2021, 22.

28. *Congressional Record–Senate,* January 31, 1944, https://www.govinfo.gov
/content/pkg/GPO-CRECB-1944-pt1/pdf/GPO-CRECB-1944-pt1–17–1.pdf.

29. Molly Guptill Manning, "Fighting to Lose the Vote: How the Soldier Voting
Acts of 1942 and 1944 Disenfranchised America's Armed Forces," *New York
University Journal of Legislation and Public Policy* 19, no. 2 (2016):
335–78.

30. Allen Drury, *Senate Journal 1943–1945* (New York: McGraw-Hill, 1963), 137,
entry for April 12, 1944.

31. Wallace OH, 3394, with diary notes of July 24, 1944.

32. "Ickes Calls Dewey Enemy of Negroes," *New York Times,* November 2,
1944, 7.

33. Editorial, *New York Times,* July 31, 1944.

34. "Sloan Sees Axe for the New Deal," *New York Times,* October 6, 1944, 13.

35. The best discussion of the "Brown Scare," a term he coined, is by historian Leo
Ribuffo, *The Old Christian Right: The Protestant Far Right from the Great
Depression to the Cold War* (Philadelphia: Temple University Press, 1988),
178–225; Ickes on lynching is in Ickes Papers (LOC), 7179,
November 8, 1942. (FDR had started the sedition prosecutions in 1942.)

36. "Tumult Is Raised in Sedition Trial," *New York Times,* May 18, 1944, 1.

37. A fair-minded analysis of Soviet espionage within the Roosevelt Administration
is by the estimable Ellen Schrecker, "Soviet Espionage in America," *American
History,* June 2010.

38. Ruth Gruber, *Haven: The Dramatic Story of 1,000 World War II Refugees*
(New York: Three Rivers Press, 2000), 4.

39. One valuable repository for documents such as FDR's speech of June 12, 1944,
is Jewish Virtual Library: https://www.jewishvirtuallibrary.org/roosevelt-tells
-congress-of-nazi-determination-to-exterminate-european-jewry.

40. Rafael Medoff, *The Jews Should Keep Quiet: Franklin D. Roosevelt, Rabbi
Stephen S. Wise, and the Holocaust* (Lincoln: University of Nebraska Press,
2019), 218; Gruber, *Haven,* 289.

41. John Culver and John Hyde, *American Dreamer: A Life of Henry A. Wallace* (New York: W. W. Norton, 2000), 283.

42. Wallace OH, 3490; FDRL, PSF, Wallace to FDR, November 30, 1944.

43. Wallace OH, 3648; Frances Perkins Oral History, Columbia University Libraries Oral History Research Office, pt. 8, session 1, p. 544; Harold Ickes, *The Secret Diary of Harold L. Ickes,* vol. 3, *The Lowering Clouds, 1939–1941* (New York: Simon & Schuster, 1955), 616, September 20, 1941. Lelyveld, *His Final Battle,* 244, doubts it was Hopkins who elevated Stettinius. From inside the White House, Sherwood observed that "there was no doubt in anyone's mind that Hopkins was largely responsible." See Sherwood, *Roosevelt and Hopkins,* 835.

44. Perkins OH, pt. 8, session 1, pp. 504, 541, 543.

45. Drury, *Senate Journal,* 332, January 7, 1945.

46. Perkins OH, pt. 1, session 1, p. 551.

47. Perkins OH, pt. 8, session 1, p. 550.

48. Wallace OH, 3637. In her much more discreet published memoir, Perkins writes only of FDR's "tears."

49. Drury, *Senate Journal,* 345, January 21, 1945.

50. Morgenthau Presidential Diaries, March 29, 1943, Vol. 5, 1370.

51. Drury, *Senate Journal,* 346, January 21, 1945.

52. Duff Hart-Davis, ed., *King's Counsellor: Abdication and War: The Diaries of Sir Alan Lascelles* (London: Weidenfeld & Nicolson, 2006), 297. Ismay quoted on February 23, 1945; "dentures" is in Lascelles's diary entry for March 14, 1945, 303.

53. Roll, *The Hopkins Touch,* 367.

54. Sergo Beria, *Beria My Father: Inside Stalin's Kremlin* (London: Duckworth, 2001), 203.

55. "Bloodlands" is the description immortalized in Timothy Snyder, *Bloodlands: Europe Between Hitler and Stalin* (New York: Basic Books, 2010).

56. Pechatnov, "Averell Harriman's Mission to Moscow," 5; On comparing Stalin and friends to big-city bosses, see Wallace OH, 3542, with diary notes for November 15, 1944, recounting dinner with Hopkins, at which Harriman was present.

57. On leverage: diplomat George Kennan, in Moscow, urged cutting off all aid to Stalin at this point. Sudden "supply chain" delays would have been cleverer. Yes, the Joint Chiefs, led by Admiral Leahy, who expected the atomic bomb to fail, believed Soviet intervention against Japan to be vital. But that was no longer General MacArthur's opinion. Moreover, chances of Stalin reaching a separate peace with Hitler were remote. Ultimately, Stalin was being placated because FDR yearned for the *Vozhd* to participate in the new United Nations.

58. Harriman interview, November 16, 1953, Harriman Papers (LOC), as referenced by Frank Costigliola, "Broken Circle: The Isolation of Franklin D. Roosevelt in World War II," *Diplomatic History,* October 2008, 29. The belief that Hopkins returned to Washington from the Mayo Clinic before FDR's

death to offer him "some assistance" is mistaken, as in Alonzo Hamby, *Man of Destiny: FDR and the Making of the American Century* (New York: Basic Books, 2015), 428. White House logs are incorrect on this matter; on Ickes and "ghost," see Steven Lomazow and Eric Fettmann, *FDR's Deadly Secret* (New York: PublicAffairs, 2009), 133.

59. "Stimson Assails Delay," *New York Times,* February 19, 1945, 1; Drury, *Senate Journal,* 351, July 26, 1945.

60. Perkins OH, pt. 8, session 1, p. 773. Truman replied, "The President is dead."

EPILOGUE

1. Robert H. Jackson, *That Man: An Insider's Portrait of Franklin D. Roosevelt* (New York: Oxford University Press, 2003), 167.

2. Robert E. Sherwood, *Roosevelt and Hopkins: An Intimate History* (New York: Harper, 1948), 881.

3. Henry Wallace Oral History, Columbia University Libraries Oral History Research Office, 3618–19.

4. "The Capital: Exit the Curmudgeon," *Time,* February 11, 1952.

5. Ickes Papers (LOC), diary, 9765, for June 2, 1945.

6. Frances Perkins Oral History, Columbia University Libraries Oral History Research Office, pt. 8, session 1, p. 749; Ickes Papers (LOC), 10, 125, November 14, 1945.

7. Ickes Papers (LOC), diary, 9938, August 18, 1945.

8. Frank Costigliola, "Broken Circle: The Isolation of Franklin D. Roosevelt in World War II," *Diplomatic History,* October 2008, 37, Harriman interview.

9. Ickes Papers (LOC), diary, 10008, October 6, 1945.

10. "Pipeline in Arabia," *New York Times,* March 17, 1944, 3, reporting the previous night's debate at America's Town Meeting of the Air.

11. Dwight Eisenhower, *At Ease: Stories I Tell to Friends* (New York: Doubleday, 1967), 317.

12. Wallace OH, 1447; T. H. Watkins, *Righteous Pilgrim: The Life and Times of Harold L. Ickes, 1874–1952* (New York: Henry Holt, 1990), 823. Truman was talking with columnist Marquis Childs.

13. Ruth Gruber, *Haven: The Dramatic Story of 1,000 World War II Refugees* (New York: Three Rivers Press, 2000), 289.

14. Wallace OH, 3653.

15. Arthur M. Schlesinger, Jr., concludes, in his three-volume masterwork, that Roosevelt possessed an unfaltering "serenity" (despite the loneliness) and historians largely agree, including Ted Morgan in *FDR: A Biography* (New York: Simon & Schuster, 1985), 408, who concludes that Roosevelt had "the happiest of souls." Perkins and the other three lieutenants would have been flabbergasted at such observations.

16. Wallace OH, 1427.

17. Professor Dunn writes of "collective leadership" in her generous blurb for this book.

18. Tatyana Monnay, "Agriculture," *Politico,* August 29, 2021, 1.

19. Economist Adam Tooze examines the importance of Keynes's April 1942

assertion here: https://adamtooze.substack.com/p/chartbook-on-shutdown
-keynes-and?s=r.

20. Perkins OH, pt. 9, session 1, p. 635.

21. Entry for "Harold Ickes," *Dictionary of American Biography—Supplement 5* (New York: Scribner's, 1977).

22. Henry Wallace, "Where I Was Wrong," *The Week*, September 7, 1952.

23. Eisenhower, *At Ease*, 268.

24. "Dime store New Deal" is Barry Goldwater's famous 1960 description of Eisenhower Administration policies, referenced even in the senator's obituary. "Barry Goldwater Is Dead at 89: Conservatives' Standardbearer," *New York Times*, May 30, 1998, 1; Ben Carson, "America Needs a Safety Net," *Wall Street Journal*, November 5, 2021.

25. Rev. Charles Hoffacker, "The Saint Behind the New Deal," *The Living Church*, May 14, 2014, https://livingchurch.org/2014/05/14/saint-behind-new-deal/.

26. Ibid. The complete article can be seen here: https://livingchurch .org/2014/05/14/saint-behind-new-deal/.

INDEX